WOMEN OF THE LEFT BANK
PARIS, 1900–1940

WOMEN OF THE LEFT BANK

PARIS, 1900–1940

SHARI BENSTOCK

UNIVERSITY OF TEXAS PRESS
AUSTIN

Copyright © 1986 by the University of Texas Press
All rights reserved
Printed in the United States of America

First Edition, 1986

Requests for permission to reproduce material from this work should be
sent to Permissions, University of Texas Press, Box 7819, Austin,
Texas 78713-7819.

LIBRARY OF CONGRESS CATALOGING-IN-PUBLICATION DATA

Benstock, Shari, 1944–
    Women of the Left Bank, 1900–1940.

    Bibliography: p.
    Includes index.
    1. American literature—Women authors—History and
criticism. 2. American literature—20th century—
History and criticism. 3. English literature—Women
authors—History and criticism. 4. English literature—
20th century—History and criticism. 5. Women authors,
American—France—Paris—Biography. 6. Women authors,
English—France—Paris—Biography. 7. Publishers
and publishing—France—Paris—History—20th century.
8. Americans—France—Paris. 9. British—France—
Paris. 10. Women—France—Paris. 11. Left Bank
(Paris, France)—Intellectual life. 12. Paris (France)—
Intellectual life—20th century. 13. Modernism
(Literature) 14. Feminism and literature. I. Title.
PS151.B46   1986   810'.9'9287   86-4124
ISBN 0-292-79029-5

This work is dedicated to the memory of my grandmothers:

EMMA CHRISTINA PETERSON GABRIELSON NELSON,

1886–1974

RUBY IRENE MOTE BARTH, 1898–1966

CONTENTS

Preface   ix

Part I. Discoveries

1. Women of the Left Bank   3

2. Secret Passages: The Faubourg St. Germain   37

3. Simultaneous Existences: Four Lives in St. Germain   71

4. From the Left Bank to the Upper East Side: Janet Flanner's Letter from Paris   99

Part II. Settlements

5. Gertrude Stein and Alice B. Toklas: Rue de Fleurus   143

6. Sylvia Beach and Adrienne Monnier: Rue de l'Odéon   194

7. Djuna Barnes: Rue St.-Romain   230

8. Natalie Barney: Rue Jacob   268

Part III. Crossroads

9. H. D. and Bryher: *En passant*   311

10. At the Sign of the Printing Press: The Role of Small Presses and Little Magazines   357

11. Paris Transfer: The 1930s   396

12. The City They Left   442

Notes   455

Works Cited and Consulted   479

Index   509

PREFACE

Women of the Left Bank examines the contributions of some two dozen American and English expatriate women to the life of literary Paris between 1900 and 1940. The diverse activities of these women—who were writers, publishers, book sellers, and *salonières*—and the double perspective of this study, which looks both at literary history and the literature of this period, are reflected in a text that marks the intersections of life and art, the crossroads of memory and history, myth and biography. Across the terrain of the Paris *rive gauche,* an undulating and uneven landscape famous for the sharp turns of its narrow, winding streets, I have traced the histories of women whose energy and intelligence nurtured the development of literary Modernism's powerful culture. The first section of the book ("Discoveries") charts this newly discovered country and places its early settlers in relation to one another; the middle section ("Settlements") directs itself to important Paris addresses and to the activities of the women who inhabited these studios, salons, and publishing houses; part three ("Crossroads") maps the intersections of various lives and investigates the changing political and cultural conditions of the Paris setting. Although several among them are accorded individual chapters, each of these women appears and reappears throughout this history, placed in conjunction with and juxtaposition to other men and women of the community. The Left Bank itself, however, assumes both a historical and a literary identity, transformed in the fiction of such writers as Jean Rhys, Anaïs Nin, Gertrude Stein, and Djuna Barnes. These women discovered themselves as *women* and as *writers* in Paris, charting experiences that were significantly different from those of their husbands, brothers, and male Modernist colleagues.

To retrace the literary history of a period is to open inevitably that history to question. The impetus for this study of expatriate women was the desire to replace them in the Paris context from which they had been removed by the standard literary histories of Modernism. With few exceptions, the women whose lives and works are recorded here have been considered marginal to the Modernist effort. Most of them have appeared in supporting roles, their contributions cataloged in footnotes to biographies of James Joyce, T. S. Eliot, and Ezra Pound or in anecdotal evidence of memoirs and literary studies of Paris between the wars. In rediscovering the lives and works of these women, however, I also confronted the ways in which our working definitions of Modernism—its aesthetics, politics, critical principles, and poetic practices—and the prevailing interpretations of the Modernist experience had excluded women from its concerns. The roots of the misogyny, homophobia, and anti-Semitism that indelibly mark Modernism are to be found in the subterrain of changing sexual and political mores that constituted *belle époque* Faubourg society, and it is here that the story of these women begins—in Edith Wharton's drawing room. This chapter of women's history closes as Janet Flanner embarks from Bordeaux to return to New York after France's entry into World War II in autumn 1939. The story of the intervening years is a tale of difference, a text signed with women's names. It writes the underside of the cultural canvas, offering itself as a countersignature to the published Modernist manifestos and calls to the cultural revolution. This female subtext exposes all that Modernism has repressed, put aside, or attempted to deny.

Women of the Left Bank emphasizes the *differences* of Modernist women's experiences in both history and literature. But it resists any effort to write literary history from a single—genderized—perspective nor does it try to define a Modernist feminist poetics. Instead, it traces differences between and within literary practices and lived circumstances in this period, choosing as one—among many—of its determining factors the difference of gender. It examines communities of women established on the Paris Left Bank without arguing for a single female community grounded on the solidarity (and commonality) of female experience. For some women expatriates, Paris offered release from American puritanism; for others the Modernist literary experiment represented a reinforcement of patriarchal values. It is not accidental, I think, that the powerful communities of women artists were established by lesbians or that heterosexual women Modernists remained in the shadows of their male colleagues—men who were husbands, lovers, or literary supervisors. Monique Wittig has written that homosexuality is not only the desire for one's own sex, "it is also the desire for something else that is not connoted. . . . this desire is resistance to the norm" ("Paradigm," 114). Modernism itself participated in "resistance to the norm," but it also—and simultaneously—reinforced the normative. Contrasting the situations of heterosexual and homosexual women Modernists reveals a resistance to and reinforcement of that which in Western society serves as the norm:

the privileging of the white, male heterosexual. The collective stories of these women map the cracks and divisions of the Modernist façade, exposing the ways in which individual contributions to this eclectic movement have been effaced in the effort to render Modernism monolithic.

Work on this project was initially supported by a fellowship from the American Association of University Women, which provided reading and research time at the Camargo Foundation, Cassis, France, in 1981–1982. It has also been supported by grants from two universities: the Research Board of the University of Illinois at Urbana-Champaign and a College of Arts and Sciences Summer Fellowship at the University of Tulsa. I owe a debt to several libraries and research institutions in helping me collect published and unpublished materials for this study: Bibliothèque Jacques Doucet, Paris; Manuscripts Division, Library of Congress, Washington, D.C.; Beinecke Library, Yale University; Firestone Library, Princeton University; Morris Library, Southern Illinois University; Humanities Research Center, University of Texas at Austin; Municipal Library, Dijon, France; University of Illinois at Urbana-Champaign; University of Wisconsin at Milwaukee; University of Maryland Library; McFarlin Library, University of Tulsa. I am grateful as well to a number of friends and colleagues who have assisted this project: Jacques Aubert, Mary Lynn Broe, Jackson Bryher, Alan Cohn, Pierre Deflaux, Janet Egleson Dunleavy, Ulla Dydo, Noel Riley Fitch, Susan Stanford Friedman, Blanche Gelfant, Sidney Huttner, David V. Koch, Maryse Mucciante, Daniele Pitavy Soukes, Michael Pretina, Alan Schaffer, David Schoonover, William Shawn, Thomas F. Staley, Paula A. Treichler, James G. Watson, George Wickes, and Russell Young. I owe special debts to Jane Marcus and Catharine R. Stimpson, who have generously shared their own research-in-progress on this period and have provided continuing friendship and collegial support. For professional advice and interest, I am grateful to the staff at the University of Texas Press. The actual writing of this book coincided with full-time teaching, administrative, and editorial responsibilities, and I am grateful to graduate students at the University of Tulsa, who discussed the work with me, read versions of the manuscript, and provided editorial and bibliographic assistance: Jan Calloway, Regina Haslinger, Susan Hastings, Mary O'Toole, Celia Patterson, Catherine Peaden, Michael Warner, and Ruth Weston. A special debt of gratitude is owed to Priscilla Diaz-Dorr, whose intelligence and kindness contributed to this book in important ways.

Bernard Benstock and Eric Shivvers, my traveling companions on the various research trips to France necessitated by this study, deserve the greatest praise. Without their encouragement, humor, and love, this project would never have been undertaken, much less completed. I owe them more than they know.

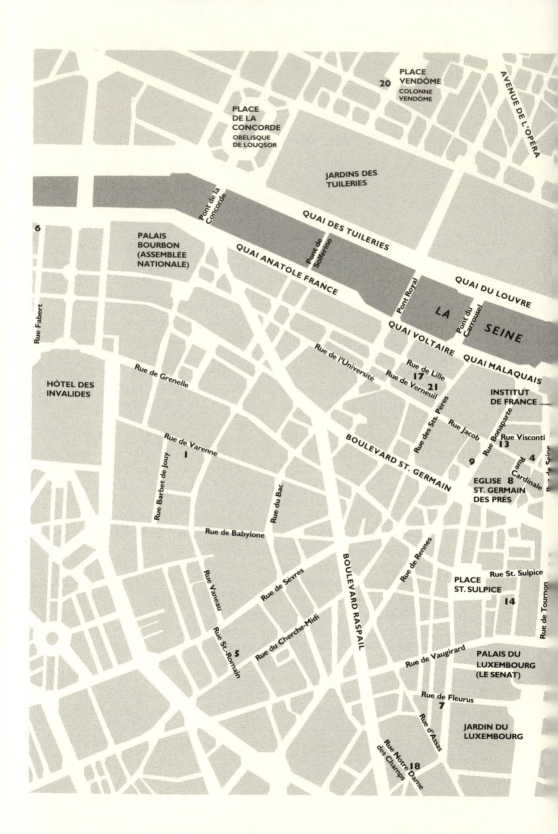

1. Edith Wharton (53 rue de Varenne) 1908

2. Adrienne Monnier (La Maison des Amis des Livres, 7 rue de l'Odéon) 1915

3. Sylvia Beach (Shakespeare and Company, 12 rue de l'Odéon) 1921

4. Natalie Barney (20 rue Jacob) 1909

5. Djuna Barnes (9 rue St.-Romain) early 1930s

6. Maria and Eugene Jolas (*transition* magazine, 40 rue Fabert)

7. Gertrude Stein and Alice B. Toklas (27 rue de Fleurus—1903–1937; 5 rue Christine—1938 until Toklas moved out in 1964)

8. Caresse and Harry Crosby (Black Sun Press, 2 rue Cardinale) 1920s

9. Janet Flanner (Hotel St. Germain des Prés, 36 rue Bonaparte) 1925 until WW II

10. Margaret Anderson (15 rue de Beaujolais) 1923

11. Robert McAlmon and Bryher (Contact Editions, 29 Quai d'Anjou) 1923

12. Nancy Cunard (The Hours Press, 15 rue Guénégaud) 1930

13. Colette (9 rue de Beaujolais—1938, her last address; corner rue Jacob and rue Visconti—1892–1895)

14. Hotel Récamier (Place St. Sulpice) setting of *Nightwood*, 1920s–1930s

15. Isadora Duncan (5 rue Danton) 1909

16. Sylvia Beach (first address of Shakespeare and Company, 8 rue Dupuytren)

17. Caresse and Harry Crosby (residence, 9 rue de Lille) 1920s

18. Dorothy Shakespeare and Ezra Pound (70 bis rue Notre Dame des Champs) 1921

19. Sylvia Beach and Adrienne Monnier (residence, 18 rue de l'Odéon) 1921–1937

20. Jack Kahane (Obelisk Press, 16 Place Vendôme) publisher of *Anaïs Nin*, 1932

21. Maria and Eugene Jolas (residence, 6 rue de Verneuil) 1924

Rue de Beaujolais
13 10
PALAIS ROYAL

Rue St. Honoré

Rue de Rivoli

PALAIS DU LOUVRE

Rue du Louvre

Pont des Arts

QUAI DE CONTI

12

Rue Guénégaud

Pont Neuf

QUAI DES GRANDS AUGUSTINS

7

Rue Christine

15

Rue Danton

16

Rue Dupuytren

3
9   2

Rue de l'Odéon

THÉÂTRE DE L'ODÉON

BOULEVARD ST. MICHEL

PALAIS DE JUSTICE

SAINTE CHAPELLE

Pont au Change

Pont Notre Dame

ÎLE DE LA CITÉ

Pont St. Michel

Petit Pont

NOTRE DAME

HÔTEL DE VILLE

Pont Louis Philippe

Pont St. Louis

Pont de l'Archevêché

Pont Marie

11

QUAI D'ANJOU

ÎLE ST. LOUIS

Pont de la Tournelle

QUAI DE LA TOURNELLE

EXPATRIATE PARIS

WOMEN OF THE LEFT BANK
PARIS, 1900–1940

Where do we meet? The geography of our friendships, the topography of the course of the relation, the spots, the fiery mountainous excitement and valleys, the silences—a steady humming when it is simply there, neither high nor low, not remarked on—all this needs a school of cartographers. Consider the point of origin, the meeting. Ancient legend recounts time after time the meeting of men somewhere in the world of nature. At a crossroads, men meet. They go forward together or they go on alone, marked by the meeting. On the battlefield. In their travels, their movement, men meet other men, but never meet women unless the women are locked in towers, because women themselves are rarely itinerant travelers.

—Louise Bernikow, *Among Women*

The young women strolled and talked; their talk is forgotten. After fifty years, though, one scrap of the master's survived.

—Hugh Kenner, *The Pound Era*

PART I. DISCOVERIES

MARGARET ANDERSON

DJUNA BARNES

NATALIE BARNEY

SYLVIA BEACH

KAY BOYLE

BRYHER (WINIFRED ELLERMAN)

COLETTE

CARESSE CROSBY

NANCY CUNARD

HILDA DOOLITTLE (H. D.)

JANET FLANNER

JANE HEAP

MARIA JOLAS

MINA LOY

ADRIENNE MONNIER

ANAÏS NIN

JEAN RHYS

SOLITA SOLANO

GERTRUDE STEIN

ALICE B. TOKLAS

RENÉE VIVIEN

EDITH WHARTON

I

WOMEN OF THE LEFT BANK

These women were part of the artistic community that formed on the Paris Left Bank early in the twentieth century. Their literary contributions—which include major works of prose, poetry, drama, critical and journalistic essays, autobiographies, *pensées*, and memoirs—display wide-ranging interests and diverse talents. In addition to their own writing activities, several of these women set up bookshops, publishing houses, hand presses, little magazines, and artistic salons through which they advertised and marketed the products of literary Paris. While certain of them are less well remembered than others, each had a particular influence on the Paris cultural scene (and was influenced by it), and collectively theirs was a formidable energy and versatility.

This study examines the lives and works of these women in the Paris context. Of primary significance is the experience of being a *woman* in this time and place. The question that predicates this inquiry is not "What was it like to be part of literary Paris?"—a question compulsively asked by both the participants and the analysts of this period—but rather "What was it like to be a woman in literary Paris?" The women included in this study provide diverse answers to this question, their collective responses suggesting rich and complex experiences that illuminate heretofore overlooked aspects of the cultural setting in which Modernism developed.

Of particular interest are the ways in which the patriarchal social and political settings of Western culture affect the subject matter and methods of woman's writing and influence the creative process from which that writing is born. The expatriate Paris experience constructed itself in ways that both challenged and underwrote this patriarchal heritage; thus it is not possible to examine the living and working situations of female

Modernists separate from those of their male colleagues or to investigate the founding principles of women's literary contributions to Modernism without questioning the assumptions in which male Modernist practice situated itself. That is, this study considers the issue of gender as an important (and all too often disregarded) element in defining the aesthetics and politics, the theory and practice, of what we now call Modernism.

Paris Remembered

Rarely has a time and place so captured the imagination as the Paris of these years. From our contemporary perspective, this period is set apart in the historical flux of the twentieth century, strangely removed from us and yet, curiously, still of interest. Our impressions of these years are marked as much by the sense of a self-indulgent hedonism as by the record of an intellectual fervor. These impressions derive from a variety of sources—from memoirs by the participants and hangers-on, from biographies and autobiographies of the great and near-great, from literary gossip disguised as academic treatise, from yellowed newspaper columns in the Paris editions of the *New York Herald* and the *Chicago Tribune*, and from Janet Flanner's "Letter from Paris" in the *New Yorker* and Eugene Jolas's editorials in *transition* magazine. In novels by F. Scott Fitzgerald, Ernest Hemingway, Djuna Barnes, and Jean Rhys, and in Gertrude Stein's autobiographies and her homage to the city, *Paris France,* such diverse figures as Josephine Baker and Kiki of Montparnasse mingle with Léon-Paul Fargue, Ezra Pound, and other Left Bank writers in startling ways.

We have romanticized those years, and so have those who lived through them. The few alive today who were part of that Paris life possess a fund of dim memories and stories too often told. The recent deaths of Djuna Barnes, Winifred Ellerman, Caroline Gordon, and Katherine Anne Porter or the publication of Morrill Cody's memoir, *The Women of Montparnasse,* perhaps took us by surprise, since we assumed all these people to be already dead. For lives so much a part of the Paris years, anachronistic later existences seem indeed displaced in time. In a recent letter to a friend, Maria Jolas (who with her husband, Eugene, founded *transition* magazine in 1926) ingenuously asked: "Did you not write, thinking I was dead? Well I'm not." Still, we feel perhaps that remnants of an age so removed from our own should be safely sealed by history, all the participants quietly at rest in Passy or Père Lachaise cemeteries. The collected letters of Alice B. Toklas, most written after the death of Gertrude Stein in 1946, are entitled *Staying On Alone.*[1] They record the painful afterlife of a lover left behind, one whose future was to be constituted by memories of the past. Alice Toklas is no longer "staying on alone," but some few still are. Something more than the malingering appearance of aged expatriates who have outlived their era, however, disturbs our notions of the "pastness" of this age.

Uneasy with the assumed historicity of the Paris years, one may question the degree to which this chapter of our cultural development is closed. One suspects that our hesitation in closing the historical door on this period is due to a sense that the shock waves these years produced are still resounding through our culture. Perhaps we also feel even more strongly now the break that such events as the publication of *Ulysses* or the presentation of the *Ballet Méchanique* made with the nineteenth century, a period that in 1920 seemed further removed in time than the nearly seventy years that separate us from the end of World War I. The war constituted a rupture in the life that went before it, uprooting those nineteenth-century values that had tenaciously persisted into the twentieth century. It is hardly likely that—had there not been this war, had there not been the resultant economic decline in Europe, had the war not provided an introduction to the very existence of Europe—those dozens of Americans with bags in hand would have determinedly found their way to the Gare St. Lazare in search of the sophistication and freedom that Paris represented. All life in Paris during these years was influenced by this influx of expatriates who appropriated the city as their own, overlaid their American values on a culture that was hardly indifferent to the vitality of such a liberated breed. The generalizations are well known to us; terms like the "Lost Generation" or the "Jazz Age" are such worn clichés that their sources are often lost to present history. Indeed, the sources of that intellectual and artistic revolt remain obscure, although the conditions of its occurrence and its consequent effects are well known to the least literary among us. Paris of the twenties and thirties continues to be both aesthetically and anecdotally available, a circumstance that constrains the effort accurately to read its social and cultural backgrounds.

Cultural Readings

But recent interest in this era is spurred by something other than the accumulation of anecdotal evidence. Two incongruent factors have structured renewed interest in the period. First is the availability of the private papers, letters, and diaries of those present in Paris during these years; these form a record that, unlike published memoirs, documents the period from a less self-conscious and self-serving perspective. The women of this study were born between 1862 and 1903, the births of Edith Wharton and Anaïs Nin enclosing three generations, their arrivals in Paris separated by almost twenty-five years: Wharton settled in Paris in 1906 (living there part of every year until her permanent residence in 1912); Nin (who had

5

been born in Paris) returned to her native city just prior to 1930. Wharton, who died at 75 (as did Sylvia Beach), was one of the shorter-lived of these women. Stein died at age 72 of cancer, but Natalie Barney lived to 96; Djuna Barnes, Katherine Anne Porter, and Alice B. Toklas to 90; Winifred Ellerman to 88; Margaret Anderson to 87; Janet Flanner and Caroline Gordon to 86; Mina Loy to 84. Maria Jolas, one of the few women of this group still living, resides in Paris, aged 93. And while Kay Boyle—in her early eighties—may still publish her memoirs, her compatriots have been consigned to posterity, their estates settled, their papers catalogued in American libraries, their private record now available to a public still hungry for more information.

A new generation of readers and critics is already at work researching these materials. Prior to 1976, only two women in the group had been accorded full-length biographies: Gertrude Stein and Edith Wharton. Since 1976, Djuna Barnes, Natalie Barney, Sylvia Beach, Colette, Nancy Cunard, H. D., and Alice B. Toklas have become the subjects of biographical studies. The past five years have produced the first full-length examination of works by Djuna Barnes, H. D., Mina Loy, Anaïs Nin, Adrienne Monnier, Katherine Anne Porter, and Jean Rhys as well as the republication of many out-of-print works by these women. Critical and biographical investigations of several others are currently in progress.

New approaches to cultural history, most significant among them feminist criticism, have provided important alternative perspectives on the Modernist literary effort and have opened avenues of approach to the diverse lifestyles and literary contributions of expatriate women. Feminist criticism directed toward rediscovery and reevaluation of the work of women writers has already altered our view of Modernism as a literary movement. It has testified to female experience in the social and intellectual settings of modern history and has examined the modes of entrapment, betrayal, and exclusion suffered by women in the first decades of the twentieth century. It has exposed the absence of commentary on women's contributions to Modernism and has rewritten the history of individual women's lives and works within the Modernist context.[2] Feminist critical practice points toward—indeed, calls for—reevaluation and redefinition of Modernism itself. Once women Modernists are placed beside their male colleagues, the hegemony of masculine heterosexual values that have for so long underwritten our definitions of Modernism is put into question. Modernism may then be seen to be a far more eclectic and richly diverse literary movement than has previously been assumed. Discovering important differences among the lives and writing of Modernist women may also suggest the heterogeneity of gender groups and shed light on differences among the lives and writings of male Modernists. Distinguishing the effects on literary practice of such determinants as

social class, education, sexual orientation, and religious and political persuasion may also reveal the extent to which the women of the expatriate
Modernist community shared a commonality of experience that often ignored such boundaries.

Feminist criticism, in the context of post-Modernist literary theory,
provides a method of discovering both similarities and differences, com-
monalities and divergences of experience. It poses a question already
asked by Sandra Gilbert and Susan Gubar: "What does it mean to be a
woman writer in a culture whose fundamental definitions of literary authority are . . . both overtly and covertly patriarchal?" (*Madwoman*,
45–46). Deconstructive critical theory suggests that patriarchal culture
is coupled with Western thought, which is structured in terms of polarities (male-female, good-evil, speech-writing), in which the second term is,
according to Barbara Johnson, "considered the negative, corrupt, undesirable version of the first" (Derrida, *Dissemination*, viii). Feminist critical theory reads the effects of patriarchal constraint on women; deconstructive practice measures those effects with particular attention to the
equivalence of "writing" and "woman" as devalued items in a hierarchical
scheme of values.

The combination of these critical methods would seem to offer a doubled
reading perspective of particular value in examining the place of women
writers in Western society, but it is precisely this mutual reinforcement of
the doubled reading that for some weakens the critical value of these
combined methodologies. It has been argued that the two practices always arrive at the same conclusions: that the patriarchy represses woman,
entraps her, subjects her to its self-reinforcing images; that in the patriarchy woman exists under erasure, absent, dispossessed of identity.
Such readings suggest that woman either apes patriarchal forms (in order
to assure a special dispensation for herself under its law) or exists in *reaction* against the forms of patriarchal repression. Thus in Gilbert and
Gubar's reading of the patriarchal psychosexual heritage (following the
work of Harold Bloom), woman finds herself locked out of the societal
power structure and locked into literary forms conceived by and written
for men. She defines the space of her world in the prisonhouse man has
constructed for her, the authority of her writing grounded in anger and
madness. This reading ultimately discovers—and even valorizes—the
effects of woman's oppression, her illness and unease the results of the
patriarchal "sentence" that condemns her to silence. Women's stories are
always the same story, the record of a seemingly eternal battle against constraint. In such interpretations, the presence of the patriarchy remains a
consistent factor, always defining itself by the same attitudes, the same
repressive practices, resistant to changes in history, politics, and culture.
Deconstructive practice reads the effects of this "Western metaphysic,"

the power and presence of the patriarchy, in woman's devalued position, equivalent to the secondary place writing plays with respect to speech. Both woman and writing lack the "presence" that underwrites power in Western civilization, and each is defined by absence.[3]

Stated in these ways, woman's plight seems overdetermined, the plot of her story too predictable, the modes of her actions and writing reductive. The authority of her experience rests in its sameness, its inability ever radically to alter its base in fact or to transform that circumstance in fiction. Woman is constantly defined as the debased "other" of the masculine norm. Yet one hopes that both feminist theory and deconstructive practice offer richer possibilities for reading women's history than this résumé suggests. Indeed, it is post-Modernist theory that has "deconstructed" the power of the Western metaphysic, that has dislodged the oppositional and hierarchical value systems that always make woman and writing derivative and demeaned. Deconstructive practice has plotted not only the differences between male and female, masculine and feminine, but the differences *within* each of these categories. Neither the biologically determined categories "male" and "female" nor the socially produced categories "masculine" and "feminine" are absolute—entirely consistent, even monolithic, within themselves. Each inhabits and is inhabited by its opposite. Here one discovers the difference *within* gender, within the experience of gender; here an alternative reading to woman's predetermined plot offers itself.

Female Expatriation: Natalie Barney and Gertrude Stein

Natalie Clifford Barney would seem to represent in the extreme the common denominators of upbringing, education, social status, intellectual ambition, and even sexual preference common to many women of the expatriate community. She was upper middle class but financially independent, a product of private schooling, a veteran European traveler at a young age, culturally advantaged and intellectually determined. She inherited sizable fortunes from both her mother and father; her education with French governesses and in private boarding schools was impeccable; she lived in Europe at various times before settling there permanently in 1902; she aspired to be and became a writer of some stature; she was the most active and candid lesbian of her day, sharing this sexual orientation with thirteen of the twenty-two women of this study. Barney never allowed herself to be consigned to the shadows of literary Paris. Indeed, her own writing may have suffered because of the prominent social role she played within the community, and commentaries on Barney have tended to focus on her life to the exclusion of her art. She was an exceedingly public figure, establishing in her home on the rue Jacob a famous literary salon that for over sixty years brought together French and Americans, intellectuals and artists. Through her salon Barney wielded considerable power among Left Bank writers, power often employed in the service of her commitment to feminist ideals, using the salon to introduce women writers and their work to each other and to the larger public.

There were important variations in individual circumstances and lifestyles among these expatriate women, but it is Natalie Barney who most often serves as the "type" for the expatriate female Modernist, a woman whose intellectual and sexual independence was secured by financial privilege and social distinction. The degree of financial security experienced by women of the expatriate community varied, however: some were born to exceeding wealth (Natalie Barney, Winifred Ellerman, and Nancy Cunard); some were comfortably middle class (Gertrude Stein, Alice B. Toklas, and Maria Jolas); some were often hard pressed to make ends meet (Jean Rhys and Djuna Barnes); and others held paying jobs, usually as journalists (Janet Flanner, Florence Gilliam, and Solita Solano). The range of economic circumstance was significantly greater among women expatriates than among their male compatriots. Except for Harry Crosby, who inherited wealth, the expatriate men of literary Paris were middle class and of modest means. Nearly all supported themselves by some kind of work other than writing literature. They were journalists, bankers, teachers, physicians, and insurance salesmen. F. Scott Fitzgerald, of course, made enough money from his writings to support himself rather well, but his case is unusual. Far more of these writers saw little financial reward from their experimental literary works. In general, the women of the expatriate community experienced greater financial freedom than the men, having arrived in Paris with small annuities or inheritances with which they purchased their freedom from America. For some of them, such support was the only form of income they were ever to know.

A few of these women came from prestigious upper-class families, but most of them came from solidly middle-class circumstances. Their fathers included prosperous businessmen (among them a railroad magnate and a publisher), a university professor, a Presbyterian minister, and two English shipping tycoons. Some of the daughters could trace family histories for several generations in American and English public life, however. Caresse Crosby—Mary Phelps Jacob Peabody before she married Harry Crosby—traced her family back one thousand years to the Isle of Wight. At least two of these women had artistically significant maternal heritages: Kay Boyle's maternal aunt painted the portrait of Susan B. Anthony that inspired the 1936 commemorative postage stamp in her honor, and Alice Pike Barney was an accomplished painter who studied in Paris with Whistler and Duran. While not all of these expatriates were privately educated, they all received similar educations—studying music, painting, or literature. (Kay Boyle differed from the majority in studying architecture.) Some of these women were graduates of the most elite New England finishing schools, while at least two of them, Gertrude Stein and Sylvia Beach, received erratic educations, shifting between schools in America and Europe as families traveled. Many of these women shared marked similarities in family backgrounds, in cultural and intellectual aspirations, and in political and even religious attitudes (Gertrude Stein and Alice Toklas were Jewish, and Winifred Ellerman reported to Robert McAlmon that her father, John Ellerman, was probably Jewish) as well as a homogeneity of childhood experience. In addition, these women appeared to share a common factor in expatriating: they wanted to escape America and to find in Europe the necessary cultural, sexual, and personal freedom to explore their creative intuitions.

Within the broad outlines of this pattern, the individual reactions to essentially conservative bourgeois upbringings varied considerably, as did the personal motivations for choosing to live in Paris. For homosexual women, the reasons for living abroad, the circle of friends developed there, and the integration of personal and professional lives were often influenced by sexual choices. In some cases, the private lives of these women reflected patterns established by the heterosexual world in which they lived. Gertrude Stein and Alice B. Toklas, for instance, established a long-standing union that in many ways mirrored heterosexual marriages, coinciding—except in the choice of a female rather than a male partner— with the conventions of their upper-middle-class upbringings. Sylvia Beach and Adrienne Monnier, Janet Flanner and Solita Solano, Djuna Barnes and Thelma Wood, however, established lesbian relationships whose only common feature was an explicit rebellion against the heterosexual norm. Only one made a public issue of her lesbianism. Candidly and openly promiscuous (indeed, committed to an ethics of promiscuity), Natalie Barney also maintained a decorous literary salon at which she served tea and cakes. The sharp contrast between Barney's public image as the leader of a lesbian community and her roles as poet and patron of the arts throws into relief the less obvious disjunction between private life and public convention evidenced in the lives of other lesbian women during these years.

Natalie Barney's place among women in the literary community has been viewed almost entirely as a function of her sexual orientation. In the gossipy biographies and memoirs of her life, Barney's lesbianism is the crucial factor, that which unites her art and life and explains her relationships with both men and women. Only very recently have feminist critics begun to reexamine the premises on which such accounts of Barney's life situate themselves, placing Barney at the center of a community of women committed to producing serious art. Barney's own writing, previously dismissed as derivative love poetry for a coterie of lesbian women, has begun to receive serious attention as critical examination plots the relation between form and content in these writings, between the shape of Barney's life and the subjects of her literary vision.[4] Lillian Faderman notes, however, that "what is generally passed over . . . is the extent to which [Barney's] circle functioned as a support group for lesbians to permit them to create a self-image which literature and society denied them" (*Surpassing the Love of Men*, 369). This literary and social self-image, as we shall see, was often a destructive and homophobic one (resting on the work of such sexologists as Krafft-Ebing, Havelock Ellis, and others). The image of lesbians in both literature and life was constructed around notions of illness, perversion, inversion, and paranoia. Natalie Barney dedicated her life to revising this prevailing image.

These interpretations of homosexual character traits among women of the Paris community still persist, even among lesbian feminist critics who rightly insist on the need for reexamination of the women in this time and place. Not only did Barney's salon operate as a support group for lesbian women; Barney herself spent a lifetime trying to revise the public and private images held by the larger community and lesbian women themselves. She provided a role model in her own behavior, she wrote poetry in the tradition of Sappho (a tradition that had been systematically suppressed over the more than two thousand years separating Barney from Lesbos), she made a pioneer effort to rewrite lesbian history and experience, to deny that guilt, self-recrimination, drug abuse, suicide, unhappiness, and psychological torment were part and parcel of the lesbian's commitment to an alternative life.[5] While Barney welcomed to her home women of all kinds (including writers, artists, musicians, and dancers, as well as music hall performers and courtesans), never discriminating on the grounds of social class or religious, political, or sexual persuasions, Barney herself objected to modes of lesbian behavior that seemed to confirm the scientific theories then prevalent. In particular, she objected to any form of dress or behavior that suggested homosexual women were really men trapped in women's bodies. Therefore, she objected to cross-dressing, to the anger, self-indulgence, and self-pity that marked the behavior of many of her friends, and to the need to mime the male in dress, speech, and demeanor.

Barney may not have realized the extent to which such forms of behavior were determined by the attitudes of a parent culture that despised evidence of sexual difference, defining it as perversion, but she fought against the effects of such attitudes with extraordinary energy. For reasons discussed at greater length below, Barney remained untouched by the prescriptions of the parent culture, her life marked in every aspect as *different from* the lesbian image ordained by society: that is, Natalie

Barney's life was significantly (and purposely) different from the lives of lesbians of her time, different most apparently from the lives of her many lovers. Importantly, the educational process Barney undertook directed itself to women and men of all sexual orientations. Although she organized a community of women in Paris (perhaps an effort to recreate Lesbos), she clearly saw the danger of forming separatist groups and made her salon an eclectic, international, and multisexual meeting place.

Important distinctions between Barney's experience and that of other women who formed her group remain unobserved, however. Crucial differences of social class and economic status are overlooked; Barney's feminism is rarely acknowledged to extend beyond the context of her lesbianism; if recognized at all, her contributions to restructuring the lesbian self-image are usually limited to the effort to rebuild Lesbos in Paris. Barney is still viewed, even by feminist critics, as the representative Paris lesbian, as though all lesbian women of the time lived out the effects of their sexual orientation in the same way, regardless of social class, religious heritage, intellectual interests, or political persuasion. The difference of sexual orientation continues to be read as sameness within the group, much as it was in Paris during these years; the expatriate community itself made a definite distinction between "the girls"—as lesbian women were referred to outside their hearing—and their heterosexual compatriots, especially those whose lives abroad reflected the conventions of middle-class life in America.[6] We assume differences in the living circumstances between heterosexual and homosexual Paris women, but we must also be attentive to differences within these two groups. For members of each group the question so frequently asked back home— "Why Paris?"—often had special significance.

Gertrude Stein reacted strongly against the American puritanism of the early years of this century and frequently addressed the issue of her residence abroad. Her stated reasons for preferring life in Europe concerned her writing: "America is the mother of the twentieth century civilization, but she is now early Victorian," claimed Stein in a questionnaire for *transition* magazine. For Stein, America was provincial, restrictive, and belonged—like Queen Victoria—to another century. Stated differently, "a parent's place is never the place to work in." Gertrude Stein found in Paris the place where she wanted to work; although her literary subject was often America, she felt the need to be distanced from it in order to write about it, believing that a writer looking at his own civilization should have "the contrast of another culture before him." (The use of masculine pronouns in this description has telling importance: Stein saw serious writing as a male activity, one to which she made claim by playing the role of the male, by seeing only male Modernists as her colleagues and competitors.) Finally, she hinted at an attitude of constraint, of forfeiture, in American culture: "It was not what France gave you but what it did not take away from you that was important."[7] The latter statement suggests a whole subterrain of resistance to having things "taken away" that Stein shared with many of her compatriots, especially women. The expatriates resented the moral and psychological restraints of America—evidenced in prohibition laws and a staunch middle-class Protestantism inherent in the work ethic—and wished for the freedom of self-determination that was provided by Europe.

Among the expatriate women of Paris was a black American writer and journal editor, Jessie Fauset, whose reasons for expatriation reveal the narrow limits of American life during these years: "I like Paris because I find something here, something of integrity, which I seem to have strangely lost in my own country. It is simplest of all to say that I like to live among people and surroundings where I am not always conscious of 'thou shall not.' I am colored and wish to be known as colored, but sometimes I have felt that my growth as a writer has been hampered in my own country. And so—but only temporarily—I have fled from it" (*Paris Tribune*, 1 February 1925). What Jessie Fauset experienced as a black woman in America was confirmed by Josephine Baker, another woman who discovered that "the French treated black people just the way they do anyone else" (Cody, *Women of Montparnasse*, 33). These women felt, to greater or lesser degrees, the continued reminders that certain forms of behavior were expected of them and certain modes of personal and professional conduct were unavailable to them: "in order to offset criticism, the refined colored woman must not laugh too loudly, she must not stare—in general she must stiffen her self-control even though she can no longer humanly contain herself" (*Paris Tribune*, 1 February 1923). One was more in need of a "stiffened self-control" in America than in Paris, where life was economically, psychologically, and politically easier.

Gertrude Stein's expatriation from America constituted an escape from a life that, rather than being constricted, seemed directionless. Even before she left America for the last time, Stein knew herself to be seeking a purposeful life; and she knew that writing was somehow a part of that purpose. Paris provided a creative stimulus not available anywhere in America, not even in New York (a city Stein hated). Prior to her arrival in Paris, she had apparently established a pattern of dependence on her brother Leo, allowing his decisions—and frequent indecision—to direct her actions. (In fact, Leo had established a prior and even more powerful dependence on his sister.) In 1903, Leo decided to take up an artistic career in Paris, and Gertrude, trying to extricate herself from a disastrously unhappy first love affair with an American woman, followed him to 27, rue de Fleurus, where they set up housekeeping. It was here that she began writing in earnest. She had found both a place and a subject that suited her. Taking her own biography as her artistic subject matter, she analyzed two important factors in her own personal development: the effects of her national identity as an American and the consequences of her sexual orientation toward women.

While it is true that Stein's most autobiographical and sexually explicit works were not published until after her death, making her lesbianism clear and her relationship with Alice B. Toklas specifically detailed, Paris nurtured the writing of these works. In October 1903, she completed *Q.E.D.* (later published as *Things as They Are*, 1950), a novella that explores an unhappy lesbian relationship; it is based on Stein's similar experience just prior to her arrival in Europe earlier that year, while she was still living in Baltimore. Exploration of such relationships occupied her at various times in her writing career, particularly in the early years of the Paris experience and in the formative years of her relationship with Toklas. Stein's own biography and the experiences of her daily life are everywhere available in her writing because for Stein *everything* in her adult life became a subject for and was subjected to her art. So when she speaks of her own experience living in Europe, of the need to distance herself from America in order to write about it, she is also suggesting the need to distance the facts of her personal life in such a way that she can reapproach them through her writing.

Paris offered Stein the privacy and personal freedom to live and write as she pleased, and it provided this valuable freedom for other members of the expatriate community as well. It was only in France that Stein was able to develop a "personal life" in which she could express her sexuality. The American experience with lesbian sexuality had led to painful self-doubts and psychological isolation. In the months prior to her arrival in Europe, she had essentially avoided the personal, directing her energies away from herself, becoming ever more lonely. James R. Mellow comments in his biography of Stein that her early life in San Francisco and her years at Radcliffe and later as a medical student at Johns Hopkins record a young woman's efforts to find friendship and emotional security: "Aside from the companionship of Leo, her adolescent years in California had been interior and introspective. . . . In Baltimore, confronted with the large and busy Stein and Keyser clans, she began 'to lose her lonesomeness.' But she felt a certain strangeness, after the 'rather desperate inner life' she had been leading in California, on moving into the 'cheerful life' of her numerous uncles and aunts" (*Charmed Circle*, 42). There is little in Mellow's portrait of Stein's psychological development to suggest the ego-ridden determination of her adult years. In fact, the ego seems underdeveloped, and there is an obvious lack of purpose and direction to her life in these early years. A definite change of personality occurred after her arrival in Paris, perhaps born of her efforts to shed the protective shell

Leo had provided for so long and to achieve a measure of independence. Initially, however, Paris offered a place in which Stein could fill the emptiness of her life.

This space was filled most obviously, and very quickly, with the dozens of people from various cultures who wanted a glimpse of the art work that Gertrude and Leo Stein were beginning to collect. Although in these early Paris years Gertrude was less in the forefront of the aesthetic discussions that took place on the rue de Fleurus than Leo, she is remembered, as is Natalie Barney, as the head of an important artistic salon. The two salons could not have had less in common: Barney's was formal, old-fashioned, almost stuffy, while the Steins' was casual, unassuming, and open to virtually anyone. Nor could these two women have seen their place in the Paris community less similarly. Natalie Barney never used her salon to further her own career as a writer, nor did she set herself up as the center of the salon. Her purpose was to bring people together, to foster the work of other artists (many of whom were women), and to embrace the cultural life of the Left Bank community. Barney's was a feminist effort that would eventually become an endeavor on behalf of lesbian literature and art. Gertrude Stein's role was quite different. She very soon displaced her brother as the spokesperson on art and literature, placing herself at the center of the Saturday evenings at home, gathering the men around her while consigning the "wives" to other rooms, where they entertained themselves or were entertained by Alice Toklas. Stein began promoting herself as the resident genius of the Left Bank. The Paris setting was soon important because Gertrude Stein was there—and she amply filled the space she had created for herself.[8]

Stein's adopted status among the men of this community reveals much about her artistic aims and psychological motivations. She instinctively realized that these men were creatively productive and intellectually powerful. As such, they were her colleagues, her rivals, and—as in the cases of Ernest Hemingway and Sherwood Anderson—her disciples. Stein wanted a place among the men of this community, and she accepted the implicit patriarchal belief that women were isolated and domesticated precisely because they were weak and nonintellectual. Stein was not able to escape the fate she feared. In fact, the militant and fiercely independent strategy she adopted ensured the very isolation she had come to Paris to escape. Stein's Paris years record her struggle to prove that she was stronger, more talented, and intellectually superior to the men. She purposely defined her literary project as separate from Modernism and superior to it; eventually, she accepted as callers to 27, rue de Fleurus, only those who swore absolute loyalty to her, men who agreed to become followers in her literary school. To understand Stein's place in Paris, then, one must understand her position among male Modernists. Specifically, it is necessary to examine the conspicuous competition and often brutal hostility that Stein felt for Joyce, an expatriate whose reasons for being in Paris were not really so different from her own. Stein thought of herself as a genius and regularly proclaimed herself to be one. Although less vocal on the subject, Joyce clearly also saw himself as a genius and set out to be the most important writer of the twentieth century.

When Joyce arrived in Paris to embark on a career as a medical student at the Ecole de Médecine in 1903, Gertrude Stein had just arrived in Paris, having given up the prospects of a career in medicine at Johns Hopkins University. Joyce also quickly abandoned his efforts in order to take up literary ventures; by the time of his return to Paris in 1920, he had published poetry, a collection of short stories, a play, and an important first novel, *A Portrait of the Artist as a Young Man*. By 1920, Gertrude Stein had published a collection of short stories, a volume of poetry, and some word portraits (much of her writing during these years, however, remained unpublished at the time). She had become in the intervening seventeen years a defender and explicator of her own experimental literary forms, something of an expert on avant-garde painting, and a well-respected if not often read writer of the Left Bank. The period of her great public renown was still ahead of her, as was Joyce's, reaching its zenith in the next two decades, after the publication of *The Making of Americans* and *The Autobiography of Alice B. Toklas*. But the Left Bank community already belonged to her: she discovered it, founded it, cultivated it, and enjoyed whatever measure of *la gloire* it provided her. By now, Paris was her "hometown," and she jealously guarded her home territory. In *Ulysses,* whose publication in Paris in 1922 was, according to Janet Flanner, the great literary event of the decade, a young Stephen Dedalus—just returned from the Left Bank—comments to his Dublin contemporaries: "You suspect . . . that I may be important because I belong to the *faubourg St. Patrice* called Ireland for short. . . . But I suspect . . . that Ireland must be important because it belongs to me" (*Ulysses,* 645). Whether the *faubourg St. Germain* belonged to Stein or to Joyce in the twenties and thirties was of crucial importance to Gertrude Stein. While she worried constantly about her position among the expatriates, Joyce abstracted himself from such local concern, more worried about whether Dubliners were adequately aware of his achievements.

By 1920, Gertrude Stein had been in Paris so long that hardly anyone remembered when she had not been there. She had sunk roots deep into the city. But despite the fact that she was a public figure—written about, talked about—she kept very much to herself. Writing in remembrance of those years, Matthew Josephson comments that "Gertrude Stein in all her years in Paris lived within her own walls so to speak" (Ford, *Left Bank Revisited*, xxiii). He seems to mean by this that she showed little interest in the French writing of the period (indeed, she read little in French, claiming that it was a language to be spoken) and that she mixed rarely with French artists and intellectuals. It is true that she showed little interest in literary experimentalism other than her own and that her relationships with other writers were often stormy, since she cast herself as a teacher among apprentices. But a long-standing relationship with Picasso developed from her quite genuine interest in modern art. This relationship had its difficulties too, as the two strong egos worked out their aesthetic premises in conversation with each other over many years. Here, however, the friendship appeared to rest on neutral ground: since Picasso and Stein worked in different media, there was no inherent competition and they met on equal terms. Stein acknowledged and supported Picasso's genius, while he often said to her *"expliquez-moi cela,"* giving Stein her lead. Like her brother, she loved to explain, and Picasso's methods and hers actually seemed almost equivalent to her at a certain point in her career. She once commented: "Well, Pablo is doing abstract portraits in painting. I am trying to do abstract portraits in my medium, *words"* (*Charmed Circle*, 202).

But Stein chose carefully those with whom she shared her views, and the scene of such exchanges was nearly always her home, where she felt comfortable among her paintings and manuscripts. She was rarely, if ever, seen in Montparnasse cafes; she seldom attended the literary occasions arranged by others. The one time she appeared at someone else's salon, she attended an evening in her own honor, arranged by Natalie Barney. An evening at Shakespeare and Company at which Edith Sitwell was asked to honor Stein by reading Stein's work nearly foundered when Sitwell began reading her *own* work. By the early 1920s, Stein's relationship with Shakespeare and Company was severely strained, because Stein could not understand or forgive Sylvia Beach for her support of James Joyce. In the early years when both Stein and Joyce were frequent visitors to the rue de l'Odéon, they managed never to encounter one another. Stein and Toklas stopped visiting the bookshop, transferring their membership to the American Library on the Right Bank when it became known that Beach would publish Joyce's *Ulysses*. Later, after Beach broke with Joyce, Stein renewed her friendship with Shakespeare and Company.

It is not surprising, then, that Stein and Joyce did not meet until 1930— and then only once. The accounts of the meeting vary, Sylvia Beach and Alice B. Toklas offering separate versions. Beach claims to have introduced them at the home of sculptor Jo Davidson, where she watched them "shake hands quite peacefully" (*Shakespeare and Company*, 32). Toklas says they met at the home of Eugene and Maria Jolas and that Joyce commented to Stein, "how strange that we share the same *quartier* and have never met," to which Stein doubtfully replied, "yes" (Ellmann, *James*

Joyce, 529; *Charmed Circle,* 300). Stein seems to have brooded over the fact that Joyce never took the opportunity to meet her, feeling that her position as the literary experimentalist was the more senior: "Joyce is *good.* He is a *good* writer. Let's not say anything about that. But who started the whole thing? My first great book, *The Making of Americans,* was published in 1905. That was long before the birth of *Ulysses.*"[9]

Implicit in this defense against Joyce is anger at his intrusion on territory that Stein considered her own: she was his elder, the precursor, and assumed it to be his duty to call upon her. Whatever Joyce thought of Stein (whose work he had not read, just as she probably had not read his) was carefully hidden by his consummate concern with his own writing. Although they were both published in the same little magazines, the *Little Review, transition,* and *This Quarter,* Joyce remained aloofly disinterested in Stein's work, as he was in the work of any other writer except himself. Like Stein, he fought tenaciously to have his writing published; although he never published it himself at his own expense, as Stein did, he suffered tremendous difficulties in finding publishers. Stein and Joyce shared a total commitment to their artistic ventures, enormous confidence in their own abilities, and egos sufficient to support years of hard work with little recognition or recompense. Also, their writing compulsively reexamined cultures they had left behind: the locus of Stein's writing was always America just as Joyce's was always Ireland. She was escaping a Protestant cultural ethic, as he was escaping a Catholic puritanism. Even their lifestyles, especially during the Paris years, were similarly bourgeois. In some sense, it matters little that hers was a homosexual union and his a heterosexual one, or that he had twenty addresses in as many years and she had one for nearly forty. The settings were similar; both were served by spouses who protected the time and energies of their mates, who preserved an intimate and private home life, who allowed these two writers to work quietly within their own walls. Their lives were exceedingly private, almost secret. They were not personally available to the public at large and were rarely seen except by close friends. Their "public" images were shadows of the real lives that were spent at home, at work.

Critics have had a particularly difficult time assessing Stein, because much about her personality, behavior, and mental attitude is uncongenial even to those who admire her creative work.[10] She presents particular problems for feminist critics because, although an important woman in twentieth-century literature and culture, she remained absolutely uninterested in supporting the work of other women or even in acknowledging herself as one of them. As a lesbian, her relationship with Alice Toklas duplicated the imbalance apparent in many heterosexual unions to the extent that Natalie Barney was shocked on feminist grounds by Stein's treatment of Toklas. In a review of the links between lesbianism and the cultural tradition, Blanche Wiesen Cook describes the Stein-Toklas marriage: "Heterosexist society is little threatened by a relationship that appeared so culturally determined. Stein wrote and slept while Toklas cooked, embroidered, and typed. Few feminist principles are evident there to challenge the ruling scheme of things. Then there is the matter of Stein's politics. And her politics, though not simple, seem on balance simply impoverished. She was not a radical feminist. She was Jewish and anti-Semitic, lesbian and contemptuous of women, ignorant about economics and hostile toward socialism" ("'Women Alone Stir My Imagination,'" 730).[11] But heterosexist society *was* threatened by this relationship, one of the best known of its kind in the Paris community (indeed, a "model" for what heterosexuals thought lesbian alliances were like), and the extent to which heterosexuals saw their own relationships mirrored in it is of central concern to this study. The indictment that Cook makes of Stein, however, extends beyond what some may consider the narrow boundaries of "feminism." It assumes in Stein an impoverished humanity.

It is important to situate Stein among the women writers of this community, even though she would argue against such an alignment. While this study focuses on how expatriate women thought of themselves as *women* Modernists, for Stein the question may be: to what extent did she think of herself as a male, and how did that self-perception affect her writing? Evidence from both her personal life and her writing suggests that she saw herself playing roles traditionally assigned to men, adopting a male persona against the feminine weakness to which her womanhood apparently consigned her. This psychological tactic has most often been read in the context of her sexual orientation (commentators note that she employed the male pronoun in her relationship with Toklas, for instance). But the implications of Stein's alliance with the masculine are more complex and more extensive than have so far been suggested. An examination of Stein's use of the adopted masculine identity sheds light not only on the ways she lived her lesbianism but on the ways in which she wrote about that experience. A careful analysis of this living/writing experience unsettles expectations about Stein's relation to women writers of the community and her place among the male Modernists. It also upsets conventional notions of the heterosexual woman writer's experience as distinct from that of the homosexual woman, revealing the extent to which Stein's presence threatened attitudes about lesbian behavior among both homosexual and heterosexual women.

Women's contributions to the Modernist literary movement have been doubly suppressed by history, either forgotten by the standard literary histories of this time or rendered inconsequential by memoirs and literary biographies. Gertrude Stein, the best known of these women, was more important in her historical context than her place in literary history suggests. Hugh Ford has commented, "Although Miss Stein continues to hold a formidable place in accounts of the Paris years, and will obviously continue to do so, she was but one of many talented American exiles of her sex who collectively comprised an extraordinary group of entertainers, artists, and writers" (*Left Bank Revisitied*, 45). Until very recently, when her writings were recovered by feminist critics, Gertrude Stein's literary reputation rested on anecdotal (and often incorrect) information about her life in Paris. Before feminist deconstructive practice provided a means of discussing Stein's writing, her works remained unread, beyond the comprehension of devoted scholars and of little interest to literary raconteurs. Considered the *doyenne* of literary Paris, Stein was a formidable presence in the expatriate community. But she was also a laughingstock, the butt of jokes that mocked her looks, her lifestyle, her relationships with her brother and with Alice B. Toklas, even her art collection; the term *doyenne*, one suspects, was as often applied in disparagement as in praise. One cannot resist the conclusion, then, that Stein's struggle to be taken seriously as a writer would have been less pronounced, her literary reputation more secure, her work more often read and taught had she been a man.

Literary Midwifery

If the powerful influence that Stein presumably wielded during these Paris years seems not to have outlived her, what of those other women who now serve as filler on a large canvas dominated by men? The editorial work and publishing efforts of these other women, the literary *soirées* they organized, their appearances in court on behalf of the Revolution of the Word, the selling, advertising, and promotion of Modernism, are usually subordinated to the literary contributions of the men whose work they promoted. These women are viewed as the midwives to the birth of Modernism, women who served traditional female roles in aiding this literary *accouchement*. Their own descriptions of their contributions often appear naive, unconsciously dissembling, cloaked by metaphors in which they serve as attendants to this literary process. In the effort to find an American publisher for *Ulysses*, for example, Sylvia Beach tried to determine what her claims as first publisher of the work were. When she was advised by a friend that she probably had no claims on the book (despite the fact that she held a contract signed by herself and James Joyce assuring her of such rights), she abandoned her search. Commenting on this decision in her memoirs, Beach wrote: "And after all, the books were Joyce's. A baby belongs to its mother, not to the midwife, doesn't it?" (*Shakespeare and Company*, 205). One doubts whether Sylvia Beach, who had risked so much on Joyce's behalf—nearly losing her bookshop because of the financial support she had given his work—really believed that she was merely the midwife to his literary creativity.[12] Even if the sentiment were true, the metaphor nonetheless reflects a strangely mixed response to womanhood. It is significant that Beach chose to describe her contribution in terms that are role-defined: even among women there appears to be an order determined by biological rights, in this case the mother's over the midwife's.

Although Joyce would surely have approved of Beach's metaphor, having often equated literary creativity with the birth process himself, it is more often assumed that it was men who created Modernism—that the event itself was a peculiarly masculine one. It was Eliot, Joyce, Proust, Hemingway, Fitzgerald, Gide, Picasso, Pound, Stravinsky, and a half-dozen others whose genius overturned cultural history. But how crucial was it to the Modernist movement—as a movement—that Nancy Cunard or Caresse Crosby published and printed books that were sold by Adrienne Monnier and Sylvia Beach (themselves the publishers in English and French of Joyce's *Ulysses*); or that Maria Jolas worked steadily, as did Margaret Anderson, Winifred Ellerman, Jane Heap, Amy Lowell, and Harriet Weaver, to publish in little magazines work so radically experimental that it could have no other outlet; or that Janet Flanner, in her "Letter from Paris" in the *New Yorker*, announced each of these publishing events to an American public eager for news of the Paris literary scene? Modernism, we should not forget, was a literary, social, political, and publishing event. And these women saw to it that this message had its medium. Their contributions differed little from those of Ezra Pound, who is remembered for similar efforts on behalf of Modernism. (He is also remembered for important literary contributions—poetry, theoretical treatises, and translations—while the literary contributions of Modernist women have been overlooked or undervalued.) Pound provided letters of introduction to other writers, secured money for them, found publishers, revised manuscripts, wrote letters to the editors of the *Herald* and *Tribune* about these writers and their writings—in short, he marketed them. These activities have not been viewed as somehow tangential to Modernism: indeed, they may seem to define the very energy and intellectual force of Modernism itself, in recognition of which Hugh Kenner has termed this movement the "Pound Era."

At the center of the vortex whose "patterned energies" he controlled, Pound directed the intellectual energies of others, defining the kinds of poetry and prose that were to be called "modern," encouraging his friends to follow his prescripts in composing this kind of literature, convincing journal editors to publish the work once it had been written. From the vortex Pound directed what Wyndham Lewis called—in a famous eponym—the "Pound Circus." Except for a brief period in which Pound actively supported and publicized the work of H. D., whose very signature as "H. D., Imagiste" he created, his efforts were directed at promoting the literary careers of men—T. S. Eliot, James Joyce, Wyndham Lewis, William Carlos Williams, among others. Pound seemed incapable of not "taking over" the literary enterprises he encountered. After being appointed as "European" or "foreign" editor on several journals—*Poetry*, the *Little Review*, and the *Egoist*—Pound quickly moved to change or solidify the literary directions of these publications. For many, it is Pound's contributions to these journals that are best remembered, suggesting that the magazines published little of intrinsic worth prior to his assistance. Harriet Monroe (*Poetry*) was thought to publish only stodgy, out-of-date items; Margaret Anderson (*Little Review*) apparently had little notion what directions she wished her magazine to take prior to Pound's appearance on its masthead. Pound eagerly took on the role of literary impresario. Kenner reports that he solicited subscribers; provided lists of people to receive sample copies; forwarded items for publication; advised on questions of layout and production; cursed faulty proofreading of copy; fussed, fretted, and controlled in his usual energetic fashion (*Pound Era*, 281–282). A glance at copies of the *Little Review*, however, reveals the persistence of Jane Heap's critical opinions (which began appearing in 1916) and Margaret Anderson's literary contributions.

What is more important than speculation about which of the two women possessed the more reliable critical eye is the realization that Pound's relationships with all women were awkward and strained. In particular, he found friendships with highly independent and forceful women almost impossible to maintain, in part perhaps because such women—Jane Heap among them—refused to capitulate to his demands. With the single exception of his long friendship with Natalie Barney, who provided him some financial support over the years, it was impossible for Pound to maintain relationships with homosexual women. Both editors of the *Little Review* were lesbian; although for a while Margaret Anderson allowed Pound's enthusiasms to direct the journal, when they later met in Paris, she found him high-strung, agitated, and "over-elaborate" in his attitude toward women. Irritated at the way he treated women and the extent to which he used the *Little Review* to aggrandize himself, she dropped him from the masthead the following year. And thereupon, argue several male critics, the journal sank into eccentric mediocrity.

The *Little Review* has been particularly ill-treated by commentators on the period. Frederick Hoffman has stated that "Jane Heap obviously did not like *Ulysses*" ("Conversation and Experiment," 3). In Margaret Anderson's personal copy of this text, she penned a note of response: "*Why* these eternal inaccuracies? Jane *loved* 'Ulysses' from the first moment, as can be easily proved by reading her *L[ittle] R[eview]* comments." In response to Hoffman's comment that Heap "had little or no perspective for a judgment," Anderson wrote, "Just what she did have!"

Writing to Solita Solano on 11 November 1972, Anderson said, "I wish, when critics write of me, they would mention what E[zra] said: 'No editor in America, save Margaret Anderson, even felt the need of, or responsibility for, getting the best writers concentrated—i.e., brought them together—in an American periodical.' It was E[zra] who influenced me to publish 'Ulysses'—he simply sent the manuscript. I published it because I loved the 'Portrait of the Artist' and because of the magic words in the first chapter of 'U[lysses].'" In the early years of the *Little Review* Margaret Anderson was often depressed at the poor quality of material the journal published, and she saw herself as heavily indebted to Pound and Joyce for having "saved" the reputation of the journal. Later she revised her reading of the early years, giving credit to her own sense of what directions the journal should take and to Jane Heap for her fine literary judgment.

Harriet Shaw Weaver's editorship of the English journal *Egoist* (formerly a feminist journal titled the *New Freewoman* edited by Dora Marsden) was virtually controlled by Pound, who devoted space to avant-garde writing. Male writers (Pound, Lewis, Eliot, and Joyce) dominated the pages of the *Egoist*, while women writers (such as Rebecca West) made fewer appearances as Pound extended his control over the magazine. In 1922, despite the legal proceedings brought against the *Little Review* for serial publication of *Ulysses*, Harriet Shaw Weaver—the woman who financially supported Joyce for more than twenty years—undertook an Egoist Press edition of *Ulysses*, disregarding the danger of police raids that threatened confiscation of the book. By that time Pound had left London (in spring 1920), having already declared in 1913 that "the important work of the last 25 years has been done in Paris." Within two years he would leave Paris for Rapallo, apparently having determined that the promise of Paris as a center of literary activity had not been fulfilled. Perhaps it is true, as Kenner contends, that "there were no more capitals" and that "the Paris decade" was one of "facilities but no city" (*Pound Era*, 387).

Kenner also argues that Pound assumed Modernism to be a thoroughly masculine enterprise because the women had no talent (or very little). Writing of the change of terminology from "Imagism" to "Vorticism" effected by Pound in the first issue of *Blast* (June 1914), Kenner states: "A Movement in part defines one's company, and Imagism, invented to launch H.D., soon entailed negotiating with dim and petulant people: Fletcher, say, or Flint, or Aldington, and eventually Miss Lowell. It is folly to pretend, in the way of historians with books to fill, that they were of Pound's stature. Vorticism implied his alliance with his own kind: Gaudier, Lewis" (*Pound Era,* 191). It is certainly open to question whether Henri Gaudier and Wyndham Lewis were of Pound's stature, just as it is open to question whether, in leaving H. D. behind with the Imagists, Pound had decided that her work was not up to his standards. His reasons for leaving her and the movement associated with her remain far more complex than definitions of literary movements might suggest. Pound's early publicity efforts on behalf of H. D.'s writing and his later silence on that writing have affected the ways in which H. D. has been read and remembered as a Modernist poet. She is still most often remembered for her early poetry, written when she was 25 years old and supposedly under his direction. Literary historians have until recently been content to leave her in the poetic cocoon in which Pound wrapped her in April 1912, "H. D., Imagiste." Retrospectively, it seems fortuitous that Pound did not continue directing Hilda Doolittle's writing. In *End to Torment,* published after her death, H. D. admitted that his presence had been restrictive, that she feared his censure, and that her fear of failing to meet his severe standards produced a writing block. What she did not seem to realize was that her mastery of Imagist forms threatened Pound, that he found her poetic practice superior to his own.

Two Modernist Interpretations: Linguistic Routes and Postwar Despair

In reading a literary movement, asserts Kenner, we give it definition. And in making Modernism a product of the "Pound Era," its theory and practice contained in the thinking and writing of a single figure who dominates all aspects of the literary scene, we render Modernism monolithic. In Kenner's definition, the literary practice of Modernism is that defined by Pound as Vorticism—a literary movement that (both Pound and Kenner agree) was brought to an untimely end by the Great War. Like many other of the "isms" that collectively comprised Modernism, Vorticism was particularly short-lived and, except as a continuing metaphor for a certain narrowly defined literary practice around which Kenner plots *The Pound Era,* the literary effects of this movement died with the second— and last—issue of Wyndham Lewis's *Blast.* In writing the story of certain Modernists within the context of such a brief literary phenomenon, Kenner's analysis points up the very real problems in trying to define a complex literary movement or to fit that movement neatly into an historical period.

For Kenner, the crucial concepts that underlie Modernism were born in the years just prior to World War I. And it was the war, in Kenner's view, that drained the energies of these early efforts, that rendered them useless, that altered the political and historical backdrop against which literature was written. Much of *The Pound Era* is deliberately anachronistic, from the Jamesian prose of the opening chapter that invokes "Ghosts and Benedictions" and follows the shade of Henry James in a Chelsea street in a year before the outbreak of the war, to its elaborate exegesis of the linguistic roots of Modernist poetry in Greek and Latin. *The Pound Era*, like Modernism itself, seems to be about language—the history of words and the principles by which sentences construct themselves. Kenner's work constructs a grammar for this literary event, interests itself in the syntax and diction of the modern. Indeed, an interest in language would seem to define the modern, and certain linguistic practices (evident in the work of Eliot, Joyce, Pound, and Williams) would characterize Modernism. The men of 1914 were schooled in the classics, shared a knowledge of Greek and Latin; men of the previous generation, of Henry James's era, had participated in the "Classics Renaissance" that began in the 1870s with Heinrich Schliemann's discovery of Troy. Pound, Eliot, and Joyce shared—as Kenner points out—a knowledge of these ancient languages and cultures, and although Pound complained that his Latin was weak and Joyce learned some Greek on his own, these men participated in an educational process that presumably demanded knowledge of the Greek and Roman cultures whose classical languages would be addressed by Modernist linguistic experiments. (Need it be noted that knowledge of Latin and Greek was not to be taken for granted among women educated in these years? H. D., Natalie Barney, and Renée Vivien learned Greek on their own in order to read the fragments of Sappho that became available in the 1890s, and the one woman Modernist whose writing consistently turns on classical sources of English words is Djuna Barnes, who received no formal education at all and who learned etymology by reading the *New English Dictionary*.)

Kenner's reading of Modernism uncovers its classical roots and recovers in the contemporary word the echoes of an historical and patriarchal past. It is noteworthy that Kenner invokes Sappho, celebrating the discovery of her work made possible by a chemical process that revealed hidden layers in the parchment copies produced thirteen centuries after her death. He reminds us that her work, like that of Catullus, had been lost because "men [could] find no way to relate their interest in it to other interests" (*Pound Era*, 557). This loss cut women off from their literary heritage; initially it was men who created a modern text from this ancient one, created a palimpsest that simultaneously revealed and rewrote the literary past. Existing under erasure in this modern text was an ancient woman, whose literary forms were barely visible under the modern chemicals used to decipher them (*Pound Era*, 5).

There is another reading of the historical situation of Modernism, however, that defines it specifically as a post–World War I phenomenon, that emphasizes the role the war played in creating the psychology of despair in which the ensuing literary movement would ground itself. This definition takes as its controlling metaphor the No Man's Land between the trenches of World War I, viewing the modern world as a landscape in which the past is not recoverable and the future offers no hope. In this definition, Modernism is grounded in the ashes of burned-out rationalism and positivism. Against a bankrupt culture, argues Susan Stanford Friedman, only through the agency of language could culture be remade:

> The starting point of modernism is the crisis of belief that pervades twentieth-century western culture: loss of faith, experience of fragmentation and disintegration, and shattering of cultural symbols and norms. At the center of this crisis were the new technologies and methodologies of science, the epistemology of logical positivism, and the relativism of functionalist thought—in short, major aspects of the philosophical perspectives that Freud embodied. The rationalism of science and philosophy attacked the validity of traditional religious and artistic symbols while the growing technology of the industrialized world produced the catastrophes of war on the one hand and the atomization of human beings on the other. Art produced after the First World War recorded the emotional aspect of this crisis; despair, hopelessness, paralysis, angst, and a sense of meaninglessness, chaos, and fragmentation of material reality. In a variety of ways suited to their own religious, literary, mythological, occult, political, or existentialist perspectives, they emerged from the paralysis of absolute despair to an active search for meaning. The search for order and pattern began in its own negation, in the overwhelming sense of disorder and fragmentation caused by the modern materialist world. The artist as seer would attempt to create what the culture could no longer produce: symbol and meaning in the dimension of art, brought into being through the agency of language, the Word or Logos of the twentieth century. (*Psyche Reborn*, 97)

Beautifully articulated, this description of the Modernist crisis is the one that underwrites virtually every study of the expatriate writing experience, that explains the presence of former ambulance drivers in Paris and explicates their literary practice.[13] This reading reconfirms earlier readings of the period by Malcolm Cowley and Frederick Hoffman, both of whom overlook (except for Willa Cather and Gertrude Stein) the very existence of women in this literary community. Their evaluations, moreover, consistently stress the masculine experience, in part because the evaluators are themselves men. Not unsurprisingly, there has as yet been no study of this period written by a woman, nor has there been a study that specifically looks at women's contributions to this literary renaissance. Of 134 entries in the biographical appendix to Hoffman's study, only 17 are women. He has effectively eliminated women from the Paris literary landscape.

Cowley and Hoffman both emphasize motives and impressions filtered through a male consciousness and take special care to protect the masculine identity in relation to the literary scheme. Hoffman places a male protagonist under analysis, consistently relying on the masculine pronoun when he poses such rhetorical questions as: "What could a young man do? . . . how could he hope to preserve himself, to keep his selfness pure?" (*The Twenties*, 13). He emphasizes the reactionary spirit of the "new man" against the Old Gang of writers, those men of late-nineteenth-century American fiction, while Cowley stresses a theme common to studies of postwar Paris, the effects of the war on male consciousness:

> It would be interesting to list the authors who were ambulance or camion drivers in 1917. Dos Passos, Hemingway, Julian Green, William Seabrook, E. E. Cummings, Slater Brown, Harry Crosby, John Howard Lawson, Sidney Howard, Louis Bromfield, Robert Hillyer, Dashiell Hammett . . . one might almost say that the ambulance corps and the French military transport were college-extension courses for a generation of writers. But what did these courses teach?
> They carried us to a foreign country, the first that most of us had seen; they taught us to make love, stammer love, in a foreign language. . . . They taught us courage, extravagance, fatalism, these being the virtues of men at war; they taught us to regard as vice the civilian virtues of thrift, caution, and sobriety; they made us fear boredom more than death. All these lessons might have been learned in any branch of the army, but ambulance service had a lesson of its own: it instilled into us what might be called a *spectatorial* attitude. (*Exile's Return*, 38)

The war became the subject of the literature of the 1920s, and women, who were assumed to be on the fringes of the war adopting a "spectatorial" attitude of their own, were thought to have experienced it at second remove. Gertrude Stein used her experience driving for the American Fund for French Wounded in some lyric poetry, and Edith Wharton wrote several books about the war: *Fighting France* (1915), *The Marne* (1918), *French Ways and Their Meanings* (1919), and *A Son at the Front* (1923). Of these, *A Son at the Front* met particular critical ridicule, but all of these works have been reviewed by men who suggest that Wharton's perspective on the war was too "removed" to be pertinent. Frederick Hoffman comments that Wharton "was but one member of an older generation that thought as she did about the war: non-participants, women for the most part, they saw the issues of the war more simply (and therefore more 'clearly') than did the writers of the so-called war generation" (*The Twenties*, 48). For Hoffman, women were unlikely raconteurs of the male war experience.

Whereas Cowley and Hoffman base the expatriate Modernist experience on a form of male bonding produced by the actual experiences of

World War I, Kenner and Friedman see the war as an apocalyptic revelation announcing the end of Western civilization in its pre—1914 form. The latter two critics see the problem of Modernism as an epistemological one that questions the relation of human experience to human knowledge. For them, Modernist writing was defined not by its use of the Great War as subject matter but by the larger issue of the cultural bankruptcy of Western civilization that the war seemed to confirm. While Cowley and Hoffman restrict their readings to American writers, Kenner and Friedman expand theirs to include English and Europeans. But the major difference in these sets of interpretations rests on the emphasis given to the role of language in Modernist writing. The common denominator among the writers Kenner and Friedman discuss is a concern with language, an exploration of the ways language constructs human experience.[14]

Both Kenner and Friedman focus on the role of the *word* in Modernist writing. For Kenner, the word is a curiosity whose ways of meaning can be explained by scientific research: first one applies to a dictionary and next one invokes grammatical systems. Friedman's Word is, rather, mystical and mysterious. Its power to shape and remake the world invokes the very power of God. This Word has powers beyond the scientific and against which the powers of scientific rationalism fail: Kenner's word can merely explain the world; Friedman's Word can remake the world.

That these two critics would generate significantly different descriptions of Modernism is not very surprising. More surprising is the extent to which the worlds they describe both exclude women. Women are denied access to Kenner's modern world because they have not learned the classical languages, Latin and Greek, on which that world is constructed. Such exclusion is not permanent, however: perspicacious women like H. D., Natalie Barney, Virginia Woolf, even the ridiculed Amy Lowell, undertook to teach themselves these languages. (There are other barriers to the Kennerian world for women, ones that will be discussed at some length later, but for the moment this problem of "classical education" suffices to remark woman's separate place in the Modernist hemisphere.) Friedman's definition denies women an experiential grounding in the world; that is, this definition in no way suggests the radical *difference* of women's experience. Claiming the war as the central factor in Modernist thinking, her definition is silent on the issue of woman's relation to that war. This silence is troubling, since it leaves the door open for agreement with another tacit assumption about postwar writing (an assumption held by Cowley and Hoffman)—that women could not participate fully in the writing of the postwar decade precisely because they had not directly experienced the war. A description of Modernism that emphasizes "despair, hopelessness, paralysis, angst, and a sense of meaninglessness, chaos, and fragmentation of material reality" excludes—for a variety of reasons—many women Modernists. These terms do not describe the visions of Gertrude Stein, Djuna Barnes, Mina Loy, Marianne Moore, or Edith Sitwell, for instance. And if it can be said that H. D. and Virginia Woolf experienced despair, hopelessness, paralysis, and a sense of meaninglessness in the world as direct effects of the postwar condition, then their separate ways of experiencing loss of hope and fragmentation—different from the male experience and distinct from each other—must be acknowledged.

We must remind ourselves, for instance, that the "reality" of these years exists today as a set of *idées reçues* constructed largely by men. We read their fiction in the literary works that have collectively defined Modernism, in the assessments of such men as Cowley and Hoffman, in the biographies—of both men and women expatriates—written by men, and in the letters, notebooks, and diaries of such writers as T. S. Eliot, F. Scott Fitzgerald, James Joyce, Ezra Pound, and William Carlos Williams and the memoirs of Morrill Cody, Robert McAlmon, and Ernest Hemingway. Frederick Hoffman, for instance, consistently employs metaphors of manliness to describe America's youth and vigor at the beginning of the twentieth century. It was a country founded on masculine values and virtues: "The American was an industrial giant, an emotional dwarf . . . he came through with ingenious inventions, processes, methods; he built bigger, better, and faster locomotives and was experimenting with automobiles and playing with airplanes" (*The Twenties*, 11). Such metaphors of experience are unhappy ones not because of their inappropriateness but because of their accuracy. In these years American men defined all that was the country's competitive (and boyish) best.

This apparent retreat to childishness was brought about by what Ann Douglas has called the "feminization of America" (*The Feminization of American Culture*). Men retreated to an earlier stage of their cultural development because women (and men associated with institutions women controlled) had become mothers to them, directing their energies toward limiting man's independence and self-will. Women were the force behind the two most powerful institutions of American life—the family, which served as a domesticating influence on men, and the church, which served to humble them. Alex Small refers to this notion of a "feminized culture" in a complaint that makes women responsible for all the worst ills of American life. Small lists as one of his reasons for preferring Europe:

> The inordinate influence in American life of public spirited women. Of course, the individual who is not poor and helpless may escape their pernicious benevolence, but the spectacle is always there and it is sickening. It is to be dreaded, too, for no one knows what forms it is going to take. These managing women (who may be of any sex) have no respect for liberty. They defend their tyrannies with the claim that all living in society is a restriction

29

on liberty, which is perfectly true, but it is a sophistical excuse for their mischief making. (*Paris Tribune*, 10 July 1930)

All that was expansive, energetic, far-thinking, enthusiastic, and driving was attributed to the masculine; all that was meddling, restrictive, manipulative, and demeaning was attributed to the feminine. Small's commentary overlooks the ways in which patriarchal dominance and the American spirit of rugged male individualism had, by the very denial of the feminine, created a particularly subversive version of it. Small denies the inevitable link between the "feminine" and the "female" in his metaphor of "managing women," thus resisting any investigation of his own misogyny. Whereas men may have seen themselves in flight from a pernicious and powerful feminine influence, women expatriates read the American myth differently, seeing this feminization of culture as an effort to control dark forces that, given their lead, would destroy the Western world.

An alternative fiction—or set of fictions—creates this world from the woman's point of view. These fictions make a claim on our interest not because women wrote truer accounts of these years (if truth is understood in the empirical sense) but because they wrote *different* accounts. These records reveal women's relation to industrial and economic growth, to war, to the dominant institutions of society; they record the constraints on women's personal growth and provide evidence that documents women's emerging independence and deepened self-awareness; they examine the effects of a cultural exchange—of American puritanism for European worldliness. Women's writings in these years demonstrate the degree to which the twenty-two women of this study were culturally freed and fettered by the expatriate experience, their roles determined, in part, by the very transitional nature of exiled Left Bank society. These accounts rewrite the myth that expatriation was always an enabling and liberating act. Perhaps most importantly, a reexamination of women's experience in this community challenges received notions about and accepted definitions of Modernism, forcing us to revise the "modern" context for the "Modernist."

Alternative Modernisms

In a recent essay, Susan Stanford Friedman has elucidated the effects of World War I on certain Modernist women writers, most particularly H. D. She argues that the development of H. D.'s postwar Modernism emerges from an identification with all those who have been "dispersed and scattered after World War I" ("Notes on Recent Writing," 10). Friedman includes H. D. among all those marginal peoples who have fled the forces of history: blacks, Jews, Indians, homosexuals and lesbians, women, and artists ("Modernism of the 'Scattered Remnant'"). Friedman argues that for H. D., as for Anaïs Nin, political activism seemed to "encode a critique of patriarchy and violence. . . . she feared that political organizations reproduce on a dangerously large scale the unresolved violence within the individual." The distrust of political activism is, as Friedman demonstrates, "part of a larger gender-based pattern that includes writers like Virginia Woolf, Gertrude Stein, Dorothy Richardson, May Sinclair, Zora Neale Hurston, Djuna Barnes, and Jean Rhys." Like Nin, H. D. was to ground her political attitudes in personal experience—in particular her experience with the Harlem Renaissance—to develop a "political syncretism, a modernism of the margins rather than the reactionary center." For some women Modernists—in particular, Virginia Woolf, Natalie Barney, Sylvia Beach, Nancy Cunard, Janet Flanner, and Adrienne Monnier—World War I solidified a commitment to liberal causes and a fear of repressive and inhumane political power structures. For each of these women, an effect of the war was a strengthened feminism in awareness of the ways women—among other marginal elements of society—were vulnerable to patriarchal violence. And for some among them, this emergent consciousness of marginalism would lead to psychological collapse (in the cases of Woolf and Cunard) and to a reversal of values as evidenced in anti-Semitism and political reactionism (Gertrude Stein and Natalie Barney). One cannot argue, then, that Modernist politics divide along gender lines—the men reactionary and the women progressive. The political attitudes of these men and women were complex, often marked by contradiction and ambivalence, composed of varied attitudes toward questions of race, social class, and religious commitment, as well as gender. But it is true, as Friedman suggests, that the distinctions between a Modernist center seen to be dominantly reactionary and a marginal political liberalism are generally constructed along gender lines in patterns mapped by this study.

The attempt to define and describe a literary movement as complex as Modernism exposes the divisions and differences among its practitioners even as it plasters over the cracks in the walls in an attempt to create a smooth facade. Kenner calls the age of Modernism "divisive," and by this he seems to mean the ways in which the disaster of World War II (which most saw as the legacy of World War I) separated "the men of the Vortex" from each other, forcing them to work alone during the latter part of their lives. The sense of community and a communal project had been lost. But the age was divisive in other ways, in the sense that it was marked by the differences among individual practices and the differences of ideologies and aesthetics. Imagist Modernism differed significantly from Surrealist Modernism or Futurist Modernism; the Modernism of Paris was

quite different from that of London. And it is this troublesome relationship between the artist and the word, between the writer and the Word,
that marks such differences in literary practice. Modernist experiments
reveal divergent attitudes toward language, one marker of which is gender: women not only experience the world differently from men, they
write that experience differently. Modernist writing by women is significantly unlike that of men, a condition that has often resulted in critical
appraisals that denigrate this writing for not meeting the "standards" of
Modernism set by and for men. But it would be a mistake to assume that
gender distinctions produce writing by women that differs from that of
men in predictable or homogeneous ways. Certainly the works of Hilda
Doolittle and Djuna Barnes bear certain resemblances, because as homosexual women both were writing to some degree against the predominant
patriarchal and heterosexual culture. Yet the writing of these women is
also individualistic, "Modernist" in quite distinct ways.

The double effort to recover the experiences of expatriate women and
to revise accepted notions of women's contributions to Modernism both
invites generalizations and exposes the internal contradictions, differences, and divisions of this literary movement. This undertaking demands
that the very suppositions supporting the investigation be put into question. The notion that Modernism is either monolithic or utterly chaotic,
that it is either private and arcane or holds within its practice a model for
social revolution, must be carefully examined. Certainly the assumption
that sexual gender *alone* can explain differences in social behavior and
literary practice of male and female Modernists requires rigorous inspection. Tempting as it might be, then, to oppose women Modernists to a
parent culture defined as monolithic or to argue that a collective female
experience resulted in a homogeneous women's literature, such arguments
force the delicate network of female relationships and individual achievements of expatriate women into preconceived patterns. Indeed, such readings produce all too predictable results: individual experience (both male
and female) is once again submitted to communal claims. For although
Modernism constituted an overtly acknowledged literary movement (perhaps the first in history), one whose aesthetic principles and literary
claims were codified in a series of manifestos, whose texts were printed in
journals specifically dedicated to the propagation of Modernist literature,
the *practice* of Modernism was highly individualistic, often anarchic, incorporating contradictory impulses under a single "ism."

One must note, for instance, that the term "Modernism" itself is of
fairly recent invention (although Edith Sitwell was using it as early as
1930), a product of the critical heritage that codified the various avant-
garde movements of the early twentieth century, placing them in relation

to one another and drawing together their presumed common elements under the rubric of the Modernist. What may have seemed highly individualistic and diverse, even divisive, in the living moment now appears to have participated in a larger—nearly encompassing—artistic movement. That there was a group of literary practitioners (most of them men) who assembled in London and Paris in these years, working in concert with each other, reading each other's manuscripts, talking and writing together about their literary efforts, is a fact of literary history. That women were rarely a party to these communal writing efforts (except to act as benefactors, publishers, and booksellers for that work) is also a fact of history. It is through the writings of Eliot, Joyce, and Pound and the critical commentaries on such writing that Modernism has been defined.[15] Although it was Ezra Pound whose commentaries on experimental writing spurred the work of his contemporary practitioners, it was the public speeches of T. S. Eliot and the editorial direction of the *Criterion* that introduced and explained what is now taken to be the expression of "High Modernism" to a larger reading public. Among his contemporaries, certain women writers—including Virginia Woolf and Edith Sitwell—took exception to Eliot's emphasis on tradition and the philosophic and moral ordering of experience. Peter Ackroyd comments that in *The Sacred Wood* (1920), for instance,

> Eliot provided literature with an order and certainty all the more potent because these were the qualities lacking in social and political life after the First World War: the older generation had lost its authority, and the younger had not found any way forward. His was not the first attempt to do so in England—T. E. Hulme had sketched out something of a similar kind, and in 1919 Clive Bell wrote a series of essays on "Order and Authority" for the *Athenaeum*. But Eliot's stance was, in the end, more influential. He reaffirmed the status of literature, as a way both of understanding the larger culture and of disciplining private feelings and experience. His own need for order reflected that which existed among his generation; his own fears of fragmentation and meaninglessness ("the Void") were also theirs. (*T. S. Eliot,* 107)

But Eliot's fears were not shared by all of his generation, nor was his obsessive need for order and discipline common to all of his contemporaries. Women especially might be expected to see in the call for order, authority, discipline, and moral certitude a further enforcement of patriarchal claims. In "Modernist Poets" (1930), Edith Sitwell made a quite different claim for contemporary writing, with special attention to women's concerns. Her views, although belated, seem to address precisely the claims made for poetry in *The Sacred Wood:* "Art is magic, not logic. This craze for the logical spirit in irrational shape is part of the present harmful mania for uniformity—in an age when women try to abolish the difference between their aspects and aims and those of men—in an age when the edict has gone forth for the abolition of personality, for the abolition of faces, which are practically extinct. It is because of this hatred of personality, that the crowd, in its uniformity, dislikes artists endowed with an individual vision" ("Modernist Poets," 78). Sitwell—and other women Modernists, including Djuna Barnes, Nancy Cunard, Natalie Barney, Gertrude Stein, and Virginia Woolf—argued an aesthetics of the individual and irrational (and perhaps even the eccentric) against Eliot's claims for tradition and logic.[16] One discovers that expatriate women participate in the Modernist enterprise often seeking to subvert and invert its cultural and aesthetic premises. This women's art is based in difference, in the difference *within* gender and genre, manifest through the inversions and diversions of Modernist logic.

Communities of Expatriates

Within the designated frames of time and place, it is the very definition of "community" that is under examination in this study. The extent to which the expatriates formed a community is, of course, open to speculation. It is not at all clear that among them there was ever a sense of community as such, or of a bonding. It is highly probable that the various relationships among these women developed haphazardly and at random. It is clear, however, that the expatriate residents of the Left Bank were intensely preoccupied with each other, living intellectually and geographically in close proximity to one another. Everyone knew about and was aware of everyone else: the Left Bank was a small town surrounded by an enormously vital large city. The American expatriates all read the same English-language newspapers, went to the same concerts and theater productions, drank and conversed in the same cafes. The privacy of Faubourg salons was replaced by the public setting of cafe life, where the rendezvous was observed and conversations overheard. Experiences were shared by the very fact of living in the same time and place.

It is important, therefore, to distinguish this Left Bank group of artists from the already well-established American colony across the river on the Right Bank. This other group was comprised of businessmen and is of little interest except as it distinguishes the peculiarly American monetary interests in Paris during these years and demonstrates the lengths to which American culture—of the middle-brow, affluent kind—could intrude upon a Paris much in need of American dollars. At the high point of activity, ten thousand Americans resided in Paris (although there seemed at the time to be more than a "mere" ten thousand), the large majority of them among the business community of the Right Bank. Moreover, this community brought with it a support group of other Americans who worked in the banks, schools, real estate agencies, bars, grocery stores, and bowling alleys established for the expatriates. Most of these people attended the American Church, joined American fraternal organizations, and used the American Library. They were on the "overseas payroll" of American businesses with European branches, and members of this group were not really expatriated—they were in residence in France for shorter or longer periods of time, but they remained staunchly American. Few could speak French even passably; a fairly decent French accent was rare.

The expatriate community of the Right Bank was served by its own newspaper, the *Paris Herald,* which kept track of its comings and goings, recounting the adventures of even the most obscure members of that community, precisely because this publicity attracted more American business and sold newspapers. While showing little interest in the Paris cultural scene, the newspaper nonetheless reported items about the "Young Intellectuals" in residence across the river. This nod to the Left Bank was due in part to the necessity for some of the Young Intellectuals to support themselves financially as journalists, working for the *Herald.* The paper considered them "earnest" (a word that would not have been used to describe the Right Bank community) and spoke of their efforts as the "Literary Revolution." That revolution was taking place in Montparnasse and in the *quartier* St. Germain, and those who participated formed a group of no more than two hundred men and women who had neither money nor business interests in Paris. But this community had a newspaper that took undisguised interest in the literary upheaval, and the *Paris Tribune* (an extension of the *Chicago Tribune*) created something of a "community" identity for the Left Bank. It devoted columns to the activities of the Young Intellectuals, the titles of which reveal the journalistic perspective: "La Vie de Bohème," "Rambles through Literary Paris," "Latin Quarter Notes," "What the Writers Are Doing."

These contributions provided a glimpse of the less earnest side of Left Bank life, made the literary revolution a human interest story. Thus some of these portraits are disquieting from the perspective of later history: Radclyffe Hall's sexual orientation is suggested by her "crisp-looking appearance" and the observation that both she and her friend Lady Troubridge wore monocles and used cigarette holders; James Joyce's painful eye illnesses became part of a local legend potentially embarrassing to this immensely private person; e.e. cummings's World War I memoir, *The Enormous Room,* was sold as a bestseller, described as "one of the topnotchers among books about the war." Nevertheless, the paper doggedly tracked the publication records of its readers, reviewed their works, provided them publicity, and paid attention to their literary experiments.

And it is here, in the pages of the *Paris Tribune,* that the women of the Left Bank play significant roles, often as the subjects of literary notes. In the daily record of these years we discover the evidence of the enormous contributions women made to the Modernist enterprise, efforts that have been largely overlooked or underestimated in retrospective evaluations of this community.

2
SECRET PASSAGES:
THE FAUBOURG ST. GERMAIN

To trace the roots of the expatriate woman's experience in Paris, we must return to a period in history that appears to share as little with Paris between the world wars as Henry James's New York shares with contemporary Greenwich Village. We must begin with James's good friend, Edith Wharton, herself a product of Old New York. On a bleak December afternoon in 1893, she stood at the door of a house on the rue Barbet-de-Jouy, a street intersecting the fashionable rue de Varenne, in the heart of the Faubourg St. Germain on the Paris Left Bank. About to ring the bell, she paused. We try to envision her there in the darkening chill, dressed in a somber velvet traveling costume, wrapped in ankle-length wool and fur against the post-Christmas chill, her head supporting a wide and heavily plumed felt hat. She is hidden by the shadows, a woman with stern jaw and sad eyes whose image is now only dimly marked in our memory. We try to trace our descent from hers, to place our experience in the context of her own, to imagine what her situation must have been, to feel the pinch of whalebone stays, the weight of brocaded shawls, the strain of buttoned shoes, to know too well the constraints of a fashionable, wealthy American upbringing. Seeing her poised on that doorstep, the driver of her hansom cab rubbing his hands against the cold as he too awaits an answer to her call, we wonder what significance this woman's experience will hold for those others who will later follow her to Paris. What worlds await Edith Wharton behind the door of the house on Barbet-de-Jouy?

The street on which Edith Wharton stood that afternoon looks very much the same today. The stately houses remain severe enclosures against the advance of the modern world. They hide private gardens that catch the meager sunlight of a December day. Behind iron-grated windows draperies conceal high-ceilinged rooms that ring with music and laughter, that hold art objects and precious libraries, that are warmed by fire-places, friendship, and excellent wines. These are rooms in which lively conversation and the art of gracious living continue to be cultivated like rare flowers, rooms where the cosmopolitan and the intellectual meet on equal footing, where all the forms of *politesse* are carefully preserved against the encroachment of a more modern, vulgar world. Society in this quarter continues to offer the chosen few a life of patrician leisure. This life remains as rigidly harnessed by social custom today as it was in the second half of the nineteenth century, when corseted and girdled women, pinned and bustled into lace and satin, presided over its famous salons. The customs may have changed in the intervening century, but their restrictions remain. On a winter afternoon in December, this Paris of another era lingers in the luminescent reflection of the pale sun on the Seine. A thickening film of frost lends the city a faint blue pallor, just as it did on that afternoon in 1893, and the lights over the bridges at the hour before nightfall glow like gaslamps.

In this twilight we see Edith Wharton, attended by her husband, waiting to be welcomed into French society by the well-known novelist Paul Bourget. A member of the French Academy, Bourget had important acquaintances in literary and intellectual circles; although not a member of the French aristocracy (he was the son of a provincial scholar who had become a professor at the Lycée Louis le Grand in Paris), Bourget could provide Edith Wharton an introduction to academicians and aristocrats alike. Visiting the Whartons in Newport on his first American trip earlier that year, Bourget had already convinced Edith that "she must alter her life to include regular and leisured relationship with the human stimulus in Europe" (Millicent Bell, *Edith Wharton and Henry James,* 56). He was prepared to open the doors of that life to her. Although she would not make her permanent home in Paris for several years, this portentous visit in 1893 would significantly alter her life. At 31 years old, not yet betraying the full range of her literary talent, she was a wealthy, cultured woman with a rare gift for conversation, a passion for elegant clothes, and a restless, unhappy marriage that would be made tolerable by the promise of a new life in Paris. This same longed-for life and her success as writer, hostess, and *femme du monde* would have deleterious effects, however, on the mental stability of her husband, Edward Wharton.

On a snowy March afternoon in 1906, Edith Wharton is again to be found waiting at the Bourget door. She and "Teddy" have returned to Paris, intent this time on establishing permanent residence there. The apartment they found, at 58, rue de Varenne, would serve for their extended visits until 1908. Now the author of *The House of Mirth,* Wharton found herself courted by the Faubourg society to which Paul Bourget had introduced her. Later, when in her own description of the events

Edith Wharton "finally settled" in the rue de Varenne, *The House of Mirth* was appearing in the *Revue de Paris*. She tells us in *A Backward Glance* that this serialization of the novel "was attracting attention in its French dress, partly because few modern English and American novels had as yet been translated, but chiefly because it depicted a society utterly unknown to French readers" (287). Finding herself something of a celebrity, she set about establishing a French life, a life that would soon exclude her husband, whose bouts with neurasthenia were becoming more serious and from whom she was to be divorced in 1913.[1] The eagerness with which Edith Wharton turned to a new European life betrays a desperate urgency, a need to escape a marriage and manner of living she found increasingly stultifying and confining. Millicent Bell comments on this decision to leave America:

> Edith Wharton turned to her life in the rue de Varenne with an eagerness born of long-felt, complex expectations. With an energy and interest that seem vulgar until we understand the motive behind them, she set herself to entering Parisian society. And to the rue de Varenne, even that first year, came new acquaintances from all of France's elite—the aristocracy of letters and the Academy as well as the old aristocracy of the Faubourg. . . . With the help of a few old Paris friends she conceived and attained the ambition of the Parisian hostess; she, a foreigner, built a salon. (127)

The Faubourg

Edith Wharton wanted a *French* life. Among the reasons she gave for her expatriation were her husband's suffering "from the harsh winds and sudden changes of temperature of the New York winter" and her own need "to find the kind of human communion I called for" (*A Backward Glance*, 257). Of the two, the second reason was the more compelling; the first was the reason she gave Teddy for taking him away from his American life. Although her husband's physical and mental sufferings continued—indeed worsened—after the move to Paris, Edith Wharton found there an intellectual, artistic, and cultural milieu in which she moved with ease. She was to spend the next thirteen years of her life in this city, later moving to the French countryside; her expatriation in France continued until her death in 1937. Before taking up official residence in France, however, she studied carefully the society she was later to conquer, she learned its history and literature, she made extensive journeys between its borders, she shed those vestiges of Americanism that her future compatriots might find *impétueux*, she practiced her new role as salon hostess, all the while summoning the courage to make an important break with her past. Aware that her success or failure would turn on the nuances of social form, Edith Wharton turned her energies in the early years of this century to

39

mastering the idiosyncrasies of French protocol in the Faubourg St. Germain. Wharton's biographer, R. W. B. Lewis, describes this area of Paris as a quarter that yielded

> less to a geographical than to a social, historical, and intellectual definition. It was the town seat of the most imposing of the French nobility; an aristocratic society slowly being penetrated by the bourgeois artists and intellectuals; the standard of social behavior for the other faubourgs in Paris; an atmosphere, a cluster of traditions, a wholly assumed but to the outsider a strangely inconsistent human world. It was the setting of those great *salons* which the thirty-five year old Marcel Proust was at that very moment beginning to contemplate exploring in a long novel, having already written half a dozen articles for *Figaro* about the most worldly of them. (*Edith Wharton,* 174)

But in the early 1890s the Faubourg had seen little of the bourgeois or of artists; it was a stronghold of upper-class French society, one that Edith Wharton was determined to penetrate. Edith Wharton was not attracted to the fashionable salons about which Proust wrote, salons in which women of the *demi-monde* mixed with aged duchesses, in which homosexual men appeared in rouge and wigs and homosexual women wore tuxedos with monocles tucked in the pockets. Not certain enough of her social standing in European society, a shy and insecure person, Wharton sought the most conservative of drawing rooms. She dared not risk exposure to a rebellious and often *risqué* modernity; she needed the protection of just those social and intellectual traditions on which Proust and other moderns cast such a jaundiced eye.

Writing of this closed salon life forty years later, Wharton displayed a distanced humor about its obsessive need to protect the sanctity of the drawing room from invasions by the masses: "In the Paris I knew . . . everybody would have told me . . . that *tout le monde* had long since come in, that all the old social customs were tottering or already demolished, and that the Faubourg had become as promiscuous as the Fair of Neuilly. The same thing was no doubt said a hundred years earlier" (*A Backward Glance,* 259). But "every convention of that compact and amiable little world" was of interest to her, was a confirmation of the aristocratic tendencies and formal bearing of her own conduct, and had become—even before her official entrance in 1910—a subject of her fiction. In 1906, her novella *Madame de Treymes,* a study of an American-born marquise, was published in *Scribner's* magazine. As R. W. B. Lewis suggests, something of herself and her own experience went into this portrait: "it was the first fruit of her dip into Parisian society, and that contradictory world is appraised with a discerning eye" (*Edith Wharton,* 164). This world, so stuffy and remote, represented to Edith Wharton a liberation from the even narrower world of Old New York, where custom enforced a rigid morality and weakened intellectual vigor. She seemed not to realize in 1906, presiding over her first dinner party, that a younger generation was already seeing her as a symbol of outmoded gentility and would openly rebel against both the values that supported salon society and the narrative forms that recorded this society.[2] Outside the Faubourg, Edith Wharton was considered *démodé* at almost the precise moment she experienced the exhilaration of success within the borders of Old World Paris.

By 1906, Marcel Proust, thirty-five years old, had left the salon world and had begun writing about it in *A la recherche du temps perdu*. Although Edith Wharton and Marcel Proust were said to be part of the same social circles in the Faubourg St. Germain for over sixteen years and were to have many mutual friends, they did not meet: "To be told that the only people who really interested him were Dukes and Duchesses, and that the only place where one could hope to find him was at the Ritz, after midnight, was enough to put me off," Wharton wrote (*Edith Wharton*, 402). Having courted a society infused with a *snobisme* supported by conservative intellectual and social values, Wharton was apparently suspicious of Proust's own peculiar brand of *snobisme*, one that valued social privilege and breeding above intellectual or artistic endeavor, that consorted with crass, rich American expatriates. For Wharton, it was not enough to be titled; one must be well read, genteel, articulate, and intellectual as well. Perhaps, however, Wharton misread Proust's need to observe those who had become his subject matter, as he might have misread her need to observe an older version of salon life. Lewis comments:

> In the high reaches of Parisian social life, they missed each other as though by divine planning. Proust entered the Faubourg world in 1894, at the age of twenty-three. After becoming the familiar of ducs and duchesses, the comtes and comtesses he would draw upon, splice, and reshape for his epic novel, he withdrew abruptly following the second trial of Alfred Dreyfus in 1899. . . . By the time, in 1906, that Edith Wharton was introduced to the aristocratic milieu, Proust had been absent from it for some years. The war and a need for broader human contact lured Proust back into the world, in particular to the center of social gravity at the Ritz Hotel. But at this stage it was Edith Wharton who had largely retired from the scene—racking personal problems had already caused her to curtail her social involvements, and her refugee work reduced them even more drastically. In addition, of course, the Ritz represented what she detested most about the changing city. (*Edith Wharton*, 401)

Wharton describes her entrance into Paris salon life in her memoirs, *A Backward Glance*. Here she introduces the reader to the various titled aristocrats and established artists and writers she met at the home of the widowed Comtesse de Fitz-James, the woman who prior to World War I conducted the most prestigious of the Parisian salons. Wharton admits that "lists of names are not of much help in evoking an atmosphere; but the pre-war society of the Faubourg Saint-Germain has been so utterly dispersed and wiped out that as a group the frequenters of Madame de Fitz James' drawingroom have an almost historical interest" (269). If such figures as the playwrights Paul Hervieu (a close friend of Proust's, a model for Swann, and an active Dreyfusard) and the Marquis de Flers, the Comte Alexandre de Laborde (a man described by Wharton as a "learned bibliophile and authority on illuminated manuscripts"), and Gustave Schlumberger (an active anti-Dreyfusard, described by Proust's biographer, George Painter, as a "bore") were already dim in Faubourg memory in 1934, the year Wharton's memoir was published, they have become virtually lost to later history. And not only because salon life was destroyed in the aftermath of the First World War, but because this closed and inbred world was, even at the moment Edith Wharton made her entrance into it, being consumed in its own death throes. Both the forms of this society and those who frequented it were *passé* by the time Wharton settled permanently in Paris.

Wharton's record of the salon life she knew, like the record of the life she lived, obfuscates aspects of upbringing and experiences that she perhaps found too difficult to articulate or too personal for publication. Thus one discovers the lapses, silences, and gaps in this autobiography to be revealing of a life that consistently wrote a fiction of itself, that sealed the ruptures in the psychic framework and overlooked the anachronistic nature of the lived life, giving priority to a consistent view of the life at the expense of troublesome introspection. Almost casually Wharton offers her husband's inability to cope with New York winters as the reason for their expatriation; she suggests by mere gesture her own need for "human communion"; she tells the story of her Paris years succinctly, with wit and verve, as though this story were a fiction. We know nothing of her more intimate relationship with Rosa de Fitz-James, a Viennese Jew who had been sympathetically accepted into Faubourg life because she suffered mistreatment by her husband. Although Rosa de Fitz-James and Edith Wharton were close friends and shared similar reasons for having adopted a life of presumed leisure and pleasant entertainments, such deeper attachments are not mentioned in Wharton's review of this period of her life. That the hectic social pattern of her days constituted an effort to escape an oppressive solitude is never mentioned; she barely hints at her steady and determined commitment to writing. She allows us to believe that the *très snob* attitude so often attributed to her, the effect of an upbringing at once constrained and privileged, accounts for her manner of living. Only through witty anecdotes does she suggest her underlying apprehension at the effort to be accepted within such a sealed, select, and anachronistic society; by side glances and hints she implies the wholesale remaking of herself that this new life required; she glosses over the ironies inherent in her place as an *American woman* in such a setting; she speaks of her old friends from this period of her life as though they were dead (as indeed many of them were by 1934), eulogizing rather than energizing them.

Of course, one would not have expected the shy, uncertain, and proper Edith Wharton to expose—in a public record—anything of her private nature. Having spent years constructing the social facade behind which she lived out a solitary existence, she could hardly be expected at age 72 to reveal the cracks in its fragile surface. Yet her keen novelist's eye and her ironic writer's voice are opposed in this account by the first-person subject, as though the writer found it too painful to look full face upon this subject. It was Marcel Proust who was able to record the ironies and inconsistencies of this world, who in fictionalizing the players in this elaborate game was able to capture their essential characters. It was precisely this aspect of *A la recherche du temps perdu* that Edith Wharton so admired, that made her more acutely aware of her limitations as a writer. It is under the guise of fiction that Madame Straus—whose favorite literary *trouvaille* was Proust—is remembered as the Duchesse de Guermantes; indeed the fictional creation has eclipsed the actual existence of this powerful *salonière*. Other women in control of the Paris social and intellectual scene in the late nineteenth century are entirely lost to modern memory: Mme Arman de Caillavet (whose lover and chief salon figure was Anatole France), Laure Hayman (an English woman who was Proust's lover and a model for Odette), Princesse Mathilde (the niece of Napoleon), Mme Aubernon (who announced conversation "themes" for her dinner table); the Comtesse Greffuhle (who entertained King Edward VII and Queen Alexandra), the Duchesse de Rohan, the Comtesse d'Haussonville, the Princesse de Polignac, the Comtesse Emmanuela Potocka. In not remembering these women or their worldly achievements we do not feel a sense of loss, only perhaps a sense of wonder that Edith Wharton could have so longed for the society they represented and controlled. One wonders, too, why she was unable (or unwilling) to make this society a more central subject of her fiction.

While Wharton thought Proust too given to dukes and duchesses, and others thought him a society writer and a snob, it was later to become clear that what he found in the Faubourg (the "Guermantes Way") was his literary subject, and he tenaciously held on to his position in salon life—against pressures by his parents to get him started on a career in law—until he had the materials necessary to begin his long novel. Edith Wharton, like most American writers in Paris over the years, continued exploiting America as the subject of her fiction, but she claimed to have found in salon circles a mental stimulation for her writing and a social set she found interesting. Although, in retrospect, Wharton herself seems far more remarkable than any of her French dinner companions, and although to a modern sensibility such a circumscribed social scene appears both arid and frivolous, one cannot underestimate the power of this setting to confer a sense of privileged acceptance on its participants. It was here that Wharton sought intellectual challenges in an environment seemingly secure against anything more disagreeable than the risk of boredom.

The salon world of the *belle époque* was, as it had traditionally been, entirely in the hands of a dozen or so women who provided French intellectuals regular opportunities to prove their social worth. Gender roles were rigidly prescribed: it was women's duty to enhance the discourse of men. Despite the power held by the women who organized such gatherings, salon culture was dominantly male. Edith Wharton was rare among the women of this world in that she was a highly successful, published writer; she was not an attendant to a famous husband or the lover of a powerful aristocrat, but rather an attraction in her own right. In this setting, however, marriage was frequently a burden, since salon invitations were not issued to couples, but to individuals who were invited on their own merits. Spouses were not necessarily welcome. Pleased to be in the company of intelligent and charming men and women, Edith Wharton played her role well. She accepted the unstated responsibility of women to retrieve dinner table conversation should it lag and redirect it should political disputes become too rancorous. A genius at conversation, an artist at covering personal feeling behind a mask of *gentillesse,* she succeeded well in a society that prized pretense as a mark of good breeding. Wharton knew herself to be an exception to the Faubourg rule that foreigners and married women (unless they were charming mistresses of artists or aged aristocrats) were never to be included in these intimate evenings. She writes that "at that time in Paris the appearance of a 'foreigner' in any society not slightly cosmopolitanized still caused a certain constraint, especially among its womenkind" (*A Backward Glance,* 290).

Nonetheless, Wharton valued the contributions made to this society by women and longed to fulfill the role of salon hostess herself, capturing in such a role the perfect blend of her Old New York upbringing and the stimulation of a new cultural setting. She describes her perceptions of this role in traditionally feminine terms that accord woman an almost innate sense of social decorum: "the only completely agreeable society I have ever known is that wherein the elements are selected and blent by a woman of the world, instinctively alert for every shade of suitability, and whose light hand never suffers the mixture to stiffen or grow heavy" (*A Backward Glance,* 290). She saw the "Frenchwoman's greatest gifts" in the "power of absorbed and intelligent attention [to male conversation] . . . a perfect background for the talk of the man" (274). Apparently she saw no inconsistency in such a view of social relations and felt no frustration at playing a conventional part. But she did take exception to the narrowness of certain salons. Finding, for instance, that few "Frenchwomen . . . can resist political or academic intrigues as an ingredient in their social mixture," Wharton nonetheless felt that by specializing in politics a salon hostess ran "the risk of making her *salon* dull" (*A Backward Glance*, 274). But Wharton underestimated the political threat—for it would be a political event, occasioned by the chance discovery on 26 September 1894 of a torn letter in a military attaché's wastepaper basket—that would intrude upon the damask-shrouded drawing rooms of Faubourg salons to disrupt the carefully cultivated friendships among aristocrats and intellectuals.

The Salon Divided: Anti-Semitism and Homosexuality

Although it seemed hardly possible in 1894, the prolonged and painful Dreyfus Affair so divided Paris salons on a question of politics that *salonières* found themselves unable to bring together their regular groupings of intellectuals and artists without turning the game of witty *repartie* into bitter dispute. Wharton and other *salonières* worked in the years of the Dreyfus Affair to preserve the fragile symbiosis of social, political, and artistic interests that the First World War finally would shatter altogether. Proust was involved in the affair early on, calling himself the first "Dreyfusard," supporting the innocence of the Jewish army captain charged with leaking state secrets, later court-martialed and exiled to life imprisonment on Devil's Island. The case stirred anti-Semitic elements in French society, elements that dominated Parisian salons. Although salons were supposedly the safe enclaves of royalist Catholics, in fact many Jews found their way into this culture (including Proust, who, although a baptized Catholic, had a Jewish mother); Rosa de Fitz-James was said to keep as a secret weapon a list of all the Jewish marriages in noble European families, on the chance that she might need to expose anyone who questioned her own presence in Faubourg society. Salons divided against each other on the question of the Dreyfus Affair. George Painter, Proust's biographer, describes the situation: "The split in society was also a split in high society. The Faubourg St.-Germain, being royalist, nationalist, and Catholic, was inevitably anti-Dreyfusist. Even the hostesses who remained neutral, whether from genuine doubt or from desire to keep their guests of both parties, were forced to choose one side or the other, for sooner or later guests would quarrel about the Affair and refuse to meet one another again" (*Marcel Proust*, 1 : 23). A whispered question around the quarter in these years was: "What are you doing with your Jews?" The question was a socially painful one, since whatever one "did with" one's Jews, there were inevitable guilts and recriminations.

As the Affair dragged on, salons chose sides, the controversy fueled by the rhetoric of those who attended the gatherings. Mme Straus's salon was from the outset a center of Dreyfusism, in part because of the presence of Joseph Reinach (himself a Jew), who led the pro-Dreyfus forces, and because of Marcel Proust, who in 1898 organized 104 petitioners to sign an appeal on behalf of Dreyfus in a call for a new trial. Proust's petition coincided with Zola's *J'Accuse* letter (also printed in the newspaper *L'Aurore*) and was supported by such major literary figures as Anatole France, as well as by many of the women who conducted Faubourg salons. Rosa de Fitz-James, in favor of Dreyfus, found herself opposing her own husband, who was one of the leaders of the anti-Semitic anti-Dreyfus forces; while Edith Wharton was strongly in favor of Dreyfus, her good friend Paul Bourget was anti-Dreyfus. More than one salon was ruined by the effects of the Affair. Certainly Mme Straus's salon died as a result of political and personal hatreds born of the case. As George Painter describes, Proust himself came to realize the essentially vapid and depleted culture that salon life represented as he labored on behalf of the Dreyfus cause: "The Dreyfus Case had broken the spell of the Guermantes Way. Proust saw his hosts stripped of the poetry with which he himself had clothed them: a duchess was only an ordinary person wearing a tiara, a duke was only a bourgeois with an exaggerated hauteur or affability. He realized that in entering the heartless and empty world of the Guermantes, in searching for something higher than himself, he had committed an absurdity" (*Marcel Proust*, 1:306).[3] On this controversy were erected the foundations of French Fascism in the twentieth century, strong support for which came from the nobility of the Faubourg, particularly among such men as Léon Daudet, Jean Lorrain, Charles Maurras, Robert de Montesquiou, and Boni de Castellane.

Salon society mixed the political Right and the intellectual Left, royalists and anarchists, Catholics and Protestants, the *haut-monde* and the *demi-monde,* government ministers and music hall singers, denizens of the Comédie Française and the Académie Française. It reflected in miniature all the contradictions and internal oppositions of the society at large, valuing certain proprieties over others. The distinctions between the conventions against homosexual practice and the actual behavior of the period, for instance, were obvious in salon attitudes: homosexuals were simultaneously protected by salon society and shunned by it—as were Jews. Both groups were feared by the larger society. The Dreyfus Affair engendered fears that Jews had entered into a conspiracy for control of the government, and homosexuals were thought to be united in an effort to corrupt the morals of French society. Thus on the question of sexual practices, salons discriminated between the kinds of sexual behavior allowed men and those permitted women. Homosexuality and drug addiction among the men were accepted (if not condoned); men attended certain of these functions disguised by powder, rouge, wigs, and heavy cloaks. But the rules for women were slightly different: they were free to have extramarital affairs, to get divorced, and to appear at the opera in seductive clothing. But display of their sexual attractions was for men; while it was assumed that some men practiced homosexuality and chose not to marry, all women were bound by patriarchal, heterosexual claims. Intimate female friendships were considered to be the result of plain or poor women's failure to attract male lovers or to be amusements that titillated male lovers. In either case, lesbianism was considered harmless, inconsequential, even pathetic.

Because the Code Napoléon had made no provision for punishment of homosexuality, however, homosexual practices were not banned by law and were a dominant feature of *belle époque* culture. Proust's writings portray male homosexual practice in Paris salon culture, while by 1900 the city itself had an international reputation as the capital of same sex love among women and was designated "Paris-Lesbos." Paris may have been tolerant of deviance, perhaps explaining the homosexual migration there at the turn of the century, but the city made fine distinctions in the ways in which female and male homosexuals were regarded, distinctions that reveal something of the moral and political priorities of the society. In salon society, married women amused themselves by indulging in erotic Sapphic practices. Same-sex love was part of the "mad gaiety" of *belle époque* life, where men and women alike sought new and exotic pleasures. As one famous salon hostess of the period commented, "all the noteworthy women are doing it" (Blankley, "Return to Mytilène," 47 and fn. 8). Salon society offered the rich and aristocratic occasions for varied kinds of sexual encounters, protecting the affairs and intrigues it engendered within the enclosure of the drawing room.

Like male homosexuality, lesbianism was not bound to class; it found practitioners in all social ranks. Female homosexual practice was evident at all levels of society, but the differences in experience between women of the Faubourg and those of the middle and lower classes were striking. The rigid structure of French life demanded varying degrees of sexual discretion according to social class: among the upper classes, women were expected to be discreet about their sexual preferences and experiences; the vulnerability of lower-class women to legal prosecution for homosexual practices guaranteed discretion. Although fashionable boarding schools for young girls provided the conditions under which homosexual experiences might occur, women of the upper bourgeoisie and aristocracy were simultaneously protected by their social status and forced by certain social circumscriptions to be less obvious in their homosexual preferences than men of their class. Also, women were bound differently by social class and convention than were men, finding it necessary to preserve themselves from scandal in the effort to protect the reputation of husbands and families and to preserve the appearance of normal married life.

Certain socially prominent Paris women made their sexual preferences public in these years, however. Among them were the *courtisane* Liane de Pougy (who announced her love for Natalie Barney in a novel entitled *Idylle saphique*, published in 1901), actress Sarah Bernhardt (who formed a couple with Louise Abbema), the Marquise de Belbeuf (who spent five years with Colette), the Duchesse de Clermont-Tonnerre, Lucie Delarue-Mardrus, and many others. There were even salons that served as gathering places for European lesbians and included "baronesses of the Empire, canonesses, lady cousins of Czars, illegitimate daughters of grand-dukes, exquisites of the Parisian bourgeoisie, and also some aged horsewomen of the Austrian aristocracy" (Colette, *The Pure and the Impure*, 69). But these women were protected against censure by their class and social standing. They lived beyond the restrictions of bourgeois society and, to a certain degree, outside the limits of the law. Female cross-dressing, for instance, was restricted by an ordinance passed in 1800 and, at the turn of the century, strictly enforced by Lépine, the Paris prefect of police. But aristocratic women cross-dressers in salon society were protected by the very fact that salons were established in private homes, beyond the reaches of legal constraints. Such women traveled to their meeting places in private rather than public conveyances and had no need to don the protective covering of long cloaks to disguise their male dress.

Women not protected in the higher reaches of society met secretly in restaurants and bars, traveled by train and hired cabs, and frequently risked exposure, if not legal punishment, should they reveal their sexual orientation through dress or publicly demonstrated erotic attachments. Some prominent women, however, openly invited censure. The Marquise de Belbeuf became an object for woman-haters, who considered her perverse and degenerate. Adopting male dress and forms of behavior, the marquise reversed the premises by which patriarchal society functioned, assuming for herself male privileges and power. Antagonizing influential elements of *belle époque* society, she put herself at risk.

On 3 January 1907, the Marquise de Belbeuf and Colette were very nearly arrested for enacting a scene of lesbian love in a pantomime skit at the Moulin Rouge. Entitled *Rêve d'Egypte,* the mime portrayed the awakening of a mummy from her eternal sleep by the kiss of a former lover. The scene incited a near-riot in the theater, making it necessary to call in the police. Further performances of the play were banned by

Lépine at the request of the marquise's ex-husband; Colette Willy's estranged husband lost his position on the newspaper *L'Echo de Paris;* and the two women were forced to stop living openly together (*Colette,* 199–201). This frequently recounted incident was significant in two ways. It illustrated the risks of any public announcement of lesbian commitment: these two women were not merely acting out a music hall skit, but were announcing to the world—in particular, to their husbands—the seriousness of their commitment to lesbian eroticism and to each other. Indeed, they reversed the premises of the male voyeurism that supported Paris burlesque shows: rather than arousing the male audience with their amorous behavior, they announced the awakening of their own sexuality to each other. The Moulin Rouge scandal also exposed the risks of openly woman-oriented eroticism to working women. Colette and the marquise were forced to work on the music hall circuit after leaving husbands who had mistreated them. Almost overnight, these women lost the allegiance of the aristocracy and upper bourgeoisie that had formerly protected them. Once the marquise was no longer screened by her husband's family and Colette no longer sheltered by her husband's power in the world of Paris journalism, the two women were exposed to possible legal as well as social censure.

Lesbian Myths in the *Belle Epoque*

In Paris of the *belle époque* at least two sets of contradictions regarding lesbianism were at work: discrepancies between the public image of lesbianism and its reality and differences between male assumptions about lesbianism and lesbian women's experience. According to Elyse Blankley, these contradictory claims often placed lesbian women in uncomfortable, if not actually dangerous, situations:

> Paris was thus a double-edged sword offering both free sexual expression and oppressive sexual stereotyping. It might cultivate lesbianism like an exotic vine, but it would never nourish it. In front of [Renée] Vivien—and, indeed, every lesbian—yawned the immense, unbridgeable chasm separating men's perceptions of lesbian women and lesbian women's perceptions of themselves. Moreover, lesbianism's public image might enjoy a certain vogue in limited circles, but for women actually living the life style, each previous freedom was extracted at a price. Few lesbian women were able to live as bravely as Natalie Barney; most, in fact, grew weary of playing the sex-role game according to Paris's rules—rules more painful because masked by many illusory freedoms. ("Return to Mytilène," 49)

Our impressions of lesbian practice in the Paris of this time have been determined by male myths—heterosexual as well as homosexual ones—constructed for a male reading audience. Homosexuality was judged against the heterosexual norm that declared "evil" or "perverted" love-making practices considered sterile rather than fertile. This normative definition of sexual practice supports the assumption that homosexuality must always express itself in the same ways, that sexual difference is a constant that admits no internal differences or discrepancies.[4] Such fixed notions of both heterosexuality and homosexuality have led to scientific, psychological, and historical misunderstandings. As J. E. Rivers suggests, the very concept of "the homosexual" becomes a means of "excusing, explaining, ignoring, or propitiating whatever we do not understand about the world and whatever we most fear and despise in our own natures, just as we have used the concept of 'the heterosexual' as an image of clarity, progress, and social and cosmic harmony" (*Proust and the Art of Love*, 311).

Women who announced their homosexuality in the *belle époque* years were not exempt from reactions of fear and repulsion on the part of the larger community. As a subgroup of an already excluded and resented societal category (women), lesbians were particularly vulnerable to abuse by both men and women. In general, heterosexual women adopted the attitudes of their husbands and fathers toward female homosexuals: they were objects of ridicule, an embarrassment to their sex. But public antipathy to homosexuality expressed itself in significantly different ways toward men and women. Although lesbianism was subject to "judicial rigor" (through laws against cross-dressing and against lesbian practices in institutions such as schools, hospitals, prisons, and houses of prostitution, all of which were under the surveillance of the law), this official stance masked "a dormant indulgence quite unlike the aversion to male homosexuality," according to Jean-Paul Aron and Roger Kempf: "Subject to an emasculating moral code, the nineteenth-century bourgeois seeks pleasure in the evocation of lesbian loves. His virility makes the best of it and even rejoices in it as laying hands on some fantasmagoric possession: he evaluates, thanks to these forbidden games, the superiority of the strong sex. A voyeur with equivocal desires, he projects into revolting scenes his uncontrollable lot of repressed homosexuality and frees himself from it, without striking a blow, through the spectacle, real or imaginary, of servile womanhood" (*Homosexualities and French Literature*, 149). Using lesbian prostitutes, the heterosexual male frees himself from the fear of his own homosexuality—his hatred of women the projection of his fear of the feminine within his own psychic nature.

As Elaine Marks has commented, images of the lesbian in society are determined by prevalent images of women in a given time and place. The same ignorant fear that attaches to more generalized images of women defines the lesbian as a social misfit, a pariah. In the male homosexual code of these years, the definition of female was one who was "weakly decorative," and the male who took her part in homosexual relationships was a "half-man."[5] For heterosexual men, lesbian women were associated with a specialized form of prostitution. These lesbian roles were enforced by nineteenth-century literature (especially in writings by Balzac, Zola, Louÿs, Gautier, and Baudelaire) and exploited by the more exotic Paris brothels where the lesbian couple was the *pièce de résistance* of erotic temptation, a form of harem lesbianism. Parent-Duchatelet, a public health doctor who wrote a famous treatise on prostitution, confirms this stereotype:

> Lesbians have fallen to the last degree of vice to which a human creature can attain, and, for that very reason, they require a most particular surveillance on the part of those who are charged with the surveillance of prostitutes, but more particularly on the part of persons to whom the direction of prisons dealing with these women is entrusted. . . . These unfortunate women have, at different moments, fixed the attention of the administrations. Thus, in 1824, it was expressly forbidden for those keeping houses of ill repute to allow their girls to share the same bed. (*La prostitution dans la ville de Paris*, I, 170–171, quoted in *Homosexualities and French Literature*, 148–149)

Prostitution was allowed, but the women who served men were punished under the law if they were discovered in erotic relationships with each other. One brothel madame, discovered in bed with one of her own young women, lost her license to keep a house of prostitution.

Homosexuality as Pathology: Trapped Souls

A primary difficulty in discussing attitudes toward homosexuality at the turn of the century rests in efforts by the scientific community to define the basis of homosexual behavior. The various theories proposed by many medical authorities were homophobic, suggesting that pathological drives led to homosexual practices. An example is the work of pioneer sexologist Karl Heinrich Ulrichs, who described the homosexual male as having "the soul of a woman enclosed in the body of a man," a theory based on the division of spirit from body. Similarly, the "mannish woman" was clinically defined as having the soul of a man trapped in a female body. Proust drew on the "trapped soul" theory to portray a certain view of male homosexuality in *A la recherche*, and Radclyffe Hall based *The Well of Loneliness* on her interpretation of this theory.[6] Although uncertain whether homosexuality was a biological accident or the product of social forces, virtually the entire medical establishment viewed it as an illness for which scientists sought a "cure."

Benedict Friedlander, a leader of homosexual rights in Germany, disputed the medical determination that homosexuals were ill and "physically inferior," an argument that attributed to homosexuals characteris-

tics otherwise defined as typical of the feminine. Friedlander attacked
what had become popularly known as the "third sex" theory and rejected
the idea of "a poor womanly soul languishing away in a man's body"
(*Proust and the Art of Love,* 193). But underlying Friedlander's impassioned plea for a cultural and historical approach to the understanding of
homosexuality there lurks a distinction between man's virile body and the
"poor womanly" soul that represents its spiritual side. His conception of
homosexuality bears little relation to classical notions, where homosexuality was associated not with weakness and "femininity" but with virility,
strength, and courage. In Greece, homosexuality was cultivated to ensure
solidarity among males in times of war (*Proust and the Art of Love,*
167–169). Friedlander's efforts on behalf of male homosexuality were
based on patriarchal definitions of woman—fixed, that is, in a prevalent
form of misogyny.[7]

Male homosexuality in the *belle époque* was overt, even flamboyant,
and was grounded in the aesthetic of the dandy that dominated the literary and artistic culture of the period. According to Martin Green, the
dandyism practiced by Oscar Wilde, Jean Cocteau, and Marcel Proust
was "preoccupied with style" and betrayed, according to Freudian psychology, a latent narcissism, rejecting the demands of the adult world that
little boys become men who accept society's responsibilities.[8] Green describes the "dominant images" of Victorian life as "those of maturity and
responsibility." These were replaced in dandyism by "young-men images"; by the onset of World War I, "life was already in thrall to the
beauty of the matriarchal mystery . . . and—less seriously—to young-
man images" (40). In this ethos, the "matriarchal mystery" allied itself to
a cult of male youth, a metaphorical alliance between powerless elements
of society (women and adolescents) that constituted a radical critique of
patriarchal power. That is, the dandy announced his opposition to cultural demands that he become a mature, adult male by exploiting (and
parodying) stereotyped images of women. The socially constructed image
of woman—her speech, her movements in the constraint of tight clothing,
her jeweled and laced adornments, her cosmetically constructed image—
formed the basis of the mime. The homosexual aesthetic that favored
adolescence over maturity and enacted misogyny in terms of matriarchal
thralldom also inscribed an artistic temperament that was feminine. Here
the "trapped soul" theory of homosexuality collaborated with prevalent
notions that those who were artistic and intellectual were also weak and
hypersensitive rather than masculine and mature. The artistic works
of such men as Huysmans, Wilde, Cocteau, Robert de Montesquiou,
and Serge Diaghilev were seen as the products of their homosexual
temperaments.

Although for men the tradition of homosexual literature extended from the Greeks to contemporary French poetry and fiction, for lesbians, the Greek tradition amounted to a few fragments from Sappho. There was no contemporary public literary record of lesbian writing, no tradition in which woman expressed her love and erotic desire for another woman. That tradition had been broken and lost due to direct censorship as well as to the historical realities of women's social condition in the intervening centuries, leaving homosexual women of the late nineteenth century to create (and recreate) their own tradition of homosexual art. Lesbianism was certainly a subject for art and openly treated in the literature of these years, but these representations of female love were constructed by men whose exploitation of the exotic and erotic elements of this love masked deep-seated misogyny. Not only did lesbian women in these years not have a literature of their own, but the images presented to them in male literature (such as Baudelaire's *femmes damnées* or Proust's portrayal of Gomorrah) only further reinforced the disgust and self-hatred apparent in medical, legal, and social attitudes toward homosexuality. Elyse Blankley provides several examples of the exploitation of lesbian sexuality by male writers of the period:

> In his "Songs of Bilitis," for example, Pierre Louÿs's description of Bilitis's "marriage" with Mnasidika, a young maiden, reads like a catalog of sensual delights. Sappho herself, pictured as a sexual predator ready to snag an unwary woman, is priestess of a sensual world composed of so many burning thighs, crushed lips, and breasts fluttering like birds. Baudelaire's "Lesbos" is a similar pageant of concupiscence. His island is a "land of hot and langorous nights" where women "caress the ripe fruits of their nubility" in their "mirrors," an act of "sterile voluptuousness." These women touch one another for the benefit of the male audience that watches, just as it might do in a Parisian brothel. Indeed, the absent male is indisputably the scene's reference point, because "sterile" caresses might define these women by what they lack (i.e., men, with whom one might share "fertile" heterosexual caresses). ("Return to Mytilène," 50–51)

The discovery of the fragments of Sappho's poetry in the 1890s provided an important opportunity to lesbian women of rediscovering their literary and historial traditions and "of redeeming Sappho from male authors who had exploited Lesbos as a form of thinly disguised pornography or as a shocking affront to bourgeois morality" ("Return to Mytilène," 49). The model of Sappho's community of women inspired several lesbian women (including Natalie Barney, Renée Vivien, and Eva Palmer) in the effort to create a modern-day Lesbos. But this attempt was inhibited by social proscription. Women were still forced into hiding, forming themselves into small groups, establishing themselves on "lesbian 'islands' . . . surrounded by treacherous waters" ("Return to Mytilène," 49). If lesbian women found safety behind the closed doors of certain Faubourg salons, it was because these homes offered security against public exposure. The drawing room became a stage for the performance of lesbian rituals later enacted, by many of these same women, in the relative privacy of Natalie Barney's Neuilly garden or in the enclosure of her Temple à l'Amitié on the rue Jacob.

This description of the threatened nature of female homosexual culture, however, does not reflect the total set of contradictions inherent in *belle époque* Paris. Despite the law against female cross-dressing (or perhaps because it forced female homosexuals to remain relatively invisible), it was male homosexuality rather than female practice that was the focus of middle-class moral outrage. In general, male homosexuality was seen to be more threatening to the moral base of society than its female counterpart: male homosexuality was treated as an evil perversion that directly threatened the family as the primary social unit of Western culture. Female homosexuality attracted the interest of men because it was viewed voyeuristically (e.g., in brothels and burlesque shows) as a sexual variant in which men had an erotic interest. Michèle Sarde comments that "the bisexual woman . . . is even more readily accepted by men who regard her homosexuality as a charming caprice, a sensual vice from which he too may profit" (*Colette*, 228), an assumption confirmed in Jeffrey Meyers's reading of *A la recherche:* "Albertine's lesbianism makes her more interesting, more desirable and more important to Marcel, and leads to greater intimacy rather than to a rupture" (*Homosexualities and French Literature,* 76). But apart from the voyeuristic pleasure it provided the male, lesbianism was considered a sign of weakness, a probable indication of mental disturbance, but an essentially harmless condition. The "inverted" behavior of lesbians was determined to be the result of frustration and fear, an attempt to escape men rather than to give evidence of a preference for women. Women who remained unmarried and perhaps lived with other women were generally assumed to have suffered a fate not at all their fault—to have been overlooked by men seeking wives. The dominant heterosexual culture in general would not have acknowledged woman's choice for a homosexual rather than a heterosexual life because this culture did not recognize woman's desire in any form.

Homosexualities in Literature: Proust's Sodom

To an important degree, our knowledge of the roles homosexuality played in this society derives from literature, particularly the work of Proust and Colette, who participated in the homosexual subcultures of Paris during these years. Proust was publicly accused of homosexuality and required to defend himself against a judgment that, although accurate, could not be admitted in public. There is evidence to suggest that the accusation itself was tied to the complicated politics of the *belle époque,* associated in some way with Proust's stance in the Dreyfus case: Proust was hated because he was a Jew who moved in the highest reaches of society and because he had taken a public stand in favor of Dreyfus. Proust's activism on the Dreyfus question put him at odds with powerful aristocratic politicians and members of the press (one of whom was Colette's husband, Henri Gauthier-Villars), men who took strong stands against Proust on this issue and would have done almost anything to have silenced his protests against the Dreyfus imprisonment.

The homosexual worlds created by Proust and Colette reflect the disparities of *belle époque* existence. And while these practices were in no way restricted to a particular social class, there are aspects of the homosexual experience of the *belle époque* that can be distinguished by class. What we know of the prevalent homosexual practices of this period we know from the upper-middle-class and aristocratic heritages that provided its record—in letters and private journals, in memoirs, in literature, drama, and politics. Lesbos may have been, as Michèle Sarde suggests, "a mixed society in which sex consciousness apparently replaced class or caste consciousness" (*Colette,* 224), but we know little of lesbianism among the working classes in these years except that it certainly existed and was perhaps more openly acknowledged there than among the upper classes. What we know of male homosexuality among the aristocracy and the *haute bourgeoisie* we know from Proust; what we know of female homosexuality among theater people, divorced aristocrats, and the *demimonde* we know from Colette, and the differences produced by social class and sexual orientation are striking.

Much as Proust was to resist admission of his own sexual preferences, finally calling Gide to his bedside to confess his inclinations ("Far from denying or hiding his homosexuality, he flaunts it, and I could almost say, brags about it" wrote Gide in his journal),[9] his fictional world examines a complex homosexual mythos. He provided for the generation of readers encompassed by this study the models of homosexuality that both reflected and structured patterns of behavior in those he saw around him. The presumed subject of Proust's fiction was the aristocratic salon, a setting that served as protective covering for the homosexuality that was his closer subject. Thus an implicit double standard is disclosed by Proust's world: two codes exist side by side—the code of the ruling class (which presumably can assimilate practices otherwise considered to be perverse and debauched precisely because it *is* the ruling class) and the code for everyone else. Proust's prejudices were as much along class lines as along lines of sexual orientation. Because he could not accept the implications of his own sexuality, his works were infused with contradictions and double standards, an attraction for and hatred of all that homosexuality connotes. Discovering in Proust's writing an inherent political and psychological disjunction, Jean-Paul Aron and Roger Kempf have noted that Proust's "statements on homosexuality remain the least obliging ones . . . because the nobility [served] him less as a mouth piece than as a subterfuge" (*Homosexualities and French Literature*, 152).

But Proust's portrayal of this world was an inherently deceptive one, resting as it did on an inability to confront his own homosexuality. It created and extended images of homosexuals as licentious, perverted, corrupted, and depraved men and women. It was Proust's vision of Sodom and Gomorrah in *A la recherche* that seemed to reveal the truth about homosexuality in the *belle époque*—emphasizing both its indulgence in the exotic and bizarre and its ritual ceremonies of repentance and remorse.[10] His portrayal of lesbian women was particularly injurious, and the descriptions of Gomorrah constitute a homosexual male fantasy of the homosexual female's world—that is, constituted by Proust's hatred of and fascination with the "woman" in himself, the spirit that accounted for his own homosexuality. Even as Proust was writing his volumes, Colette and others were living the experiences of Gomorrah, and her impressions of this world differed radically from his. The extent to which relationships among women threaten both homosexual and heterosexual men is a difficult issue, one whose internal complexities form an almost impregnable defense against investigation of such complexities. But Proust's misreading of women's responses to other women tended to confirm the suspicions the larger reading public had of lesbian practices and to fulfill the latent expectations and fantasies in which both homosexual and heterosexual men indulged.[11]

Colette's Lesbos

The trajectory of sexual degradation and perversion, marked by choice of homosexual partners along a descending social scale described by Proust in *A la recherche*, did not have its counterpart in Colette's study of lesbianism, *The Pure and the Impure*. The netherworld of lesbian practice described in Colette's work is defined less by its depravity than by its enforced secrecy, the need to play doubled roles—inside and outside the lesbian community. If the male homosexual relationships described by Proust show a disparity marked by social class (the "Prince and the Pauper" syndrome), those in Colette's work follow a model established by mothers and daughters. Older women supported and nourished younger, less secure women, providing them affection and tenderness absent in heterosexual relationships. This women's world was, in fact, a refuge from the dominant heterosexual culture in which women served men's needs, in which women were under both the protection and the dominance of the patriarchy; this women's world recalled maternal dependence, as Colette suggests: "you will give me sensual pleasure, leaning over me, your eyes full of maternal anxiety." In this view, only another woman could help repair the effects of heterosexual experience, which often endangered the woman's relation to her own body and psyche. As Michèle Sarde notes, "To Colette—and particularly during this period— the male represented otherness, separation, jealousy, suffering, slavery, emotional alienation; the female was relationship, contact, fidelity, independence, emotional harmony" (*Colette*, 230–231). Women of the lesbian community sought maternal protection, meeting in darkened, discreet places away from "intruders and the idly curious."

George Painter draws distinctions between the world of Sodom and Gomorrah and suggests an underlying patronizing attitude toward lesbians. He writes that lesbians were spared "the unjust stigma which condemned the natives of Sodom to a furtive and defiant criminality . . . [lesbians] seemed to the world, as indeed they were, an innocent, proud, eccentric, indispensable leavening in a monotonous society" (*Marcel Proust*, 2:327). Proust's own terms fix Biblical associations with homosexuality, suggesting the moral stigma of the behavior they encompass. Although Painter's description of the women in Proust's Gomorrah is not accurate (Proust's condemnation of these women is apparent, although— like the church fathers—he makes distinctions between the effects of male and female homosexuality on its practitioners), Painter's view does coincide with a prevalent *belle époque* attitude toward lesbians. Apart from legal restrictions against lesbian practice, many in French society thought lesbians embodied an innocence that encompassed both naivete and moral purity. This set of contradictory opinions regarding female homosexuality coexisted precisely because the society made distinctions between the behavior of bourgeois females and that of lesbian prostitutes. Painter's description, as Michèle Sarde has noted, makes woman's choice of relationships with other women not "the result of freedom, but of frustration, of attempt to compensate" (*Colette*, 227–228).

Colette's world is not nearly as simple or as "innocent" as Painter would portray it. Even its name—Lesbos—suggests the need to discover another tradition of women's love for each other, a model based on freedom of choice, reinforced as healthy and enabling, occupying a place unmarked by societal notions of evil and corruption. It is Sappho who is invoked by "Lesbos," not a wrathful Old Testament God, and Colette's selection of names implies her participation in a movement by turn-of-the-century women to rediscover an alternative tradition for their sexual orientation. Nonetheless, Elaine Marks describes the Lesbos of Colette's making as a society that "abounds in contradictions and paradoxes," a work where "ambiguity is sustained on all levels" (*Homosexualities and*

French Literature, 366). If Proust was ambivalent about his homosexuality, Colette was no less ambivalent about hers, and there is some doubt whether she thought of herself as lesbian. But Colette, and other women of the Paris community, took particular exception to Proust's portrayal of "Gomorrah":

> Since Proust has thrown light on Sodom, we feel respect for what he has written of. We would no longer dare to meddle with these hunted creatures. . . . But—was he misled, was he uninformed? When he assembles a Gomorrah of unfathomable and vicious young girls, denounces a frenzy of bad angels, we are only amused and care little, having lost the consolation of the overwhelming truth which guided us through Sodom. Because, with due respect for Marcel Proust's imagination, there is no Gomorrah. Puberty, college, solitude, prison, aberration, snobbism, are meagre nursery-gardens, insufficient to engender and store a manifold and well-established vice, and its necessary solidarity. Intact, enormous, eternal, Sodom contemplates from on high its puny, underdeveloped imitation. (*The Pure and the Impure,* 131)

Indeed, Proust suggested that Gomorrah was an imitation of Sodom, a miniature mirror image of the vaster and more evil parent culture. The patriarchal cultural norms that structure heterosexual life are operative as well in the two homosexual worlds of *A la recherche,* based on strictly enforced stereotypes of male and female behavior. Colette, however, seemed to accept without question the accuracy of Proust's portrayal of Sodom; she raised no questions about the ambivalence and discrepancy within this cosmic vision, just as she seemed unaware of the degree to which her own ambivalence toward female homosexuality was recorded in her own remarks. She worked within the culturally constructed male and female stereotypes, uneasy with the need of some lesbian women—including her lover, Missy—to dress and behave as men. Colette desired a female community in which femininity, of the culturally composed sort, is reinforced and where all that is male—instructive, demanding, aggressive, repressive—has been exorcised.

Colette's text is important to an understanding of lesbian practice in this period because it displays uneasiness with the polarities of male and female sexuality. It displays this discomfort with such oppositions not by questioning them or decentering them, but by trying to work within them. As Marks suggests, Colette constructed her text as a test to determine whether or not she was lesbian, according to the definitions of the day: "It is as if the narrator were testing herself against the portraits of these women in order to determine whether or not she was a lesbian, in order to determine the limits of her understanding and her compassion. 'Colette's' central obsession is with the women who imitate men . . . and thereby violate what would seem to be the narrator's fantasm of an exclusively woman's world." Marks concludes that for Colette "the woman who imitates a man, either in love or in literature, is not an acceptable model for a woman who loves women" (*Homosexualities and French Literature*, 368). Like Natalie Barney, Colette was disturbed by transvestism; although she herself cross-dressed in these years, she never fully comprehended the psychological and sexual impulses for such role reversals. Indeed, she may have experimented with cross-dressing in the theater and in private life in order to understand its causes.

The radical difference in tone and point of view between Colette's visit to Lesbos and Proust's to Gomorrah reflects their individual attitudes toward women and toward their own sexuality, and their consequent sympathy or antipathy toward the events they observed. Colette was not interested in sexual "perversion" as it was societally defined, nor was she trying to present a moral treatise. She was interested in the various possibilities for women's survival. The problem with Colette's text, however, is that it revolves on a culturally determined "male/female, masculine/feminine" axis, grounding itself in (and unable to reconcile) socially constructed male/female polarities except by implying, in Marks's words, an "equivalence between textual and sexual androgyny" (366).

From this contradictory world, in which repression and licentiousness served as reverse sides of the social code, emerged the beginnings of a feminist movement. Included in its ranks were lesbian writers who preserved the record that we now have of women—and lesbianism—of this era; in addition, literary aspiration itself became a subject of lesbian literature. Natalie Barney, for example, not only wrote a prolific record of her own lesbianism (as did Colette, Renée Vivien, and Radclyffe Hall) but also served as a fictional model of lesbianism in an astonishing number of works by other writers of the *belle époque*, appearing in works by Liane de Pougy, Renée Vivien, Ronald Firbank, Remy de Gourmont, Colette, Djuna Barnes, Radclyffe Hall, and Lucie Delarue-Mardrus. Without historical models, this writing was forced to take upon itself the double burden of creating a model of lesbian behavior while recording the personal experience of that behavior. With few exceptions, however, these novels tended to reflect scientific thinking about homosexual behavior that cast lesbian women as sexual deviants—men trapped in women's bodies. These works portrayed women who wanted to be men, lesbian marriages that took their models from heterosexual unions, and visions of lesbian existence as fraught with pain and suffering, disguised by makeup and clothes, eased through drugs and alcohol, carried on in the dark, in secret, and in fear. Renée Vivien's case may serve as the most extreme example of this pattern, but hers was not an isolated case. The story of Renée Vivien's death from drugs, drink, and slow starvation was well known among Left Bank expatriates, among heterosexuals and homosexuals alike, and its tragic end tended to confirm the belief that homosexuality constituted both moral and psychological deviancy that could only end in mental illness or death—more often, both. Both male and female homosexuals were seen as victims of self-hatred, their sufferings thought to be produced in part by disgust at their own depravity.

The Decadent and the Bourgeois

While male homosexuality was openly accepted—even flaunted—in certain salons, there were strong social pressures against it in many of the more bourgeois salons. In the salons that Edith Wharton attended, male homosexuality would indeed have been regarded as a sign of the moral bankruptcy of contemporary culture, and the subject of female homosexuality would probably not have arisen even as a topic of conversation, since in polite circles it was generally considered not to exist. Jean-Paul Aron and Roger Kempf have outlined three forms of homosexual "discourse" in this period, none of which would have been entertained in the more conservative salons: "a common discourse, scarcely spoken; a scientific discourse which is systematized only during the Second Empire; and a literary discourse which is applied to sapphism but more or less freezes over on the subject of male homosexuality" (*Homosexualities and French Literature*, 150). According to Aron and Kempf, the mere existence of these discourses did not mark an "overthrow of values"; rather, they translated themselves in a "slackening-off of bourgeois severity." Some strongholds of "bourgeois severity," however, were to be found in the seventh *arrondissement*—in precisely the drawing rooms in which Edith Wharton met her friends.

Thus a Robert de Montesquiou frequented the most prominent and worldly Faubourg salons, but would not have been present at the bourgeois and less fashionable evenings attended by Edith Wharton. An eccentric aesthete and the model for Huysmans' des Esseintes and Proust's Charlus, Montesquiou was a poet devoted to artists, writers, and salon hostesses. He perfected the decadent pose, hiding behind the facade of the aesthete the reality of his homosexual life, an existence that included liaisons with salon celebrities as well as with waiters, servants, and actors. Because homosexuality was considered a vice as well as an illness, it was thought to follow a cycle of decadence by which the homosexual male was brought low in "the pit of Sodom." Describing Proust's descent, George Painter repeats all the conventional notions about the consequences of homosexuality. Proust "began with love for his equals . . . progressed through platonic affection for social superiors . . . to physical affection for social inferiors, and now ended, disillusioned with all, in a sterile intercourse with professional catamites" (*Marcel Proust*, 2: 266). [12] When male homosexuals crossed the barrier of social class to seek out relationships with working-class men, they were considered to be irretrievably lost, morally and physically corrupt. That the male homosexual experience was thought to result in degradation that crossed lines of social class and economic structures marked it as significantly different from the perception and experience of female homosexuals.

Had Robert de Montesquiou been a woman, his homosexual practices—both inside and outside the salons—would have been bound by a quite different set of social codes. He would have been expected to marry, but marriage would have allowed certain sexual freedoms, even same-sex experimentation as long as it was done discreetly. Marriage would have served as protection against the effects of gossip injurious to the woman's reputation or to the possible threat of damage to her husband's reputation. Because women were—to a far greater degree than men—forced into sexual secrecy and deception, it was possible to pretend that lesbianism did not exist within the borders of the Faubourg; its existence elsewhere—among theater people and prostitutes—was taken as evidence of degeneracy to which the moral conservatism of the Faubourg opposed itself. In general, prescriptives against certain forms of social and sexual behavior were determined by a heterosexist society that enforced the male prerogative. The Comtesse de Noailles and Edith Wharton, for instance, counted Jean Cocteau among their closest friends; neither would have anything to do with Natalie Barney or Renée Vivien, the comtesse once having remarked that she was not "interested in such people" (Wickes, *Amazon of Letters*, 106). This attitude reflects the more conservative Faubourg notions, prejudices that could be put aside to serve practical purposes (the poet Princesse Marthe Bibesco, for instance, chose to call upon Natalie Barney when she wanted an introduction to Remy de Gourmont, with whom Barney had recently established a close friendship). And while it may be true that the Comtesse de Noailles held such opinions in the early years of her friendship with Wharton, she later explored lesbian relationships herself and, with Colette, was a regular at Natalie Barney's afternoons "for women only."

Although Edith Wharton believed nonetheless that the Faubourg manner of living also encouraged a certain experimenting with life that she simultaneously felt the need of—the assertion of one's individuality, an expression of the self—never would she have extended that "freedom and experimentation" to include lesbian sexual choice, not for herself and not for those she knew. In Wharton's part of the Faubourg, homosexuals were offered no hiding place. Persons accepted into Faubourg society played by its rules, however inconsistent and interminably complex those rules might have been. And the salon culture of these years preserved aristocratic prejudices close to Edith Wharton's sense of taste and decorum. While certain salons courted the more frivolous elements of Paris society and experimented with pleasure more *risqué* than dinner-table conversation, we can assume that Wharton refrained from such pleasure, preferring not to acknowledge its existence within the quiet enclosures of the Faubourg; for her, the drawing room was itself a barrier to such behavior. Neither would her group of friends have found a place for the more flamboyant, revolutionary, and often unwashed and impolite of artistic and literary innovators, and these young rebels would have found the atmosphere stuffy, *recherché,* even dull. Decorum and *politesse* were the hallmarks of salon living as Edith Wharton defined it.

Salons in Retreat

The institution of the salon itself, of course, was under attack by those who wanted to create modern art. The world of the Faubourg, like that of Mayfair-Belgravia in London in these years, embodied "tradition" as entrenched social and cultural codes that would need to be swept away in order for a new generation and a new century to come into being. Modernism would mount an assault on every aspect of Faubourg life, from the ornate antiques in the drawing room to the facile conversation of the dining table. Ezra Pound, of course, never entered a Faubourg drawing room (the closest he came was attending Natalie Barney's salon for a short period), but we can imagine what his reaction would have been to the society that surrounded Edith Wharton. Everything about her life, her values, the subject matter of her writing, the magazines in which her short stories appeared, would have horrified him. Doubtless, she would have been shocked by his behavior and language; indeed, he would have done his utmost to offend her. Had he been able to take her seriously enough to explain the reasons for his disgust at the society she frequented, and had she been willing to listen, he would have argued that the style of her writing, like the style of her dress (which was corseted and fussy), was derivative, clichéd, old-fashioned—old maidish. The subject matter of her writing—with its primary emphasis on women's intellectual and psychological isolation—would have provided yet greater evidence that her work was of limited interest to a larger reading public. That Wharton's novels were consistently at the top of the American bestseller lists would have further confirmed Pound's suspicions that she had "sold" her talents on the open marketplace. He would have described her friends as second-rank intellectuals and literary *poseurs.* The very comforts of their life, the accepted conventions of their social class, constituted obstacles to any thoroughgoing critique of the culture. For her part, Edith Wharton seemed entirely unaware in the prewar years that it was she and her old friend Henry James who were the targets of young Modernists. Indeed, neither of them seemed aware that a new and revolutionary literary movement was already overturning the culture Wharton and James had created.

The one French thinker Pound could have made an exception for in his critique of nineteenth-century intellectuals was Remy de Gourmont, editor of the *Mercure de France,* whose work Richard Aldington and Pound would later translate. Had Gourmont frequented society at all, he would have frequented Faubourg society, and Edith Wharton might well have met him. (Instead, he became the great friend of Natalie Barney, who met him secretly at Gourmont's apartment around the corner from her rue Jacob home.) Pound had tremendous respect for Gourmont, wrote about him frequently, and praised him for a comprehensive intelligence that lacked prejudice. Pound carefully distinguished Gourmont's mind from that of Henry James (whom Ford Madox Ford called "an extraordinary old woman"), on the grounds that "on no occasion would any man of my generation have broached an intimate idea to H. J. [Henry James] . . . with any feeling that the said idea was likely to be received, grasped, comprehended. . . . You could, on the other hand, have said to De Gourmont anything that came into your head; you could have sent him anything you had written, with a reasonable assurance that he would have known what you were driving at" ("De Gourmont: A Distinction," in *Little Review Anthology,* 255). Wharton would probably not have recognized what Ezra Pound was "driving at," but on at least one issue her cultural liberalism outdistanced his intellectual liberalism: never would she have been sympathetic to anti-Semitic behavior, while Pound's anti-Semitism was to shape his personal philosophy.

There were no occasions, then, for Edith Wharton to meet in the circles in which she moved those who were to become the great literary experimentalists of the twentieth century. It is ironic, and perhaps sad, that the Faubourg society that an Ezra Pound would have considered a stultifying anachronism served to stimulate Wharton's intellect, fed her craving for enlightened conversation, and provided a place where her talents were praised and where she herself was valued. We can read in the enthusiastic embrace of her Paris life the narrow limits of her marriage, the restrictions of her adolescence, the constraints of an American upbringing that insisted on social success and decried intellectual pursuits. She was perhaps unaware that in the closed circle of the Faubourg she was culturally isolated from the most interesting of the literary innovators living in Paris before the war. Perhaps she had heard of Picasso, Stein, Apollinaire, Valery Larbaud, LaForgue, as she knew of Proust, but took no interest in their work. Only Jean Cocteau, whom she met at the home of the painter Jacques Emile Blanche after her divorce, proved an exception to this pattern. The two seem as odd a pair as the Henry James and

Ezra Pound who traverse Church Walk in the opening pages of *The Pound Era*. Twenty-seven years older than the young poet, Wharton seems to have had strong affection for Cocteau (whose personal excesses distressed her), while the young French poet seemed genuinely to admire this representative of an older American generation. She attributed his sad and short life, however, to the effects of a certain kind of Parisian salon. Wharton discovered both Proust and Gide as writers but not as friends, although her own good friend and literary mentor Walter Berry was close to both men and could have provided her the necessary introductions. Instead, Edith Wharton preferred the elegant warmth of Henry James, a man whose breeding, good manners, and refined intellect were safely to her own liking—and whose literary reputation would, unfortunately, dominate and define her own for several decades of this century.

Edith Wharton among Men

It is interesting and important that Edith Wharton's closest friends were men, that the reticence that so marked her public life was put aside in her friendships with Henry James and Walter Berry, two men who served as artistic advisors and confidants. "What is one's personality, detached from that of the friends with whom fate happens to have linked one?" she asked in *A Backward Glance*. "I cannot think of myself apart from the influence of the two or three greatest friendships of my life, and any account of my own growth must be that of their stimulating and enlightening influence" (169). She isolated Walter Berry, thought by more than one critic to have been her secret lover in the years preceding her divorce,[13] as the single most important friend of her life: "I suppose there is one friend in the life of each of us who seems not a separate person, however dear and beloved, but an expansion, an interpretation, of one's self, the very meaning of one's soul" (*A Backward Glance*, 115). Rather than suggesting a romantic liaison in these words, Edith Wharton implied a relationship that was, to her, more important. Walter Berry served as her mentor, the one who gave her the courage to write: "He alone not only encouraged me to write, as others had already done, but had the patience and the intelligence to teach me how" (116).

Although Wharton and Henry James discussed the patterns and limits of fiction almost endlessly over a friendship of some forty years, they both avoided any detailed discussion of Wharton's writing. James felt an embarrassed reticence in the role of critical authority on her work, and she feared his honest, possibly brutal, appraisal of her methods. Walter Berry, however, read with care the various manuscript stages of her writing—a privilege no other was allowed—and commented freely and courageously on her developing strengths: "When he could follow my work in manuscript he left no detail unnoticed," she commented in her memoirs (117). And, by Edith Wharton's own admission, Walter Berry found her when her "mind and soul were hungry and thirsty, and he fed them till our last hour together" (*A Backward Glance*, 119). Wharton met Berry in July 1883, two years before her marriage to Edward Wharton, but Berry assumed the role of confidant and counselor in the painful years following her marriage, when she tried—by measures that resulted only in exhaustion and nervous depression—to "adjust" to the emotional and social demands of her married life. It was Berry who gave support and encouragement in writing an early story, "The Greater Inclination," publication of which "broke the chains which had held [her] so long in a kind of torpor" (122).

While Wharton turned to Berry for practical advice on her writing, she turned to Henry James for good conversation, finding him especially interesting company in travel or at the salon dining table. She counted James in the group of "beloved guests" that included Bay Lodge, Gaillard Lapsley, Robert Norton, and John Hugh Smith—all of whom she loved having "under her roof." She counted James, as well, among those "masters of fiction" who served to stimulate her creative energies. James was perhaps the last of a series of such male models first discovered in the "gentleman's library" of her New York childhood home where Wharton—like Virginia Woolf in Leslie Stephen's London library—was first to discover the patriarchal literary heritage she tried to make her own. Even in Edith Wharton's adult life, she persisted in keeping the "masters" within easy reach, cultivating their friendships, seeking their advice, looking to them for confirmation of her personal worth and verification of her growing self-confidence. Even excluding James and Berry from among her intimates, the list of close male friends is a formidable one, including Bernard Berenson, Theodore Roosevelt, Jacques Emile Blanche, Charles Eliot Norton, Howard Sturgis, Egerton Winthrop, and—late in her life—Kenneth Clark. It was in friendship with these men that she developed her political and aesthetic senses, extended her study of art and music, and refined her literary skills.

Edith Wharton's Feminist Commentary

Perhaps more than any other expatriate included in this study (with the exception of Natalie Barney), Edith Wharton sought to define herself by the standards of French culture; in doing so, she consciously put aside aspects of her American heritage and upbringing that she found self-seeking, unrefined, and chauvinistic. In her fiction, private writings, and memoirs, she obsessively replayed the elements of the American experience she thought to have stunted and impeded her intellectual and spiritual growth: "I have often wondered, in looking back at the slow stammerings of my literary life, whether or not it is a good thing for the creative artist to grow up in an atmosphere where the arts are simply nonexistent" (*A Backward Glance,* 121). In her volume *French Ways and Their Meanings,* a collection of "disjointed notes" on French reaction to World War I, Wharton isolated those elements of French character and culture she most respected, contrasting them to the American life that she had left permanently behind her. She spoke in general terms of courageous French efforts to preserve a long-standing and important culture, admitting her attraction to the French sense of continuing tradition, with its emphasis upon taste and aesthetic values and its homogeneous and stable consistency. But she wrote at length—incorporating a wealth of anecdotal evidence—on the important differences between French women and their American counterparts.

Marriage is isolated as the institution toward which Wharton directed her most discerning commentary. She argued that from the day of her marriage the American woman "is cut off from men's society in all but the most formal and intermittent ways. On her wedding-day she ceases, in any open, frank and recognised manner, to be an influence in the lives of the men of the community to which she belongs" (*French Ways,* 116). Such isolation forced American women into a social context dominated by other women: "It is because American women are each other's only audience, and to a great extent each other's only companions, that they seem, compared to women who play an intellectual and social part in the lives of men, like children in a baby-school." She compared American education of women to a Montessori-method kindergarten in which girls developed "their individuality . . . in the void without the checks, the stimulus, and the discipline that comes of contact with the stronger masculine individuality" (*French Ways,* 102–103). According to Wharton, such isolation of one sex from the other was destructive to the very notion of civilization, which, in order to survive and prosper, must be "based on the recognised interaction of influences between men and women."

While the roots of this argument for equality of the sexes—for which she sought confirmation among the French—would seem to be located in traditional notions of the differences between them, Wharton ultimately argued that women of her time stood in need of the stimulating male intellect because American society had, by separating women from the world, limited their intellectual and aesthetic capacities.

> It must be remembered that a man who comes home to a wife who has been talking with intelligent men will probably find her companionship more stimulating than if she had spent all her time with other women. No matter how intelligent women are individually, they tend, collectively, to narrow

down their interests, and take a feminine, or even a female, rather than a broadly human view of things. The woman whose mind is attuned to men's minds has a much larger view of the world, and attaches much less importance to trifles, because men, being usually brought by circumstances into closer contact with reality, insensibly communicate their breadth of view to women. (*French Ways*, 119)

Wharton always articulated her notions of the "feminine" in the context of the "masculine," seeing women in relation to men, emphasizing the cultural (and, for her, possibly innate) superiority of the male mind to the female consciousness. She did not hold men responsible for "narrow[ing] down" women's interests, but rather focused her attention on the effects of such narrowing in women's lives. Thus her praise of a French society that allowed women an equal part in social interaction and offered a cooperative partnership in marriage was founded on resentment of the restrictions imposed upon American women by marriage, an institution she did not immediately identify as patriarchal.

Wharton acknowledged that French women were accorded a status and power in the family that remained unacknowledged by the law. Because French women of the commercial classes, for instance, were always business partners in the family enterprise, they enjoyed more real freedom in practice than they were granted under the law:

> The French wife has less legal independence than the American or English wife, and is subject to a good many legal disqualifications from which women have freed themselves in other countries. That is the technical situation; but what is the practical fact? That the Frenchwoman has gone straight through these theoretical restrictions to the heart of reality, and become her husband's associate, because, for her children's sake if not her own, her heart is in his job, and because he has long since learned that the best business partner a man can have is one who has the same interests at stake as himself. (*French Ways*, 105–106)

Acknowledging the self-interest in such an enterprise, Wharton nonetheless made clear that at every level of French society women participate in extraordinary social freedom: "In France, as soon as a woman has a personality, social circumstances permit her to make it felt" (117). Although such statements are not without their contradictions, Wharton nevertheless captured an essential component of French societal attitude, one that gives priority to adults (whether male or female) and rejects the childishness, insecurity, and immaturity that Wharton saw as intrinsic to the American woman's condition. In this context, the French see themselves as adults, the products of a long and sophisticated culture. Americans, by contrast, are children, the product of a culture too young to be civilized, still imprisoned in "perpetual immaturity": "*Ce sont des enfants*—they are mere children!" (*French Ways*, 95).

In Wharton's view, the Anglo-Saxon heritage in America resulted in keeping women childlike, irresponsible, and socially segregated. The root of the problem rested on the inevitable link in American marriages between "fidelity" and "family responsibility." The French, to their credit, separate these two incompatible but necessary components of human relationships, thus providing the needed stability for the family while allowing women (and men) the option of love outside the boundaries of the marital law: "The French marriage is built on parenthood, not on passion," concluded Wharton. Whatever degree of accuracy one may accord these observations, it seems obvious that Wharton's insistence on bringing her argument around to questions of love, marriage, family responsibilities, and woman's place in society illumines the effects of her own marriage on her adult development. She sought in every form of French life—but particularly in its social and cultural norms—to escape the crudity and constraint of American life as she observed it and lived it in her own marriage. She saw marriage as the social contract that forced the woman's "withdrawal from circulation," that sealed her fate in loneliness, vanity, sentimentality, and—often—mental illness. If American marriage contracted the woman to a life of isolation, the French marriage assured her a life of social influence. Discarding her own marriage, accepting her responsibilities as "a real factor in social life," Edith Wharton spent thirty years in France attempting to shed the vestiges of her puritan New World heritage in the French salon. Defining it as "the best school of talk and of ideas that the modern world has known," Wharton saw the prime virtue of the salon to be its nourishment of "stimulating conversation . . . between intelligent men and women who see each other often enough to be on terms of frank and easy friendship" (*French Ways*, 117). It was the French salon that provided Wharton an escape from a marriage that for the previous thirty years had seemed to provide no exit.

It was not in the French salon, however, that Edith Wharton met women artists and writers who could influence her developing sense of independence and self-confidence. Just as she did not meet young Modernists in Faubourg drawing rooms, neither did she meet women who could provide her a radically altered conception of woman's place in French culture. Within the salon Wharton played an exceptional role as an intellectual woman, but she remained isolated from friendships with women that might have nurtured her art and life. Her encounter with Anna de Noailles, a countess of Rumanian-Greek background, was almost accidental. The comtesse was not part of the Paris salons Wharton frequented because, according to Wharton, her "dazzling talk was always intolerant of the slightest interruption" (*A Backward Glance*, 275)—a suggestion that the comtesse would not easily have settled into a conventional role. In fact, the Comtesse de Noailles was very active in the salon circles frequented by Proust.

Anna de Noailles was an unconventional woman, one with whom the sometimes shy and socially stiff Edith Wharton assumed an immediate intimacy. By the time she met Wharton at tea in early April 1907, the comtesse had been honored by the French Academy for her poetry and was an accomplished novelist whose works examined the psychology of women in love. Wharton found her "quite exceptionally interesting," and—as R. W. B. Lewis describes—something in the comtesse's demeanor suggested a hidden and silent existence to which Edith Wharton was attracted: "Something in Edith responded at once to the young woman's passion for life and for letters, to the rush and gaiety of her talk, and to what Edith intuited as an undercurrent of sadness and dissatisfaction. She was, as well, 'indescribably' attracted to Anna de Noailles' poetry, fusing, as it did, romantic evocations of natural landscapes with expressions of erotic desire and the subtle disclosure of the wounded heart" (*Edith Wharton*, 162). As in her attraction to the writings of George Sand and George Eliot, Wharton was to feel in the poetry of de Noailles "an affinity that was almost a self-revelation" (*Edith Wharton*, 169). In the dark days of worry about her husband's mental health and in the uncertainty about the relationship with Morton Fullerton, Wharton considered writing an essay on the poetic imagination of Anna de Noailles. One suspects that the desire to examine the psychological sources of her friend's poetry—a project never completed—was occasioned by Wharton's need to inspect her own emotional state. That she would choose the critical essay as the form for such a commentary is both interesting and ironic: Wharton may have been unable to deal with the powerful suggestiveness of her friend's poetry from anything other than a distanced perspective. Although Wharton's own emotional sufferings often found their way into her novels and short stories, they were carefully disguised by the fiction.

Apart from an acquaintance with Vernon Lee, Wharton's friendship with Anna de Noailles was the first extended relationship she had with a woman author. Although twelve years younger than Wharton, Noailles was a powerful influence on her thought, giving the support and friendship Wharton desperately needed. Anna Noailles provided intellectual support to male writers as well, including among her close friends Proust and Cocteau. It was perhaps to the Comtesse de Noailles that Proust owed the development of his genius, as she helped him see that his pattern of life in the *belle époque* was a subject worthy of fiction. She shared his political views (as did Wharton) and, with Proust, was a fiercely ardent Dreyfusard. She too had watched the Dreyfus Affair disrupt the imposed politeness of the salon, raising tempers and voices, displacing elegance with passion. Her refusal to renounce her lover, Maurice Barrès, because of his anti-Dreyfus sentiments nearly destroyed Mme Bulteau's salon. (The story is recorded in Painter, *Marcel Proust* 2: 19–22.) And she knew, as Edith Wharton surely must have suspected, that this life was soon to be replaced by a more egalitarian one.

Did Edith Wharton foresee the death of the salon culture she so wished to enter as she stood at the door of the house on the rue Barbet-de-Jouy that cold December afternoon in 1893? She longed for the setting the Faubourg St. Germain might offer her, the comfort and security of a physical space in which to discover her individual relation to traditions that had sunk deep roots in French culture. It would not have seemed possible in the last decade of the nineteenth century that such cultural history could be so easily and quickly uprooted or that she herself would be seen as a representative of a culture already attenuated and dying. In December 1893, Wharton had already experienced a physical longing for this city, for its sounds and smells, sunrises and sunsets. She sought both the pleasure and privacy the city could offer. She was to discover—perhaps sooner than other women of the Left Bank—that Paris could offer independence without the accompanying penalty of isolation, could afford her "the sense of continuity and the sense of personal freedom" (Lewis, *Edith Wharton,* 176) she so desperately sought.

3
SIMULTANEOUS EXISTENCES:
FOUR LIVES IN ST. GERMAIN

The second phase of the *belle époque,* between 1900 and the Great War, was marked by advances and retreats, by an emerging Modernism and a clinging to old ways. The twentieth century was ushered into France with the Paris Exhibition. Among the technological advances on display for the world's fair were the first stone bridge (the Alexandre III), completed just in time for the exhibition, the Paris Metropolitain, which gave underground rides across the city, and two glass exhibition halls, the Grand Palais and the Petit Palais. Seen today, these monuments display a rather quaint and Old World quality, suggesting that the nineteenth century was difficult to cast aside, and its customs and styles, its social and moral restrictions, deeply ingrained in the French character. The emphasis on forms and formalities assured the safe passage of French civilization, or so it seemed at the time. In retrospect, the two decades preceding the war have an aspect of the unreal about them, as though they were suspended in time, existing as an extension of a previous era, the lingering malaise of a former century. Gentility and social ease were preserved, especially for the middle and upper classes, but the underlying tensions of personal and political life strained the polite facade. At the time, the period gave a false sense of its "unshakable stability, even of permanence." But the exterior calm of this period was at odds with a terrible internal unrest that was to result in World War I:

> The arts were flourishing as never before, and with them the theaters, galleries, bookstalls, cafés, and music halls. In fiction, it was a time of work as varied as the psychologizings of Paul Bourget, the delicate eroticism of Colette in her "Claudine" novels, and the adventures of Maurice Leblanc's attractive gentleman-rogue Arsène Lupin. Poetry had fallen below the peak of the previous generation, but poets swarmed across the literary foothills. In

drama, Rostand and a host of others; in music, Debussy and Saint-Saens; in painting, Impressionism was giving way before the achievements of Cézanne, Matisse, Picasso, and Gauguin. It was a time, too, of great performers, from the aging but still formidable Sarah Bernhardt and Coquelin to Mistinguette and the young Maurice Chevalier with his cane and bowler hat. (Lewis, *Edith Wharton,* 126)

This résumé of *belle époque* culture does little to reassert a sense of the period's permanence, however.[1] With the exception of advances in painting, by painters who achieved little public acceptance during these years, the arts of this era belong to the nineteenth century. The fiction, poetry, drama, and music were trapped in a time warp of the prewar years, and the cane and bowler hat were a lingering anachronism. Even now it is difficult to recall that behind the gay facade this society was crumbling; life was affluent, peaceful, and predictable despite the constant changes of government, the proliferation of strikes, the various bomb threats and assassinations.

Cultural Collapse: World War I

This world collapsed on 1 August 1914. On this date, wrote Gertrude Stein, the twentieth century was born. At the first posting of mobilization orders in France the nineteenth century died, taking with it to the grave the attenuated decadence of the *belle époque*. To Pearl Adam, an English woman journalist then living in Paris, wife of George Adam, the *Times* Paris correspondent, the false security of the summer of 1914 seemed "positively fantastic. It [was] as droll as a cardboard farm supplied with cardboard animals and tin trees and just about as real." Left behind as her male colleagues followed the troops to the front, she kept a diary of the war years, a chronicle of disillusionment. She writes about the last Sunday afternoon at the fashionable restaurant, Armenonville, in the Bois de Boulogne just outside Paris:

> A week before war broke out, I spent an afternoon at Armenonville which was typical of those days. It was hot and sunny, and numbers of girls in thin black frocks of satin, silk, chiffon, or all three, with shady hats, were collected in a canvas-shielded quadrangle outside the restaurant proper. . . . A wooden floor had been laid and a tail-coated orchestra discoursed the latest . . . syncopations. The trees stretched overhead, and from without came the subdued murmur of those aristocratic vehicles which used to haunt such spots at that hour. The black-garbed girls were not in mourning; black and white were the fashionable colours that year. Their skirts were very narrow, their hats very wide, their sunshades very frilly. . . . The young men wore dark grey mourning coats, light striped grey trousers, abundant ties, with

scarf pins negligently poised to the left of the main mass, and left beneath their chairs, when they came into the centre to dance, glossy tall hats. . . . Comic things, tall hats.

The afternoon drew on; lemon squashes followed tea, and those subtle small drinks which entail straws began to appear on the tables. A hint of freshness floated down from the trees to the dust-laden air. The high-heeled shoes of suede and velvet and satin (these materials were then dearer than kid, and consequently were fashionable; now the work-girl wears them and the Duchess demands calf) ceased to tap the improvised floor. The little crackling crush of landaulettes on gravel sounded more and more often behind the canvas screen. The orchestra went to take its collars off for an hour before dinner, and we all drove back through a golden haze out of which rose the enormous and solemn bulk of the Arc de Triomphe, grey as Gibraltar. Beyond it, we bowled down to the Louvre, drowned in a valley of twilight, and so returned to prepare ourselves, perhaps for a dinner and more tango at the same Armenonville. (*Paris Sees It Through,* 3–4)

These young people dancing away the afternoon in a fashionable Paris suburb no longer resembled figures in a Renoir painting. Fashions had changed radically since Renoir painted similar Sunday afternoon scenes in the Bois de Boulogne, but the social customs he captured had been hardly touched by the birth of the twentieth century. There is little in this scene to suggest the ways that technology left the nineteenth century behind. We recall with surprise that at this time Paris already had an underground system transporting thousands of workers to all parts of the city; that there were more than 54,000 cars in France (1 to every 8,000 residents of Paris), which led the world in production of motor cars; that 210,000 French had telephone service; that the aircraft industry, in its infancy, would soon develop in response to the needs of the war; that the cinema was a favorite pastime; that the tango had replaced the waltz.

Nearly all aspects of French life in this period were decreed by some authority—the fashions in painting or in dress were officially decided by the *salons* and *maisons de couture.* What one read, ate, traveled in; how one danced, courted, made love; and where one entertained, conducted business, or gossiped were all controlled by tradition and public sentiment, if not by actual law. Art and literature were rigidly controlled by the academies (which, for instance, allowed only male students to draw nude figures, using females to pose at a minimal fee for the drawings). Of primary importance to the expression of this culture was its language, which was an essential component of French identity (Zeldin, *France,* 2: 17). In response to a question concerning French individuality, Paul Valéry replied, "the first thing to examine if one wants to appreciate the mental life of this people and its evolution, is its language, the first intellectual fruit of a nation" (Zeldin, *France,* 1: 19). Thus in introducing new concepts (such as "heterosexuality," which came into the French language in 1911) and technologies, the first problem was always "how to call it." The Académie Française frequently debated such issues and was often caught in contradictory stances: it took a decree from the Conseil d'Etat to decide that the word *automobile,* like the word *voiture* that it would eventually replace, should be feminine. When Edith Wharton bought her first Panhard in 1904, the Conseil had not yet met; when Gertrude Stein bought her first Ford in 1915, her *voiture* was officially an *automobile,* declined in the feminine and christened "Auntie" for Gertrude's aunt Pauline.

At this period two contradictory elements were influencing French society and moving it in opposite directions simultaneously: there was an increasing move toward individualism (in behavior, dress, taste, politics, and cultural preferences) countered by strong pressures on the part of the general public in favor of conformism. While these concurrent pressures were evident in all aspects of society, especially in literature and the arts, they caught in their wake the more marginal and fragile elements of French society; they had, for instance, great effect upon women. French women in the early years of the century lagged far behind their American and English peers in their efforts to gain political and legal equality. They did not receive the vote or equal pay until 1944. Except, perhaps, for poets and salon hostesses, most middle-class French women were highly influenced by the church and preferred traditional values of home and family.

French Women and Their Ways

By the early 1900s, a reaction had set in against the George Sand model of sexual and artistic liberation, which appeared to be out of date. The church played a significant role in this retreat, angry at the new clothing styles that allowed women greater freedom of movement. Church proclamations declared such apparel "indecent and provoking" (Zeldin, *France,* 1:353). Indeed, fashions and popular new dances indicated to arbiters of moral standards an increasing immorality, especially among French women. One of the new talents in the fashion industry just prior to World War I was Coco Chanel, the illegitimate daughter of a factory worker. Instigating reform in dress, Chanel designed clothes that were affordable and less restrictive, creating a style called the *genre pauvre.* Chanel had taken as her model Colette, who very early in the century cropped her ankle-length hair and began wearing the less restrictive clothing typical of the music hall where she worked. Both Colette and Chanel symbolized for many French the deterioration of feminine virtue: Chanel's clothes were considered by many to be unseemly and Colette was thought to be a prostitute, displaying herself for male audiences. Chanel found her clientele among working women, and although her style would eventually become the symbol of French *haute couture*, at the outset her simple clothes were shunned by the majority of young women, whose encumbered feminine dress was a mark of social distinction. These women rejected the strident militancy of the British suffragettes; they put aside the move by women poets like Anna de Noailles and Marthe Bibesco to revolt against custom and practice. Marriage and motherhood were popular. Etiquette became very important again as middle-class women copied the manners of the upper classes, aping the more formal elements of salon culture. In etiquette guides, which sold in huge numbers at the turn of the century, women were encouraged to find satisfaction in the social amenities and adherence to the rules of *politesse*.

While the First World War had little effect on the lives of most French women, who continued the same familiar patterns even after husbands and sons went to the front, its ultimate consequence was to make bourgeois women more aware of the problems of working women. Before the war, France had a higher percentage of working women than almost any other European country, twice as high as that of England. But the war meant that even middle-class women sought employment because their private incomes were vanishing. And although one would think this change might have meant a change in attitude on the part of French women, it did not. A member of the British Expeditionary Forces in France writes in 1918 about French women's self-conceptions: "The Frenchwoman is no feminist as yet. She has little faith in the political systems devised by mere men, and thinks she wields far more power in her informal way than she could ever exert if she was an elector. This war, however, by forcing so many women to leave their home occupations, and take their chances in the modern world of labour, has slightly accelerated the tendency of working women to group together and obtain more equitable salaries, calculated not upon their sex, but upon their actual output and requirements" (Saillens, *Facts about France*, 276). In the small family business that constituted the backbone of French middle-class economy, however, the *petit maman* was always at the cash register and it was she who managed the family economy: "the influence of our women over all our activities in literature, business, art, daily life, has always been very great, and very seldom combatted. It is often the case with us, that the wife, having more leisure, or doing less exhausting work, is the accountant, cashier, manager, and scholar of the household" (*Facts about France*, 276).

The status of French women has always been deceptive. In their homes, in society, and in the church, their position has remained secure, provided that these institutions found no reason for disapproval—the price for which has traditionally been banishment. But in terms of real political, professional, economic, and legal power a French woman at the turn of the century was marginal, often overlooked by the system altogether. Everything about her existence—from economic security to social status—depended on the benign protection of a system created for and controlled by men. At the same moment, these women strained to be free of a past that weighed upon them; they needed freedom from cumbersome clothing and long hair, from unwanted pregnancies and unhappy marriages, from the persistent mythology—propounded by men—that women were innately and biologically inferior to males. Exceptions to these implicit restrictions were made among the upper classes, where greater economic freedom ensured a less restrictive existence. It is not surprising, therefore, that writers came from these privileged classes (Colette is in all ways an exception to this pattern), nor is it surprising that women of the bourgeoisie and proletariat felt it safer to seek whatever security the patriarchy could provide than openly to challenge the system.

Expatriate Women Writing

For the women of this study—and for many more whose work never found a public hearing—writing was a remedy for a life that was all too rigidly controlled by tradition. Writing allowed the momentary release of the bonds society tightened around women. In France particularly there was a strong tradition of women writers who kept accounts, journals, diaries, and commentaries on daily life; these ledgers gave a form and shape to lives that were warped into the conformity dictated by both church and state. Through these writings we discover the discrepancies, the huge gaps, between the exterior life of preserved gentility and the interior life of passions, frustration, and unused energy. Colette's life of writing began during her courtship with Willy, a two-year period when she wrote him long letters. After their marriage, Willy directed her to "jot a few of your recollections down on paper," claiming that money was short and such remembrances might provide material for a novel. Four months later she presented him with a 656-page manuscript—he had hardly thought her capable of such dedication. Nonetheless, he saw no immediate use for her remembrances, and she temporarily stopped writing. Colette admits, "Relieved, I returned to the divan, to my cat, my books, my new friends" (*My Apprenticeships,* 19). As we know, Willy later resurrected those early writings and published them under his name, and "Claudine" became famous. Perhaps it would never have occurred to Colette to write if her husband had not told her to do so, but once she discovered the pleasures of writing, she continued.[2]

But Colette's example is again not typical of patterns established by women writers, most of whom began writing for themselves, in secret. In 1873, when Edith Wharton was 11 years old, she tried to write a story. Her subject matter was well known to her—the social patterns of her own mother's life—and she constructed her plot around an unexpected social call: "'Oh, how do you do, Mrs. Brown?' said Mrs. Tomkins. 'If only I had known you were going to call I should have tidied up the drawing-room.'" But when young Edith Wharton showed the first page to her mother, she confronted rejection: "drawing rooms are always tidied," her mother told her (Lewis, *Edith Wharton,* 30). Wharton temporarily abandoned fiction for poetry, which was further removed from the facts of everyday life, but three years later completed (in secret) a 30,000-word novella, *Fast and Loose,* whose very title belies the personal and social constraints of her upbringing.

Gertrude Stein was told by all her teachers that she could not write, that she demonstrated a faulty knowledge of English grammar, that her prose was unruly, ill-directed, and often incomprehensible. Stein was eventually to turn her supposed weakness to her favor, insisting on a prose style that was oral in its intonations and inflections rather than "literate." Despite discouragement from teachers and college professors, Stein wrote for herself, beginning as a university student to comment on her personal life and, in particular, upon the disquieting realization that she was sexually and emotionally attracted to other women—a disclosure that would have produced immediate disapprobation in her middle-class home. Natalie Barney's poetry explored a similar subject, but placed it in the tradition of French verse—formalized and balanced. The traditional forms of this love poetry helped to disguise its radical otherness from the heterosexual poetic tradition, the narrative voice often taking what might have been assumed to be the traditional male stance of the wooing lover. When as a young adult she tried to write serious love poetry to other women, she chose as her literary confidant a man—Jules Cambon, the French ambassador—to read and comment on her work. (Whether Cambon realized the unusual nature of the poetry he read or whether Natalie confessed it to him is not known.) Because Natalie Barney was not emotionally tied to men, a male perspective was safely removed from the realm of the feminine that her poetry most often probed. She was to continue her reliance on men as first readers and evaluators of her work throughout her life, testing her literary efforts on such men as Remy de Gourmont and Ezra Pound before she made her writings "public" by reading them aloud or sending them to women.

The occupation of writing is demanding precisely because it requires privacy, solitude, time for reflection, and a place set apart for such a special activity. In the early years of the twentieth century, Paris was able to offer these necessities to a host of would-be writers seeking privacy within the larger context of a social and intellectual setting sympathetic to the literary effort but not directly involved in it. These people needed a place in which to write; as Gertrude Stein wrote in her homage to Paris, "so the twentieth century did need France as a background." Women particularly required the freedom from external restraints, from the cultural expectations that kept women locked into social forms or placed them in the service of husbands and children and denied access to the wellsprings of their own creativity. Despite its emphasis on propriety, etiquette, forms, and politeness, France offered the perfect background for such creativity, for several reasons. The societal pressures that forced French women into preconceived roles did not affect the lives of American women who resided there. French society was closed, even to women like Edith Wharton and Natalie Barney, who participated as guests of a culture whose secret heart they never really penetrated.

For expatriate women this separate place outside the bounds of French society was absolutely essential; it allowed them to dismiss the fear of rejection, the weight of inhibition, the constraint of traditional attitudes and roles. Gertrude Stein correctly observed that "everything is private and personal in France"—by which she meant that the usual communal expectations and restraints, those found in America for instance, were absent. But the personal and the private in France continued to exist within the confines of the family, and to Maurice Sachs "the necessity of living *en famille*" represented "a torment which equals that of purgatory":

> With an attentive eye that lets nothing escape, each watches the other closely. Everything the world counts most private becomes most public: it is impossible to love or stop loving, to write or stop writing, to paint with blue or pink, without all of Paris taking a hand. Each book that appears is a cause of scenes, each exposition of painting a reason to fight. An overwhelming confusion of words and arguments wherein the persons involved have almost no voice covers everything with a thick fog, like that which rises at times in the country at dusk. (*Decade of Illusion*, 4)

Although this dust surrounded and enveloped the Americans who were in its midst, it never suffocated them. Indeed, it allowed them to breathe more freely. They were not French, they were not part of this society, they were not affected by French mores and prejudices, they were not participants in French antagonisms. They were separate.

It was this very need for separateness that brought them to Paris. And while it has always been assumed that the occasion for this expatriation was intimately connected to a masculine ethos—and directly attributable to World War I—such an assumption is necessarily refuted by the experience of women expatriates, whose motivations for living abroad were importantly different from those of their male compatriots. Despite differences in age, social class, sexual orientation, and artistic goals, the reasons why Edith Wharton, Gertrude Stein, and Natalie Barney chose Paris are strikingly similar, and their experiences there are not entirely unlike those of Colette in the years following her marriage to Willy. These four women lived within close proximity of one another, although in the years they occupied residences in the sixth and seventh *arrondissements* they were not aware of one another's existence.

Natalie Barney: From Neuilly to Rue Jacob

When Natalie Barney arrived in Paris in 1902 hoping to find a place among the cultured aristocracy, more than her American birth presented a barrier to acceptance into French society. As a woman whose lesbianism was the subject of her literary efforts and the outstanding feature of her public demeanor, she was *persona non grata* with certain Paris society matrons. But her revenge, if such it was, against the closed doors of the Faubourg was swift. She began with garden parties on the lawn of her Neuilly home to which she invited her literary and aristocratic friends. Her good friend Lucie Delarue-Mardrus introduced her to her own friends, among whom were such aristocrats as the Princesse de Polignac and the Duchesse de Clermont-Tonnerre (with whom Natalie Barney was to have a long love affair). Soon she was able to number among her guests the most distinguished artists in France, including Paul Claudel, Auguste Rodin, Anatole France, André Gide, Marcel Proust, Paul Valéry, and others. Although Barney was never to be accepted by the Faubourg, she lived out her adult life in its very shadow. In 1909, she moved to 20, rue Jacob, almost at the border of the seventh *arrondissement,* which houses the Faubourg St. Germain, and there established the most powerful literary salon in Europe, which was to endure for almost sixty years. If some of her neighbors would not speak to her, there were perhaps some who envied her famous Friday evenings, and a few—notably Anna de Noailles—who eventually left the enclosure of the Faubourg to join Barney's salon.

George Wickes has described Barney's salon as located "in the heart of the Faubourg Saint-Germain" (Rood, *American Writers in Paris*, 4: 23). In fact, it was just beyond the eastern limits of the old Faubourg. The distinction is an important one: Barney did not live within the borders proper of old French society. Although she was to count among her friends and salon guests some residents of this old quarter, her real conquests in Paris were French intellectuals who were often lionized by Faubourg salon hostesses but were not themselves of that society. Barney's address is important, however, for another reason. It was located in the heart of the intellectual and artistic quarter of Paris, a place whose traditions are associated with the classical divisions of learning—philosophy, letters, the arts—rather than with inherited titles and property. Even today, the rue Jacob maintains its links with an artistic bohemia rather than with the staid propriety of the seventh *arrondissement* a mile or so to the west.

Natalie Barney arrived in Paris at the height of the *belle époque*, when salon society was its most powerful; these years encompassed the Dreyfus Affair (1893–1906), years that were coincidentally those of the first marriage of Colette Willy, who serves as another important link to the Paris of the prewar years. Colette began writing in a fourth-floor apartment in the rue Jacob, in "a dismal and dreary house" that overlooked the rue Visconti, just steps away from Natalie Barney's future home. Although the street had literary associations—Prosper Mérimée, Adrienne Lecouvreur, and Laurence Sterne had all lived there—these ghosts were, undoubtedly, unknown to the 23-year-old bride from Burgundy. Her life in this street was solitary and painful, and she was only later to learn that the gardens she could see over her back window belonged to a famous literary recluse, Remy de Gourmont, and that her future friend Natalie Barney was a frequent visitor there.

Colette: Rue Jacob

The apartment to which Colette was consigned for more than sixteen hours a day, alone with her cat Kiki-La-Doucette, had been lived in for the previous fifty years by a tenant with odd tastes in interior decoration: "175,000 pieces of confetti . . . lozenge shaped, multi-colored bits of paper, had been glued all over the doors, the cornices, the columns, the niche behind the porcelain stove, the moldings, the closet shelves, and large areas of the walls. Colette had the sensation of being shut up in a dark and cheerless space over which brooded the interminable energy expended by a madman" (Sarde, *Colette,* 119). During the day she wrote long letters to her mother, who still lived in the tiny village of Saint-Sauveur en Puisaye, and drafted *Claudine à l'école,* which was begun between May and November 1894. In this year she sank into a depressive illness that brought with it fevers and respiratory problems (resulting from the poor heating in the apartment) and was nursed back to health by her mother, who arrived to discover a daughter she thought was dying. This was the beginning of "la vie de Bohème" for Colette Willy. Interestingly, Colette displayed the same maladjustment to marriage as did Edith Wharton, perhaps for some of the same reasons. Both women endured periods of serious physical illness in the years immediately following their marriages; both of them were unprepared and ill-equipped for the sexual initiation of the marital state. They both recovered from physical illnesses and eventually gained independence from marriage through writing.

Colette's husband, Henri Gauthier-Villars, was thirteen years her elder and a well-known journalist and critic for various Paris newspapers who wrote under the pen name "Willy," a name Colette was to take for a while as her own. He was, as well, a notorious womanizer, and his charm, quick wit, and good looks made him a favorite of salon patronesses. Every evening, after completing his theater and music reviews, he took his young bride into the fashionable world of Proustian nightlife. With her long hair braided around her head, her eyes staring out of an innocent country face, she was hardly prepared for these ventures into the *haut-monde,* nor would her presence have been tolerated there except as a concession to her husband's charm. She is remembered by those who knew her in these years for her wide-eyed, and often sleepy, silence. But these evenings were important to Willy, who cultivated his subjects in the drawing rooms of the Faubourg; his presence was crucial to hostesses who wanted their particular brand of culture to be touted in his newspaper columns: "in such surroundings," writes Colette's biographer, "Willy could meet the people with connections and could polish the urbane aura that would help him create his reputation as a music critic, a reputation that he actually owed to the musicians with which he surrounded himself. In literary circles, his strategy was the same" (Sarde, *Colette,* 135–136).

Colette and Willy were regularly seen at salons such as those of the Comtesse Greffuhle and the Princesse de Polignac, but they were also included in other salons that drew people who specifically shared Willy's interests. Debussy, for example, was often at the salon of Mme de Saint-Marceaux, and Anatole France was a regular (because he was her lover) at the salon of Mme Arman de Caillavet. It was here that Colette met Anna de Noailles, who was to become her lifelong friend. But it was at Rachilde's Tuesday evenings that Colette's secret status as the author of the *Claudine* novels, to which Willy signed his name, was discovered. Rachilde was also a woman from the provinces who began writing under a man's name. When she came to Paris at age 21, she was variously a journalist, playwright, and fashion writer. She eventually became a critic for *Mercure de France* and later married its editor. She was particularly kind to Colette, knew well her insecurities and fears, and suspected that this young woman was the spirit behind Claudine, not Willy. Rachilde was to write in *Mercure de France* about *Claudine à l'école:* "By Willy, the book is a masterpiece. By 'Claudine', the same book is the most extraordinary work ever to be hatched from the pen of a beginner" (Mitchell, *Colette: A*

Taste for Life, 52). In a note of thanks to Rachilde, Colette confirmed Willy's collaboration and gave him credit as the one who "pruned and thinned the Claudinish crudities."

Although Willy was brutally jealous of any associations Colette had with men other than himself and was also threatened by her friendships with women, he soon came to learn that his wife's innocence and youth were a drawing card that he could use for his own success in the salon world. Gradually, Colette learned how to conduct herself in such situations and was able to tell witty stories and to converse with her sophisticated elders. Consequently, she was protected by people Willy could ill afford to reject. In this way Colette found means to escape Willy's overbearing protection and to cultivate a group of people who supported her through the most difficult period of her life.

For a period of almost six years, however, Colette carried the secret that she was the author of the successful and very lucrative *Claudine* series. By the turn of the century Willy was the most powerful music critic in the city (so powerful that an enraged Erik Satie once attacked him in front of a concert hall, resentful of the reviews that Willy, under the heading *Ouvreuse,* had written about him). But Willy's highly prodigious output had never been his own; he kept a stable of ghostwriters who prepared his material. He paid his staff little, worked his stable hard, and reaped all the social and financial benefits for himself. In 1894, Willy began exploiting his wife's talents, but when he realized that Claudine was the darling of all Paris, that his wife from the provinces was making him rich, he drove her harder, forced her to write faster, pushed his *risqué* plots further, exploiting the best ghostwriter he had ever found. Colette's innocence and natural wit were exotic in a world inured to the sophisticated and refined.

The shocking disjunction between Willy's real character and his public image reflects perfectly the oppositions inherent in the *belle époque,* a world that no longer distinguished between courtesans and countesses, that was more interested in hoaxes than in scientific discoveries, that erected a glittering artifice to cover the sordid, the fake, the ludicrous. This era produced Huysmans' *A rebours* and Oscar Wilde's *Salomé;* it was a period of dandyism, of drug-induced eroticism, of exotic fashions and overstuffed drawing rooms, of sexual indulgence. In the Bois de Boulogne, the women of virtue rode the same paths as the *grandes horizontales,* often making it difficult to distinguish one kind of woman from another. It was here that Natalie Barney made some of her most famous "conquests," including the most beautiful courtesan of the era, Liane de Pougy, an actress welcomed in the most aristocratic European society. It was also here on an afternoon in 1900 that Barney first saw Colette, who was to become one of her most intimate friends. In these prewar years, before motor cars were common, "there was an opportunity to exchange long glances, half smiles, as one drove from the Tir au Pigeons to the Cascade, passing and passing again most of the fashionable courtisanes, actresses, society women and *demi-mondaines;* none of them had a glance as lovely as Colette's" (*Souvenirs indiscrets,* quoted in Sarde, *Colette,* 149). The discrepancy between Colette's character and her surroundings was immediately evident to so astute a judge of women as Natalie Barney.

This incident in the Bois de Boulogne preceded by some years the period of Colette's lesbian attachments, between 1906 and 1911, but the glance shared with Natalie Barney in the woods that afternoon was to be remembered by both women. In 1906, at age 33, Colette left Willy and moved to 44, rue de Villejust, on the Right Bank in the area known as Passy. Behind her ground-floor apartment and connected by two gardens was the house of Renée Vivien, the lover of Natalie Barney. Vivien's early death, a long wasting away from depression and drugs, was in part brought on by the difficulties of this relationship. Renée Vivien could not adjust to Barney's code of sexual conduct, which separated the issues of fidelity and monogamy, and wrote sad love poetry to the lover she thought unfaithful. From her apartment Colette observed the increasing morbidity and illness of this young English poet, whose life gave evidence of all the discrepancies and ambiguities of this period: Vivien was young, beautiful, and—to outward appearance—smiling and vivacious; her name suggested a romantic spirit and a sophisticated heritage. But Renée Vivien (her mother was American, her father English, and her real name was Pauline Tarn) was consumed by the notion of death. According to Barney, who was Vivien's lover for several years, and to Colette, her neighbor, Vivien had no will to live. Natalie Barney claimed that Vivien's life was "a long suicide" from which she tried to save her, and Colette, whose will to live and survive was so strong, could not understand the nature of her young neighbor. Her visits to the darkened apartment where pale candles burned at mid-day against a dark velvet interior in which the odor of lilies and incense hung in the air horrified Colette. In this cloistered world Renée Vivien wrote sad poetry about her lost loves, pined for Natalie Barney, drank, drugged and starved herself to death in 1909, not yet 32 years of age.

Renée Vivien's sufferings seemed to lend credence to the assumption that homosexual preferences were the result of mental illness and psychological deviancy that, left unchecked, would eventually ruin the lives of their victims. There is little doubt that Willy's worst suspicions about lesbianism were confirmed by Vivien's circumstances, which he found to be laughable rather than tragic. When Colette went on stage after having left him, she became involved with the Marquise de Belbeuf (Missy), who herself had left an intolerable marriage. In the view of Willy and his salon society friends, Colette was thought to have fallen into the clutches of a sexual deviate, although Willy himself had promoted the fiction that Colette and Polaire (the woman who played Claudine on stage) had been in their youth and were as adults lesbian lovers. He dressed the women as twins and paraded them in Paris salon society. The Marquise de Belbeuf, however, was not one of Willy's fictions. Her lesbianism was real, and she derided bourgeois society by making a burlesque of male dress and mannerisms. (She did to men what dandies did to women in hateful mockery.) A cruel observer of the marquise, Willy delighted in satirizing her masculine mannerisms and her transvestism: "for his part, Willy felt no need whatsoever to speak well of her and preferred to indulge in his usual gross witticisms. One of his favorite games was to travel in train compartments marked 'For Women Only.' When someone would finally complain of his presence, he would reply, 'But I am the Marquise de Belbeuf'" (Sarde, *Colette*, 221). It was the marquise, however, who protected Colette from Willy's continued domination and who helped erase the effects of his physical and psychological abuse.

For these reasons, Willy hated her, insisting that under the marquise's influence Colette, too, would succumb to depression, drink, and early death. But it was not from concern for his former wife that Willy struggled against the marquise, but because his vanity had been injured. Soon after the divorce Willy was exposed as a literary fraud and was to die, ill and alone, without the support of friends.

Gertrude Stein: Rue de Fleurus

When Gertrude Stein arrived in Paris in September 1903, she was taking her first steps toward survival as a woman. Although the move itself entailed a continued dependency on her brother Leo, and although it did represent at the time a retreat into the safety of a patriarchal relationship, it also offered Stein the opportunity for self-discovery. In these early years in Paris she was to discover her sexual identity, her creative talents, and to establish—under Leo's initial direction—the most important artistic salon on the Left Bank. It was Leo who had discovered the apartment with its attached artist's studio at 27, rue de Fleurus, just off the Luxembourg Gardens. At this address, he hoped to take up painting. At age 31, Leo "had come to the end of his professional options," according to James R. Mellow. "History, philosophy, biology had all been tried and found wanting. His latest venture, art history, had also been abandoned" (*Charmed Circle*, 69). Options seemed to be narrowing for his sister as well: at 29, Gertrude found that her unsuccessful career as a medical student at Johns

Hopkins University no longer interested her. At loose ends, she was looking for a new life.

The studio at number 27 became, then, the focus of new directions in the Stein lives. Soon it was filled with the bright colors of Matisse and Cézanne paintings and by the Cubist angles of works by Picasso and Braque. The beginnings of one of the greatest art collections of the twentieth century were modest enough, however, purchased from the monies Leo and Gertrude saved by setting up household together. When the news came from their brother Michael in late 1904 that they had an unexpected 8,000 francs in their account, they quickly spent it at the art dealership of Ambroise Vollard on two brightly colored Gauguins, a pair of small Cézanne compositions of the *Bathers,* two more Renoirs, and a small Maurice Denis—a gift from Vollard. Within a short time the "collection" was to cover virtually every available inch of wall space in the studio and to overflow into the two-story *pavillon* adjacent (*Charmed Circle,* 83–84).

The salon that was to be associated with the rue de Fleurus address came about almost as accidentally as the art collection that was initially its focus. It began with friends, often the artists who painted the pictures that hung on the walls. It expanded to include almost anyone who knocked on the massive double doors on a Saturday evening. Although Gertrude Stein traditionally inquired of the visitor *de la part de qui venez-vous?* she rarely turned away anyone who could not provide a reference or an introduction. The Stein salon was open to anyone interested in modern art, and it required none of the elaborate inspections of social credentials needed a few blocks away in the Faubourg. Only after the fact were these informal evenings to take on the trappings of the salon. Even so, they bore little resemblance to the aristocratic gatherings in the homes of comtesses.

One was not required to speak French at these evenings. One certainly did not need to "dress," since Gertrude and Leo were comfortably attired in lookalike brown corduroy robes and leather sandals made for them by Raymond Duncan, who lived across the courtyard. Gertrude tended to squat rather than sit on a low Renaissance chair while Leo paced the studio, talking and smoking. One was guaranteed here an introduction to unconventional and controversial artwork and to the artists themselves, who were both less and more unconventional than their canvases. Guests frequently included Matisse and his wife (who served as his model), Picasso and Fernande Olivier (his mistress and model), and Georges Braque, as well as the poets Max Jacob and Guillaume Apollinaire, accompanied by Apollinaire's mistress, the painter Marie Laurencin. To fill out the numbers there were always American writers and artists in whom

Gertrude and Leo had a special interest. Although there were occasional visits from members of the upper classes or even European royalty, the usual group was neither titled nor monied. Thus Gertrude Stein's experience as a salon matron was far removed from that of Edith Wharton or Natalie Barney, although the careers of Stein and Barney were eventually to coincide. These three women did not share the same Paris, even though they lived quite close to one another. They did not even share the same epoch: Wharton belonged totally to the nineteenth century, although she spent thirty-seven years of her life in the twentieth. Barney, who lived in the twentieth century for seventy-two years, was always caught in the afterglow of the *fin de siècle*. Gertrude Stein stood squarely in the twentieth century with absolutely no interest in anything but the "continuous present."

Natalie Barney and Edith Wharton in the Sixth and Seventh *Arrondissements*

The similarities and differences among the three women are striking. Two of them were monied, Wharton and Barney having fortunes large enough to support expansive Paris lifestyles. Although by far the wealthier of the two, Barney lived rather modestly. Continuing to earn considerable royalties from her writing, Wharton spent money more ostentatiously on clothes, large houses, and frequent travels. Barney had a staff of two in her little house on the rue Jacob; Wharton had a staff of six in her second-floor apartment on the rue de Varenne. Wharton also had the very aristocratic Old New York upbringing that was not quite matched by Barney's railroad fortune and Washington political connections. But by the general terms of birth and breeding, these two women had much in common. As children they traveled extensively in Europe, even living there for long periods. They were drawn to European culture by education and instinct, but while Natalie Barney became equally at home in French and English as a young girl, Edith Wharton resumed the serious study of French in her mid-forties. Natalie Barney was 26 when she arrived in Paris in 1902, but she shared Wharton's aspirations: she was seeking a stimulating intellectual climate; she wanted to be part of the European cultural tradition; she hoped to continue her literary activities and practiced writing poems in the French mode; she intended to make a place for herself among the French in Paris. Edith Wharton wanted to be accepted by a society that was a separate and closed place on the Paris Left Bank.

These two women found places for themselves in this city, discovering social circles that overlapped. They skirted each other's company, knowing people in common but never knowing each other. Edith Wharton would have found friendship with a woman like Barney unthinkable, almost certainly because of Barney's flamboyant sexual activities. Perhaps not thoroughly aware of Vernon Lee's lesbianism—or politely refusing to recognize it—Edith Wharton pursued in these same years a friendship with Lee, a woman who had written studies of Italian art that Wharton treasured and who was a frequent visitor at Natalie Barney's rue Jacob salon. When Wharton needed support and encouragement for her own interests and self-development, someone to provide friendship and a model for her own ambitions, she "took to the older woman at once, as she would to other women over the years who, like Vernon Lee, combined gifts of mind and imagination with a somewhat unorthodox private character" (*Edith Wharton*, 72). Lewis's comments on Lee suggest a hesitancy to define the source of this "unorthodox private character," yet Vernon Lee was a well-known lesbian in her time, a woman who rode to hounds in the fashion of Radclyffe Hall and who left England in order to escape the censure of family and friends. Wharton, however, was not at all tolerant of lesbianism, although she pretended to a certain forbearance of male homosexuality. Lewis writes:

> She was less discerning and less tolerant of the Sisterhood. Looking back, she suspected her girlhood friend Emelyn Washburn of what she called "degeneracy," but at least in the early days she failed to intuit the latent tendencies of the mannish Vernon Lee. The habit of several well-born Parisian ladies, like Anna de Noailles, of experimenting sexually in both directions also seems to have escaped her—or perhaps not to have interested her. When Radclyffe Hall's autobiographical novel about lesbian experience, *The Well of Loneliness*, was published in France—after having been banned in England and fiercely condemned in America—Edith Wharton dismissed it as "dull twaddle."
>
> Edith Wharton made a point of steering clear of Natalie Clifford Barney. . . . Mme de Prevaux would remember that Edith looked upon Mrs. [*sic*] Barney as "something—appalling" (433–434).[3]

Natalie Barney's "private character" was, no doubt, too unorthodox and too public for Edith Wharton. Among all that these two women might have shared, the barrier between them was really one of social mores—Barney was determined to escape her stuffy, Protestant upbringing. Unlike Radclyffe Hall—and many other lesbian women who frequented her home—Barney did not suffer guilt because of her sexual orientation; she fairly rejoiced in her lesbianism, making it both a political and artistic *cause célèbre*. Wharton was determined to preserve the vestiges of endowed propriety and to protect the social facade she had so painfully erected around her. Natalie Barney was beautiful, but dowdy; Edith Wharton was not beautiful, but always elegantly dressed. Barney possessed a warm, open, and hospitable personality; Wharton's manner was frequently cold and reserved, apparently the result of intense shyness.

Wharton lived in houses that were perfectly designed, artistically appointed, with gardens she arranged in the eighteenth-century manner. Barney's rented houses were drab, furnished with items her mother did not think worth transporting back to America, cluttered with bric-a-brac, their gardens overgrown and unkempt. Wharton loved fast motor cars and traveled all over France in them. Barney kept a glass coach and horses and resented the day—well after World War II—when she was forced to buy a car. While Wharton belonged to the world of Henry James, Barney belonged to the world of Marcel Proust. Even so, as the two women advanced in age, they began to look rather like one another, representatives of an era consigned to the past.

Although Natalie Barney did not find a place for herself in the Faubourg, she certainly brought to her salon every important French writer of the period (including André Gide, Jean Cocteau—who was a close friend of Colette as well—Paul Valéry, and Colette herself). Barney's salon was unusual in that it freely mixed the French and American communities. Indeed, her greatest contribution to Left Bank intellectual life may have been in insisting that the two groups meet on the neutral territory of her drawing room. Pound was a frequent visitor, as were Ford Madox Ford, Carl Van Vechten, Sherwood Anderson, Thornton Wilder, Edith Sitwell, Romaine Brooks, Dolly Wilde, Janet Flanner, Solita Solano, Esther Murphy, Djuna Barnes, and many others. Barney was a particular supporter of women writers and often arranged meetings for women only that would allow a new writer to read her work to a sympathetic audience.

Spatial and Temporal Cross-References

If Barney was able to reach only the outskirts of the aristocratic enclave of the Faubourg, establishing herself on its borders, Gertrude Stein made no effort to reach it at all. Stein possessed none of the essentials required for entrance into this society. She was not from an upper-class American family. She was Jewish. Although well-educated, she was not rich. She did not arrive in Paris with letters of introduction to influential people, nor did she have her heart set, in autumn 1903, on becoming head of an artistic salon. The role she found for herself in Paris developed by chance, coming almost as a surprise to her. Once she found it, however, she exercised its power, enjoying herself immensely. Like Edith Wharton, Gertrude Stein found herself in Paris because she was lonely and seeking a life enriched and unencumbered. Like Natalie Barney, Stein found in Paris a setting that would allow her to act upon her love for women and to make her lesbianism a subject for her writing. If in certain ways Wharton and Barney trailed with them into the twentieth century all the encumbrances of the nineteenth, Stein's goal was to create the new era.

For Stein, America held the potential for the twentieth century, but Paris was required to develop that potential. Stein was not, therefore, interested in finding a place in French society, but in making a place for her own creative endeavors: "so Paris was the place that suited those of us that were to create the twentieth century art and literature, naturally enough" (*Paris France*, 12). Her inspiration in this effort was Henry James's brother, William, with whom she had studied at Radcliffe, and it was his theories of psychology that she applied in her early writings. She was later to say that only she and Henry James embodied the tradition of writing in America—modern writing, that is—but in her early years in Paris James was making his last visit to the city—to see Edith Wharton—feeling that he no longer had the strength to keep up with a city and a century changing so fast. Before Stein was known as an experimental writer of some repute, but not before the paintings she owned had attained their initial regard, both William and Henry James were dead.

It is doubtful whether any of these women pondered at great length the ironies of her temporal and spatial proximity to others. Nonetheless, the lives of Edith Wharton, Natalie Barney, Gertrude Stein, and Colette represent a continuum of experiences among Paris women. In physical space, these women encircled Left Bank literary Paris. In lived experience, these women's lives formed the circumference of an unacknowledged (and, to some extent, unrecognized) common center of feminine consciousness. Differences of social class, educational levels, religious upbringing, political attitudes, sexual preferences, age, and even nationality served to enrich rather than eliminate definition of such a consciousness, counteracting the myth that the Paris of these years was homogeneously masculine, chauvinistic, and self-destructive. But the inherent, and essential, disparity among individual lives has often suggested that such women as these had nothing in common with each other, that their consciousness of themselves *as women* was a factor of little or no importance. Yet the coincidence of their Paris residence, the tangled web of common friendships, and the accident of missed acquaintances invite examination.

What, then, did these women share? Each of them found herself in Paris because of an important male figure in her life. Edith Wharton came to Paris to escape the constraints of a marriage that Paris eventually destroyed. Natalie Barney came to escape an overbearing and puritanical father, whose early death would provide the means by which she could continue her expatriation. Gertrude Stein followed a brother to Paris in an effort to escape an unhappy lesbian love affair in New York. Colette came to Paris in bondage to a husband whose unwilling accomplice she became. Each of these women eventually overcame obstacles to independence and self-fulfillment, separating themselves psychologically as well as physically from the men who would entrap them, turning their collective energies toward writing as a means of liberation. Often these works concerned the lives of women like themselves and examined the relation of women to writing, placing it in relation to the writer's own biography. Only one among them *had* to write, had to accept a vocation she did not initially desire and for which she felt she had no inherent talent ("No, I never, never wished to write," wrote Colette). But in the strange circumstances of Colette's first marriage, this vocation she did not want became the means of freeing her from a marriage that very nearly destroyed her will to live.[4]

Colette discovered what the others already seemed to know—that writing was an essential act of creativity bearing direct relation to her womanhood, a way of discovering herself as a woman. Colette's experience was, in important ways, the reverse of Edith Wharton's, and these two women's lives as writers bear an odd relation to each other. Colette is the only member of the group from a rural background, the product of a *bourgeoise déclassée* family that could provide a daughter no skilled training and no dowry to ensure a comfortable marriage. Perhaps the choice of Willy turned on just these economic factors, making Colette a victim of a form of white slave trade, in bondage to her own husband. Michèle Sarde comments:

> The appearance of true literary pandering assumed by Willy's exploitation of her literary talent could be perfectly studied from a feminist perspective. I see no better point of reference than that of pandering: instead of prostituting his wife's body, Willy prostituted her literary talent, drew from it the financial and moral profit (for it was he who was famous and recognized) and, in exchange, ensured conjugality (that is, a type of vague protection and even vaguer emotional security). . . . Colette is therefore doubly alienated from her position, *both* as writer-proletarian in her husband's workshops *and* as unpaid writer-wife. (In Eisinger and McCarty, *Colette: The Woman, The Writer,* 7–15)

But Edith Wharton's economic circumstances and the demands of her social class suggest that she also had little option on the marriage market: it was imperative to marry someone of her own rank and breeding; in Old New York society, this meant the choice of a socially well-placed but unintellectual husband. Thus Wharton's writing threatened her marriage and her place in the society to which she was born: "I remember once saying that I was a failure in Boston (where we used to go to stay with my husband's family) because they thought I was too fashionable to be intelligent, and a failure in New York because they were afraid I was too intelligent to be fashionable" (*A Backward Glance,* 119). If Wharton's literary royalties allowed her the freedom to decide where she would live, to buy and redecorate houses, to take upon herself decisions usually left to husbands, Colette's economic dependence on Willy—despite the profit her writing was making him—doubly bound her. When it was recognized that Colette rather than Willy was the author of the *Claudine* series, however, she—like Wharton—became a threat to her husband. Colette received her divorce in 1910, Edith Wharton hers in 1913.

That Natalie Barney and Gertrude Stein avoided the marriage trap had less to do with economic factors than with sexual preference. Barney barely escaped a marriage arranged by her father as a "cure" for her lesbian tendencies, while Stein, having lost a father, set up housekeeping with a brother to allay her own suspicions about her sexual orientation. Three of these women were suffering acutely from repressed sexuality at the moment of their arrival in Paris. The fourth arrived to announce— and continued to celebrate for sixty years—the sexual preference she had known for some time. Their fiction and poetic writings recapitulate this period of sexual repression and awakening. Three of them make explicit reference in their memoirs and autobiographies to the psychic trauma resulting from such sexual repression. Edith Wharton, of course, censored such concerns from her autobiography, hiding them in her private notebooks and diaries. Writing for these women was a process of self-discovery: what they discovered, in all cases, was a *sexual* self. What is most significant is that they survived the traumas of self-discovery, writing through their own biographies the history of sexual and intellectual liberation in the twentieth century. Each fashioned from the materials of her life a chronicle of woman's reliance and recuperative power. All acknowledged that Paris itself served as a source of inspiration in these efforts. In a sense, each of them discovered a different city upon her arrival. Each was to structure a space for herself within its larger boundaries, but the undercurrent of woman's durability—of her ability to survive under patriarchal repression—unites even the most disparate among them.

At Home: 1909

If we choose 1909 as the year in which to visit each of these women, we can better fix them in terms of each other. Although they share no explicit set of relationships, the absence of manifest connections is striking evidence of the range of choices available to women within the Paris literary community. In 1909, these women continued to live in their individual orbits, ignorant of the larger patterns their private histories would make, unaware of the specific temporal and spatial relations among them that history would trace. If we look in on them "at home" in this year, the properties of their separate lives become more available. We find Edith Wharton living in an apartment at 53, rue de Varenne. Her husband had left for America, suffering from the neurasthenia that would eventually incapacitate him. Wharton remained in Paris, determined to separate herself from him permanently and "to find a place in the Faubourg where, with or without Teddy, she could settle more or less permanently" (Lewis, *Edith Wharton,* 258). This was the first year in thirty that she spent entirely in Europe, and it was a decisive one for her.

The apartment she found was across the street from number 58, where she had resided periodically for several years. The new apartment was larger, with a series of balconies along the street, the interior facing a private courtyard. It stood at the top of the street, near the rue du Bac, next to the Cité de Varenne (a "close"), and adjacent to the gardens of the Doudeauville *hôtel.* The apartment was large and unfurnished:

> In addition to the library, the spacious, high-ceilinged drawing room, the elegant dining room (all in a row above the court), and a good-sized kitchen and pantry, there were a half-dozen bedrooms of various sizes, another sitting room—probably for Gross [Wharton's housekeeper] and Edith's personal maid—and several inadequately equipped bathrooms. The apartment contained what amounted to a guest suite: a bedroom and bath, and for private access a back stairs leading down to the courtyard. . . . Happily, and in a leisurely manner, Edith began to rummage through the Paris bazaars and the Faubourg antique shops in pursuit of one of her favorite occupations—and keeping an eye out, too, for that most urgent necessity, a porcelain bathtub. (*Edith Wharton,* 258)

This apartment provided sanctuary for Wharton during a year filled with emotional highs and lows. In part because of her increasing marital unhappiness, Wharton was between publications, concentrating on poetry and short essays rather than long fictional works. Psychologically, her energies were directed toward a permanent separation from her husband. Acquiring the apartment at number 53 was the first step in this direction.

On 3 July 1909, at the Charing Cross Hotel in London, Edith Wharton experienced the first night of sexual passion in her entire life—in the arms of her lover, Morton Fullerton, who had replaced George Adam as the Paris correspondent for the *Times* of London. She was 47 years old. The following morning, before Fullerton had left the hotel to catch his train from Waterloo station, Wharton had already begun the poem describing the event. She sat propped up in bed, a lapboard before her, writing the verses in longhand. Writing in bed in the morning was common for her, a daily activity of her life even when she traveled. Wharton's desire for Fullerton, who spent the next several months in America, sustained her through a summer in which she received reports of her husband's oddly manic and overstimulated behavior in Boston. His physician warned of the possible ill effects to his mental balance that a return to Paris ("an environment that does not appeal to him") might bring him. Upon his return in October 1909, Teddy Wharton was plunged into acute depression, followed by the admission to his wife that he had speculated with large sums of her money, had purchased a "small flat" in Boston (a purchase that also included a piece of land with buildings on it), and had established a young mistress there. Although certain aspects of the story were exaggerated—that he had let out rooms in the building to chorus girls, for instance—it was clear that his illness had reached a point where it could no longer be overlooked. In the autumn of this year Edith Wharton decided eventually to divorce him, thereby leaving herself free for the attentions of (and hoped-for marriage with) Morton Fullerton—a dream that was not to come true.

In the autumn of 1909, Natalie Barney moved to an address about a mile and a half from Wharton's—20, rue Jacob. She was to occupy a house that Maréchal de Saxe had built for Adrienne Lecouvreur, the very popular eighteenth-century actress, a house "with a leafy garden in which Racine and his mistress La Champmeslé had strolled together" (Wickes, *Amazon of Letters,* 104). The address was not prestigious, but the setting was—and remains—intellectually interesting, located in the most artistically active part of the sixth *arrondissement,* an area known to la Rochefoucauld, Saint-Simone, Voltaire, and Fénélon. Barney's house, however, separated her from the busy life of this quarter, situated as it was "in a world of its own":

> Actually, the house she lived in is off the street. . . . The building on the street at 20 rue Jacob is a four-storied affair divided into apartments, like most of its neighbors. A large gateway leads into a cobblestoned courtyard, and at the end of the court is the two-storied *pavillon,* a little house that stands by itself in a garden. The garden is quite spacious for this section of Paris and completely wild, with thin, reedy trees growing very tall, creating a shadowy atmosphere of subaqueous greenery. . . .
>
> The most distinctive feature of the property she rented is a small Doric temple tucked away in a corner of the garden. There are all sorts of legends about this temple, chiefly centering on the great actress Adrienne Lecouvreur, who was the idol of eighteenth-century Paris and the love of some of its greatest men, and who died under mysterious circumstances, probably poisoned by a jealous rival. But contrary to legend, the temple was not a trysting place or a tomb of love, nor are its origins so ancient. The inscription on its pediment dedicates the temple *à l'amitié,* "to friendship," and official records show that it dates back only to the early nineteenth century. (*Amazon of Letters,* 104)

Barney's two-story *pavillon* located behind this weedy and mysterious garden fit her character as appropriately as the spacious and elegant apartment on the rue de Varenne fit Edith Wharton's personality. Barney was to occupy this apartment until her death in 1972 at the age of 96. She shopped at the market on the rue de Seine, as did Alice B. Toklas, both bringing home fresh fruits and flowers to their lovers. Barney was often seen arriving and departing this address in her glass coach (complete with footman), as the middle-class residents who mingled with Sorbonne students and neighboring artists looked on astonished. When the 1968 student riots took place outside her window, she continued her salon, as impervious to these events as she was to the progress of time. She remained transfixed by history, like the medieval streets on which she trod.

Natalie Barney moved to her new house in an effort to win back Renée Vivien, the lover with whom she had spent tempestuous years in Passy. She rented the apartment on the rue Jacob hoping that she could welcome Vivien—who for much of 1909 was away on a voyage around the world with relatives—to a place removed from the painful associations of the Bois de Boulogne. Instead, the house proved to be Barney's refuge against the grief over Vivien's death in November. She spent the end of that year— the time when Edith Wharton suffered the news of her husband's financial disasters and evidence of his worsening health—mourning Vivien. Only the following year did her life brighten with the publication of three volumes of poetry and an important new friendship with Remy de Gourmont.

The year 1909 was an important, and happy, one for Gertrude Stein because it saw the publication of *Three Lives,* which she had completed in 1906, as well as the propitious development of her relationship with Alice Toklas. In the autumn she declared her love to Toklas on a hillside outside of Florence, asking her to be her "wife" and to move in with her at 27, rue de Fleurus. Like Wharton, Stein during this year needed to be rid of the male who for years had been her companion and closest friend, but who now was perhaps threatened by her new commitment—her brother Leo. In the spring she asked if Alice Toklas could move in with them. More than one year later—September 1910—the move was effected; in the following months Leo felt increasingly uncomfortable in the house and eventually moved out of it forever.

Although this address is now associated with Gertrude Stein's life there—the blue plaque on the front of the house marking her thirty-five-year residence—the *pavillon* and studio were chosen by Leo to suit his own special needs. The address was close to 58, rue Madame, where he later found an apartment for his older brother Michael, and the studio annex was a choice that acknowledged Leo's hope, in 1902, that he was headed for a career as an artist:

> The marvel was that the studio at 27 rue de Fleurus—large by ordinary domestic standards but small for such a public function—should have held so

many paintings, so many people. The Steins had set about collecting so industriously that the three available walls of the studio—the fourth was cut by the double door and oddly shaped windows that let in the northern light—were crammed with pictures hung row above row. In the dim and fluttering gaslight, only the lower ranges of art were clearly visible. Visitors had to shade their eyes from the glare of the low-hanging fixtures in order to pierce the gloom in which many of the pictures hung tantalizingly above. . . .

The room was a jumble of furniture as well, crowding guests into a sense of intimacy. A long, sturdy Florentine table [where Gertrude wrote] surrounded by Renaissance chairs was drawn close to the cast-iron stove at the back of the room. There were sideboards and buffets and bulky chests and little tables settled along the walls and in corners. . . . There were cheap porcelain figurines, costly Renaissance plates, tiny alabaster urns with alabaster doves balancing at the rims—objects Gertrude bought when she visited curio shops. Leaning against the walls were large portfolios of Japanese prints and Picasso drawings. (Mellow, *Charmed Circle*, 17–18)

Although furnished by the efforts of both brother and sister, this room was to become famous in pictures and in the memories of hundreds of people who visited there because of Gertrude Stein's presence, her black eyes peering out of a cheerful face, her short, squat body mounted on one of the Renaissance chairs.

The neighborhood around the rue de Fleurus is less interesting than that of the rue Jacob and not nearly as well preserved as the street on which Edith Wharton lived. This neighborhood is newer than either of the others, its streets dating from the late eighteenth century, and further removed from the intellectual and artistic activity of the sixth *arrondissement*. But much about the area was congenial to Stein's work habits and general lifestyle. The neighborhood is quietly respectable, if not elegant, its tree-lined streets cut by small parks and enclosed gardens. The rue de Fleurus leads directly into the Luxembourg Gardens, a place where Stein walked frequently and the setting of her first afternoon alone with Alice Toklas in the autumn of 1907. It was here that her anger at Alice's tardy arrival at the studio cooled as they walked among the flowers, statuary, and children at play, observing governesses and nurses with starched white caps minding infants of the nearby Faubourg. In later years, after Stein's death, Toklas continued to walk their white poodle through the gardens, remembering the happier hours she had spent there with her companion.

There was nothing sophisticated or elegant about Stein's house. It was spacious, quiet, and comfortable. It provided her the work space she needed. When she wrote about this first Paris residence in *Paris France* (1940), she was living in the rue Christine, a one-block street in the heart of St. Germain des Prés, made famous by an Apollinaire poem, "Lundi, rue Christine." The move to this house, which had supposedly belonged to Queen Christina of Sweden, was not by choice but by decree of the landlord of the rue de Fleurus property, who needed the apartment for his newly married son. Stein tried to make the best of it, writing to a friend: "We were tired of the present which also was the past because no servant could stand the kitchen, there was no air in the house, the garage they had built next door had made it uncomfortable." Nonetheless, to leave the old quarter was "awful." It was this first Paris neighborhood that was "hometown" to her:

> We none of us lived in old parts of Paris then. We lived in the rue de Fleurus just a hundred years old quarter, a great many of us lived around there and on the boulevard Raspail. . . .
> So from 1900 to 1930 those of us who lived in Paris did not live in picturesque quarters even those who lived in Montparnasse like Picasso and Bracque [sic] did not live in old houses, they lived in fifty year old houses at most and now we all live in the ancient quarter near the river, now that the twentieth century is decided and has its character we all tend to want to live in seventeenth century houses, not barracks or ateliers as we did then. (Paris France, 15, 17)

Without being at all definite about specific places and people, with no reliance on facts, Stein offers a memoir of Paris that is accurate in its sense of time and place. We know that Stein knew intimately what it felt like to live there, and her impressions of the city tell us what it felt like for *her* to live there.

By 1909, Colette had dropped out entirely from the salon world she had known with Willy and was in her third year of traveling performances with a music hall group. She had exchanged the social life of the *haut-monde* for that of the *demi-monde*, a life lived on the margins of society, her daily existence dominated by work and by relationships with other women. Ironically, it was Willy who had first suggested this means for an independent life, initially encouraging Colette's interest in the music hall. She began by taking a series of dance and mime lessons with George Wague, who was later to become her mime partner. Her first appearances were in Paris at the popular café-concert (the *caf' conc'*), where she sang provocative songs and danced in various stages of undress. Audiences at the *caf' conc'* were always in need of cheap thrills (the price of admission was one drink) and the subject matter of the skits often revealed interest in variant sexual practices. Burlesque, striptease, and bawdy musical varieties were the fare at such theaters as the Ba-Ta-Clan in Montmartre, where Colette often appeared.

Colette's professional life during the years that followed her divorce were spent in vaudeville, among proletarian theater people whom she had not known prior to her separation from Willy. The penury of these years brought her dangerously close to prostitution as a method of self-support. Instead she followed a seven-day-a-week routine of hard labor in the dance hall. These years are described in *L'Envers du music-hall,* about which Michèle Sarde comments:

> It was a glimpse into a working-class world more varied than the usual pro-
> letariat, one in which the female element was considerably more important.
> In a certain way, Colette lived as a working-class woman. She did not ap-
> proach her life as a militant, she had no ideological prejudices, but from it
> she gained a clear realization of class and sex consciousness. The rapidity
> with which she moved from one stratum of society to another also makes us
> realize how socially mobile women are, and how fragile that mobility is.
> Yesterday, she had been a respectable middle-class woman; today, she is a
> semiworking-class actress; tomorrow she will be a baroness. Women were less
> strictly tied to one social class than men, to an unalterable hierarchy. The
> wheel of fortune could drop her in an instant from the heights to the bottom
> of the rickety social ladder. (*Colette,* 253)

More obviously than the lives of Wharton, Stein, or Barney, Colette's existence during the years before World War I illustrated the insecurity of social place for women. Of the four, she was the only one not protected by some kind of inheritance. Thus she was totally independent and forced to support herself by her own resources. Edith Wharton was heir to a large fortune that included several houses and some land in New England, so her life—inside or outside her marriage—would have been comfortable. She essentially supported her husband through many years of marriage; he had no great wealth and no profession other than managing her estate. But in the years before the war Edith Wharton earned an enormous income from her writing, particularly from *The House of Mirth,* which for several months was on the bestseller list in America. In the three-year period between 1906 and 1909, she earned $65,000 from her writings (the equivalent, perhaps, of $650,000 today). Colette's writing was also earning huge sums in these years, the *Claudine* novels selling at a fantastic rate and the stage performances derived from them also meeting with great popular success. But Colette never saw any of the money she earned from her writing. Willy kept all of the royalties and, needing money in 1910, sold the rights to various publishing companies, effectively closing Colette out of any proceeds from her early novels. (Colette eventually did succeed, in 1926, in having her name put on the *Claudine* novels and in receiving royalty rights; Sarde, *Colette,* 206–207.) From her music hall work she earned barely enough to pay the 1,700-franc yearly rent on the Villejust apartment and to feed herself while on road tours around France. She was frequently ill and underfed; she suffered from overwork, the effects of living in underheated lodgings, depression, and the pressures of constant travel.

During these years Colette lived in a world populated almost entirely by women—the world of the *caf' conc'* and of Lesbos—and by comparison with the years of Willy's oppression, these were happy and productive ones. She was freed from the confinement of place, from the apartments in which, under lock and key, she had written for his economic gain. In 1909, when Wharton, Stein, and Barney took refuge in their Paris apartments, protected from the outside world by the interior worlds they created for themselves, Colette was exposed to the public, traveling from one small town in France to another, sleeping in train stations or in hotel rooms with four persons to a bed. Still, she worked on *La vagabonde,* her memoirs of these years (to be published under her own name), and traveled through Brittany with Missy looking at country houses that they might buy with Missy's money. Finally, in December, the two women took an apartment together on the rue Saint-Senoch, finding a private world of their own. Not yet officially divorced from Willy, and still publishing her work under the name "Colette Willy," she played Claudine on stage, a role that Willy had made famous for her. On 21 June 1910, her divorce was final and she at last became "Colette."

Paris had given Colette—under circumstances very different from those that brought Edith Wharton, Gertrude Stein, and Natalie Barney to the city—a place to write: indeed, it was in this city that each of these women discovered the necessity to write. When Stein commented, "I write for myself and strangers," she might have been summarizing the writing situation of each of these four women. Each discovered that a room of one's own in this city of light could provide a window on a very special world. Wharton's world was an enclosed, luxurious space: "From her bedroom, as she sat writing the final pages of the novel called *The Fruit of the Tree* . . . she could look down not onto the street but onto a wide courtyard protected by a heavy iron gate: a somberly handsome enclave in which she could feel luxuriously shut off from the world about her" (Lewis, *Edith Wharton,* 176). Colette discovered that, pen in hand, she could fly away from the dark, narrow, chill room high above the rue Visconti to discover the lush fields of the Burgundy of her childhood. Barney recreated Lesbos as she looked out on her overgrown garden in the rue Jacob and composed a sonnet to Renée Vivien; Stein sat at a long writing table, her window overlooking the interior courtyard of a *pavillon,* and closed the pages of *Three Lives.*

4

FROM THE LEFT BANK TO THE UPPER EAST SIDE: JANET FLANNER'S LETTER FROM PARIS

The Early Years (1925–1932)

Much about the Paris described in previous chapters was unknown to the Americans who invaded the city following World War I: these newcomers were little interested in the "French" aspect of Paris. They sought respite from an America they found to be politically naive, puritanically restrictive, and culturally deprived. For some, the need for escape was itself a sign of self-destructive tendencies. For others, expatriation meant real liberation. For women, America was a particularly oppressive environment, and among the expatriate women were those who took up Edith Wharton's "argument with America" on "the woman question," finding in their personal sense of alienation from their native land important literary themes. Exploring Edith Wharton's reaction to the predominant optimism regarding woman's situation in America toward the end of the nineteenth century, Elizabeth Ammons comments:

> Relentlessly she examined the disjunction between popular optimism and the reality as she saw it. Typical women in her view—no matter how privileged, nonconformist, or assertive (indeed, often in proportion to the degree in which they embodied those qualities)—were not free to control their own lives, and that conviction became the foundation of her argument with American optimism for more than twenty years. She agreed that the position of women in American society was the crucial issue of the new century; she did not believe that change was occurring. In her opinion the American woman was far from being a new or whole human being. (*Edith Wharton's Argument with America,* 3)

Although Ammons makes a strong case for Wharton's feminism and for the transformation of Wharton's own painful experiences as daughter,

99

woman, and wife into her fiction, she does not explore the relation between the desire to live abroad—that is, the choice of living in Paris—and either Wharton's feminism or her writing. And it was away from America, from the vantage point of Europe, that Wharton was able to gain a perspective on American woman's experience and to contrast this experience with that of the French. This topic constitutes the narrative thread of Wharton's *French Ways and Their Meanings,* published after World War I.

A major problem in reconstructing Paris of the postwar period arises from the limited perspective of source materials commonly used in such an investigation. Not unexpectedly, the accounts of these years focus on the expatriate community as an entity separate from and tangential to the French capital that encompassed it. For the most part, these accounts have been constructed by the expatriates themselves, people who maintained their status as outsiders regardless of the length of their residence in France or the influence of Paris on their lives. It is a commonly held assumption, for instance, that members of this literary community made little effort to learn about French culture, to meet the French, or to do anything beyond the effort required for survival in the parent culture. This premise has well served critics and chroniclers who evoked the Paris setting as a fertile but undemanding culture in which the expatriate Modernist experiment prospered.

Consequently, we know very little from these accounts about Paris as a French city after the war. And we know less about the French: their economic worries, their cultural tastes and artistic preferences, their customs, habits, and daily routines remain mysteries. Nevertheless, it was just this Paris—the city of the French—that Harold Ross wished to define when he asked Janet Flanner to contribute a "Letter from Paris" for his fledgling magazine, the *New Yorker,* in 1925. He sensed a special relationship between New York and Paris, between the French and the Americans, and he was curious about the cultural basis of this accord. In the succeeding fifty years, Flanner documented Paris life for American readers, tracing the cycle of events, both ordinary and spectacular, in "the most capital capital of the world."[1] Her accounts ceaselessly detailed a pattern of Paris life that went unobserved by the casual tourist and also remained, perhaps, unknown to the expatriate resident.

These letters are so wide ranging in their interests, so inclusive in their accounting of events and people, that they miss virtually nothing of interest to later researchers. Moreover, they include information and impressions that could not now be reproduced by the most scholarly activity, even if all the principals in this cultural drama still lived. It is a record that is experienced, not remembered. Its perceptions are not dusted over with the span of years, nor do they serve as belated repayment for disappointments, injustices, or youthful errors—as do many memoirs of the period.

More importantly, this chronicle is not a reflection upon an individual life in the context of literary Paris, but a narrative in which Paris itself serves as the central figure. Nonetheless, Flanner's intellectual presence in the letters is undeniable. Indeed, her presence is essential to the success of this venture. It was she who breathed life into this portrait of Paris and, as her confidence in the project grew, flaunted her opinions, her perspective, her artistic and political interests. As an observer she was not without ego and personality or devoid of sensitivity and sophistication. She chose carefully what was observed and ignored anything that did not hold her interest. But reading the letters retrospectively, one is overwhelmed at the sheer amount of activity that attracted Flanner's interest and commentary.

The Paris Letters are put to the service of this study of expatriate experience as the narrative chronicle through which an analysis of a woman's place in literary Paris can be focused. Of course, these letters were not intended to serve such a purpose. It is, perhaps, an accident of history that this record was constructed and articulated by a woman, one who shared with other women writers resident in Paris similar reasons for expatriation and similar goals for her literary experiment. She knew everyone in this community. There was no event—no concert, opera, horse race, fashion show, ball, art opening, poetry reading, or salon tea—where she was not welcomed. And to document such events was her professional calling.

Such documentation was admittedly subjective and specialized, even as it appeared to be descriptive and generalized. The tone of the letters is consciously witty, their organization casual, and the subject matter (particularly in the early years) often inconsequential. Especially at the outset, the special perspective of an American woman journalist is not always easily apparent, whereas the constraints of the journalistic form and the cycle of activities that are its subject matter are often rather obvious. But these constraints, like the convention of the letter itself, are turned by Flanner to her advantage. Although the letters chronicle real events, they serve almost fictional, extrahistorical roles, as if they were the product of literary endeavor rather than journalistic report. Consequently, there is a perceptible space between the language of the letters and their subject matter, a space in which Parisians and Americans move about a mythical city constructed by a woman who continually places herself midway between expatriates and Europeans.

Flanner's only published novel, *The Cubical City*, recreates the cultural life of New York in the 1920s. As its title suggests, the basic metaphor is architectural, but the thematic concerns of the novel turn on American sexual puritanism—in particular its double standard of behavior for men and women—and it contrasts life for a modern woman set "in the midst of a mechanical civilization" (New York City) with that of "ancient females, who in small select numbers had received in absentia grain, prayers, milk, worship or hyacinth buds placed on credulous rural shrines." This novel is about women and reflects their struggle to free themselves from patriarchal constraints and restrictions on "natural" behavior: "The world has always had lovers. And yet as near as I can observe, for thousands of years the concentrated aim of society has been to cut down kissing. With that same amount of energy . . . society could have stopped war, established liberty, given everybody a free education, free bathtubs, free music, free pianos and changed the human mind to boot" (366). The novel displays Flanner's characteristic humor, but it also reflects her determined effort to break free of midwestern puritanical thought. She shared this determination with several other women of the expatriate community, including Edith Wharton.

The Paris Letters negotiate a delicate territory: they had to make Paris and its citizenry available to an American public that was both physically and psychologically removed from the subject. In the beginning, Flanner knew little about her prospective audience, just as the *New Yorker* knew little about its intended readership. She assumed herself to be writing for those of her own kind—literary, cultured, curious, sophisticated readers—who were genuinely interested in the idiosyncrasies of a foreign culture. In the early letters she frequently commented on the kinds of information her fellow New Yorkers were receiving about Paris, carefully preserving the double perspective of an American resident in Europe. These accounts often occasioned a self-reflexive response to their own composition and defined—by their ironic tone—the readership they addressed. They succeeded by casting the unknown in terms of the known. Paris was always introduced by way of New York, and American attitudes were firmly imbedded in the various vignettes presented in the letters. The writer frequently appears as someone who lives simultaneously in New York and Paris:

> "The Paris That's Not in the Guidebook," by Basil Woon, has reached and excited this American city. It is written for our compatriots who, already familiar with the Louvre and Mona Lisa, are more interested—so far as Paris is concerned—in the Ritz bar and Mrs. Jean Nash. Besides two chapters devoted to Mrs. N., invaluable information is included for art-lovers on how long it takes Boni de Castellane to dress each morning, why Anthony Drexel closed his house on the Rue de Grenelle, how Viola Cross-Krauss launched new styles at Lanvin's, why Ganna Walska mourns, etc., etc. Splendid "don'ts" are also given for worried Ciro-lunchers. As we recall it, No. 1 said you mustn't appear before one-thirty, and we disremember No. 2, but it doubtless forbade you bringing a basket lunch. The book is a gold-plated mine of private information now made public, of wholesale accuracy and

shrewd observation. Unfortunately, not a face, fact, facet nor fortune of inter-national Paris society escapes the wonderful Mr. Woon. Lacking the literary grace for permanent memoirs, the book is only garrulously apt for 1926. But by 2026 it should be regarded by Parisian history-students as a tender classic. (23 October 1926)

Woon's book, no doubt, was intended for the sort of American tourist who needed no guide to identify Mrs. Nash, Anthony Drexel, or Ganna Walska, and who already knew the proper hour for lunch at Ciro's. Flanner's incisive wit cuts in both directions in her commentary, as she disdains the audience for which this book was written while finding herself engrossed by the type of information—if not the kind of society—such a work defined. And the description of the book's working method is almost—but not quite—a commentary on her own Paris Letters, her literary style, and the presumably ephemeral quality of such a record. Her letters take special interest in making private information public; they are based on fastidious accuracy and shrewd observation; they make no effort to capture anything but the contemporary scene.

Flanner, too, presents a cast of characters assumed to be already known to her readers (if we do not recognize Boni de Castellane, the letters will not help identify him) and employs a narrative method that eschews exposition, explanation, or analysis of local events. No event, however portentous, is blatantly "covered" by these early letters. Rather, the event is fixed in its social and cultural context, woven into a narrative that carefully orders plot lines through periodic installments. Genuinely interested in people, Flanner was put off by "personalities." She was especially contemptuous of the American interest in expatriate "society" and would have taken little interest in Edith Wharton's dinner menus or the table conversation of her dining companions. (As her memorial essay on Wharton makes clear, however, Flanner was very interested in Wharton's intelligence, her feminism, her writings, and her contributions to French-American cultural exchange.) When Flanner reported the social scene, it was almost always with a malicious eye. She wrote that "it was also unusual in the recent round of Parisian parties . . . that [this one] was given by a French woman and featured only good food and good friends. Among the latter was Miss Dolly Wilde in the habiliments of her uncle, Oscar Wilde, and looking both important and earnest" (16 July 1930).

Janet Flanner knew well the multiple attractions Paris held for her compatriots, but only rarely do her Paris Letters articulate these qualities. Instead, they endeavor to render the essential nature of the city, concentrating on what is particularly and peculiarly French in its landscape. While they seem to assume a broad readership, in fact the letters are intended for a very specific audience, one that the letters themselves create: this correspondence addresses middle-class New Yorkers who share Flanner's interests, attitudes, and politics. While preserving only the barest forms of the epistolary convention, these letters nevertheless imply both a writer and a reader. The speaker is hidden by a pseudonym ("Genêt," a totally androgynous name chosen for Flanner without her knowledge by Harold Ross, who apparently thought it the French equivalent of "Janet"), and the letters address Flanner's editors—Harold Ross until his death; William Shawn thereafter. Flanner shared important professional and personal relationships with both these men. These two friends characterized the kind of reading audience the *New Yorker* (still under the direction of William Shawn) continues to have; thus their interests were her interests and also those of other readers. Increasingly, she relied on Shawn's judgment, feeling that he allowed her to be serious about her work in a way that Ross did not. The relationships among various writers for the *New Yorker* have often been described in memoirs that suggest an intimacy and good humor among the staff. Except during World War II, however, Flanner never worked in the New York office. Like Mollie Panter Downes, who took up the "Letter from London" following World War II, Flanner was always at long distance from her immediate supervisors and her readers.

Nevertheless, relationships were carefully cultivated and preserved, and the Paris Letters reveal the extent to which Flanner instinctively knew both her subject and her intended audience. Her letters serve friendships as well as journalism, constructing a subterrain of common viewpoints, frames of reference, and implicit understanding; often, they contain private jokes and personal messages. Like all letters, these are occasioned by the moment and are locked into a specific historical context, one that is seen in retrospect to be comprised of much that is trivial, daily, and no longer worthy of note. In their public and literary status, however, they have ensured a future for much that was inherently without a future—and in doing so, they allow us the privilege of a contemporary perspective on a period now only partially recuperable. More importantly, the letters have ensured a literary future for Janet Flanner. Those ephemeral occurrences that caught her eye are of interest to us now because they were part of *her* world.

But what, precisely, constituted Janet Flanner's world? Her response to a somewhat different question posed by the *Little Review* (May 1929) defines the perimeters of her interests.

> What should you most like to do, to know, to be? (In case you are not satisfied.)
> I should like to be a traveller proper to this century: a knapsack and diary [are] no longer enough. A voyage suitable to the 20th century is like no exploration into visible space ever taken before, must be conducted with elabo-

rate knowledge, scientific data, vaccinations and most particularly, the superb modern mechanics which only a millionaire can rent. Poor people should not travel now. The day of pilgrims is over.

The questionnaire includes other interesting information about Flanner: she wanted to be writer (to be "Sterne or any of the Brontes"); she wanted to be a modern writer like Hemingway—"to be even Hemingway, since he is better at being Hemingway than any of the other Hemingways." Her closest male friend, Hemingway served for Flanner as model writer and journalist, one who took the profession of writing very seriously.

Flanner *was* the "traveller proper" to the century she describes, although her travels began carelessly enough. In 1922, she left America and brief posts on American newspapers to join others on the Left Bank. She had a small income and no stated professional intention. By 1925, her personal letters from Paris to Jane Grant, whose husband founded the *New Yorker,* had earned her a post on its staff. Grant encouraged Flanner to "write newsy letters like you've been writing to me—about anything except fashion . . . you need to get to work." The first Paris letter appeared on 10 October 1925 and was enthusiastically praised by Jane Grant for being "chatty and instructive, angled for the prospective tourist." Later Flanner was to feel embarrassed by these early efforts, sensing in them a naivete belied by her later, more blatantly political writings. She took these concerns very seriously. Writing to William Shawn about a proposed collection of prewar letters, she said:

[the collection] contains appalling illiterate holes and omissions where French books are concerned and French writers of major importance to American readers today, whether the writers are alive or dead now, being in any case famous and part of the trans-Atlantic cultural scene as at present recognized. Instead of reviewing books by Gide, on Gide, by Camus such as *L'Etranger* and *La Peste* or by Sartre such as *L'Etre ou le Neant,* etc. I wasted our pages with such trivia of ephemeral quality that it is enough to make an intelligent bookloving reader's gorge rise, in 1966. I have no idea why I wrote so rarely about books; I only know it is an omission that is now a shocking error which since I notice it will most certainly be noticed by others, who in criticising me, will be criticising the magazine in a way, which would make my grief even more real. . . . What can we do? If you have already started to look through and cut those early letters you must be as shocked as I am at how little is worth saving and how tawdry even when you will have cut out, as you certainly will, the worst of it; you will also be equally shocked with me at the omission of literary news which give the Letters an intellectual emptiness that is sad, that is light-minded, that is so regrettable that I cannot understand why I never noted what I was *not* doing over the years . . . what I wrote in the late 1920s and thirties—nothing but the ephemeral politics of the fleeting scene (often done well enough but with no greatly conscious historic sense constantly maintained). (31 April 1964)[2]

Although Flanner herself presents a rigorous critique of her own past work (with which many might, from the vantage point of a later perspective, agree), she underestimates the difficulty of the task assigned her or the value of just those "fleeting" impressions of the literary and political scene. Because she was in later years lauded for her political writing—collected in several separate volumes—she may have felt regret for the lack of demonstrated literary analysis. She was, most importantly, a writer to whom writing was of supreme importance. Her agonies over sins of omission in neglecting acute analysis of Gide or Sartre perhaps reveal the extent to which her own ego and interests were involved in literary efforts. Even at the outset, however, Harold Ross expressed only cautious enthusiasm for Flanner's efforts, asking her to "remember that *The New Yorker* is a magazine of reporting and criticism"—an apparent effort to urge her toward less frivolous subjects and flippant manner (see Grant, *Ross, The New Yorker and Me*, 223–225). In later years, when security in her subject matter and methods had grown strong, Janet Flanner extended Ross's dictum: reporting gave way to analysis.

Harold Ross's directive led, in fact, to a sweeping and long-term professional assignment. Flanner was given a subject—the French—without limiting prescriptives. She was left to define the emphasis and scope of such an undertaking, to fill in the tabula rasa, to unwind the narrative thread. The reader is always aware that this record is written, that its effects are both comic and literary. It offers recognizable echoes of Dickens ("I have observed a curious phenomenon lately which I put down to a bad dinner I had last week") and Lewis Carroll ("As for the clothes, they are getting curiouser and curiouser"). And should readers wander from the subject, the inattentive will be unexpectedly jolted to attention by what appears to be a misplaced comma, or the sudden reversal of a complex phrase, or even the apparently absentminded repetition of a favorite word (like "curious").

The evocation of time and place in the letters is often highly poetic, even lyrical. At these moments the comic mask slips slightly to reveal a speaker genuinely enraptured with the landscape she describes: "The chestnut trees on the boulevards have not yet turned, on account of the continued hot weather, but Paris knows its business better than nature. The city properly reflects the last slackness of summer." But the underlying tone of this commentary suggests irony rather than nostalgia: "There are present here too many tourists and nude revues and not enough Parisians and good plays. Indeed, activities usually indigenous to Paris alone and its winter season are being developed outside the city and before the season starts, in order to assure for them some degree of the Gallic spirit submerged by the overflow of sightseers here" (25 September 1926). These were the years when Americans provided much-needed economic support for a city still feeling the effects of the war. But the presence of these "sightseers" was not a comfortable one, either for Parisians or for Flanner. The ambivalence she felt toward the tourist community is often apparent in the tone of her language, frequently accounting for sudden shifts in attitude and style—shifts that mark a classic epistolary method.

The letters are always conscious of their form and structure, never casual or inattentive to their own design. Their effects are achieved by the appearance of random cataloguing that is, in fact, a judicious juxtaposition of subject and style. One can appreciate the Flanner perspective best by aligning it against the more commonplace observations by her journalistic peers, most of whom were men, and some of whom—like Ernest Hemingway and Eugene Jolas—were extremely talented writers for whom journalism was a matter of earning a living rather than a professional calling. By contrast, Flanner's journalism assumed a literary status precisely because it constituted her profession. On 15 November 1928, for instance, the *Paris Tribune* ran a brief note on the anniversary of Marcel Proust's death.

> More than one character from Marcel Proust's monumental *A la Recherche du Temps Perdu* was present in flesh and blood at the little church of St. Pierre de Chaillot yesterday morning when a mass was said on the occasion of the sixth anniversary of the famous writer's death.
>
> To many of those present the Chaillot church evoked that of Combray, destroyed during the war but immortalized in *Du Cote de Chez Swann.* Among those attending the ceremony was Mme de Chevigny, whom he is believed to have taken for the original of his Duchess de Guermantes.

As such, this item is "literary" only in the pretext of its writing. It is recognizable as the kind of journalistic filler that serves as a footnote to history. A year earlier Janet Flanner had dealt with the remembrance of things past on the anniversary of Proust's death in a quite different way:

> In this month has passed the fifth anniversary of Marcel Proust's death. The final two volumes of "Le Temps Retrouve," along with "Chronique," rather tiresome reprints of his *Figaro* contributory days, are now available. In "Le Temps" one finds that the glory of the Guermantes has passed. Gilberte is presented as the widow of St. Loup, killed in the war, Charlus is declasse, Mme. Verdurin has married the old prince, Oriane and the duke are divorced. The glamorous style with which Proust established his dynasty and theirs is lacking in his arid descriptions of their decline. Himself dying, he wrote of their end, he was too weak to ornament their epitaphs. Proust has been dead since 1922, yet the annual appearance of his posthumous works has left him, to the reader, alive. Now there is nothing left to publish. Five years after his interment, Proust seems dead for the first time. (24 December 1927)

The strength of Flanner's prose is evident even in so short a piece as this, the opening sentence ringing portentously. Flanner's mourning here is for the death of Proust's prose, a sadness that the latent expectation of another volume of *A la recherche* is no longer to be fulfilled. She is little interested in the verisimilitude of living counterparts to fictional characters or in the real-life demise of their creator. She laments the "arid decline" of the style that marked the first French Modernist.

A striking quality of the Paris Letters is the frequency with which they announce the death of artists and writers. As a commentator on this period, Flanner was often a eulogist and a compiler of obituaries, a role she played for Rainer Maria Rilke, Juan Gris, Jean Cocteau, Erik Satie, Marie Curie, D. H. Lawrence, Isadora Duncan, and—in later years—for nearly every member of the Paris expatriate community. In addition, she often marked the death dates of important political and literary figures, using the occasion to comment again on their contributions to modern culture. Because history has the power to restructure all events, to bring writers and artists into a later flowering of interest or to reduce contemporary favorites to "period pieces," one forgets that the historical moment creates its own contextual ordering of event and circumstance.

Janet Flanner was highly aware of this process even as it was happening, was constantly intrigued by the repetitions and reversals that constituted historical cycles. That her perceptions of the moment still agree with history's assessment of this era suggests a *déjà vu* effect, as though her commentaries derived their impetus from a later perspective. History has rarely proven her wrong in the analysis of artistic movements or political developments. Nonetheless, it is surprising to remember that it was Gide (now little read), not Proust, who served as the literary *monstre sacré* of this period and that his announced homosexuality and his conversion to Communism, for instance, influenced a whole generation of French readers. It was Matisse, not Picasso, who was *cher maître* for young French artists. It was Edith Wharton, not Gertrude Stein, who was the most famous and longest-resident American expatriate of the Paris Left Bank. Flanner, of course, made mistakes, as she herself was only too well aware. She wrote to Solita Solano in September 1964:

> Lunched with Bill (the famous Shawn, world's best editor) today at the Algonquin, packed with nobodies in pretense of being somebodies. He had already edited and cut my Paris Letters from Sep[tember] 1925 through 1935. . . . He added his surprise on having noted what he described as my dual personality, juvenile and adult—the meretricious early glitter which Ross's lack of culture imposed and then my own maturing style and thought over this last two decades. I am very relieved, very happy, that my critical faculties in discarding my earlier trash had already also occurred to him

(put more tactfully) and of the post War II work he said he would be proud,
I should be proud, to have it published.

This letter reveals two important aspects of Flanner's professional demeanor. Like nearly every other woman writer of this period, she relied
on men's judgments about the quality of her work. (She often relied on
women as well—especially on Solita Solano and Katherine White, whom
she described as "always my closest-to-the-heels critics.") Like many another, she consistently discounted the importance of the "juvenilia" to the
later work; she did not see that the writing of the early years bore important relation to the writing of the later years. Oversights, missed opportunities, good intentions are recorded in these early letters along with
more expected occurrences. In cataloguing the year's recipients of literary
prizes and bemoaning the silly but predictable choices of the critics, Flanner reminds us that Mazeline (whom we have forgotten altogether) took
the coveted prix Goncourt from Céline in 1932 (probably because the
exhausting analysis of corruption in *Voyage au bout de la nuit* was too
much for public consumption); that the prix Fémina rarely went to a
woman; that Buñuel intended in 1933 to make a film of *Wuthering
Heights* (an intention never fulfilled); that the best French film of the year
was based on a 1931 Simenon novel, *La tête d'un homme,* which itself
was "built around a chance remark of the late Harry Crosby at a Montparnasse bar" (8 March 1933).

Flanner's attention to every conceivable nuance of daily French life sustains the retrospective impression that the period was simultaneously
alive and dead, both flourishing and diminishing even as it occurred, embodying contradictions and cross-currents that revealed the extent to
which the era was at odds with itself. How strange that Gertrude Stein's
experimental prose fiction should have coincided in time with the French
penchant for American cocktails (spelled, provisionally, *coquetèles*), that
the publication of early portions of *Finnegans Wake* should have been
contemporaneous with the first Hollywood "talkies" starring Maurice
Chevalier, or that the Académie Française should ever have debated at
great length the gender of the automobile. The major figures of the period, of course, survive such anachronisms, but Kiki of Montparnasse is
rarely remembered today, except perhaps by Hemingway's introduction of
her. How odd to discover that she was a real woman with a real name
(Alice Prin) and a profession other than that of artist's model. Alice Prin
was a painter whose first exhibition at the Sacre du Printemps, the Paris
Letters tell us, created an "impression of simplicity, faith, and tenderness."

Whatever else Flanner's world encompassed, it provided a central place
for women, whose activities are described, promoted, and analyzed at
length. This is a world defined by a woman's perspective—Flanner's own—

and it is often doubly focused, first through Flanner's prose and second through the women subjects she chose to write about. A striking example of this technique is a review of Berenice Abbott's 1927 exposition of photographs at the Sacre du Printemps. Abbott was one of the foremost photographers of the period, and her portraits, like those of Gisèle Freund, captured many of the major figures of the Modernist literary movement from a Modernist perspective:

> With her lens she has portrayed Caillaux, Gide, S. Huddleston, Marie Laurencin (hand to jaw), Djuna Barnes (proud and romantic), a potent and bandaged James Joyce, etc. . . . The frippery of lights, false and stimulating, is not Miss Abbot's [sic] genre. Stolidly, as if almost accidentally, she arrives at a posturing of her subject so that mind and matter are clothed and balanced against a sensitive plate. Her new studies of Cocteau—faceless; only his hands to be seen rising like Medusa's locks from a white mask he holds—are poetic and brief. The poet himself has been eliminated. (16 April 1927)

Flanner's sensitivity to Abbott's work no doubt arose from a sympathy for her powers of observation, powers that Flanner shared.

If we see the major figures of the Modernist period through the lens of an Abbott or Freund, we see the more ordinary figures of French life through Flanner's prose. It is tempting to assume that this egalitarian attitude was the product of Flanner's strong feminism, although it may have been the product of her journalistic instincts. By today's standards, the means she employed to include women in her world may seem rather old-fashioned and stereotyped, sometimes even frivolous, since the new feminism dictates that we take ourselves seriously as women. The issue of whether fashion was an appropriate woman's concern, for instance, was one with which Flanner did not grapple for long. She studiously ignored Jane Grant's admonition that she write on any topic "except fashion" and placed this topic in a more serious context by aligning it to French economics. In this, Flanner was to anticipate Gertrude Stein, another woman unabashedly interested in fashion, who—in her later years—had her clothes designed by Pierre Balmain. In *Paris France* Stein places her notions about fashion in the larger area of cultural concern ("fashion is the real thing in abstraction"):

> In Paris around 1900–1914 the men were elegant and had almost more beauty of elegance than the women. When we came to Paris the men wearing their silk hats on the side of their head and leaning heavily on their cane toward the other side making a balance, the heavy head the heavy hand on the cane were the elegance of Paris. The women were plain, fashionable more than elegant in contrast with the men. As the century progressed the war came. The horizon blue and the black uniforms of the aviators continued the tradition of French elegance among the men. The women for a while did lose fashion and slowly then the men lost their elegance and the women retained

their fashion and then they were no longer plain they were pretty and for a while, it was another idea. (111)

Stein's commentary on clothes, what they do to the human shape and how they record reality, sustains a narrative thread in *Paris France*. She analyzed French society through a reading of its fashion; clothes became the measure of economic success or failure, a record of the shifting male and female roles, a signature to cultural identity.

Flanner supported her interest in fashion through an analysis of the deleterious effects of World War I on the national dressmaking industry and the need for its economic recovery in 1918. With the influx of foreigners following the war, Paris found a new public for its fashions, among them American women. In 1925, for instance, the failing economic situation in France spurred a bizarre fashion trend—evening dress from the "mint," made from "cloth of gold, cloth of silver, or cloth of copper, at least, or lead, and pewter maybe, and highly colored" (21 November 1925). The women who wore these ostentatious creations were wealthy and usually foreign, a reminder that in France there was not "much money" any longer: "Paris will go on being gay, at least for the foreigners, for another thousand years if there are any foreigners left by that time. Most of them seem to be coming to Paris to live forever. It will always be gay for them, but for Parisians, not so funny" (21 November 1925).

Flanner was genuinely and seriously interested in fashion, and when Paris fashion was not interesting, she made her views clear: "women have looked the same for two years. By day they look like boys and by night they look like female impersonators" (17 April 1926). But she had economic rather than aesthetic reasons for preferring the *garçonne* look, created by Chanel and effected by certain models and show business personalities: "Daniel Vincent, Commissioner of Commerce and Labor, has succeeded by government pressure in forcing the big dressmakers to revive the use of embroideries as a means of giving employment to midinettes whose hands have been idle during the last few plain years. The garconne and her severe style have been accused of killing one of the oldest industries in France, *les passementeries,* which is, of course, greatly in the garconne's favor" (25 September 1926). Flanner's politics emerge on the question of exploitation of women in the labor market, especially in the fashion industry, where many women worked long hours for little money in demeaning conditions to support the indulgent whims of a few wealthy women. The social and political complexities of the fashion issue in France, where Coco Chanel (who herself had started out as a day laborer in the fashion workhouses) was considered to be the country's most important economic commodity, are not easily resolved, and Flanner's interest in the topic is not without a certain ambivalence. She was, of course, obliged to devote space and a certain degree of interest to the well-known couturiers, who were mentioned and often reviewed in the letters. Chanel made frequent appearances and was later, with Elsa Schiaparelli and members of the staff from Worth et Cie, accorded her own Flanner "Profile," while Lanvin, Chantal, and Lucien Lelong received honorable mentions. For those who could not afford such extravagances, Flanner shopped at the Galeries Lafayettes and the Trois Quartiers (where Gertrude Stein regularly shopped), reporting on styles, prices, and the women she encountered there. She pointedly reminds us of what we know retrospectively to be true, that the women of this era looked shockingly unlike contemporary women and nothing like the Modernist portrayals of women seen at avant-garde art openings: "the *vernissage* of the Salon d'Automne is permanently invaluable as a final fashion index. Against a background of cubism and nudes were visible the curves and clothes of the most fashionable two hundred Parisiennes" (3 December 1927).

In establishing the "Letter from Paris," the *New Yorker* exploited an existing economic bond between New York and Paris. Rereading copies of the magazine, one can see the various ways in which the link between the two cultures was forged. The only clues readers had to the gender (if not the identity) of "Genêt," for instance, were the sketches that began appearing as part of the headnote for the letters of the 1930s. These often portrayed an elegant woman posed in front of a recognizable Paris landmark like the Eiffel Tower, which Flanner was able to see when she later lived in the Hotel Continental. If the fashion and travel industries were often subjects of Paris Letters, they were also visible in the advertisements that lined the pages on which the letters appeared: clothes, shoes, furs, perfumes, jewelry, and lingerie—much of it imported from France—claimed the attention of the reader, forming an extratextual commentary on Flanner's own message. Indeed, Parisian firms took out advertising space in the magazine, and one suspects that the placement of advertising copy was not without purpose. Among the more bizarre effects created by the marketing device were letters that discussed Nancy Cunard's literary activities in Paris framed by advertisements for the Cunard Line cruises to Europe.

Such juxtapositions reflected the internal ironies of Flanner's own commentaries, where analyses of fashion trends followed hard upon notices of avant-garde art, where Coco Chanel and Sylvia Beach might share the same paragraph or Colette and Cole Porter the same sentence. The world of the *New Yorker* during this period was one of women's fashions and transatlantic crossings, a vision incorporated by an American woman artist in a letter that included mention of fundraising activities for the Isadora Duncan School of Dance, a review of Jane Marnac's performance in Somerset Maugham's *Pluie* (Rain), the announcement of a new journal of film and photography, *Schemas,* edited by Germaine Dulac ("the only woman director and one of the best known in France"), notice of new illustrated editions by Marie Laurencin, and the latest work of the near-blind lithographer Hermine David: "More skeptical, more critical, less blind are the etchings of the American, Madame Eyre de Lanux, privileged to illustrate Paul Valery's 'Le Pauvre Chemisier,' excerpted from his 'Barnabooth.' Madame de Lanux's line is poetical, practiced, ironic. In perfect economy she assembles a woman's hand, a steamship, and a ten-dollar bill. These, with an ocean, can constitute for her a version of modern life" (2 April 1927). Indeed, these might comprise a cover for any issue of the *New Yorker* in which the "Letter from Paris" appeared. If the contrast of women's interests and accomplishments in this particular letter is almost painfully apparent, Flanner closed her commentary with the remark that of the 80,000 then unemployed in France, one-fourth were women. This figure alone constituted a version of modern life often overlooked in between-wars France.

The images of women vary considerably in the letters and include among the various portraits women of all social and economic ranks, political persuasions, and professions. Flanner expressed concern about working conditions for women in French industries, analyzed the work of women in the world of cinema, theater, and art, recorded activities of society matrons (for whom she felt little affinity and less affection), commented on women in sports and other traditionally male pursuits such as boat racing, airplane building, and horse breeding, and often acknowledged the more traditional roles of women as mothers, cooks, seamstresses, and housewives. Women figure prominently in the news she recorded, and she used the letters to bring women and their work to public attention. An announcement of the appearance in *transition* of a portion of Djuna Barnes's novel *Ryder,* describing it as a "brilliantly stylized eighteenth-century recrudescence," led Flanner to a discussion of the peculiar printing and publishing history of this work, a subject to which she devoted longer essays on the deluxe editions prepared by Nancy Cunard at the Hours Press and Caresse Crosby at the Black Sun Press for French readership. Flanner had a strong interest in the printing, publishing, and marketing of literary materials, and the activities of many women in the expatriate community in just such enterprises made them good copy for her letters.

While documentation of literary events, especially those involving women of the Left Bank community, assumed major importance in the Paris Letters, Flanner's interests continued to be aesthetically and politically wide-ranging. Loïe Fuller's return to Paris for the production of her ballet at the Moulin Rouge gave Flanner the opportunity to mention that "between politics Miss Fuller has been directing a fantasy film," while display of embroidery work at La Maison des Amis des Livres provided the occasion to introduce Marie Monnier—sister of Adrienne Monnier, the owner of this Left Bank bookshop—whose embroidered tapestries were purchased by the Louvre. Women whose work did not please Flanner's critical tastes, however, were not spared her acerbic assessments: she expressed reservations over the sentimentality of Claire Goll's poetry, called Gertrude Beasley's "naughty book" *My First Thirty Years* "perfectly frightful," and concluded that Marie Laurencin "shows humans . . . who never seem to grow stale though they have no infinite variety." Certain women of the Paris community—Mistinguette, Josephine Baker, Spinelli, Hermine David, Mme Piteoff, Chanel, Schiaparelli, Colette, Edith Wharton, and Gertrude Stein—were favorites of Flanner and made repeated appearances in the letters (several among them accorded the honor of a Flanner "Profile"). Others of the community discussed at some length by Flanner included Margaret Anderson, Sylvia Beach, Anna de Noailles, and Alice B. Toklas.

Flanner's comments about Edith Wharton are interesting in that she speculated on the possible reasons for Wharton's expatriation and the circumstances of her residence in the Faubourg:

> It was in this aristocratic Parisian quarter that Mrs. Wharton, more than a dozen years ago, began her expatriation. Twice only she returned to America, once to witness a marriage, and once for a ten days' retreat to the Hotel St. Regis, where she prepared to receive her honorary degree from Yale. Her withdrawal from America had been her most American act. . . . so from the Rue de Varenne she finally started her frigid conquest of the *faubourg,* in company only with her mother, who had been Lucinda Rhinelander, and an iron hostess in her day, but was now disgusted with the way Newport was going. Mrs. Wharton was perhaps too formal even for the *faubourg.* As one duchesse complained, "*On est trop organisé chez elle.* One can't so much as forget one's umbrella at Madame Wharton's with impunity." (*Paris Was Yesterday: 1925–1939,* 174)

Although Flanner herself seems to have been a victim of Wharton's cold, austere, aristocratic public image in this "Profile," she nonetheless suggested the underlying sense of constriction that Wharton's American life presented: "Moving in high society at this time meant moving but little indeed." And Flanner admitted that Wharton "always suffered the disadvantage of being an outsider" (171–172).

The subtleties of Flanner's wit may escape the inattentive reader, but to those who read carefully, her attitudes are crystal clear. For instance, she was for many years a close friend and strong supporter of Nancy Cunard; she approved of Cunard's politics, her publishing ventures, and her poetry. When Cunard's massive study of black culture, *Negro,* was published in 1934, Flanner gave it careful attention, cataloguing its complex research and hailing it as an important contribution to political sociology.

Nancy's mother, Lady Emerald Cunard, did not approve of her daughter's relationships with black men and hardly approved of the publication of this book. For her, Flanner reserved polite understatement, referring to her as "one of London's greatest American hostesses." In Flanner's ethic, little was more socially useless than such a claim to fame.

Although one might have expected Flanner to express a certain degree of sympathy and sisterly support for Radclyffe Hall, there is little evidence that she had read carefully *The Well of Loneliness* (although she devoted some space to it in more than one letter) or that she was in any way responsive to Hall's treatment of the lesbian psyche. She confines her comments on Hall's book to recording its sales history: it apparently sold well at the Gare du Nord news cart nearest the *Flèche d'or,* the deluxe express train for London, the city where the book was first banned as obscene. When word came that a stage version was planned in Paris by a woman who specialized in "banned plays" (Wilette Kershaw), the news upset Radclyffe Hall, who claimed to know nothing about the intended production. Flanner was quick to comment that "her—well, loneliness was greater than one supposed" (4 October 1930). One suspects that Flanner was annoyed, perhaps embarrassed, by Hall's emotional and stylized reenactment of lesbian relationships and that, as a lesbian, Flanner resented being typecast as a guilty, unhappy "invert." Flanner shared something with Natalie Barney in her attitude toward lesbianism. Like Barney, she was a happy person, not given to guilt and self-recrimination because of her sexual orientation. She apparently rejected the prevalent scientific and medical theories about the reasons for lesbianism and did not take heterosexual unions as the model for her relationships with women. Like Barney, Flanner demonstrated an attitude toward homosexuality well in advance of her time, but the Barney-Flanner model of lesbian behavior constituted a minority opinion among homosexual women of the Left Bank community, most of whom demonstrated that they had internalized both homophobia and misogyny.[3]

That Flanner herself was a lesbian is carefully hidden behind her professional role as a journalist and beneath a smooth and sometimes ironic prose style. She succeeded in keeping her private life separated from her public career during her own lifetime and in securing a certain silence on the more intimate details of her Paris years after her death. Among her letters and memorabilia left to the Library of Congress there is virtually nothing that betrays her sexual orientation, for instance, or that reveals anything about her long-term association with Solita Solano. It is evident that Flanner was part of the Paris community of lesbian writers—she frequently attended evenings for women writers at Natalie Barney's and with Solano was a character in Djuna Barnes's *Ladies Almanack.* That she maintained friendships with heterosexual women as well and was accepted and loved by women of both groups is obvious from memoirs and letters of various women. Flanner apparently served as an important feminist role model in this community, yet nothing of her more intimate relationships among these women is revealed. An observer of this community, Flanner rarely pictured herself as one of its participants.

If women receive ample space in Flanner's literary record, their contributions are weighed with the same demanding precision as those by men. In fact, Flanner's feminism could have a sharp edge. In reviewing the state of art in spring 1927, she commented that "the women's show is as good as most men's shows. . . . There is still a lot of talk in non-feministic France about women never being men's equals. In the matter of good mediocre painting, they unfortunately are" (19 March 1927). But the review of the "remarkable exposition of old lace" that follows in this letter lauds this lost art as a "delicate feast." Nor did Flanner miss the chance to remind readers that France had badly exploited women in the lace trade: "Real lace was not made in France until the seventeenth century, when Louis XIV imported thirty female Venetian laceworkers in the hope of saving governmental expenses on his previously imported cuffs and cravates. Today's superb collection of French lace at the Grande Maison de Blanc, and incidentally the French Revolution, are both indirect results." Flanner gave solid support to the artistic contributions of her compatriots and contemporaries, provided their work passed her stringent critical tests. Her review of the 1932 American Women's Show reminds us that a number of talented American artists were then active: "The work of Lillian Cotton, Gwen Le Gallienne, Janet Scudder, Ivy Troutman, and Lillian Fisk, among others, showed an amazonian quality of strength that did not surprise or fail to please. As a group, theirs was by all odds the best amalgamated work of the year" (22 June 1932). This same letter included an assessment of work by Salvador Dali, Jean Cocteau (ink drawings), and Francis Rose, the newly discovered protégé of Gertrude Stein.

In summer 1932, Flanner wrote an uncharacteristically long analysis of French feminism for the benefit of her American readers. The commentary was occasioned by the French Assembly vote on the question of suffrage for French women (which failed to pass):

> It would seem a little late to bring up the question of votes for women if the French men weren't a little late in bringing it up themselves. Never has a struggle for civil liberties been so calm. Outside of the aviatrix's having dropped feminist pamphlets on the roof of the Senate to influence the senators' minds, no one would guess that the French sexes are in danger (well, not very much) of being equalized. There is none of the excitement that marked the London and Washington campaigns—nothing, except the hunch that the French women won't get it. Nor do they seem to care. France is still a country given to marriage and little to divorce, where in small shops *Maman* is tradi-

tionally the powerful cashier. And if, as feminists aver, she can't call her soul her own because, whether she loves and honors her husband or not, she must obey, at any rate she can call her wages her own. Furthermore, laws are even now being modified to permit wives to open bank accounts and leave the country without their spouses first signing a visa and deposit slip, a humiliating restriction which up till now seems not to have humiliated much, since the French never travel and, unless millionaires, don't fuss much with cheques, preferring to pay cash and bank in the sock.

Apparently the flatness of the whole suffrage campaign lies in the fact that, in being originally classed among those humans unfit for suffrage, the French women were not properly insulted. Where American women were excluded from the ballot along with idiots and their own children, the French ladies are merely lumped as pariahs along with policemen and soldiers. It seems not to be enough. (July 1932)

Beneath this satiric résumé of the French woman's political status one detects Flanner's understanding and latent disapproval of a French consciousness much in need of education on the question of women's rights. Her feminism and her own belief in the necessity of equal rights for all underscored this commentary. In general, Flanner's feminist politics reflected her political notions on the broader questions of human rights and human responsibilities: she concerned herself with that which was socially just, and she was sympathetic toward those who were socially useful. In this regard, a certain midwestern puritanism colored her political thinking, much as her personal and professional behavior attempted to escape this remnant of an American upbringing. The "socially useful" for Flanner encompassed diverse categories, including the writing of experimental prose and the painting of avant-garde pictures. It included lacemaking, fashion design, gourmet cooking, filmmaking, and any number of other intellectual and cultural pursuits that a stricter puritan would have found frivolous, if not actually subversive. But it did not include self-indulgence, excesses of money and bad taste, waste of time or intellectual resources, or inhumane acts. Although the Paris Letters may seem an unlikely political forum, they nevertheless reflect a consciousness that was politically motivated. And it is not surprising to find among them eloquent support for those whose work was undervalued, misrepresented, or even suppressed by the very puritanism that Flanner so much hated, including artists such as Charlie Chaplin, Isadora Duncan, and Paul Robeson.

In the early letters Flanner's politics are most apparent on issues that have an economic rather than a moral basis, however. The underlying tension between the French and Americans could not be overlooked by someone living among them: the French economic structure was badly damaged by the costs of World War I, and the French in the 1920s were poor; Americans living in France were rich by comparison. As the years passed and the French felt more threatened by the American demand that the war debt be paid, as they watched the franc sink lower in value while Americans flourished at the expense of Parisians, the whole question of the invading American hordes with their fat bankrolls and big cars led to ambiguous threats and the potential for ugly street scenes. But November 1929 brought an end to the excesses of that life, and Flanner's report of the event betrays her loyalties:

> The recent unpleasantness in Wall Street has had its effect here. In the rue de la Paix the jewelers are reported to be losing fortunes in sudden cancellations of orders, and at the Ritz bar the pretty ladies are having to pay for the first ten rounds themselves. In the Quartier de l'Europe, little firms that live exclusively on the American trade have not sold one faked Chanel copy in a fortnight. . . . In real estate circles certain advertisements have been illuminating: "For Sale, Cheap, Nice Old Chateau, 1 hr. from Paris; Original Boiseries, 6 New Baths, Owner Forced Return New York Wednesday: MUST HAVE IMMEDIATE CASH: Will Sacrifice." (14 December 1929)

In fact, the stock exchange crash remained merely an "unpleasantness" for some time in Paris: its effects were not directly felt until 1932, when "the suicides of men as rich as Kreuger and Eastman left Paris a little more shaken in the Bourse and in its beliefs" (9 April 1932). But in 1930 the French were only aware of the Depression to the extent that there were fewer Americans visible in Paris (many of whom complained that the prices were too high, that the French were unfriendly, and that the government still owed America repayment of the war debt). There were many more French visiting America, which had suddenly become cheap for them. Early that year Paul Morand published his guide New-York, a book that supported Flanner's own views about the city, confirming much about American life that expatriates already knew too well: "To Morand, New York is a 'city of contrasts, puritan and libertine, double image of a continent policed and at the same time savage, contains the prettiest women in the world and the ugliest men, will ruin you in an afternoon after having made you rich in eight days'" (22 February 1930). Both cynical and accurate, this view of the city captures a life that Flanner had long ago left behind, unable to live among such blatant contradictions. At the moment of the Wall Street crash she seemed to have little sympathy for either the rich American investors and their pretty ladies or the French firms that lived off their wealth.

Indeed, the capacity for sympathy that was to become so evident as the Paris Letters moved toward the events of 1939 had always been directed toward Europe. Whatever sense of Americanism Flanner might have felt, she had become a European during these years in Paris. By the mid-thirties, when the mass of Americans had repatriated and the French were involved with the threat to European stability posed by Fascism, Janet Flanner's perspective had quietly but markedly changed: she assumed that her reader shared her concern for European stability, shared her own liberal politics, shared her interest in the Spanish Civil War and Picasso's reaction to it, respected her right to have chosen a new landscape that she now observed as a participant rather than as a bystander. By 1933, the Paris Letter had changed its focus and intent. Janet Flanner was no longer writing a commentary for someone across the waters whose New York perspective she shared. She was writing the Paris Letter for herself. The lively and audacious opinions of the early years became caustic, her style marked by humor of the bitterest sort. Discussion of fashion previews, automobile shows, flower exhibitions, art openings, and cinema spectaculars gave way to an obsessive analysis of several apparent forms of Fascism. The later letters constitute political commentary more in the style of Samuel Pepys than of Jonathan Swift. The subject may be daily life, but the analysis examines the effects of political threat on a populace that remembered too well the costs of World War I.

The Later Letters (1933–1940)

If the tone of the Paris Letters prior to 1933 displayed a marked levity, the letters leading up to the occupation of Paris were ominously foreboding. By 1933, events outdistanced Flanner to such an extent that the letters became a political chronicle, ending with her own forced return to America during the war years. It is doubtful that her political judgments would ever have surfaced so directly or that the dark tone and penetrating thought of these commentaries could have developed had it not been for Mussolini, Hitler, and the Spanish Civil War. As the chronicle of these years approaches 1939, the letters focus on only two subjects—politics and literature—and it is frequently difficult to separate one from the other.

There were marked absences on the Paris landscape after the stock market fall in 1929. The cultural scene shifted significantly by the early 1930s. Paris was losing its status as the center of the arts to New York, and Flanner's commentary often reflects a mixed sense of loss and hope: "Another proof that brighter days and nights are coming back was Kristians Tonny's smart evening *vernissage* at the Left Bank Galerie Pierre, once famous for introducing all the important young men who have since gone Right Bank. . . . The Tonny evening was more like the nineteen-twenties than anything seen in the nineteen-thirties for a long time" (28 April 1934). Many of the artists and writers of the 1920s had moved farther from St. Germain than the Right Bank: some had gone to London, but many were on the Riviera, where coastal villages such as Cagnes-sur-Mer, Juan-les-Pins, Cannet, and others housed colonies of writers and painters seeking escape from the hectic and high-priced life of Paris. Even those who were still in and around Paris, like Eugene and Maria Jolas or Gertrude Stein and Alice B. Toklas or Nancy Cunard, spent great periods of time away from the city in an effort to avoid interruptions and distractions.

But many of the former expatriates had rediscovered America, a process analyzed at length by Malcolm Cowley in *Exile's Return*. After a thirty-year absence from her homeland, Gertrude Stein returned in glory in 1934—following the publication of *The Autobiography of Alice B. Toklas*—for a six-month lecture tour. Others who were "away" for more extended periods during these years included Margaret Anderson (whose *Little Review* had died in 1929), Kay Boyle, Malcolm Cowley (now overseeing the literary section of the *New Republic*), Hart Crane (who committed suicide on his return from Mexico in 1933), Harry Crosby (who committed suicide in New York in 1929), Caresse Crosby (who lived at an old mill north of Paris), Nancy Cunard (who was living at Réanville, where she had set up the Hours Press), e. e. cummings and Mina Loy (both in New York), Hilda Doolittle and F. Scott Fitzgerald (both in Switzerland), Ernest Hemingway and Matthew Josephson (both in America), Robert McAlmon (who had announced in 1928 that "the good days of the Quarter" were finished), Katherine Anne Porter (in Mexico), and Ezra Pound (in Rapallo). Those who were still firmly planted in Paris were those who had first discovered it—Natalie Barney and Gertrude Stein—and those who came later—James Joyce, Henry Miller, Anaïs Nin, and several (including Janet Flanner) who made their living there. The Left Bank was quieter now. Those who stayed on were at work: Djuna Barnes on *Nightwood* (1936), Natalie Barney on a second series of *pensées*, Nancy Cunard on *Negro* (1934), James Joyce on *Finnegans Wake* (1939), Anaïs Nin on a prose poem, *House of Incest* (1936), Gertrude Stein on *Everybody's Autobiography* (1937).

In the 1930s, the Paris Letters became more markedly European in their interests, in large part because the theater of political events had widened and there were fewer expatriates left to serve as literary subjects. Flanner introduced a new cast of characters—almost entirely male—who played roles unfamiliar to them and to us as readers. France was experiencing an exchange between literature and politics, with key figures from each domain assuming places in the territory of the other. Flanner wrote in April 1933: "The politicians here are giving lectures like *litterateurs* and the literary gentry are settling into politics. Within the past fortnight Leon Blum (Socialist), Leon Daudet (Royalist), and Eduard Herriot (Radical) have given the *causeries* that ordinarily go with authorship;

while André Gide has taken over the frontpage spot that usually belongs to such fallen solons by addressing a friendly message to the young folks on the Soviets." Blum, Daudet, and Herriot were to become major figures on the Paris political scene during the thirties, while Gide's ambivalent love affair with Communism and with Soviet Russia provided an artistic/political melodrama.

Although literature and politics had always merged in France, with figures from each group appearing under the auspices of the other, this period was particularly interdisciplinary. Even where art was allowed space of its own in the later Paris Letters, it often found itself in the context of larger political concerns. Flanner's left-wing tendencies, formerly submerged on questions of aesthetics and artistic methods, now emerged as inextricably tied to a culture that was, like Flanner's ethic, in a situation of growing political consciousness. By 1933, her letters reflected the enormous French curiosity about the state of Soviet Russia. It was a period when various French political and artistic leaders (André Gide, for instance) made trips to the Soviet Union and when information about any aspect of life there was of great interest in the French capital. In this year Flanner provided a long, if eccentric, review of a small collection of "Soviet Paintings Relative to the Execution of the Five-Year Plan." These paintings were important because they were among the first products of the collectives to be shown in the West, their collaborative production a distinct contrast to the cult of the single egotistical artist that had existed for some years in Paris:

> Painting has become such a personal ballyhoo in Paris that impersonal talent seems as pure as a silent prayer. In this manner, the Moscow show is meditative and the propaganda devoted more to painting than to politics—with aquarelles of pink Dnieperstroy derricks that are as delicate as apple blossoms in spring, a gouache oil well in Baku that rises, with its flood, like the framed carving on a muezzin's tower, and a "Cycle of Civil War" which at close range doubtless deals with death, but dreamily, distantly seen consists of tender water colors of sad men of action seen by one sadder, with talent and paint.

Flanner's description of the show tends to romanticize its effects, if not its content, suggesting an effort to argue the aesthetics of political art. She was later to employ a similar method of description, relying on metaphor and image, in the assessment of Picasso's political paintings produced in the aftermath of the Guernica bombing. Although Flanner's aesthetics might sometimes be questioned, her politics were consistently liberal, increasingly influenced by the polarization of European politics during the 1930s.

The rising tide of Nazi anti-Semitism provided another arena for aesthetic and political conjunction, since all art by Jews—or those suspected of being Jewish—was systematically banned in Germany and its occupied territories. This move placed in jeopardy the German film industry, until the early 1930s the most avant-garde and liberated in the world, where women and Jews dominated creative filmmaking. Mistakenly thinking that Fritz Lang was a Nazi, Flanner suggested that his film *Das Testament des Doktor Mabuse* was censored because "his backing was Jewish." In fact, Lang himself was half-Jewish, and his film was banned in Germany in 1933 because of its openly anti-Nazi bias. Lang fled to France, leaving behind his wife, an ardent Nazi from whom he was later divorced. It was indeed true, however, that the emphasis on German nationalism that had brought Hitler to power had made the film industry vulnerable to political manipulations. Women, Jews, and avant-garde filmmakers were forced underground, a situation that Flanner decried: "with the best cinematic talents and organizations of Berlin disrupted, from now on there will apparently be no more of those excellent films coming out of Germany, except maybe some featuring Friedrich der Grosse with a little up-to-date moustache." As often, Flanner's prediction was absolutely correct.

Among the best German cinematographers of this period was Leni Riefenstahl, who had apparently supported Nazism out of expediency in order to continue acting in and making films. At one time a confidante of Hitler, possibly even his mistress, Riefenstahl was a rare talent whose energies were exploited by the Nazi party for propaganda purposes. Flanner's comment on seeing Riefenstahl's *Triumph of the Will* appeared to be flatly apolitical, concentrating on the film shots and cutting techniques in the final version. Flanner focused on the film's subject—Nazi rallies—much as one might discuss a halftime performance at a football game: "It gives two hours of Hitler, fabulous flags, acres of marching men, shovellers, trumpeters, etc.—undoubtedly the best recent European pageant" (27 April 1935). Although by 1933 Europeans were taking Hitler seriously as the head of the German state, it was still unclear how his plans would affect Europe. Flanner, like many other political commentators of this period, adopted a "wait and see" attitude, hoping that her worst personal fears were not to be realized. But the Paris Letters of these years display Flanner's morbid curiosity about Hitler: in this particular letter, the review of *Triumph of the Will* is imbedded in a long recital of recent German events that articulates the frightening implications for a film summary that seems to make Hitler an innocuous lover of parades and pageants. Clearly an admirer of Riefenstahl's work, Flanner was particularly unwilling to commit herself to commentary on this woman's politics and her place in German political life or to raise the issue that must by then have been apparent to Flanner—that Riefenstahl had sold out to Nazism to preserve her film career. For a woman with Flanner's ethical principles, such a decision spelled collaboration of potential victims—particularly women—with their victimizer.

An aspect of Hitler's rise to power that most intrigued Flanner was the role that women, especially ones with great wealth, had played in his political career. In her three-part "Profile" of the Führer written in 1936, she concentrated on his inconsistent attitudes toward women, commenting that although he was personally charming and overly polite to them, he was nonetheless "chief of the political party which doctrinally enforces the domestic submission of women to 'men's natural rule as illustrated by the Wagnerian heroes like Wotan and Siegfried.'" His relationships with men were equally flawed, making for constant jockeying among his advisors for favoritism. In the totally male world of the Third Reich, Leni Riefenstahl was a solitary female figure: "At the tremendous opening Shovel Parade of the *Arbeitsdienst*, she was not only the sole motion-picture director, she was the only woman on the great parade field—one white linen skirt moving freely before fifty-four thousand, green-woolen, mechanical men, one professional woman on her job." Flanner's description of Riefenstahl in this setting would seem to overlook political links between her profession and her presence on this particular parade field. If Riefenstahl was a lone woman in a man's "profession," so was Flanner, and the common experiences and contrasts between the two women must have provided Flanner some interesting self-analysis. How did Riefenstahl see herself in this setting? Was she aware of the multiple ironies of her place and power within the Third Reich? To what extent had she placed professional commitment above political concerns? Riefenstahl herself might have seemed an apt subject for Flanner's "Profile" series, allowing Flanner the space to speculate on answers to some of these questions. For whatever reasons—and one suspects that they had to do with Flanner's unwillingness to expose a woman to the kind of scrutiny she had undertaken with male political figures—Flanner never made public an analysis of Riefenstahl's professional politics.

For Flanner, the decade of the 1930s was one of self-examination about her own professional commitments, however, and her relation to the political and cultural scene about which she wrote. If she had previously taken for granted her role as a woman reporter, never questioning the set of circumstances that had brought her into a peculiarly male domain, political events in Europe were to force the issue. She had secured her place as a respected commentator on European events. She no longer merely promoted the work of others: she was a journalist experimenting with the genre for her own professional purposes. She had learned how to make the Paris Letters serve her own highly developed political interests as well as her literary ambitions. She was no longer adapting her strategies to someone else's expectations. She had found her voice, her method, and her subject. Thus the relation between gender and genre in this later writing is more subtle. If the world Flanner portrays is almost totally male, dominated by figures of fear, then these letters constitute an analysis of a psychopathology of patriarchal authority that was to assert its will on a global scale. This is a record of victimization, and if the victims—Jews, women, children, the poor, the aged, the ill—are not centrally located in the historical narrative, it is because they were seen by tyrants such as Hitler and Mussolini to be marginal, and therefore expendable. The potential effects of a political purge on such as these is first implied and later made totally explicit in Flanner's narrative. By the 1930s, Flanner was expatriated. She was herself a potential victim, as journalist, as American, as woman. If Leni Riefenstahl's collaboration with Fascism was apparent in her professional filmmaking, Flanner's resistance to Fascism was evident in her professional writing.

The argument has already been made that women saw World War I differently than did men. Most often this "seeing differently" has been cast in the pejorative, suggesting that women who had no direct experience of the war were little able to comment authoritatively on it. Sandra Gilbert, however, suggests quite another reading of women's activities during the war years. She argues that women found productive and well-paying work when they replaced their husbands, sons, and brothers in factories and businesses so that the men could join the forces at the front, that many women were sad to see this newfound freedom end in 1918, and that women began to write about war and women's relation to it. Many of these women writers—Mrs. Humphrey Ward, May Sinclair, Edith Wharton, and Willa Cather—actively solicited support for the war through their fiction ("Soldier's Heart," 422–450).[4] Edith Wharton, for instance, not only wrote about the war, but visited the trenches, maintained an active and knowledgeable interest in the progress of the war, and used the immense powers of her organizational abilities and her contacts in Faubourg society to set up an *ouvroir* on the rue de l'Université in Paris where seamstresses produced clothing sold all through France and America. In recompense these women were paid for their work and given free lunches, medical attention, and a supply of winter coal. Later Wharton raised the money to set up American Hostels for Refugees, which she administered and which by the end of 1915 had cared for 900 persons, 750 of them children (Lewis, *Edith Wharton*, 363–383).

Although it might be possible to argue that because of their separation from the confined trench warfare of the Great War women could experience only at second hand the fear, the sense of betrayal, the understanding of loss the war produced, it is not possible to make such an argument about the decade preceding World War II. The destructive possibilities of

a masculine ethic of domination and authoritarianism were acknowledged in the writings of every female writer of the period and were a subject of major concern to such women as Virginia Woolf, Hilda Doolittle,
Gertrude Stein, Bryher, Natalie Barney, and Colette. Sandra Gilbert has
argued that World War I contributed in various ways to the liberation of
European women, who used the war as subject matter for fiction and po-
etry and used the war years to produce first-rank Modernist literature
("Soldier's Heart," 433–443), but Louise Bernikow argues that World
War II destroyed a community of women in Paris dedicated to literary cre-
ativity and the rejection of patriarchal, authoritarian values. Writing of
Virginia Woolf's reaction to the rise of Fascism as recorded in *Three
Guineas,* Bernikow says:

> Imagine the effect of an ideology that insisted that a woman's world was hus-
> band and children on women who had rejected both. It is not an ideology
> that arose in the 1930s—since it describes most of world history—but it did,
> then, thunder as it had not for some twenty years. It did cut off the routes of
> escape from that ideology that women had relied on those twenty or more
> years. It weakened the walls around a women's community within which
> women might be heretics against this particular ancient religion. Woolf says
> that the fight against this aspect of the Dictator must wear down a woman's
> strength and exhaust her spirit. (*Among Women,* 189–190)

Decrying the effects of Fascism on women, Bernikow describes the particular female response to the Second World War: "There was no culture
in exile. Everyone retreated to her private life, cut off from common
life. . . . The fathers not only dictated, but bombed and invaded. A
woman would feel this as rape." She recounts the resulting deaths and
severe illnesses among women writers, describing the wasteland that replaced the flourishing community of women on the Left Bank:

> In addition to historical and economic considerations, in addition to the fact
> that Europe was altogether devastated by that war, that most aspects of the
> culture were wiped out, there is one important and concrete phenomenon in
> the obliteration of women's culture that calls for attention. These were not
> women who married or had children—with the exception of Woolf and
> Colette. . . . Without husbands, without children, what are the roads of con-
> nection to culture? To posterity? They are, to learn something from what
> happened in the twenties, collective roads built by women who refuse to dis-
> perse. (191–192)

As we shall see, many of the women who participated in a "women's community" in Paris between the world wars refused to leave Europe, even if
they were forced into hiding and isolation during the war. When the war
had ended and the women were free to reopen their Paris homes, however, they were old and ill. Some, like Gertrude Stein, died almost im-

mediately; some, like Adrienne Monnier, soon committed suicide. Others lived on their memories of that earlier and less threatened period.

Although many of the Modernist women writers of this time turned to issues posed by the threat of yet another world war, for none of these women was the political arena of the 1930s the explicit subject of her writing. The American audience had for some years been intentionally uninterested in European politics; it had spent a decade rejoicing in the victory of the Great War and by 1930 was too far in the depths of the Depression to think of anything other than its own plight. During the 1930s, political analysis became Janet Flanner's specific professional commitment, and it forced her to develop skills that had lain dormant under Harold Ross's leadership at the *New Yorker*. Events conspired to make this shift possible, allowing her to test her analytic skills on historical and political events in process.

To succeed in this effort, Flanner drew parallels between literature and politics, using the letters as examples of the ways in which political analysis could be formulated to advance the plot of a realistic historical novel. She created characters, giving life and breath to the major participants in the battle between Fascism and democracy, often using her "Profiles" to extend analysis of those she found most intriguing (e.g., Adolph Hitler, François Coty, Henri Pétain). She paraded the tyrants, co-conspirators, and freedom fighters across the pages of the *New Yorker*, drawing out the physical, psychological, and behavioral oddities of each. She consistently undercut the images of authority and power by making the Führer, the Duce, the Maréchal and others subjects of caricature and parody. Under Flanner's scrupulous prose Hitler became the victim of his own poorly integrated personality, Mussolini was reduced to a shouting, stamping child—and such effects only rendered these figures of domination all the more frightening. She sustained an ironic style that often occasioned the personal "aside"; she specialized in understatement and satiric contrast in developing her theme and plot. Her letters were important links between a Paris that feared becoming another European battleground and an America increasingly eager for on-the-scene reporting.

The desperate effort to know the news, to keep abreast during these years, became a constant theme in Flanner's narrative. She was frustrated by the time difference between Paris and New York, thwarted by the two-week delay between the writing and the reading of the letters. She was often curious about what American readers already knew and what interpretation of the news they were receiving. The transatlantic distance seemed greater in these years, and the necessity to communicate feelings as well as events became more pressing. She was increasingly irritated with the two American Paris newspapers, the *Herald* and *Tribune*, which seemed to lag further and further behind events. She humorously complained that to find news of America one had to read the *London Express* ("for original news of the Pacific Coast's wooden nickels, and now rumors of Middle West Secession"), the *Paris-Soir* ("for warning months ago of America's failing banking system"), the (Frankfurt) *Zeitung* ("for the first news of the Morgan-Rockefeller feud"): "in getting the news hot from home over here, one also gets a dandy big reading vocabulary in French and German, plus a fine London accent" (April 1933). The 1930s was a decade of frantic newspaper reading, even though events outdistanced journalism to such an extent that it was necessary to read several newspapers a day and to rely on the radio, which circulated news reports of changing events in Europe in four languages. America's role, which was uncertain and ambivalent, became crucial for the English and French, who were frightened of another struggle against German aggression. The worsening economic situation in Germany, France, England, and America tied the fates of these countries in a complicated web. Flanner negotiated this webbed terrain by serving as both the Paris and London correspondent for the *New Yorker*, shuttling between the two cities, keeping one eye on Germany and another on her reading audience at home.

As early as November 1933, the French were frightened over the possibility of impending war ("there is constant talk of, fear of war") and were outraged by Hitler's methods for attaining power. A year later, however, French attention was focused closer to home in an incident that seemed unrelated to the growth of Fascism, but reminded the French of recent earlier political upheavals. When the Stavisky scandal broke, the government was left in turmoil and Stavisky mysteriously died by suicide or murder, probably the latter. A Russian Jewish émigré, Stavisky had made a fortune in bonds held against nonexistent credit through a municipally owned pawnshop in Bayonne. He escaped prosecution by the French due to his connections with influential politicians. The scandal further polarized the Left and Right factions, further raised fears of Communist infiltration and the level of anti-Semitic rhetoric. The Dreyfus Affair was not far from French memory, and the ironies and reversals of that earlier scandal made the Stavisky story doubly painful.

Flanner documented the scandal in installments, trying to draw from it the personal and political idiosyncrasies that would make it interesting for a foreign reading public. While hardly anyone admitted in January 1934 to having known Stavisky (by then dead), Colette, a fellow lodger at the Hotel Claridge, agreed to describe him to Flanner: "he excelled at having no face; at counting, when he chose, only as a silhouette. . . . He was at an age which in women is called menopause—marked by neurasthenia, capricious weakness, doubts" (18 January 1934). Although the Stavisky affair did not bring down the government, it nearly resulted in a Fascist coup d'état. A bloody riot on 6 February 1934 led by Jeunesses

Patriotes, Action Française, and Solidarité Française (all Fascist or near-Fascist organizations) was a frightening image of things to come. These groups hoped to discredit the government and to solidify their strongly national and anti-Semitic support base. The events surrounding the Stavisky case added to the growing suspicion that right-wing extremism was not confined to Germany and Italy. Flanner covered the riots and the Communist violence the following Friday at the Place de la République, commenting that although the Third Republic would not fall, "never in its history has there been so much soiled linen and so little washing" (10 February 1934). Like many of the French, Flanner was disgusted by the entire episode.

By 1936, political threats were apparent on three sides: from Germany, which moved to reoccupy the Rhine; from Spain, where the Spanish Civil War broke out; and from America, where Roosevelt tried to maintain a stance of American neutrality in Europe. French journalism was stirred on each of these issues, and Flanner's letters detail the kinds of reports available in French newspapers of all persuasions—*Le Temps* ("government organ"), *Figaro* ("aristocrats' sheet"), *Vendredi* (the New Left, intellectual publication under the auspices of the *Nouvelle Revue Française*), *Le Populaire* ("Leon Blum's Socialist newspaper"), and *Le Matin* ("usually pro-American"). While these newspapers were often divided on issues, the Roosevelt speech in January 1936 announcing a policy of "no aid" in future European wars stirred a new wave of anti-Americanism. Flanner reported *Le Matin* as stating: "we have had directed economy from the United States. Now we are having directed history." In fact, France was hoping for help from both England and America against the ever-closer threat of Hitler's troops, and the reoccupation of the Rhineland in March 1936 led to a new panic. Flanner's report on French attitudes in the 11 April 1936 letter summarized national feeling:

(1) The French still feel that Germany started the last war. . . .
(2) The French still think that Germany was beaten in 1918. . . .
(3) The French still think the loser must pay, this being customary in cutthroat bridge, not to mention brutal blood games. . . .
(4) The French think Hitler is a medieval maniac; they think his Germany now is not twentieth-century civilized Western Europe but tenth-century tribal and northern hinterland. (This is the one item of the four about which the French may be completely right.)

In spring 1936, both Spain and France elected Popular Front governments, coalitions of the Left that were carefully and delicately held together. It was the issue of the Spanish Civil War, which broke out that summer, that drew together the French Left against Léon Blum's decision to preserve the nonintervention agreement that France had made with

England, preventing any aid to the Spanish Republicans. Flanner's own sympathies, like those of Nancy Cunard, who also covered the Spanish Civil War as a freelance journalist, were strongly for the Republicans, and she devoted long columns to discussions of the issues of the Spanish struggle and its relation to the larger European political struggle. A central figure in her cast of characters was Léon Blum, the French prime minister hated by many for his Socialist politics, his liberal economic policies, and his status as a Jewish intellectual—hated for all the reasons that Flanner loved him. Blum was a controversial political figure and a convenient scapegoat of French anti-Semitism. He was a particular villain for Céline, for instance, who blamed Blum's economic policies for weakening France and making it ripe for Communism. Especially, however, Céline hated Blum because he was a Jew. In 1936, Blum was forced to devalue the franc, making France even more vulnerable to other European powers and throwing the country into a period of mass confusion. Flanner commented at the time: "with the reliable instinct of a nation in discomfort, France has been constantly talking about crises because she needs the relief of having one. She has had it in devaluation." In 1941, Céline wrote: "Do you remember the pisspool of 36? We are still drinking it, the Popular Front! The Yid's portion!" (McCarthy, *Celine*, 163).

Blum was first introduced to readers of the Paris Letters in June 1936. Flanner emphasized his human qualities, describing him as an "odd man," whose educational background and upbringing seemed more appropriate to Paris intellectual circles than to politics. She adored him, particularly because he represented the combination of broad-minded politics and intellectual prowess with interests in literature and the arts that suited her temperament and tastes. He was, in fact, ill suited for the role of prime minister, a truth that Flanner was not long in discovering:

> Apparently we are alone in thinking Blum has been a remarkable progenitor, if a poor politician. To our mind, he has fathered more needed social reforms than any of his predecessors, who for years glibly promised to beget some such ideas. Clearly because he is too brainy, he has been a poor politico, and under pressure he is constantly becoming more cerebral. He said the other day, "I should have been a writer." He should have remained in the Chamber minority, where his heckling voice made volumes of trouble for the majority. Now his assets make major trouble for him. Nevertheless, this remarkable Judaic intellectual will surely, some day, be historically appreciated as a magnifying glass which valuably clarified the difference between two of this century's major faiths, Socialism and Communism, and led France to see which social image, rightly or wrongly, it hoped to select. (September 1936)

Flanner lived long enough to see this reevaluation of Blum's contribution come about and to see that many of her perceptions about the man were correct. He stood alone in her narratives as a father figure committed to protecting his offspring, hated by the elements of French society who thought that those who were politically weak, socially expendable, physically ill, or aged were a drain on the national energy and should be eliminated.

Not all agreed that Blum's image as father figure was an appropriate one. In this same year Gertrude Stein wrote:

> There is too much fathering going on just now and there is no doubt about it fathers are depressing. Everybody now-a-days is a father, there is father Mussolini and father Hitler and father Roosevelt and father Stalin and father Trotzky [sic] and father Blum and father Franco is just commencing now and there are ever so many more ready to be one. Fathers are depressing. England is the only country now that has not got one and so they are more cheerful there than anywhere. It is a long time now that they have not had any fathering and so their cheerfulness is increasing. (*Everybody's Autobiography*, 133)

Stein was unfair in placing Blum in the same category with Stalin, Mussolini, Hitler, and Franco, but her perception of the patriarchal order of the 1936 world was nonetheless correct.

By early 1937, "father Franco" had succeeded in focusing European attention on the conflict between his rebel forces, which by now had support from Hitler and Mussolini, and the Republican government, which was supported by English and French flying squads. This was a conflict about which everyone had an opinion and in which dozens of artists and writers, fighting on the side of the Republican forces, would die. Flanner wrote: "a Paris letter about Paris at this moment wouldn't be worth the stamp it cost to post it. For right now—and don't be mistaken about it—what makes French news is what's happening in Spain." What had made the difference was the belated realization that the "nonintervention pact" engaging England, France, Russia, Germany, and Italy had been broken, and many felt betrayed. The news broke in various French newspapers, and, relying as usual on information that was already in print from the news services, Flanner relayed to New York reactions of the French upon reading the reports:

> All is known here now: the thousands of German male "tourists" touring Spain in Nazi boots; the thousands of Italian "trippers" who landed in Cadiz; the five hundred to a thousand English volunteers; the Russian-paid Red French flying corps, known as the Escadrille Espana, and supposedly organized by the author of "La Condition Humaine," Andre Malraux; and the White French flying corps, which the Fascist *Le Jour* brightly says is killing its opponents "*en bons sportifs*." . . . The anger, fright, and cynicism of Parisians are as disquieting as the news itself. (January 1937)

By April, a bizarre connection between Spanish art and the war surfaced in the Paris Letters. Although art expositions had continued to open in Paris on a regular basis, Flanner rarely had space enough to cover them and political events as well, but two art events that spring drew her interest:

> It seems sad that war in Spain should make the Jeu de Paume's Catalan Art Exposition the chic exhibition of the spring season. Even the fact that Catalonia's art is, as shown, almost exclusively religious and abounding in distorted wooden Christs has not lessened its vogue. . . . There is considerable gossip here about Spain's art treasures in general; there is question whether the Catalonian show is not merely a ruse (which every art lover should applaud) to get the objects safely out of—with no idea of sending them back into—the war-stricken land.

Just days after she wrote this piece Guernica was bombed, killing 1,654 people, mostly women and children on afternoon shopping, and wounding 889 others. The killers were German military personnel, armed with the most modern equipment. The world was horrified and European countries were frightened, reading in this act the possible future subvention of liberty by Fascist forces. When Picasso heard the news in Paris, he was overcome. On the first of May—four days after the attack—he began working at furious speed on his *Guernica,* having decided that this mural would be Spain's contribution to the Paris Exposition that had begun that day. He later stipulated that he would require Spain to be a true republic before allowing the mural to be shown in his homeland. (*Guernica* has only recently been returned to Spain.)

Flanner did not publish her "Profile" of Picasso until December 1939, after she had returned to America following the outbreak of the war, but her portrait of him included a discussion of the extent to which his leftist politics were solidified by the events in Spain and crystallized by the Fascist atrocities at Guernica:

> The Spanish war profoundly affected Picasso, theretofore politically indifferent. His patriotism, previously visible principally in the nostalgic Spanish shadows of his Blue Period, became passionately republican. He refused to shake Italians by the hand because they were bombing his land; his broadsheet, "Songes et mensonges de Franco," he sold in postcard format for charity; he gave "Guernica" for propaganda to the Spanish Pavilion in the Paris Exhibition; in optimism, he gave big sums to the Spanish government to buy planes; and finally, in defeat, he gave money to the Spanish refugees in the French border camps. The Spanish war furnished a terrible, trite human tableau which distracted Picasso for the first time from a pre-occupation with his own vision. (9 December 1939)

Although it is unclear that Flanner's assessment of Picasso as a self-absorbed artist and a "politically indifferent" human being prior to Guernica is entirely accurate, it is clear that the Spanish war affected him deeply, as it did other artists and writers from various European countries. Among the women discussed in this study, Nancy Cunard was importantly involved in the war. Some suspected, among them Janet Flanner, that Cunard's slide into irreversible alcoholism, anorexia, and eventual death were in large part due to the effects of the Spanish Civil War and the Fascist takeover of Europe (Chisholm, *Nancy Cunard,* 308–349). By 1937, even the most self-absorbed could not avoid the overwhelming evidence that Europe was in the grip of Fascism.

During these years just prior to the occupation of Paris, Flanner analyzed the specific kind of journalism required by political upheaval such as Spain was then experiencing. In January 1938, she reviewed André Malraux's *L'espoir,* a book that offered little hope. It put forth an analysis of the ideology of political violence, whose roots were sunk deep in the male character. In her critique, Flanner revealed much that she usually hid about herself, including her desire to participate in the kind of journalism usually reserved for men such as her friend Hemingway, whom she once confessed she wished to be, men who were able to observe the more violent aspects of political events firsthand. The difficulties Malraux's book would cause for women readers precisely because its subjects were war and man's participation in it were of concern to Flanner: "It is, first, a handbook about civil war as practiced by practical fighting men, and, second, a book written about war in general from a philosophical man's ideological standpoint." That Europe was on the brink of war, that Communism was locked in a battle with Fascism, that the French people regarded Malraux as a revolutionary are reflected in Flanner's commentary. She accurately diagnosed French reaction to the book by focusing on its "academic romantic tone . . . devoid of humanness as well as of hate" as that which "disappointed Communist noncombatants here, who, safe in Paris, wanted more fire and fewer mottoes." Two months later, in March, Hitler captured the Republic of Austria, making it a German province; five months after the takeover, Flanner visited Austria to observe firsthand the consequences of German occupation. In Austria, and later in Perpignan when she observed the escape of Spanish refugees into France, Flanner participated in the excitement of the on-the-scene reportage for which she often envied her male colleagues.

But for all Flanner's desire to practice the profession of journalism as a man would, she admitted to having little talent for it. Her feelings about the various practices of journalism were always ambivalent, and she remained unsure of her own skills even late in her life. Writing to Solita Solano on 3 January 1944, she said: "I failed to send second letter to *New*

Yorker [for the] first time: Nearly went mad doing it, it was dull, incoherent, introverted. I have been scooped on Gertrude Stein returned, on Sylvia Beach doing piece on underground writers. . . . Solita, I am a failure at this sort of huntsmans [*sic*] reporting. Shawn says take it easy, rest, wait: I must or I shall return." Indeed, Shawn set Flanner's talents quite apart from traditional reporting and journalism methods. Her gift was to analyze news already in print, to report reactions to news rather than the news itself, to sift and sort items for coverage—in short, to place European events in a context. Whether Flanner was ever consciously aware of the importance of this kind of writing or her particular talent for it is doubtful. Often in letters to friends or to her editor she disparaged her own abilities, found fault with her writing style and reporting technique, discounted the worth of what she wrote. She spent a professional lifetime learning how to do better what she did. She never talked or wrote about herself as someone with special writing abilities, although she was especially talented at evaluating the writing of others, at knowing exactly how to encourage their analytic talents.

The reports from Austria form a particularly valuable record, since little was known at the time of daily life under the new regime or the response of the people living in Salzburg or Vienna. Even to those who had no sympathy with Nazism (and these were few in Austria), Hitler represented hope for a strengthened economy; not unsurprisingly, the enormous support for Nazism in Austria came from the lower and working classes, with Austrian peasants being Hitler's most passionate followers. Nevertheless, Flanner's account of the new "order" revealed the extent to which Austro-Germans were still in shock over the radical turn of events in their country. They felt both terrorized and protected: "No foreigner except a fool could expect to get at the inner politics of a city which has just been through what it still calls a revolution. And no democrat except a dolt would deny that the Germans have a talent for organization, the lack of which apparently gave the Austrians their charm. And surely no Marxian to whom Communism had become a theology should fail to comprehend that to millions of Austro-Germans, Nazism is revered as the new order's savior and the exterminator of the opposing cult" (August 1938). Flanner's analysis defines the polarized condition of European politics, where only two choices—Fascism or Communism—seemed possible. As these two giant forces played out their big brother battle for control, promoting individual images of brute strength and omniscient power, promising economic revival and renewed stature in the political sector, many—including Flanner—were left to wonder whether a third, more humane and cultured, possibility existed as a political alternative. Her record suggests that in 1938 Europe was a pawn between two cruel and uncompromising masters, one bent on destruction of the other.

In Germany, as in Russia, economics had been the central issue; under the new Fascist economic policy, the plan was to rid the German-speaking world of Jews, to destroy Jewish control of wealth that had, according to Hitler, left non-Jews economically disadvantaged. The Nazi campaign against Jews went well beyond economic concerns, however, as is only too well known. But in 1938, even before the death camps were suspected, the propaganda campaign against Jews was shocking in its audacity. While in Vienna, Flanner toured a display entitled "The Eternal Jew," described by her as "the largest anti-Semitic demonstration, aside from pogroms, held in Christendom. It is the Nazi's first exhibition here. . . . Prints, photographs, models, electric signs, graphs, fine typography, and sales talks are used not to make consumers buy a product but to make the public boycott a race." Flanner's report made little effort to explicate inconsistencies in Nazi thought as it pertained to Jews, but recorded those inconsistencies and the public reaction to them. It was unclear how the new Nazi measures were to help the Austrian economy, for instance, since it survived primarily on tourism and international trade—both of which were restricted by nationalistic measures in 1938. Moreover, Hitler had put Germans rather than Austrians into high government positions and in the more lucrative directorships of banks and other large businesses: "As a defeated German people, they are proud of it, and think that if there is a war, this time they will be on the winning side, since they believe that no matter what it is that Herr Hitler plans to do (and they don't know what it might be any more than if they didn't belong to him), nothing can stop him now. The psychology of the defeated nations has as much as economics to do with their trends today" (17 September 1938). And it was the psychology of defeated peoples—or those who might potentially be defeated—that interested Flanner after her visit to Austria. It was difficult in 1938 for the French to accept that they were a second-rate European power, having been outdistanced by the country they presumably defeated in 1918. Flanner used the brief respites between crises of the French government and in international politics during these months to comment on the French psychology and the stronghold of Fascism within its own borders. The concept of democracy had been called into question by Hitler, Mussolini, and Franco; according to Flanner, democratic governments were ill-prepared for war because their forms of government were too slow-moving: "The practice of democracy dates from the last part of the eighteenth-century and the time of the stage coach. The functional speed of democracies is still that of the vehicles that bore the first argumentative democrats around liberty-loving lands. Fascism dates from the first third of the twentieth-century. Like all startling political innovations, it reflects its period, and thus takes its tempo from the airplane" (22 October 1938). Unwittingly, perhaps, she had struck at a major gap in the thinking of those who opposed Fascism—that it would reveal itself in entrenched belligerence of the kind that marked World War I. Unfortunately for France, the speed of Hitler's methods was the *Zeitgeist*, not the shovel. But economic and military problems in France in 1938 turned on the question of how a war with Hitler might be fought, the answer to which sealed the fate of the Popular Front:

> Since the Front Populaire's stay-in strikes of 1936 in the automotive industry and the Front's idealist forty-hour-week program are now held responsible for France's unpreparedness in the air, and since it has been the Socialists and Communists who have demanded aid for Czechoslovakia (which France could not fight for since she had no planes to fight with), popular feeling is now against the defunct Popular Front. As a reform, it came high; peace will cost a fortune in further armaments, and France is in for more money difficulties, as usual. (22 October 1938)

As the months passed, the reality of the European situation became increasingly clear in its broad outlines, even if its specifics were still only rumor and speculation. In Flanner's post-Christmas letter of January 1939, she commented on the self-centered and indulgent escapism that this particular Christmas celebration had meant for the French ("perhaps because of the general relief at having peace, maybe because of fear of war"). The Parisians had spent an unprecedented amount on food, drink, and entertainment during this holiday season. Even so, "*le plus beau cadeau de Noël*" that year was the undiluted escapism of Walt Disney's *Snow White*, which was given, according to Flanner, "a reception unique in the cinematographic history of France." Hardly had the season passed, however, before Flanner was analyzing the past year's political failure:

> The wishful thinking of the past six years—choosing to believe that Hitler was only funny, that Germany was bankrupt, that the Nazis were slipping, that their whole setup was a bluff—has, since Munich, given way before undesired reality. Hitler is the most important figure in Europe today. Germany, by using its people's faith as a form of credit, has been able to afford the costliest war machine of our time. The Nazis have slipped farther into extremes, and apparently the only bluff was England's and France's promise to stand by their allies. Being crass individualists, the French now see the situation as it is; what they fear is that the English still view it only with the eyes of gentlemen. Since Mussolini's March on Rome, England has accepted anybody's Fascism in order to avoid Russia's Communism. France, after its recent Socialist phase, seems fluid, modern, and adult compared with an England demode and jejune.

Events had forced Flanner to a greater revelation of her own personal responses in a worsening situation, and the shuttles between Paris and London had allowed her a double perspective on the two major forces in democratic Europe. But these observations also meant that her political and personal responses favored France, toward which she was now clearly partisan. In these months she was unable to hide completely her discomfort at English attitudes, particularly their bias against the French. Although she continued to cover the English political scene, one feels through her writing a lack of enthusiasm about this journalistic project and senses that her own attitudes prevented her from remaining objective.

For months the Spanish Civil War had been in the background of political concerns, but in January 1939 Barcelona fell to Franco, and the extent to which he was aided in his efforts against the Republicans became clearer. At this time, Léon Blum, who had held to a strongly non-interventionist line when the Spanish Civil War broke out in 1936, called for a motion of intervention—which the Chamber defeated. But it was too late for interventions. (Flanner pursued the ironies of these events, reporting in the same letter that recounted Franco's victory the announcement of a Picasso retrospective.) Throughout the spring Spain dominated Flanner's commentaries. Spanish refugees, mostly women, children, and defeated soldiers, poured into France. A group of French—including Cardinal Verdier, Henri Bergson, Jacques Maritain, François Mauriac, and Paul Valéry—signed a poster that called on France "to accept the honor of relieving the frightful misery of the Spanish population" by giving goods, money, and clothing to refugees. Again, Flanner interpreted French reaction through the press. Unlike the government, the French press and the French people were interested in the Spanish crisis: "When Barcelona fell, the Communist paper here made no announcement. The Fascist journal not only announced the event but added that under Franco's civilizing regime the Barcelona police immediately began wearing white gloves. Such bigotries still mold the news reports, though all Catalonia has fallen and peace of a sort is perhaps in sight" (February 1939). In March, Flanner visited Perpignan and sent a letter from there observing firsthand the exodus of Catalonians toward a France that hardly knew what to do with this exhausted, frightened, and poverty-stricken group. She observed two of the largest French concentration camps for refugees and described at some length daily life there, the lack of food and sanitary facilities, and the high rate of disease and illness. This was "peace."

By April, her attention had turned to another quarter of Europe, this time to the Balkans, which now seemed to hold the fate of all Europe. In March, Hitler broke the Munich Accord, and Britain and France secretly agreed to support Poland if Hitler invaded, an action that seemed imminent. The hope for peace still flitted in the air, but developments occurred so quickly that Flanner wrote: "any news dispatched from Europe to America these days can be false by the time it is put into print." Communications were again of concern, with radio—"the youngest form of communication"—furnishing

> the only dignified, staid political tone in Europe today. . . . newspaper cartoons and caricatures have lately developed a fever of wit, cruelty, and crassness. . . . the newspapers' texts have displayed vocabulary unseen since the worst pamphleteering days. . . . Excerpts from the frenetic German press attacks are carefully studied here, not because the French are interested in reading that they are sadists and degenerate war-mongers but because they feel that perhaps they will be able to discern in the shrill, planned overtones the moment where mongering might stop and war begin.

As the moment war might break out drew closer, radio propaganda was increasingly sophisticated:

> Probably the neatest device in the increasingly tense radio propaganda war is the German Zeesen station's use of an English-speaking man, who begins by saying "Some may think me a traitor" and then goes on to explain why he loves being a Nazi. To the British ear, the regular English-speaking Hamburg announcer is less painful, despite his murdering the King's English. He rudely refers to Mr. Chamberlain's silly "con*tro*versies, for which the Chermans have *ree*gistered their contempt," thinks that "clothes" has two syllables and that the plural of "geese" (of which, he announced, Germany has a nice new Rumanian lot) is "geazes," and always commences his bulletin of triumphant information by saying, "Today the news are . . ." It's true, alas, that the news doesn't seem to come singly any more. (29 April 1939)

This brief and rather nasty return to Flanner's former wit offers a faint smile in a spring of bad news and misinformation. Again the French deluded themselves with false theories and frantic hopes that Hitler would not do what they dreaded he would. With a million French already mobilized, the country tried to speculate a continued peace. After much prodding from France, the English finally accepted conscription, however: "for months many of the French have been frankly wondering," wrote Flanner in May 1939, "whether the English were simpletons or sly fellows, secretly bent on anything so naive as appeasement but rather on a sympathetic alliance with the new Germany, the only nation since the nineteenth century which has showed anything like England's talent for imperialism." A later letter that month suggested a certain pathos in a belated English effort to mobilize, conscript, and train an army. Sadly, the trenches in Green Park, leftovers from World War I, were now to serve as air-raid shelters.

But the summer in France was a strangely lighthearted one, like the summer of 1914, celebrated "in a fit of prosperity, gaiety, and hospitality: there have been money and music in the air, with people enjoying the first good time since the bad time started at Munich last summer." Even at this moment it seemed ironic that the French exports were so strong: "the gaiety in Paris has been an important political symptom of something serious and solid, as well as spirited, that is in the air in France today" (July 1939). In the midst of this revelry, however, Flanner suspected a grim turn of events and turned her attentions of the history of European tensions:

> The more acute the so-called ideological tension in Europe becomes, the less does it appear that the difference between the various nations really lies in their politics. . . . Certainly the Germanness of the Germans has been the most persistent phenomenon in Europe over the last hundred years. Any foreigner living in Berlin in 1912 found basically what he finds there today—a mustachioed absolute ruler, hailed as the genius of his time (Kaiser Wilhelm, Adolf Hitler); a society worshipping arms (the Imperial Army, black-shirted S. S.); a rank-and-file population unequipped for liberty, talented for efficiency, and with the helot heart, obedient to statesmen restlessly determined on a domineering empire (a Place in the Sun in 1914, *lebensraum* today), and having neither the oldfashioned "*Gott Mit Uns*" or today's "Gross Deutschland Uber Alles" as a psychological backing for this strange, shrill superiority complex that does not, alas, soften or change with the calendar. Had Hitler become interested in Marx rather than in Mussolini (surely it was much a question of chance), Germany today would be trying to Sovietize instead of swastikatize Europe and the world. (July 1939)

Again, Flanner suggests that the only two options open to Europeans at that moment—Fascism and Communism—were the product of chance, that only by chance was it a Fascist Germany rather than a Communist Germany that was attempting a takeover of modern Europe. Flanner, like many others, tended to see little difference between the restrictive authoritarian measures of Fascism and similarly restrictive, authoritarian measures in Communism. This dilemma, the choice between two powers, led to terrible frustration and political crisis for many liberal Europeans. By 26 August, however, France's attention turned to Germany directly as England and France tried to secure an agreement with Hitler over Danzig and Poland. These efforts failed, of course, and Germany invaded Poland on 1 September, bringing England and France into war.

Flanner began cabling her letters to America immediately after the official announcement of the war and herself sailed from Bordeaux on 4 October. These last letters record the sense of "being there" in the days of a crisis that reproduced the various crises of the previous two years. On the weekend of 26 August, the frustration again was in having no news: "on the whole, one of the dreary agonies of these past days has lain precisely in the fact that there has been little relieving excitement—nearly no news, no discussion, no facts, no arguments; nothing but waiting and watching men march off to what may be Sunday's, Monday's, or Tuesday's war." By

10 September, she commented that "this is a queer war so far—thank God!" There was still no news ("maybe it does not exist"): "All that can be truthfully and properly reported from France today is that what is going on in no man's land is strategically strange. . . . Certainly this must be the first war which millions of people on both sides continue to think could be avoided even after it had officially been declared." And for the first time since 1934, there was again direct mention of women, who had until now been submerged by the events of a male political world: ". . . women of *sangfroid,* as the appeals describe them, have been requested to register with the various passive defense organizations. American women who own automobiles have been aiding the evacuation of the lame, halt, and blind. The American Committee for Devastated France, which functioned so well in the last war, is being reorganized in Paris . . . as the Comite Americain pour le Secours Civil." For expatriates, the difference between the two world wars was principally the occupation of Paris that forced enemy aliens into concentration camps. This war had the effect of driving women into retreat; many others fled before Hitler's troops arrived. By 16 September, the war was a reality, one that forced censorship:

> Though newspaper readers haven't yet complained of the blank spaces which constantly appear in their journals, the writers are up in arms against the censorship, which recently censored part of England's White Paper as being something the French had better not know. . . .
>
> The London *Times* carries more news than the Paris *Temps,* and the Paris *New York Herald* has more than the Paris *London Daily Mail,* and all the journals in England and France combined have less than those in New York, where information is still one of the unhappy luxuries of peace.

By 4 October, Flanner's own last letter was censored. Her comments on the evacuation in Bordeaux were particularly painful:

> This period has brought about the greatest, most terrible, and most destructive migration of modern times, a movement of men, women, and children trekking across Europe in flight from other men, women, and children, hurrying because there have been bombs in the air, running with their bundles or sitting stagnant in slow trains, sleeping in strangers' garrets or haymows, and eating bitter bread anywhere because they are democrats or Jews or Christians or libertarians or just plain people, trying to save their sanity, their children, and what is left of their lives. Whether they go north, south, east, or west, they head toward poverty.

Two years earlier, writing from Budapest following her trip to Salzburg and Vienna, Flanner commented almost as an aside that "history looks queer when you're standing close to it, watching where it is coming from and how it is being made." Undoubtedly that statement had validity not only for Flanner the journalist, but for anyone caught up in the rush of events. That she should have been able to state so succinctly the exact measure of her success as a writer concerned with history is ironic. It was precisely her ability to capture the "queerness" of history observed close up, her instinctive knowledge of "where it is coming from and how it is being made" that is revealed in retrospective reading of the Paris Letters. The letters take us into what feels like a fictional world, precisely because we feel the immediacy and the irreality of the events they describe. So immediate are these impressions that we forget the ways in which they are filtered. We overlook a highly subjective intelligence that has directed both the events and our responses to them by its special focus.

In some ways, the world Janet Flanner described was truly a fiction, much of it shaped by women who sought personal freedom and intellectual liberation in Paris. When Edith Wharton stood at the door of a house on the rue Barbet-de-Jouy that chill December afternoon, she looked beyond her present shadowed existence to a bright future. She was not to be the only woman whose hopes brought her to Paris, whose fears left her trembling in the winter cold. But she and two dozen other women, many of whom she would not know personally, were to create the culture they sought. As poets, novelists, publishers, booksellers, journalists, and salon hostesses, they invented and sustained one of the richest literary communities in history. Wharton was the first to arrive, and when the door at which she knocked opened, it was to welcome her. Janet Flanner was one of the last to leave, and when she fled Paris on the afternoon of 4 October 1939, she ran from encroaching darkness augured by the sounds of military aircraft and marching armies. The door of the culture she helped to create on the Paris Left Bank closed behind her. We turn now to another series of arrivals.

PART II. SETTLEMENTS

Edith Wharton, Paris, about 1908 (Photography Collection, Harry Ransom Humanities Research Center, University of Texas at Austin).

Colette during her years in the music hall (Photography Collection, Harry Ransom Humanities Research Center, University of Texas at Austin).

Right: *Janet Flanner,* Little Review, *1929 (McFarlin Library, University of Tulsa).*

Below: *Gertrude Stein at her desk, rue de Fleurus (Yale Collection of American Literature, Beinecke Library).*

Gertrude Stein and Alice B. Toklas (Yale Collection of American Literature, Beinecke Library).

Left above and below: *Gertrude Stein at her desk, rue de Fleurus (Yale Collection of American Literature, Beinecke Library).*

Sylvia Beach reading the plan of Ulysses *(Photography Collection, Harry Ransom Humanities Research Center, University of Texas at Austin).*

Left: *Sylvia Beach in front of Shakespeare and Company at its first location, 8 rue de Dupuytren (Sylvia Beach Collection, Princeton University Library).*

U L Y S S E S

by

J A M E S   J O Y C E

will be published in
the Autumn of 1921

by

"SHAKESPEARE AND COMPANY"

— *SYLVIA BEACH* —

8, RUE DUPUYTREN, PARIS — VI°

Advance Press Notices.

— Mr. EZRA POUND in — *Instigations* — His profoundest work . . . an impassioned meditation on life . . . He has done what Flaubert set out to do in Bouvard et Pécuchet, done it better, more succinct.

— Mr. RICHARD ALDINGTON in — *The English Review* — A most remarkable book . . . Bloom is a rags and tatters Hamlet, a proletarian Lear . . .

— THE TIMES — . . . . . . of the utmost sincerity . . . complete courage.

— Mrs. EVELYN SCOTT in — *The Dial* — A contemporary of the future . . . His technique has developed unique aspects that indicate a revolution of style for the future . . . This Irish artist is recreating a portion of the English language . . . He uses the stuff of the whole world to prove one man.

— THE NEW AGE — . . . "One of the most interesting literary symptoms in the whole literary world, and its publication is very nearly a public obligation".

— Mr. VALERY LARBAUD in — *La Nouvelle Revue Française* — Avec *ULYSSES*, l'Irlande fait une rentrée sensationnelle et triomphante dans la haute littérature européenne.

ULYSSES suppressed four times during serial publication in "The Little Review" will be published by "SHAKESPEARE AND COMPANY" complete as written.

This edition is private and will be limited to 1,000 copies.

100 copies signed on Dutch hand made paper	**350** fr.
150 copies on vergé d'Arches	**250** fr.
750 copies on hand made paper	**150** fr.

The work will be a volume in-8° crown of 600 pages.

Subscribers will be notified when the volume appears, which will be sent to them by registered post immediately on receipt of payment.

All correspondence, cheques, money-orders should be addressed to :

Miss SYLVIA BEACH

"SHAKESPEARE AND COMPANY"

8, RUE DUPUYTREN, PARIS — VI°

ORDER FORM

Please send me ULYSSES by JAMES JOYCE

NUMBER OF COPIES *	
	Edition on Dutch hand made paper with signature of the Author **350** fr.
	Edition on vergé d'Arches . . . . **250** fr.
	Edition on hand made paper . . . . **150** fr.

I will pay on receipt of notice announcing that the volume has appeared.

Name . . . .   *Signature:*

Address . . . .

* Please cancel editions not required.

107

Advertisement for James Joyce's Ulysses *in* Little Review, *autumn 1921 (McFarlin Library, University of Tulsa).*

Above: *Sylvia Beach and James Joyce at Shakespeare and Company, 12 rue de l'Odéon (Sylvia Beach Collection, Princeton University Library).*

Left: *F. Scott Fitzgerald and Adrienne Monnier in front of La Maison des Amis des Livres in 1928 (photograph by Sylvia Beach; Sylvia Beach Collection, Princeton University Library).*

Above: *Mina Loy and Djuna Barnes (Copyright by Man Ray; Sylvia Beach Collection, Princeton University Library).*

Right: *Djuna Barnes,* Little Review, *spring 1929 (photograph by Berenice Abbott; McFarlin Library, University of Tulsa).*

Djuna Barnes, Little Review, *December 1919 (McFarlin Library, University of Tulsa).*

Natalie Barney (George Wickes Collection).

Right: *Natalie Barney, the lady and her page (George Wickes Collection).*

Left below: *Eva Palmer (George Wickes Collection).*

Right below: *Renée Vivien, portrait by Alice Pike Barney (George Wickes Collection).*

Above: *Natalie Barney and Romaine Brooks, about 1915 (George Wickes Collection).*

Romaine Brooks, La France croisée, *1914 (National Museum of American Art, Smithsonian Institution, Gift of the Artist).*

Natalie Barney, "l'Amazone," by Romaine Brooks, 1920 (Ville de Paris, Musée de Petit Palais, Paris).

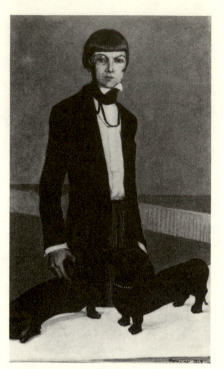

Una, Lady Troubridge, by Romaine Brooks, 1924 (National Museum of American Art, Smithsonian Institution, Gift of the Artist).

Sketch of the Temple à l'Amitié, by André Rouveyre (George Wickes Collection).

5
GERTRUDE STEIN AND
ALICE B. TOKLAS:
RUE DE FLEURUS

Gertrude Stein before Expatriation

Gertrude Stein wrote in *Paris France* that "every century has a beginning and a middle and an ending. . . . it begins that is it has a childhood it has an adolescence it has an adult life, it has a middle life and an older life and then it ends" (116). The birth of the twentieth century coincided with Stein's emergence into adulthood; by the time the twentieth century reached its middle age, Stein was dead of cancer in Paris. When she arrived in that city in 1903, the nineteenth century was in its death throes; Paris, like other European cities, was still governed by the outdated and meaningless conventions of an earlier culture. Stein's residence in Paris would result in freedom from those conventions, but the initial move in 1903 did not mark an immediate break with her past. Although she had no intention of returning to America to live, she did travel there several times before staying on permanently in Europe. The effort to resolve her insecurities and indecision, to escape the ethics of her middle-class up-bringing, and to discover her potential as a creative writer was to require, as Catharine R. Stimpson has explained, ten years of work, during the same decade in which the twentieth century labored to be born ("The Mind, the Body, and Gertrude Stein"). By the time the first gunfire was heard along the Somme, Stein had resolved the personal conflicts that troubled her youth and had entered into maturity. Later, she claimed her maturity was marked by giving birth to the twentieth century in her writings.

Stein's adolescence was prolonged, as was that of many other women of her time, by cultural norms that made women both dependent on and in the service of the family. Thus the move to Paris was less a step toward independence than a temporary retreat to the security of a relationship with her older brother Leo. Having just abandoned a career in scientific research and having survived a painful love affair that scarred her self-confidence, Stein was the victim of vague fears. At 29, she was not yet ready to give up the tormented safety of adolescence to embark on independent adulthood. A decade later, however, she had ended her relationship with Leo and entered into a satisfying and enriching union with Alice B. Toklas and had fought through the tentative stages of her writing and embarked on a radical critique of the linguistic structures produced by Western thought. Why had it taken her so long to liberate herself from youthful dependencies? How did she free herself from childhood constraints to emerge at 40 to a life of directed intellectual energies, sexual passion, and psychological stability?

A number of seemingly disparate factors characterize Gertrude Stein's experience in the years just preceding her expatriation, factors denied by her later descriptions of this difficult period in her life. Adopting a narrative perspective that filters all experience through the eyes of the lover, for instance, *The Autobiography of Alice B. Toklas* leaves obscure aspects of life at the rue de Fleurus prior to Toklas's arrival or that she herself did not witness: "There are a great many things to tell of what was happening then and what had happened before, which led up to then, but now I must describe what I saw when I came."[1] The lingering impression of the *Autobiography* is that Gertrude Stein fell into the center of an exciting art movement about which "the outside world at that time knew nothing" (26). Other, more private, sources tell a different story, as Leon Katz notes in his introduction to the collection *Fernhurst, Q.E.D., and Other Early Writings*: "The notebooks and her letters of the first months in Paris—in fact of her first four years there—suggest that Stein underwent a period of the most relentless despair, surrender of ambition, and psychological disorientation. She became passive, cynical; she was moved to do nothing. The picture that she herself offers in her autobiographies of an eager, not to say bouncing, enthusiast for Parisian art, for friends, for her new life, was written from the happily distant perspective of the 1930s" (xxix). If we are to understand something of the contrast between the mature public persona of Gertrude Stein, the woman simultaneously accused of having "one of the great egos of all time" and of effecting a "great withdrawal into the closet of private art" because of an "isolation that she herself could never understand,"[2] then we must look closely at the construction of this adult personality. In the first years of her Paris residence, Stein by acts of stubborn will forged the dissonant elements of her adolescent personality into an imposing and authoritative persona that submerged the frightened, often bitter, woman within. The factors contributing to this casting of a public image included her simultaneous dependence on and resentment of Leo; the fear that his assessment of her as a "basically stupid" person might be accurate;[3] her experiences as a medical student at Johns Hopkins University; the early suspicions and later confirmation of her homosexuality; her desire to participate in the wholesale effort of the twentieth century to free itself from the constraints and moral imperatives of the nineteenth century; her efforts to come to terms with a childhood that left her emotionally orphaned; her need to be appreciated, loved, admired, and—perhaps most important of all—listened to.

Gertrude Stein's ambivalent relationship with Leo has been assessed at some length by almost every critic who has made an effort to understand her. The story of their mutually supportive early relationship and the later disintegration of that union has been told by each of her biographers. James R. Mellow attributes the dependency of sister on older brother to the deaths of the Stein parents: "She seems to have trailed after him, like a satellite after a superior planet. Without him she grew restive and unhappy" (*Charmed Circle*, 42). The two youngest children in the Stein family, Leo and Gertrude became mutually dependent, opposing themselves to the older children in the family and striking out together to discover lives outside the family confine. Richard Bridgman's reading supports such an interpretation of the relationship, suggesting in the chronology attached to the study that Gertrude decided to attend medical school at Johns Hopkins because Leo was already there doing work in biology (*Gertrude Stein in Pieces*, entry for 1897, 360). But this assumption is contradicted by Bridgman's text, where evidence is cited that Leo may have decided on the year's graduate work in biology because his older brother, Michael, had done the same: "Leo was working for his A.B. when Gertrude made up her mind to attend [Johns Hopkins]. He received it in 1898, then, like his elder brother, continued as a graduate student of biology during the academic year 1898–9" (34). This set of statements is particularly confusing, since Bridgman's own chronology has Leo Stein receiving his A.B. from Harvard in 1895. The suggestion is that Leo received a second A.B. from Johns Hopkins that allowed him to do graduate work in biology. Mellow's reading of this crucial period is quite different: "Gertrude had decided to pursue her medical career at Johns Hopkins University School of Medicine, in Baltimore, which had recently opened its doors to women students. . . . Furthermore, Leo—perhaps stimulated by the example of Gertrude's published laboratory work—had decided to pursue some independent research projects in biology there" (*Charmed Circle*, 55). Indeed, it seems that Gertrude's interest in science, developed while Leo was in Japan on a world tour, gave him the idea to take up a scientific career—in which case, he followed his sister to Baltimore not only geographically but also intellectually.

That Leo Stein may have needed to be central to Gertrude's life, rather than she to his, calls for a rereading of the decision-making pattern these siblings adopted. For instance, Leo transferred from the University of California to Harvard University in 1892, the year Gertrude was sent to live with her aunt in Baltimore. Gertrude later decided to attend Radcliffe and to take up the study of philosophy because Leo was already there studying philosophy. Her decision to study medicine, however, had nothing to do with Leo's later decision to study biology at Johns Hopkins (he followed her back to Baltimore); rather, hers was an effort to continue the experiments in the psychology of the brain that she had begun at Harvard under William James. Stein apparently never had any desire to practice medicine (in fact, the practical emphasis in the coursework in the last two years of medical school was repugnant to her), but her discovery at Hopkins of a role model for her intended career in research was crucial to her attitudes as a medical student. Claribel Cone also had a distaste for medical practice, had turned her efforts to laboratory research, and later became a well-known research scientist (Mellow, *Charmed Circle*, 59). More importantly for Gertrude's life, Claribel Cone was to serve as a role model long after Leo had been put aside; her friendship with Cone constituted the first important relationship she had yet had outside the family.

Like her decision to work for the medical degree, Stein's decision to leave medical school seemed to rest outside the more common reasons given by women who forsook their studies (e.g., the lure of marriage and family, the physical and mental exhaustion of the work). When Leo abandoned his study of biology and moved to Florence to pursue an interest in art and aesthetics (Mellow, *Charmed Circle*, 60) Gertrude Stein's interest in medicine suddenly seemed to wane and her scholastic achievement began to falter, suggesting to some that Leo's absence somehow motivated her decision to give up her studies. But too much credence has been given the notion that it was Leo's absence from Baltimore that contributed most directly to Stein's failure in medical school. Mellow has argued that "there is little doubt that Leo's defection contributed to the failure of Gertrude's medical career. She lost interest in her studies, failed to do her classwork, and, when asked questions in class, responded by saying she did not know the answer" (*Charmed Circle*, 62). But this was not the first time Leo had been away from America while Gertrude was in school. During her undergraduate career at Harvard he had taken a world tour (1895–96). Janet Hobhouse describes Gertrude's earlier reaction to Leo's lengthy absence, a reaction quite different from the later one that presumably led to her withdrawing from medical school:

> For the first two years at Harvard, Gertrude remained for most of her acquaintances as "Leo's little sister." She followed him in her choice of friends, as she had in her choice of studies. When in 1895, Leo graduated from Har-

vard and left America to join his cousin Fred Stein on a trip around the world, Gertrude's work at the university began to take direction. In the following year she published, together with her colleague and friend, Leon Solomons, the result of their work in experimental psychology. With the appearance of the paper on "Normal Motor Automatism" in *Psychological Review,* her professors, always admiring . . . now began to take her seriously. (*Everybody Who Was Anybody,* 16)

Actually, Stein's interest in medicine had dropped off sometime before Leo's departure, her grades showing a marked decline in 1899–1900 (see Bridgman, *Gertrude Stein in Pieces,* 358). Efforts by the teaching staff to extend her course of study failed, and she later thanked the professor who had refused to approve her unsatisfactory work for sparing her a profession that she detested (Mellow, *Charmed Circle,* 63). It is interesting to speculate on what might have happened to brother and sister had Gertrude actually finished her medical studies at Johns Hopkins and gone on to practice medical research. Her brother seems to have encouraged these efforts, expressing concern when she wrote in February 1901 that she would not be able to finish. In Leo's 3 February 1901 letter to Gertrude (*Charmed Circle,* 62), he expresses concern about the termination of her studies. However, one might assume from his later reactions to her success that, whatever purposeful direction her life might have taken, Leo—unable to find purpose in his own life—would have found fault.

Stein seems to have discovered sometime in the third year of medical school that her initial interest in psychological research, influenced as it was by her devotion to Professor James, was in reality not suited to her own habits of mind. An ill-suited career choice, however, did not entirely account for Stein's unhappiness and confusion. In the following year, during which she failed four of her senior courses, Stein formed a friendship that both excited and disturbed her. By summer 1901, when she again traveled with Leo in Europe, she had discovered her sexual attraction to someone of the same sex, a discovery that disoriented her (see Katz, "Introduction," *Fernhurst,* xiv). Stein returned to America in autumn 1901 and "settled down to a year of purposeless improvisation" ("Introduction," xv). After an interim period marked by travel and moves from one apartment to another, Stein eventually abandoned her studies and took up permanent residence in Europe, moving in with Leo at the apartment he had rented on the rue de Fleurus. Rather than a sister's search for a brother, however, these shifts in intellectual allegiances and the prolonged search for a permanent residence constituted the circuit of sexual discovery.

The affair with May Bookstaver, on which *Q.E.D.* is based, began sometime in 1900, the year Leo left Baltimore for residence in Europe. Although the chronology of the affair is speculative, it appears that Stein met her and Mabel Haynes after Leo left.[4] One wonders, then, whether it was by chance that these friendships followed Leo's departure, whether his departure allowed Gertrude opportunities to establish her own social life, even whether Leo's absence allowed Gertrude the psychological freedom to fall in love with another woman.

Leo's expatriate travels commenced with a summer vacation in 1900 when he traveled throughout Europe with Gertrude and a friend, Mabel Weeks. When Gertrude returned to the states to continue her education, Mabel stayed on in England to study, and Leo remained abroad, resident first in Florence and later in Paris. In her senior year of medical school, Stein's record demonstrated a lack of effort, in part no doubt due to the effects of the love affair, but also due to Stein's decided distaste for the practical application of medical knowledge. In particular, courses that dealt with obstetrics and with sexuality were stressful to her. The simultaneous study of the body, especially the parts of it involving sexuality, and the pressure to act on her feelings of physical passion for May Bookstaver may well have converged in the decision to drop out of medical school (see Stimpson, "The Mind, the Body, and Gertrude Stein," 494–495, especially fn. 13). *Q.E.D.* commences with the boat trip to Europe in 1901, the summer following Stein's decision to leave school. In the story Stein—the Adele figure—travels with her two companions, Helen Thomas (May Bookstaver) and Mabel Neathe (Mabel Haynes). In fact, Stein traveled that summer, as she did the next, with Leo, retreating to the safety of this known relationship in respite from the tensions of the more compelling love affair.

Between the onset of the affair in 1900 and the completion of *Q.E.D.* in October 1903, Gertrude Stein made four voyages between America and Europe, alternately trying to escape the stalemated relationship with Bookstaver and to effect a reconciliation. The completion of *Q.E.D.* did not end Stein's involvement with May Bookstaver, and the tensions arising from Mabel Haynes's position in the three-way affair continued. In March 1904, Stein returned again to America, apparently to try once more to reconcile with May Bookstaver, but the effort was a failure; "when she returned to Europe that summer, sailing with Etta Cone, it represented her last trip to America in thirty years" (Mellow, *Charmed Circle*, 81). As Richard Bridgman notes, it took Gertrude Stein nearly a year and a half after the completion of *Q.E.D.* to overcome the effects of the affair: "recording it had been insufficient therapy" (*Gertrude Stein in Pieces*, 45).

It is the period between completion of *Q.E.D.* in October 1903 and the beginning of *Three Lives* in February 1905 that remains something of a mystery. Gertrude was living at 27, rue de Fleurus, but the occupation of her time is unclear. There is some suggestion that she was trying to overcome the last emotional effects of the affair with Bookstaver. Documentary evidence is not fully available, since Alice Toklas destroyed Bookstaver's letters to Stein and Stein's letters to Bookstaver have not survived (*Charmed Circle*, 79–80; *Gertrude Stein in Pieces*, 40), although there are letters from Stein to friends and family suggesting that the first months of her residence in Paris were marked by depression, even despair. We know, and have known for some time, as much of this story as available factual evidence permits. It is the interpretation of the story that remains open to revision. Stein's return to Johns Hopkins in fall 1901 to do brain research probably suggests both a need to be nearer Bookstaver and an effort to salvage something of the eight years of scientific training she was to abandon in spring 1902 when she began selling her medical books (*Gertrude Stein in Pieces*, 37–38). Once having left America to take up residence in Paris, Stein commenced her expatriation by writing out the story of the unhappy love affair that was, importantly, the reason for her expatriation. The decision again to take up life with her brother represented a regression to the patriarchal fold and suggested as well that Gertrude Stein had nowhere else to go.[5]

The Composition of Q.E.D.

Written when she was 29 years old, *Q.E.D.* represented Gertrude Stein's first effort at writing fiction and, apart from college essays, her first effort at sustained writing. Following *Fernhurst* (written in 1904, another effort at clarifying the relationships explored in *Q.E.D.*, this time using the story of Mary Gwinn, Alfred Hodder, and Helen Carey Thomas, the president of Bryn Mawr), she was to emphasize the twenty-ninth year as a turning point toward adulthood:

> It happens often in the twenty-ninth year of a life that all the forces that have been engaged through the years of childhood, adolescence and youth in confused and ferocious combat range themselves in ordered ranks—one is uncertain of one's aims, meaning and power during these years of tumultuous growth when aspiration has no relation to fulfillment and one plunges here and there with energy and misdirection during the storm and stress of the making of a personality until at last we reach the twenty-ninth year the straight and narrow gate-way of maturity and life which was all uproar and confusion narrows down to form and purpose and we exchange a great dim possibility for a small hard reality. (*Fernhurst*, 29)

The events recorded in *Q.E.D.* constituted Stein's difficult passage through the "straight and narrow gate-way of maturity." In *Q.E.D.* she addressed her own sensual and acquiescent nature, explored the tensions between her dreary somnolence and the internal emotional strife aroused by sexual stirrings, and discovered her morality—which had heretofore been characterized by a kind of "assertive naivete" ("Introduction," *Fernhurst*, xi)—to be a product of the middle-class upbringing that must necessarily be put aside. Adele's strife in *Q.E.D.* results from two aspects of this middle-class morality: mistrust of physical passion and disgust at Mabel's ability to buy Helen's affections. Unlike Adele, Helen is wealthy (although she apparently has niggardly parents); she is unable to break off the affair and commit herself to Adele because of her own susceptibility to the material comforts that Mabel's money can provide her. Sexual acquiescence and economic dependency appear to be linked in the story: although a victim of Mabel's manipulation, Helen cannot break free: unable to bring about a resolution to the deadlock, Adele is both disappointed and frightened. It is also interesting that for both the other women in this triangle, lesbianism seems to represent a stage of sexual experimentation to be replaced by heterosexuality. Rather than suggesting a marked preference for heterosexuality, however, their marriages, which took place shortly after the events recorded in *Q.E.D.*, may reveal the pressures brought about by the heterosexual parent culture. (May Bookstaver was married in August 1904 and Mabel Haynes a year later.) By leaving America, Stein removed herself from the intensity of such pressures, an action that may have allowed the survival of her attraction to other women.

Q.E.D. marks Stein as the outsider, one who by social class, upbringing, and lack of experience is separated from others. In the story Adele is described as "queer" (perhaps original, interesting), accepted by her wealthy, indulged friends because she is different from them. But the story makes clear that Adele never successfully negotiates this territory of difference, that her emerging self-understanding does not allow her to comprehend Helen and Mabel. Her movements are ponderous, her thoughts confused, her sexual instincts slow to arouse. Adele seems lumbering and almost stupefied (sometimes stupid, as Stein at this time was convinced she was); she is unable to take action, remaining at the story's end outside its central dynamic. Indeed, as interpreted by most critics the story is articulated through a series of oppositions that display a polarized emotional landscape. Adele is seen to be engaged in a struggle between "revulsion and respect" (*Q.E.D.*, 87). But the opposition of Adele to Helen is made possible only by the presence of Mabel, who at all times represents the obstacle separating the would-be lovers. By the close of the story Mabel's power has become evident rather than implied, and she prevents the resolution of the tensions undergirding the plot and ensures the "dead-lock" on which *Q.E.D.* closes. One year after the completion of the novel, Stein commented on the emotional economy it traced, drawing a distinction between the French analysis of the *ménage à trois* and the American understanding of love relationships that exclude the third party: "It is the French habit to consider that in the usual grouping of two and an extra which humanity so constantly supplies it is the two that get something from it all who are of importance and whose claim should be considered—the American mind accustomed to waste happiness and be reckless of joy finds morality more important than ecstasy and the lonely extra of more value than the happy two" (*Fernhurst*, 38). Because Stein played the "lonely extra" in the affair, the one whose presence suggested excess in an otherwise limited economy, her instincts for self-preservation encouraged the American interpretation, to find herself of "more value than the happy two." Moreover, her overriding concern with "morality" in its typically American manifestation assured her the cold comfort of the morally superior position. It is not clear that Stein was ever able to put aside entirely her American morality, which linked itself to her sense of intellectual superiority (Mellow, *Charmed Circle*, 58). In her next, and only, other important relationship—with Alice Toklas—Stein made very certain that she would not play the part of the lonely outsider.

Stein used *Q.E.D.* in much the same way she had used her undergraduate themes at Radcliffe—to comprehend her own emotional states.[6] It seems to have allowed Stein access to the submerged confusion and conflict of her sexual desires. The "emotional disaster" of the affair with May Bookstaver had made Stein painfully aware of her vulnerability to sexual and emotional manipulation. The autobiographical importance of the work is in providing a portrait of the artist as a young woman doubly imprisoned—first, by the contradictions of emotional commitments to her own sex and, second by the resulting isolation of those attachments. Although the author of *Q.E.D.* had not completely extricated herself from the relationship she described and used the writing of this text to understand her situation, Adele's story was already part of Gertrude Stein's past. Reviewing the drama from a certain physical and psychological distance, Stein survived its crisis. The long-term effects of this painful experience, however, were to be found in various contradictory elements of her personality and behavior: her intense love of Alice Toklas and the simultaneous exploitation of Alice's need to serve; her mistrust of the public and her craving for *la gloire*; her seclusion among the Left Bank writers and her continued claims to centrality in the Paris literary world.

Two plus One: Gertrude, Leo, Picasso

Although some critics have suggested that during the years 1897–1907 Gertrude and Leo had developed a relationship based on frankness about their private lives (Mellow, *Charmed Circle*, 256), it seems almost certain that Leo did not immediately surmise that *Q.E.D.*'s subject was the literal record of a failed lesbian love affair. He may not even have known that in the first weeks of her residence at 27, rue de Fleurus, Gertrude was composing this piece. When he speaks of *Q.E.D.* in his own autobiography, he writes as though it were an early draft of the "Melanctha" portion of *Three Lives.* (Indeed, "Melanctha" is a version of *Q.E.D.*, rewritten into a heterosexual rather than a homosexual triangle.) Just when he read *Q.E.D.* and whether he was openly critical of the manuscript is uncertain, although he comments in his autobiography, *Journey into Self:* "If I hadn't known that Gertrude was in her pre-'cubist' days a barbarian in her use of language (it was rather interesting she should have 'forgotten' that early manuscript [*Q.E.D.*] which I was the only person to have read and which, stylistically speaking, or rather more than that, as literature, as objective writing was impossible)—if I hadn't known that Gertrude couldn't write, though she then had something to say, I might be inclined to take her more seriously" (141).

One assumes that Leo was aware that his sister was writing shortly after her arrival in Paris when she took over the atelier he was no longer using. From a later word portrait (*Two: Gertrude Stein and Her Brother,* written after Alice Toklas moved in to 27, rue de Fleurus, and before Leo Stein moved out) we can surmise that Leo Stein was amused by and often critical of his sister's writing effort, which he was later to call an "abomination." Leo Stein and many who came after him were to conclude that Gertrude's experimentation with linguistic convention was the result of her inability to deal effectively with language, so that she made her greatest weakness into her most "remarkable" strength. The knowledge of her brother's opinion may well have been enough to curtail Gertrude's desire to share her work with him. She claimed in *Everybody's Autobiography* that as early as the drafting of *The Making of Americans,* she did not show her work to her brother: "I was writing in the way I was writing. I did not show what I was doing to my brother, he looked at it and he did not say anything" (*Everybody's Autobiography,* 76). That Leo "looked at" the work even though Gertrude did not "show" it to him may also suggest that he continued to take (silent) liberties.

Undoubtedly Stein's unwillingness to show Leo this more experimental work was based on fear of further ridicule from him. Her decision to write during the night while other members of the household were asleep seems to have been taken early in her Paris years. She gave as the reason for this practice the reassurance that she would not be interrupted; she would begin to write at that moment in the evening when she felt certain no one would come to call (Mellow, *Charmed Circle,* 92). Yet one wonders whether another, unspoken and perhaps unacknowledged, reason for these nightly vigils was the certain knowledge that Leo Stein was asleep. His repressive presence safely removed, she perhaps felt free to explore her own consciousness and to continue the experiments in writing that were to lead to *Three Lives* and *The Making of Americans.* In the years before Alice Toklas's arrival in Paris, Stein took advantage of Leo's frequent absences to outline her writing efforts; she wrote in the Luxembourg Gardens, made mental compositions as she walked back from Picasso's studio. In later years, when Alice Toklas was present in the house and Leo Stein was no longer resident, Gertrude apparently did not feel it necessary to restrict her working hours to the dead of night, although she used odd moments, often while seated in the car, to jot down her impressions. In support of this interpretation of Stein's working methods, Edith Sitwell recalled in her autobiography that Stein "had a remarkable ability to work in the midst of any amount of noise. She had been known to sit in a garage while her motor was being repaired, writing with complete concentration" (*Taken Care Of,* 136).

What Gertrude Stein needed desperately in the early Paris years was an intelligent, sympathetic friend with whom she could discuss her theories of art and the literary experiments she was undertaking. She found this person in Picasso, for whom she sat for her portrait during the months in 1905 and 1906 when she was composing *Three Lives* and continuing *The Making of Americans.* Gertrude had been almost immediately drawn toward Picasso and his group, although Leo rarely thought highly of his work, seeing him as a dilettante rather than a serious painter. While Leo resented his presence, Gertrude discovered she could discuss with Picasso matters that she could not discuss with Leo. Unlike her brother, who did not allow her to talk and who was not interested in her writing, Picasso apparently took Gertrude's work seriously, and the two established a method of dialogue that allowed each to discuss artistic method in terms of the other's métier. In *Everybody's Autobiography* she wrote: "My brother needed to be talking and he was painting but he needed to talk about painting in order to be painting, he needed to understand painting in order to be painting" (*Everybody's Autobiography,* 75).[7] Leo talked about painting in relation to his own work; Picasso and Gertrude Stein discussed the larger issues of aesthetics. She used these discussions to hone her literary theories and allowed her mind to range freely over the material that after dark, in the silence of the atelier, she would later commit to paper. She gained confidence in her insights in Picasso's presence and felt inspired to continue her experiments. Picasso served as a substitute brother in these crucial years, one who helped her discover the power to speak, to voice her thoughts and opinions.

Neil Schmitz comments, however, that the relationship with Picasso was not without its difficulties for Stein. He represented a droll, enchanting, and exotic practitioner of experimental art and a friend who would listen to her. But he was still a male who, by assuming the male prerogative of leadership and independence, placed her in a dependent position, not altogether unlike the position her brother forced her to assume.

In the *Autobiography of Alice B. Toklas,* for example, it is Alice's perspective that grants Picasso a central place. Stein is not central to the *Autobiography;* indeed, she claims not even to be present there. Alice Toklas, for instance, says she wishes to speak of "three geniuses . . . Gertrude Stein, Pablo Picasso, and Alfred Whitehead" (5—6), but according to Schmitz, "only two geniuses matter in the *Autobiography* [Stein and Picasso] and their relation is the problem of the text" (*Huck and Alice,* 211).

The sign of Gertrude's emerging independence from Leo was the observation in *Two* of sound. In this word portrait, Leo's methods of analysis are contrasted and compared with those of his sister-in-law, Sally Stein: sound is first "coming out of him," then superseded by sound "coming out of her." The effects of this incessant sound are registered by the third party to the situation—Gertrude. In this portrait she draws the philosophic link between the state of being and the ability to express being through speech: "In sound coming out of her she was expressing all of feeling all she was feeling and asking all of saying what she was saying" (*Two,* 9).[8] *Two* records Leo's insistent self-expression in speech that tired his sister and left her in later years easily fatigued by the sounds of voices talking. In a probable reference to Leo's need to lecture her, she commented in *Tender Buttons* that "sound is sickened" ("Rooms," 75). Stein was very sensitive to the sound of spoken English, and she preferred to be surrounded by people who did not speak the language (Mellow, *Charmed Circle,* 256). *Two* records Leo's inability to hear his sister (he was, as Stein noted in *Everybody's Autobiography,* 72—73, becoming increasingly deaf in these years) and her insistent need to declare her independence from him through speech, to keep him silent by means of her own voice. Although Gertrude Stein had apparently always been an enthusiastic talker, eager for argument and controversy, as the relationship with Leo continued she became increasingly silent and introspective. Alfred Stieglitz—a visitor to 27, rue de Fleurus, in the early years—was impressed by her unwavering silence under provocation by visitors who were appalled by the paintings and her silent acquiescence to Leo's taste and declarative manner (Brinnin, *The Third Rose,* 54).

In *Everybody's Autobiography,* Stein commented that she had nothing to say at this period in her life ("there was nothing to say because just then saying anything was nothing," 76). She suggested that her brother was responsible for her silence ("we were together as much as ever") and that when he had something to say about her writing he began "explaining": "Now and then I was not listening. This had never happened to me before up to that time I had always been listening." When Leo claimed that Gertrude's writing was not marked by genius but by her presence (the "I"), she rebelled: "it destroyed him for me and it destroyed me for-him" (77).⁹ It is significant that the mature Gertrude Stein, who was willing to hold forth on almost any subject whether or not she seemed to be expert in it, lost her voice in her late twenties and early thirties. She was silenced by her brother, but continued to analyze forms of expression in her writing.

Three minus One: Gertrude, Alice, Leo

The shifting significance of the word "two" in the literary portrait of Gertrude Stein and her brother records the disintegration of their relationship and the emerging alliance between Gertrude Stein and Alice Toklas (Bridgman, *Gertrude Stein in Pieces*, 113). Indeed, the numerical significance of one versus two and the mathematical possibilities held captive in the combination of these numbers to make three diagram the basic dimensions of Stein's early literary subjects. These works often examine the difficulty of establishing the self as a member of a couple. This concern with the dynamics of coupling suggests the residual effects of the May Bookstaver affair and increasing unease in the relationship with Leo. After 1903, Stein could not overlook her sexual orientation or dismiss her need for an emotional and physical union with another woman. The desire for such a coupling and the barriers to it provide a constant refrain in the poetry of the early Paris years. Afraid of isolation, shaken in her self-confidence, she stayed with her brother until the longed-for lover arrived. But Alice Toklas's arrival was not the cause of the break between Gertrude and Leo: her presence merely confirmed the suspicions Gertrude was afraid to face. *Two* tracks the brother-sister alliance to its dead end ("She was changing. He was changing. They were not changing," 19); Leo is portrayed as one whose character is marked by stipulation and denial (97). His unmitigating sense of "oneness," his need to impress himself on others, to make someone else's life contingent on his own, led to the break: "He was one who was not one of the two of them" (99). In focusing so relentlessly on Leo's inability to play the role of partner in the couple, *Two* effectively displaces Gertrude's fears about her own failures in such circumstances.

Two testifies to the degree that Stein had learned well the lesson of *Q.E.D.* Unlike the former triangle, this later relationship did not remain deadlocked, in large part because Gertrude, Leo's once docile and undemanding sister, insisted that he play the role of outsider. She dared not take any chances with the occasion for future happiness; with Alice's help, Gertrude connived to remove all obstacles to their growing intimacy. In the interim period of their residence together, Alice provided a buffer between Gertrude and Leo Stein. John Malcolm Brinnin describes Leo's eventual disappearance from the household as an action taken by

Leo, who "cut himself off from a *ménage à trois* in which, he felt, his life was marginal, sterile, and where his problems were met with little sympathy" (*The Third Rose*, 198). Leo's decision had been encouraged by Gertrude and Alice, who forced a change in the domestic balance of power. When his position in the household evolved into the one that Gertrude had played for him for years, he moved out, unable or unwilling to play subordinate to Gertrude's evolving dominance. Leo wrote Mabel Weeks that "one of the greatest changes that has become decisive in recent times is the fairly definite 'disaggregation' of Gertrude and myself" (Mellow, *Charmed Circle*, 246). Leo saw his departure from 27, rue de Fleurus, as a flight toward freedom.

Whereas Gertrude Stein felt "that mixed dependence and resentment for Leo that a prisoner feels toward his guard," as Richard Bridgman states, she found in Alice Toklas someone openly interested in every aspect of her life. No longer an outsider in her brother's home, Gertrude assumed centrality in Alice's life, and Alice came to occupy the "interior space that [was] the site of Gertrude Stein's text" (Schmitz, *Huck and Alice*, 174). In her role as lover, Alice's first obligation was to attend to Gertrude Stein, to fulfill her need to be heard. In her role as textual subject, Alice entertained Stein with funny stories, thus serving as Stein's literary subject matter: "Someone who was living was almost always listening. Some one who was loving was almost always listening. . . . The one who was loving was telling about being one then listening. That one being loving was then telling stories having a beginning and a middle and an ending" ("Ada," *Geography and Plays*, 16). When Alice took her central place in Gertrude's life and in her texts, Leo's existence became marginal and contingent. In the *Autobiography of Alice B. Toklas,* for instance, he is consistently referred to as "Gertrude Stein's brother." From Alice's perspective, Leo was marginal and Gertrude central. From Gertrude's perspective, Leo was forced to play for her text the role she had so long played for him. In *Everybody's Autobiography* Stein again placed Leo in relation to herself ("my brother"), employing a technique often used by men to keep women in their "place" ("my wife," "my mother," etc.).

When Alice Toklas came to live at 27, Gertrude noted that "the closet was not holding all the clothes that had been made," but after Leo's leave-taking the rooms seemed empty and needed to be filled again (*Two*, 141–142). The apparent emptiness of the house was, however, only temporary. Leo's removal from 27, rue de Fleurus, provided the occasion for major renovations, badly needed repairs, and refurbishing (Mellow, *Charmed Circle*, 250–251). The two women set about making their own the house that Leo had discovered and in which he had served as head of household. The change in living arrangements led to changes in Gertrude Stein's writ-

ing, which became openly sexual and erotic as well as increasingly domestic after her brother moved out. Examining the daily events and common objects of her home life, Stein made her homosexual marriage the
subject matter for art, describing it in terms that suggested the heterosexual pattern for its roles: Gertrude as husband and Alice as wife. After
1910, the year Alice moved to the rue de Fleurus, the elements of the
living situation became subjects of virtually all of Gertrude Stein's writing, not only all her openly erotic poetry—but many of the ensuing word
portraits and meditations. As Elizabeth Fifer remarks, after Alice's arrival, Stein's writing became joyful and capricious, a celebration of the
women's love for each other and for their life together in Paris ("Is Flesh
Advisable?").

Just as Stein may have found it necessary in the early Paris years to have
Leo safely asleep in order to write, she became increasingly aware of the
necessity to separate herself from America in order to write about it. Exploring in *The Making of Americans* the history of her family and her
place in it, Stein examined the relation of family history and cultural heritage to sexual identity. Such probing was painful, and it is doubtful that it
could have been carried out closer to "home." Stein needed distance from
America in order to gain perspective on herself; more importantly, she
needed the security of emotional attachment in order to carry out this
self-analysis. She was aware, for instance, that the establishment of a domestic homosexual relationship in Baltimore would have required subterfuge beyond the customary discretion practiced in the Stein-Toklas
marriage in Paris. Nor would Stein have been able in America freely to
examine the sensual and emotional spectra of that relationship in her
writing.

Although separation from America liberated Stein's personal and professional lives, it also isolated her from her readership, from Americans
who were both her subject matter and her intended audience. One is
tempted to speculate on the coincidence in Stein's career of the enforced
separation from both the writing subject and its audience and the decision to break "the discursive pact" that had traditionally bound writer to
reader (Schmitz, *Huck and Alice*, 189). Stein's project would expose the
underlying assumptions of language by making linguistic forms a critical
tool. A literary project that stripped language of its natural associations
necessarily frustrated its readership and alienated the writer. That Stein's
subjects were often domestic, that she set out to divorce literary language
from its etymological history, that her writing was devoid of allusions and
the extratextual referents so common to Modernist writing, that the
writing comically mimicked itself, making claims to childishness rather
than intellectual pretension, virtually assured the kind of mockery

to which Stein fell victim. Stein's project was the most radical of any twentieth-century writer, and the resulting isolation became the problematic of both her art and life.

Stein created within the boundaries of the Left Bank community a culturally rich and emotionally rewarding separate existence, but the question remains: was this seclusion born of necessity or choice? Stein simultaneously portrayed herself as a public person, the head of an important salon, and an artist exiled by the Modernist fathers. She was discriminated against, as a woman and as a lesbian. Her "enormous ego" apparently developed in reaction to a community of artists who refused to take her work seriously. Stein did not become bitter; she appeared unscathed by the mockery and maintained a persistent charm that disarmed even her most voluble critics. She waited, with infinite patience, for the moment of public acclaim (which arrived in the year of her return to America, when she was 60 years old). She told the cheering crowds on American campuses that artists are always misunderstood in their own lifetimes. But while she waited, she was alone, attended to by Alice and a few close friends.

Stein's "Agency of Language"

To understand something of Stein's isolation within the expatriate community we must examine the principles of Modernist art that displaced Stein's own radical and highly personal literary project. Modernist writing focused on the "agency of language" as a vehicle of meaning. To whatever degree other defining characteristics of Modernism operated in juxtaposition to each other, in contradiction to each other, in uneasy alignment with each other, the determined emphasis on the Word or Logos overshadowed all other divergences among Modernist practitioners. The one sacred belief common to all was what seemed to be the indestructibility of the bond between the Word and its meanings, between symbol and substance, between signifier and signified. Multiple linguistic experiments—juxtaposition of unlike words, typographical experimentation, translations of language into the dreamworld of the night or the language of the mad—only reinforced the linguistic claims on meaning. The Word was the only thing in this modern world that remained sacred. It survived wars, resisted the claims of materialist culture, could serve to mask despair or expose cultural hypocrisy. The Word held within it the possibilities of restructuring, rewriting, the world: the writer would succeed, as Susan Stanford Friedman has explained it, where God had failed (*Psyche Reborn*, 97–98). A James Joyce could exclaim in writing *Finnegans Wake* that he was able to do anything he wanted with language: he had learned the principles by which language worked, broken its "code," mastered its secret and harnessed its energy for his own creative vision (Ellmann, *James Joyce*, 702). Joyce realized his early dream of becoming an author, a priest of "eternal imagination" and a "God of creation," the absent center of a linguistic universe.

Perhaps Gertrude Stein was a slow learner, as Leo had accused her of being, or perhaps she was just a silly woman whose midnight writings were a childish game to counter boredom. Whatever the reason, Stein never discovered she could do anything she wanted with language. She never mastered the principles by which language worked, she never broke its code or harnessed its energy. She always stood resolutely outside the mystery of language, just as she stood outside the gate of Modernism, outside the boundaries of the expatriate literary community. For more than sixty years critics have read failure of communication in Gertrude Stein's nonsense writing.[10] Even those who wanted to read her, to understand her, discovered in applying the age-old tools of literary exegesis that they reaped only minimal results. Interest in Stein followed the track of her personal charisma (and its opposite: hatred of her egotism). The difference between Joyce's writings and Stein's is telling, an opposition that goes well beyond personal jealousy on her part or benign disregard on his. When Stein called Joyce "old-fashioned," she was not referring to his Old World manner that clashed so obviously with her American brusqueness but rather to the literary values that inhabited his work. He still believed in the Word, in the power of the Logos, in the immutable and undeniable link between form and substance, word and meaning. She no longer believed in the power and immutability of this relationship. Indeed, when Leo called her writing "nonsense" and her prose an "abomination," it was to just this underlying disbelief that he referred. As Richard Kostelanetz has noted, Stein asks "her readers to pay particular attention to words rather than to the content and motives that might lie behind them" ("Introduction," *Yale Gertrude Stein*, xxiii).

Rather than trying to master the movements of language, to discover the perfect match of word and meaning through image, metaphor, and symbol, Stein began by careful observation of linguistic nuance and submitted herself to the rhythms and sounds of language, listening carefully to the speech around her, allowing herself to be educated by language. She did what no other writer has had quite the courage to do: to relinquish the right to make language submit to the writer's will. Instead, she submitted her will to a linguistic power play that she recognized. Because Stein insisted on seeing language as autonomous from her rather than a part of her that she herself could control, language outwitted her—and she loved being outwitted. As Kostelanetz notes: ". . . words become autonomous objects, rather than symbols of something else, rather than windows onto other terrain. They cohere in terms of stressed sounds, rhythms, alliterations, rhymes, textures, and consistencies in diction—linguistic qualities other than subject and syntax; and even when entirely divorced from semantics, these dimensions of prose have their own powers of effect" ("Introduction," *Yale Gertrude Stein,* xxi). Such experiments began at Radcliffe, and there is evidence in those early themes of the direction her linguistic studies would later take. The really concentrated effort to learn the language *of* language was taken up in Paris. Although such an experiment can be, frequently has been, dismissed as an effort at "automatic writing," a kind of self-induced hypnotic state, the method demanded the concentrated effort to *resist* mastery and control of linguistic operations.[11] Stein used this method in writing *The Making of Americans,* a text that analyzes the minute differences in spoken phrases and circles around its subject in almost endless repetition and revision. More than any other Stein text, *The Making of Americans* has been considered an unreadable white elephant—an experiment interesting only in the abstract and certainly not in the reading experience. Stein had already proved before completing this particular experiment, however, that she could write perfectly "acceptable" and "readable" English in the stories comprising *Three Lives.* And this text, because it is less radically experimental than her later works, has most frequently been the subject of critical work on Stein, precisely because it is still possible in *Three Lives* to deduce "meaning" from language.[12]

Stein admittedly paid a high price for continuing a linguistic venture so open to misunderstanding. In the years when she worked at night in the rue de Fleurus, isolated from the larger literary community growing up around her, she was learning something about her methods from the visual arts, by watching the practice of the Cubists, who divorced painting from representation and broke the visual subject into its component lines and dimensions. Stein knew that her experiments with language were similar to Picasso's efforts in painting. Picasso's portrait of Stein, completed during the year she was finishing *Three Lives,* shares something in artistic method with Stein's early work: portraiture is maintained, the subject is recognizable, although slightly distorted to suggest the effects of character. Stein's word portraits coincided with Picasso's Cubist period and resisted characterization altogether. Later efforts, in particular *Tender Buttons,* seemed at first absolutely arbitrary and unthinking juxtaposition of words on the page. Only later were they recognized as an interrogation of the very method that produces "characterization" or the rendering of the representational. In discovering the limits of the representational, Stein discovered, according to Kostelanetz, the "nonrepresentational," discovered that " 'meaning' . . . lies wholly within language, rather than beyond it" ("Introduction," *Yale Gertrude Stein,* xxiii–xxiv). Stein's radical project led her to the discovery that "meaning" lies not in linguistic representation or reference, but within its own principles of operation.

Stein's contribution to literature was decidedly different from Joyce's. Joyce always worked within the limits of grammatical and syntactical constructs, shoring up meaning through etymology and reinforcing it through multilingual puns. Stein's experiment revealed something quite different—that language, when given its free play (outside the boundaries of grammar and syntax), tends toward apparently arbitrary alignments of sign and substance, alignments that often result in the comic and always produce *meaning*, no matter how arbitrary the combinations: "I took individual words and thought about them until I got their weight and volume complete and put them next to another word and at this same time I found very soon that there is no such thing as putting them together without sense" (Stein, quoted in "Introduction," *Yale Gertrude Stein*, xxii). Stein's writing gives evidence of a move toward the independence of the word from prescribed and coded meanings, a move away from the easy equation of sign and substance. Her writing first revises the relation between word and a determining world of objects (*The Making of Americans*, *Tender Buttons*, the word portraits) and later breaks entirely the assumed connection between word and world (*Lucy Church Amiably*, *Stanzas in Meditation*, *Four Saints in Three Acts*, etc.). In the view of many of Stein's critics, such a break between language and objective, external reality renders literature "irrelevant" and nonsensical. Certainly Stein's most experimental writing was seen as irrelevant for many years.

Stein's project, then, was radically self-destructive. Her writing put into question the determinacy of meaning in language, suggesting that if meaning was not determinant, then perhaps the opposite must be true. Her critics were quick to agree that Stein's writing was gibberish precisely because it could not be decoded and explicated. If such writing was not entirely nonsensical, then it was the expression of an enormous ego that consumed the external world. As Katherine Anne Porter commented after Stein's death: "Wise or silly or nothing at all, down everything goes on the page with an air of everything being equal, unimportant in itself, important because it happened to her and she was writing about it" ("Gertrude Stein: A Self-Portrait," 521–522).

The Lesbian Text

Against the claim by Porter and others that Stein's writing was egotistical silliness has been the recent counterclaim that Stein's language renders meaning if one is familiar with an essentially lesbian code. Once the code is broken, meaning spills out, showing the link between word and meaning to be the same as in all literary works—overdetermined, multiply self-reinforcing.[13] Such critics argue that the Modernist patriarchy did not recognize in this writing a sexual confession for the simple reason that the patriarchy can only read heterosexual confessions, of the kind written by Joyce or Lawrence, for instance. Katherine Anne Porter was able to recognize Stein's lesbian behavior (for which she chastised her) but was unable to read Stein's lesbian texts because her reading was bounded by patriarchal assumptions. Stein's position as an alienated, misunderstood writer was due not only to her status as a woman writer in a highly patriarchal environment but also to her status as a *lesbian* writer. Her writing constitutes both the expression of the social (the lesbian writer writing against the dominant culture) and the negation of the social (Stein's language denies the claims of the patriarchy by writing a different language—what Catharine R. Stimpson calls Stein's "antilanguage," one that the patriarchy can only read as nonsense).[14] In this reading of Stein's work, she was not doing something different from Modernism; she was writing lesbian Modernism. The Word, once its meanings are made available, is the agency through which symbol and meaning are joined, by means of which the culture is rewritten. Word and meaning maintain their predictable and indissoluble links once the reader knows the social code that releases meaning. And here the "social code" is lesbianism.

Stein's earlier, rather conventional, writings suddenly became radical the moment she was released from the constraints of her home life—the moment she could freely act on her sexual impulses. Alice Toklas became the agent of Stein's liberation, and the *Autobiography* returns compulsively—and lovingly—to her arrival in Paris. George Wickes sees Alice's arrival in Gertrude's life as the reason behind the disrupted chronology of the *Autobiography:* "By this means she keeps the narrative returning to one pivotal point, the moment of Alice B. Toklas' arrival in Paris and the beginning of their twenty-five years together" (*Americans in Paris,* 62). According to Neil Schmitz, once Alice was safely taken into the fold at 27, rue de Fleurus, Stein's writing passed from the philosophic to the poetic, from painful self-examination to humor (*Huck and Alice,* 12). The transitional work is *Tender Buttons,* which bridges the early word portraits and the later theoretical writings (begun in the mid-twenties and added to in the mid-thirties) by composing a grammar of lesbian domesticity. (Alice, of course, had already made her first appearance in the word portrait "Ada," written in December 1910.) In *Tender Buttons* Stein creates a woman's world; she renames and thereby reacquires the objects that surround her, including Alice Toklas, who has now become an object (of love) in this homemade universe. *Tender Buttons* creates a new language for a new life. It erases Leo's pernicious influence—his insistence on calling things by his names for them, of appropriating everything for himself. In putting aside the domineering and pestering brother who had made her feel stupid and insignificant, Gertrude Stein put aside the language by which that brother had imprisoned her in silence. In accepting Alice's love, Stein learned a new language (or rather rediscovered a language she had known in childhood) and exchanged monologue for dialogue, preaching for joking. Her writing suddenly ceased imitating the patriarchy.

Alice Toklas's arrival may have spurred Stein's announced intention to write primarily about women (see Bridgman, *Gertrude Stein in Pieces*, 104; for an alternate reading of Stein's literary development, see Dydo, "Must Horses Drink"). Many of the works from this period specifically treat the nature of women's relationships with each other—for example, "Two Women," "A Kind of Women" (in *Two*), "Ada" and "Miss Furr and Miss Skeene" (in *Geography and Plays*), "A Long Gay Book" and "Many Many Women" (in *Matisse Picasso and Gertrude Stein*)—and to a greater or lesser degree explore a language that is often opaque, difficult to summarize or explicate. Both Edmund Wilson and James R. Mellow have argued that the opacity of Stein's writing in this period was an effort to disguise its lesbian elements through an impenetrable prose. This theory rests on a belief that in the first decade of this century it was essentially impossible to discuss homosexuality openly in literature and that Stein's linguistic disguises were necessary if she wanted these pieces to be published. In fact, none of these pieces was published contemporaneously with its composition. Although Stein struggled to publish these poems, most of them were printed very late in her career or after her death.

It seems more likely that the radical nature of Stein's language was linked to her lesbianism in a different way than has been traditionally perceived. To acknowledge a preference for women not only involved Stein in a renunciation of her previous beliefs, but urged her toward acceptance of various ways of loving. There was no one way that was "right" and all others "wrong." Expression of this rich plenitude of loving possibilities required language that had previously been inaccessible, unthinkable to Stein. Her writing is marked by two erotic periods—the first, the early years of her relationship with Alice; the later, the period just following World War I. This second return to eroticism seems to suggest a certain "wandering" of Stein's affections, a period concluded with *A Novel of Thank You* (1925), which presumably returned Stein to her lover. In both cases, the erotic elements of Stein's writing seem to open the way to more radical investigations of language, serving to liberate her thinking and to guide her writing to another, higher, theoretical stage of development. Sexual expression is intimately linked to linguistic expression.

Alice's presence in Gertrude's life influenced her writing habits long before Leo's disappearance from the house in Paris. From the earliest days, Alice effected important alterations in the rhythm of daily life at 27, rue de Fleurus. In autumn 1907, the two women began to spend their after-noons together, either shopping or walking about the streets of Paris—one of Stein's favorite occupations. Prior to Alice's arrival, Leo had often accompanied her on these excursions, trips that sometimes took them to Vollard, the art dealer, or to *broquante* shops where the two looked for items with which to furnish the house. When Gertrude began sharing her afternoons with Alice, the nature of these walks changed. The women often shopped for clothes—both were addicted to buying clothes and at-tracted to new Parisian fashions—and talked about Gertrude's writing. As Gertrude worked on *The Making of Americans,* she sat with Alice in the Luxembourg Gardens discussing the system of character analysis that she hoped to demonstrate through the book (Mellow, *Charmed Circle,* 161). By 1908, the two women were spending their evenings together as well, usually discussing Gertrude's writing. When Alice returned to her own apartment, Gertrude would go to the atelier and begin writing in the quiet of the Paris night.

The daily discussions with Alice allowed Gertrude something she had never had before—the possibility of serious discussion about her writing with a woman, with someone who was not only a good listener and a supportive reader but capable of aiding the writing effort. Alice was not a competitor; her loyalty had already been assured. And it can be assumed, I think, that Alice served as something more than a silent ear patiently attending her lover. She was, as all the evidence from the early poetry sug-gests, capable of asking pointed questions, of giving opinions on narrative structure and poetic methods, of participating in a dialogue of ideas. The two women apparently employed a question and answer exchange with each other, a pattern of communication that transferred itself into all of Stein's writings after 1907. This new writing was double-voiced; it ad-mitted the heretofore forbidden voice of irreverent, humorous erotic love. This second voice punctuated the narrative, exposed pretense, corrected the storytelling, offered advice and opinion—and the voice belonged to Alice (Schmitz, *Huck and Alice,* 197). As Alice's knowledge of Gertrude's writing methods increased and as she was taken into greater confidence by her lover, her opinions became more markedly evident, and Gertrude relied more heavily on her insights. More importantly, Gertrude found in Alice her most desired writing subject.

Alice Toklas's influence on the formation of Gertrude Stein's adult char-acter was undoubtedly more important than any other single force in Stein's life: Alice's presence allowed Stein to break with an unhappy past; her demeanor allowed Stein to make a wife of her, to exploit her willing-ness to serve as spouse, lover, sister, muse, stenographer, social secretary, housekeeper, cook, gardener, and domestic servant; her love buoyed Stein's self-confidence; her humor cheered Stein during periods of doubt.

It has been suggested, by Ernest Hemingway among others, that Alice's public subservience transposed itself in private moments to a jealous manipulation that demanded Gertrude's fidelity as the price for Alice's continued servitude. While friends of the two women (Natalie Barney, Sylvia Beach, Margaret Anderson, among others) repeatedly declared their pity for Alice's situation, Alice Toklas's own published comments made clear her happiness in the role she created for herself in the marriage. Catharine R. Stimpson comments on the complexities of this relationship, remarking that "to oversimplify the Stein/Toklas marriage and menage is stupid":

> Toklas was also a willful woman whom Stein sought to please. In "Bonne Annee," Stein has Toklas say, "This must not be put into a book." If this shows Toklas's linguistic inhibitions, the line's imperative mood also marks her power. So does a phrase . . . of "Lifting Belly," the most audacious, pungently lyrical, witty text ever published about lesbian sexuality: "Husband obey your wife." If Toklas appeared to be "Pussy," the guardian subordinate, the salon keeper, the watchful servant of "Lovey's" needs, she chose that role. She knew that in that role she would have something to guard, a salon to keep, a way to serve her needs as well. ("Gertrice/Altrude," 130)

Such apparently disparate attitudes of lover to lover and wife to husband may well suggest the sadomasochistic elements of the relationship, but they also signal the decisive split between the public and private roles fashioned by Stein and Toklas. Indeed, these apparent contradictions may well have constituted the very fabric of this union, wrapping Alice's central importance to Stein's private life in the shroud of her public demeanor.

Mapping the set of contradictions that defined this relationship is difficult, since the only record that survives is Stein's, a record in which Alice is central to observations that rest in Gertrude's perceptions. After Gertrude's death, Alice loyally attested to the accuracy of this record; if there were discrepancies, they were never admitted. In 1950, Toklas wrote to Carl Van Vechten about her interview with John Malcolm Brinnin: "Then I got him to exclude me from his book because the atmosphere of Baby's home was a private matter—that if my existence had even made the slightest difference to her work it was nothing to equal the effect—for example of landscape—and was he in a position to put his finger from what he knew or from internal evidence when and how that was. It was agreed that my name could not be ignored in connection with Plain Edition but not elsewhere" (27 September 1950). Separating Gertrude Stein's life into various categories—home, work—Toklas carefully avoided admitting that "home" had ever become a subject of Stein's "work"— whereas, in fact, she knew her own voice, if not her very presence, was central to Stein's writing.

The advantage had always belonged to Gertrude, however, who even prior to her first meeting with Alice Toklas had occasion to learn about her through Alice's letters to Annette Rosenshine. Looking for a way to examine the various character types that interested her, Stein asked her friend to let her read these documents (see Faderman, *Surpassing the Love of Men,* 402–403). Toklas became a subject of Stein's analysis, a character to be fit into an established system of character types. But Stein may have learned more about Toklas than she might have hoped for, since the letters provided evidence that Toklas had had prior attachments to two other women, who became the specific referents of "Didn't Nelly and Lilly Love You." When Alice appeared at 27, rue de Fleurus, to meet Gertrude Stein, she was unaware of Stein's prior knowledge of her. In that first fateful meeting Stein was in control of a situation that left her visitor from California at a certain disadvantage. One wonders whether Stein had already made a decision in favor of Alice Toklas, whether having learned from her letters Alice's sexual orientation, her need to serve and to love, Stein had already drawn Alice to her. And at the second meeting, when Alice turned up late to meet Gertrude's anger, the measured power that Stein had over her lover—because it seems clear that she had already decided to love Toklas, as Toklas had decided to love her—was considerable. One suspects that Stein already knew enough about Alice Toklas's character to know that Alice would both love and fear her.

It may not be so surprising, then, to discover that the shift in affections from brother to female lover brought with it an enforcement of patriarchal domestic privileges. The prescribed roles that Gertrude and Alice played with each other indicate that the model for their marriage was a paternal and heterosexual one that duplicated the authority and submission patterns found, for instance, in the relationship of Stein's own parents (the domineering husband, the submissive wife) or the power structure of her more recent relationship with Leo. No sooner had Leo left 27, rue de Fleurus, than his sister began to imitate some of his worst habits. Like him, she was self-absorbed, self-indulgent, childish, tyrannical, opinionated, and domineering. While Leo may have kept Gertrude silently dependent on him in their early years together, he had never made a servant of her. The routine established after his departure from 27, however, effectively made Alice a domestic.

The model for the Stein-Toklas union seems to have been the strange sisterhood of Claribel and Etta Cone, who were probably both homosexual. The reasons behind the fierce loyalty of the younger sister for the older are suggested by Claribel's need to dominate and to be waited upon, by the power she wielded as a factor of her superior education and her public role as a woman physician and researcher. Claribel Cone, having served as a role model since Johns Hopkins days, was admittedly an object of fascination for Stein, who was intrigued by the methods Claribel employed to ensure her own comforts and the insistence with which she got her own way. Etta seems to have established a relationship of her own with Stein and was perhaps secretly attracted to her. As Carolyn Burke comments, "during the time she had known" the two women, Gertrude's own perspective had undergone "a crucial shift": "If initially she saw herself as an Etta, in the shadow of an older, more brilliant sibling, she now was moving toward the substitution of lover for brother and toward the creation of a new kind of couple. The Cone sisters' duo and her 'marriage' to Alice were like hinged mirrors set at different angles; they permitted related perspectives on the puzzle of female friendships" ("Gertrude Stein, the Cone Sisters," 553). Before Alice Toklas's arrival in Paris, Etta Cone served for a time as Stein's typist. Stein treated her in the same peremptory manner as did her sister, and Etta responded with continued patience in her effort accurately to transcribe Stein's difficult handwriting. When Etta saw herself replaced by Alice Toklas (and there is a suggestion that she was replaced not only as typist but in Gertrude's affections as well), she endured her resentment silently (Mellow, *Charmed Circle*, 156).

Although Alice began tirelessly to wait on Gertrude in the same ways that Etta waited on Claribel, thus duplicating aspects of the Cones' sisterhood, the relationship between the Cone sisters already mirrored aspects of the relationship between Gertrude and Leo. Claribel, like Leo, was not attentive to Etta's need to be heard (Mellow, *Charmed Circle*, 166). Stein's early portrait, "Two Women," in which Etta Cone is given the name "Ada" (already assigned to Alice in "Ada," *Geography and Plays*, 14–16) and in which Martha (a name Stein had chosen for herself in *The Making of Americans*) is the authoritative and dominant character, suggests that Stein understood very well the power structure of the Cone union and attempted to duplicate it in her own life. As Carolyn Burke remarks, Stein commented on the Cones in "Possessive Life" that "a revolving life is a sad sad life." What she apparently desired with Alice was an "evolving life" ("Cone Sisters," 553), but the early stages of their relationship were marked by Gertrude's need to establish her power over Alice, a strategy perhaps to bind Alice to her more closely. After Leo's departure, Gertrude exercised a growing sense of importance in the household, and she was aided in this effort by Alice, just as Claribel Cone was aided by her submissive sister. The initial pose of self-assurance that covered doubts, fears, failures, and the scars of prior relationships composed itself in imitation of Claribel Cone and in defiance of Leo Stein. Marking Stein's painfully purchased liberation, this public image was a necessary element of survival, one that could not be put aside once survival was assured.

The impression of Alice Toklas as a silent and ministering partner to Stein's egotistical theorizing is in large part the product of Alice's hard work. Those who were allowed glimpses of the intimacy between the two women suspected that Toklas was the more powerful of the two figures, that Gertrude was dependent upon her in ways that gave Toklas dominance in the relationship. But few people were taken into intimate relation with these two women, and Alice's role as attendant lover allowed her the privilege of privacy. These lovers were discreet, private women, who kept the intimacies of their bourgeois marriage intimate (Catharine R. Stimpson notes that "not surprisingly, given the period, the marriage was Victorian," "Gertrice/Altrude," 130). Privacy was particularly privileged in the early years of their relationship, when the women were cautious in their choice of friends. No longer was 27, rue de Fleurus, open to anyone who might knock at the front door.

The salon for which Gertrude Stein is so famous continued for several years after Alice's arrival in Paris, but by 1913 it no longer existed. It was never resurrected. In the eight years of its existence, its emphasis had shifted from art to literature. In 1908, no longer able to hold forth against his sister, Leo ceased attending, claiming that these evenings now belonged to Gertrude, that she dominated the conversation. Leo's jealousy of his sister's presence accounts only in part, however, for this alteration in lifestyle. Never comfortable at large dinners and casual parties, Alice restructured Gertrude's social life according to her own dictates. She insisted on decorum (something the early Stein parties had displayed in only the slightest degree); she prepared elaborate foods and served them elegantly; she privileged the select few. Although Stein blamed the war for changing the quality of Paris life, for ruining old friendships and displacing members of the early group, major shifts in alliances had already taken place prior to World War I. Those who came to 27 came by invitation only. They came singly or in pairs. They talked at length with Gertrude while Alice served cakes and tea. They did not intrude on Gertrude's working life. They did not interest themselves too obviously in the relationship of the two women. When Stein and Toklas returned to a social life in Paris after the war, Stein was a cult figure among American expatriates. The doors of 27, rue de Fleurus, which were always open to American soldiers, were closed to curiosity seekers. Alice carefully screened those who were entertained in the Paris and country homes, providing an atmosphere in which "Stein talked out her ideas and received stimulus and esteem" (Stimpson, "Gertrice/Altrude," 132). The social life of these two women was, like all else in their life together, an intimate part of Gertrude's writing. Alice saw it to that Gertrude received "stimulus and esteem" when she needed it and was left alone to write when she desired. As Stimpson comments, Stein "husbanded" her energies; she had assistance in this effort from her wife. After the war, Stein entered the first stage of her public renown. She became an "absent presence" in Paris, working quietly on her literary project, seeing only those who could foster her career, demanding absolute loyalty of all who were privileged to enter her private sanctum.

The Flowers of Friendship

Gertrude Stein's close friendships divide themselves into clearly distinct periods. In the decade between Stein's arrival in Paris and the onset of World War I, her close friends included Claribel and Etta Cone, Mildred Aldrich, Picasso, Apollinaire, Matisse; in 1910, Stein met Mabel Dodge, primarily responsible for creating the first interest in Stein's writing in America at the Armory Show in 1913, this publicity initiating new friendships that included Marsden Hartley, Alfred Stieglitz, Francis Picabia, Carl Van Vechten (whose friendship was to last until Stein's death), Henry McBride, and Juan Gris. By the time Stein and Toklas left France for Spain at the outset of the war, some of these earlier friendships—with Mabel Dodge and Matisse, for instance—had already disintegrated, and the war created a hiatus for all the others. New friendships were made with American soldiers—namely, William Rogers—during the war, and when the two women took up their Paris life again in 1918, a new set of alliances was formed. These later friendships included Sylvia Beach and Adrienne Monnier, Sherwood Anderson, Ernest Hemingway, Jacques Lipchitz and Cocteau (both of whom she had known before the war), Jo Davidson, Lincoln Steffens, and Janet Flanner. When the fall of the New York stock market sent Americans in Paris back across the Atlantic, Stein was relieved, grateful to have her French city French again. In the 1920s she took up a set of younger friends that included Virgil Thomson, Pavel Tchelitchev, Georges Hugnet, René Crevel, and Bravig Imbs, and in the 1930s Francis Rose, Pierre Balmain, and Donald Sutherland. It is evident in this list, which attempts to single out those who had especially close relationships with Stein, that men outnumber women almost three to one. Although all the women on this list were lesbian, only two maintained true, long-term friendships with Stein: Mildred Aldrich and Janet Scudder. Among women of the Paris lesbian community, Janet Flanner was the best-known friend to Stein (and she did not count herself as one of Stein's confidantes). Stein's other friendships with women of this group tended to be established on professional grounds rather than those of intimacy. Apart from Alice Toklas, Stein had no close women friends. Like Claribel and Etta Cone, these two women were everything to each other.

In later years, when Stein's career was established, she was less restrictive in her social life, although no less demanding of loyalty. She was particularly open to the young, to those whom she might influence, to those who could carry her cause to the younger generation. A younger friend of her later years, Donald Sutherland was allowed to observe the Stein-Toklas marriage closely. His friendship with Alice continued after Gertrude's death, and in his later recollections he comments that "Alice was not accustomed to kindness and did not expect it, so she had to question it in any degree. Gertrude had not been good to her, and in the course of their long life together the quarrels and broken friendships with writers and artists of all kinds had surely resulted in her having far more enemies than friends" ("Alice and Gertrude and Others," 295). For it was Alice who was given the responsibility of narrowing friendships to the select few with whom Gertrude felt comfortable, and Sutherland suggests that Alice paid a high personal price for undertaking such jobs. But Alice herself had strong preferences among friends, and those who did not meet her approval did not long remain in Gertrude's good graces. Those who found themselves no longer registered on Stein's list of intimate acquaintances blamed Alice; those who continued to see Gertrude admired Alice, remembering her as kind and hospitable. Impressions of Alice were as contradictory as those of Gertrude, and as predictable.

One famous alliance that did not survive, of course, was Gertrude Stein's friendship with Hemingway. All parties to the friendship gave different accounts of the split (which probably took place in 1926), but only Hemingway's account hints at Alice Toklas's jealousy of his attentions to Gertrude as the cause of the ruptured friendship. Hemingway's revenge for Stein's remarks about him in *The Autobiography of Alice B. Toklas* has been read as a particularly vicious attack on her sexuality, on her role as the "male" lover to a wife who secretly controls and manipulates her. In *A Moveable Feast* Hemingway records his reactions to overhearing an intimate argument between the two women. Appalled at the language he heard Alice use, at her apparent power over Gertrude, at Gertrude's fawning dependency, Hemingway slipped out of the house to which he had been invited that morning. Hemingway's account never specifies the cause of the quarrel, but it might well have been Gertrude's attraction to him and Alice's resentment that Gertrude continued to open her home to someone Alice detested. Hemingway's anger makes Alice Toklas, who was his rival for Gertrude's affection, the target of this nasty story. Gertrude, like Hemingway, becomes Alice's victim.

Alice Toklas's version of what happened between Stein and Hemingway is somewhat different, but it acknowledges Hemingway's admission that he had been sexually attracted to Gertrude. In a conversation with Donald Sutherland in 1966, Alice Toklas admitted that she "made Gertrude get rid of [Hemingway]" ("Alice and Gertrude and Others," 297). And Sutherland acknowledges having known that

the relationship between Gertrude Stein and Hemingway was more than literary comradeship at one time or even maternal and filial affection. I had heard
that Hemingway had not infrequently said in conversation and once at least
in a letter that he had always wanted to lay her. I could well believe it, for the
second time I met her she came too close and my sexual response was both
unequivocal and, considering that I was nineteen and she sixty, bewildering. . . . There had been less difference in age between her and Hemingway,
and as she had been some fourteen years younger than when I knew her, her
sexual attraction must have been more alarming. At least her attraction and
her being attracted had alarmed Alice. (297)

Sutherland's admission is an extraordinary one, since it testifies to an aspect of Stein's sexual power generally assumed to have been effective only
with other women—that is, it has been assumed that only lesbian women
would have found Stein attractive. Indeed, many men have made jokes
about her girth, her Roman haircut, her heavy masculinity, suggesting in
their jests that Stein was a matronly and ridiculous imitation male, under
whose skirts was the lumpy body of a female with misplaced sexual impulses. Such a view marks Arthur Lachman's remembrance, "Gertrude
Stein as I Knew Her," recalling Stein as a student at Harvard when "she
was about 24 years old": "She was a heavy-set, ungainly young woman,
very mannish in her appearance. Her hair was cut short at a time when
this was by no means the fashion among the fair sex. She always wore
black, and her somewhat ample figure was never corseted. She was, in
fact, frequently untidy in appearance and her garments were not always
neat" (typescript in Yale Collection of American literature). The impression that Stein was a "mannish" looking young woman who went without corsets and wore untidy clothes may be as inaccurate as Lachman's
memory of Stein's short hair in her years at Harvard. (Photographs confirm that she wore her hair long, in the fashion of the day, and that she
wore clothes and hats that looked very much like those worn by other
young women at Radcliffe.) However, such impressions of Stein are fixed
in the public mind and difficult to dispel.

That men might have been sexually aroused by Stein or that she might
have been attracted to men is surprising only to those who assume the
rigidity of sexual identity. *A Novel of Thank You*, written as the intense
friendship between Stein and Hemingway was fading, would suggest that
the "wandering" from which the novel marks a return to the marital fold
might well have been Stein's attraction to, even mutual desire for, Hemingway—for whom she always admitted to having had a "weakness." A
letter from Hemingway to Janet Flanner on 8 April 1933, just prior to the
publication of *The Autobiography of Alice B. Toklas* in late summer of
that year, however, reveals the ambivalent nature of his attraction to Stein
and his reaction to the knowledge that she was lesbian. A close friend of

Flanner, Hemingway seems to be seeking her assessment of the situation, but his comments about lesbianism suggest that he was either unaware of Flanner's own lesbianism or chose to place it in a different category from Stein's:

> Nancy [Cunard] I never liked. Gertrude S. I was very fond of and god knows was loyal too until she had pushed my face in a dozen times. Last time I saw her she told me she had heard an incident, some fag story, which proved me conclusively to be very queer indeed. I said You knew me for four or five years and you believe that? Oh it was very circumstantial, she said. Just how completely credible and circumstantial it was. Poor old papa. Well I'll probably read it in her autobiography that you had a piece about in N[ew] Yorker. I never cared a damn about what she did in or out of bed and I liked her very damned much and she liked me. But when the menopause hit her she got awfully damned patriotic about sex. The first stage was that nobody was any good that wasn't that way. The second was that anybody that was that way was good. The third was that anybody that was any good must be that way. Patriotism is a hell of a vice. Mabel Dodge is a hell of a rival. America's legendary women sweepstakes.
>   The only way, I suppose, is to find out what women are going to write memoirs and try to get them with child. The hell of it is that the women that I feel, shall we say, drawn to don't write their memoirs. It is a mistake to ever meet a legendary woman indoors. Some misinterpretation will be placed on anything you do. . . . Never encounter a legendary woman anywhere except in the open and then bring your own witness. (*Selected Letters*, 387–388)

It would seem that Stein's hint at Hemingway's own latent homosexuality had struck the mark, and his admission of attraction to her may be a defensive effort to maintain his heterosexuality. This defensiveness also hints that, in order for Hemingway to maintain his own precarious sense of sexual identity, it was necessary for him to believe that *all* women were sexually attracted to him. Had there been no admission of "weakness" for him on Stein's part and had Alice Toklas not been so threatened by Hemingway's presence in Gertrude Stein's life, we might accept his account as just another attempt to justify his own self-importance. But the dynamics of this episode indicate something other than one-sided attraction.

In this letter, Hemingway seems particularly angered that he has been displaced by a woman (and he suggests, oddly, that the woman is Mabel Dodge, who had also been removed by Alice from close proximity to Gertrude Stein—and for the same reason—some dozen years earlier). His notion that Stein's lesbianism became more marked at menopause would seem to be an uninformed evaluation of female sexuality, a feeble effort to explain Stein's resistance to his charms. The threat to save public embarrassment by impregnating all potential female memoirists is a particularly desperate effort on Hemingway's part to keep the patriarchal assumptions of heterosexuality in place. But Stein had used against Hemingway the weapon she knew he most feared, and it is clear that he was frightened by her innuendo concerning his own sexual ambivalence, that he understood little about Stein's relationship with Toklas and less about the dynamics of the friendship Stein had for him. Flanner's response to this letter is not available, but her perspective on the situation would be interesting, since she was a close friend of all parties involved and her sexual orientation was toward women. Even more interesting is the evidence that Hemingway found his two closest women friends among lesbians. The implications of this observation are by no means clear. It is possible that the knowledge of these women's sexual preferences reduced Hemingway's heterosexual tensions. The desire, even the need, to seduce them could not figure as a dominant feature of the relationships. But the importance of these two friendships for Hemingway may lie in the other direction—that lesbian women (no doubt without his conscious knowledge) affiliated him with his feared and repressed other, the Hemingway whose womanizing was the means by which latent homosexuality was repressed.

Paris-Lesbos

We may pause here to consider our lingering impressions of Paris lesbians, of the images that come to mind when we think of the women of this period, and of the place Stein and Toklas held among them. The most pervasive image of lesbianism in these years is of women who appear at first glance to be male: Radclyffe Hall, Romaine Brooks, or the Marquise de Belbeuf—monocled, tuxedoed, hair cropped short, cigarette in hand. The assumption, too, supported by the scientific work of nineteenth-century sexologists, was that such transvestite tendencies signaled a sexual disorder in which men's desires inhabited women's bodies, resulting in lesbian alliances that were markedly promiscuous, unhappy, destructive, and manipulative. In describing the historical circumstances of such women, Esther Newton has argued that "[Radclyffe] Hall and many other feminists like her embraced, sometimes with ambivalence, the image of the mannish lesbian and the discourse of the sexologists about inversion, primarily because they desperately wanted to break out of the asexual model of romantic friendship" ("The Mythic Mannish Lesbian," 560). The term "inversion," used by these women to describe their own sexual inclinations, meant for them not only the desire for someone of the same sex, but the more pervasive need to duplicate heterosexuality within the homosexual relationship and to play out the sexual ambiguity of a woman in man's clothing seducing another woman to lesbian love. As

C. A. Tripp explains, "inversion . . . implies nothing about the sex of the partner; it refers to a reversal of the commonly expected gender-role of the individual" (*Homosexual Matrix*, 22–23). By her masculine dress and mannerisms, the "mannish lesbian" drew attention to her sexual orientation, and particularly to erotic lesbian sexuality (as distinct from the asexual "friendships" of an earlier period), and in doing so she played, as Esther Newton describes, an important role in the development of lesbian culture. In the Paris of the twenties, the mannish lesbian was perceived—in the heterosexual parent culture and often in homosexual culture—as a doomed misfit, a product of genetic malfunctioning.

An alternate version of the Paris lesbian experience was characterized by "attic abandonment," according to Bertha Harris, the free-spirited play of upper-class homosexual women who saw their lesbianism as another mark of their select birth ("The More Profound Nationality of Their Lesbianism," 79). As the leader of this particular group of lesbian women (many of whom were her current and former lovers), Natalie Clifford Barney created a "female world of ritualized love" according to Jane Marcus ("Liberty, Sorority, Misogyny," 81), encouraging their pleasures, helping them create their own mythology (or rediscover a female mythology in Greek culture), and fostering a happy and (more importantly) guilt-free revel in their own sexuality. In this myth of Paris lesbianism, to be lesbian was to be elegant, beautiful, dressed in the most feminine of costumes, self-indulgent, and artistically talented. Bertha Harris argues that for contemporary lesbians, this Paris culture is the only record that exists, all previous records having been destroyed by a dominant heterosexual patriarchy.

But Harris's description of Parisian lesbians erroneously suggests that most of these women were rich and indulged: "From the turn of the century and into the Twenties, they escaped the American Gothic with huge hunks of papa's fortune stuffed in their pockets . . . spent by these women solely on themselves and each other; and they took immense pleasure in the spending" (79). It is true that for Natalie Barney, for instance, immense wealth was an important factor in her rise to leadership in the lesbian community. But for many other of these women—for instance, Colette, Djuna Barnes, Sylvia Beach, Janet Flanner, as well as Stein and Toklas—there were no family fortunes to support elegant Paris lifestyles. Those women who had some money—like Stein and Toklas—had it in small amounts and carefully dispensed it, sometimes on themselves, sometimes on others. Stein claimed, for instance, always to have "lived simply" in France, whether in Paris or in the country. She was in no way a spendthrift. A pervasive misconception about these Paris women rests in the insistence on their similarities. Natalie Barney is thought to be typical of all lesbians, Anaïs Nin to be typical of all heterosexual women. Such typecasting along lines of gender and sexual orientation erases the important differences among them, marking a division according to sexual orientation that is itself sexist.

Gertrude Stein and Alice Toklas, however, did not participate in either of these lesbian mythologies. While they knew women from both of these "groups"—and participation in one did not rule out participation in the other—they did not count any of these women among their close friends. That is, Stein and Toklas appear to have carefully avoided relationships with women of the Paris lesbian communities for reasons that point toward an unwillingness to participate in a larger lesbian culture or in a more public display of their attraction to women. Their marriage was grounded on fidelity to each other, and they would have been threatened and made uncomfortable by these ritualized group activities. Stein and Toklas shared assumptions about female relationships that were, in fact, antithetical to those on which these two groups were based. Yet Stein and Toklas remain the best known lesbian couple of the Paris years, their marriage considered by many to be typical of domesticated homosexuality. And Gertrude Stein's place as the best known lesbian of the expatriate community is rivaled only by Natalie Barney, whose public behavior shocked Stein.

Analysts of this period have tacitly assumed a bond of sisterhood among lesbians of the Paris community that transcended all other differences among them. But lesbianism did not, I think, represent "the more profound nationality" that Bertha Harris describes (79). Although it is difficult to generalize about these women, and especially dangerous to generalize about them on the grounds of their sexual orientation and practice, it would seem that the commitment to art represented a common bond of experience at least as strong as sexual orientation. Virtually every one of these women was either a writer or a painter, and it is certainly true that their ritualized dress and love often provided material for their art. The treatment of the lesbian subject matter, however, varied tremendously among them: there are few common denominators of literary technique or perspective among Hall's *The Well of Loneliness*, Barnes's *Nightwood*, Barney's *Pensées d'une amazone*, Colette's *The Pure and the Impure*. (For several other lesbian writers—Margaret Anderson, H. D., Janet Flanner—lesbianism was not a subject immediately related to their work.) Among the painters and sculptors, lesbian themes were treated variously as well: Thelma Wood's silverpoint drawings or Djuna Barnes's woodcuts and sketches for *Ladies Almanack* and *The Book of Repulsive Women* are nothing like Romaine Brooks's portraits, for instance.

It can safely be said that Stein's artistic rendering of her lesbianism differed significantly from that of any of her Paris counterparts. In her writings, lesbianism provided neither the occasion for tortured, introspective examination of the psychological dimensions of her sexual orientation nor the material for sophisticated satire. Stein's relationship with Toklas was the occasion for linguistic experimentation, exploration, and the expression of childlike joy. For Stein and Toklas, the assumption of an artistic priority is particularly important in understanding the personal dimensions of their Paris life. Until very recently, the erotic component of Stein's writings was not a subject for critical discourse, the portrayal of lesbianism in her writings having been entirely overlooked. Now the lesbian element of her writings is a subject under discussion, one that poses a considerable risk—that the poetry will be read as disguised biography, that works like "Lifting Belly" and *Tender Buttons* will undergo critical interpretations equating life and art, assumptions that have characterized readings of *The Well of Loneliness*, for example. As Catharine R. Stimpson warns, "Perhaps the danger now is not that we will avoid their wedding and their bedding, but that we will linger there too long. Confusing attention and voyeurism, we will inadvertently extend the error that defines women either as chaste creatures, incapable of sex, or as promiscuous creatures, capable of nothing else" ("Gertrice/Altrude," 128). It would be equally dangerous to generalize from this lesbian marriage to others in the expatriate community. Among the misapprehensions such a method might propagate is the mistaken assumption that all such alliances were imitations of heterosexual marriages or that all lesbian relationships were based on a power struggle that oppressed one partner.

The model for lesbian marriages was less often the heterosexual union than popular opinion would have us believe, and the daily pattern of lesbian relationships among expatriates varied to a greater degree than among their heterosexual counterparts. Long-term alliances often were established on the grounds of common professional and intellectual interests. The friendships uniting Sylvia Beach and Adrienne Monnier, Jane Heap and Margaret Anderson, Janet Flanner and Solita Solano, H. D. and Bryher manifested common bonds of bookselling, publication, journalism, and the writing of poetry. The Stein-Toklas marriage, by contrast, was characterized by the commitment to Stein's writing career, and the combined energies of the union were focused on gaining for Stein the recognition she claimed had been unjustly denied her. But if Gertrude Stein's writings were far in advance of the Modernist aesthetic, her domestic arrangements were Victorian, the union with Alice Toklas privileging fidelity and enforcing assumptions about "male" priorities outdated among both the heterosexual marriages and lesbian unions of Paris.

In a community in which many women rejected traditional models of behavior, flouted convention, and overturned patriarchal norms, Stein and Toklas were set apart. Stein, for instance, was unconventional in her choice of a sexual partner, in her dress, and in her writings, but the co-incidence of these oddities did not constitute a subversive feminism. Indeed, it is difficult to find a common ground for the unconventional aspects of Stein's life. She seemed to have resolved the heterosexual oppositions that presumed male authority and female submission, that divided a woman's mind from her body, by appropriating the masculine role for herself. In how many ways *was* Stein a "male"—only in her marriage, or in her writing, in her dealings with other women and men? What can we make, for instance, of her choice of clothing? Susan Gubar has argued that Stein's dress masked an "ambiguous eroticism" that made "a travesty of sexual signs" ("Blessings in Disguise," 488). She reads a complex relation among sexual choice, social class, role identification, and intellectual endeavor in Stein's idiosyncratic dress code.

Costume as Metaphor

Soon after her arrival in Paris, Stein shed the tight-waisted dresses of her Radcliffe and Johns Hopkins years and adopted looser clothing—Greek sandals, heavy woolen stockings, and large overcoats. This apparel allowed her the freedom to walk, an activity that took up as much as six hours of her day in Paris, and with few changes over the years this attire served her to the end of her life. A costume that in some ways disguised her ample physique, this uniform never made her look masculine, but instead seemed to enhance her solid yet supple girth. The metaphors frequently applied to Stein, even those used in jest, suggest that, rather than giving the appearance of being a man, she appeared to most as a maternal figure (e.g., she became the Mother of Us All and Mother Goose of Montparnasse). Even with her cropped hair (cut in early 1927, when she was 53 years old), Stein remained recognizably a woman, something that Radclyffe Hall—in her guise as "John," in man's suit and haircut—did not. Alice Toklas, as if to accentuate her diminutive and supportive role, dressed in ever more feminine costumes, affecting a gypsy look, complete with flowered, flowing dresses and long earrings. But if Toklas's dress was always entirely feminine, Stein's was never altogether masculine. Like much else about their life together, the dress adopted by these two women was nonconformist, even among Paris lesbians.

In her study of female Modernist cross-dressing, Susan Gubar argues that "female modernists escaped the strictures of societally-defined femininity by appropriating the costumes they identified with freedom." She links cross-dressing to both the scientific theories of female homosexuality (the "third" sex notion of Krafft-Ebing and Havelock Ellis) and the suffragist movement, making cross-dressing part of a feminist effort to "di-vest conventional forms of legitimacy." For Gubar, cross-dressing constituted an intimate link to the radically experimental art of some female Modernists:

> As a metaphor that flourished when the success of the suffragists paradoxically and tragically marked the temporary destruction of the women's movement, cross-dressing was closely related to lesbianism and expatriation in the art of female modernists. On the one hand a sign of self-division, even self-contempt, on the other an effort at expressing love for other women (and, by extension, for the female self) cross-dressing reflected their anxious sense of transition and uncertainty, even as it demonstrated their remarkably self-conscious experimentation with sexual role-playing. ("Blessings in Disguise," 501)

Stein's individualistic use of costume, which according to Gubar "transcend[ed] the limits of gender," also very nearly defied classification: "Stein managed to create herself as a 'being of its own kind,' neither masculine nor feminine. Her inversion is a radical form of conversion, for she seems to transcend . . . the limits of humanness" ("Blessings in Disguise," 493). Pictures and sculpture of Stein portray her as a cross between Buddha and Julius Caesar, but both as religious icon and as Roman emperor she wears skirts. The disruption of expectations in masculine/feminine distinctions emphasized by Stein's odd dress poses difficulties for the analyst's effort to determine the precise effect Stein tried to create.

Distinguishing Stein's original forms of dress from that of other female Modernists, Gubar suggests that such originality informed Stein's art as well: "Claiming the right of self-creation with great wit and relish, Stein evaded the gender categories that obsessed so many of her contemporaries. But contempt for the secular classifications of culture also led Stein to create radically innovative art" (495). Certainly Stein evaded gender categories in her choice of dress, which was original in extending the boundaries of traditional female costuming, but both in her life and in her writing, Stein remained within the socially constructed dichotomies that distinguish the masculine from the feminine. In her personal relationships Stein assumed male authority—importantly, without having to adopt male dress as a sign of that authority—while her writing explored the polarities of a male-female dialectic in which the female labors under the male prerogative inherent in grammar itself. That she rewrote the story of a lesbian triangle (*Q.E.D.*) as a heterosexual triangle ("Melanctha"), taking the masculine persona for herself, suggests Stein's difficulty in moving outside the gender dialectic. Although her writing does not duplicate either the tone or the content of patriarchal language, it demonstrates the ways in which the masculine prerogative of language is reinforced in the most unexpected ways. For Stein it was not clothing that marked a break with patriarchal rules, but language, and for her there is no easy equation between her form of dress and behavior and her literary and linguistic experiments. As Stimpson argues:

> In brief, when Gertrude and her brother Leo were little, they grasped, grappled with, and broke the rules of language *as children*, each with his or her individual being. As they grew up, they entered an adult world. As Stein knew, it gave men more power than women—including greater power over and within the female body. . . . Stein's sense of her own monstrosity in this world—as a sexual being, as a marginal cultural citizen—influenced her writing, and her somagrams. However, laboring with language in this world, Stein came to believe that women were in many ways more capable than men. Women could assume power over and within language; over and within their bodies. ("Somagrams," 78–79)

Conflating feminism, cross-dressing, and Modernist experimentalism, Susan Gubar does not adequately distinguish the various uses of and motivations for cross-dressing among Paris expatriates. Although Gubar calls attention to cross-dressing as "a political statement that exploits the rhetoric of costuming to redefine the female self" ("Blessings in Disguise," 498), she does not separate cross-dressers by social class or political persuasion, nor does she carefully trace the effects of scientific theories that suggested women homosexuals were males trapped in female bodies: "'Inversion'—as the psychologists of the period call it—is most simply an attempt by women to invert the traditional privilege system that lends primacy to men. But inversion goes through a series of displacements, as it is translated into a synonym for per-version and a means of con-version and sub-version" (479). Although Gubar makes note of the confusion between transvestism in this period, and what we would now call transsexuality, her discussion nonetheless situates itself within the heterosexual norm, reading lesbianism as a perversion of that norm to conclude that lesbian cross-dressers invert sexual stereotypes. This interpretation assumes that all lesbian behavior has in common its *reaction* to the norm of compulsory heterosexuality and that all lesbians act out their sexual orientation in the same way—here, through cross-dressing.[15]

Commentators have often conflated several importantly different sets of behavior patterns among members of the Paris lesbian community, however: the use of costuming in ritual celebrations to honor female goddesses (documentary evidence of such practices at Natalie Barney's Temple à l'Amitié shows women dressed in tissue-thin Greek robes, their long hair entwined with flowers); the use of male clothing in masquerades (again, evidence is provided from Natalie Barney's photograph collection); the adoption of male clothing and the assumption of a male identity as part of a homosexual code; the use of male clothing as a sign of masculine authority. Distinct as these forms of behavior would seem to be, there is evidence that some women in the Paris lesbian community variously adopted such costumes according to the occasion, their choices apparently depending on whether the "audience" for such practices was heterosexual or homosexual. And certainly these various reasons for costuming and cross-dressing differ entirely from efforts by women to "pass" as men (behavior that has its own set of distinguishing characteristics, motivated variously by psychological and practical considerations) or requirements in which male dress may have been a professional signature, a mark of professional identity, as well as a sign of sexual preference.

For many Paris expatriates, participation in attic rituals or male dress masquerades was the mark of upper-class wealth and intellectual and artistic superiority. Even this statement must be qualified, however: Colette, Isadora Duncan, and Janet Flanner—to name only three who participated in these occasions—were exceptions because they were not born to upper-class wealth. For such women, evenings at Natalie Barney's provided occasions for pretense, but the prevailing assumption that 20, rue Jacob was the setting for public declarations of lesbianism and open efforts to shock the bourgeois sensibilities of the heterosexuals who attended such gatherings is a mistaken one. The Friday evening poetry readings were decorous to a fault and, by Paris salon standards, rather staid and often boring occasions.[16] Less inhibited displays of lesbian behavior and varieties of lesbian dress were restricted to gatherings at the Temple à l'Amitié behind Barney's house, to which only women were invited. Here lesbian women dressed for each other, their choices of costumes displaying a wide and imaginative diversity. They staged ritual observances to Sappho and goddesses of the moon, and at these times some women might have been dressed as Greek goddesses, pale and ethereal against a backdrop of spring flowers, while Colette danced naked. At other times, one might see Dolly Wilde dressed as her uncle Oscar or Janet Flanner in top hat and tails.

But again we need to make distinctions between evenings of "attic abandonment" and occasions for male masquerade, since the occasions for these forms of dress were importantly different; and a further distinction must be made between those women who might dress as men for a costume party and those who wore male attire consistently. For those women who adopted male clothing as their daily costume (Radclyffe Hall and the Marquise de Belbeuf), female cross-dressing was not only a mark of aristocracy, it was sister to the dandyism of the period and shared, ironically, in the misogyny that supported the dandy's burlesque of the female. Female cross-dressing was indeed the mark of self-contempt, as Gubar argues, but it was decidedly not an "effort at expressing love for other women (and, by extension, for the female self)" ("Blessings in Disguise,"

501)—quite the opposite. Cross-dressing served as a public announce-ment of a commitment to lesbian relationships, but it registered this com-mitment in a code that specifically denied an allegiance to womanhood as societally defined (e.g., the feminine). Cross-dressing constituted a simul-taneous denial of the feminine and a taunting of male authority, a de-meaning of the forms of male authority—the most obvious of which was male clothing. Although cross-dressing was an antisocial act that called attention to societal definitions of female homosexuals as "inverts" and "perverts," it nonetheless was not a sign of liberation from heterosexual norms or patriarchal domination. Cross-dressing reinforced the power of such constraints. Cross-dressing, moreover, did not acknowledge women's oppression—indeed, just the opposite. These aristocratic women cross-dressers flaunted their right to live and dress exactly as they pleased. They were protected in their behavior by the privilege of social class, and they assumed a superiority over all others, men and women alike.

The distinction in social class is an important one. In general, those women who indulged in costuming were outside the bounds of social de-corum dictated by economic necessity; they had no need to maintain a "straight" public image. For the group of women who needed to dress "straight" in their public, daytime lives, who at night covered their male dress in long wraps and made their way to lesbian bars where they played out their sexual fantasies, cross-dressing represented an escape from the demands of a heterosexual world that would have exacted an economic price for the knowledge of their homosexual desires. For this group, cross-dressing held implications of a far different, and more serious, import than for women of wealth and social distinction. And for those women who affected male dress to take on male prerogatives, masculine authority, and to share in freedom given only to the male in this society—that is, to "pass"—the issue of cross-dressing was something quite differ-ent. Its founding assumptions were ones to which heterosexual as well as homosexual women might give support.

To the extent that adoption of male clothing declared a separation of women from traditional roles and societal expectations of marriage and motherhood, unconventional modes of dress tended to segregate cross-dressers from the heterosexual world. The desire for this segregation, like the reasons for choice of dress, varied enormously—from the need to sig-nal women of similar sexual orientation to self-divisive doubts about sex-uality and gender identity. Thus a number of the portraits and photo-graphs of the period reproduced for Gubar's study picture women in postures of tense isolation ("Blessings in Disguise," 487–488, 508). (These photographs and self-portraits by such Paris artists as Frida Kahlo and Romaine Brooks affirm the self-contemptuous psychological subter-rain supporting cross-dressing but do not illustrate other forms of costuming that reinforce feminine attire for women, particularly the veiled or nymphlike costumes adopted by Natalie Barney, Renée Vivien, Eva Palmer, and others.) It is significant that another mark of the aristocracy was the long, lean female body—small-breasted and slim-thighed—that inhabited these feminine clothes. Although it has been assumed (by Radclyffe Hall, among others) that male clothing more appropriately fit this female frame, Natalie Barney demonstrated that the same body was highly feminine, although its contours differed from the norm of feminine beauty at the time.[17]

Stein's Iconography of Costume

Gertrude Stein, of course, stood outside all the definitional boundaries just enumerated. She was not aristocratic; neither did she possess a long, lean body that fit naturally into a tuxedo or was seductive beneath gauzy veils. More than the clothes that covered it, it was Gertrude Stein's body that marked a certain originality, as Catharine R. Stimpson suggests:

> In a subtle maneuver, to picture Stein as fat also deflected the need to inscribe her lesbianism fully and publicly. One could offer a body, but not an overtly erotic one. One could show some monstrosity, but not too much. Although people refer to such "mannish" characteristics of Stein's as her sensible shoes, no one spoke openly of her lesbianism until after her death in 1946. Her friends protected her desire for privacy. Her detractors evidently found the taboo against mentioning lesbianism stronger than their desire to attack. Moreover, a popular icon of the lesbian, which *The Well of Loneliness* codified—that of a slim, breastless creature who cropped her hair and wore sleek, mannish clothes—did little to reinforce an association between the ample Stein and deviancy. She may have cropped her hair, with Toklas her barber, but she wore flowing caftans and brocaded vests and woolen skirts. ("Somagrams," 68–69)

Moreover, Gertrude Stein can never be said to look solitary or outcast in the pictures we have of her. The photographs of her prior to the Paris years invariably show her in groups (usually in the middle, a little toward the back), looking out with dark, soft eyes. In the Paris photographs she is often with Alice Toklas, the double image of their womanhood demonstrating the strength and the endurance of their coupling. In the several portraits of her, especially in Picasso's famous painting, the mass of her body fills the frame. She appears intelligent, relaxed, comfortable both in her body and in her clothes. These visual images in no way suggest a woman who felt herself to be either psychologically or sexually "incomplete." Unlike Radclyffe Hall, whose portraits often emphasize her ambiguous sexual identity and painful isolation, Stein seems not to have harbored doubts about her sexuality or her creativity. The separateness Stein experienced in the Paris community was due less to her sexual orientation than to the radical difference of her literary project from Modernist norms. Although her sexual choice may have made her a "marginal cultural citizen" as Stimpson argues ("Somagrams," 69), Stein was clear about her sexuality and took strength from her position as the "male" within a same-sex union. Acknowledgment of her sexual orientation (rather than adoption of a dress code) seemed to release in her the very creative abilities that the patriarchal culture in which she grew up had nearly stifled. Acceptance of her sexuality coincided with changes in her dress. While Stein never entirely escaped the imperatives of sexual stereotypes, she avoided enforcing them through her dress, using the force of her own personal magnetism to achieve the authority and the *gloire* that she sought.

This is not to say that Stein was not aware of the clothes she wore or the effects they created. She enjoyed being gazed at and loved shopping for clothes. She was quick to notice the change in women's dress following World War I (in *Paris France,* for instance) and Alice Toklas, like Janet Flanner, noted the relation between economics and fashion brought about by Chanel's introduction of the "sheath" in 1918: "It was not a creation, merely a revival of the Middle Ages when the poor wore them. A little courage—a little work and one was effectively dressed" ("Collections and Couturiers"). In fact, in releasing women from corsets and petticoats, Coco Chanel effectively destroyed the force of cross-dressing, which achieved its most significant impact in the first decade of the twentieth century when nineteenth-century conventions of women's dress still prevailed. In France, changes in women's costume were brought about by the entrance of women into the work force during the war and the interruption to the French fashion industry from 1914 to 1918. After the war, the elegant differences in male and female dress that had marked the *belle époque* had almost entirely disappeared, so that women who continued to cross-dress (in the fashion of an earlier period) did so for reasons that had little to do with adopting the forms of male authority, since those forms had radically changed.

In their last years in Paris, Gertrude Stein and Alice B. Toklas were dressed by Pierre Balmain, then one of the leading young couturiers in the city. Gertrude and Alice attended Balmain's openings, modeled his fashions, and were photographed in his creations. Stein even wrote an article for *Vogue* about Balmain's costuming genius.[18] She was acutely aware of the sensual qualities of clothing, the feel of textured fabrics, the effect of such "feminine" additions to costumes as sequins, rhinestones, and other adornments. In her later years, when she had money, Stein set store on being fashionable, a trait she may perhaps have adopted from Alice, who always took great care with her clothing. "The rhetoric of clothing" was, indeed, central to Stein's concerns, but displayed itself—like the rhetoric of her experimental art—in ways that unsettled conventional notions about the appropriate and prescribed. To have dressed as a male, to have given the illusion of masculinity as a mask for the feminine, would not have served Stein's purposes. Indeed, her intentions inverted traditional notions in just the opposite direction. Like Adrienne Monnier, Stein assumed the habit of an abbess; unlike Monnier, she assumed the rights and privileges of the abbot.

The Language of Patriarchy

Recent studies of Stein that have examined the links between her sexual orientation and her art suggest that the relationship with Alice Toklas was important not only because it provided stability and a supportive framework in which Stein could explore her literary experiments, but because it allowed her to play the male, to assume masculine authority in her private life. These studies point to the occasions when Stein referred to herself as a man to argue that Stein was uncomfortable with her femaleness, was convinced that women were inferior and unable to do "great things," and that her earlier unhappiness had been the result of self-hatred for having been born female.[19] Important questions concerning the link between Stein's lesbianism and her writing still nag. Was Stein's lesbianism a refusal to play the patriarchal game or was it yet another version of the patriarchal code overlaid on a same-sex marriage? Can it be said that Stein refused to play by the patriarchal rules, even as she interrogated those rules in her later, more theoretical, writings? While it now seems increasingly clear that Stein's writing was a systematic analysis of the patriarchal linguistic code, a resistance to the forms of conventional writing, it may be less clear that Stein's lesbianism was a form of resistance to patriarchy.

The question of Gertrude Stein's position among twentieth-century writers, especially her place among Modernists, for instance, situates itself on the issue of language. David Antin has written that he sees Stein's interests in language as significantly different from others of her generation:

> Of all the writers in English only Gertrude Stein seems to have had a thorough understanding of how profoundly Cubism opened up the possibilities of *representation* with this analysis. But then she was the writer in English with the deepest interest in language, the only one with an interest in language as language. I know almost everybody will object to this, but I've never understood why anybody thought Joyce, Eliot, Pound, Stevens or Williams were innovators in language. Essentially all of their interest was concentrated at the level of rhetoric. ("Some Questions about Modernism," 13)

Agreeing with Antin's initial premise, we might then ask a question not posed by his discussion: did Stein's interest in language *as* language have anything to do with her lesbianism? If her works are homosexually coded, how does such a code operate?

We might begin with Stein's meditation on grammar in "Arthur A Grammar," a work whose title suggests that grammar belongs to the patriarchy: Arthur both "names" the work of grammar and performs that work. Arthur is serious, and his business—related to mathematics ("Grammar. Our account. On our account") and based on scientific principles—is to produce meaning in the sentence. Thus grammar is "substantial," not frivolous, capricious, or fickle like the flourish of "style" that would adorn its meaning. Assigning gender to "grammar" (a serious male) and "style" (a frivolous female), Stein places them in libidinal proximity to one another: "A grammar has nothing to win her as foliage is priceless." The sentence, working along the logic of grammar, joins male and female principles into "meaning": "A sentence refers to wedding weddings." Arthur A Grammar joins noun to verb, subject to object, to produce meaning. Grammar produces meaning by enforcing its own linguistic law—a declaration of what parts of speech shall be joined to others—a law not unlike the one that enforces societal couplings and declares the male to be "substantial" and the female to be "inessential."

In the more fashionable terms of Saussurian linguistics, Stein's "male" ("Arthur A Grammar") is that which is signified through the grammar. He is simultaneously the agent by which meaning in language is produced and the constituent of that meaning. The female is the signifier that refers (and defers) to the male signified. The movement through grammar to meaning is "inevitable" ("Natural sentences exist in arithmetic"), the sentence the unit presided over by Arthur A Grammar. And it is the "inevitability" of the sentence, of the referential notion of meaning implied by the equation *signifier* + *signified* = *sign*, that Stein tried in various ways over the years to disrupt and redirect. She tried to stop the naming process ("There is this named him") and to redefine the noun ("now" is a noun). She even gave the noun adverbial qualities ("a noun is not only a name it is a manner, and a reply") in order to suggest the arbitrary nature of grammar, whose "sense" was not implicit in an algebraic logic. Indeed, Stein discovered that the equation supporting Western logic (signifier + signified = sign) always produces a remainder, that which is left over and unused: "Remain for grammar. To remain for grammar . . . Tomorrow is grammar. Allow" (*How to Write*, 80–81). Stein found a form of inequality in the grammatical system presumably based upon mathematical equalities. She discovered that one of the terms supporting this system—the signifier, the female—was devalued and considered unreliable. Thus it was necessary for "grammar," a guardian of the values imbedded in the sign system, to act as policeman within the system, enforcing a set of arbitrary rules to keep the signifier from wandering away from the signified to which she was attached.

In short, Stein arrived at readings of language that have more recently been attributed to deconstructionist thought (and Stein's early training in philosophy is significant here). Stein discovered inherent inequalities in linguistic principles that mirrored similar inequalities in the world in which she lived. She found a discomforting reflection of the "world" in the "word" and made grammar a method for discussing and illustrating the effects of patriarchy in language and life. In a poem significantly entitled "Patriarchal Poetry," Stein meditated upon and restated some of her earlier discoveries: "Patriarchal poetry makes no mistake makes no mistake in estimating the value to be placed upon the best and most arranged of considerations of this in as apt to be not only to be partially and as cautiously considered as in allowance which is one at a time. At a chance at a chance encounter it can be very well as appointed as appointed not only considerately but as it as use" ("Patriarchal Poetry" in *Yale Gertrude Stein*, 124). It was the "chance encounter" that fascinated Stein, the "wandering" (sexual and linguistic) of a Melanctha Herbert, the movement of the signifier from its "appointed" place, and the equation between "arranged considerations" and the "estimated value" of the properties that constitute patriarchal poetry. In Stein's investigation into language, she placed herself not with the signified (semantic content), that which is usually privileged in literature, but with the sign itself as it operates in the syntactical system. In other words, she watched the sign move; she both tracked its movements and insisted on its movement; she anticipated all the ways in which the sign could block rather than reveal meaning, could redirect meaning, could operate outside the set of binary oppositions that we have always assumed contained within its division the source of grammatical effects.

Stein discovered that the equation between sign and substance, between form and meaning, on which Modernism staked its claim was not sacred. Although she shared her work with other Modernists and gave a series of lectures in America in the mid-1930s to explain her work, her discoveries were systematically overlooked—misread—by her literary colleagues. Within the Modernist movement, Stein herself took the part of the "wandering" signifier that dislodged and overturned accepted meanings, that turned up in odd places and disrupted heterosexual patriarchal assumptions. Even when she adopted the "patriarchal" notion of referential relation between signifier and signified in her lesbian writings—when she made "cows" and "Caesars" *stand for* parts of the female body and homosexual erotic acts—the patriarchy could not "read" her. Perhaps Stein's most radical act as linguistic experimenter was just this—using the father's tools to rebuild the father's house in another's image. Although the "house" in *Tender Buttons* is constructed in imitation of its Modernist model, it cannot be read as Modernist poetry. Having broken the Modernist code, Stein was free to use it against those who oppressed and denied her, who mocked her and ignored her. If the Modernist fathers declared her writing to be unreadable, devoid of sense (nonsense), she could rejoice in the secret knowledge that she had joined sexuality and textuality to refute the conservative patriarchal assumptions underlying Modernism's experimental claims. Indeed, Stein's writing gave evidence that avenues of acceptance by the Modernist fathers were closed. Rather than waiting for acceptance by the patriarchy, Stein placed herself among its most prominent members, insisting not only that she was one of them, but that she had already outdone (and redone) their artistic efforts.

The Language of Lesbianism

This reading suggests that Stein's perverse literary style was intimately allied to her sexual identity, that her lesbianism was itself a motivating force for her investigations into language and produced a private, coded language at odds with accepted forms of meaning. Stein's reading of the "language of language" further hinted that language itself may be prevented from "wandering," from forming unwanted and "deviant" alliances between words and meanings, by the policing structure of grammar, whose rules for right reading are grounded in patriarchal claims to authority. To put that policing mechanism at the service of a deviant sexuality, to use the very patriarchal structure that would deny lesbianism as a means of encoding lesbianism in the literary work, became a secret but important goal of Stein's later writings. She made style—that never-to-be-trusted-garment that clothes linguistic operations—serve as a mask for her lesbian subject matter, an "envelope," a "tricky disguise of Nature" as Katherine Anne Porter would call it, that hid her real self, the American Amazon:

> she was of the company of Amazons which nineteenth-century America produced among its many prodigies: not-men, not-women, answerable to no function in either sex, whose careers were carried on, and how successfully, in whatever field they chose: they were educators, writers, editors, politicians, artists, world travelers, and international hostesses, who lived in public and by the public and played out their self-assumed, self-created roles in such masterly freedom as only a few early medieval queens had equaled. Freedom to them meant precisely freedom from men and their stuffy rules for women.

They usurped with a high hand the traditional masculine privileges of movement, choice, and the use of direct, personal power. They were few in number
and they were not only to be found in America, and Miss Stein belonged with
them, no doubt of it, in spite of a certain temperamental passivity which was
Oriental, not feminine. ("Gertrude Stein: A Self-Portrait," 522)

Porter's analysis of American lesbian practice reveals anger at its "high-
handed" freedom, its privilege, its use of power, its "usurpation" of the
male prerogative, and—worst of all—its success. Stein denied her sex in
the secret heart of lesbianism. Her writing denied the claims of intelligibility enforced by patriarchal language through an encoding of lesbianism *as* its secret heart. Gertrude Stein, it turns out, was a linguistic cross-
dresser. Unlike a Natalie Barney, however, who cast her message of lesbian love under the sign of heterosexual desire, using the forms of love
poetry to inscribe her desire for woman, Stein dressed her celebration of
lesbian eroticism in the garment of heterosexual grammar. The result was
that for more than sixty years Stein's work was read as having *no* meaning, not read as having *double*—and exclusionary—meanings. Certainly
no one suspected that this language simultaneously exposed the patriarchal assumptions of linguistic practice as it produced overdetermined
texts according to that practice.

The oppositions and contradictions at work in Stein's life were at play
in her linguistic experiments as well. Stein differed from many other
women of the Paris community by publicly refusing to be marginalized.
Survival in this environment meant that Stein had to deny any suspicion
that on the basis of gender alone she might be refused the fruits of her
artistic efforts. In short, she had to renounce her womanhood in order to
acknowledge a genius that was grounded *in* her womanhood. Expression
of that genius would trace the opposed psychological and artistic forces
through a language that served Stein as a smoke screen. Stein hid behind
the language of her fictions, as she hid behind the "male" persona she
created for herself in her lesbian marriage. Stein's lesbianism involved her
in a complex psychological game that simultaneously demanded that she
disavow and acknowledge both her gender and her sexual orientation. In
accepting her lesbianism Stein committed herself to one other woman—
Alice Toklas. In accepting her artistic endeavor, Stein was forced to distinguish herself from all other women.

As Marianne DeKoven has remarked, Stein distinguished herself from
other women by making herself appear to be a man: "With Alice Toklas
as her wife and Pablo Picasso as her peer, Stein was able to live fully the
male identification which allowed her to accept herself. . . . the fact that
she was Baby needn't undermine her power as long as Mama was also
subservient wife rather than dominant father or brother. Once her liaison with Toklas was established, Stein made the following remark in her

notebook: 'Pablo & Matisse have a maleness that belongs to genius. Moi aussi, perhaps'" (*A Different Language*, 136, fn. 31). Catharine R. Stimpson also charts the relationships between Stein's masculinity and her male language: "consistently the language of self was male and masculine. Stein was 'husband' to Toklas' 'wife.' . . . Speaking of the female as male/masculine, she reverted to old patterns to meet the new dilemma of the feminization of the mind/body problem" ("The Mind, the Body, and Gertrude Stein," 496–497). Unable to step outside the heterosexual cultural imperative, Stein clothed her homosexuality in heterosexual forms.

Consequently, Gertrude Stein's place in the Paris literary community was the most anomalous: she had separated herself from the community of women and she was a powerful threat to the community of men. The proclamation of her genius and the claims for the importance of her own work were threatening to the patriarchal hegemony of the Left Bank community in far more ways than either her sexual orientation or the implied mockery of gender differences in her unusual dress. Stein's goal was not to gain acceptance of women's writing, but to proclaim the superiority of *one woman's writing*. She needn't have been feminist to mount such an attack; she needn't have been a "masculine" lesbian; she needn't have been confused or tormented about her sexual identity or convinced of the inferiority of women to do so. She need only have put aside the traditional modesty and reticence of women, a modesty and reticence that she abandoned when she slipped out from under her brother's protective influence. Stein's actions were enormously threatening, precisely because her behavior suggested that the only alternative to male dominance was the assumption of masculine authority.

The Paris experiment, which seemed to offer the promise of sexual and artistic freedom for women like Stein and Toklas, proved—ironically—to be but another version of patriarchal convention, one that perhaps only seemed less restrictive and binding. The Paris that Stein discovered in 1903 was transformed after World War I by the presence of a strongly masculine American expatriate culture in revolt against those conventions that still held sway back home. To the extent that Left Bank culture was dominated by men, the distinction between male authority and female subservience was precisely the convention that would not be put aside in this new environment. Expatriate women found themelves fighting in Paris the same kind of conventional attitudes toward women that were more strictly enforced back home. To a certain degree the Paris environment was perhaps more frustrating than that of Baltimore, for instance, because it promised a freedom that it could not entirely ensure. Stein's reaction to this unfilled promise implies that she both exploited the cultural norms of this patriarchal community (by taking for herself the role of the "male" in her marriage to Toklas) and tried to undermine them (by asserting for herself the unique contribution of her experimental literary effort). Indeed, the relationship with Toklas allowed Stein to assert her individual contribution to literature because it established a boundary of significant experience, a separate, interior space within the larger world of Paris.

Stein could isolate herself from the world of patriarchal power outside the walls of her apartment, but she could not divest that world of its power to ignore her work. When she did finally manage to draw the attention of the outside world, her public image eclipsed her art, making her writing seem to be the product of an enormous ego. That she was locked in a battle with the patriarchy that joined the dual concerns of her writing and her womanhood, and the complex links between them, seems to have been overlooked, even by Stein herself. Only rather late in her career—in 1936 with the publication of *The Geographical History of America*—did Stein publicly state her cause as a woman, calling attention to the fact that the "only literary thinking in this century was done by a woman." Had Stein's personal life been tormented and self-destructive, had her art consisted of a few desperate poems written in honor of Sappho, had she not proclaimed her talents to all who would listen, she would have become a lesbian cult figure and been patronized by a heterosexual public that considered her pathetic. Instead, she was resented by her brother and others for surviving so well. Survival for Stein included surviving as a Jew, and some have questioned the means by which that survival was effected.[20]

Gertrude Stein: Expatriated American

It was immensely important for Stein to survive as an American in a foreign clime. In her stout, good-humored presence, she blocked out the backdrop of literary Paris against which she had carved out both her life and her writing: "And so I am an American and I have lived half my life in Paris, not the half that made me but the half in which I made what I made." Although this statement seems to take the Paris setting rather for granted, giving America credit for having made Gertrude Stein, its syntax also suggests that the Gertrude Stein who made her art also invented herself. As Catharine R. Stimpson has recently commented, Stein's work and literary identity remain inseparable from her American being, and her work traces an "ideology of and about America."[21] Although Stein consistently took credit for all that was herself, denying in her rhetoric literary models and outside influences, and set herself to writing a new (literary) history of America, that history defined itself in her conception of *herself* as an American. Importantly, Stein preserved herself as American by living in a city that in no way threatened to "take away" or reshape that identity.

One of the gifts Paris gave her was the sound of the French language. Particularly aware of spoken language around her, Stein admitted that in order for her to investigate the complexities of the English language she needed to remove herself from contexts in which English dominated. It was a relief to her to hear French in the streets, to approach the English language fresh because she need not live in that language. She wanted to be "left alone with my eyes and my english": "I do not know if it would have been possible to have english be so all and all to me otherwise. And they none of them could read a word I wrote. No, I like living with so very many people and being all alone with english and myself" (Harrison, *Gertrude Stein's America,* 13). Stein claimed to write "entirely" with her eyes: "The words as seen by my eyes are the importance of words, and the ears and mouth do not count." In *Everybody's Autobiography,* Stein revealed that in 1931 her older brother Michael decided to sell his Paris residence and return to America. Gertrude was horrified at the prospect, unable to fathom Michael's reasons for wanting to move. He responded by saying, "you don't understand . . . I want to say in English to the man who brings the letters and does the gardening I want to say things to them and have them say it to me in American" (13). In his older years he wanted to live in his own language. His sister, however, wanted to write in her own language. In order to do so, she found it necessary to live in a country where English was not spoken, in part perhaps because the sounds of spoken English set up rhythms in her head that she found it difficult to control.[22]

Stein's comments on language have always seemed odd—for instance, her explanation for not reading French: that it was meant to be spoken not to be read. She drew a sharp distinction between English as spoken by the English, with its accumulated history of meaning and usage, and the efforts of Americans to make a new, fresh language, one that emphasized words: "if you arranged and concentrated and took away all excrescences from them you could make these words do what you needed to do with them" (*Gertrude Stein's America,* 97). She argued that the American effort was to destroy the heritage of the English language and to make a new language, one of its own—one that eradicated the notion of "having a beginning and a middle and an ending" and one that moved, rather than contained certain specified, residual meanings. To hear English put pressures on her creative processes, distracted her from her linguistic project, deflected her attention. The major advantage of her expatriate experience, then, was linguistic and was totally unknown to her in 1903 when she arrived at the rue de Fleurus, an advantage that undoubtedly spurred her investigations in English and became the primary cause for her special undertaking.

Residence in Paris removed Stein from a patriarchal American literary heritage whose acknowledged practitioners were suspicious of openly experimental writing. Removed from that literary heritage, Stein did not suffer an anxiety of influence. Having put aside her American fathers, Stein found herself having to play both father and mother to the writing subject, assuming the authority invested in the male in order to explore the troublesome interior world of her femaleness. Stein's "anxiety of authorship" was particularly complex: she needed to deny her predecessors; she wanted to create herself and the new century through her writing; she refused to acknowledge that her womanhood was a factor in the rejection of her experimental work. The relationship of her sexuality to the textuality of her works was openly denied by her. The painful labor of her early writing was linked to its subject matter: her place in the family; the place of her sexuality in her life. She tried to come to terms with her own upbringing in the writing of a family history and to understand her early lesbian experiences by writing about them. Once family influences were set down as "history" (in *The Making of Americans*), they were set aside; when she had worked out the psychological dynamics of the affair with May Bookstaver (first through *Q.E.D.* and then in "Melanctha"), she was able to accept her sexual orientation and act on it in her love for Alice Toklas. By autumn 1911, all that remained was to separate herself from her brother. When this was finally accomplished, Stein retreated from the busier and more public world of literary Paris (living away from the city for most of the war) and looked only to herself for inspiration and to her immediate surroundings for subject matter. In fact, the choice of a more private and homely subject matter was itself radically experimental and served to separate Stein from the Modernist fathers who explored grander literary themes and who linked their artistic subjects to the past through literary allusion. But until Stein reemerged as a public figure in the 1930s, as someone not only discussed by the public but present to it, her writing located itself close to home—her Paris home.

It was Stein's investment in her Paris home and the life she created there that allowed a complete break with the past that "made" her and offered her a second birth. With Alice as her wife, Stein was able to reinvent herself (as "Baby"); she also proclaimed herself the mother of the twentieth century, her experimental writing marking the birth of the "continuous present." In this private mythology of the writer's life cycle, Stein linked her own rebirth—as a modern woman writer who had struggled free from the oppressive restrictions of the nineteenth century—to the moment she gave birth to the twentieth century. She embodied everything that this new century might come to represent, the emerging genius of the century evident in her own writings. The mind/body split that the nineteenth century had enforced for women, the split that painfully divided many other women of the Paris community, sealed itself (and healed itself) in Gertrude Stein's life as she took for herself all the parts in the mythological family she had constructed: she was husband to Alice, the baby their marriage had produced, and the Mother of Us All. Her status as genius allowed her to subsume gender distinctions and ignore them; consequently, she was the only woman of this study to assume a central place in the literary hierarchy of the Paris community.

6

SYLVIA BEACH AND
ADRIENNE MONNIER:
RUE DE L'ODÉON

One Woman Reading

In May 1938, the owner of La Maison des Amis des Livres at 7, rue de
l'Odéon, broadcast over Radio-Paris a "Letter to Listeners." Adrienne
Monnier began her spoken letter with a hypothetical objection from the
male listening audience: "'les Ami-es des Livres' . . . they do not exist, of
course. Women are incapable of loving books; far from being their friends,
they are their natural enemies" ("Les Amies des Livres," in *The Very Rich
Hours of Adrienne Monnier,* 183).[1] More than twenty years earlier, Monnier had opened the first lending library ever established in France. In the
front room of her small, sparsely furnished shop potential readers were
encouraged to expand their reading and to experiment with their literary
tastes. Like Sylvia Beach, who owned the English-language bookshop
across the street at number 12, Adrienne Monnier's accomplishment depended in large part upon her personal love of books and of the adventure
of reading. While both women successfully imparted to others their enthusiasm for books, Monnier dedicated herself to changing the reading
habits of the French and to overturning the lingering assumption that
women were impervious to the claims of books.

An unabashedly feminist analysis of women's relation to books, "Les
Amies des Livres" examined the historical circumstances that had traditionally prevented women from becoming part of the reading public.
These conditions included differences in education between males and females, but more important were the circumstances of family and marital
life that made the home the place of woman's work rather than of leisure:
"Women are asked to take care of their persons and their homes above
all; they are not praised for devoting themselves to housework and it is

not considered proper for them to become lost in books, whether these books be frivolous or serious" (184). Monnier carefully differentiated the reading habits of men and women in this essay, focusing on those special traits that a woman brings to the reading situation:

> She will not experience the need, like a masculine reader, to own her favorite authors in beautiful and lasting editions—at bottom it is true that she is not a bibliophile in the sense in which this word is generally understood. She will prefer to keep the ordinary editions that were the very ones she read first, and she will surround them with kind attentions; she will cover them with fine patterned paper, she will put in as a frontispiece a portrait of the author that she has cut out of some magazine, she will sometimes slip in a flower. If the book pleases her intensely she will copy passages from it. It is not she who will have that nasty habit of writing in the margins, except perhaps as far as her school books are concerned. The fact of writing in the margins is further-more specifically masculine. Yes, it is curious, a man and above all a young man, often corrects the author, he underlines, he denies, he opposes his judg-ment; in fact, *he adds himself to it*. A woman remains silent when she does not like something, and when she detests something *she cuts it out*. I know women who are not at all stupid who cannot stop themselves from removing or covering up such and such a displeasing passage of a book; they do that above all for the benefit or to the disadvantage of a work that they admire but that offends them in places, just as to suppress the ugly traits in the characters of the men they love. (185)

These acute observations of the differences between men and women readers were based on Adrienne Monnier's own experience as a woman and reader. They informed both her desire to become a bookseller and her insistence that Les Amis des Livres not encourage men's love of books at the expense of women's relationship with books.

Indeed, Monnier's own practices as a bookseller were the product of her notions about various kinds of readers and, in particular, her reac-tions as a woman to the male-dominated world of books. For instance, her shop did not carry expensive leatherbound editions of classic works of literature; thus it did not encourage "bibliophiles." She could not have afforded to stock such items, nor did she admire the "masculine" men-tality that desired to use books for economic profit. In fact, her bookshop was directed less toward the sale of books than to the reading and lending of them. Monnier remained convinced that the French would only buy books that pleased them, works that they already knew well. Her shop encouraged people to browse, to sit near the potbellied stove and read, to take tea with her and discuss the novels, volumes of poetry, and reviews she stocked. She herself knew well every book in her shop and had chosen the individual items because of her own interest in them. She encouraged customers to take books home with them, to live with them for a while before making a decision to buy them.

La Maison des Amis des Livres was, as its name suggested, a house for all of those who loved books. In order for Monnier to succeed in her own terms—to bring people to a love of books—it was essential that she define in advance the kind of person she wished her shop to attract. In "Number One," the first essay in Monnier's *Gazette des Amis des Livres* (published January 1938), she explicated the particularly French attitude toward books, later noting that "a French person does not lightly engage in the purchase of a book" (145). Admitting that among Europeans the French were not avid readers, she set herself to determining what might spur them to place a higher value on the reading experience. She noted that the French prefer paperbound books, for instance, because the hardbound variety remind them of the years at school when books were for study rather than for pleasure. They want books that fit in their pockets, whose pages they can bend back a bit, whose weight and size feel comfortable in their hands. Although the French continue to be sensitive to the value of a "pleasing volume," to the quality of paper, they do not particularly prize beautiful papers or wide margins, both of which seem to them to be unnecessary extravagances. In short, if the French love books, they love to *read* them. (Monnier's observations on French reading habits were later confirmed by Colette; see "Occupation" in *Looking Backwards*, 110–111.)

From the perspective of the paperback age of books, Adrienne Monnier's ideas about the place of books in her life and the importance she placed on Les Amis des Livres as a reading room and lending library seem quaint. The great success of the Monnier-Beach endeavor in Paris was due, in part, to the absence of similar bookshops in that city. Although in England and America public lending libraries came into existence in the nineteenth century, they were unknown in France prior to the appearance of Monnier's own bookshop on the rue de l'Odéon. But the success of Les Amis des Livres and Shakespeare and Company was more significantly due to the refusal of these two librarians ever to purchase a book they had not read and loved. Thus the two bookshops represented the reading habits of its two *patronnes,* women who were not merely lenders or sellers but readers and lovers of the books they chose. These shops were for those who could not afford personal libraries, for whom the purchase of a book was a significant expenditure.

The Americans who came to Sylvia Beach's shop and the French who came to Adrienne Monnier's, however, came for rather different reasons. Many of the Americans in Paris were transients who had left private libraries back home. They had difficulty finding English-language books in Paris (as one still does), and many were longing to read works in their own language by authors well known to them. Shakespeare and Company proved to be an important way station on the expatriate tour. But the Parisians had different needs, in part because the French, who according to Monnier "love books" ("Number One," 145), were not the best customers for books and because the city offered more exciting temptations than reading. Monnier's idea was to establish a place, a country, in which the French would be encouraged to explore their love for the written word, to discover the pleasures of reading. In establishing her bookshop Monnier created such a world; later, she aided Sylvia Beach in a similar effort. When the two bookshops faced each other across the street leading to the National Theater, they stood at the entrance to a country Monnier called "Odéonia."

Odéonia

Specifically situated in time and place, Odéonia nonetheless formed an interior landscape, described by Monnier as a "Country of Memory, where the Mothers lull us and ever smile at us" ("Number One," 139). This was not only a country that welcomed women, but one that recalled the pleasure in the sound of a mother's voice reading to a small child. The physical boundaries of Odéonia were the sixth *arrondissement,* but its spiritual boundaries were almost limitless, including all those who loved books. The defining feature of this country was its welcoming spirit. Included among the memorials in the *Mercure de France* on the occasion of Beach's death, Stein's poem "Rich and poor in English" (written in the early years of their friendship and dedicated to Sylvia) suggests the spirit of this country:

> Not a country not a door send them away to sit on the floor.
> Cakes. This is not the world. Can you remember.
> ("Sylvia Beach," *Mercure de France,* 95)

When Adrienne Monnier first established her shop, the rue de l'Odéon was known primarily to students at the nearby Sorbonne and to those who came, in the evening, to performances at the National Theater. Because of La Maison des Amis des Livres and, later, Shakespeare and Company, the street became one of the most famous in Paris, a street on which even today one meets the ghosts of all those who regularly walked up the slope toward the twin bookshops. Behind the large windows that displayed the latest works by French and American writers, the two women waited to welcome any who paused at the threshold. In later years, each of these women used her shop for poetry and prose readings, occasions when well-known and unknown writers presented their work to a Paris audience. At these times, the shop became a small salon—people crowded in to hear Joyce or Eliot, Gide or Larbaud, read; aperitifs were served with small snacks and the tiny rooms were filled with laughter and conversation. A superb cook and hostess, Adrienne often entertained groups of writers in her apartment, at 18, rue de l'Odéon, which she shared with Sylvia for almost seventeen years. For these women made no distinction between their professional and personal lives; their public and private interests were integrated to such a degree that it was difficult even for them to say how their professional alliance was different from their personal and intimate relationship.

In important ways Adrienne served as guide for Sylvia Beach's own efforts to establish herself as a bookseller in Paris. Adrienne drew upon her already extensive experience, and, without her help, the chances for Sylvia's enterprise would have been dim. Adrienne helped her obtain the necessary permit to set up business, found the building, and convinced the landlord to rent it to a foreigner. She gave advice on both the intellectual and business concerns of such an undertaking. Adrienne served as sister and muse, as helpmate and financial advisor, and—perhaps most importantly—as the model librarian and bookseller in whose image Sylvia would fashion her own. Although five years younger than Sylvia, Adrienne Monnier always appeared the more matronly and older of the two. Like Gertrude Stein, Adrienne was plump and motherly; Sylvia, like Alice Toklas, was small and wiry. It was Adrienne who showed Sylvia the possibilities for a free and independent life in Paris, who shared her clientele when Sylvia opened Shakespeare and Company, who provided emotional stability and introduced Sylvia to the pleasures of their long life together.

In March 1917, when Sylvia came into La Maison des Amis des Livres in search of Paul Fort's review *Vers et Prose*, Adrienne already had established her bookshop as significantly different from others in the sixth *arrondissement*. She had weathered the initial traumas of setting up a business about which, she later admitted, she knew little. She had no previous business experience, was unfamiliar with even the rudimentary elements of bookkeeping, and felt uneasy in the world of tradespeople and businessmen. It was not common for a woman to establish herself as a bookseller—far more appropriate for her to be a proprietress of a *maison de couture* or a seller of baked goods or candies. And even as a bookseller, Adrienne Monnier was strikingly different from her colleagues—the difference born, in part, of necessity:

> Our first idea was very modest: we sought only to start off a bookshop and a reading room devoted above all to modern works. We had very little money, and it was that detail that drove us to specialize in modern literature; if we had had a lot of money, it is certain that we would have wanted to buy everything that existed in respect to printed works and to realize a kind of Na-

tional Library; we were convinced that the public demands a great quantity of books above all, and we thought that we had much audacity in daring to establish ourselves with hardly three thousand volumes when some reading-room catalogs announced twenty thousand, fifty thousand, and even a hundred thousand of them! The truth is that only one of our walls was furnished with books; the others were decorated with pictures, with a large old desk, and with a chest of drawers in which we kept wrapping paper, string, and everything we did not know where to put; our chairs were old chairs from the country that we still have. This bookshop hardly had the look of a shop, and that was not on purpose: we were far from suspecting that people would congratulate us so much in the future for what seemed to us an unfortunate makeshift. ("La Maison," 71)

It was precisely because her shop hardly had the look of a place of business—its worn chairs invited those who entered to sit and read or chat—that Adrienne Monnier achieved such success. "Business" for her had a "moving and profound meaning." She thought of a shop as a "place of transition between street and house" and of her own shop as a "magic chamber" where the "correspondence between [the] external attitude and [the] profound self" of those who entered could be revealed to her. Monnier loved books, and made them her business, but she was an eager and intelligent student of human nature, and La Maison des Amis des Livres provided the setting for her studies.

Adrienne Monnier was not satisfied, however, with merely watching her clientele discover the modern literature with which she stocked her shelves; she was also concerned to discover young writers in need of a reading audience. In an early essay, Monnier addressed herself to a fictional poet of her own creation who wrote to her for assistance in finding both a reading public and a "road to posterity" ("A Letter to a Young Poet," April 1926). She responded as a woman, emphasizing at each turn in the essay her own particular situation as a reader and writer. She claimed that her womanhood, defined as "passive by nature, accustomed over several centuries to attach little value to my mind and its 'paltry productions,'" had given her a detachment, a perspective from which she could comment on poetry. Responding to this young poet's great desire to see himself "in print," she suggested that he take various of his rejected, unpublished poems to a good printer, choose the kind of typeface that pleased him, and prepare a small printing of his work. These copies he could give as gifts to friends and circulate to critics, libraries, booksellers, and reviewers in hope of being noticed by some of them. In outlining such a plan of action, Monnier described precisely the desire for publication that led other women friends to set up handpresses to print their works and those of their friends.

Monnier saw in the young poet's particular sense of loneliness and discouragement at continued rejection by publishers and lack of acknowledgment by reviewers a condition common to women, who exist, she claimed, outside the boundaries of the established literary community. To find a place among intellectuals, women often chose to serve the interests of men at the expense of their own development. In their "capacity for being smitten with genius and loving to serve it," French women, wrote Monnier in 1940, do disservice to their own creative and intellectual energies ("Lust," 172). Rather than imitate her countrywomen, Monnier set about to undermine the established principles by which women became handmaidens to male genius, disguised their own intellectual aspirations in the pursuit of men, and gave in to male assumptions that women were capable of reading and writing only the most banal literature. Monnier never lived on the margins of the Paris literary community: she embodied the spirit of that community, made the bookshop the locus of its activities, and continued for almost forty years to enlarge its intellectual and literary boundaries. She was always more than the proprietress of La Maison des Amis des Livres—she was also a chronicler of her times, a gifted essayist, a bibliographer, a publisher, and a reader.

With few exceptions, the writers who were supported and encouraged by Adrienne Monnier and Sylvia Beach have paid tribute to the combined genius of these two women. Literary history has acknowledged that each of these women was far more than a mere "bookseller" (they made an "ordinary" profession "extraordinary," as Leslie Katz remarks), yet their accomplishments have been judged to be practical and personal rather than intellectual or artistic ("Meditations," 81). Because they lived together and worked in close association with each other, it has often been assumed that their accomplishments were almost indistinguishable. Yet a closer examination of their interests, their personal situations, their daily working lives suggests that Adrienne Monnier and Sylvia Beach saw their professional commitments in distinctly different terms. And the combination of their individual talents constituted an assertive and articulate force among Left Bank intellectuals. To understand something of this special combination of energy and intellectual drive, one must examine the circumstances under which they became booksellers and librarians. Each wanted an independent life, outside marriage. For Sylvia Beach, such a life was possible only by living away from her family, putting as much distance as possible between herself and her mother, a woman who came to her daughters with various emotional needs, and separating herself from her father's professional circumstances. Monnier, however, preferred to stay in Paris—her birthplace—to maintain a close but separate existence away from her parents. Both of these daughters were encouraged to be independent, to interest themselves in the arts and literature, and to establish for themselves fulfilling professional and personal lives. The adult relationship they established with each other ironically extended the values of their upbringing and constituted a reaction against those values.

Sylvia Beach: Princeton and Paris

When Sylvia was 15 years old, her father became associate pastor of the American Church of Paris with a special mission to the students of the Latin quarter. The family moved to Paris from Bridgeton, New Jersey, in 1902. Each of the three Beach daughters was affected by the experience of living and being educated in Europe, but of the three it was Sylvia who eventually made her home in Paris, in part because she wanted to experience the city on her own. She felt restricted during this first three-year stay with her parents: "I was not interested in what I could see of Paris through the bars of my family cage," she wrote in a suppressed version of her memoirs (Fitch, *Sylvia Beach*, 25). The later decision to take up a life abroad was also an effort to establish her independence and to separate herself from the tensions of her parents' marriage. Sylvia Beach was the product of a family torn by conflicting values: those belonging to her father were "orthodox," and those of her mother "heterodox":

> From Eleanor [her mother] she learned to love Europe, particularly France, to seek pleasure and individual freedom, to admire bold and creative artists above all others, and to shun sexual contact with men. From Sylvester [her father]—whose ministry was less a devout call to service than a prestigious profession—she learned social respectability and congenial good manners. From her grandmother Nancy Orbison [for whom she was named] and her missionary heritage, she learned dedication to a cause beyond self-gratification. Prudence and good taste would temper the personal freedom she enjoyed by living in Paris. (*Sylvia Beach*, 22)

Despite the increasing physical and psychological distances in Sylvia's relationships with her parents, she maintained strong loyalties to both of them. After the family's three-year stay in Paris, Eleanor Beach spent much of her time in Europe or in California with her daughters, in part to escape the unhappiness of her marriage. Sylvia followed the creative interests of her mother, who was an accomplished musician and painter; it was her mother's money that allowed her to set up Shakespeare and Company. Yet, she maintained powerful—if complex—loyalties to her father. In her adolescence, she stopped using her given name, Nancy, and adopted the name Sylvia, a variant of her father's name, suggesting that she psychologically allied herself with him. Her memoir, *Shakespeare and Company*, begins by introducing her father. Sylvia's rather difficult relationship with her parents is mirrored in the relationships her sisters maintained with them. Interestingly, both her sisters altered their names as well—her youngest sister, Eleanor, changed her name to Cyprian for the stage; her second sister, christened Hollingsworth, after the family name of a close friend, shortened hers to Holly. Both sisters felt the burden of their mother's increasing dependency on them; each was to feel the need to distance herself from Sylvester Beach.

The Paris experience of 1902–1905, although a rare opportunity whose implications for the lives of the Beach daughters would only later become evident, circumscribed a difficult period in Sylvia's life. Already a young woman whose education had been interrupted by ill health (she suffered from incapacitating migraine headaches that plagued her all her life), Sylvia Beach claimed that the few months she spent in a private school in Lausanne constituted the only schooling she ever had. "Owing to the curious notions of the two ladies who directed it," Beach explained, discipline at the school "was better suited to a bunch of incorrigibles in a reformatory than to a lot of meek maidens." After a few months in residence at the school she asked to return to Paris. Upon her return, she claimed she would have been completely happy had it not been for the memory of Holly, who continued on as a student in Lausanne, "still walking out twice a day in twos, never allowed to look out of the window at the Lake of Geneva, or to address a word to anyone except on the walks, and singing with a cork between her teeth to keep her mouth open" (*Shakespeare and Company*, 6). Rather than a doctrinaire education, Sylvia received brief intervals of tutoring; shortly after her return from Switzerland, she was sent to live with an American family at their country place near Bourre, a spot she came to love, devoting herself to long hours of reading and walking in the woods. Sylvia established the most important friendship of her Paris years with the daughter of this family, Carlotta Welles, whose father was an American businessman in France. Carlotta too had been taken out of school on the advice of the family doctor, who prescribed outdoor exercise. This prescription fit Sylvia's needs admirably. Away from the tensions of her family and pressures of a rigid school atmosphere, her health improved.

Although Sylvia struggled her entire life against tension headaches and eczema, she seemed determined not to repeat her mother's alternating mood swings between the desire for freedom and independence (almost always the reason behind her flights to Europe) and neurotic dependencies. In 1918, a year before the opening of Shakespeare and Company at number 8, rue de Dupuytren, Sylvia was under considerable pressure from her mother to return from Europe. She had been in Europe since 1915, having spent the first two of those years in Spain with her mother. Now her mother wanted her closer to home. In 1918, Eleanor Beach was physically ill from the misery of her marriage and the pressure of social and professional obligations as the wife of the pastor of the First Presbyterian Church in Princeton. She had been recalled from Europe in

1916 as the result of an item that appeared in New York's *Town Topics* broadly hinting that her husband was carrying on a rather public affair in her absence. The accusation led to a meeting of the church board at which Sylvester Beach had to defend himself, a defense that suggested his anger at such meddling in his personal affairs. Writing to Sylvia, he avoided mentioning the particular complications of his relationship with his wife, concentrating instead on their mutual commitment to their daughters: "Since we went to Paris 15 years ago, it has not been possible for the family to be together much of the time. Our first duty is to the children. We owe them the best possible chance in life. In lieu of money, which we do not have, we can give them a little travel and experience to fit them for the career they may choose . . . I wish people would understand that and LET US ALONE" (Fitch, *Sylvia Beach*, 29).

Eleanor Beach had waited a full year to return, arriving in Princeton in 1917 in an effort to "keep up appearances." The parsonage in Princeton, however, was the only home she had. By fall of 1918, she was writing her daughters that she could not "live without" them. Sylvester Beach, apparently, had been complaining to her of the young women's expenses. At last, the oldest sister, Holly, made the decision: she urged Sylvia to stay in Europe and sent back Cyprian, whose film career in France was just beginning to succeed. Cyprian would never again find success in a career. Feeling guilty, Eleanor Beach "begged the forgiveness of her three daughters for hurting them with her pressuring and complaining" (*Sylvia Beach*, 32). By luck or design, Sylvia had been spared the return to the family fold. She was now free to find a career, and her newfound friend, Adrienne Monnier, was ready to help her do so.

Sylvia's effort to find a satisfying career had been delayed by World War I. Listing herself on her first adult passport as a *journaliste littéraire*, she actually published only one article (on the Musée Rodin in Paris) and did various odd jobs. She had served as a *voluntaire agricole* in Tourraine and, after Cyprian's return to America in 1918, she set out for Serbia with Holly to work for the Red Cross. Six months later, she returned to Paris with the gift of an engraved cigarette lighter for Adrienne and plans to open a bookshop in London. After spending one week in London and learning from Harold Monro that there was no market for such a shop in London, she returned to Adrienne, who very quickly found appropriate housing for what was to become Shakespeare and Company (*Sylvia Beach*, 38–39). Although Eleanor Beach still wanted her middle daughter to return to America—perhaps to set up a bookshop in New York— she provided her the initial $3,000 that allowed her to open her shop on 17 November 1919. Chiefly a lending library, like La Maison des Amis des Livres around the corner, Sylvia's bookshop included books from *Beowulf* through the nineteenth century. Soon it would also display radi-

cal experimental Modernist writing, the publications of avant-garde journals and local small presses.

Adrienne Monnier: Right Bank/Left Bank

By the time Sylvia Beach returned to America in 1908, following her adolescent Paris experience, Adrienne Monnier was nearing completion of
her *brevet supérieur* that would accredit her for secondary school teaching. When she received the degree in 1909, she did not begin teaching
but followed Suzanne Bonnierre, her childhood friend and the woman
with whom she would later establish her bookshop, to London, where
Suzanne had a teaching job. In order to be near the woman with whom
she was passionately in love, Monnier worked as a lady's companion and
as a French teacher in Eastbourne (*Very Rich Hours,* 10). When she later
returned to Paris, she studied to become a literary secretary and in 1912
became secretary to Yvonne Sarcey, founder of the Université des Annales
and editor of *Le Journal de l'Université des Annales.* After three years of
working for Sarcey, Monnier decided that editing an academic journal
did not interest her. But in the three years of working on the *Annales,*
Monnier had made another important discovery that was to affect her
professional life: she had discovered that the Right Bank, where the offices of the *Annales* were located, in no way appealed to her. She was to
write in her "Souvenirs de l'autre guerre": "In that stronghold of the
Right Bank I had made myself no relationship, no relationship that I
wanted to keep and maintain. The authors that I loved did not frequent
the place. . . . My taste and my ideas had been formed in complete independence; the milieu had nothing to do with them. . . . The Left Bank
called me and even now it does not cease to call me and keep me. I cannot
imagine that I could ever leave it, anymore than an organ can leave the
place that is assigned to it in the body" (*Very Rich Hours,* 10–11). Years
later, following a lunch with Colette, Monnier wrote in a note to the July
1939 number of the *Gazette des Amis des Livres,* "At bottom, what I am
for her: a little provincial of the Left Bank!" Colette too had begun her
years in Paris as a "little provincial of the Left Bank." When Monnier met
her in the 1930s, however, Colette was one of the greatest literary figures
in France, resident in the Palais Royal, where Cyprian and Sylvia had
lived in the year 1918, when Eleanor Beach had forced her youngest
daughter to come home. And by the time of this meeting, Adrienne
Monnier herself was a well-known person, a leader of the Left Bank literary community. The two women shared provincial roots—one of a family
from Savoy and the other from Burgundy—despite their intellectual distance from each other in Paris. Colette's success had taken her across the

river to Right Bank respectability, whereas Adrienne's success had tied her more firmly to Left Bank intellectuals.

There was another, unacknowledged, link uniting these two French women, a link that might well have remained unknown to them. In 1913, while still working for Yvonne Sarcey, Adrienne Monnier visited the Left Bank offices of the *Mercure de France* at 26, rue de Condé, because she claimed that this journal, which she had discovered at age 10, had altered the direction of her literary reading. At the offices, she met Rachilde, the French novelist and the wife of the *Mercure* editor, Alfred Vallette. It was Rachilde who discovered Colette to be the secret author of the *Claudine* stories, who befriended the young provincial woman in the years of her marriage to Willy, urged her to leave her taskmaster, and supported her both financially and emotionally at a period in her life when Colette was considered *persona non grata* by friends of Rachilde and Vallette. Monnier was looking for a literary occupation on the Left Bank, something that would allow her to use the literary experience she had already gained, and she went to Rachilde in hopes that she might provide an introduction to her husband. Although nothing came of this meeting (the editorial staff of the *Mercure* was, in Monnier's terms, "disabused" of her youth, enthusiasm, and illusion), the decision to find a place for herself on the Left Bank was confirmed by this visit.

In less than a year, because of a tragic accident to her father, Adrienne Monnier's wish to have a bookshop on the Left Bank was fulfilled. Badly injured in a train accident, Clovis Monnier received an indemnity for his injuries, a sum that he gave to his eldest daughter to establish a bookshop (*Very Rich Hours*, 11). It was Adrienne's father who provided the capital for La Maison des Amis des Livres and Sylvia's mother's money that helped establish Shakespeare and Company, although traditionally such gifts were given to the sons rather than the daughters of middle-class families. Without brothers who might have had first claim on their families' rather limited means, Adrienne and Sylvia were the natural choices for this kind of "financial aid." And the assistance Adrienne and Sylvia initially received from their families continued over the years, in the form of numerous loans to Sylvia from her mother and in the weekly rations of vegetables and farm products that the Monniers provided for both "daughters."

According to Adrienne Monnier's memoirs, she was twice favored in 1915—first by the surprise gift brought about by her father's accident and second by "the terrible goddess" of war. Had Monnier been male, she would have been fighting in the trenches. Instead, she was a young woman in search of a profession at a time when those businesses still in operation in Paris were in the care of wives, sisters, and daughters of fighting men. Many businesses had been forced to close, and "shops were available at reasonable prices. . . . Competition could not slow me down because most of the booksellers were in the army. As life was slowed down, I did not lack the time to learn a profession whose practice I was completely ignorant of. I loved books, that was all" (*Very Rich Hours,* 12). La Librairie A. Monnier, as it was first called, opened on 15 November 1915, four years ahead of Shakespeare and Company. Monnier thought of her shop as an "ark," a little ship that sailed the literary waters of the Left Bank. Morrill Cody called Shakespeare and Company "the cradle of American literature" ("Shakespeare and Company—Paris," 1261). If Adrienne Monnier's hand was the one that guided *Le Navire d'Argent,* it was Sylvia Beach's that rocked the cradle.

Professional Interests and Personal Allegiances

Just as the terms in which Adrienne and Sylvia described their literary enterprises differed, so did the ways in which they thought of their professional service to literature. Adrienne Monnier worshipped books and served the word rather than the writer. Sylvia Beach defined her duty in other terms: she interested herself in both writers and readers, fostering the word by supporting and aiding both. Although many who have written about the two women have used religious metaphors to describe their efforts on behalf of literary Modernism, Monnier's French Catholicism should be carefully distinguished from Beach's American Presbyterianism. Monnier actually thought of herself as someone who had taken religious orders; she described herself as a *religieuse ancienne* (nun of other times), who "established a house . . . half convent and half farm" (*Very Rich Hours,* 13). Indeed, both in dress and demeanor she resembled a combination nun and farmwife. In the uniform of her work—a white blouse, waistcoat, and long gray skirt over which out of doors she wore a full-length cape—she resembled an abbess; in her wide girth, prodigious appetite, and hearty laughter, she might have been a provincial farm woman.

But if Adrienne was the abbess of the avant-garde, Sylvia was the patron saint of literary experimentalism. By contrast to Adrienne's quiet determination, Sylvia exuded energy and missionary zeal. Morrill Cody has described Shakespeare and Company as a "character store," with Sylvia Beach as the "primary character" ("Shakespeare and Company—Paris," 1262). She combined seriousness with "witty intelligence" and a sense of humor that kept herself and others laughing. In looks as in demeanor the two women differed greatly. Adrienne was an earthy, Rabelaisian figure. Sylvia was ascetic, combining the looks of a pre-Raphaelite androgyne with a distinctly American demeanor. If Adrienne appeared motherly,

Sylvia appeared boyish—even into her old age. If Adrienne indulged her gourmet appetite and enjoyed an occasional evening at the Folies Bergère, Sylvia denied her own impulse to pleasure, uninterested in "entertainment," new clothes, or any of the usual comforts of life. Describing the differences between the two friends, Noel Riley Fitch writes:

> Adrienne had a religious temperament—her ancestors were Catholic; she was drawn to Buddhism, her mother to Theosophy. Sylvia, though reared in an established church, was agnostic. If Adrienne was French and mystical, Sylvia was American and pragmatic. Sylvia bobbed her hair, never wore makeup, and insisted that her skirts be made short for ease of movement and built with pockets—a working person always needed pockets, she insisted. Whereas Adrienne spoke deliberately and philosophically, Sylvia was gifted with an understated and swift wit. She delighted in inventing puns, quoting comic verse, and playing practical jokes. If Adrienne was contemplative, Sylvia had a nervous, restless energy. (*Sylvia Beach*, 34–35)

The contrasts between Monnier and Beach were as important as the similar loves for literature and intellectual pursuits that united them personally and professionally. During their many years together, they adapted themselves to each other, Sylvia taking strength from Adrienne's quiet supportiveness, Adrienne finding adventure in Sylvia's enthusiasms.

Only a few months after the opening of Shakespeare and Company, a sudden death changed the relationship that had until then existed between Sylvia and Adrienne. Not a year after her marriage to Gustave Tronche, the administrator for publications of the *Nouvelle Revue Française*, Suzanne Bonnierre—who, Adrienne admitted, had never returned Adrienne's love in the measure that it was given—died suddenly. Commenting on Adrienne's relationship with this young woman, Jules Romains says that Suzanne "visibly submitted to her empire, received her spiritual orders, participated as best she could in that state of mastered exaltation in which literature sustained Adrienne. This companion separated from her rather quickly, in order to go back to those regions of life in which more ordinary emotions and duties prevail" (*Very Rich Hours*, 14–15). The shock of Suzanne's death, coming as it did upon Adrienne's loss of her in marriage, exposed certain tensions between Sylvia and Adrienne, most importantly a subtle competitiveness between their two establishments and a marked resistance on Sylvia's part to continuing as Adrienne's willing pupil in the bookselling business. Adrienne had a propensity for playing "the boss," as she herself admitted (*Very Rich Hours*, 14), her relationship with Suzanne having suffered from similar tensions.

Adrienne had already become a very fine businesswoman and developed her business skills as the years progressed. She later advised Sylvia on the publishing ventures of Shakespeare and Company. Since Adrienne consistently tried to protect Sylvia's financial interests in the bookshop,

James Joyce often found her a formidable influence, a woman sometimes capable of strengthening the resolve of the more acquiescent Sylvia. He bore Adrienne a grudging respect, however, referring to her in a letter to Harriet Weaver as Sylvia's "more intelligent partner" (*Sylvia Beach*, 322)—a remark that exposed the underside of the *politesse* he adopted with Sylvia. One senses, however, that in the early years of her professional relationship with Adrienne, Sylvia strained at Adrienne's determined guidance and set about defining her own terms for the literary enterprise that Shakespeare and Company was to become. Having introduced Sylvia to the literary world of the Left Bank, Adrienne had a difficult time letting Sylvia set her own course and make her own mistakes. Adrienne apparently wanted Sylvia to become an astute businesswoman, like herself. But such a dream was never to materialize, in part because Sylvia's generosity of spirit refused commercial constraints. Although both bookshops were intellectual rather than commercial successes, La Maison des Amis des Livres never skirted bankruptcy to quite the same degree as Shakespeare and Company—for reasons that were not entirely Sylvia Beach's fault.

Suzanne Bonnierre's death brought first a confrontation between the two women ("a sort of set-to," as Sylvia described it, *Sylvia Beach*, 53) whose resolution led to a deepening friendship. A disagreement that rested in professional concerns, the presumed reasons for this confrontation between the two women may well have masked the underlying tensions of their sexual attraction to each other. Sometime in the months following Suzanne's death, the two women became lovers. Suzanne Bonnierre's death may well have forced them to acknowledge their attraction for each other. Gertrude Stein, who might have sensed the tensions of sexual attraction in this relationship, posed the question in "Rich and poor in English," "do you care for Suzanne?" Within a few months Sylvia moved in with Adrienne in her apartment at 18, rue de l'Odéon, a residence she kept until 1937. As with other aspects of the relationship between Sylvia and Adrienne, however, the younger woman took the lead, probably seducing Sylvia to sexual love. Adrienne took the initiative in love as she had in professional pursuits.

We do not know whether Sylvia Beach had had earlier love affairs or whether she ever felt jealousy in the knowledge of Adrienne's earlier lesbian pursuits. It is possible that prior to her relationship with Adrienne, Sylvia was entirely naive about romantic love between women. Such relationships often begin at school, which she had not attended, but two earlier friendships—the first with Carlotta Welles and the second with Marian Mason, whom Sylvia accompanied to Florence for a year in 1907—might have offered occasions for her to discover her sexual interests. In her relationship with Monnier, Sylvia was silent on the subject of their shared sexual orientation, remaining reserved even with women friends—like Gertrude Stein and Alice Toklas—who were also lesbian. Adrienne Monnier was typically more open about her preferences, writing about her attractions to women, especially her relationship with Suzanne Bonnierre, with some degree of candor. Playing both wife and mother to Sylvia, she cooked for her, looked after her health, protected her interests, and took her into the bosom of a French family that loved Sylvia as their own daughter and helped heal the hurt that Sylvia had experienced with her own family. It is unclear whether Sylvia's parents knew the nature of her friendship with Adrienne, but Sylvia certainly took her sisters into her confidence, in particular Cyprian, who was also a lesbian.

Because neither Adrienne nor Sylvia wrote about their relationship, the intimate aspects of their friendship remain hidden by the natural discretion that marked both women. Letters written during their infrequent separations over the years reveal the depth of their commitment to each other, and Adrienne's letters in particular employ pet names for her adored Sylvia, urge her to protect her health, and express the desire to hold and kiss her. Sylvia's own prudence, developed from years of parsonage life, displayed itself in a discretion that masked sexual repression. Even her own sister Cyprian suggested that the relationship between Adrienne and Sylvia may not have been a sexual one, since she surmised that Sylvia was too repressed to express a latent sensuality.[2] For Adrienne—who was by everyone's admission a highly sensuous person—such an arrangement seems unlikely. There is some slim evidence for the sexual nature of their union in its early years (through 1921) in the relief Sylvia experienced from the debilitating headaches that she regularly suffered. These headaches may well have been the result of her efforts to repress certain aspects of her personality; later, under pressure from Joyce's demands and worries about the financial future of the shop, the headaches worsened. Sylvia had been educated to fear, repression, and pain by a mother who detested the physical nature of heterosexual love and who suffered terribly from the demands of her heterosexual union. In an unpublished portion of her memoirs, Beach wrote: "Whether from my puritan ancestry or puritanical upbringing—once when I was in my early teens my mother told me, 'never to let a man touch me'—I was always physically afraid of men. That is probably why I lived happily so many years with Adrienne" (*Sylvia Beach,* 367). Earlier Eleanor Beach had confided to her daughters that shortly after Cyprian was born, she began to sleep separately from her husband (*Sylvia Beach,* 21). As Noel Riley Fitch explains, Sylvia embodied the contradictions inherent in her early homelife, so that her spiritual libertarianism did not extend itself to the physical world, which was still for her marked by puritan morality and reserve (*Sylvia Beach,* 22).

If Sylvia suffered from apprehensions about physical lovemaking or puritan guilt concerning love between women, it seems likely that Adrienne Monnier—less dominated by contradictory values—worried little about the consequences of physical passion. By her own admission, Adrienne was enchanted with the pre-Raphaelites, an enchantment that "was mingled with that of Eros. I do not say this lightly, you are going to see why." The face of her first lover, Suzanne, "resembled one by Rossetti, the very one that he painted in all of his pictures, with a strongly modeled mouth and a long neck that swelled at the base—a beautiful face that might have been virile without the sweet animality of its look and its tresses. Was it possible for me not to be smitten with that face?" ("Memories of London," 315). Her later, and more constant, lover had a pre-Raphaelite figure whose slim, boyish quickness delighted Adrienne. It is far less easy to define the nature of role playing in the Beach-Monnier friendship (which was never described as a "marriage") than in other relationships between women of the Paris community, most notably the Stein-Toklas union. Although Sylvia often wore rather severe, practical clothes that might at the time have been thought to be "mannish," she—like Gertrude Stein—was particularly sensitive to fabric, choosing for her professional uniform tailored skirts and Edwardian-style velvet jackets accented with a silk foulard tied in a droopy bow. Like Gertrude Stein, Sylvia loved to work outdoors chopping wood; although she referred to herself as "he," she did not play the male in her relationship with Adrienne. She was the pursued object of Adrienne's affections, not the pursuing lover. And although Adrienne was the cook and housekeeper, who served as both mother and sister to her lover, she did not play the "wife" in any traditional way with Sylvia.

Perhaps because this relationship was founded on strong intellectual and professional commitments, joining lives of dedicated service to others, Adrienne and Sylvia were not forced into choosing between the two most prevalent models of contemporary lesbian sexuality. Their friendship was not modeled on heterosexual unions, neither was it given to male masquerade or "attic abandonment." Like the Stein-Toklas marriage, this friendship sought fulfillment in literary activity. Unlike the Stein-Toklas union, Beach and Monnier sought equality in their relationship, seeking support *from* each other through support *of* each other. Perhaps because both partners were strong feminists (Sylvia's Socialist feminism was adopted from the English suffragist movement, its politics not necessarily shared by Adrienne), women who had committed themselves to independent and mutually rewarding lives, this long friendship demonstrated an egalitarianism unusual in either homosexual or heterosexual relationships of the period. It was not marked by self-destructive behavior, neither was it given to self-indulgence. Indeed, this union might well serve as an alternative model to the more popular view of Paris lesbian experience, in particular the belief that by inheriting the dominant-submissive structure of heterosexual marriages, such companionate relationships were doomed to unhappiness. Neither of these women lived out in adult life the patterns established by the parental relationships of their childhoods: Adrienne Monnier avoided duplicating the rigid conventions of French marriages and Sylvia Beach openly resisted repeating the behavior of either of her parents. This friendship succeeded, perhaps, because it established itself on equality and mutual esteem.

Although there is evidence that Sylvia thought of herself professionally in masculine terms, often referring to herself as a "tired businessman" or a "tired working man" to suggest the pressures under which she labored in her professional life, there is no indication that she "supported" Adrienne or saw herself as head of their personal household. To the contrary, Sylvia seemed to rely on Adrienne's expertise in financial affairs, to be in constant need of her support, both financial and psychological. Sylvia had found her earlier war work in the Tourraine region of France invigorating, allowing her to wear khaki culottes and a pith helmet over her bobbed hair. As Noel Riley Fitch notes, the pictures of Sylvia from this period show "a woman who is brave, free, and proud of the work she has been doing." But the war delayed her choice of a career "limited by the options tradition dictated to her" (*Sylvia Beach,* 31). Ironically, for Adrienne, who had stayed in Paris during these years, the war had offered opportunities she might not otherwise have so easily come by. Thus she was from the beginning able to serve as a role model for Sylvia, to direct her friend's interests along paths she had already traversed. Depressed at the prospect of a future that was "useless" by comparison to her war efforts, Sylvia found in Adrienne an image of usefulness, saw in her the model of an alternative womanhood. But Sylvia would never become as self-assured as Adrienne; neither could she endure the solitude so essential to Adrienne's self-composure.

Intellectual Contrasts

To a far greater degree than Adrienne, Sylvia pushed herself beyond the limits of her physical and psychological strengths in order to make Shakespeare and Company the center of expatriate literary life that it became under her direction. Unlike Adrienne, Sylvia was never able to subordinate the needs of her customers and friends to her own needs; she lacked Adrienne's ability to separate the personal from the professional, to keep her customers' demands in check, to set priorities for the bookshop over the personal concerns of her friends. Sylvia detested confrontation, would avoid it at all costs, while Adrienne often used confrontation successfully, placing the stamp of her personality and intellect on all her professional transactions. Able to argue passionately for the rights and privileges of others, Sylvia was far less forthcoming about her own situation and, consequently, was taken advantage of by her clientele. For many, Sylvia's refusal to separate the personal from the professional was the mark of her genius. Writing in tribute to Beach after her death, Malcolm Cowley comments that for him "the truly fascinating chapters of *Shakespeare and Company* [were] those in which this publisher describes her most unbusinesslike relations with her author and divinity [James Joyce]" ("When a Young American," 58). Sylvia's difficulties with Joyce may well have made interesting reading in her memoirs (and many wished she had been more candid than she dared); more often, however, readers have equated Sylvia's reticence in setting limits on Joyce's demands with weakness. Others—including Joyce himself—assumed that her silent acquiescence masked hostility. However one reads the history of Sylvia's personal commitment to the patrons of Shakespeare and Company, it is clear that her industrious cheerfulness was the result of an iron-willed determination to repress anything that might undermine the public identity she had so carefully assumed.

The enormous differences in background and upbringing, in religious and secular education, account for both the attraction of Beach and Monnier to each other and their ensuing tensions. While commentators often suggest the significant physical differences between the two women, less often acknowledged are the even more important differences of intellect and taste. Unlike Sylvia, Adrienne had received a complete, highly structured, and demanding French education. She knew both Latin and French, had studied philosophy and mathematics, knew thoroughly the history of Europe and Asia, and had had her tastes moulded by the rigidly patriarchal system of the French *collège*. Sylvia's education, like that of many of her female expatriate counterparts, had been uneven and haphazard. She learned French, Italian, and Spanish on her own and constructed her own reading program during the years she should have been at school. Like Virginia Woolf, she was essentially self-taught. She learned the necessary mathematics to keep the accounts at Shakespeare and Company and to juggle the complicated rates of exchange on book purchases, but, like Virginia Woolf, she never was certain of the multiplication and division tables and often resorted to counting on her fingers. She found bookkeeping burdensome, never developing anything more than a rudimentary accounting system that amounted to little more than recording lists of orders and sales. No prices were marked on the books for sale in the shop; at the time of sale Sylvia worked out the price based on the current English or American exchange rate. Her business arrangements with the several customers for whom she served as banker were equally simple. T. S. Eliot, a banker as well as a poet, admitted surprise at Joyce's dependence on Sylvia for such matters, claiming that he "never knew" what "the financial arrangements may have been between those two" ("Miss Sylvia Beach," 10).

While the bases of logic and the formal expression of literary and philosophical principles in writing became consistent and dominant features of Adrienne Monnier's verbal and written expression, carried over from her school years to her adult life, Sylvia Beach was never able to conduct an ordered critical argument. Her comments on the people she met, like her analysis of the books they wrote, were anecdotal, suggestive, and exceedingly charming. Like Alice Toklas, Sylvia was a mimic, an excellent storyteller, and was able to use both French and English with enormous facility. It was just such qualities of mind and spirit that attracted Adrienne to her:

> This young American displayed an original and most attaching personality. She spoke French fluently with an accent that was more English than American; to tell the truth, it was not so much an accent as an energetic and incisive way of pronouncing words . . . words never failed her; on occasion she deliberately invented them, she proceeded then by an adaptation of English, by a mixture or extension of French vocables, all that with an exquisite sense of our language. Her finds were generally so happy, so charmingly funny, that they at once came into usage—our usage—as if they had always existed; one could not keep from repeating them, and one tried to imitate them. To sum it up, this young American had a great deal of humor, let us say more: she was humor itself. (quoted in *Sylvia Beach*, 100)

Maurice Saillet, executor of Adrienne Monnier's estate, has catalogued a number of "Sylvia-isms" in French, expressions that combine French and English or that transport well-known French expressions into a new context. Many of these invented forms expressed Sylvia's ability to survive in difficult circumstances: *nous ne sommes pas à vendre* (we are not for sale, are not selling ourselves), in regard to the perilous state of Shakespeare and Company's finances; *jusqu'à tous à terre* (until all have fallen, a fight until the end) suggests her determination against all odds ("Mots et locutions de Sylvia," 78, 81).

The lack of formal education may well have been an advantage for Sylvia Beach. It allowed her to find literature on her own, to learn languages in their natural setting rather than in the classroom, to substitute wit and inventiveness for more studied intellectual poses. But the lack of traditional and disciplined education, against which she had rebelled as a young girl, seemed to bother her in later years. Corresponding with her editor about her memoirs, Beach wrote: "About my education, the less said the better: I ain't had none: never went to school and wouldn't have learned anything if I had went. You will have to copy what goes for T. S. Eliot: say I have degrees from all those places, same as him" (*Sylvia Beach*, 25). Making her untutored condition a situation for humor, Beach often mimicked herself.

But it was not merely that Adrienne possessed a traditional French education while Sylvia had escaped the American equivalent that accounted for such differences in quality of mind. Sylvia came to an interest in French literature and in the Gallic mind by living in Paris. She discovered her first French literature in bookstalls along the *quais* of the Seine and helped organize poetry readings and musical evenings for American students when her father was a pastor in the Latin Quarter. Adrienne, on the other hand, was passionately interested in and well read in American literature without ever once visiting the United States. Her earliest conversations with Sylvia centered on furthering her knowledge of English-language literature—a language she could neither read nor speak—and she depended on Sylvia to open up new literary works to her: "It is not only the brilliance of a great interpreter that can correct the imperfection of a translated work, but also the ardor of an impassioned commentator. So it was that I could enjoy Eliot's poetry through the spirit of Sylvia; she revealed it to me just as she revealed *Ulysses* to me" ("A Visit to T. S. Eliot," *Very Rich Hours*, 201). As a young woman, Adrienne wanted to be a poet; as a mature woman, she continued to write poetry and essays that combined criticism and fiction.

The selection of essays from Adrienne Monnier's various literary reviews suggests an interest not only in the people of her time (Reverdy, Breton, Cocteau, Gide, Joyce), but a facility in analyzing their works and an interest in the aesthetic and cultural developments they helped create. These essays address a formidable range of topics, from the circus to film, from art appreciation to literary criticism, from social and political concerns to attitudes toward women. Monnier's essays combine anecdote with analysis; they address themselves to the unseen intellectual elements of daily events in the bookshop; they analyze the political and literary realities of France, the reading and writing habits of the French, political issues such as war and anti-Semitism, individual works by Shakespeare as well as Shakespeare in performance, and the role of women in European society. In her *Gazette*, Adrienne Monnier was able to create a fictional country—Odéonia—and to populate it with the figures, real and imagined, of her years there. Her sketches and occasional essays are the French counterpart to similar efforts by Virginia Woolf to record the literary and social pulse of her time.

Adrienne Monnier's essays begin in anecdote and extend themselves into critical analysis and philosophic speculation. Her letters and journals continue this effort, whereas Sylvia's correspondence—apart from chatty letters to her mother or to Adrienne—stays firmly within the demands of her professional commitment. Perhaps because she lacked the time, Sylvia did not keep a journal or write on a regular basis. But there is also a suggestion that she felt uncomfortable in the writing situation. Sylvia's letters give the impression of an efficient businesswoman pressed for time; she shows herself to be an active person, but not at all a contemplative one. Most of her business correspondence is little more than acknowledgment of payments or announcements for book orders. Adrienne, on the other hand, found the leisure to recount events, to analyze circumstances, and to reflect on the nature of her profession. Adrienne carefully considered avant-garde thought, analyzed the literary movements in which she had engaged herself, and scrutinized the intellectual abilities of the participants in Modernism. Adrienne's analyses of her contemporaries, like those of Janet Flanner, are both lucid and humorous and have been proven correct. Writing of André Gide in her diary of 2 September 1921, she said: "We also had a discussion about the influence [Gide] has on the young writers. Sylvia thinks that it is he who influences the new generation most. I do not think so. His influence is more superficial than real; they acknowledge it all the more because little trace of it will be found in their works. Besides, it is rather *chic* to like Gide" ("With Gide at Hyères," 94–95). Adrienne's opinion coincided with Flanner's on the subject of Gide, both women opposing the contemporary assessment of his literary stature and influence. Upon his death, Monnier wrote a moving eulogy for him for the newspaper *Combat,* a memoir in which she carefully sidestepped the issue of his genius: "Posterity will know better than ourselves the degree of genius that his work attains, but we know that he had the genius of Literature, that he was in his own home there, that he possessed there a discernment that is perhaps without precedent. Never have we seen such a master for apprentice writers as he was—as much through the teaching of his books as through what he gave from person to person with an extreme kindness." This tribute left open the possibility that Gide might influence younger generations, while her more personal speculations suggested that his contributions would be lost to later audiences. Thus far in literary history, there are few traces of his influence.

Monnier tacitly acknowledged Gide's powerful literary presence in her journals, however, frequently mentioning him and addressing her opinions to him. In July 1939, she commented in her *Gazette* on the publication by Gallimard of Gide's *Journal* (in which Gide records Proust's confession of his homosexuality). She looked for references to herself, discovering that on 16 October 1926 she had told Gide that she disliked his recently published *Les faux-monnayeurs,* asserting that "the fundamental coldness and *unkindness* that this book reveal[ed] must be the basis of my nature." Gide commented, "I do not know what to say, what to think. Whatever criticism is addressed to me, I always acquiesce" (quoted in *Very Rich Hours,* 476). For her part, Adrienne noted, "the devil if I remember that. That October 16, 1926, I was not really too wicked. Unkindness—I knew then perhaps what it is. Do I know now?" ("Unkindness," 174). In April 1942, she published in *Le Figaro Littéraire* an open letter to Gide on the subject of the young. Perhaps still thinking of his possible influence on the next generation of writers, Monnier analyzed the work of Gide's contemporaries (Joyce, Valéry, Faulkner, Prévert) and described the altered looks and moods of contemporary youth. This letter, like several others she wrote during the war, was addressed to those living in the Free Zone, its tone suggesting somehow that those who stayed behind in Paris were truly in another country, one little understood by those residing in the relative safety of Vichy. Her essay described the youth not yet old enough to serve in the war, those who might live to discover the influence of Gide, assuring him that "as for youself, dear great Friend, do not doubt that they love you as intensely as ever. Our young people run all over Paris in order to find your *Journal,* which has been out of stock for about a year" ("A Letter to André Gide about the Young," 410). The tone of this letter is particularly difficult to assess, perhaps due to the necessary precautions of passing under the censor's wary eye. The letter simultaneously asked Gide to take comfort that the young search for copies of the out-of-stock *Journal* and reinforced the reality of his estrangement from Paris. Monnier's relationship with Gide was always ambivalent, this letter revealing (perhaps in ways she could not acknowledge) the depth of that ambivalence.

A woman capable of forming almost instantaneous—and asserted—assessments of those who entered her shop, Adrienne Monnier's powers of observation were well developed. She claimed that, allowed to observe unaware the approach of someone unknown to her shop, she could "know him in his truth." She maintained that in such an unselfconscious moment "he reveals all the good will with which he is endowed, that is to say, the degree to which he is accessible to the world, what he can give and receive, the exact rapport that exists between himself and other men" ("La Maison," 69). André Breton, among others, revealed himself to her in that first unguarded moment and was never afterward able to recover her loyalty and friendship.

She was immediately antagonistic, not only to the literary movement he was to head, but to the man himself. Taking Breton as the subject for an essay, Monnier examined the principles upon which the Surrealist movement in literature based itself and the differences between the poetic stance of Breton and his mentor, Apollinaire. She opposed the philosophy that undergirded the movement, even as she made the official organ of the Dadaist movement, Breton's journal *Littérature,* part of her lending library and encouraged discussion among members of the group around the large table in her shop. Adrienne may well have sensed the underlying misogyny of Surrealism, a subject Anne Chisholm discusses at some length in her biography of Nancy Cunard, who was—briefly—Louis Aragon's mistress:

> Apart from personal difficulties, there were other reasons why having Nancy as his recognized mistress cannot have been easy for Aragon. Women played a small part in the Surrealist scheme of things. For all their desire to live unconventionally and to shock the bourgeoisie, the Surrealists had highly conventional, even traditional, ideas about women. No woman writer or painter emerged to join their activities or sign their manifestos. They found it thrilling to visit brothels and befriend prostitutes but at the same time there was a strong romantic, almost puritanical streak in their sexual attitudes. The ideal was an exclusive, reciprocated love with the perfect woman. Foreign women were fashionable in the group, perhaps because they tended to be more independent and available than middle- or upper-class Frenchwomen; but Nancy was all too obviously someone, a person in her own right, with more money and freedom of movement than seemed safe or appropriate. Breton in particular disapproved of Nancy and feared her influence on Aragon. She represented the rich, fashionable world that he despised. (*Nancy Cunard*, 150)

The attitudes toward women that marked Surrealism suggest something more than the accidental alliance of literary movement and personal behavior. Adrienne Monnier would have been sensitive to the "puritanical streak" in these sexual attitudes as well as the efforts to manipulate women. Like Sylvia, however, she gave encouragement and support even to those literary movements to which she was unsympathetic and was often called upon carefully and tactfully to negotiate the territory between rival factions or competing philosophies.

The Joyce Years

Once her loyalties were engaged, Adrienne's commitment knew no boundaries. When Sylvia told Adrienne in 1921 that Joyce had asked her to publish *Ulysses*, following his frustrated efforts to get it published in England and America, Adrienne most enthusiastically endorsed this venture. She encouraged Sylvia to take the risk in publication and gave her necessary support during the difficult months that followed. In these months, Sylvia's time was almost entirely devoted to Joyce's financial and publication difficulties. She organized the postal and banking services that her bookshop undertook on Joyce's behalf, spent her nights reading proofs of the text and her days dealing with Darantière, the Dijon printer. As soon as Valery Larbaud began reading *Ulysses* (Sylvia having loaned him copies of the *Little Review* serial publication), he was taken with the idea of a

French translation, for which he would become the official translator. Adrienne wrote that she too was taken with the idea for such a project, offering to publish it under the sign of La Maison des Amis des Livres. The first fragments of the text were not published until 1924, in *Commerce,* a journal whose administration Adrienne had undertaken at great cost to her health. She too suffered from editing and administration labors on Joyce's behalf, and when it became clear in 1931 that Sylvia's health had been broken by the demands of publication and that Shakespeare and Company was on the verge of bankruptcy because of Joyce's continued loans and advances against royalties, Adrienne wrote to Joyce asking him to release Sylvia from her labors.

Until publication of Noel Riley Fitch's biography of Sylvia Beach, it was not possible to track the financial history of Shakespeare and Company. Although Richard Ellmann's biography of James Joyce suggested his state of continual need and Beach's continuing generosity, that biography did not make a meticulous study of Joyce's finances or of Beach's. Fitch, however, undertook to give an accounting of the Joyce-Beach finances, and the results demonstrate incontrovertibly Joyce's indebtedness to Beach. In 1929, she paid him "between 7,000 and 10,000 francs a month on *Ulysses* royalties," and she negotiated "large advances for portions of *Work in Progress,* for the second German and the second French editions of *Ulysses,* for Polish and Czech translations of *Ulysses,* and for productions of *Exiles* in Berlin and Milan" (*Sylvia Beach,* 301). Nonetheless, Joyce was building up greater indebtedness to Shakespeare and Company—a record 13,000 francs per month by February 1930. Sylvia's business in that year following the stock market crash was on the verge of bankruptcy, and her health, weakened from worry and overwork, was on the point of collapse. But the letter Adrienne wrote to Joyce as a result of this crisis did nothing to ameliorate Sylvia's situation. Indeed, it may have made it worse. By summer 1931, the finances of Shakespeare and Company were so precarious that Sylvia was forced to dismiss her assistant, sell her car, and give up plans for a vacation. By February 1932, she was forced to release all the Shakespeare and Company publishing claims to *Ulysses.*

Joyce was apparently upset by the letter, but did not act upon it. He assumed that it derived from Adrienne's jealousy over his attentions to Sylvia rather than from Adrienne's unhappiness at his continued dependence. In this year both bookshops were facing financial difficulties due to the fall of the French franc. The problems were made worse for Shakespeare and Company by the effects of the stock market crash of 1929, which not only devalued the American dollar, but took large numbers of Sylvia's clients back to America. Because Sylvia certainly would not have confronted Joyce on the matter, he might have claimed to be unaware of the severity of the financial constraints on Shakespeare and Company, unaware that she was in danger of losing the bookshop. He appeared, however, to be fully aware of the emotional and physical toll his demands were putting on her. On various occasions he wrote joking apologies or made teasing mention of his constant needs. On 17 March 1927, for instance, he wrote: "It is a grand thing, so I am told, to be a 'genius' but I do not think I have the right to plague and pester you night, noon and morning for money, money, and money. You are altogether overworked without my rapping at the door. I am almost inclined to let the bailiffs in and watch them walk off with the furniture and animals in the ark" (*James Joyce*, 651). As this letter testifies, Joyce was indeed a genius at turning a gesture of sympathy for Sylvia into yet another request for her help. By spring 1931, Sylvia was taking out loans from friends and from her mother and members of her family in order to pay Joyce's escalating debts.

According to Maria Jolas, the letter Adrienne sent Joyce was intended to constitute a *rupture finale*. In it, Monnier began by suggesting that André Gide might suppose Joyce indifferent to success and money, but that she and Sylvia knew better, and that they had been put upon in order to assure his financial and literary success:

> What Gide doesn't know—and like the sons of Noah we put a veil over it—is that you are, on the contrary, very concerned about success and money. You wish others also to go the limit [for you]; you lead them by rough stages to some Dublingrad or other which they're not interested in, or rather, you try to lead them.
>
> In Paris rumor has it that you are spoiled, that we have ruined you with overwhelming praise and that you no longer know what you're doing. And there isn't one of your Seventy, beginning with [Paul] Léon—St. Peter, who doesn't acknowledge everywhere, at all times, that he understands nothing of Anna Livia.
>
> My personal opinion is that you know perfectly well what you are doing in literature, and that you are quite right to do it, especially if it entertains you, life isn't so funny in this vale of tears, as Mrs Bloom says, but it's folly to wish to make money at any cost with your new work. I won't say you can't make any, everything is possible, but it is most unlikely. The three pamphlets which have been published by Crosby Gaige, Harry Crosby, and Kahane have scarcely sold more than two-thirds or at most three-fourths. . . .
>
> We haven't the slightest desire, Sylvia and I, to become associated with Kahane. Times are hard, and the worst isn't over. We're travelling now third class and soon we'll be riding the rods. (*James Joyce*, 651–652)[3]

The tone and rhetoric of this letter suggest the degree of anger that Joyce's behavior toward Sylvia had elicited from Adrienne. The letter is an extraordinary document, perhaps the only one of its kind in Joyce's correspondence. Always employing a mode of extreme gentility with women, in particular with "Miss Beach" and "Mademoiselle Monnier," Joyce was famous for securing the continued assistance and financial support of women who believed in his genius. Following the publication of *Ulysses*, Joyce's genius was so admired, his personal problems and physical sufferings so well known, that none would have dared breach his defenses. That Adrienne Monnier undertook to do so, that she failed in her effort, that she engendered the wrath of Joyce's friends and hangers on, suggests powerful motivations behind the composition of the letter. Did this letter expose the "Sapphic heart," as Maria Jolas suggests, or were there other reasons for its blunt accusations and bitter rhetoric?

Adrienne Monnier's letter and the circumstances surrounding Sylvia Beach's renunciation of her publication rights to Joyce's text have been variously interpreted. Like much else about the relationship between Joyce and Beach, these incidents are clouded with ambiguity. Given to reticence and indirection, the two principals required intermediaries who had strong allegiance to the individuals on whose behalf they intervened. Joyce's own personal situation was fraught with worry over illness, and his energies were devoted to the composition of *Finnegans Wake* in these years. During 1932 and 1933, Joyce was estranged from the two women who had provided his most consistent and solid financial support, Harriet Weaver and Sylvia Beach. Although Joyce and Beach were later to establish an *entente cordiale,* the relationship never recovered its early enthusiasm. Joyce discovered other, younger supporters, and Sylvia slipped into less public roles, concentrating her efforts on the bookshop and renewing old acquaintances. Meanwhile, Joyce felt that Beach had mistreated him and convinced a number of his friends that she had. For her part, Beach was forced to swallow her anger and hurt, a situation that made the writing of her memoirs, even thirty years later, very difficult for her.

An understanding of this incident and the reasons Beach and Monnier withdrew their support of Joyce depends less on the "Sapphic heart" than on drawing careful distinctions between the kinds of investment that each woman had in the "Joyce enterprise" and their quite distinct views of the contributions their bookshops and their publishing efforts made to the intellectual life of the Left Bank. Adrienne Monnier had the advantage of being French and working among the French. The success or failure of her bookshop was not tied to any particular resident community in Paris; it could—and did—survive all manner of economic hardships, changes in governments, states of war, and shifts in literary tastes. Shakespeare and Company was from the outset in a far more precarious position, dependent on an essentially transient community. The aims of the American bookshop were different from those of La Maison des Amis des Livres just as the interests and special talents of Sylvia Beach were significantly different from those of Adrienne Monnier. In part because their lives, like their bookshops, were so much a part of each other, the individual contributions of these two women have never been carefully distinguished. The differences between them are nonetheless apparent, most obviously in the kinds of things they wrote about themselves and their literary experiences.

Sylvia Beach in Retrospect

It has often been claimed that Sylvia Beach would not be remembered today had it not been for her courage in undertaking the publication of *Ulysses*. It was Joyce's text that brought her fame and—many thought—fortune. Without his book, she would have remained what she was before and after his arrival in her life—a Left Bank librarian and bookseller. That she herself was convinced of the truth of such an assessment is evidenced in *Shakespeare and Company,* her memoir of the Paris years. Little more than a catalogue of anecdotes about the now-famous writers who frequented the bookshop, Beach's memoir is disappointing, most particularly because it is so successfully self-effacing that we are left with little sense of the woman who played such a pivotal role in Modernism. Unlike the memoirs written by others who experienced these years (most of them written by men), *Shakespeare and Company* does not make Sylvia Beach the heroine of her own story. Indeed, the memoir is not of her, but of the bookshop, and its title suggests the patriarchal literary heritage of England rather than a woman's contribution to an American expatriate literary enterprise. For reasons that are not clear, the memoir begins by tracing the clerical history of her father's family, perhaps suggesting Sylvia's need to identify with him. Its opening pages discuss Sylvia's family members—father, mother, sisters—and the balance of the book focuses on the personalities that frequented Shakespeare and Company. Beach employed this indirect autobiographical technique in order to deflect interest from herself. She was always a bit outside her own story, seeing the experiences it recorded from an angle. *Shakespeare and Company* gives little sense of the person responsible for the events.

Other remembrances of Sylvia Beach—most notably those in the special issue of *Mercure de France* in homage to her—portray quite a different person, one of great strength, wit, self-determination, a woman given to enthusiastic passions and intense loyalties. Marianne Moore writes: "Sylvia Beach,—how do justice to one with impact so great as hers, and unfailing delicacy? Who never allowed logic to persuade her to regret over-charity to a beneficiary; ardent, restive, forever exerting herself, to advantage and give pleasure to one who had, as she felt, benefitted her. During sixty years and more, this has been my impression of her" ("How do justice . . . ," 13). Bryher, one of Beach's closest friends, captures subtleties of Sylvia's character unremarked by other commentators. Returning to the rue de l'Odéon apartment after Sylvia's death, Bryher feels Sylvia's presence there: "There is not an object that is not soaked in memories and I realise (half consciously, perhaps, as in a dream) that she, more than many of my friends, stamped a strong and living sense of her being upon inanimate objects. What will be their future now? However well librarians or friends may care for them, what will they be but wood, canvas or paper, away from these three rooms?" ("For Sylvia," 17). Bryher suggests Beach's ability to make books "live." In part, Beach was able to rescue books from the "inanimate" because she was so committed to those who wrote and read them. Bryher's comments surprise us with their emphasis on the "strong and living sense" of Beach that is retained after her death. Our impressions of her, filtered through her own memoir and through the memories of others, have been of a woman somehow lacking the stamp of personality. Her self-effacing attitude, her discretion, her service to others have often been read as weakness or reticence in the face of the overpowering egotism, for instance, of a Joyce or Stein. Bryher's comments restore the luster to that faded photograph, suggest a woman of strong will and determined energy, a woman sure of her own sense of "self." Bryher's memoir also makes clear that Joyce was not the only one for whom Sylvia served as "a shield . . . at so many difficult moments" (19). Her energy, intelligence, discretion, and kindness were given freely to all who frequented her shop, and there is ample evidence that her contributions to literature went far beyond her efforts on behalf of Joyce.

If Adrienne Monnier was suited to her chosen profession by her own literary interests and a continuing desire both to read and to write, Sylvia Beach possessed special characteristics of personality and intellect that allowed her to make a unique contribution to the Modernist movement. Janet Flanner's memorial essay to her suggests that the reasons for Beach's tremendous success as librarian, bookseller, and literary diplomat may be found in the fact that she was not "literary" in any traditional sense. Beach made a profession of being an "amateur" bookseller and publisher:

> Sylvia herself did not have a literary mind or much literary taste though in time a certain sense of literature rubbed off into her from the people around her. What she instinctively recognized and was attracted to was merely literary genius or flashes and fractions of it, or of tremendous great talent—men like Joyce, Hemingway and T. S. Eliot or Gide and Valery. . . . Sylvia had a vigorous clear mind, an excellent memory, a tremendous respect for books as

civilizing objects and was really a remarkable librarian. She loved the printed word and books in long rows. ("The Great Amateur Publisher," 48–49)

On the surface, Flanner's assessment is not a particularly complimentary one. It reveals a woman comfortable with "books in long rows" on the shelves rather than one who—like Adrienne Monnier—wanted to feel the weight of the book in her hand as she read. Sylvia appeared to value books for their social uses (as "civilizing objects"), to value writers for their "flashes and fractions" of genius, to let literature rub itself "into her from the people around her." Sylvia's interest was clearly in the people who visited her bookshop, whose lives and anecdotes fill her memoir; she directed herself to analysis of their personalities and qualities of mind rather than to analysis of the literary works they wrote. Beach is present in this story only as a *raconteuse*. The central portion of the story she tells belongs to Joyce and his modern Odyssey. Beach's history of literary Paris makes it clear that she owed a great deal to James Joyce and that he owed little to her: "I understood from the first that, working with or for James Joyce, the pleasure was mine—an infinite pleasure; the profits were for him. All that was available from his work, and I managed to keep it available, was his" (*Shakespeare and Company,* 201). Shakespeare and Company published eleven printings of *Ulysses,* amounting to total sales of several thousand copies.

Joyce himself placed a higher value on Sylvia's contribution to his literary reputation than she herself did: "All she ever did was to make me a present of the ten best years of her life," he told Maria Jolas ("The Joyce I Knew," 86). To the same friends to whom he admitted his indebtedness to her, he let it be known that Sylvia had volunteered to publish *Ulysses* for him. Yet a portion of her self-censored memoirs reveals that Joyce had asked her to publish his book: "I accepted with enthusiasm Joyce's suggestion that I publish his book" (Fitch, *Sylvia Beach,* 78). One day after Sylvia had made her decision, in conference with the woman Joyce referred to as "Shakespeare and Company's adviser," she wrote her mother the news, adding in a postscript: "*Ulysses* means thousands of dollars in publicity for me." Indeed, for many years commentators on the Joyce-Beach publishing operation have assumed that Beach made money on the publication, if not in actual royalties from the sale of books then from the publicity it brought her shop. The legend has been virtually impossible to dispel, and even those who do not believe the myth that Sylvia Beach made fantastic sums on the publication of Joyce's novel think that she would have had no right to any royalties. Beach's own memoirs confuse the issue, as they continue yet another popular myth—that Joyce received $45,000 from Random House on the sale of the American rights (see Jolas, "The Joyce I Knew," 86). Beach believed him to have received that amount, none of which he shared with her, and her comment, "I know how desperately he needed the money," suggests a charity on her part that may not have existed at the time: "As for my personal feelings, well, one is not at all proud of them, and they should be promptly dumped when they no longer serve a purpose" (*Shakespeare and Company,* 205). In fact, as the expurgated portions of the *Shakespeare and Company* memoir make clear, Beach was bitterly angry over Joyce's treatment of her, but she was forced to repress rather than voice her anger, a repression that cost her painful migraine headaches and divided her against herself. Adrienne, who had taken a more direct approach with Joyce, now refused to see him and drew Sylvia back into a life among their French friends in Paris (*Sylvia Beach,* 320).

Until 9 December 1930, six months before the letter from Adrienne Monnier to Joyce, a contract for the publication of *Ulysses* had never existed. As Sylvia stated in her memoirs: "Contracts didn't seem important to either Joyce or myself. At the time I published *Ulysses,* I did mention the subject, but Joyce wouldn't hear of a contract and I didn't care, so I never brought up the question again" (*Shakespeare and Company,* 204). Almost ten years after the first edition of *Ulysses* was printed in Paris, a contract was drawn up at Joyce's insistence with Sylvia, giving her "exclusive right of printing and selling" *Ulysses.* This contract included a clause that the publisher would "abandon the right to said Work if, after due consideration such a step should be deemed advisable by the Author and the Publisher in the interests of the AUTHOR, in which case the right to publish said Work *shall be purchased from the Publisher at the price set by herself*" (*Sylvia Beach,* 308; emphasis mine). On the basis of this contract, she asked the representative of Curtis Brown in New York for a payment of $25,000 to Shakespeare and Company, a 20 percent royalty to Joyce and an additional $5,000 cash payment to Joyce upon signing the contract. Meanwhile, she signed a contract in Paris with a German firm, the Albatross Press, which gave her 25 percent royalties on all sales of *Ulysses* for the next five years and 7½ percent for life. Because no future European editions of *Ulysses* were published, she received nothing on this second contract. The requested $25,000 on the American sales was never paid—in fact, the request was never formally made. Working through his friend Padraic Colum, Joyce eventually forced Sylvia to give up any claim to her publishing rights, invoking the "interests of the AUTHOR" clause. Once she had abandoned her rights, the Random House American edition of *Ulysses* proceeded. Sylvia Beach resigned as Joyce's publisher almost exactly ten years after handing him his first copy of *Ulysses;* the "thousands of dollars" of publicity she had hoped the publication might bring her bookshop never materialized. Although it is impossible to say with any precision how much Sylvia earned as a publisher, it seems unlikely that she earned more than a few hundred dollars over a decade.

Les Amis des Livres in the 1930s

It is ironic, then, that Adrienne, who had rebelled against the toll that the publication of *Ulysses* had taken on Sylvia's health and the financial state of Shakespeare and Company, should herself have received a cash payment for the French translation of Joyce's *Ulysses*. In fact, the payment of 22,000 francs to Adrienne from Gallimard allowed her to pay outstanding debts and to undertake the publication of her *Gazette,* a project that she had had to delay for almost a decade due to lack of funds. The sale of the French *Ulysses* saved Adrienne's business in a year when her outstanding debts were 3,000 francs, and she calculated that after twenty years in the bookselling business she earned 1,500 francs a month on the average ("Number One," 149). In 1921, Sylvia had calculated that Shakespeare and Company earned a total of $100 for the entire year. The financial crises that both women faced in the early 1930s were due less, however, to any claims that Joyce might have made on them than to the effects of the American stock market crash. Sylvia's business was immediately hurt, since the dollar was devalued against the French franc, forcing many Americans to return home. It took almost three years for the more general economic depression that affected all of Europe to jeopardize La Maison des Amis des Livres, and when it did Adrienne was saved by the payment from Gallimard.

Although the first and last customers at Shakespeare and Company were the French, it was hardly possible for Sylvia's bookshop to survive without her American clientele. Shakespeare and Company's margin of profit was so slim that any reduction in the numbers of customers immediately put the shop into financial jeopardy. Although Sylvia had become a valued member of the Left Bank literary community, negotiating the distance between the expatriate community and the resident Paris population, her bookshop had always been dependent on a resident, English-speaking population. In the years when all of her energies were consumed by attention to the publication of Joyce's text and worries about his health and financial status, she was torn between her loyalties to him and the demands of the bookshop. Indeed, she eventually ended her relationship with Joyce out of concern for Shakespeare and Company. If it was unclear to her at the time that Joyce's demands represented a drain on her resources rather than a boon to them, it is even less clear today. Her earlier hopes that a professional association between author and publisher might accrue to the benefit of Shakespeare and Company seem to have misfired in ways she could not have foreseen in March 1921, when she agreed to become Joyce's publisher. A decade later, however, as expatriate Americans left for home from the Gare du Nord, Sylvia was brutally reminded that Shakespeare and Company had always depended on the presence and goodwill of expatriate Americans and English.

The clientele of La Maison des Amis des Livres however, had consistently been the resident French population in Paris. Like Sylvia, Adrienne had spurred interest in her bookshop by arranging poetry readings there, providing occasions to bring the work of both unknown and well-known writers to public attention, and by publishing a journal, writing essays for Paris publications, and later giving radio talks. The publication of the French *Ulysse*, then, was only one of several publishing ventures in which Monnier had interested herself. Alone, it did not serve radically to alter the direction of her professional life or the quality of intellectual life in her bookshop. Apart from *Ulysse*, Adrienne had involved herself from the summer of 1924 with the literary review *Commerce*, sponsored by Marguerite Caetani (the Princesse de Bassiano), an American who had married an Italian prince. The journal was born of the princesse's salon (which met in various Paris restaurants and at her home in Versailles), and it filled an enormous need among French intellectuals following the war. *Commerce* published the first fragments of the French *Ulysse*, overseen by Adrienne Monnier, who had to resign her position as administrator of the journal in August 1924, due to overwork. Monnier's exhaustion was due not to Joyce's demands on her time, but rather to Léon-Paul Fargue's strange working habits. He claimed he could contribute poems to the review only by dictating them at night, after Adrienne had spent a long and fatiguing day in the bookshop.

A year later, Monnier began her own review, *Le Navire d'Argent* (the Silver Ship), which took its name from the emblem of the city of Paris. Valery Larbaud's opening essay, a tribute to the way in which Paris survived the war, explains the title of the review and extends the metaphor of the city as a ship. During the year of its publication, *Le Navire d'Argent* included poetry by Adrienne, a translation of Eliot's "The Lovesong of J. Alfred Prufrock" by Adrienne and Sylvia, and, in addition to avant-garde writing by various French intellectuals, a section devoted to critical comments and clippings from reviews of important works in Paris newspapers and journals, a bibliography of French translations of foreign-language literatures (beginning with English), and a "Gazette" in which Adrienne wrote about the people she knew and the events she witnessed and called for comments from her readership. *Le Navire d'Argent* described itself as a journal of "general culture," its subjects including letters, philosophy, science, history, moral questions, and politics. Its bibliography was of particular interest, because it listed the first dated translation into French of English-language works, offered a listing of copies signed by famous people, and noted those editions that first appeared in the nineteenth century and now were available from the bookstalls, as well as those owned by La Maison des Amis des Livres (for these, Monnier listed the sales price from the bookshop). Adrienne was forced to stop publication of *Le Navire d'Argent* because of the expense. Upon publication of the French *Ulysse* in 1929, Adrienne ended her professional association with Joyce and two years later ended her personal association with him. In the next decade, she devoted herself to her bookshop and to publication of her own writings: the catalogue of her lending library, her *Fableaux* (1932), the journal *Mesures,* which she managed from 1935 until 1940, and her *Gazette des Amis des Livres.*

Given that Adrienne maintained strong literary and intellectual associations apart from Joyce, it is no wonder that she was able to preserve a certain distance and perspective on his involvement with Shakespeare and Company. While Sylvia admitted that she "worshipped" Joyce, Adrienne cast a colder eye on him—and he on her. In a letter to Harriet Weaver in 1931, Joyce catalogued his complaints against Adrienne, resentful of her influence over Sylvia. He focused on the difficulties caused him by Sylvia and the women around her: Adrienne, whom he called Sylvia's "more intelligent partner"; Sylvia's mother, who had recently committed suicide; Cyprian, whom he claimed to be in poor mental health; Sylvia herself, who was suffering badly at the time from migraines. Some time after receipt of Adrienne's 1931 letter, Joyce moved his professional enterprise to the home of Paul Léon, a former St. Petersburg jurist, whose presence in Joyce's life occasioned the snide "Dublingrad" reference in Adrienne's letter. It was Léon who brought the negotiations with Random House to completion (Jolas, "The Joyce I Knew," 86). Sylvia, Adrienne, and Joyce would "keep up appearances" over the next decade, but the professional and personal relationships that had sustained them since 1920 had come to an end.

In a letter to his son Georgio of 19 February 1935, Joyce wrote of Sylvia's sale of valuable items from her shop, including Joyce manuscripts. As the years advanced, Sylvia was feeling the effects of the general European depression and the loss of American clientele even more keenly and was forced to sell precious items in order to keep the shop going. Adrienne was also forced to sell similar items as the Depression of the 1930s continued: "A propos of the S. B. sale of my MSS (of which I am still officially ignorant), I am journalistically informed that the rumor is current over there [in New York] that she, by her generous sacrifice of all her rights of U to me, resigned herself to absolute poverty. Frailty thy name is woman" (*Letters,* 3 : 345). It is doubtful that Sylvia herself used the term "absolute poverty" in referring to the perilous economic state of Shakespeare and Company or that she described the resignation of her contractual rights with Joyce as a "generous sacrifice." Such terms belonged to friends and associates who felt that she had been badly used by the man and the work she had served so well. Among these friends, Janet Flanner, who advertised the 1935 Shakespeare and Company sale in the *New Yorker,* concluded that Sylvia "always gave more than she received." Joyce would certainly have agreed with Flanner's assessment. But, according to Flanner, Sylvia Beach's "generous sacrifice" was not in terminating her contractual agreement or in the sale of her Joyce materials—which included, among manuscripts, Sylvia's personal first edition copy of *Ulysses*—but rather in what Flanner called her "greatest act of generosity," the publication of *Ulysses* ("Great Amateur Publisher," 51).

Bryher commented in her tribute to Sylvia Beach that the "difficult ending" of her life—which included internment by the Nazis during the war and the closing of her bookshop—"seems richer to me personally than the triumphant beginning" ("For Sylvia," 18). If the 1920s was the decade of Sylvia Beach's success as the publisher of *Ulysses,* the time when hundreds of expatriates flocked to Shakespeare and Company, the 1930s was a decade of frustration, often despair, and a great deal of sadness. Beach's professional life, which had always been central to the literary life of the Left Bank community, now began to seem marginal. Adrienne too was pressed with financial difficulties, but her friends remained in the city they had always known. Adrienne involved herself with younger writers and with new literary movements while Sylvia struggled to survive. This decade saw not only the enforced return of a number of Sylvia's close friends to America, but the breakup of marriages and the disruption of long-term friendships.

Sylvia herself was to face such a crisis in 1937. She left Paris in July to visit her father on his eighty-fourth birthday, her first return to America in twenty-two years. Returning from her California visit to the east coast, she became ill and learned that she must undergo a hysterectomy, which required several weeks of rest before her doctor allowed her to return to Paris. When she did finally return to the rue de l'Odéon in mid-October, she discovered that she had been replaced in Adrienne's apartment by Gisèle Freund, the young German photographer. The previous winter, Gisèle—who had been ordered out of France and who had no passport to return to Germany—was taken in by Adrienne and Sylvia and spent increasingly more time with the two women. Adrienne helped her make a "marriage of convenience" to a Frenchman in order to continue living in the country. Whatever the reasons for the move to 18, rue de l'Odéon, Gisèle Freund represented a threat to Sylvia's relationship with Adrienne, and the evidence suggests that in her absence Adrienne had replaced

Sylvia with a younger lover. Within days of her return Sylvia had moved into the rooms above Shakespeare and Company; although she still took her meals with Adrienne and Gisèle (there being no proper kitchen in her own apartment) and continued her professional relationship with Adrienne, their long-standing union had effectively been terminated.

Gisèle Freund was forced to leave Paris with the advance of the Germans in 1940, but Adrienne and Sylvia did not take up their former intimacy. Each stayed in her apartment; each continued her professional life. Sylvia closed her bookshop in December 1941, after an unpleasant incident with a German officer who wanted to buy her only copy of *Finnegans Wake,* which she had displayed in the window. The officer threatened to confiscate her books; with the help of friends, Sylvia moved the books four flights above the bookshop premises, removed the shelves, and had the name of the shop painted over. Within a few hours, Shakespeare and Company no longer existed. In July 1942, Sylvia was taken to an internment camp south of Paris. Although she returned to live in number 12, rue de l'Odéon, after the war, she never reopened Shakespeare and Company. After a long and very painful illness that affected the inner ear, Adrienne Monnier committed suicide in 1955. In the years following Adrienne's death, Sylvia was to maintain two close and long-standing friendships. The first was with Bryher, whom Sylvia had known since the early days of Shakespeare and Company; their friendship had intensified during the war. They corresponded frequently in the 1940s, and after the war Bryher regularly sent Beach money. In these years Sylvia also spent a great deal of time with Camilla Steinbrugge, a woman who had shared a friendship with Adrienne Monnier as well, spending vacations with the two women before Adrienne's death. It was Steinbrugge who filled the space in Sylvia's life left by Adrienne.[4]

7

DJUNA BARNES:
RUE ST.-ROMAIN

If there was an intellectual center to the expatriate experience in Paris, it existed on the rue de l'Odéon. Sylvia Beach and Adrienne Monnier made major contributions to the life of this literary community in providing a focus for its social and artistic interchange. Shakespeare and Company and La Maison des Amis des Livres became the hub of expatriate literary life from which all other activities radiated and to which all participants—male, female, rich, poor, known, unknown, talented or mediocre—were drawn. During the day, the rue de l'Odéon was a busy thoroughfare as poets and novelists, dramatists and translators, scurried to and fro between the twin bookshops. On most evenings, however, the street became silent, echoing only the sounds of solitary individuals taking a shortcut from the *quais* to Montparnasse.

The Expatriate Myth

Although well known to the rue de l'Odéon group, Djuna Barnes probably spent little time in either of the bookshops. She was part of McAlmon's "crowd," as Sylvia Beach called it, known to all those expatriates who had formerly been part of the Greenwich Village group. She is mentioned in nearly every memoir of the period, her beauty and caustic wit the best remembered of her characteristics. She passed frequent afternoons and many evenings at the cafes along the Boulevard du Montparnasse; she was apparently well known at the Dome, the Coupole, and the Rotund, but preferred the less Americanized Café de Flore on the boulevard St. Germain des Prés. Dressed in a long opera cape originally owned by Peggy Guggenheim, Barnes spent long hours lost in her own thoughts, watching street activity. Although she later claimed to have wasted these years, in fact she wrote regularly. Barnes propped herself in bed in the mornings at the Hôtel Angleterre, balancing a writing pad on her knees. Some blocks away, at the rue de Varenne, Edith Wharton (whose work Barnes detested) was also writing, propped in a similar pose. In her long life, Djuna Barnes published seven books and experimented with a variety of genres—including poetry, short stories, plays, short essays and journalism, and theater reviews—and was both a portrait painter and an illustrator of her own work. Among these works only *Nightwood* was remembered and read, in part because T. S. Eliot's introduction (about which Barnes was ambivalent) suggested to students of literature that it should be taken seriously and because the novel attracted an underground following, becoming part of the "camp" culture of the Paris twenties. Her own reputation as a cult figure of this period was probably enhanced by the fact that her work, like that of many other expatriate Modernist women writers, was variously in and out of print for many years. In 1962, the *Selected Works of Djuna Barnes* became available, and by the mid-1970s scholars began to publish book-length studies of Barnes's work.

Like the myth of the expatriate experience itself, the myth of Djuna Barnes "expatriate woman writer" has been the creation of a male culture. Her closest relationships in Paris were with women, most of whom protected her need for privacy by not commenting on her at length in their memoirs. The men, who knew her less well, nonetheless found her beauty and caustic wit the occasion for commentary. She has often been recalled in relation to James Joyce, with whose work hers is often compared. She was perhaps the only other writer in Paris with whom he would discuss his work at length and the only person other than his wife who was allowed to call him "Jim." Barnes treated Joyce as her equal, refusing to bow before his awesome genius, but finding in it a source of artistic inspiration; he treated her with great respect. Because Joyce apparently took Barnes seriously as a writer, others were forced to do the same. Still, there were jokes about the *hauteur* that masked her shyness, her sexual preferences, and her writing style. Walter Winchell's comment that "Djuna Barnes, the femme writer, can hit a cuspidor twenty feet away" ("About New York," 5 June 1929) characterizes her as a tough, vulgar, butch lesbian whose masculine wit struck its mark. This comment, like many made about Barnes and other women of the Paris community, says far more about the writer than it does about Barnes. The comments of Robert McAlmon, who published Barnes in the Contact Editions series and who knew her in Paris, admits a similar, if less antagonistic, view of a woman whose beauty attracted men but whose wit made them uneasy. McAlmon's description is defensive in its polarized view of Barnes the formidable *femme* and Barnes the Irish sentimentalist:

I had known Djuna slightly in New York, because Djuna was a very haughty lady, quick on the uptake, and with a wise-cracking tongue that I was far too discreet to try and rival. It seemed, however, that once I had written a letter to *The Little Review,* asking how came it that Miss Barnes was both so Russian and so Synge-Irish. Some comment in the letter Jane Heap apparently used frequently to cow Djuna, and Jane kept assuring her that McAlmon was not taken in by her cape-throwing gesture but understood her for the sentimentalist which she was. In the end Djuna had gathered the idea that I disliked her, and I was a very sarcastic individual. She was wrong about the first idea at least, for Djuna is far too good-looking and witty not to command fondness and admiration from me, even when she is rather overdoing the grande dame manner and talking soul and ideals. In conversation she is often great with her comedy, but in writing she appears to believe she must inject metaphysics, mysticism, and her own strange version of a "literary quality" into her work. (Knoll, *McAlmon and the Lost Generation,* 167–168)

McAlmon's version of Djuna Barnes is typically clichéd, his view of her as a beautiful but "haughty" woman given to theatrical gestures a confirmation of Ezra Pound's assessment. Following a failed effort to seduce her, Pound described Barnes to friends as a woman who "weren't too cuddly" (Field, *Djuna,* 107). Like some other men of the community, Pound seemed uncomfortable with a woman in control of her sexual responses and not given to his rather inept attentions. Describing a similar incident with Pound, Bryher commented that under such circumstances "an Elizabethan would have screamed or snatched up a dagger, but I decided to be wary and calm" (*Heart to Artemis,* 191).

Perhaps because Pound sensed the phallophobia of Barnes's writing, he had little sympathy for her work, felt that her later reputation was exaggerated and "in need of deflation." In 1937, the year after *Nightwood* was published by Faber and Faber with Eliot's introduction, Pound included a nasty (and poorly written) limerick about Barnes in a letter to Eliot:

> There once wuzza lady named Djuna,
> Who wrote rather like a baboon. Her
> Blubbery prose had no fingers or toes,
> And we wish Whale had found this out sooner.

Ford Madox Ford, who had published Barnes's work in *Transatlantic Review* and who introduced her at a special evening in her honor held at Natalie Barney's in 1927, is the "whale" whose literary aesthetic is called into question by Pound (*Djuna,* 107–108, 122). By implication, Pound also disparaged Eliot's critical taste, since Eliot had already publicly committed himself to the value of Barnes's work and was to remain one of her most loyal supporters. As Andrew Field has suggested, "Pound's reputation for energetic concern on behalf of writers and poets whom he sometimes scarcely knew and whose art could be quite antithetical to his own" (*Djuna*, 107) did not extend to the support of women artists. His brief professional alliance with Natalie Barney was established in order to help James Joyce and T. S. Eliot. Neither of these ventures succeeded. The exception Pound had made for H. D. in their London years together was reversed when he took a new lover and H. D. stopped taking his literary advice. Pound never forgave H. D. for leaving his literary fold, and until recently most critics have agreed that her best work was done under his tutelage. Pound undoubtedly resented both Barnes's independent sense of her own literary directions and the regard that other writers—namely Eliot and Joyce—held for her.

Most commentators have had little idea what to say about Djuna Barnes's life and less notion what to do with her writings. As Louis Kannenstine has pointed out, although Barnes's work displays certain affinities with the major literary movements of the early years of the twentieth century, it cannot be said to wholly conform to any of these movements (*Art of Djuna Barnes*, xvi). The perception that Barnes's art refuses to constrain itself to the demands of genre has resulted both in praise of its diverse efforts and in lack of understanding of its experimental methods. Because the better known of Barnes's writings—*Ryder, Ladies Almanack, Nightwood,* and *The Antiphon*—include characters and situations drawn from her own biography, particularly of the Paris years, there is a tendency to read her fiction as a record of her life. The mysterious unreality of *Nightwood* has translated itself into accounts of Barnes's life, so that the self-imposed seclusion of the later years is linked to the apparent hedonism of her ten-year residence in Paris. Cultists of the period take pride in being able to identify the various Paris characters who appear in her work, focusing on the *roman à clef* aspects that tie her writing to a specific time and place. Djuna Barnes becomes a pathetic victim of the Parisian nightworld, her "basic heterosexuality" undermined by the evils of a lesbian community, her beauty lost in drunken brawls, her wit turned acid. She is read as a participant in the Paris lesbian community portrayed in *Ladies Almanack;* she is Nora in *Nightwood,* a victim of the drugged, alcoholic, sexually ambiguous Paris nightworld. Such an interpretation of Barnes's Paris years has now become the standard material of expatriate accounts.[1] It has been difficult to rewrite this myth, to place Djuna Barnes in a community of serious women writers in Paris, to suggest that the informing despair of *Nightwood* might be interpreted beyond the biographical details of her own life, to discuss her seclusion as a deliberate act of devotion to her writing, or to offer alternatives to the crass efforts at psychoanalysis indulged in by most commentators on her life and work.

Writing to Natalie Barney on 31 May 1963 concerning her literary reputation, Barnes pointed to the discrepancy between the praise her work received among her contemporaries and the consequent lack of critical attention from later writers and scholars: "There is not a person in the literary world who has not heard of, read and some stolen from *Nightwood*. The paradox that in spite of all the critical work flooding the press since 1936, not more than three or four have mentioned my name. I am the most famous unknown of the century! I can't account for it, unless it is that my talent is my character, my character my talent, and both an estrangement." The relation between character and talent is indeed a problematic one in Barnes's work. Reading the writer through the work, critical response has maintained that the element of estrangement that at first appears idiosyncratic in Barnes's writing is in fact symptomatic of the underlying *malaise* of the Modernist period and of the expatriate experience in general. Louis Kannenstine calls *Nightwood* a "distillation of the despair and estrangement of expatriation" (*Art of Djuna Barnes,* 104). Such a reading limits the scope of the novel to the time-frame of the expatriate experience and makes the estrangement of woman's talent and character odd quirks of Djuna Barnes's nature rather than possible common features of woman's situation. That Barnes herself seemed puzzled by the relation of her character and talent suggests a starting point for a reevaluation of both her life and work.

In Retrospect: The Early Years

Like many other expatriate women, Djuna Barnes seemed peculiarly trapped in the supposed glamour of the Paris years. Photographs from this period capture her elegance and style, her eyes always directed away from the camera, her pose often in silhouette. The late photographs expose the effects of ill health and show a woman no longer at ease with the camera, her eyes frightened, her fragility all too apparent. To read late Barnes correspondence with her friends is a painful experience. Having outlived the expatriate situation, these women share their memories of each other, report progress on their memoirs, and recount in shaky handwriting the various difficulties of their old age. They seem all too aware that if they are remembered at all by others it is for the roles they played in the Paris community. The peculiar sense of estrangement from their own pasts and the difficulties of an anachronistic present are common to all these women's lives.

Memoir writing became a means of constructing the present by reconstructing the past; it staved off death and invited a renewal of public interest in these lives. Although Djuna Barnes refused to write her own memoirs, she was a careful reader of the remembrances of others. Responding to Peggy Guggenheim's wish to know what she thought of Sylvia Beach's memoirs, Barnes wrote on 9 November 1960: "I think it very like her—kind and modest—probably too much of both." She wrote Natalie Barney that she was "depressed by reading Kay Boyle's re-edited . . . 'Being Geniuses Together' by Bob McAlmon. Re-hash of our twenties . . . all out of shape, it seems to me, and an egregious display of Miss Boyle herself. If you can't make the passage of time as it was, or better than it was (in the rough sense) by quality not much short of superb artistry, then why at all?" In 1972, she wrote to Barney about the unreality of the Paris years: "I think of all of us with amazement and antique amused affection—what a far-off-unlike our present that world was . . . or like too, if I think back far enough . . . long hair and all, capes, our polemics for and against freedom and love!" Among the women of this study Barnes was particularly conscious that she had outlived her own myth. "Should old ladies, 'under death's whittle,' send lines about the matter to each other?" she wrote Natalie Barney on 15 September 1965. "I think it well when after all, the news is small, and the world worn flat!" Natalie Barney's old age was unusual in that her world was not "worn flat"; she, like Maria Jolas, maintained her joy of living, while Barnes became increasingly acerbic and dour. At the end, Barnes complained that she would die at least forty years too late.

A refugee from the moribund literary culture that had been Greenwich Village, Djuna Barnes had come to Paris as a journalist on a *McCall's* magazine assignment that took her nearly five years to complete. Facing financial difficulties that were never successfully resolved in her lifetime, Barnes chose Paris, and later Berlin, as places that could provide her a subsistence income and the leisure and privacy to pursue her own work. When she arrived in Paris sometime in 1919 or 1920 (she had difficulties remembering the precise date), it was still unclear to her whether she would continue painting and drawing or would turn her attention to writing. In 1915, in New York, at the age of 23, she had published in pamphlet form *The Book of Repulsive Women,* a collection of poems and explicit drawings on the subject of female sexuality. In 1923, in Paris, she compiled a series of poems, stories, plays, and drawings as *A Book,* a collection that drew attention to her as a serious artist. The 1928 publication of *Ryder* provided a fictionalized history of the Barnes family in mock-Elizabethan style; the same year, the *Ladies Almanack,* a *roman à clef* to the Paris lesbian community, was privately printed by Darantière of Dijon. Her most famous and enduring work, however, was *Nightwood* (1936), a work that was to become a cult guide to the homosexual underground nightworld of Paris that Barnes shared with her lover, Thelma Wood. Barnes left Paris in 1931, living variously in New York and London, traveling on the continent, returning in 1937 to sell the rue St.-Romain apartment the two women had earlier shared. In 1941, she took up residence in Patchin Place in Greenwich Village, where she lived until her death at age 90. In the forty-one years of residence in the one-room apartment in Patchin Place, Barnes published only one other full-length work, *The Antiphon*, a play in which a mother and daughter act out their hatred of each other.[2]

Barnes was considered to be the most important woman writer of the Paris community, her work generally thought to be second only to that of Joyce, with whom she shared certain literary methods. Her work was taken seriously by the male literary community. She never suffered within the expatriate environs the combined ridicule and lack of attention to her work endured, for instance, by Gertrude Stein. Barnes rarely spoke of her writing, did nothing to increase her literary reputation, and made no compromises in either her subject matter or her style to attract a reading audience. She was revered by this community—and also feared—her vicious wit often turned on those who intruded upon her solitary mood. In her early New York days and during the Paris years she participated in a community of primarily lesbian women who supported her both psychologically and financially. In New York she knew Mabel Dodge, Jane Heap, Margaret Anderson, the Baroness Else von Freytag-Loringhoven, Edna St. Vincent Millay, Mary Pyne—with whom she was probably in love—and Peggy Guggenheim, who consistently, but parsimoniously, supported Barnes throughout her life. In Paris, her closest friends were Janet Flanner, Solita Solano, and Mina Loy. Although Natalie Barney probably had a brief affair with Barnes in Paris, helped support her in later years, and frequently invited her to her salon, the two women did not know each other well. Strained as the friendships with women might become, women were allowed a degree of intimacy in Barnes's life that was never offered to men, although she had many male friends—most of them homosexual or bisexual—and lived for two years with Greenwich Village script editor Courtenay Lemon. The longest, and most damaging, love affair in her life was with the American sculptress Thelma Wood.

The effort to write *Nightwood*, which is most often characterized as a record of the love affair with Thelma Wood, constituted the beginning of Barnes's exile from the Paris community and the gradual disengagement from the outside world that distinguished the second half of her life. Always uncomfortable with the claims of the human community, Barnes seemed in her later life to have little need of human contact. Her earlier relationships with several women of the Paris community had already suggested that she was sought out by others toward whom she made little effort to continue friendship. Often in need of financial support, she made only minimal efforts to continue long-term relationships with Peggy Guggenheim, Natalie Barney, or Samuel Beckett—all of whom provided financial assistance. She was loved by others in spite of her announced intention to live outside the boundaries of love. Her years in seclusion in New York, reflected in her late works—*Nightwood,* the *Antiphon*—wrapped both her life and work in mystery. She was rumored to have been an alcoholic and drug-addicted lesbian in her early life and known to be an eccentric and surly recluse in her later years. Barnes's later writing became increasingly angry and embittered, her retreat from the world misunderstood. She shared with Nancy Cunard a hatred of her family and all that her parent culture represented, a hatred that surfaced more readily and openly in her later years. Unlike Cunard, who died an anorexic alcoholic, Barnes stopped the self-destructive pattern of the Paris years and ceased to drink, smoke, and involve herself in wearying love affairs in order to write. The last thirty years of her life were spent at work on a long poem, the manuscript for which was found among her belongings at the Patchin Place apartment when she died in May 1982.

Djuna Barnes led various and dissimilar lives, each new artistic interest or professional calling a matter of conscious choice. In the early Greenwich Village years, Barnes was a writer of light essays and journalistic commentaries. These short pieces, published in little magazines and periodicals such as *Charm, Vanity Fair,* the *New Yorker,* and *Theatre Guild Magazine,* as well as in numerous New York newspapers (the *Press, Telegraph,* and *World*) have been virtually forgotten—in part because Barnes herself did not take them seriously. At this period of her life, she involved herself with the public, often seeking out subjects that required acts of courage: she was hugged by a gorilla, jumped into a fire rescue net from a skyscraper, was force-fed in order to comment on the use of such coercive measures against English suffragists. Such "participatory" journalism even by men was rare in that time and was virtually unheard of for women. Andrew Field comments that "certainly no other woman journalist was doing the sort of things [Barnes] was doing prior to World War I" (*Djuna,* 54). She conducted interviews and investigated vaudeville and the circus, reporting for the daily press and preparing literary and theater reviews. By the time Barnes arrived in Paris, she had developed a sure eye for portraiture and a witty style of reporting that would have made her noteworthy had she never written the more "serious" pieces to which she was devoting her spare time. The style, sensitivity, and ironic humor of these pieces share something with the work of Janet Flanner.

Many of these early essays demonstrate what has come to be known as the distinctive *New Yorker* style. But for Barnes, journalism was only a means of maintaining herself in order to write poetry and plays of a more demanding and less compromising nature. Barnes is importantly different from many of the expatriate women writers in that she never experienced financial security; she did not come to Paris with even a minimal inheritance as a cushion against poverty. Barnes managed to give the impression of elegance and financial stability even when borrowing money for rent and meals. She consistently took financial risks for her art. In the early years she refused to make concessions to either publishers or the public in the choice of subject matter or style of her serious writing. As Douglas Messerli has noted, Barnes supported herself rather well in the early New York years because city newspapers, even one that "marketed itself as New York's 'racing sheet,'" published her peculiar and radically experimental fictions ("The Newspaper Tales" in *Smoke*, 8–9). In later years, she maintained a subsistence living on small gifts from friends in order to write without interruption.

The subjects of Barnes's early journalism show a marked interest in women's place in modern society. Adopting a feminist viewpoint, Barnes examined the sexual exploitation of women. Her feminist politics, however, were marked by her own sense of woman's struggle. She eschewed group causes and refused to become part of a "sisterhood," probably from fear of jeopardizing her individuality. Although the tone of some of these early articles on suffrage might suggest that Barnes was not sympathetic to the movement, it seems clear that she felt the issue of women's equality was so important that she had little sympathy with any public act that misrepresented or limited feminism's goals. An article for the *Brooklyn Daily Eagle* on a Suffrage Aviation meet in 1913, therefore, is mocking and condescending; an article for the *New York World* a year later on the force-feeding of suffragists constitutes a feminist manifesto: "If I, play acting, felt my being burning with revolt at this brutal usurpation of my own functions, how they who actually suffered the ordeal in its acutest horror must have flamed at the violation of the sanctuaries of their spirit?" Commentators have usually seen little affinity between these early writings and her later literary work, but the anger at the "brutal usurpation" of woman's functions reappears in *Ryder, Ladies Almanack*, and *Nightwood* in the form of a literary theme rather than as political argument.

In these years, Barnes's life was divided between the professional and public (journalism) and the private and creative (poetry and painting). In a rare interview for the *New York Times* in 1971, she described these years as "desperate" ones: "Years ago I used to see people, I had to, I was a newspaperwoman, among other things. And I used to be rather the life of the party. I was rather gay and silly and bright and all that sort of stuff and wasted a lot of time. I used to be invited by people who said 'Get Djuna for dinner, she's amusing.' So I stopped it" (Raymont, "From the Avant-garde of the Thirties," 24). The desperation behind this public persona and the irritation with the superficiality of social popularity—in particular the use of women as "amusing," decorative items—inform the works of the Paris period and account, perhaps, for Barnes's decision to avoid social involvement, to stop talking. Although the decision to re-place the public with the private was made when Barnes was 40 years old, it is forecast in an early piece written under her pseudonym, Lydia Step-toe, in a 1923 essay in *Vanity Fair* entitled "What Is Good Form in Dying?" In this piece Barnes distinguished a protocol of female death ac-cording to hair color. It is the redhead, interestingly, who is able to spare herself the public perusal of her decline toward death: "Seclusion, for in-stance, far, far from the madding crowd; countries one may visit; fourth and fifth dimensions one may overtake. There are . . . all manners of black and white magics, and timeless regions, and faiths that take a red-haired woman out of herself" (Kannenstine, *Art of Djuna Barnes*, 11). Djuna Barnes had red hair and became a recluse. Margaret Anderson dyed her red hair blonde and also became a recluse, shutting herself up in a small house on the French Riviera to write her memoirs of the Paris years. Although Barnes hated Anderson in the early Greenwich Village period for having taken Jane Heap away from her, the last stage of their lives—lived out half a world apart—shared certain similar features. Both women detested the physical debility of old age; both were vain about being seen without makeup. Barnes used to write propped on her bed, dressed in a black negligee, highly rouged, her hair done—a pose made famous in her depiction of Matthew O'Connor. Both women maintained their former relationships by letter, refusing to meet new people and oc-casionally avoiding old friends from the Paris years. Margaret Anderson wrote to Janet Flanner in the 1960s:

> No, no, NO, I can't, I CANNOT see new people: even the thought of it makes me so nervous that I can't work. But in order not to hurt your friend's feelings (and your own) you must explain for me.
>   For at least two years I have stopped seeing ANYONE but old friends—people who knew me before I became a ruin. I'm too ugly, look too much like an invalid, can't talk without losing my voice, and have NOTHING to say to anyone new. Besides, the doctor won't allow me to think of such *dérange-ments*—knowing that I would soon become a nervous wreck. The only thing I can do to preserve the little energy I still have is to keep writing, which pleases and excites and keeps me going.

Djuna Barnes would have found it a bitter irony that she and Margaret Anderson—for whom she had little respect—should have decided to live out their old age in similar fashion. For her part, Anderson was surprised to learn from Janet Flanner in the late 1960s that Barnes was still alive.

The Early Poetry

Barnes's noncommercial writing (mostly poetry) composed during the period in which she wrote journalistic essays has for the most part been lost. The poems that survived—from prestigious magazines and journals that continued publishing—suggest the dark side that was the complement to the often breezy wit of her commercial writing. Of greatest interest are the poems included in *The Book of Repulsive Women*. These slight, rather macabre, verses are important, however, for reasons usually overlooked by commentators. In tone and style they seem derivative of the *fin de siècle* poetic school of Wilde and Symons, and the drawings that accompany them have often been described as Beardsleyan (Kannenstine, *Art of Djuna Barnes,* 23). Carolyn Burke comments that these poems and drawings were an effort to "kill off the old images of women," so that "a different vision might become possible" ("'Accidental Aloofness,'"). The poems are thin and appear to address a highly select audience, as their appearance in a few numbered copies in the "Outcast Chapbook" series suggests. They may even have been intended, as some of Barnes's later work seems to have been, for an audience of women.

What is most striking about *The Book of Repulsive Women* is the implicit relation between women's physical and psychological states. The degeneration of women's bodies in the aging process is placed in the context of "degenerate" acts of lesbian lovemaking, the juxtaposition of these images suggesting an unstated relation between degeneration and the degenerate. The woman in "From Fifth Avenue Up" is "spreading," "strangled," "lang'rous," "leaning," "oozing":

> See you sagging down with bulging
> Hair to sip.
> The dampled damp from some vague
> Under lip.
> Your soft saliva, loosed
> With orgy, drip.

The woman "Seen from the 'L'" is simultaneously "chain-stitched" and becoming "unstitched." (The metaphor of the woman "sewn up" will be taken up again in *Nightwood*.)

> Still her clothing is less risky
> Than her body in its prime,
> They are chain-stitched and so is she
> Chain-stitched to her soul for time.
> Ravelling grandly into vice
> Dropping crooked into rhyme.
> Slipping through the stitch of virtue,
>   Into crime.

In "Twilight of the Illicit" the aftermath of lovemaking provides the occasion to comment on the slack heaviness of aging and to figure the implicit violence of the love act ("Your dying hair hand-beaten / 'Round your head"). "Great ghastly loops of gold" have "snared" the ears of the woman reclined upon the bed—the ornaments a mark of woman's servitude to man's desire, their loop the "snare" by which she is caught. The drawings that accompany the poems show woman variously as disjointed, grotesque, and abstract. She is robbed of identity, beauty, and humanity; her body signals her "repulsive" condition. Carolyn Burke notes that "it is impossible . . . to separate Barnes's fascination with the dissolute and the decadent from her implicit critique of the very attitudes she would satirize" ("'Accidental Aloofness'").

Louis Kannenstine describes these poems as participating in "stylistic excess" and argues that they represent the "iconoclastic side of the author, subversive of meaning and traditional literary decorum to the point of affirming only the pointless and perverse" (*Art of Djuna Barnes,* 32). Blind to the crucial position that the relation of style to substance, of ornamentation to perversion, holds in Barnes's writing, Kannenstine reads *The Book of Repulsive Women, Ryder,* and *Ladies Almanack* as aberrant and misdirected efforts rather than as part of a developing critique of woman's place in modern society. The decadence and depravity of city women portrayed in *Repulsive Women* is an *effect* of woman's situation in patriarchal culture, not its cause. The fall from innocence into "a sort of death in life" results from the realization that woman in Western society is defined by her *difference from* the masculine norm. She is estranged from a society that sacrifices her body on a patriarchal altar. Woman survives in psychic withdrawal from the knowledge of her condition ("mouthing meekly in a chair"); she loses her tenuous grip on identity ("A vacant space is in her face"); though ambulatory, she is dead: "Somewhere beneath her hurried curse, / A corpse lies bounding in a hearse." These walking dead of Barnes's youth foreshadow the "Walking-Mort" (a 1971 poem published in the *New Yorker*) of her old age. Images of smiling skulls, of wombed tombs, of shrouded corpses, of insanity, of hysteria and speechless mumbling abound in these fragments. Of the two corpses considered in the last poem of the series, "Suicide," the second receives as little kindness in death as she did in life:

> They gave her hurried shoves this way
>   And that,
> Her body shock-abbreviated
> As a city cat.
> She lay out listlessly like some small mug
> Of beer gone flat. (*Book of Repulsive Women,* 100)

If *Nightwood* forms an "interior landscape . . . an anatomy of the night," as Kannenstine suggests (*Art of Djuna Barnes,* 21), *The Book of Re-*

pulsive Women exteriorizes the most frightening images of women—images that are both produced and repressed by a patriarchal culture for which the city provides a squalid landscape.

This vision of woman as the particular creation and victim of the depersonalized modern city was to become a major theme of Barnes's work. *The Book of Repulsive Women* and certain poems from *A Book* forecast, accurately and ironically, the repulsive nature of her own old age as one of "those living dead up in their rooms." Contrasting childhood with later life in "Lullaby," Barnes wrote in her early thirties of the inexorable boredom of living: "There will be a morrow, and another, and another"; and in "Six Songs of Khalidine," she described love in the midst of death: "Yet think within our hair / The dusty ashes that our days prepare" (*A Book*, 145–146). In an uncollected poem written in 1918, "The Lament of Women," she wrote of "this flesh laid on us like a wrinkled glove" (quoted in *Art of Djuna Barnes*, 30), an image that holds within it woman's particular horror at the aging process.

The Poetics of Style

All of Djuna Barnes's writing can be read as a critique of woman's place in Western society. But until recently, her work has been placed against the Modernist tradition, where it has suffered a neglectful misreading. Both her prose and poetry have been seen as eccentric, almost inverted, forms of the Modernist aesthetic. They have been read as private and highly peculiar writing that addresses itself to a select audience, drawing its subject matter from Barnes's life and in form and imagery composing a pastiche of earlier literatures. But it is precisely Barnes's relation to literary tradition that so troubles assessments of her work: readers do not know where to "place" her. She has simultaneously been berated for not attending enough to the work of the major writers of this period—in particular the poetics of Eliot and Pound—and for imitating, unsuccessfully, the Joycean mode.[3] Kannenstine, for instance, admits that the most important direction of Barnes's work was not found in the Joycean model, but he fails to see in *The Book of Repulsive Women* and *A Book* intimations of her particular contribution to the feminist literary tradition:

> Taking alone these personal, muted lamentations, still essentially ornamental, that Djuna Barnes continued to publish through the twenties one might have assumed that she was unaware of the distinctive new poetics evolving from *imagisme* through Eliot's *The Waste Land* and Pound's experiments with transliteration and juxtaposition. But it would soon be apparent in two unusual novels that a modern voice was developing, along the lines of Joyce's, in the rhythms of a prose expanded, not according to the dictates of a current

aesthetic rationale, but by a new application of abandoned traditions. (*Art of Djuna Barnes*, 31)

Indeed, Barnes's poetry did not seem to follow the currents of the most recent American and English poetry—and there is no reason why it should have. Kannenstine's remark about Barnes's "application of abandoned traditions" refers both to her interest in earlier historical periods and to the use of outmoded and antiquated verbal forms. But Barnes was also at work reconstructing the "abandoned traditions" of woman's culture. This effort simultaneously searched for woman in the patriarchal culture that had abandoned her and sought to give back to woman the voice that had for so long been silenced. Such an enterprise, as we have already discovered, was a risky one. Although well respected by her contemporaries, Barnes's work has fallen prey to the same set of received notions that until very recently informed studies of Gertrude Stein: both women have been chastised for being significantly different from their Paris colleagues and for failing to master the Modernist enterprise.

While similarities between the work of Gertrude Stein and Djuna Barnes may not be immediately apparent, *Ryder* does take up a theme common to Stein's *Making of Americans*. In these works, both writers pay particular attention to the fates of their female forebears, exposing the ways women are made to suffer for the patriarchy. Barnes's novel, like Stein's, has been described as a "plotless exercise in technique" (*Art of Djuna Barnes*, 33); Barnes like Stein has been accused of elaborating the "irrelevant" (*Art of Djuna Barnes*, 37). Whereas Stein's work remained unread, *Ryder* became a bestseller in 1928, despite critical quibbling with its methods and the marked inability of reviewers to comprehend its subject. The *New Republic* assumed it to be a "tragedy of women," while the *Saturday Review*—for reasons unstated—claimed it was "the most amazing book ever written by a woman" (*Art of Djuna Barnes*, 39). It was less on the grounds of subject than on the matter of style, however, that these two novels met resistance by critics. Like *The Making of Americans, Ryder* was initially seen by reviewers as a family history whose chronology was radically, but perversely, undone. Stein's style was considered boring in the extreme, while Barnes's style was thought to be unnecessarily arcane. The style of a work like *Ryder,* in particular, served to block the reader's entrance to the text, posing nearly insurmountable obstacles to reading it. The technique was by no means accidental or a literary "fault," but a purposeful endeavor to set the reader at odds with the text. As Annette Kolodny has suggested about *Nightwood*, a text that blocks the reader from entering in ways significantly different from those employed in *Ryder,* Barnes's method "places its readers in precisely that situation in which the main characters of more recent women's fiction find themselves: that is, embroiled in the hopeless task of trying to decode or decipher a strange and incomprehensible reality" ("Some Notes on Defining a 'Feminist Literary Criticism,'" 44).

It is significant that critical attention to these two writers has focused on style. Rather than being a tactic intended to divert attention away from the subversive subject matter of the Barnes-Stein texts, this critical move suggests that readers did not understand the subject matter. The attention to style, however, constituted a way of sidestepping ideological questions that discussions of subject matter might have entailed. Moreover, a focus on the "style" rather than "substance" of these works allowed critics to mask their own ideological and political biases. Katherine Anne Porter claims, for instance, that in matters of style "Miss Stein had no problems": "she simply exploded a verb as if it were a soap bubble, used chthonian grammar long before she heard it named (and she would have scorned to name it), was a born adept in occult hypnosis of language without even trying. . . . Wise or silly or nothing at all, down everything goes on the page with the air of everything being equal, unimportant in itself, important because it happened to her and she was writing about it" ("Gertrude Stein: A Self-Portrait," 520). Porter's assessment of Stein's method joins that of many others who suggest that the oddly nongrammatical form of her writing was the result of "hypnosis," a free play of the mind. Not only was this style "mindless," it was perhaps the supreme manifestation of Stein's egotism: all that was "unimportant in itself" became important because it happened to Stein. This argument suggests that Stein was revealed in her writing style, yet Porter wishes to argue precisely the opposite: the writing style that seems so silly and innocuous is actually a cover-up, a cloak hiding the self.

For Porter, Stein's style functioned as a sign of her insurmountable passivity, the mark of her overpowering ego. Stein possessed the freedom "not to decide, not to act, not to accept any responsibility for anything—one held the pen and let the mind wander. One sat down and somebody did everything for one" (522). Thus Stein's early claim to be "a modern girl, a New woman, interested in scientific experiment, historical research, the rational view" (522) was an elaborate lie constructed to deceive herself. She was, according to Porter, reduced to worrying ("worrying and thinking were synonyms to her"), feeling "very lonely in the awful singularity of her confusion" (522). Eventually, only gross avarice could ease the pain of loneliness, doubt, and self-deception (523).

Reading Stein through her style, Porter uncovers an insidious and deadly division among women of the expatriate community, a division based on sexual orientation. For heterosexual women of this community, the choice between standing in the shadows of the male literary giants or forming an alliance with the "Amazons" was no choice at all—better to be a footnote to the history of these years than to "usurp with a high hand the traditional masculine privileges of movement, choice, and the use of direct, personal power" ("Gertrude Stein: A Self-Portrait," 522). According to Porter, Stein's matronly appearance served as a "tricky disguise" for homosexuality—in some cases a disguise so successful that the lesbian center of the writing was never fathomed. Barnes's treatment of lesbianism was overt, however, and readers could not read past its presence in the text. Instead, they insisted on reading Barnes's texts as confirmation of the degradation and innate depravity of homosexuality, turning these texts against themselves. If the heterosexual Paris community did not feel comfortable with Stein (they knew she *was* lesbian, even as they tried to claim she did not *write* lesbian), Barnes was taken in by the heterosexual community and considered to be one of their own. For them, it was inconceivable that a woman as beautiful as Barnes might be lesbian. And it was difficult even for Barnes to admit that the lesbianism of her writing bore a relation to the sexuality of her life. Darryl Pinckney, who worked for her briefly in the Patchin Place years, reports that she proclaimed to him that "she was never a lesbian, could never abide 'those wet muscles' one had to love to love women" ("Sweet Evening Breeze," 37). Andrew Fields quotes Barnes as saying, "I'm not a lesbian. I just loved Thelma" (101), but on 12 November 1936, Barnes responded to a letter from Ottoline Morrell, who had suggested publicly that Barnes was lesbian: "Please do not think of it—I was not offended in the least to be thought lesbian—its [sic] simply that I am very reticent about my personal life, a little English perhaps." If Barnes successfully negotiated both sides of the division in sexual preference and personal style that marked the expatriate experience, it may have been because she worked hard at keeping her personal life private. Her writings, however, divided themselves along lines of sexual orientation: her journalism, short essays, and certain fictions (*Ryder,* for instance) were directed toward the larger heterosexual community, while other writings, including much of her poetry and the *Ladies Almanack,* were intended primarily for a lesbian readership.

The question of audience suggests again the problem of style, which may act as a protective covering for that which might otherwise be censored. Style becomes code: available to those who "know," unavailable to those who do not. It was Edmund Wilson who first suggested that Stein's opaque style was made necessary by the impropriety of her subject matter ("Gertrude Stein Old and Young," 581). Barnes's early critics thought her style "perverse," only to realize that her subject matter was perversion itself—specifically, what has been termed female sexual perversion. Recent feminist criticism has made the works of both these women more accessible, providing corrective readings to the earlier ones. Specifically, the "problem of style" has been shown to be the effect of an interpretive strategy that disguises misogyny in the distinctions between style and substance and in the operations of criticism itself. The text has been likened to a woman's body whose envelope (style or code) must be broken in order for the substance to be recovered and explained. Reading is rape, a submission of the text (woman) to patriarchal (critical) priorities. Such a method produced antilesbian readings of *Ladies Almanack,* suggesting that lesbian practice itself is ridiculed by this text, and made Robin Vote the perpetrator of evil in *Nightwood* rather than its victim.[4] That *Ryder* was a scathing critique of precisely the ideology informing a critical practice that places woman under man's interpretive power was overlooked by critics altogether.[5] In *Ryder,* man is made "the agent of woman's suffering" through the power of the puritan marriage ethic. In *Ladies Almanack,* the world's pain belongs to woman and is "rooted in sexual difference" (Kannenstine, *Art of Djuna Barnes,* 42, 53). *Ryder* exposes the power of sexual difference, correctly reads the priority that Western civilization has assigned to the male over the female, writes a commitment to a feminist literary method.

The Lesbian Other

In the same year that *Ryder* became a bestseller in America, a slim chapbook entitled *Ladies Almanack* was published in Paris under the imprint of McAlmon's Contact Editions. Published in 1,050 copies, *Ladies Almanack* contained twenty-two pen and ink drawings by Barnes, who handcolored the first fifty numbered copies of the edition. It is interesting to note that McAlmon underwrote the project with part of the alimony he received from Bryher's family, so that Bryher—who was among the Paris lesbians who read the almanack—indirectly had a part in the printing of it. The almanack addressed itself to the particular readership of "ladies," underwriting a class association with lesbianism. If *Ryder* situated itself in the space of sexual difference, this volume, "written by a lady of fashion," made man its avowed enemy and glorified love between women. In important respects, this almanack served to counter Proust's version of Lesbos in *Sodome et Gomorrhe;* indeed, it was probably written as a corrective to the Proustian vision (Wickes, *Amazon of Letters,* 179). Using "a lady of fashion" to address other "ladies," the language that invokes these privileged women in their art of loving conspires with the language of psychoanalysis, deconstructive practice, and feminist critical theory: "Neap-tide to the Proustian chronicle, gleanings from the shore of Mytilene, glimpses of its novitiates, its rising 'saints' and 'priestesses,' and thereon to such aptitude and insouciance that they took to gaming and to

246

swapping that 'other' of the mystery, the anomaly that calls the hidden name. That, affronted, eats its shadow" (n.p.).[6] This commentary points toward the mystery that is woman—the mystery that the male tries to penetrate, that confounds his efforts at explication, that irritates his daily life. The "other" eerily forecasts Lacan's rereading of the Freudian Other— the mystery of the unconscious that directs our conscious lives but eludes our knowledge and our explanations. The "other" is the object of desire, the beloved, the woman of man's dreams. Wendell Ryder's efforts to possess this elusive object of desire lead him to polygamy, make woman "a perfect prostrate tapestry of fecundity," and force him to "gaming and to swapping that 'other' of the mystery" (Ryder, 50). The Ladies Almanack provides an alternative to this tale of heterosexual aggression, offering a lesbian creation myth in the birth of "the first Woman born with a Difference" (Ladies Almanack, 26). That "difference" is marked by the return of woman's sexual self, the part of her forced to "eat its shadow" in the savage ritual of the heterosexual world. In the patriarchal world, woman is denied her own desire as she becomes the object of man's lust. Carolyn Allen argues that the "difference" here is lesbian sexuality: "in their love of the same sex, they . . . admire their non-conformity, their sexual difference from the rest of the world" ("Writing toward Nightwood"). Ladies Almanack, several stories from the Spillway collection, Nightwood, and The Antiphon explore the nature of female sexuality. In particular, these works examine the difference within sexual difference, within gender. Under the patriarchal law, not only are the male and female decreed different from each other ("the little Difference which shall be alien always," Ladies Almanack, 57), but each is discovered to inhabit the other. Barnes's examination of internalized sexual difference, common both to the texts that addressed a heterosexual audience and to those written for other women, becomes the primary subject matter of her writing.

In mapping the inversions and subversions of sexual difference under the law that would enforce heterosexuality, Barnes's work anticipates (and simultaneously puts into question) the Lacanian notion that heterosexuality unwrites the very law of difference it would seem to put into place. That is, heterosexuality in Western culture is really a form of what has previously been defined as homosexuality: as a search for an image of the self, a search for the twin, a search for confirmation of one's identity through the double, a reinforcement of sameness under the guise of difference.[7] Barnes's work also puts into play the prevalent scientific theories of homosexuality of her own day: that the homosexual crime constituted an "inversion" of sexual roles, an attraction to one's own sex, to a "twin." Homosexuality was seen as narcissistic, a need constantly to gaze upon the self: "woman tears her Shift for a Likeness in a Shift, and a Mystery that is lost to the proportion of Mystery" (*Ladies Almanack*, 57). As Katherine Anne Porter's comments on Stein suggest, homosexuality could be viewed as a condition born of immense egotism. Barnes examines all of these stereotyped notions of sexuality, both heterosexual and homosexual, with special concern for the underlying equation of "invert" and "inversion." *Nightwood* demonstrates the entire range of inversions brought about by sexual orientation toward one's own sex. This text purposely—some have said perversely—insists on conflating notions of sexual practice and role reversal.[8] If *Nightwood* has been read as an analysis of lesbianism that damns its practices and *Ladies Almanack* as a satire of lesbian communities, it is perhaps because Barnes is so successful in inverting expected values, in putting the author at an odd angle to the literary work so that her own attitudes are simultaneously concealed and revealed by it.

The shadow presence of the other appears frequently in *Nightwood*. Guido, Robin and Felix's mentally deficient son, is called "the shadow" of his father's anxiety, one who "eats a sleep that is not our sleep" (120); he is a child who, like his mother, is described as "estranged" (108, 121). Nora sees in Robin her "other self" and thinks that in walking beside Robin she is "beside herself," seeing her own image in her lover. Robin Vote carries the past about her like a former but undiscarded self; she is described as "gracious and yet fading, like an old statue in a garden" (41). In the final scene of "Night Watch" Nora looks down on the garden in the moments before dawn, searching for Robin. Seeing a "double shadow" falling from a garden statue, she does not at first see "the body of another woman swim up into the statue's obscurity," held in Robin's embrace. Moments later, Nora meets the "double regard" of the women's eyes and shuts her eyes against the double vision, hoping that "they will not hold together" (64). Nora discovers that she can possess Robin, have her undivided loyalty, only when Robin is "dead drunk." At other times Robin's divided identity makes her a presence "in her own nightmare": "I tried to come between and save her, but I was like a shadow in her dream that could never reach her in time . . . she was like a new shadow walking perilously close to the outer curtain" (145). This double image of woman that "holds together" a fractured female identity and sexuality is first explored in the homocentric world of *Ladies Almanack*, where woman's lesbian lover represents her "second self" and together the two discover the joys of woman's sexuality. In *Nightwood* that second (sexual) self is suppressed by society, forced to live in the secret nightwood of the unconscious, where it threatens to rob woman of her sanity. *Ladies Almanack* expresses the joy of woman's double presence and examines the richness and diversity of her character. *Nightwood* makes woman's double a "negative presence." Unable to understand this presence, woman tries to control it—as Nora tries to control Robin—and when she discovers it cannot be appropriated, she flees from it into alcoholism or insanity.

The Almanack

Ladies Almanack was one of several underground "lesbian" documents of the Paris expatriate community. In histories of the period it is mentioned in passing as a satire on Natalie Barney's company of women, the Académie des Femmes, which met regularly in the garden at 20, rue Jacob, to read women's writing. In his life of Natalie Barney, George Wickes recounts that in January 1928 Barney wrote Richard Aldington to inquire whether he might be interested in publishing this little book: "All ladies fit to figure in such an almanack should of course be eager to have a copy, and all gentlemen disapproving of them. Then the public might, with a little judicious treatment, include those lingering on the border of such islands and those eager to be ferried across" (*Amazon of Letters,* 180). Even Barney's lighthearted tone cannot disguise her perceptive reading of the *Almanack*. It is Dame Evangeline Musset, the heroine of the *Almanack* based on Natalie Barney, whose lifelong commitment is to rescue women from the perils of heterosexuality. The community Dame Musset creates is one in which women are not estranged from themselves—from their identity and sexuality—falsely mirroring the images created for them by the men who desire them, but a community in which women have value in and of themselves—because they *are* women, not merely because they behave as men have determined they should. The community of women celebrated by the *Almanack* is one where women revel in the pleasures of their newfound freedom. As Susan Sniader Lanser has suggested, "the *Almanack* creates a lesbian-feminist culture mythology and even suggests a radical critique of patriarchy by recognizing the personal/sexual as political. As it rewrites scripture, documents lesbian rituals, muses about women's condition, and tells the mock-heroic story of its patron saint, Dame Musset, *Ladies Almanack* offers both a mockery of patriarchal values and institutions and a vision of women turning to women in pleasure and joy" ("Speaking in Tongues," 41). A document by a woman for women, *Ladies Almanack* was one of the best-known pieces of "coterie" literature of the period. Apparently not taken seriously by its author, who referred to it both as a "piece of fluff" and as a "slight satiric wigging," it has not been taken seriously by commentators. (One might argue that such disclaimers by Barnes should not be taken at face value, that the comic cloak may hide a more serious subject.) But if this work is comic satire—as its author claims—it is certainly *not* a satire at the expense of lesbianism or of such groups as Natalie Barney established. Rather, it deplores the treatment of women in the heterosexual world, suggesting the same reasons for woman's "estrangement" from herself that *Nightwood* further explores. In telling the story of Dame Musset, the *Almanack* overturns patriarchal mythologies and creates a counterculture for women; it makes love between women a radically subversive act ("Speaking in Tongues," 40–41). If, as Louis Kannenstine observed about *Ryder*, "the man of *virtu* became the homosexual O'Connor. . . , in *Ladies Almanack, virtu* becomes a Sapphic trait, the property of women alone" (Kannenstine, *Art of Djuna Barnes,* 50).

The frontispiece drawing shows Dame Evangeline Musset (whose name suggests her evangelistic intentions) walking on what is described as "exceeding thin ice," a long pole extended to prevent the surrounding women, who are pictured in various stages of drowning, from "sinking for the third time." Dame Musset is called "a wonder woman," whose efforts are on behalf of that "which it has pleased God more and more to call frail woman." The *Almanack* itself is not only a tribute to Dame Musset—whose life is recounted through the twelve months and who is elevated to sainthood at its close—but a collection of poems, stories, and rituals designed to provide psychic support as woman endures the hardships of life among men. Woman is given a calendar that celebrates her accomplishments and places her works in an historical context. She is provided goddesses to protect her, a zodiac whose signs describe her, and a lullaby to soothe her. Her calendar is an intimate description of her "distempers"—the signs of her "fallen" condition; it also lists her "tides and moons," her "spring fevers, love philters and winter feasts." The chapbook provides a woman's history, rewrites woman in patriarchal culture and myth, explains the workings of her body and the directions of her sexuality, and—most importantly—analyzes the reasons for her frequent unhappiness, the difficulties of her situation, and accounts for man's simultaneous hatred and love of her. *Ladies Almanack* helps woman understand her longing for the lost Eden of her existence, when woman was praised and venerated rather than belittled and despised; she learns that it was her strength, her "impudence," her beauty and knowledge that affronted man, in punishment for which "the Earth sucked down her generations, Body for Body" (62).

Woman's body—which has been made the vehicle by which man satiates his lust—is returned to woman's control. Discovering its pleasures, the ladies of the *Almanack* celebrate woman's sexuality, writing the lesbian body. The almanack also discovers the pleasure of woman's speech, finds a language in which to express woman's desire for herself—a language that encompasses both heterosexual and lesbian women, that can accommodate the difference *within* womanhood As Susan Sniader Lanser has discovered, this woman's language speaks in "tongues." The tongue is glorified as a subtle sexual instrument (Dame Musset's tongue continues "flicking" through the ashes of her funeral pyre), an "antidote to the ethos of phallic supremacy and clitoral insufficiency of a newly Freudian age" ("Speaking in Tongues," 44). Woman is taught how to please herself, is encouraged to find "the Consolation every Woman has at her Finger Tips, or at the very Hang of her Tongue" as even Duchess Clitoressa becomes a character in the story (*Ladies Almanack*, 7). The signs of the zodiac correspond to a part of woman's body, each addressed in an attitude of sexual desire: "the longing leg," "the twining thigh," the "seeking arm," "the hungry heart." Woman's womb becomes "the spinning Centre of a spinning World" (*Ladies Almanack*, 52).

But even as woman is taught to love herself, to reject the image man has given her and love the one she herself creates, to seek a spiritual and physical soulmate in another woman, she learns that her unconquerable shame and despair is the result of patriarchal education. Entering "through the masculine Door," women have been taught that a strong, independent woman was not a woman at all, but a version of man. In the annals of history such a woman was thought to "have had a Testes of sorts, however writed and awander; that indeed she was called forth a Man, and when answering, by some Mischance, or monstrous Fury of Fate, stumbled over a Womb, and was damned then and forever to drag it about, like a Prisoner his Ball and Chain, whether she would or no" (*Ladies Almanack*, 53). The comic and antique language of this description cannot belie the seriousness of the accusation embedded here. Barnes is expressing a familiar argument—made by men and women alike—that proud, independent, intelligent, strong women are often accused of not being women at all: they are rather men in "drag." This was Katherine Anne Porter's argument against all the women of Natalie Barney's salon; it was also evident in Colette's comments on the sadism of the *Amazones*, "these mannish women [who] were able to break in and subjugate a horse, and when age and hard times deprived them of the whip and the hunting crop, they lost their final sceptre" (*The Pure and the Impure*, 72). When woman frees herself of the image of femininity by which man has constrained her, sheds the clothes he has fashioned for her, she exchanges his image of her for her image of him: she remakes herself in his image. No other possibility is available for woman under the law of the patriarchy because the law can only "admit [woman] to sense through the masculine door" (*Ladies Almanack*, 53). Such "inversion"—of behavior, of dress—is an effect of the patriarchal law. In trying to discover her own true self, she only discovers man's image of her. The *Almanack*, therefore, charts a double course: to illustrate the effects of man's effort to define woman and to provide a series of *different* images for woman. The almanack subverts the masculine image of woman by putting another in its place, one that reflects woman's diversity.

The price woman pays for displacing the patriarchal law, however, is a painful one, as the September entry, "Her Tides and Moons," illustrates. The *Almanack* suggests the complex condition of woman in the world, the illustration portraying woman as a mermaid stranded on land: "she is a fish of earth" (55). Woman is displaced in both time and place, as this entry in the calendar makes explicit: "The very Condition of Woman is so subject to Hazard, so complex, and so grievous, that to place her at one Moment is but to displace her at the next" (55). Man's jealousy of his wife does not reflect his high regard for her, but rather his fear that she will betray him with another's child, make a mockery of his masculinity, place the cuckold horns on his head. And worse awaits the woman who turns to another woman for sexual satisfaction: "see how vain is Man's suffering, change it how you will, for though that Prick is nowhere in the Flesh of Sister for Sister, they cry as loud" (57). Unable to comprehend sexuality in terms other than the phallic, man rages at his loss of woman, weeps for his wounded pride. But woman, when she remains the rib in man's side, submissive to his heterosexual law and defined by his desire, weeps "for Loneliness estranged—the unthinking returning of themselves to themselves" (58). Woman seeks the consolation of her sisters, desires the community of women, but is ashamed in betraying the master who would confine her, afraid to leave the world of patriarchal convention. The patriarchal scheme has not succeeded in reducing woman to nothing, in making her a "non-person" within the legal definition. Rather, she has been divided against herself, man has made her a fish out of water, a creature who cannot walk on land, who has been taught how to hate herself. The bizarre forms—neither man nor woman—that haunt Barnes's short stories (particularly those collected in *Spillway*) and form the company of grotesques that populate *Nightwood* are less Barnes's inventions than the creations of a world in which woman is a weaker, degraded version of man—"unmanned." Woman's gifts are wasted; she becomes waste: "She fouls everything she touches with the Droppings natural to her lost Condition!" (49). When her strength and independence have been returned to her in the company of women, she is a threat to man, who defines her as the "phallic woman."

The Book of Repulsive Women and *Ladies Almanack* exploit what has often been termed by male critics "the bawdy." This is a specifically female "bawdy" that admits no males, but nonetheless may have initially awakened a prurient male interest in the frank (and funny) emphasis on woman's sexuality. These works provide contrasting views of woman's body: the first its repulsive form, seen through the eyes of women who see themselves as a man would see them; the second the eroticized form woman sees when she has recaptured her sexuality from the patriarchal culture that appropriated it. The divided loyalty to the female body is an effect of woman's position in Western society: she quickly learns that man's desire for her body is the measure of its worth. Once that body "sags, stretches, becomes distorted" (*Ladies Almanack,* 56), it is cast aside by man. If that body is not desired by man or if its virtue is retained in chastity, woman weeps for the body's uselessness or subdues its carnal longings. As the woman ages, her body can only serve as a reminder of her lost worth—and the momentary nature of that worth, as Susan Sniader Lanser comments: "The 'September' section is the most overt in this recognition; the narrator complains that woman's 'very Condition' is 'so subject to Hazard, so complex, and so grievous' . . . that by middle age her body has been distorted and her mind 'corrupt with the Cash of a pick-thank existence'. . . . She suggests that although a woman may spend 'half her duration' 'upon her Back' . . . it will never be her preference" ("Speaking in Tongues," 43). Woman's body becomes in middle age the measure of her worthlessness, and as such, she despises it to the same degree as does the male who has abandoned it. Woman learns the bitter lesson that not only can the body be discarded, but it existed only to serve man's pleasure—never woman's own pleasure. It is noteworthy that Dame Musset, most unusual of women in never submitting to man's definition of her or in serving his sexual desire, recounts that she was deflowered "by the Hand of a Surgeon" when she was a child of ten (24), exclaiming that "I, even I, came to it as other Women." The notion that woman could teach herself the pleasures that her own body could afford her, could value her body beyond—indeed, apart from—the interest that man would have in it is one of the many lessons of *Ladies Almanack.* It is a lesson that Djuna Barnes herself desired to learn, but perhaps could not; it is a lesson that Natalie Barney seemed always to know—even into her old age.

Double Images of Womanhood

In a community of beautiful women, Djuna Barnes was considered to be the loveliest. Although apparently indifferent to lingering glances at her remarkable features, she nonetheless took great care with her appearance, was always dressed stylishly despite her recurrent financial difficulties, always wore dark red lipstick and blood red nail polish. Among the women Modernists, Barnes, Mina Loy, Jean Rhys, and Anaïs Nin all address in their fiction the question of woman's relationship to her body; in Barnes's work the various and frequently contradictory views she held about her own body are reflected through her heroines. The women of *Ryder* are victims of natural female processes—of menstruation, of pregnancy. They seem unable to escape their bodies or to control them.

Ladies Almanack argues for an acceptance, even a celebration, of the functions of the human female body. *Nightwood* shows woman divided against her physical being. She has been taught to revile the body and to be revolted by its functions; society makes her the instrument of her own destruction. At various times in her life Djuna Barnes held each of these perspectives on female anatomy. As a woman aware of the power of her own beauty, she realized that she could use it to manipulate others, but also that her beauty could be manipulated. In a brief encounter with Gertrude Stein, for instance, Barnes's appearance assured the jealousy of Alice Toklas, at the same time confirming for Stein that Barnes was not someone to be taken seriously: "Do you know what she said of me? Said I had beautiful legs! Now what does that have to do with anything? Said I had beautiful legs! Now I mean, what, what *did* she say that for? I mean, if you're going to say something about a person . . . I couldn't stand her. She had to be the centre of everything. A monstrous ego. Her brother—what was his name? Leo. Leo Stein. Poor thing. He was a nice boy. She simply ate him up!" (Field, *Djuna*, 104). Stein reduced Barnes to the "merely" beautiful, set her aside as a decorative *accoutrement,* made an object of her. Stein's reaction to Barnes reinforced the metonymic economy of the heterosexual world in which women's value for men is measured by certain parts of their bodies (breasts, buttocks, legs, hair), reducing the complete woman to her sexual parts. As a beautiful woman, Barnes was particularly aware of the ways in which she became the object of the desirous glance of men and was inspected by the sweeping gaze of women. Barnes's profound insecurity and ambivalence about her own body is obvious in photographs of her, which are nearly always taken in profile, emphasizing the ways in which she was divided against herself. She resented the claims her body made on her, the ways in which it proclaimed a sensuality to which she could not respond. Immensely vain, Barnes affected a pose that drew attention to her beauty, yet resented the notice taken of that beauty and resisted the effects of vanity, in particular the sexual trap. She was always aware that her style might be confused as her substance (as it seemed to have been with Stein), that her intellect might be successfully hidden by her own beauty. Barnes's beauty made her vulnerable; her protection was a haughty disregard.

This vulnerability under scrutiny by the human eye becomes a central trope in *Nightwood* and a feature of the narrative method, which operates by indirection, as though the characters were seen at a double remove. As Carolyn Allen has suggested ("'Dressing the Unknowable'"), this method results in narrative passivity that is directed by a hidden viewer ("Here he had been seen ordering details for funerals . . ."; "he would be observed staring up at the huge towers," *Nightwood,* 29). The characters of *Nightwood* are constantly the victims of society's vigil over them, seen when they think they are not observed, caught unaware by another's glance. An example of the power that such "unseen seeing" can hold is apparent in the scene where Robin Vote is first present, being revived by Dr. O'Connor from her faint. Although a "sham," a doctor who is not really a doctor, O'Connor serves as a fallen version of society's representative. Robin is unprepared to meet his gaze, is vulnerable to that gaze: "The woman who presents herself to the spectator as a 'picture' forever arranged is, for the contemplative mind, the chiefest danger. . . . Such a woman is the infected carrier of the past: before her the structure of our head and jaws ache—we feel we could eat her, she who is eaten death returning, for only then do we put our face close to the blood on the lips of our forefathers" (37). The doctor's gaze and ours prey on this woman, her vulnerable beauty a reminder that in the past she has been forced to submit to man's will, has been "eaten" by him, her blood dripping from his lips. (Here the image of blood is reinforced by the fact that Dr. O'Connor has used the occasion of tending to the ill woman to borrow her lipstick to replace the "line of rouge across his lips"; this image of "blood on the lips of our forefathers" recalls the male fear of female power—of the mother as a devouring vampire.) Juxtaposed against Barnes's claim that Stein "ate" her brother, the image of eating those who are vulnerable is particularly barbarous. We remember too Natalie Barney's horror at the vision of Alice being consumed by an ever larger and less mobile Gertrude Stein. Vampire women are frequent characters in Barnes's work; they have learned their methods from the patriarchy (as Gertrude Stein learned hers). Robin Vote, unfortunately, has too often been mistaken for a vampire woman, a representative of the world's evil. This victim, however, has been mistaken for the victimizer. Rather than a "depraved nymphomaniac," Robin Vote is, as Jane Marcus has argued, "Our Lady of the Wild Things, savage Diana the huntress with her deer and dogs, the virgin Artemis roaming the woods with her band of women" ("Carnival of the Animals," 7). She stands *outside* society's definitions, and that is her salvation; Nora Flood, society's representative in this novel, tries to keep Robin within society's reach—in her life, in her bed— and that is her damnation.

There is little evidence from Barnes's writing that her own body ever gave her much pleasure. The celebration of human female sexuality offered in *Ladies Almanack* belongs to Evangeline Musset, not to Djuna Barnes. Although *Nightwood* explores the painful psychic realities of a destructive love between women, it does not portray the physical relationship. Indeed, there is no enactment of the love between the two women—only a statement of its existence as a powerful force. The same silence on the pleasures of physical love between women marks Barnes's own relationship with Thelma Wood. The record of their affair states the fact of their love for each other without demonstrating the reality of that love. It is a record marked by anguish, by fear that the statement of love is not a true one, the fear of loss. Remembering that relationship, Natalie Barney wrote Barnes on 15 October 1966: "Is our memory a second life—when the past becomes the future? What have you done with yours now? And after 'Nightwood'—where Thelma proved rather a rough guy? As for 'Charles'—what poor materials for the richness of love. Have you nearer and better friends now, as I have—and always Romaine. Do you recollect the evening when we wanted to carry you off from Cagnes—and you told us it would be of no use: that you would only weep and return there." Barney's letter recalls the painful time when Barnes followed Thelma Wood as Nora Flood follows Robin Vote. The reference to Thelma as a "rough guy" suggests that Thelma (who was "Simon" in the relationship) used Djuna ("Irine") as a man would (Field, *Djuna*, 155). As Barney perceives in her letter—written when she was 90 years old—Djuna Barnes had not been well treated by either her male or female lovers. In an undated letter (probably 1927), Simon promises his "Dearest one" that he will try to be better to her: "You said something just as I was leaving that makes things seem a little less terrible—maybe you didnt mean it—you said it so softly—that we could meet in New York and maybe Simon would be different. But you see how Silly Simon must clutch on anything to make him stronger—you see I can't think of anything ahead that doesn't mean you—I keep saying 'Simon you've got to be a man and take your medicine'—but then always in my head goes 'there is no Simon and no Irine' and I cant bear it and go crazy." The letter goes on to promise that "Simon will not touch one drop" more of alcohol, blaming the liquor for his violence and infidelity. Barnes endured four more years of suffering with Thelma Wood before the relationship died.

The writing of *Nightwood* was an act of revenge and an attempt at exorcism—each achieved its end. Thelma was angered by the portrayal of her as Robin Vote, and refused to talk about the novel. In the years prior to the publication of *Nightwood,* Thelma had apparently held out hope that the affair could be resumed, but Djuna had categorically put an end to it, turning away not only from Thelma but from lesbian alliances. In the years following Djuna's departure from the rue St.-Romain apartment that she had purchased in order to live with Thelma, she was involved in several heterosexual relationships, underwent an abortion at age 41, and fell in love with a man living in England during the time she stayed at Peggy Guggenheim's country house. He betrayed her in various ways—including an affair with Dolly Wilde—and she was reminded of similar treatment she had undergone in the relationship with Thelma. There was at least one more brief heterosexual affair before Barnes gave up efforts to find a suitable lover. Years later Barnes responded to an announcement by Natalie Barney that she had taken a new *petite amie* that no "little friend" existed in Barnes's life: "If I saw one I would jump into the river" (24 October 1966). At 92, Natalie Barney wrote Barnes (then 76) to inquire: "Have you no 'mate' to torment and exalt you? Love is a better drug than drink. So I lift this glass of hope to you" (letter dated "day after Easter, 1968").

The life that Djuna Barnes led in New York beginning in the 1940s was as far removed from the life at 9, rue St.-Romain, as possible. In New York she was able to establish the "simple and ordered domestic situation" she had apparently always desired (Field, *Djuna*, 111). That in old age Barnes became increasingly confined to her own home, and that she preferred the monastic life of her tiny apartment to any alternative that New York City might offer, suggests a desperate need to establish control over her daily life. In the Patchin Place apartment she pared the necessities of existence to a minimum; the St.-Romain apartment, by contrast, had been characterized by a certain lushness and bohemian warmth. The list of contents from that apartment corresponds in almost every detail with the apartment described in *Nightwood* (with the exception that no circus roundabout horses flanked the bed on St.-Romain). The walls were hung with ornate mirrors and ecclesiastical pictures, Venetian chandeliers hung from the ceiling, rooms were furnished with large couches and tapestried chairs on which lay liturgical pillows in yellow and red. There was a church runner over the fireplace, satin-covered chairs in the bedroom, a china Virgin, Venetian mirrors, and a religious scene painted on glass. The apartment was a veritable *broquante* shop. The juxtaposition of the sacred items with the secular and the contrast between the spiritual trappings of the apartment and the profane union this home supported are ironies that Barnes undoubtedly enjoyed, indeed insisted upon. Decadence inhabited the domestic; the apartment was a world in which moral and sexual codes were reversed.

The decadence—even depravity—of such ornamentation becomes the motif by which *Nightwood* is known. The standard interpretation of the novel discovers depravity itself under investigation. Louis Kannenstine writes that "the novel's fantasticality persistently yields an impression of beauty and barbarity or degradation" (*Art of Djuna Barnes*, 101–102). Yet as Matthew O'Connor tries to explain to Nora Flood in "Watchman, What of the Night?" that corruption is an effect of lighting: what seems frightening and perverse under darkness of night seems less diabolical by daylight. The combination of beauty and barbarity that has been so often noted in the novel, however, rests in the dark and mysterious regions of womanhood that *Nightwood* exposes to the light. Nora Flood seeks out Matthew O'Connor—a man in woman's clothing who often refers to himself as "an old lady"—for information about the nature of woman-hood. She learns that she is estranged from her own womanhood (a form of which is embodied in Robin), is unaware of its complexities and myste-ries, is doomed to misunderstanding its processes. Nora is a "type" of woman caught by the double bind of the patriarchal law. She is the object of desire but is allowed no desire of her own. Heterosexual desire acts itself out on woman's body, that body is a commodity in an economy of sexual desire, but the body belongs not to the woman who inhabits it but to the man who desires it. By definition under the patriarchal law, woman is estranged from her own body, divided from it and against it. Nora cries in despair at O'Connor's revelation ("I'll never understand her—I'll al-ways be miserable—just like this," 85), but never realizes that she is not only a victim of the patriarchal law but an agent of it.

Nightwood constructs a society doomed to misread itself and to misin-terpret the signs of its own operations. Nora Flood cannot "read" Robin Vote because Robin's behavior, appearance, and efforts to communicate are not inscribed in the societal code to which she is asked to conform. A product of a culture that has suppressed female *difference,* Nora Flood sees Robin as a man would see her: as an object of desire. Like a man, Nora constructs Robin in her own image. Thus Robin simultaneously serves as a "sign" of female difference repressed by Western culture and is misread by Nora into conformity with the cultural code. Every time Robin's actions make obvious the strain of conforming to the operations of this society, every time she draws attention to Nora's "misreading" of her, Nora suffers, claiming that Robin—rather than Nora herself—is the cause of the ensuing misery. Nora both loves and fears Robin, but she loves her own "re-made" image of Robin and fears the Robin who signals woman's difference, the Robin who stands outside the sexual economy of this culture. Woman's eroticism is linked to death, her womb the center of a dark, threatening mystery (157). This culture has tried to expunge woman's presence, has washed itself clean of her "with every emollient and *savon,*" as O'Connor tells Nora. The mystery of woman's sexuality is thus hidden from her; it cannot be read because it cannot be seen. It is enclosed in the dark moist regions of her own body: woman's nature, according to this ethic, is the root of all evil. And that aspect of the womanly that inhabits man—his sensitivity and sensuality—must be sup-pressed, its only form of expression the fantastic parody of womanhood presented by the rouged, wigged, nightgowned Matthew O'Connor. O'Connor transforms himself into a woman by adopting her adorn-ments—her powder, lipstick, nail polish, perfume—and in doing so calls attention to woman's role as *ornament* in society: she is decorative (and expected to be decorous—that is, to hide her desire), inessential, an adornment that in its beauty calls attention to its very depravity. The debauchery *Nightwood* exposes is the product of a moral code that attempts to root out debauchery and depravity, to punish it under God's law. Woman is the sign of that debauchery, her womb the vessel that protects its holy elements.

So it is that Nora Flood "becomes hopelessly fascinated by the depravity suppressed by the Puritan ethic" (Kannenstine, *Art of Djuna Barnes*, 119): she is fascinated by the depravity that now inhabits her, a depravity she had never known until it exposed itself in her love for Robin Vote. Nora's love is both homosexual and incestuous, a form of self-love and self-discovery. Her attraction to Robin rests in that which society has suppressed in herself; she sees in Robin both the alien and the known: "She is myself. What am I to do?" (127). But the source of attraction is also the cause of fear, as Robin's presence puts into question all of the moral and ethical assumptions Nora has learned to accept in society. Nora's nightwatch reveals precisely this relation of the estranged and the familiar, brings the realization that Robin is an earlier form of herself, one unconscious of puritan moral values. In fact, Robin is Nora's unconscious, repressed self: "A man is another person—a woman is yourself, caught as you turn in panic; on her mouth you kiss your own. If she is taken you cry that you have been robbed of yourself" (143). But the discovery that another "woman is yourself" does not lead to a reinforcement of woman's "self," a doubling of the power of womanhood. The discovery leads, ironically, to yet another form of self-alienation. Nora discovers that she has been robbed of the difference *within* gender, of the difference within woman and between women. That difference is signaled by Robin's erotic abandon and promiscuity. When woman's sexuality cannot be appropriated and thereby contained within the patriarchal norm, woman's sexuality becomes her destruction: the penalty for sex is death. Promiscuity is a man's right, not a woman's. Under the law, sexuality is phallic and is the mark of male priority. Thus women are interchangeable; women are the "same" from the male point of view. Nora transgresses this law by constantly calling attention to her difference, by refusing to conform to the dictates of the law. Indeed, she seems to be a "throwback" to an evolutionary period that preexisted the law.

Ladies Almanack offers a form of consolation against the effects of this violence and provides remedies against the self-destruction that is often its end result. *Nightwood* explores the very roots of such injustice and follows the route to an earlier existence, one in which women were, as Jane Marcus describes, "in command of their own sexuality, free from domination and submission and the moral implications of sin and guilt related to monogamy" ("Carnival of Animals," 7). In such a culture the control that Robin Vote exercises over her various lovers is not the sign of cruelty, bestiality, and depravity, but rather a recognition of control over her own sexuality. In a society in which women are estranged from themselves, from their sexual appetites, their sexuality becomes depravity: they become organisms "surviving in an alien element" (*Nightwood*, 13). Western society has (almost) managed to unsex women, to make them the lifeless playthings of the patriarchal culture.

Nightwood: The Puritan Perspective

Perhaps the only item from the rue St.-Romain apartment that Djuna Barnes did not sell along with her other belongings in 1937 was the broken doll that Thelma Wood had given her. Propped on their bed with its legs spread, the doll was smashed by Thelma in a fit of rage against Djuna. In *Nightwood* that doll appears as a symbol of childishness, of innocence, but also as an image of a dead child. Nora knows she has found Robin's new lover when she discovers the doll on Jenny Petherbridge's bed: "We give death to a child when we give it a doll—it's the effigy and the shroud; when a woman gives it to a woman, it is the life they cannot have, it is their child, sacred and profane; so when I saw that other doll. . . . What part of monstrosity am I that I am always crying at its side!" (142). This "dead" child is not only the child that a lesbian relationship cannot produce, but an image of the self that has been killed in Nora. It is one of several "dummy" images of woman in the novel that include the garden statue, the doll, and the trapeze artist who is sewn into her trapeze costume: "The stuff of the tights was no longer a covering, it was herself; the span of the tightly stitched crotch was so much her own flesh that she was as unsexed as a doll. The needle that had made one the property of the child made the other the property of no man" (13). Man loves not the living woman but her deathly image; he remakes the living in the image of the dead, taking away her life and breath, sewing up her sexuality.

The garden statue that is gazed upon, the doll that is played with, the trapeze artist who performs, all symbolize woman as object. The doll, however, serves one other function in the iconography of the novel: its "unsexed" condition suggests the genderless state of the boy-girl who is neither one thing or the other, "answerable to no function in either sex" as Katherine Anne Porter observed ("Gertrude Stein: A Self-Portrait," 522). Representing the homosexual female in the doll, Barnes played out the myth of the third sex in which female sexuality is "dead" in ways different from the death prescribed for female sexuality by the heterosexual code. Here woman's sexuality is "dead" because it is not procreative. The eroticism of homosexuality constitutes a trick of nature: the sexuality it would arouse is no sexuality at all, a poor substitute for the supposed potent eroticism of heterosexuality. Thus the homosexual woman is once again denied her body: she discovers an erotic form that can only remind her that she is "sexless," permanently estranged from her body, from self; a sexuality whose act constitutes a "misgiving." Such beings are the property of no one: they belong neither to each other nor to man. Thus they are outside man's law. Unable to "perform" for man, they cannot be possessed by him: "The last doll, given to age, is the girl who should have been a boy, and the boy who should have been a girl! . . . The doll and the immature have something right about them, the doll because it resembles but does not contain life, and the third sex because it contains life but resembles the doll. The blessed face! It should be seen only in profile, otherwise it is observed to be the conjunction of the identical cleaved halves of sexless misgiving!" (148). Matthew O'Connor's explication of the correspondences between the unsexed doll and the ambiguously sexed boy-girl can be—and often has been—read as an indictment of homosexuality. In acknowledging the doll to be the symbol of the child the lesbian relationship cannot produce, Nora Flood articulates the primary reason homosexuality stands outside the patriarchal law: the homosexual act is not procreative. In claiming that Robin is the image of herself, her own double, Nora again offers a reason that homosexuality is "unnatural." A product of the puritan ethic, Nora gives the standard objections to such unions, which view homosexuality as a bond of death, according to Louis Kannenstine: "Robin can only finally be possessed in death. And lesbianism is the absorption in the mirror image, which amounts to the foreswearing of generation" (*Art of Djuna Barnes*, 121). The doll is, then, the image of lesbian death.

As Annette Kolodny has noted, *Nightwood* "is not a novel written to explore the world of perverts, as some of its earliest critics insisted, but instead a novel which explores the psyches of those who inhabit and perceive what is to the 'normal' reader an inverted version of his own highly conventionalized sexual and social reality. The characters come alive most fully at night, prowling the streets of European cities, and harbor within their gendered bodies an inverted (or opposing) sexual identity" ("Some Notes on Defining a 'Feminist Literary Criticism,'" 44). That early readers of the novel should have "misread" it is not at all surprising, since the narrative method of *Nightwood* locates its reading in Nora Flood, herself trying to read the iconography of the landscape into which her love of Robin has taken her. Her interpretation of the people and events she encounters is a "normal" one—that is, an interpretation infused with Western puritanism. She is caught in an interpretive act that forces her to read perversion in her own actions, to interpret herself as a pervert. Louis Kannenstine and others overlook Nora's role as representative of American culture—a woman puritanized and purified. What she is experiencing in her agonized love for Robin is, indeed, a love of self—for a self that has been denied her, suppressed in such a way that she can only see its shadow, can only glimpse its form at night. If Robin is "innocent" of the moral values that inhabit modern culture, Nora's very naivete—the unknowing state that produces her misreading—results from cultural efforts to deny her access to knowledge of and pleasure in her own body. Robin possesses this knowledge and acts out this pleasure instinctively, but Nora remains blind to it, confused by the ways in which Robin seems both alien and allied to her, unable to see that Robin is her own self, a former prelapsarian self. Nora discovers herself in the boy-girl Robin, sees herself in the doll splayed upon the bed, but she misperceives that vision, thinking it to be a sign of an hermaphroditic self—neither one thing nor the other; instead the deathly doll is an image of her own sexual desire, of her womanhood. These have been destroyed by the very patriarchal forces that would possess them. That the self Nora discovers *seems* to be depraved nymphomania, that such discoveries can only be made under cover of darkness, is a trick of perspective. The discovery is seen through the eyes of puritanism, the force that has produced the very depravity it abhors.

The world of the nightwood does not liberate those who wander its groves, nor does it provide release from the constraints of the day world. To the contrary, rather than being liberated from the *dis-ease* of gender by his nightly transvestism, Dr. O'Connor sees this behavior as a symptom of his diseased condition. Nora does not find in Robin a counterpart of her lost self or achieve a union that would produce sexual and psychological integration for her; rather she discovers an alienation *from* herself and *of* herself that she had not previously recognized. Even at the novel's close, however, Nora does not realize the source of the alienation in herself or in the social code she embodies. Barnes's feminist discovery that such suffering, such discomfort and disease, is societally produced—that nightwood is produced by the puritan ethic that would expose its deadly effects—in no way alters the darkness of her vision. Indeed, such a reading further darkens the world *Nightwood* exposes.

The very subject of *Nightwood* is a product of its narrative effects. Its "trans-generic" qualities and "generic mutability" (Kannenstine, *Art of Djuna Barnes,* 96, 109) are produced by the search for form. But it is the notion of "forms" and definitive categories that is put into question by *Nightwood*. Definitions of gender and sexuality are shown to be socially produced rather than biologically determined, but the directions of sexual orientation are also discovered to be at odds with social norms. The literary artifact reflects the inversion and subversion of sexual coding through the dislocation and disruption of literary genre. Although it is Robin's experience that figures the contradictions of sexual gender (reflected in inconsistencies in literary genre), and it is she who stands outside the patriarchal code, calling it into question, she is forced by the narrative perspective of *Nightwood* to serve as the object of the narrative investigation, not as its subject. Robin is the product of the various reactions revealed by those who observe her—she is controlled by her circumstances, never in control of them.

That woman's sexuality is made man's object (his plaything), that woman is observed rather than observing, that she is defined by society in her ornamental aspect, suggests Robin Vote's tragedy to be the impossibility of her becoming a subject of her own discourse. Of course, Robin does speak in the novel, and when she does her anger is directed at Nora, who inverts her words and accuses her of lying. Robin calls Nora a "devil" who "make[s] everything dirty" (143). Later, in the street outside the apartment, Robin makes Nora give her money for "a poor wretched beggar of a whore." Seeing herself in the beggar woman, Robin speaks to her using the term "they" to refer to women like Nora: "These woman—they are all like her. . . . They are all good—they want to save us!" (144). Like other "good" women, Nora imposes her moral principles on all women. She becomes the unknowing instrument of the patriarchy. Unaware of the patriarchal crimes against her own nature, she allies herself with her oppressors—the church (whose ecclesiastical draperies hang in her bedroom), the law, the medical community—in trying to "save" Robin, to make her answer to society's claims. Nora thinks her tragedy lies in loving a woman who is faithless and drunken, a liar and a cheat; she does not realize that she herself is an instrument of Robin's tragedy: Nora's "crime" is her effort to make Robin conform to a moral code based on patriarchal self-interest and misogyny. At the end of the novel, Robin knows the crime against her but cannot speak it (she barks "in a fit of laughter"); Nora can speak but does not yet realize her part in the crime.

The perversion *Nightwood* exposes is not the depravity of homosexuality, the horrors of transsexuality, or the ugliness of woman's hidden nature, but the tragic effect of woman's estrangement from her own self. Woman has been made to think her sexual nature is perverse; men who display the sensitivity thought to be endemic to the feminine nature "recall . . . a degraded form" (30). Matthew O'Connor's transvestite needs mark the pathos of his situation ("he dresses to lie beside himself, who is so constructed that love, for him, can be only something special," Nora thinks as she enters the abominable room he occupies, 80), but also parody woman's role as sexual object: "I'm a lady in need of no insults," O'Connor tells Nora (151). Matthew O'Connor is a construct of the patriarchal, forced into his "perversion" by society's perversely rigid definitions of sexuality. But *Nightwood* neither celebrates nor condemns perversion: it reveals "difference from" arbitrarily imposed norms and exposes the roots of that which society has defined as the perverse, uncovering "sin" as the transgression of sexual difference. Appropriate

punishments are meted out for crimes against the heterosexual imperative: Robin, who does not want to be married or to be a mother, gives
birth to a mentally deficient child; Nora, whose sin is loving another
woman, is made to comfort other women whom Robin has abandoned;
Matthew O'Connor, who requires woman's dress to perform onanistic
rites, describes himself as a "permanent mistake" of nature (132).

The Patriarchal Vision

The patriarchal vision of *Nightwood* offers only debased images of
womanhood. The forms of manhood—in Felix Volkbein (the Jew trying
to prove himself a Gentile) and O'Connor (a male trying to become female, a doctor turned medicine man)—parody masculinity's priorities.
All those who do not fit the arbitrary categories of this system are displaced by it, estranged from themselves by the very act of trying to conform to the system's demands. Woman's particular estrangement from her
sexuality and sensuality is a condition suffered not only by lesbian women
(or by male homosexuals who want to be women), but by *all* women.
Nor is it homosexuals who display a more radically perverse manifestation of this estrangement by trying to unite with an image of themselves.
Indeed, as *Ladies Almanack* satirically suggests, it may well be heterosexual women who play out the most damaging perversion—pretending for
themselves and for their lovers that the desire they feign is their own, that
they possess it (rather than being possessed by another), that they can
direct it and act upon it. If, as Adrienne Rich and others have argued,
sexual identity displays itself along a continuum, then all women are part
of the lesbian community celebrated in *Ladies Almanack*—and all men
share in Dr. O'Connor's transvestite rituals. In *Nightwood* lesbianism
displays certain affinities with the unconscious operations of the mind,
which direct the body's responses even as the conscious mind tries to suppress them. Nora never understands her love for Robin (which does not
display itself in the novel as lesbianism, if lesbianism is defined by sexual
acts). Indeed, she is horrified by its nature ("I see the night does something to a person's identity," she tells O'Connor, 81). The day "is thought
upon and calculated," according to O'Connor, whereas "the night is not
premeditated." The Bible is the book of the day world, whereas the night-
gown is the dress of the night realm (80).

Pretense and artifice—lying—become part of *Nightwood*'s scheme of
inversion not because the characters are innately corrupt but because
their very survival in society demands that they lie. The effects of this perverse principle are played out in the actions of Jenny Petherbridge, perhaps the most accomplished liar in the cast. As O'Connor describes her,

she is a "little, hurried decaying comedy jester, the face on the fool's-stick, and with a smell about her of mouse-nests": "She is a 'looter,' and eternally nervous. Even in her sleep I'll pronounce that her feet twitch and her orifices expand and contract like the iris of a suspicious eye" (98). O'Connor correctly sees that Jenny "has a longing for other people's property, but the moment she possesses it the property loses some of its value, for the owner's estimate is its worth" (98). Jenny's "sin" is the sign of her capitulation to the patriarchal code in which woman possesses no intrinsic value, only the value attached to her by her "owner." Seeing a woman desired by another is a stimulus to desire and an excuse for stealing her away—once she has been stolen, her value is debased. Jenny plays out the evils the system produces precisely because she is trapped within the system's code, a victim.

The moral point of view the novel holds produces the very "evil" the novel examines. Whatever unity or centrality *Nightwood* achieves results from the imposition of this viewpoint. Such unity—of character, of theme—is yet another pretense, however, a form of storytelling (or lying) arbitrarily imposed. The "evidence" the novel uncovers is that the human personality is multiple, often divided against itself, contradictory, and enigmatic. The consistency of a public persona is achieved only at great cost. Such demands that the diverse (and perverse) elements of one's nature be suppressed make a *somnambule* of Robin Vote, a vulture of Jenny Petherbridge, an imposter of Felix Volkbein, and a transvestite of Matthew O'Connor. The dictates of this society are that one be male, Gentile, and heterosexual: women are tolerated only if they submit themselves to male privilege. It is true that *Nightwood* is not a well-wrought, unified work of art. It eschews artistic synthesis, exposes the malicious philosophy that calls for unity and decries diversity. It is little wonder that T. S. Eliot initially thought the doctor the central character or that he found the final chapter "superfluous" (xii). Reviewers and commentators have had difficulties in situating this work in the literary tradition, within a single genre, or in agreeing on whether it is an artistic success, and if so, *how*. And to concentrate on *Nightwood* as a woman's novel—as a work that examines the situation of women—does little to argue artistic unity. In fact, the psychic fragmentation that is the effect of woman's hopeless effort to deny her own internal diversity is present in the metaphors critics have used to discuss the "splits" in *Nightwood:* beauty and bestiality, sacred and profane, daylight and darkness, duality and damnation. No synthesis of these doubles is achieved by *Nightwood*, since the oppositions that inhabit the moral structure of the novel are artificially produced in society by the very effort to suppress one component in the series of doubles. The puritan ethic has allied woman's sexuality with bestiality, profanity, darkness, and damnation in order to channel that sexuality toward forms of expression that served man's interests rather than woman's needs.

Nightwood is distinctly different, then, from other works of the Paris period. It is not a minor Modernist masterpiece, a shadow to Joyce's *Ulysses,* but a singular undertaking that addresses woman's place in the patriarchal construct. As Sandra Gilbert has suggested, "For Lawrence, as for Eliot and Joyce, the 'cybernetic' patterns of dominance/submission associated with paradigms of gender were not only inevitable but necessary, not just irrefutable but consoling": "That a male modernist should have wanted the consolation of orthodoxy is not surprising, for it is, after all, only those who are oppressed or repressed by history and society who want to shatter the established paradigms of dominance and submission associated with the hierarchies of gender and restore the primordial chaos of transvestism or genderlessness" ("Costumes of the Mind," 416). Djuna Barnes did not see transvestism as a restoration of "the primordial chaos," nor did she envision a "genderless" world of androgyny: for her, the "third sex" was a patriarchal creation that further bound homosexuals—men and women alike—to the heterosexual paradigm.[9] Only *Ladies Almanack* might be seen as a predictive text, one that envisions a world where women are able to take control of their sexuality and sensuality in order to derive pleasure rather than pain from their bodies, to free themselves of puritanic guilt. But the "vision" of *Ladies Almanack* was a contemporary reality for only a small number of expatriate women, a community in which Barnes herself participated but through which she did not find release from the constraints of gender roles dictated by the larger society. She apparently did not discover there the sexual freedom of expression the *Almanack* celebrates; she did not find in lesbianism a release from the patriarchy. *Nightwood* displays the horrors of oppression and repression, but it offers no solutions to them. *Ladies Almanack* was an effort to make woman the *subject* of her own discourse, to find a language that could articulate woman's experience separate from patriarchal linguistic forms. *Nightwood* returned woman as *object* of the patriarchal fiction, robbing her of a language through which to articulate her passion and anger. Playing the grandmother, bewigged and rouged, Matthew O'Connor parodies woman's language, steals her stories and her images in order to teach her about herself. Gossipy and garrulous, he renders Nora mute. Unable, finally, to explain herself, Robin howls like a dog.

"Censor the body and you censor breath and speech at the same time," claims Hélène Cixous ("Laugh of the Medusa," 280). Five years after the publication of *Nightwood,* Barnes left Paris permanently, taking up a new residence and a new life: her last forty years were marked by celibacy and silence. This decision was as carefully considered as any other in her life and should not be seen (as it usually is) either as an inability to live in the world or as an elaborate eccentricity. It was a choice: a self-imposed censorship of sexuality and speech. Now that the body, which for many years had been the object of sexual desire by both men and women, was no longer on display and no longer vulnerable to sexual involvement, Barnes began to care for it. She stopped smoking and drinking, put herself on a high protein diet, and took vitamins. Years of abuse, however, had produced in Barnes (as in Margaret Anderson, another expatriate Modernist who left Paris) a chronic emphysema, so that she found speaking enormously difficult in the last years of her life. In the mid-1970s, she rebuked a young man who commented in a telephone conversation with her that her voice sounded strong and good: "The voice is the last thing to go, after the eyes, ears, and legs have betrayed you." Betrayed by her body in almost every conceivable way, Djuna Barnes finally refused to acknowledge her body, refused photographs and mirrors, refused to be seen. Only her voice, rarely heard by e. e. cummings, her neighbor in Patchin Place, revealed her continuing and anachronistic existence among the living.

8
NATALIE BARNEY:
RUE JACOB

If among the expatriate women of Paris Djuna Barnes suffered most intensely the effects of her upbringing in a puritan culture, Natalie Barney was least affected by American Protestant morality. Barney seems to have existed entirely apart from certain aspects of Western culture, escaping the pervasive guilt from which most of her generation suffered. Her knowledge of organized religion was minimal (she took communion only once and claimed uncertainty about whether Christmas marked the birth or death of Christ); her interest in pagan cultures was in part a reaction against Christian insistence that bodily pleasures be sacrificed to preserve the soul. At a young age Barney realized the trap Western culture held for all women and refused to surrender her body, independence, or feminism to marriage. Like Sylvia Beach, Barney became increasingly aware in her adolescent years of the unhappiness of her parents' marriage. Jealous of Alice Pike Barney's interest in painting—and her proximity to the handsome models who posed for her—Albert Clifford Barney turned more frequently to his mistresses and to alcohol. Natalie saw in her father's behavior a model of the duplicitousness she assumed to be an inherent part of patriarchal culture. When her mother decided to spend periods away from Albert Barney, Natalie and her sister followed their mother to Paris while their father spent time in London. The difference between the cultures of these two cities is of crucial importance to understanding Natalie's later decision to live out her adult life in France. She saw in English culture an extreme form of patriarchal power and described England as a country "where nothing is provided for women, not even men" (Chalon, *Portrait of a Seductress,* 15).

A Privileged Life

At the time Natalie Barney discovered the hypocrisy of her parents' marriage, she also realized her sexual interest in women. Her "escape" from the marriage trap and her refusal throughout her life to abide by the terms of fidelity and discretion dictated by Western society were carefully considered decisions. In almost every respect, Natalie Barney *chose* the life she led; no aspect of her life was left to chance. She turned her intelligence and common sense to constructing a life that would itself be a work of art, an aesthetic as well as a sensual experience. It would be a mistake, then, to read Natalie Barney's life as merely a rebellion against patriarchal forms. Rather, one needs to follow Barney's own suggestion that her life was consciously constructed outside and beyond the dictates of Western culture. This lived record was Barney's most perfect artistic achievement.

Most commentators on Barney's life begin by listing the various rich resources with which she was endowed: beauty, intelligence, charm, wit, sensuality, and kindness. Perhaps the most important factor in the development of these qualities, however, was the freedom from social stricture provided by financial security. Natalie Barney's fortune was comparable only to that possessed by Winifred Ellerman (Bryher), a woman who, like Vita Sackville-West, had been denied by English law the right to inherit her father's property and the bulk of his shipping fortune. Although Bryher showed an aptitude and interest in her father's financial affairs, the Ellerman fortune (about $800 million) went to her brother, John, who was unable to manage it successfully. In 1934, a few months after her father's death, Winifred Ellerman inherited a small portion of the estate, £1,200,000, then about $6,000,000. Like Albert Barney, young John Ellerman had little interest in increasing the family wealth and eventually sold the business interests. Albert Barney also sold his father's business: when he was about 30 years old, he sold the Barney Car Works, a producer of railroad cars, to the Pullman Sleeping Car Company. Barney "retired" on the profits, and on his death at age 52 left his daughters $2,500,000 each. When Alice Pike Barney later married one of her models, a young man who resented the implication that he had married a woman more than twice his age for her money, Natalie and Laura Barney inherited another $1,500,000 each from their mother. Although difficult to compute in terms of real economic value, this fortune today would be worth perhaps twenty times its value in 1902.

Considering the extent of Barney's financial independence, she lived rather modestly all her life. The staff at her residence at 20, rue Jacob (a house she rented for sixty years, although she easily could have afforded to buy it), was smaller than that maintained by Edith Wharton at her rue de Varenne apartment—and Wharton's means, although comfortable, were in no way comparable to Barney's fortune. Like Ellerman, Barney supported the work of other writers and artists, but unlike Ellerman she did not usually give direct monetary gifts or provide ongoing financial aid. Instead, she encouraged the intellectual development of individual artists, introducing them to more established writers, found publishers for their work, and through her salon developed an audience for their art. Virgil Thomson, who set several of Barney's short lyrics to music and who had received support from Barney in his early Paris years, reports that she "was not a woman of facile generosity" or an "easy touch" (Wickes, *Amazon of Letters*, 249–250).

In using her money to establish a cultural community in Paris and to support artists whose work interested her, Natalie Barney followed a direction already set by her mother, who had abandoned the responsibilities of marriage—especially the social demands of her husband's position—to continue her own painting and to establish Washington, D.C., as a center of the arts. Shortly after her husband's death, and with money she inherited from his railroad fortune, Alice Pike Barney built Studio House to house theatrical and musical entertainments. (Studio House, now owned by the Smithsonian, still provides a forum for the arts.) Released from the bondage of her marriage by the early death of her husband, Alice Barney devoted her energies to art, especially to amateur theatricals, some of which were considered too *risqué* for Washington tastes. Her later life overturned all the conventions honored by her husband in the years of their marriage. If Alice Barney's life was "very correct, conventional and decorous" before her husband's death, her later life was "openly bohemian" to the extent that she stood "on the verge of social ostracism" in polite Washington society (*Amazon of Letters*, 23). Alice Pike Barney served as a role model for her daughter in two important ways: the suffering she endured in an unhappy and highly conventional marriage served to warn her daughter of the threat marriage posed to woman's independence; in Alice Pike Barney's devotion to art and in her disregard for social conventions, Natalie discovered a model for her own unconventional behavior.

Natalie Barney's father would no doubt have been appalled at seeing a portion of the Barney fortune dispensed on the Académie des Femmes, on afternoon entertainments that included Colette sliding naked through the wooded garden at 20, rue Jacob, or for the private publication of lesbian poetry. Since adolescence, however, Natalie had been successfully evading Albert Barney's authoritarian and highly puritanical strictures. Without ever openly rebelling against him and while always appearing to meet his expectations, Natalie had cleverly escaped her father's design for her life. Like Edith Wharton, Natalie appeared on the debutante circuit for several seasons. Unlike Wharton, Natalie Barney seems to have enjoyed the dances, the dressing up, the flirtations. Whereas Wharton succumbed to the pressure to marry someone of her own kind, Barney chose as her future spouse Lord Alfred Douglas (Oscar Wilde's infamous "friend"), a choice her father was sure to veto—as he did. Barney successfully deferred the moment she might be forced into open rebellion against her father, procrastinating long enough that at age 26 she found herself accompanying her father's ashes back to America after his death in Monte Carlo. When she recrossed the Atlantic in 1902—not to return to New York until 1946—she was a fabulously wealthy woman who no longer needed pretexts for a continued residence in France. It was no longer necessary for her to claim a desire to improve her French or to study French versification as reasons for staying on in a permissive city, a city that honored women. By 1902, Natalie Barney spoke perfect French and could duplicate French versification in several classical forms. A city dedicated to aesthetic and sensual pleasure, Paris provided an inviting setting for Natalie Barney's desire to make her life a work of art, and it was the only lover to whom she would remain faithful for the next seventy years. She discovered in this city a spirit that perfectly matched her own: "Paris has always seemed to me the only city where you can live and express yourself as you please" (Wickes, *Amazon of Letters,* 44).

The Rebellion against Patriarchal Norms

Paris was the only city in the world discreet enough to allow Natalie Barney her indiscretions. In choosing—and being chosen by—this city, she was more fortunate than she has subsequently been in those who have commented on the life she led in Paris. The two book-length studies that examine this Paris life portray Natalie Barney as a lover whose literary contributions, whatever their merit, played a secondary role to the amorous adventures they recorded. The title of Jean Chalon's book betrays its perspective as a *Portrait of a Seductress,* while George Wickes's study, *The Amazon of Letters,* concentrates on the "life and loves of Natalie Barney" rather than her "letters," which he says are "downright bad" (10). She is described by both men as a "female Don Juan" (*Amazon of Letters,* 8; *Portrait of a Seductress,* 66). Her "emancipation" is evidenced by her blatant lesbianism, the manifestations of which constitute the thread that weaves together both readings of her life. Both studies reduce Natalie Barney's life to the succession of love affairs that made her, in Wickes's terms, "unquestionably the leading lesbian of her times" (7). Wickes also calls her a "latter-day Sappho" (8), but a Sappho known for her sexual appetites rather than the excellence of her literary work or her very significant efforts to bring women writers together in an artistic community. To date, Natalie Barney's life has been rendered as gossip—

lesbian gossip rather than literary gossip. Her work remains unread, most of it untranslated, and her autobiography has not yet been published. Because her writing has not been taken seriously (if read at all, it is read as confirmation of her sexual and social exploits), commentaries on Barney have constituted remembrances by those who knew her or knew of her. Chatty and gossipy, these impressions open themselves to analysis of the truth they would represent. Both the statements Natalie Barney made about her life and those made about her by others are open to inspection. Although Barney's "loves" are central to a record of her life and letters—and it would be a disservice to these intricately balanced components to separate them into mutually exclusive categories—it seems possible to read this record differently, to read both her life and her writings as works of art and to unbalance the assumption that Barney was "a gifted dilettante rather than a dedicated writer" (*Amazon of Letters*, 12).

Even as a child Natalie Barney read the script of social and sexual interaction as one based on hypocrisy. Well-bred, she learned not to reveal the duplicities she observed (for example, the *maître d'hôtel* surprised in the act of stealing cigars, *Portrait of a Seductress*, 10), but she determined not to practice such deceits herself. She set for herself a standard of conduct few were able to duplicate: "To live openly, without hiding anything" (*Portrait of a Seductress*, 10). Coupled with the resolution to act on her desire, this code of behavior placed Natalie Barney outside the bounds of societal norms. Barney refused to accept the paternalistic notion that women were innately deceitful. She suspected that men created the conditions for the deceitfulness they found so charming and irritating in women. When men were deceitful to women, as Natalie Barney's father was with her mother, women were expected to remain silent about the injury. Thus women were made complicit in their own victimization, expected to protect the institution that simultaneously sheltered them and exposed them to psychic and sexual injury. Women were not allowed to act on their sexual desire: they were sought after and chosen as the objects of man's desire, never in possession of their own sexuality. Although Natalie Barney did not flaunt her resolve to "live openly" before those who might be hurt or embarrassed by it, neither did she ever allow her desires to be mediated by others. In her adolescence, she carefully managed her sexual liaisons so that her parents were unaware of their essential nature. She not only protected herself against the inevitable objections of her father, but also guarded her parents against the censure of friends.

But Natalie Barney's own sexual rebellion against obligatory heterosexuality coincided with her mother's efforts to free herself from the pressures of an unhappy marriage. Between the years 1894 and 1902, when her father died, Natalie Barney was very much the victim of his efforts to marry her to someone of her own social class. She evaded what appeared to be the inevitable role as wife of an important political or business figure by traveling abroad with her mother, who—although she may not have been aware of Natalie's more intimate friendships in these years—supported her announced reasons for living in France: to improve her French, to learn more about French poetry, to learn Greek in order to translate poetry from the Greek. That these announced intentions, which may have served as something more than a ruse to escape the demands of an impatient father, have not yet been taken seriously by any commentator on Barney's life suggests the degree to which her efforts at self-education and intellectual development have not been accorded significant importance.

In the early stages of her relationship with Liane de Pougy, Natalie Barney used the pseudonym Florence Temple-Bradford so that society rumors and newspaper reports would not give away her real identity. It was under this name that she appeared in Liane de Pougy's novel about their affair, *Idylle saphique,* published in 1901 in Paris and quickly a bestseller. The previous year, however, Natalie had published her first volume of poetry, *Quelques portraits-sonnets de femmes,* a book that sent her father into such a rage that he bought up all available copies and the typesetting plates—in an effort to destroy the evidence of his daughter's sexual orientation. This collection of poems was illustrated by several portraits done by Alice Pike Barney of Natalie's Paris friends and included as a frontispiece the Carolus-Duran portrait of Natalie as a Renaissance page. Apparently, Natalie's mother was unaware of the use to which Natalie intended to put the portraits or of the exact nature of her liaisons with the women who were their subjects. Natalie's father, however, was already aware of Natalie's affair with Liane de Pougy, having caught Natalie in 1899 reading a love letter from her friend. By 1900, Natalie had escaped her father's wishes that she marry; indeed, by the beginning of the twentieth century Alfred Barney's wife and two daughters seemed beyond his jurisdiction.

Alice Pike Barney had never cooperated in her husband's efforts to restrain the impulses of their eldest daughter. By the time Natalie was a teenager, both mother and daughter were making efforts to escape his irritable authority, Alice Pike Barney no doubt in sympathy with the sentiments Natalie expressed in an early letter to Eva Palmer on the subject of Albert Barney: "As a result of a scene caused only by my father's bad mood, I feel horribly oppressed by a murky cloud and engulfed in the world of evils: pettiness. His snobbish thinking shocks me and his hard, egotistical words, his power to heap injustice on a world that is already filled with it, disgusts me with everything and poisons me on this magnificent night. Only your presence and the certainty of all I believe in could change my feelings" (Chalon, *Portrait of a Seductress,* 13). There is more than a suggestion here that Natalie Barney took her father seriously, that she recognized his power—over herself and others—and felt "oppressed" by his victimization of her. Albert Barney represented all that Natalie could not tolerate—social snobbery, authoritarianism, arbitrariness, the inability to control one's temper, and an insistence on seeing women as possessions; his philosophy of life was in direct contradiction to that of his wife and daughter—he refused to "live and let live." Following her mother's example, Natalie adopted a strict moral and ethical code based on an entirely different set of principles than those that informed her father's thought and determined his conduct. Her feminism was formed in the family, a social structure she found to be constraining and debilitating. She saw in marriage an institution that legalized the victimization of women and children to the whims of male sexual desire and the necessity of social conformity. In her view, Albert Barney's life was shaped by an effort to maintain pretenses of respectability and honesty that disguised deceit and dishonesty.

If the institution of marriage secured man's comforts in the home, the institution of the *demi-monde* assured his social comforts in the public world. And while Natalie Barney's father was eager that she make her debut in Washington society, she apparently desired a debut in the Parisian *demi-monde* (*Portrait of a Seductress,* 23). The dress for her debut was designed in Paris by Worth, who also designed clothes for the most famous of the *demi-mondaines,* including Liane de Pougy. But it was less to the world of high fashion that Natalie was drawn than to a social subculture of powerful women who were beyond society's dictates. An elite group of prostitutes, the women of the *demi-monde* did not pretend to be something more than they were; instead, they were recognized by polite society to be intelligent, witty, beautiful, and very influential women. If Natalie objected to the familial constraints imposed by a tyrannical father, she did not immediately recognize the institution of the *demi-monde* as another manifestation of patriarchal privilege, another avenue by which men kept women in social and economic servitude. What Natalie observed as she rode in her carriage in the Bois de Boulogne were women openly displaying their beauty and charm. Natalie was initially attracted by the apparent independence and power of such women as Liane de Pougy, who quickly became the object of Natalie's desirous attentions. Natalie succeeded where men had failed—Liane fell in love with her—but the increasing intimacy of the two women revealed the extent to which Liane lacked control over her existence. She was courted by princes and heads of state, but she nonetheless served at their pleasure. She was rewarded with jewels, furs, houses, carriages, and riches, but these gifts only further bound her to her profession: she could not escape her own economic dependency on those who courted her.

All of Natalie Barney's efforts to release Liane de Pougy from her economic subjection failed; inevitably, the relationship turned from passion to friendship. Liane betrayed Natalie, however, not with one of the many lovers to whom she was indebted (it was assumed by both women that Liane's heterosexual attachments constituted professional obligations), but with the wife of an Italian count, a man for whom Liane served as courtesan. Deeply hurt by this betrayal, Natalie Barney nevertheless decided to overlook the personal injury of Liane's behavior and to continue her efforts to secure Liane's release from the servitude of prostitution. Natalie hoped to convince Liane to flee the heterosexual world so that the two women could create an alternative culture in which they would live as equals, sharing their love and literary interests. Natalie recognized in Liane a woman divided against herself, a woman imprisoned by "the world, society, life" (Chalon, *Portrait of a Seductress*, 38), and came to see that the *demi-monde* was a situation in which women only *appeared* to control themselves and others. In fact, Liane de Pougy was controlled by the need for comforts and riches, a need both created for and catered to by the powerful men who directed the *demi-monde*. While Natalie wrote of her desire "to freely love the one whom one loves," Liane answered by saying that "a courtesan does not have the right to be or to feel like other women" (*Portrait of a Seductress*, 44). Natalie was forced to conclude that the *demi-monde* offered no alternative to the conventional social world of her parents:

> So long as I live, the love of Beauty will be my guide. . . . Did my parents create me to deny myself? This allusion to my parents' chagrin managed to trouble me, however. The friend of the family [who had reported to Natalie's parents details of her affair with Liane] may thus be assured in any case that for me society seems preferable to the demi-monde, but that neither can ever suit me. I therefore have to find or found a milieu that fits my aspirations: a society composed of all those who seek to focus and improve their lives through an art that can give them pure presence. These are the only people with whom I can get along, and communicate and finally express myself openly among free spirits. . . . let's discover real values which alone can inspire us or make us comprehensible. I will submit to their much stricter laws than the social obligations which shield their egotistical inclinations by a cold philanthropy, proving that they have never really come face to face with anyone. (From Natalie Barney's unpublished autobiography, quoted in *Portrait of a Seductress*, 47–48)

This long statement of her disappointments and desires is the closest that Natalie Barney came to expressing a creed by which she lived.

Although Natalie Barney did not herself succeed in rescuing Liane de Pougy from her fate (Liane later married Prince George Ghika, who took her away from the *demi-monde*), Natalie did succeed in getting Liane radically to alter her perceptions of the world. Natalie could not save Liane from the effects of her existence in the *demi-monde,* but she did educate her to the seductive lie imbedded in the warning sent to Liane by her mentor in the *demi-monde,* the Valtesse de la Bigne: "The day I became a courtesan, I gave up what they call the soul's sensitivity. For me, there are no more duties, nor any responsibility except toward myself and my desire! What independence, what intoxicating freedom! Think about it a little Liane: no more principles, no more morals, or religion. A courtesan can do everything out in the open, without feigning or hypocrisy, without fearing the slightest reproach or blame, for nothing can touch her. She is outside of Society and its pettiness" (*Portrait of a Seductress,* 44–45). Indeed, the *demi-mondaine* existed outside the pettiness of society, able to "do everything out in the open," but she was bound to an even more deceptive code that confused expression of woman's sexual desire with the obligation to meet man's sexual needs. What appears as "independence" and "freedom," even power, is really servitude under a more exotic and fashionable guise. The call Natalie made to Liane was one that placed desire under the terms of art, one that demanded a moral commitment to the principles of the beautiful—the "Ethics of Beauty." Natalie had seduced Liane by linking sexual desire to aesthetics, introducing Liane to her own sexual desire (as distinct from her response to men's desire for her) and to her own considerable talents as a writer. It was Natalie who had encouraged Liane to write *Idylle saphique,* who provided her both the subject and the literary method, who even wrote portions of it for her, as Jean Chalon convincingly argues in *Portrait of a Seductress.* Nonetheless, Liane could not escape her situation, could not step outside patriarchal conventions.

Natalie Barney's failure to save Liane de Pougy from a fate she apparently both resisted and desired was followed by another failure: to save Renée Vivien from suicide. One of Renée's many notes to Natalie proclaiming her love pleaded that Natalie forgive her for having "saddened" her, saying "I love you *differently*" (*Portrait of a Seductress,* 63). Natalie was Renée's first female lover (their relationship began in winter 1899), as she had been Liane's first, and Natalie tried to teach each of these women to love *differently*—to instruct them in the ways of physical pleasure, to teach them that sensual enjoyment has nothing to do with fidelity of spirit, to educate them to erotic joy rather than romantic sadness, to discover with them a relation between love and literature. They were to be awakened to the power of their own desires through the gift of Natalie's love. For neither of these women, however, was this awakening of desire the liberating experience Natalie had hoped it might be. Rather, these women quickly bound themselves to Natalie's independent strength, prescribing a code of behavior that duplicated the power structure of marriage, especially in its emphasis on fidelity. It was Natalie Barney's fate never to find a lover who could escape the psychological need for monogamy. Even Natalie herself expected her chosen lover to be true to her, but only for the duration of her own passion.

Sappho's Circle

Jean Chalon is not correct, however, in declaring that Natalie Barney was "a perfect example of the feminine Don Juan, conquering and holding on to her captives, while the masculine Don Juan runs from one victim to the other" (*Portrait of a Seductress,* 66). She did not make "captives" of her loves; indeed, each lover in her way tried to make a "captive" of Natalie. And if Natalie "bound" her lovers to her, it was through friendship rather than through the pretense of continued sexual attraction. Natalie cherished friendship above all else, and her opinions on her own abilities to befriend others are well known. Although she claimed not to work at friendship ("when it comes to a friendship I am very lazy; once I confer friendship, I never take it back"), she in fact dedicated herself to the cultivation of this art: "I have sometimes lost friends, but friends have never lost me" (Wickes, *Amazon of Letters,* 9). And it was in this context that Natalie suggested forming a Sapphic circle, one dedicated to the love of beauty and to the love of sensuality. Like Sappho, Natalie wanted to be free to love as she chose. In principle, each of her lovers embraced this philosophy. In practice, each was to betray its central premise. Ironically, the lover most committed to Sappho—as poet, feminist, lover—was the one least capable of living up to the Sapphic ideal. Renée Vivien's life was, according to Barney, "a long suicide" (*Amazon of Letters,* 67). Some have suggested that it was Natalie's infidelities that drove Renée to her death. Others have noted that it was a combination of Christian and Romantic attitudes, an inability to escape the psychological as well as the societal binds that made a "moral issue" of bodily pleasures, infusing sexuality with morbidity (*Amazon of Letters,* 59; Colette, *The Pure and the Impure,* 79–97).

The influence of Greek culture on Natalie Barney's life and work should not be underestimated. It was probably Eva Palmer, heiress to the Huntley and Palmer biscuit fortune, who first seduced the adolescent Natalie to lesbian love (although Natalie was aware of her sexual orientation from an early age). It was certainly Eva Palmer who introduced Natalie to Sappho's poetry and to an appreciation of a Greek culture that provided an alternative to the heterosexual imperatives of the Christian world.

These two young women spent their vacations together at Natalie's house in Bar Harbor, Maine, and there discovered the delights of the rivers, their bodies, and poetry. Natalie's second book of poems, *Cinq petits dialogues grecs* (published under the pseudonym Tryphé), restated this interest in Greek love and art. Here she seemed to dedicate herself to reliving Sappho's life in a contemporary setting, and she stated for the first time the aesthetic principle that was to guide her life and art: "[Sappho's] poetry and her music are but the accompaniment of her loves. . . . When she speaks, she seems to exist only for art; when she loves, one knows that she lives only for love" (Wickes, *Amazon of Letters*, 52). Art and love are inextricably bound in this statement. The aesthetic of art finds a counterpart in the ethics of love. It is precisely here, in the delicate balance established between art and love, between aesthetics and ethics, that most commentators on Natalie Barney's life and work have stumbled. Was Natalie Barney's interest in Greece only a product of her lesbian inclinations, as George Wickes suggests, or did she find in Sappho a poet who touched her aesthetically? Did Sappho serve her as the pretext for an elaborate game of seduction and betrayal or did she serve to support Barney's feminist commitment?

In attempting to find possible answers to these questions, we must begin by examining Barney's education. Like most women of her social class—Edith Wharton, Winifred Ellerman, Nancy Cunard, Vita Sackville-West—Natalie Barney's education began at home under the tutelage of a French governess. By the time the governess arrived at the Barney home in Cincinnati, however, Natalie was already fluent in French, having learned it from her great-aunt Louisa, who was born in Louisiana in 1803. When Natalie was 10 years old, her mother decided to spend two years in Paris studying painting. After the first months of travel, Natalie and her sister were placed in a boarding school, Les Ruches, near Fontainebleau, where they spent the next year and a half being educated in the various arts of a French finishing school—learning to sing, dance, ride horses, draw, and memorize French literature.[1] At Les Ruches, Natalie mastered the French language, the language that would become for her the means of artistic expression. Totally bilingual, Natalie Barney divided her world between English and French, the former used for practical and commercial matters, the latter the language of love and the imagination. In these years Natalie learned the forms of poetic French expression, so that her own literary expression would always be dictated by the strict conventions of French poetry, her writing "confining spontaneous impulses within strict forms," as George Wickes has noted (*Amazon of Letters*, 47).

Over the next fourteen years, until her father's death in 1902, Natalie Barney divided her time between France and America, completing her formal education at age 17 in America at Miss Ely's School for Girls in New York, where she met Eva Palmer. In summer 1894, she traveled to Europe with two women friends, Miss Ely serving as chaperon, studying German and taking violin lessons in Dresden. In 1896–97 and 1898–99, Natalie accompanied her mother and sister to Paris. In autumn 1901, Natalie and Renée Vivien followed Eva Palmer to Bryn Mawr, where she had entered college. Her friends were allowed to attend the literature courses of feminist Mary Gwynn. During this time, Natalie was engaged to a Philadelphian, William Morrow, which served to deflect Albert Barney's suspicions about his daughter's sexual inclinations and to protect her against her father's interventions in her European life. Nonetheless, she was summoned to Washington more than once during this four-year period to be kept under the watchful eye of her father, who encouraged an early marriage to Morrow; in May 1897, Natalie was presented as a debutante in Washington; and Renée Vivien, age 20, was presented in England.

The early interest in Greek poetry and drama, awakened through Eva Palmer's love of this civilization while the two young women were schoolmates together in New York, was reawakened in 1899, this time with Renée Vivien's participation, when Natalie met Professor Charles Brun in Paris. A classical scholar, he educated Natalie in both Greek poetry and the French Romantics. The effects of the Romantic vision—as inscribed by Lamartine, Vigny, Gautier, and Baudelaire—is most obvious in *Quelques portraits,* where the poems tend to link love with death and employ exotic metaphors drawn from nature, exploiting a lush, rich imagery. Here the portraits and sonnets are addressed *to* women, Natalie taking the traditional male role of poet-raconteur. In this, Natalie employed standard forms of love poetry whose premises she inverted, addressing herself to a female lover. George Wickes describes this slight (and perhaps unfinished) volume of poetry as "frankly, apprentice work," the acknowledged effort of "an American who has been struggling to master the strict rules of French rhyme and meter in order to please a pedantic schoolmaster":

> The poems themselves, mostly sonnets, reveal that the author was an apt pupil whose schoolmaster had curbed every effort to experiment with versification and had probably stifled every attempt at original expression. The style, the imagery and the language of love are all familiar to anyone who has browsed through conventional nineteenth-century French verse. The most daring departures from the commonplace occur in a dedication to the memory of Mallarme and in a poem echoing Baudelaire, describing kisses as "flowers of evil." But in 1900 it was not too shockingly modern to admire Mallarme and Baudelaire, both safely dead. The style of Natalie's poetry was never to progress beyond this point. Though she had obviously made a great

effort to master French verse, she was never to strive for much more than competence. (*Amazon of Letters,* 45–46)

Wickes's assessment calls for further commentary rather than a dismissal of Barney's early work. If, as Barney's preface seems to suggest, these sonnets exist as student exercises whose forms were to be learned by rote, then we need to examine the conditions under which she was studying this literary tradition.

Like Virginia Woolf, Natalie Barney learned Greek and studied poetic form with a tutor (whereas Woolf's tutor was female, however, Barney's tutors were Frenchmen).[2] When these two women were working at their studies, a knowledge of Greek was a mark of "the intellectual aristocracy" ("Liberty, Sorority, Misogyny," 86). As Jane Marcus has demonstrated for Virginia Woolf, women were not eligible for the kinds of educational experiences that their brothers took for granted—an education founded on the study of Latin and Greek—but were forced to attain such skills in secret, since, for women, learning to read classics constituted a radical act, a rebellion against the patriarchy. Thus women were marked by the situation in which they learned foreign languages and literary history, their learning taking place outside an ongoing educational experience, separate from a classroom shared with others of their age and social class, not as part of fraternal organizations or select and secret Cambridge societies (such as the Apostles, to which Virginia Stephen's brothers belonged), but alone with a tutor. For Virginia Woolf, this method of learning undermined the very concept of a "female intellectual aristocracy," since the notion of such an aristocracy is founded on a group identity, not on the experience of an individual female working alone with the text and a tutor. The English "intellectual aristocracy" constituted itself, in Jane Marcus's terms, as a "Cambridge homosexual hegemony," a group of men that included Virginia Stephen's brothers, men who proudly bore the stamp of the institution that had shaped their thinking. At the core of this intellectual brotherhood was a fear of women, a barely suppressed misogyny, and an elitism that was both the product of and the protective covering for the patriarchy. In *Moments of Being,* Woolf comments on the ways the institutions of family and university shaped this intellectual aristocracy: "All our male relations were adepts at the game. They knew the rules and attached immense importance to them. Father laid enormous stress upon schoolmasters' reports, upon scholarships, triposes and fellowships. . . . What would have been his shape had he not been stamped and moulded by the patriarchal machinery? Every one of our male relations was shot into that machine and came out at the other end, at the age of sixty or so, a Headmaster, an Admiral, a Cabinet Minister, a Judge" (132). This fraternity proclaimed the superiority of the male sex, reveled in a Greek culture that joined male homosexuality to literature and art, and could trace its philosophic roots from Plato to G. E. Moore. More than mere knowledge of a language, command of Greek gave these men the keys to Western civilization.

Virginia Woolf and Natalie Barney had similar reasons for desiring to learn Greek: they wanted to recover Sappho from male professors who either had pictured her as a seducer of young girls or had denied the existence of a Sapphic sexuality altogether.[3] Nineteenth-century male writers (many of them homosexual) had appropriated Sappho as a figure of concupiscence and equated Sapphic love with female decadence. In England, Swinburne's Sappho called for repudiation; in France, Baudelaire's required correction. The recovery of Sappho as a woman's poet whose writings celebrated female love and friendship constituted an important lesbian feminist enterprise toward the end of the nineteenth century. For women on both sides of the channel, Lesbos offered itself as a female utopia; efforts were made to create London and Paris equivalents of Mytilène. The latter fared far better than the former, not because Paris was a more open and indulgent city than London (although it was) or because Paris intellectual circles were less in the grip of a male homosexual hegemony that excluded women on misogynist grounds (although this was also true). Rather, the notion of lesbian eroticism had, by the 1890s, permeated the Parisian imagination: it offered a form of sexual diversion for women and provided men a new voyeuristic medium. As Elyse Blankley comments, "in the lowest terms of encoded international erotic language, 'lesbian' at the turn of the century signified a Parisian erotic refinement" ("Return to Mytilène," 49). The "islands" of lesbian sorority that developed in Paris during these years were less a sign of advancing French feminism than a by-product of Parisian prurience. In London, Virginia Woolf studied Sappho's culture in an effort to understand the social conditions that gave women the necessary freedom to function as artists. In Paris, Natalie Barney discovered in Sappho the promise of an alternative lesbian culture, one defined by women themselves rather than by a dominant patriarchy, one that repudiated the view of lesbianism as "sick" and "perverted," its members outcast as "the third sex."

While Virginia Woolf achieved a certain mastery of Greek, able to read *Antigone, Oedipus Coloneus,* and the *Trachiniae* in the original language, Barney, it has been suggested, was a lazy although intelligent student, one more interested in acting on her sexual impulses than in reading lesbian poetry in the original Greek. It is not certain, however, that either woman was able to read Sappho's dialect, even though both of them took Sappho as a model for specifically lesbian authorship. For Virginia Woolf and Gertrude Stein, experimental linguistic forms often coded and disguised the lesbian content of the writing. Whereas Stein's work celebrated explicit lesbian desire for an identifiable lover, Woolf's lesbian writing celebrated female community and friendship, embedding its eroticism in a language less coded than fluid and sensual. Natalie Barney's lesbian writing addressed both the specific female lover and a larger lesbian community; while her writing was not "coded," it did conform to strict rules of poetic rhyme and meter and cast itself, as well, in a language other than her mother tongue. While Sappho had chosen her native dialect for poetic expression, Natalie Barney consciously chose an outdated form of French prosody in which to declare her commitment to female eroticism. George Wickes has suggested that the decision to write in the forms of a "tyrannical French prosody" revealed a fundamental contradiction in her nature, one that "always characterized Natalie's style of living as well as her style of expression, confining spontaneous impulses within strict forms. Her life was American in its unplanned casualness; her speech, French in its controlled precision. She wrote mostly in French because that language expressed her essentially classical temperament. No matter how tempestuous her love affairs, she remained incurably rational, regarding the emotions with a detachment and irony that many took for cold cynicism" (*Amazon of Letters,* 47). The impression here is that Barney adopted French literary forms because of their balanced precision and symmetry. These forms, which Wickes has already suggested Barney learned none too well, worked against creativity and experiment. They were, as Barney herself often seemed, self-consciously anachronistic.

Why would a woman so philosophically, sexually, and politically in advance of her time revert to older forms for poetic expression, especially when the subject matter might seem to call for an equally radical and unconventional form of expression? Perhaps because the forms of her education, which took place primarily in France, had "stifled every attempt at original expression" as Wickes claims. Or perhaps, like Stein, Barney wanted to cloak the real intentions of her words (if so, she seems to have failed: Wickes reports the content of these poems to be "scandalous," 45). More likely, though, the use of traditional forms constituted an effort to summon literary authority, to place her poetry in a long and respected tradition. Rather than being "facile and derivative" (*Amazon of Letters,* 50), Barney's poetry addressed a subject that has been denied a literary tradition of its own. Although the external forms of this poetry were traditional, even clichéd, they enclosed a radical sentiment.[4]

The Erotic Subtext

Among Barney's mentors in Paris was Pierre Louÿs, a young, well-respected writer of erotica. With *Les chansons de Bilitis* (1894), Louÿs had perpetrated a very successful literary hoax in creating a female poet contemporary with Sappho whose work he "translated" in a volume that included a biography of Bilitis as well as an accompanying bibliography and scholarly notes. At Barney's request, Louÿs read her writing, including poems and an unpublished novel about her affair with Liane de Pougy entitled *Lettres à une connue,* and offered advice about her work that she did not follow. Barney's disregard of his advice is part of a consistent pattern: she most often turned to literary men for assistance—Remy de Gourmont, André Germain, Ezra Pound—and then disregarded their suggestions. But the relationship with Louÿs is particularly troublesome, since it appears that Barney was not uncomfortable with the image of Bilitis that Louÿs created in the erotic poetry he invented for her. She questioned neither the methods nor the motives of this male homosexual who wrote lascivious works about women's sexuality. She did not pose questions that a contemporary feminist would ask: what does it mean when a homosexual male describes erotic acts in the voice of a homosexual female? What unexamined psychological motives are implicit in such an act? What is the readership for such work? Barney was honored by the attention Louÿs gave to her work, finding him gracious and erudite. She apparently did not read into his writings a form of misogyny or see in them a possible male homosexual fantasy of female sexuality or sexual stereotyping. Instead, she seems to have admired his success in publishing such works, saw an affinity between his interests and hers, talked openly with him about her lesbianism and the need to express its erotic desires, and hoped to solicit his support in an effort to publish her own writing.

In these early years, Barney wished to have her poetry and fiction published; later in her life, publication of her work seemed less important to her, although she continued writing for herself and friends. And while writing served her as an important form of lesbian expression, perhaps signaling a need to announce herself as a lesbian, her writing was not openly erotic and certainly not lascivious. Her poetry was neither shocking nor sexually stimulating; it addressed itself implicitly, if not explicitly, to an entirely different audience than the one Louÿs found for his writings. As Elyse Blankley has commented, "the proliferation of lesbian disguises—whether of Zola's Nana, Gautier's bisexual Mademoiselle de Maupin, or Balzac's Marquise de St. Real—set [women] in motion to cavort in front of the male eye poised at the keyhole" ("Return to Mytilène," 48). Like the vision of lesbian experience expressed in the poetry of Renée Vivien, Natalie Barney's writings proclaim the delicacy and tenderness of lesbian love and demonstrate a subtle eroticism excluded by phallic notions of sexual desire. While Louÿs "catalog[s] sensual delights" and makes Sappho "a sexual predator" ("Return to Mytilène," 50), the work of Vivien and Barney redefines female sensuality. What is "scandalous" in this work is not a language of sexual enticement—as George Wickes's description would suggest—but rather that women are writing about their own sexuality, outside the terms of the heterosexual norm. Moreover, in proclaiming their lesbianism, these women refuse traditional roles as the objects of male desire and rewrite the dynamics of desire in an art of their own. In addressing the loved one from the position normally assigned to the male in courtly love poetry, Natalie Barney is not announcing herself as a "masculine" lesbian, one who plays the role of the male lover in her sexual encounters with women; rather, she displaces the male as the one who has the right to write of his passions and longing. Barney adopts male literary forms for her own purposes, thereby inverting and subverting the very premises on which those literary forms rest. In its own way, this act of literary seizure was as radical as Stein's encoded lesbian grammar or Woolf's construction of a feminine sentence.

Almost without considering the consequences of her actions, Barney turned to Sappho as a subject of her poetry: the first of the *Cinq petits dialogues grecs* is in praise of Sappho, the Greek poet's noteworthy attributes recognizable as belonging to Barney herself. Like Barney, Sappho follows her nature; is brave, daring, and irresistible; her passions are fleeting, but she is faithful in her inconstancy; she is an elemental force, a "flame which destroys and glorifies"; she is both goddess and mortal woman, "subject to all the torments of love" (*Amazon of Letters*, 51–52). It may be that Barney's recreation of herself in Sappho arises from lack of more specific biographical information about the poet. But it may also be that she needed in these early years of her writing to speak through the voice of an ancient, lost sister; she needed to identify herself as both lesbian and poet, making Sappho fit her own psychological and artistic needs. In making Sappho a subject of her writing, in making Sappho's image reflect her own, in attempting to recreate Lesbos in Paris, however, Natalie Barney was trying to verify the authenticity of her own experience.[5] Hers was an important first effort to reclaim lesbianism from its place among male erotica, to situate it in the context of a female community. Whether or not Barney was aware of the degree to which lesbian women were degraded by the images of them in works by Baudelaire, Louÿs, and others, whether she was aware of the extent to which the reawakening of classical interest in the late nineteenth century was controlled by men, whether she was attentive (as Virginia Woolf would have been) to the irony of her education in literary history and poetic forms under the tutelage of men, whether she realized that in seeking friendship and support from Louÿs she was in fact collaborating with a specialist in lesbian pornography, Barney nonetheless charted her course differently from her male predecessors and educators. She made them accomplices in a project that was perhaps more subversive than even she imagined. Moreover, when her tutors and mentors had served their function, she set aside their advice, ignored their cautionary directives, and continued in the direction she herself had determined.

Contrasting Poetics: Vivien and Barney

Barney, for instance, probably did not allow herself to be as influenced by Louÿs as did Renée Vivien, who developed a particular attraction to the decadent alliance of homosexuality and evil. As Lillian Faderman has suggested, Vivian found in Baudelaire and his followers "both the language and imagery of lesbianism. Her poetry most often associates lesbian love with vice, artificiality, perfume, and death" (*Surpassing the Love of Men,* 362). Faderman catalogues references in Vivien's poetry linking love and death, bitterness and ecstasy, the attraction and repulsion of lesbian love, and uses a quotation from "Modern Naiad" to illustrate the pattern of contradictions revealed by Vivien's language. In the poem, the speaker declares, "You attract and repel me like the unseen abyss / Hidden by the churning waves" (362).

A quite different impression of Vivien's concerns and her poetic style is given by Elyse Blankley, whose reading concentrates on Vivien's effort to recreate Mytilène and recall Sappho in her poetry. These poems do not speak of the soul's despair or "impure caresses," but rather imagine a world of female freedom in which lesbian love is cut free of the morbidity implicit in the Symbolist model. Full of light and warmth that oppose the dark oppression of the Symbolist vision, these poems provide an important counterstatement to the decadent/aesthete pose that Vivien also adopted. This view of lesbianism offers an alternative to the familiar conclusion that "Vivien's verse—and life—sadly burlesques an aesthete model" ("Return to Mytilène," 46). According to Blankley, this alternate vision contradicts the Proustian model and rewrites the versions of lesbianism produced by Baudelaire and Louÿs in "favor of an authentic metaphor for the glorious possibilities of women loving women" (50). That is, Vivien set out to reclaim Sappho from male authors and to reconstruct Lesbos from a matriarchal rather than a patriarchal viewpoint. In part, this effort aided Vivien in constructing a version of herself as a lesbian writer separate from dominant literary images of lesbian women. In Blankley's terms, Vivien "reappropriate[d] the pen of Baudelaire, Zola, or Gautier" (57), rewriting her Paris lesbian experience through her vision of Mytilène. She also discovered a female literary tradition that included "glorious queens who stretch from antiquity to the present—Lilith, Eve,

Cassiopeia, Aphrodite, Bathsheba, Cleopatra, Lady Jane Grey"; Vivien herself joins this sisterhood, speaking "through a female genealogy that is reborn in her body" (58).

In short, Vivien's poetry imagines a refuge for lesbianism outside the patriarchal construct, establishes a female literary tradition, and redefines the female body. The vision constructed through Mytilène, as Blankley has suggested, presented enormous difficulties to Vivien precisely because its "ideal [was] recognized *through* the body and emerge[d] from the body's needs" (64). The poetic project—which attempted to reclaim reality, join art and life, body and spirit—failed. Its end was marked, ironically, by the simultaneous wasting of body and spirit in the anorexic starvation that finally killed Vivien.

Just as it has been important to separate the two contradictory poetic stances reflected in Vivien's poetry—one combining images of morbidity, exoticism, and enclosure; the other transforming these images to ones of fertility, independence, and the freedom of a liberated female body and spirit—it is just as important carefully to distinguish Vivien's vision of Mytilène and Sappho from Barney's. The fundamental difference between the two rests in the quite separate ways these two women saw the relation of poetry to life, spirit to body. While Vivien tried to unite in poetry orders that had not only been divided by Western culture but whose relation had been defined as hierarchical (art superior to life; body submitted to spirit), Barney's writings preserved the hierarchical order in reverse. Thus Barney's declared intention to live a beautiful life, to make life itself a work of art ("my life is my work, my writings are but the result," Wickes, *Amazon of Letters*, 48), is not merely an excuse for producing derivative and second-rate art (as commentators have suggested), but a signal of her aesthetic and ethical principles. Such a philosophy was antithetical to the suppositions that informed Symbolist and decadent art forms.

Barney was opposed to the notion that sexuality was linked to sin and death; to the contrary, she saw homosexuality as a perfect expression of love, a celebration of health and vitality. Her effort was to preserve the body, to express oneself *through* the body, and she rejected both the guilt and fear ingrained in the dominant definitions of female homosexuality. Barney's artistic expression was grounded in a celebration of the body, particularly of its health and beauty. She was dismayed by the self-destructive quality of decadent art and life, frightened by the evidence that Renée Vivien mistreated her body. Vivien wanted to share Barney's vision, journeyed to Lesbos to try to find the sources of that vision, and sought fulfillment of that vision in poetry. But Vivien failed in her effort to escape the sentence of her own guilty morbidity—a fate to which the patriarchy had sentenced her in dividing her against her own body. She recognized the effects of Western puritanism (for which decadence is the dark underside), and in her autobiographical novel *A Woman Appeared to Me* constructed an ideal self, her alter ego, the androgynous San Giovanni, who angrily protested against this ethic: "I was aroused on behalf of women, so misunderstood, so made use of by male tyranny. I began to hate the male for the base cruelty of his laws and the impurity of his morals. I considered his works and judged them evil" (15). It is ironic, then, that some of Vivien's poetry exploits the very images of female sexuality enforced under "the base cruelty of [man's] laws." For example, the poem "Lucidity" opens by equating woman's sexuality with sin ("You fill your leisure with the delicate art of vice") and ends by declaring tombs to be "less impure" than the lover's bed. It is only this lover, however, this woman who "feign[s] sweetness" beneath which a "watchful reptile lies," who can "quench the lover's thirst" (*Muse of Violets*, 26). This poetry envisions lesbian love as the incarnation of evil, but if it were read without the knowledge of its homosexual base, one would assume the perspective of this poem to be the traditional male articulation of woman's body as the corrupt vessel through which he acts out the ritual of his own corruption. (When Vivien's first book of poetry was published under the name R. Vivien, it was assumed that the author was a young man addressing his mistress, Wickes, *Amazon of Letters*, 57.) In other words, this lesbian poetry simultaneously repeats and reverses the patriarchal code, but both visions frame woman in a patriarchal definition. It is such versions of woman—divided against her own self, her sexuality appropriated by the male—that the Mytilène poems try to rewrite. "Let Us Go to Mytilène" is an invocation to a place in which the "soul soars" to the "welcome of the adored virgins," where "the shadow of Sappho . . . will smile," and where the lovers "re-sing to an intoxicated earth / The hymn of Lesbos" (*Muse of Violets*, 61). While this poetic effort to "formulate major cultural revisions" in the conception of Sappho (Blankley, "Return to Mytilène," 51) was successful, the personal effort was not. Perhaps the poetic success of this reformulation prevented its success in life. The Renée Vivien whose poetry invoked delicate sensuality and a subtle eroticism was in life apparently unmoved by her lover's caresses, unable to join the sensuality of her poetry to lived experience.[6] The poetry may well have served as wish fulfillment, outlining a dream landscape in which women's bodies no longer responded to the power of the patriarchy and heterosexual demands, but served women's passions.

Vivien's poems in praise of virginity do not repeat and reverse the patriarchal code of her "decadent" verse. Rather, these poems are allied in both subject matter and method with the "Mytilène" poems. Here Vivien declared her intention to preserve a virginity that acted as a shield against the ravages of eroticism ("Eros today has torn my soul, / wind which in the mountain fells the oaks," "Eros Today," *Muse of Violets,* 43). In "I shall be always virgin" (*Muse of Violets,* 44), Vivien argued that her virginity allowed her to remain serene ("I shall remain virgin as the serene snow"), unsoiled ("I shall flee imprint and soiling stain"), and distant ("I shall remain virgin as the distant moon"). And in "Virgin," she countered the prevalent heterosexual notion that a virginity that extended into woman's old age was a debilitating, withering force. Vivien approached this cultural concept only to reject it:

> as a sweet apple reddens at
> the extremity of the branch,
> at the distant extremity:
> the fruit-pickers have forgotten
> it or, rather, they have not
> forgotten it, but they have
> not been able to reach it. (39)

Virginity rests at the "distant extremity" of the apple tree, out of man's reach. Allowed to ripen there, the apple becomes "blushed and golden-skinned," preserves its distant viewpoint, "mocking the vain cupidity / Of the covetous passerby," and keeping "the fruit of [woman's] body beautiful / And inaccessible" (39). Susan Gubar has argued that Vivien "praises female virginity as virility" ("Sapphistries," 50), but Vivien's concept of virginity, like Natalie Barney's Ethics of Beauty, does not emphasize its active potency. Rather it suggests a serene inaccessibility: virginity serves as a protective device, a screen against male virility.

Vivien's search for an idyllic exile separate from dominant Western culture was far more determined and desperate than Barney's. Vivien apparently needed to return to Mytilène at frequent intervals, to rediscover the land of Sappho and her lost heritage. To a far greater degree than Vivien, Barney was able to separate herself from the patriarchy that surrounded her and to construct in her writings a woman-identified world. Vivien's life and poetry are marked by contradictions; Barney's are not. Vivien's work divides itself between a vision of corrupted female-centered love (poetry identified with the London-Paris axis of Romantic decadence) and poems in praise of a female-identified eroticism that joins the physical to the spiritual through the invocation of Sappho and Mytilène. Vivien's world is divided between Paris and Lesbos; Barney's world finds a place for Lesbos in Paris. It is Barney's aesthetic, then, that privileges the virginal, that consistently finds in lesbian love a method of honoring and preserving the female body. Barney's poetry praises the female body as virtuous and glorious *in and of itself.* Put to the service of man's desire, undergoing the childbirth that can result from woman's submission to male desires, woman's body is degraded; often, her body is divided from her spirit. Whereas Vivien sought through her poetry to undo patriarchal patterns, to seal the split in her own psyche, Barney had no need to practice a poetics of reintegration. She had never experienced self-doubt or self-division.

Barney's *Cinq petits dialogues grecs* praise virginity, suggesting that "purity" and "sensuality" need not be opposed constructions, but rather that lesbian sensuality simultaneously celebrates and preserves (celebrates *by* preserving) woman's body. If the male organ is the instrument with which the patriarchy divides the woman against herself, separates psyche from body, from Barney's viewpoint lesbian rituals reconfirm woman's body intact. If late-nineteenth-century society read in lesbian eroticism a double estrangement of woman—first from the heterosexual norm and next from herself, in guilt and retribution for her "abnormal" behavior—Barney's reading of female homosexuality offered a double confirmation of woman's separateness and wholeness. Ironically, the belief in sexology theories that considered lesbianism to be caused by "cerebral anomalies," that made it the sign of an inherited diseased condition of the central nervous system and defined its practitioners as abnormal, may have allowed Barney more easily to accept her sexual orientation as a factor of nature, thus eliminating the need to consider contingent moral or philosophic issues. She considered the world "a distorting mirror which makes [lesbians] appear unrecognizable." Writing in her autobiography, she commented:

> albinos aren't reproached for having pink eyes and whitish hair, why should they hold it against me for being a lesbian? It's a question of nature: my queerness isn't a vice, isn't "deliberate," and harms no one. What do I care, after all, if they vilify or judge me according to their prejudices? Their "taboos" have bowed heads way beyond them, clipped the wings of enough enthusiasm for them to be despised. The so-called virtuous make the mistake of pitying those who are different, of feeling compassion for the fate of those they censure. (quoted in Chalon, *Portrait of a Seductress*, 47)

Whereas society condemned homosexuality as evil because it was not procreative and viewed lesbian sexuality as barren and infertile, Barney saw lesbianism as a "natural" state—that is, produced by nature. Its nonprocreative sexuality, for instance, freed Barney and others from the fear of unwanted pregnancies. This sexuality left women "pure" and allowed them the possession of their bodies. They could enjoy sensuality without risking consequences they could not control. For Barney, lesbian eroticism was defined by a sharing of sensual experiences, each of the partners taking pleasure in the other's body. This sense of equality and sensual exchange distinguished itself from heterosexual practice, in which a woman was "taken," "possessed," or "ravished" by the male. The heterosexual act made woman a victim of man's desire; lesbian sexuality allowed her to direct her own desire and discover through her body her own sensual purposes.

The women of Natalie Barney's Sapphic circle believed that lesbian love preserved and honored the female body, beautified it, sanctified it, and kept it safe against the ravages to which heterosexuality subjected it. That love between women freed the participants from the fear of pregnancy was a powerfully seductive force—especially for women who wanted to lead independent lives. Woman could relax to her own sensual experience without fearing possible consequences. A practice of lesbian love that defined itself in spontaneity—as Natalie Barney's did—was itself a liberating and invigorating force in women's lives. At the time in her life when she wished to enter the *demi-monde,* Barney was extremely interested in the precautionary measures courtesans used to protect themselves against unwanted pregnancies. She wished to know their secret methods. She apparently never received answers to her questions, but the continuing concern that pregnancy made woman the victim of her own bodily processes, that the fear of pregnancy inhibited woman's sensuality and forced her to repress her own sexual desires, was a subject of her writing. In *Scatterings,* the first volume of Barney's *pensées,* she commented on maternity: "If maternity worked backwards, beginning with the pains of childbirth, there would still be mothers, but they would be willing heroines, not victims of a mistake or wretched martyrs or one of nature's tricks. When will man be borne for the child's sake, not the child for the man's" (quoted in Wickes, *Amazon of Letters,* 115–116). It is the violence implied by heterosexuality—violence against the woman's body and, often, against the child who becomes "nature's trick"—that Barney opposed. If woman is to preserve her sensual and artistic life, she must also preserve her body against the risks posed by heterosexuality. Thus, for Barney and others of her group, lesbianism signified not only a sexual orientation but a feminist position, a radical denial of heterosexual dominance. Lesbianism was defined by Barney as the essential component in what she termed the Ethics of Beauty. The forms of its lovemaking—the caress, the kiss—were themselves forms of art, the synthesis of a sensual as well as an aesthetic experience in which woman's body was celebrated rather than abused.

The Aesthetics of Barney's Sexual Ethics

Barney's emphasis on the aesthetics of Sapphic love not only suggests the inseparability of art and life, but directs us to a consideration of a lesbian aesthetics. If we are to take Barney's cultural revisionism seriously, we cannot overlook the various ways Sappho served her efforts. That is, we must take Barney's reading of Sappho seriously. In *Actes et entr'actes* (1910), a set of theatricals written to be enacted in Barney's garden, Barney took up the issue of woman's entrapment in patriarchal society. In *Equivoque,* the fourth of the plays, Barney's feminist views are linked to an understanding of Sappho's writing. The play itself is an original drama that rewrote male-authored legends that Sappho committed suicide because her lover, Phaon, was to marry Timas. In Barney's version, Sappho leaps off the cliff, apparently out of jealousy for Phaon. But the poems she leaves behind reveal that she loved Timas, who is then left at the marriage altar. Barney's text incorporates quotations from Sappho's writings and includes footnotes and critical commentary (see Jay, "Disciples of the Tenth Muse," 95). George Wickes has commented that *Equivoque* "is a scholarly tour de force," incorporating as it does fragments of Sappho's writing with footnotes (in Greek) provided by Barney (*Amazon of Letters,* 94), but it is also a feminist treatise, a work in which Barney's opinions are made to coincide with Sappho's and endowed with her authority. Life is seen to be a celebratory work of art, a "most beautiful poem."

Perhaps the most interesting facet of Barney's Sappho is the Greek poet's renunciation of fame and immortality through her writing. Barney not only endowed Sappho with an opinion that she herself shared (that trying to assure one's immortality through the written word was a vain and self-indulgent act) but in so doing offered an explanation for the absence of Sappho's writing from the Western literary tradition. In Barney's version of the story, the writings are not merely "lost" to history; they are prevented from becoming part of that tradition by Sappho's own decision. This reading of Sappho's life returns to her a measure of control over both her present and future life, allowing Barney to emphasize the importance of life over art. In this version Sappho not only renounces poetry, but renounces any claim to posterity, telling her disciples: "I sang for you, not for posterity. Fame for its own sake is vain, and what do I care for praise after death?" (quoted in *Amazon of Letters,* 95). Barney's drama, however, constitutes an epitaph in which Sappho sings again.

But Sappho's decision to sacrifice her art is not as unassuming or as selfish as it might first appear. The decision underscores a tenet of her philosophy that Barney saw to be of particular importance: the emphasis upon communal art, a joining of art and life. *Equivoque* was presented in the garden of Barney's Neuilly home in June 1906, with Marguerite Moreno playing Sappho and Eva Palmer playing the bride who leaves Sappho's circle to marry. (Eva Palmer herself was to leave Barney's circle for marriage: she wed the Greek brother-in-law of Raymond Duncan and dedicated her life to the rediscovery of Greek arts.) Of significance, then, is Barney's belief in the use of artistic performance as a method of communal education, a practice she learned from her mother. Natalie used theatricals, masquerades, ballets, and poetry readings differently than her mother, however, since her declared intention was to bring women together, to encourage feminist dialogue and intellectual exchange. In addition, these performances were teaching devices in which the principles of Barney's feminism were given public acknowledgment. She hoped to create a contemporary Sapphic circle, a proposal she had first shared with Renée Vivien.

Although it was with Renée that Natalie first visited Lesbos in 1904, and even though Renée continued to maintain a villa there, returning several times a year, it was Renée who found it impossible to live up to the Sapphic ideal defined by Natalie. Central to that ideal was the freedom to love as one chose, but Renée felt betrayed when Natalie took other lovers and shared her life with other women. Barney separated the sexual act itself from the spiritual notion of "love"; the body (through which the sexual act was performed) and the soul (through which fidelity was defined) remained discrete entities in Barney's code of ethics. Such a division seems a contradiction in her otherwise consistent philosophy that the body and spirit should be joined in a single lived life. It was a contradiction that Renée was never able to resolve, either for Natalie or for herself. She could not accept Natalie's insistent separation of fidelity from sexual faithfulness: for Renée, one implied the other; for Natalie, the two were divided from each other on philosophic grounds. Renée was not only bound to a morbidly idealized Romantic temperament, but was a victim of a Western morality that demanded fidelity in love as the price of sexual and sensual pleasure.

Natalie's refusal to bow before Western tradition (precisely because it reaffirmed the superiority of the spirit to the body) evidenced itself in a distaste for sentimentality and a hatred of hypocrisy often read by her friends as a form of callousness. Natalie established for herself standards of behavior and morality that few could meet; although she appropriated Sappho as her most important model for the kind of artistic and intellectual life she wished to lead, Barney was ultimately to trust her own instincts and to develop her own standards for developing ethical principles and making aesthetic judgments. Her life is distinguished by a remarkable emotional maturity and the absence of self-destructive impulses, but she was surrounded by women who turned against themselves by internalizing patriarchal values. Barney's effort to create a Parisian Lesbos constituted an effort to reverse the effects of self-hatred, an attempt to act on her own definition of Sapphic culture. The effort carried with it, however, the seeds of its own failure: unaffected by the particular form of homophobia from which many of her friends suffered, she was considered someone set apart from the world, a kind of amazon—a representative of an earlier, matriarchal, civilization whose expectations could not be met by others. Thus each of her lovers felt betrayed by her fierce independence, and Renée Vivien pictured her in *A Woman Appeared to Me* as the coldly beautiful Lorely, a woman associated with ice, winter, and moonlight.

If Natalie Barney's philosophy of life placed itself at a purposefully oblique angle to the mores of *fin de siècle* France—simultaneously classic and modern in its views—her art has always been considered *passé* and oddly anachronistic. If her life has been read as self-indulgent and self-serving, her writing has been thought silly. Unfortunately for Barney, the twentieth century quickly set itself against the various movements that shaped her intellectual development in the 1890s. Romanticism became a foil for Modernism; the decadent movement, based in the aesthetics of Pater and Baudelaire, seemed to represent the last vestige of nineteenth-century individualism; classic materials rediscovered in the final years of the nineteenth century were reinterpreted by a cynical twentieth century. The very forms of Natalie Barney's art—Romantic poetry and the epigram—were considered slight, occasional, sentimental, glib, and clichéd. The Modernist enterprise would strip such forms of artificiality and convention in order to expose an essentially banal and outmoded core of thought. Barney's use of such forms to express a radical lesbian feminism has been the excuse for dismissing both the subject and its method. Quick-witted, she was called facile; committed to expressing love of women, she was accused of producing coterie literature; interested in the social function of the arts, she wrote works judged to have only occasional interest; joining life and art in a feminist aesthetic, she was thought to have devalued art at the expense of life; refusing to revise her work according to the dictates of her male mentors, she was considered lazy; writing in a variety of forms and genres, she was judged to be a dilettante; placing a high value on the indiscreet, she was immediately adopted as a worthy subject of gossip.

But Barney herself did not confuse gossip with indiscretion, nor did she discredit the indiscreet by the terms she used to discuss it. Under the pretext of discussing indiscretion, for instance, she turned her attention to aesthetics. Indeed, Barney revealed a commitment to the aesthetics (and ethics) of indiscretion:

> in blaming indiscretion, it seems we forget the good things that derive from it. All expression, art itself, is an indiscretion that we perpetrate upon ourselves. It stems from an excess of riches, not from "poverty." For this is the way we make the few hours of our lives last beyond themselves. Faced with our past, when it is really over with, discretion is merely oblivion, sterile, valueless. I think that it is an act of devotion to honor our dead with a few words by which they may continue to outlive themselves; instead of mute

forgetfulness, we can give them some inspiring and courageous epitaph describing what they were. For are we not perhaps more guilty if we allow these prodigies who have created masterpieces out of life itself to vanish, without voice, without song. The history of their loves, devotedly recorded, adds to the beauty of our world; it is this that we inherit from their riches, their unique patrimony. Silence too can be indiscreet. Would it not rather be proof of our own irremediable poverty if we should permit the dead to die? (from *Scatterings,* quoted as the epigraph to Chalon, *Portrait of a Seductress*)

If art itself is a form of indiscretion, as Barney claimed, then her own "indiscretions" might best be placed within the definition of art that she herself constructed. She urged in this contemplation of the indiscreet that art be joined to life and history, that the past be honored in the richness of language rather than through the poverty of silence. Barney emphasized that it is the response of others to the artist's life and work rather than the artist's individual efforts to ensure a position in history through the written word that is significant. This consideration of the uses of the indiscreet provides important guideposts for those who would look at Natalie Barney's life and work: she urged us to look not at the indiscreet nature of life itself but rather at the indiscretion that constitutes the commentary on the life. She asked us to look at her writings. She drew a subtle but important link between indiscretion—an attribute often assigned to women—and art. By its very indiscretion, art belongs to woman. It is shown to participate in that which has most often been discredited in Western culture: woman's experience and her commentary on it. The terms that have been most often used against Barney's writing—that it is facile, occasional, indiscreet—or that have described her unworthiness as an artist (she was lazy, inconstant, a dilettante) might well be turned in a feminist aesthetic toward the *difference* of her art. She not only loved differently, she wrote differently—that is, she loved and wrote as a woman. For Natalie Barney, as for Sappho, woman's art was the product of shared experience among women, a social and collective effort by a small group of extraordinary women who separated themselves from society in order to love and write literature. Literary effort was inseparable from love, inseparable from the occasion that provided its impetus: art was not separate from life but was defined by it.

Writing in Difference

One of the reasons, of course, that it has been so easy to dismiss Barney's writing and to concentrate on the indiscretions of her life is the very inaccessibility of her writings. Most of her early work was printed in limited editions through small Paris publishing houses. Her later writings, although reaching a wider reading audience at the time of publication, have not remained in print. A large portion of Barney's literary *oeuvre* remains in manuscript, and—with the exception of *The One Who Is Legion* and "Memoirs of a European American"—all of her writing, including the autobiography, is in French. Although Barney wrote consistently throughout her life, she published her work infrequently, gathering together selections from her journals and diaries to be included in memoirs and *pensées*. The generic range of these writings—poetry, drama, gothic fiction, epigrams, biography, and autobiography—attests to her varied literary interests, but these works divide themselves between writings in fixed literary forms (poems, plays, and fiction) and those that exist almost by definition outside strict generic limits: *pensées*, memoirs, and various autobiographical accounts. This work divides itself almost too neatly between the poetry that utilizes standard Romantic structures (work written prior to 1920) and the later, more personal and less formal, writings. The single exception to these discrete categories is *Scatterings*, a series of meditations on art and life, published in 1910.

Because Barney's writings have never been fully available to those who have written about her, and because she herself placed restrictions on both letters and unpublished writings, it has been difficult to assess the pattern of her literary development. Nonetheless, it seems that she became increasingly interested in forms of writing most often associated with women: diaries, letters, and memoirs. These occasional writings have traditionally been considered "appropriate to" the shapelessness of the female mind, to woman's inability to master more demanding generic forms, and to woman's interests and capabilities. In each of these forms, Barney turned to traditionally feminine topics and exploited those aspects of literary form most often associated with women. Her *pensées* may well belong to the classic tradition of epigrammatic form as practiced by Pascal, La Rochefoucauld, and Oscar Wilde, but the subject of these thoughts is woman's situation in Western society. They illustrate the ways in which the feminine constitutes an aberrant form of the masculine norm; they develop a feminine (and feminist) wit by which woman preserves both her identity and her independence against male efforts of appropriation; they comment on love from the woman's perspective, observe society from the point of view of one who is rigidly circumscribed by its demands, summarize feminist logic, and comment on the role of art and literature. Rather than closing subjects, offering a final word on the situation, Barney's *pensées* open the world to a different perspective and radically alter accepted perceptions. These thoughts provide a record of Barney's developing philosophies of life and art. She saw love not only as the subject for art but as that which generated art, and although she was not spared disappointments in love and friendship, the initial bond she had established between the ethics of love and aesthetics of art supported her own writing throughout her life.

Barney's commentary on the Western tradition of love that makes woman the object of man's pursuit was often bitter. She entitled the opening section of her first volume of *Pensées d'une amazone* "The Adverse Sexes: War and Feminism."[7] Her argument was less that feminism is engaged in war—against oppression and prejudice—than that war represents an extreme form of masculine aggression apparent in all male relationships. The feminine principle that opposes this dominant masculine ethic defines itself in love and a sense of community. Because love does not strive for mastery, however, it is often assumed to represent weakness and vulnerability. Barney commented, for instance, that "if love existed among men, they would already have found the means of proving it" (18), and she suggested as well that in war—man's sport—"the choice of arms is not equal, for it is the aggressor who chooses them" (26). During both world wars, Barney elaborated arguments that claimed women were made the unwilling victims of the male need to fight. For her, marriage itself constituted a battleground on which men hold the advantage over women, in which the choice of arms always belongs to the male aggressor.

Barney was particularly sensitive to the inequality inherent in the notion of the "couple," an institution that fostered woman's dependence on—and therefore her vulnerability to—men. She argued that men have a "double right to life and death in the world," since they make the decisions to which women must silently consent. Taking up the theme of Lysistrata, Barney argued that it is man who is the real enemy, that through war (which she labeled an "involuntary and collective suicide ordained by man"), he "destroys woman's work," kills the children she has produced, and "without her consent" (8–9) ruins the life she has constructed. Although Barney called the Amazons to resist men who appropriate women's lives and take their children into the fields of death, she also argued that woman's courage is demonstrated when she silently watches the wounding and killing of the sons she brought to life. She concluded that although men insist that they fight for an "ideal," in fact they fight out of "false valor or for pleasure" (33).

The series of observations that constitute the *pensées* construct themselves around seeming oppositions (love/war; birth/death; sensuality/brutality). The commentary unsettles the expected relation between the oppositional forces, showing them to be a "couple," united in unexpected ways. Barney commented, for instance, that "the infant and the lover are born simultaneously from the sorrows of the disappointed and mutilated female lover [*l'épouse*]." Here the female body is mutilated by experiences that supposedly would give her pleasure and joy. Barney's comment that "feminism can not be a question of sex, since the Frenchman is more a woman than the Englishwoman" (7) continued her argument with England, a country whose treatment of women appalled her. Yet the remark seems to cut both ways: the Frenchman was derided for feminine qualities and the Englishwoman satirized for her masculinity. Many of Barney's comments on womanhood suggest a certain ambivalence about the female situation. The exclamation "this catastrophe: to be a woman!" (11) can produce contradictory readings. Was she bewailing her biological state? Or was she suggesting that womanhood is a "catastrophe" created by man's definition of woman? Or was she suggesting a relation between biological womanhood and the social situation in which woman finds herself? When she proclaimed that the notion of "lady" erased the presence of "woman," she revealed the ways in which the social definition and placement of woman can eradicate and displace the very womanhood on which such definitions base themselves. The comment that "equality" is "a level of inferiority" forces a relation between apparently mutually exclusive terms to argue that instead of expunging the notion of inferiority, the idea of equality writes the concept of inferiority into its operating principle.

Included with the *pensées* is a section ("What the Men Think") that cited reviews by male readers, among them some of Natalie Barney's close friends. Dr. Joseph-Charles Mardrus, for instance, commented that Barney participated too much "in this unhappy feminine humanity," a terrain he described as almost "impermeable." Barney's commentary reminded him of a story of hopelessness from the Great War. Told by a man, the story concerned women typesetters in a Paris printing shop who had taken the positions of the men sent to war: "Oh, sir, these women workers, full of good will in the face of this strenuous work. They worked even harder than the mobilized men they replaced. But what can you do with women: they aren't men. No sir, they aren't men!" (xii). Dr. Mardrus felt that the *pensées* lacked something, and he defined the lack as the feminine. For this, he said, Natalie Barney would not become a literary goddess. His comments suggest the very kind of misreading that the text not only invites but that is its subject. Barney's analysis of woman's situation produces the predictable patriarchal response (a "misreading" of her text) as well as a critique of the patriarchal misreading. The two readings are not mutually exclusive—one incorrect, the other correct—rather, each reading participates in the other. Most male commentators found Barney's remarks shrill and motivated by moral disgust. Writing in the *New York Evening Post*, Vincent Sullivan commented that Barney's thought was "governed by her emotions rather than by her intelligence, but her emotions are so completely sterilized that this discovery cannot be immediately made" (xvi–xvii). Although no commentaries by women were provided (perhaps because Barney was particularly interested in male response), one can imagine similar conclusions: rather than supporting the cause of women, Barney abandoned her sex and suppressed her own womanhood. Behind these commentaries lurks the suspicion that Barney tricked her reading audience: the form her comments take belies their seriousness. Presented as slight, witty, and ephemeral comments on the human condition, they concealed their very serious and pointed critique of Western culture. Consequently, the *pensées* produce oppositional readings, readings that resist conclusions and that contain within them the tensions between form and content apparent in the *pensées* themselves. Put in an uncomfortable position, readers assumed their discomfort to be the fault of the author rather than inherent in the civilization under analysis.

The One Who Is Legion

If some readers assumed the *pensées* to be a bitter denunciation of Barney's womanhood, the strange text she produced and had privately printed by Eric Partridge in 1930, *The One Who Is Legion, or A. D.'s After-Life,* constitutes an effort to recover through language the feminine in Western culture. It is exceedingly important that this effort to "make good the failure" is undertaken through writing, since it suggests an equivalence between woman's situation in society and the place of writing in Western culture. Because the work is almost impossible to place in a literary genre (it is, perhaps, a kind of gothic novel, as George Wickes suggests) and because it had a limited reading public (only 560 copies were issued), it has generally been overlooked in discussions of Barney's work. Djuna Barnes tried to find an American publisher for it, and Romaine Brooks provided illustrations. Wickes suggests that because *The One Who Is Legion* exploits a "weird . . . and dreamlike atmosphere," the product of a tormented psyche, it owes more to Brooks's imagination than to Barney's. In form, the work is unique among Barney's writings, but its story examines the effects on women of societal constraint, a theme common to all of Barney's writings. In particular, the story concerns the resurrection of a suicide who appears as a sexually ambiguous hermaphrodite; a poem introducing the story pays a debt to Balzac's *Seraphita,* a work Barney had long admired:

> A double being needs no other mate—
> So seraphita-seraphitus lives;
> Self-wedded angel, armed in self-delight,
> Hermaphrodite of heaven, looking down
> On the defeat of our divided love.

Incorporating self-division in the hermaphroditic body, the resurrected suicide suggests both the possibility of a "self-weddedness" that will dissolve division and the permanent state of self-division. The story opens in a graveyard opposite the Longchamps racecourse in the Bois de Boulogne, a place where nuns were buried after the destruction of their abbey. The suicide is resurrected in the moonlight when a powerful woman breathes life into "the pinched nostrils that expanded to her breath" (19). The resurrected being is then taken to a small house surrounded by a heavily wooded garden in central Paris (the description of the house matches that of Natalie Barney's own house on the rue Jacob) where the suicide discovers in a small temple behind the house the book of her own life. Entitled *The Love-Lives of A. D.*, the book is arranged by epigrams: "It comprised hymns, quotations; poems threw out their antennae for individual comprehension" (29).

The story seems to combine commentary on Natalie Barney's own writing with her efforts to understand the motivations for Renée Vivien's suicide. Although time and place are often unclear, the story begins in the period of horse-drawn carriages and ends with airplanes flying overhead. A listing of *dramatis personae* in the text includes A. D.'s horse, and the notes indicate that the time of the story is "beyond time." In an author's note Barney explained ". . . for years I have been haunted by the idea that I should orchestrate those inner voices which sometimes speak to us in unison, and to compose a novel, not so much with the people about us, as with those within ourselves and cannot a story arise from their conflicts and harmonies?" (159). Resurrected from her grave, A. D. "is replaced by a sponsor who carries on the broken life, with all the human feelings assumed in the flesh, until, having endured to the end in A. D.'s stead, the composite or legion is disbanded by the One, who remains Supreme." The One who remains supreme (a being defined as "A. D.'s angel") incorporates in her own self all the other "characters" in the tale.

The One Who Is Legion traces the effects of self-division in women: A. D. is identified as "self-destructive. A lover." While the sources of internal conflict are not made explicit in this text, they are powerful enough to lead to the suicide on which the story is premised. We never learn why A. D. committed suicide, but the story suggests that the immediate reasons concerned disappointment in love. What is important about the death, however, is its very resistance to explanation, suicide registering itself as a traumatism whose causes are never understood, least of all by the victim of its self-destructive aggression. This version replaces the suicide victim with a guardian presence who is able both to subsume contradictions and to overcome them, the doubled sex of the resurrected A. D. marking this division and union of opposites. The "legion" are described by Barney as "low characters, spirits—a hierarchy of selves," who surround the resurrected corpse and register the complex contradictions of the life that destroyed itself; they are dispersed by the "One," who both encompasses them and eliminates them through her own being. Although the text hints that it is love that causes self-torment, the various ways that self-division manifests itself through the story suggest a more complex set of contradictions. Woman, for instance, is divided into the component parts of body and spirit: the Glow-woman is described "as a beauty of the flesh that we have only met in the flesh," whereas Stella is "a beauty of the spirit that we have met in many ways, and loved and lost, and loved and found again in losing." Two male characters point to the possible sources of woman's self-division in patriarchal definitions of her. Duthiers serves as the "third person in all situations" and the "boyhusband" is one "who only exists through others." These two characters participate in the self-division of others, both registering that division and acknowledging the ways in which initial division leads to fragmentation.

At one level, *The One Who Is Legion* suggests that lovers can only be fully united after death, that the loved one is only truly loved after she has departed: "we are so obtuse that we could not even feel the presence of the Beloved until a higher medium joined us to her" (152). The "higher medium" is represented as both death and the "One" whose presence is only available *after* death. The terms of the love relationship are heterosexual, the hermaphrodite representing sexual counterparts: although sexual identities shift and merge, the suggestion that lesbian love causes a special kind of torment leading to self-destruction is never specifically acknowledged. Instead, woman's self-division is seen to participate in sexual difference, in the division of humans into males and females. A. D. is brought back from the dead to reread the text of her life, a life that has been sacrificed to the terms of sexual difference. Her death was an *effect* of this difference. Seated before her own writing, in the library that is termed a "dead-letter office," she reads the text of her life, a letter composed by one part of herself and directed to another self. Here she "unfold[s] pages hardly meant for us" (46). The writing is disorganized and contradictory, and we are told that its meaning rests in its aftereffects: "we can judge of nothing while we are in it. Even happiness is an aftermath. . . . A choice—a lead from the unconscious. Its dictates at loose ends" (45).

The writing in A. D.'s book is the trace of her former life, marking the very divisions of that life. Rather than erasing or eliminating the contradictions, the writing cannot help but expose them, so that the text of the life marks—by its own oppositions and self-denials—the inevitable death of its subject. The letter A. D.'s sponsor reads in the library is A. D.'s death warrant, written and signed by her own hand. But the letter is also a love letter addressed to the beloved, a text that can apparently only be read after death. We are told that "A. D. made us realise that the love-stories we live are hardly ever our own, that their significance dwells in what they lead us to express, or awaken within ourselves" (28). Thus the love story has a happy ending: the lover is not lost, dispersed within the text of a dead life, but recuperated through the presence of the One who, after the fact of existence, can resolve the very differences that brought an end to the life.

One is tempted to read in this story Barney's own effort to complete Renée Vivien's broken life, to resolve the contradictions of that life by subsuming and overcoming them in her own life. Yet the story also invites a rereading of Barney's life and writings. In its very resistance to telling a story, an effort that would require an elaboration of the life it represents, A. D.'s book avoids coherence and explanation. A. D.'s life is refracted through the text rather than reflected in it. A similar observation might be made of Barney's own writing, which gives evidence of the ways that it resisted development. The total body of writings suggests a work in progress, left incomplete in the hope that its author might someday return to rewrite it. If Vivien's life did not develop because it was cut short, Barney's long life would seem to invite commentary on its development and change. Yet the record suggests that she was caught in a turn-of-the-century moment, never able fully to live in the modern world. *The One Who Is Legion* simultaneously marks timelessness and time's inevitable change: Barney's life also marks these apparently contradictory states. Although the world changed around her, she did not perceive any major changes in the human situation.

The Ethics of Beauty: Pre-Raphaelite Forms

Barney devoted energy and intelligence to imagining forms of love and beauty that would remain unmarked by the effects of time. Barney's writing never acknowledges the ways love might be affected by aging. She always captures her lover in a moment outside time; the beloved remains youthful, unchanging. A. D. returns from the grave as a beautiful young woman, unaffected by the corrosive powers of death or the changing patterns of the outside world. Barney's effort to stop time by creating an existence that denied the march of time manifested itself in two ways: her Ethics of Beauty took as its model figure the pre-Raphaelite form of the androgyne, a form as yet unmarked by signs of the maturation process; Barney discovered in the garden at 20, rue Jacob, a kind of green world that sheltered her against the modernized and mechanized urban civilization of Paris. The garden became a place in which androgyne beauty was celebrated, where slim-hipped, long-legged, small-breasted women danced for each other, paying homage to the aesthetic ideal that Barney both worshipped and embodied.

Barney was always sexually attracted to women who embodied the female aesthetic celebrated in nineteenth-century paintings by Rossetti, Burne-Jones, and Sandys. Such paintings presented an enigma of gender, illustrating figures that were not clearly female or male. Often portraying lovers who seek their own image in the lover, these paintings provide doubled images of ambivalent sexuality: lover and beloved offer mirror images of one another. Joseph Kestner has argued that such portraits of androgynous females reveal an anxiety about women that was to emerge in the nineteenth century as misogyny. He cites comments by Graham Hough, who in *The Last Romantics* suggests disturbing psychic forces that underwrite such conceptions of women:

> Any full treatment of the culture of the period would have to explain the lavish and eccentric display of erotic symbolism that made its appearance on both sides of the Channel after the middle of the century—the obsession with various illicit alliances between love, pain, and death; the femme fatale or the vampire; homosexuality, male and female; hermaphroditism, and all the rest of it. No doubt some of the mythological embodiments of these states of mind, notably the conception of women as some sort of mysterious fatality, were . . . personifications of forces and ideas buried deep in the human psyche. (191; quoted in "Burne-Jones," 119, fn. 4)

Susan Gubar has argued that in calling up a "satanic Sappho," who morbidly sings of the "sinful delights of Lesbos," Renée Vivien reclaimed for women the decadence so exploited by the masculine literary and artistic tradition of the nineteenth century: "Vivien suggests that the 'unnatural' longing of the decadents' Sappho turns the lesbian into a prototypical artist, for her obsession with a beauty that does not exist in nature is part of a satanically ambitious effort against nature to attain the aesthetic par excellence" ("Sapphistries," 49). Gubar claims, then, that Vivien demonstrated decadence to be "fundamentally a lesbian literary tradition" (49). To the extent that this claim is true for Vivien (and to make her argument Gubar must overlook important aspects of Vivien's essential ambivalence toward Sappho as woman, as lover, and as lesbian poet),[8] it is equally untrue for Barney. Barney never conceived of Sappho in the terms used by Vivien, never thought of her as "satanic" or her delights as "sinful," never linked eroticism to morbidity. The terms of Barney's aesthetic, moreover, were drawn from nature: woman's place was among trees, flowers, rivers, and streams. In the Paris years, Barney's wild and overgrown garden served as a creative source for her writing,[9] the inspiration for *The One Who Is Legion,* a work that examines the "mysterious fatality" associated with womanhood, probing its source in the male psyche and suggesting that such a vision of woman is a creation of the masculine imagination. It was precisely the morbid fear of women, the association in the male mind of the "femme fatale" with the "vampire" figure, that Barney attempted to overturn—not by tapping the energy of the "decadents' alienated lesbian," as Gubar argues Vivien might have done ("Sapphistries," 49)—but by divesting the image of the lesbian of its homophobic implications. Rather than replacing the masculine image of the androgynous female with another model of female beauty, perhaps one more representative of the acknowledged model of late-nineteenth-century beauty—the short, stocky, buxom women who lived outside the imaginations of pre-Raphaelite artists—Barney attempted to recuperate the pre-Raphaelite image of women. That is, she celebrated this female figure, separating it from the morbidity and misogyny that underwrote the male conception of it. For her, this effort was part of a larger attempt to disassociate woman's self-conception from the dark misogynous vision inherent in societal notions of homosexuality.

Radclyffe Hall exploited the androgyne female image to compose the figure of the "mannish lesbian" whose ambiguous sexual features reflected the sexologists' assumption that the androgyne bodies of lesbian women contained the souls of men trying to escape the female form. Natalie Barney feminized this body, draped it in Grecian robes or photographed its lithe contours by moonlight and celebrated the very sexual ambiguity that, in the vision of a male artist like Burne-Jones, outlined a deep-seated fear and hatred of women. Joseph Kestner has noted that such androgyne figures in late-nineteenth-century art constitute a form of masculine repression of the female as a castrating figure and offer a representation of the castrated and androgynous male-female ("Burne-Jones," 113). These representations demonstrate a reversal of masculine sadism inverted to masochism: they image the results of female power. Rather than resisting women who reflected the Burne-Jones vision, Barney found herself attracted to them, eroticizing and feminizing the very bodily features (lithe limbs and small breasts) that marked for male artists of the period a castrated and ambiguous sexual identity. If male artists used such figures to portray the feared effects of female power, Barney found in such figures an eroticized and highly feminine beauty.

Prior to World War I and during the years that Barney's own body conformed to the ideal of feminine beauty she so praised, her garden offered a setting for the contemplation and glorification of this female image. André Germain comments that by 1909—the year she moved to the rue Jacob—the era of "pagan nudity" had already come to an end and that an aura of "mysterious austerity" surrounded the "little pavilion" where Barney "enshrouded" herself (*Les fous de 1900*, 158–159). Surely this change was brought about by the death of Renée Vivien, the woman who had symbolized for Barney the perfection of female beauty. Within a few years, of course, the war itself would disperse the community of women Barney had assembled, marking the end of an era that had defined itself in Sapphic celebration and attic abandonment. When the women of Barney's circle returned to Paris following the war to meet in the garden at 20, rue Jacob, changes in clothing styles—brought about by the war—revealed the extent to which Barney and her androgyne friends had aged. They had cropped their hair, become stocky, large-breasted, and full-hipped. Their hair was now gray and their skin sagged along the fine bones. In 1918, Barney was 42 years old, and she no longer resembled the wood nymphs, shepherdesses, or court pages that constituted the poses of her youth.

Visual Disjunctions: The Portraits of Romaine Brooks

Although Barney's writings never comment on the aging process, never discuss the disjunction between the ideal and real, Romaine Brooks's portraits reveal the women in her circle in their maturity. Brooks met Barney in 1915; they became lovers when each was in her early forties and were to spend the rest of their lives in close proximity to each other. Unlike Barney, Romaine Brooks had suffered both psychological and physical deprivation, had been persecuted and eventually abandoned by her mother, had made a disastrous marriage to John Brooks, a pianist, had nearly starved during her years as a student artist, suffering from a pneumonia so serious that she was forced for the rest of her life to spend much of every year in a warm climate. These experiences had left her in need of love but ignorant of the conventions through which love expressed itself. Brooks was bitter, cynical, suspicious, and highly neurotic. She disliked social occasions (rarely attending Natalie's salon) and had little in common with the women who frequented Natalie's garden or who formed the Académie des Femmes. Such gatherings, with their musicals and masquerades, must have seemed childish indulgences to Brooks. If Natalie's memoirs picture a group of ageless androgynes whose lesbianism preserves the female body against the ravages of patriarchal culture, Romaine's portraits provide a different set of visual images, which reflect the souls of these women through their amazon bodies. These portraits do not reveal the strength and pride of women warriors; the figures are rather angry and self-tortured. Only Natalie is spared a hard, tight-lipped, and angry mouth; only Natalie is given eyes that are dark and soft rather than small and piercing. No one else is spared Romaine's dark vision, not even herself. Una, Lady Troubridge, represses a snarl in her portrait, her mouth twisted and her right eye enlarged and made unreal by a monocle, producing an asymmetrical and frightening gaze. Elizabeth de Gramont, the Duchesse de Clermont-Tonnerre—Romaine's rival for Natalie's love—has a clamped mouth, a weak chin, and sad dog's eyes. In her own self-portrait, Romaine's eyes are shaded by a hat, her mouth forming a grim line across the bottom of the face.

In this series of studio portraits of the Barney circle, Brooks's subjects adopt stylized poses and costumes. Although each of the subjects is identifiable as a woman, only Natalie Barney herself is dressed in something approximating customary female clothing. All the others, Brooks included, are portrayed in tuxedos, morning coats, and capes: they are amazons in drag. The portraits expose devastating self-divisions presumably hidden by external poses, attesting to rather than disguising the divided psyche. Susan Gubar has commented that Brooks's paintings portray "the pain the male costume produces on and in the female figures." Cross-dressing frees these women from culturally enforced roles as sex objects for men, but it also "expresses the mutilation inextricably related to inversion when it is experienced as perversion. . . . the cross-dresser is no longer a woman warrior. Instead she is a self-divided, brooding Byronic figure who dominates the center of [the] canvases, hinting at power diminished or fallen" ("Blessings in Disguise," 486). Whereas the canvases of Burne-Jones and Rossetti repressed fear of women, portraying it in a lithe, elongated female form, the effects of such misogyny emerge directly in Brooks's work, where the portrait reveals the painful results of self-castration. Suffering the effects of self-division, Brooks captured "in the tension between costume and body" the evidence of a psychic split ("Blessings in Disguise," 488). Under Brooks's observant eye, these women no longer represent Barney's notion of ideal female beauty, but rather betray that ideal by choosing male costuming in which to cloak the effects of psychic castration. Brooks employed traditional art forms to render her subject matter. She did not turn a Modernist eye on her subjects, did not strip them of pretense to expose with ironic humor the gaps between pose and reality. Instead, she faithfully preserved the poses, allowing the pose itself to reveal the ways in which posture had become reality. The *démodé* style of these paintings reveals, more precisely than Picasso's brush might have, the internal adjustments that shaped external reality under the force of psychological constraint.

The irony of Brooks's portraiture is that Natalie Barney felt discomfort in the presence of masculine women, yet was surrounded by them in her salon. According to Meryle Secrest, "even Romaine considered that Natalie had lived 'years in dank unhealthy houses among many dank unhealthy people'" (*Between Me and Life*, 334). Barney never acknowledged the extent to which self-division registered its effects in the costuming of such women as Radclyffe Hall and Elizabeth de Gramont, choosing perhaps to overlook these manifestations of self-hatred among her friends while simultaneously providing them with alternative self-images recuperated from Greek culture. Barney's project failed for all but herself. The pursuit of beauty through the androgyne body to which Barney dedicated her art was destroyed by the modern, mechanized world. After World War I, women cut their hair and shortened their skirts, a situation Barney deplored. The beautiful bodies she had worshipped throughout the *belle époque* were now disfigured and denuded: "These short skirts: so many women showing their legs without being asked, their twisted columns which no one even suspected. Poor legs one meets in the streets, knock-kneed, wanting in padding and training. What has become of that dance, that rhythm, the gait?" (Chalon, *Portrait of a Seductress*, 139). For Barney, this change of style marked not a liberation of the spirit but an obscene disfigurement of the human body. Although she herself eventually cut her hair and wore short skirts, she was never happy with the change. Like other women of her social class, she was dressed by Paul Poiret in the boxy dresses and close-fitting hats of the period. She discovered after the war that clothes were no longer interesting, so she adopted a uniform in gray, white, and black (the three shades most loved by Romaine Brooks, who painted her portraits in these neutral tones). The women Barney knew were transformed by the modern world; they no longer embodied her remembered images of them. They were no longer beautiful in the ethereal, spiritual way they had once been.

Lesbos Divided

The mythic world of Parisian Lesbos over which Natalie Barney had presided, and which in certain measure she had created, was not one in which all lesbian women celebrated their sexual orientation. For most of these women, lesbianism did not offer a release from the code of compulsory heterosexuality of the modern world but rather bound them in continued opposition and imitation of that code. The vision of a modern Sapphic circle remained very much Barney's personal vision, one that she recreated for her own pleasure within the enclosure of the garden at 20, rue Jacob. In her presence, all jealousies and personal conflicts among her friends were temporarily set aside; within the garden walls, safe from the intrusion of the outside world, the divided female spirit healed itself, rejoicing in short-lived freedom from patriarchal constraint. Natalie Barney's lesbian feminist vision and Radclyffe Hall's homosexual anguish represent diametrically opposed views of woman's culture in relation to the heterosexual norm: Hall's vision was dominated by the norm, while Barney's denied the power of heterosexuality. Barney's dream of a separate culture is appealing precisely because it denies reality; Hall's anxiety and self-hatred represent too dramatically the power of the parent culture.

Indeed, the two forms of female separatism did not live comfortably with each other. Radclyffe Hall feared Barney's distanced judgment and, like many others, interpreted her independence and self-assurance as callousness. Barney was put off by Hall's assumed identity as "John," an image of denied womanhood that Barney both pitied and despised. The nymphlike creatures draped in gauze who danced in Barney's garden inhabited a world different from that of the monocled women in tuxedos. Barney was democratic enough to encourage the participation of both types of women, just as she invited men, both heterosexual and homosexual, to her salon, but she preferred her highly feminized image of womanhood. This image— embodied in Liane de Pougy, Eva Palmer, Colette, and Renée Vivien— belonged to the prewar period. Lucie Delarue-Mardrus, Elizabeth de Gramont, Romaine Brooks, Janet Flanner, Dolly Wilde, Radclyffe Hall, Una Troubridge, and Janine Lahovary belonged to a later generation, one that had been "liberated" to dress, talk, smoke, and act like men. These women reacted to the heterosexual norm by aping its forms; Barney preferred to ignore those forms altogether, to deny the effects of time on her body or the evidence of a modernized world that surrounded her wooded garden, and to pursue the elemental, sensual, feminine. Barney's vision emphasized the *otherness* of womanhood, its *difference* from the masculine norm.

PART III. CROSSROADS

Hilda Doolittle (Morris Library, Southern Illinois University, Carbondale).

*Hilda Doolittle in the 1920s (Yale
Collection of American Literature,
Beinecke Library).*

*Hilda Doolittle and Bryher, 1920
(Rosenbach Museum & Library).*

Hilda Doolittle in Egypt, 1923 (Yale Collection of American Literature, Beinecke Library).

Left and right above: *Margaret Anderson and Jane Heap (Sylvia Beach Collection, Princeton University Library).*

Jane Heap, Little Review, *spring 1929 (photograph by Berenice Abbott; McFarlin Library, University of Tulsa).*

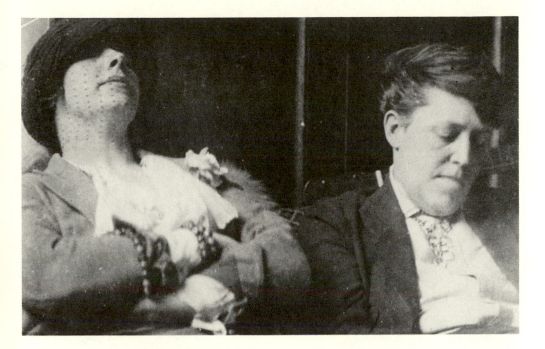

Above: *Margaret Anderson and Jane Heap, early 1920s (Sylvia Beach Collection, Princeton University Library).*

Cover of Little Review exiles' number, spring 1923 (McFarlin Library, University of Tulsa).

Maria and Eugene Jolas at their country house in the late 1920s (Morris Library, Southern Illinois University, Carbondale).

Left: *Kay Boyle (Morris Library, Southern Illinois University, Carbondale).*

Cover of transition, *number 14 (McFarlin Library, University of Tulsa).*

Gertrude Stein in the 1930s, transition, *number 14 (McFarlin Library, University of Tulsa).*

Nancy Cunard, London, 1930s (photograph by Cecil Beaton; Morris Library, Southern Illinois University, Carbondale).

Left above: *Nancy Cunard at the Hours Press, Réanville, France (Morris Library, Southern Illinois University, Carbondale).*

Above: *Nancy Cunard with an Hours Press publication (Morris Library, Southern Illinois University, Carbondale).*

Left: *Nancy Cunard,* Little Review, *spring 1929 (Copyright by Man Ray; McFarlin Library, University of Tulsa).*

The American Moron and the American of Sense—Letters on the Negro

It is necessary to explain to the English reader (I think ?) that "caucasian" in the U.S. is used as a self-awarded title of white man's superiority. It has no more to do, geographically, with the Caucasus than "nordic" (same meaning) has to do with Scandinavia.

I should like to print all the raving, illiterate, anonymous letters—some are very funny indeed, mainly from sex-maniacs one might say—but what is to be done? They are obscene, so this portion of American culture cannot be made public.

Of course there were other letters as well—some 400 or 500—from Negroes and friendly whites, commending the stand I took and the making of this anthology. Of the anonymous threats, etc., some 30. Most of them came in a bunch, just after the press outcry, May 2, 1932.

LETTERS

Mrs. Nancy Cunard take this as a solemn warning, your number is up. You're going for a ride shortly. You are a disgrace to the white race. You can't carry on in this country. We will give you until May 15th. Either give up sleeping with a nigger or take the consequences. This is final. X 22. P.S.—We will not only take you but we'll take your nigger lover with you.

* * * *

Miss Nancy Cunard repair to pay ransom 25,000 dollars will be demanding kidnaping H—B kidnaping inc.

* * * *

Miss Cunard, this is one of the rare instances where we have found it necessary especially among intellectuals to deal drastically with those who would impair the fundamental principles of the Caucasian race of peoples. Since you have evidently found it expedient to disrespect your Aryan birthright and as we are conscious of that which might result from your present environment while in this country or your previous associations in Europe you will please be governed as below.
We shall call for you just as soon as the necessary plans have been completed for your reception.
The secretary of the second society of Caucasians of America.

* * * * *

Miss Nancy Cunard, you are insane or downright degenerate. Why do you come to America to seek cheap publicity? you have not gained any favor but a whole lot of hatred. If I saw one of your publications I would be the first to suppress it. Furthermore I and a committee are appealing to the U.S. department of labor to have you deported as a depraved miserable degenerated insane. Back to where you belong you bastard. If you dare to make any comparison you had better look out for your life wont be worth the price of your black hotel room. You for your nerve should be burned alive to a stake, you dirty low-down betraying piece of mucus. [Here follows a sentence which might be considered obscene and which is not, therefore, printed.] K.K.K. 58 W 58.

(I suppose this purports to come from the Ku Klux Klan, or possibly the writer only stole their " signature.")

* * * * *

Of the other side it is only fair to quote as well. There are *indeed* many white people who have a liking for Negroes ; some are afraid to say so, others are not. (I must perforce exclude in this count entirely the followers of the Communist Party, with whom it is a *sine qua non* to stamp out all race " inferiority "; this has not exactly *come of itself* to some of those who have joined the Communists, and there have been cases of trial and exclusion of members who have been taken back into the Party after their admission of guilt in race-prejudice, and conditional on their eradication of it in themselves and in others.) This type of letter is from people who are presumably not yet aware that all race-prejudice has a distinctly economic basis, that the Negroes in America are looked down on primarily because they were once slaves ; the more so in the South because these slaves were taken from them by the result of the Civil War in 1865. Though it is out of place nowhere when talking of the Negro and slavery to repeat that the vast bulk of Southern State Negroes are as enslaved as ever ; the name only has gone, the condition is the same, and worse.

LETTERS

NEW YORK, *May* 2.

MY DEAR MISS CUNARD,—It's with a great deal of pleasure that I read about you in today's papers. I might say also that I am proud of you when you come out and defend the Negro race. It has been my good fortune to know some very fine people of the Negro race. I went to public school with Negroes, they were no different than any other children, perhaps better than some others. I'm staying in New York tonight, so after dinner I went up to the Public Library at 103 West 135th St. to read a book by a Negro. I could not find any fault with the people there. In fact I found it a very pleasant place to be. The book I wished to read was looked up

198

Letters objecting to publication of Nancy Cunard's Negro, *printed in the published text (McFarlin Library, University of Tulsa).*

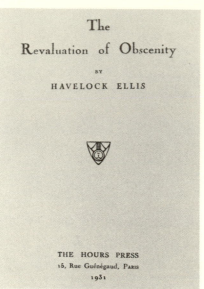

Title page of The Revaluation of Obscenity, *the Hours Press, 1931 (McFarlin Library, University of Tulsa).*

Advertisement for books from the Black Sun Press (McFarlin Library, University of Tulsa).

Caresse and Harry Crosby, Paris, about 1927 (Morris Library, Southern Illinois University, Carbondale).

Caresse Crosby and Narcisse Noir (Morris Library, Southern Illinois University, Carbondale).

Solita Solano, Little Review, *spring 1929 (Copyright by Man Ray; McFarlin Library, University of Tulsa).*

Anaïs Nin in the 1960s (Morris Library, Southern Illinois University, Carbondale).

Jean Rhys (photograph by Pearl Freeman; McFarlin Library, University of Tulsa).

9

H. D. AND BRYHER:
EN PASSANT

Hilda Doolittle and Winifred Ellerman made significant contributions to the expatriate Modernist movement without living in Paris. H. D. consciously chose not to live there, finding the city too demanding of her psychic energies and feeling herself an outsider among the expatriates, all of whom seemed to have arrived in France with letters of introduction to the most important Modernist figures. Bryher, an heir to her father's shipping fortune, had been counseled by him to take up residence in Switzerland as a tax shelter. Consequently, both women spent most of their adult lives living in London and Switzerland, making brief visits to other European cities, among which Paris was not their favorite. That H. D. should have discovered London in 1911 as a setting that both stimulated her work and provided a comfortable atmosphere in which to live sets her apart from all the other women of this study. Her Anglophilia contrasts sharply with the Anglophobia experienced by Gertrude Stein and Natalie Barney, both of whom found London depressingly unsympathetic to women. Like Virginia Woolf, H. D. commented at length on the ways in which London stimulated her writing, and her analyses provide an important balance to the notion that Paris offered the only agreeable environment for Modernist women. H. D.'s preference for London over Paris forces us to distinguish significant differences among women Modernists who lived in these two cities and, in particular, challenges us to look closely at H. D.'s early experiences as a writer living in London.

The Poetics of Marginalism

H. D.'s ambivalent relationship with the city of Paris, where—according to Ezra Pound—everything of importance in modern literature was happening, reflects a similar unease with Modernism itself, and she purposely situated herself well beyond its boundaries. Not only physically displaced from this literary enterprise, she was also psychologically troubled by its concerns. High, formalist Modernism was specifically a masculine, heterosexual phenomenon that excluded those who did not share the mores of its dominant culture. For H. D., the patriarchal and heterosexual features of Modernism constituted a trap, forcing her to efface the issue of her own sexual difference, which was problematically bisexual. Homosexual women were constrained by Modernist aesthetics in a variety of ways: they could remain silent on the subject of their lesbianism and its relation to their art; they could adapt Modernist forms (as Gertrude Stein and Virginia Woolf did) to disguise the lesbian viewpoint of their poetry and fiction; or they could translate love of women into the dominant heterosexual code. Susan Stanford Friedman and Rachel Blau DuPlessis have argued that H. D. practiced all three forms of such disguised disclosure, dividing her art between poetry and fiction, between public and private texts. Their argument rests on the belief that H. D.'s lesbianism was the creative wellspring of her art, necessarily forced into hiding by the dominant culture. But all of H. D.'s writing displays an uncertainty of sexual identity, making the writing moment highly traumatic for her. Although these texts dissimulate, even encode sets of double messages, the sexual identity out of which they are composed oscillates between the heterosexual and the homosexual. H. D.'s most important contributions to Modernism—her radical rewriting of the Doctrine of the Image, the creation of palimpsests, and her reappropriation of woman-centered myths—are allied to the complexities of her own sexual difference and to the question of sexual identity. In this, her situation is significantly different from any other woman Modernist: she was pulled toward contradictory worlds— the paternal and heterosexual world of Modernism (exemplified in her relationships with Ezra Pound and Richard Aldington) and the maternal and homosexual world of Bryher. Ultimately, she was never able to choose between the two, and the writing moment always brought with it this crisis of sexual identity.[1]

Both Bryher and H. D. lived between two worlds: the dominant heterosexual culture and a marginal homosexual culture. But for Bryher the negotiation of this space of sexual difference was significantly different than for H. D.: Bryher knew from adolescence that she was lesbian, but to protect herself from the inevitable censure of her parents she was forced to hide her sexual self. Her first marriage, to Robert McAlmon, permitted her to escape parental boundaries; her second marriage, to Kenneth MacPherson, served to screen H. D., whose affair with MacPherson H. D. wished to hide from her husband, Richard Aldington. It was precisely Bryher's lesbianism that enforced the division between public and private lives (an experience explored in her early novel, *Two Selves*): privately she supported the work of lesbian Modernists, contributing to support of Sylvia Beach's bookshop, Djuna Barnes's poetry, and Dorothy Richardson's fiction. Publicly, Bryher's money was dispensed by her husband, Robert McAlmon, in support of various Modernist publishing efforts, including McAlmon's Contact Editions, and in direct support of such Modernist writers as James Joyce. Bryher's own self-knowledge, however, made questions of sexual difference more complex for H. D., who felt the tensions between the public and the private spheres, between psychic reserves and physical strength, between dominance and submission, between heterosexual and homosexual desires, between efforts to resist a culturally determined feminine destiny and the need to explore a specifically female creativity, between Modernist aesthetics and modern ethics, between poetry and fiction, between Paris and London. During the 1920s, the period of High, formalist Modernism, H. D. separated herself physically and psychologically from the literary movement that might have claimed her as one of its foremost practitioners. Susan Stanford Friedman suggests that H. D. purposely placed herself on the Modernist margins, perhaps in order to develop an aesthetic of the marginal (see "Modernism of the 'Scattered Remnant'"). In order to understand something of this marginal aesthetic and to see the shape of her career, we must examine the simultaneous need to express herself in writing and to repress that writing—the psychological situation of that writing.

Dialectical Tensions

When H. D. withdrew from Bryn Mawr in 1906, the reason given was her failing health. In fact, her return home was occasioned by failing grades, including a failure in English literature, and a feeling that she had disappointed her parents. As with Gertrude Stein, H. D.'s academic difficulties were the product of a lessening interest in her studies, itself a camouflage for internal tensions that divided her. H. D.'s biographer, Barbara Guest, has suggested that "the truth was that she was facing dual worlds: an authoritarian institute of learning, and an equally authoritarian poet. It was either Ezra Pound or Bryn Mawr" (*Herself Defined*, 5). H. D. had established an intimate relationship with Pound five years earlier when she was 15; the interim period had been fraught with family tensions over Pound's role in her life, her parents disapproving of the young bohemian poet. He was to remain an important influence on her life for several more years, however, directing her reading and thinking in the five years following the Bryn Mawr disaster, during which time she lived with her parents and attempted to recover her health. Beautiful and talented, H. D. nonetheless saw herself as "a disappointment to her father, an odd duckling to her mother, an importunate overgrown unincarnated entity that had no place here" (*Herself Defined*, 22). She lacked self-confidence, felt marginalized, and was emotionally torn by the diametrically opposed claims of family respectability and sexual desires—desires she already recognized as problematically heterosexual and homosexual. Pound encouraged her to write, serving as both teacher and critic. Directing her reading, he tried to introduce her to a dynamic intellectual world beyond the boundaries of Upper Darby, Pennsylvania. The world Pound opened to H. D. was an exciting one, but the price of admission to it was exacting: it required meeting Pound's intellectual expectations, responding to his sexual desire, fulfilling his hopes. In these years, the two were engaged to be married—despite the ambivalence of Professor and Mrs. Doolittle—awaiting the return of Hilda's health and the realization of Ezra's hopes of becoming a major modern poet before making their relationship official.

In January 1908, Ezra Pound was dismissed from a teaching job at Wabash College in Indiana and departed for Europe on a trip that would result in his permanent exile from America. He was to return to America in June 1910 with several literary successes to his credit, the publication of *Personae* and *Exultations* among them, having made the acquaintance of key poets and literary editors in London during his eighteen-month stay there. Feeling that he had conquered the London literary scene, Pound wished to secure his American reputation and wrote H. D. in 1910 that he was coming to New York. She immediately went to New York in an effort to find a job, partly in anticipation of Pound's arrival but also to escape an increasingly difficult family situation in which her relationship with Frances Gregg, a young woman who had become Hilda's lover, was at issue. The months in New York were among the most unhappy of her life, and she returned to Upper Darby in defeat, again retreating to the family fold. As Barbara Guest reports, "she had made no contacts, had found no work" (*Herself Defined*, 25). Unlike Pound, H. D. was never able to make her way alone in new places. She always retreated to isolation, unable to find new friends, to make literary contacts, to survive alone in unfamiliar surroundings. The New York experience, following the earlier failure at Bryn Mawr, frightened her and undermined an already threatened self-confidence, leaving her vulnerable to the attentions of those less intimidated by new situations.

In spring 1911, Hilda Doolittle embarked on her first trip to Europe, accompanying Frances Gregg and her mother. When the Greggs returned to America, Hilda stayed on, taking an apartment at 8 Duchess Street in London. In the months that followed, Pound introduced her to all his London acquaintances, including Ford Madox Hueffer, William Butler Yeats, Harold Monro, May Sinclair, and the poets who would form the Imagist movement—F. S. Flint (whom Hilda called, in a letter to Ezra

Pound's mother, a "derelict poet," *Herself Defined*, 29) and Richard Aldington (Hilda Doolittle's future husband). Earlier in the trip, H. D. had spent several days in Paris, where she encountered unexpected discomforts and disappointments. She had wanted to see the Venus de Milo at the Louvre, but discovered the museum closed due to a burglary; she thought her hotel too far from the Left Bank quarters that interested her. Little about Paris appealed to her: she was afraid to walk for fear of being run down by taxis; she did not speak the language and had no confidence in her ability to communicate even the least of her needs; the tensions with Mrs. Gregg over her relationship with Frances had greatly intensified during the trip. London, the next stop on the itinerary, was a welcome relief. She spoke its language and assumed a commonality of culture that she was only later to discover did not entirely exist; she adapted quickly to its customs and became dependent on her afternoon tea (a dependency she shared with Bryher). She discovered the Elgin marbles in the British Museum; she was admired as a friend of "the leading poet in London," Ezra Pound (*Herself Defined*, 32).

While there was "no equivocation in her love for London," as Barbara Guest tells us (28), there was great ambivalence and misunderstanding in her relationship with Pound. Did Hilda think she and Ezra were soon to marry? Had she followed him to London for that reason? Had she attempted, in the four-month journey with Frances Gregg, to put an end to that troubled female relationship? Interpretations of H. D.'s behavior during these months vary: Barbara Guest reads the trip to Europe as H. D.'s effort at rebellion. This leave-taking marked her apparent guilt at having failed her family's expectations, but it also marked a further and more radical form of rebellion: an effort to continue, away from her parents, an erotic involvement with another woman (*Herself Defined*, 27). Janice S. Robinson reads the pattern of H. D.'s life in an elliptical arc that traces both her attachment to and need to separate herself from Ezra Pound. According to Robinson, H. D. went to Europe having decided to marry Pound against the wishes of her parents (*H. D.*, 23). Perhaps there is some truth in each of these interpretations, their contradictions marking H. D.'s own confusion about her sexual directions and emotional attachments. In the nearly five years since she had left Bryn Mawr, her life had been held in suspended animation: still not knowing precisely which direction to take, she nonetheless acted on a strong desire to live away from her family, a decision that would lead to a permanent separation from America.

Under the emotional strain of her relationships with Frances Gregg and Ezra Pound, H. D. found relief in a new friendship with Richard Aldington, who studied Greek culture and discussed poetry with her. He immediately recognized her poetic talent, knew her to be more creative than

himself, and, although he fell in love with her soon after their first meeting, was tolerant of her other emotional commitments. Six years older
than Aldington, H. D. was attracted to his youth, his energy, and his desperate need for conversation that matched her own. More importantly,
she was attracted to his Englishness: "he was a twentieth-century Englishman, and she wanted to remain in England" (Guest, *Herself Defined*,
35). Hilda herself felt not only that she belonged in England but that a
return to the United States was not possible. It meant retreat to the over-
protectiveness of her family and to the disparate expectations of her parents. When H. D. moved to 6 Church Walk, to an apartment across an
interior courtyard from Ezra Pound's, Aldington followed her, taking
lodgings on the floor above. Here, in April 1912, the three began discussing their poetic theories in earnest, and either in these rooms or in the tea
room of the British Museum the Imagist principles were conceived and
drafted. Although the poetry movement that Pound would label Imagism
had already been developing in the work of T. E. Hulme and F. S. Flint
since 1908, the April 1912 meeting established Pound as the propagan-
dist for a poetry movement he hoped would revolutionize English verse.
Initially an English poetry movement that attempted to counter French
Symbolism, Imagism was to find in a young American woman its most
talented practitioner. By autumn 1912, H. D., who so recently had felt
herself to have "no place here," stood at the center of an exciting literary
movement, her poetic gifts and sexual attentions contended for by two
other important figures of the movement—Ezra Pound and Richard
Aldington. Again, H. D.'s affections and loyalties were polarized. There
seemed no alternative to the oppositional pull between Pound and Aldington, as Frances Gregg sent news that she was soon to be married in
America.

Those who have examined H. D.'s role in the Imagist movement against
the London literary scene of the Georgian period have usually emphasized the crucial role Pound played in providing introductions and in soliciting interest among the English for H. D.'s work. Her sudden appearance as a poet of some importance in this group has often been read as
the magical effect of Pound's presence and his careful editing of her early
work. The older generation of writers—represented by Harold Monro,
editor of *Georgian Poetry*, and Ford Madox Hueffer, editor of *English
Review*—were indeed powerful among the English, but outside that
country their work was virtually unknown, and Pound quickly discovered
the necessity of overturning the principles on which Georgian poetry
rested. He convinced Hueffer to support the work of younger poets, specifically the Imagists, over the views of older, more traditional writers.[2]
With the exception of W. B. Yeats and T. S. Eliot, none on the London
scene would be able to compete with the later Modernists who were to

group themselves in Paris. Very quickly the English world that had seemed so alive and exciting to Pound began to pale. Within the year he would redefine Imagism in terms of Vorticism and shift his literary attention from London to Paris. Through Vorticism Pound hoped to counter the "melange of satin and talcum powder" of French Symbolism, an effort that was guided by his contacts with young avant-garde writers in Paris in 1913. In that year he published two accounts of Parisian efforts, drawing attention to those poets associated with the magazine *L'Effort Libre*. In the January issue of *Poetry* he claimed that "the important work of the last 25 years has been done in Paris"; his seven-part series "The Approach to Paris," an analysis of contemporary French poetry, was published in the *New Age* in autumn 1913.[3] Vorticism was Pound's last effort to bring London into the twentieth century. The effort failed for several reasons (not the least of which was the coming of World War I); the ideological and aesthetic revolution to which Vorticism sounded an early call was to be carried out on the continent—not in London—and would transplant itself to Paris following the war. Obsessed with this revolution, Pound seems to have forgotten H. D.—perhaps even to have abandoned her. Certainly she felt herself abandoned by him.

Imagism marked the break between nineteenth-century Romanticism and twentieth-century Modernism. In order to succeed in revolutionizing literature, however, the Imagist movement needed to be known internationally. Such a possibility was inconceivable in an England separated from the most important developments in art and music occurring on the continent. Prewar London was still caught in the conventions of Victoria's reign. By comparison, Paris had already experienced the shock of the *fauves,* had read Huysmans' *A rebours,* had seen Alfred Jarry's *Ubu Roi,* and was soon to be overwhelmed by Stravinsky's *Rites of Spring.* London was a quaint backwater, "a rather prissy milieu of some infernal bunshop full of English spinsters," as Richard Aldington was later to recall bitterly (*Life for Life's Sake,* 122). Never one to be associated with the prissy or to associate with spinsters, Ezra Pound reinvented Imagism, replacing its emphasis on direct treatment of the thing with Vorticist insistence on "movement, energy and intensity" (Zach, "Imagism," 236). Importantly, according to Richard Sieburth, this new literary movement, "embodied . . . an entire style of revolt—pugnacious, irreverent, militantly intolerant of all the stagnant *idees recues* of bourgeois culture" ("Ezra Pound," 322). That is, Vorticism preserved that which was masculine about Imagism (its hard, clear, concrete, and unsentimental treatment of subject) and welded it to the dynamic force of the Vortex. In setting aside Imagism, Pound privileged energy and conflict over stasis and fixity and rejected an aesthetic that appeared to be passive and "feminine" for one that was aggressive and "masculine."[4]

Although World War I would destroy the London that H. D. had come to love, forcing her into a "permanent, rambling exile" (Guest, *Herself Defined,* 73), the loss of this literary world and her place in it was presaged by Pound's desertion of her—first by his marriage to Dorothy Shakespear, which secured for him powerful literary alliances (Dorothy's mother, Olivia, had introduced Pound to Yeats, who actively encouraged Pound to marry Dorothy: see Robinson, *H. D.,* 25–26), and next by his dismissal of Imagism in favor of Vorticism (*Herself Defined,* 64). These initial leave-takings would be repeated by Aldington, whose enforced separation from H. D. during the years of his duty in World War I aggravated tensions in the marriage that led to his taking Arabella Yorke as his lover. Never able to maintain a truly independent course in her life, H. D. lived most of her adult years under the protection of stronger, more powerful, allies. The first of these was Ezra Pound; the last was Bryher. Although such relationships inhibited H. D.'s struggle toward self-identity and emotional stability, and even though she herself made attempts to escape them, she remained an essentially dependent person, never able successfully to chart her own course, always in need of nurturing and therefore always vulnerable to disappointment.

Between London and Paris

In this H. D. shared less with Gertrude Stein and Natalie Barney than with Virginia Woolf, who was also plagued by emotional and physical illness during the years of her greatest productivity as a writer. A comparison of these two writers rests on a series of similarities in their lives and work, not the least of which was their intense and abiding love for London, the city that served as literary inspiration for both. In the years when Pound, Aldington, and H. D. were participating in a new and exciting literary movement in Kensington, Virginia Woolf was playing an important role in Bloomsbury—a world from which H. D. would have been excluded by the fact of her American birth. Aldington's bona fide English credentials would have done H. D. little good, since Virginia Woolf did not care for Aldington, describing him in her diary as "a bluff, powerful, rather greasy eyed, nice downright man, who will make his way in the world, which I don't much like people to do" (vol. 2:326). But Virginia Woolf's situation in the Bloomsbury setting and H. D.'s in the Imagist group shared important common factors as well as significantly dissimilar ones. In each, the women were surrounded by men to whom they initially listened, carefully following the direction of masculine wisdom. For Virginia Woolf, the Cambridge intellectuals she came to know through her brothers were to provide her the university education she had never received. For H. D., Pound's English friends were to open an intellectual world to her that had been unavailable in her protected family environment. With the exception of Leonard Woolf and Roger Fry, the men who surrounded Virginia Woolf were homosexual. H. D., however, was the desired object of attention among men who competed with each other for her affections.

The sexual dynamics of these two literary groups mark differences in the experiences of two women whose sexuality was defined by a high degree of ambivalence. One experienced sexual denial, the other sexual threat; both felt the absence of understanding and affection among literary colleagues. For a complex set of reasons that shaped their sexual and artistic orientations, both women were to become increasingly isolated in their respective groups, charting in their writings an interior territory of linguistic experiment, following the psychological implications of their sexuality, taking risks in the patterns of their expression, fearing the publication and exposure of themselves through their writing. Virginia Woolf's history of recurring mental and physical illness followed the predictable and obvious directions established by the publication of her writing. H. D. also feared censure, and kept back the most experimental of her writings (her prose work) to prevent disclosure of a more private, and divided, self. Although both Virginia Woolf and H. D. developed strong dependencies on individual women—Virginia on her sister, Vanessa Bell, and H. D. on her companion, Bryher—neither of them participated in a larger community of women. They worked alone, in private, sharing their work with men whose censure they feared, but whose praise they desperately needed.

While in Paris communities of women artists developed alongside the male Modernist enterprise, in London Woolf and H. D. remained outside the circle of that effort, beyond the boundaries of its expressed intentions. Of the two, H. D. found—in part through Pound's early efforts on her behalf—women friends and literary supporters who continued to encourage her work. These early friends included May Sinclair, "who took on Imagism with the same stalworthy air with which she espoused suffragism" (*Herself Defined,* 30), and Brigit Patmore. H. D. wrote to a later friend, May Sarton, in 1941 concerning Virginia Woolf's suicide: "The general attitude was 'poor thing—she went through such a lot' but having been through so much, I myself, did feel stricken to think she got away like that, just when really everything is very exciting and one longs to be able to live just to see all the things that will be bound to happen later—think of not being here to look at France, to watch the whole shift of civilization" (*Herself Defined,* 265). Having conquered her own battle with suicidal tendencies, H. D. may have considered Virginia Woolf's death an indulgence that should have been avoided. For both women the onset of World War II brought back painful memories of the First World

War, but their experiences in that earlier war were decidedly different. For Woolf, the First World War meant the continued fear that she would lose those who were close to her, and her efforts were directed at keeping Leonard, Clive Bell, Lytton Strachey, Duncan Grant, and other male friends from conscription. For H. D., the war meant the loss of a stillborn child and the disintegration of a relationship on which she was totally dependent but about which she was nonetheless ambivalent. She had married Aldington in reaction to the news that Pound was to marry someone else.

In 1912, H. D. made two separate trips to Paris, the first of these with Aldington in May of that year. Pound had already left London to spend the summer in Paris studying the troubadour traditions in the Bibliothèque Nationale and later traveling from Paris to Poitiers and Chalais following the routes of the troubadours. In October of that same year, H. D. left London alone and took a pension on the rue Jacob; here she tried a third time to discover Paris. Unhappy at her absence from his life, Aldington gave up his job in Fleet Street to follow her, although she had not as yet promised to marry him. Indeed, the confusion of her reactions to him, her depression at the prospect of having to make such a choice, may well have spurred her decision to spend time in Paris. But she made no contacts there, spending her time with Walter Rummel, whom she had known in London, or with Aldington when he joined her. Although Aldington would later translate Remy de Gourmont's essays from the *Mercure de France,* following Pound's interest in the French writer, he had not yet discovered this French intellectual and seemed generally uninterested in French literary developments. Absorbed with her own problems, H. D. moved through the city taking little note of Parisians or their city. Writers she would later come to know and appreciate, especially women writers in the circles of Gertrude Stein and Natalie Barney, remained unknown to her in 1912. Years later, when Sylvia Beach could provide introductions and her bookshop was the setting in which literary discussions took place, H. D. felt more comfortable in the Paris milieu.

But this particular Paris trip resulted in the decision to marry Aldington, and it was here that she learned of the suicide of Margaret Cravens, a young American woman who had apparently been in love with Pound, who took her own life at the news of his engagement to Dorothy Shakespear. As Barbara Guest reports, "The Margaret Cravens incident assumed all sorts of proportions for Hilda, who almost believed that she herself might have been the one to commit suicide, as she had been 'dropped' by Pound too. She identified with Margaret, who had appeared to live the kind of life Hilda would wish for herself—an elegant apartment, many friends, independence from her family" (*Herself Defined,* 49). Such a life of financial and social comfort was provided later by Bryher, who used her father's money to purchase an easy and secure existence for H. D. In the meantime, H. D. turned to Aldington for emotional support, having finally realized that Ezra Pound would not—undoubtedly could not—meet the demands of her dependencies. In some ways this Paris trip signaled another moment in H. D.'s life when the hoped-for and sought-after independence was not to be accomplished. This time the return to London constituted yet another retreat rather than the liberation it had seemed to promise only a year earlier.

Had H. D.'s relationship with Ezra Pound not been part of a developing literary movement, had he not spent ten years directing her reading and thinking, teaching her Greek and Latin and taking her education in hand, the dissolution of their sexual and emotional bonds might not have been so traumatic for her. Had there not been a literary context for this love affair, however, there probably would have been no love affair. It is Pound's role in the development of "H. D., Imagiste" that captures the attention of anyone trying to understand the link between H. D.'s developing literary talents and the continuing ambivalence of her sexual and emotional orientation. H. D. had begun experimenting with poetry in 1910 in New York as she waited for Pound's return from Europe. She modeled these early pieces on Theocritus, but labeled them translations (from the German, based on Heine). She continued writing poetry after her arrival in England, the poems she composed in summer 1912 marked by a "laconic speech" that was, according to Pound, unmistakably Imagist. Indeed, Pound would later remark that the "whole [Imagist] affair was started not very seriously chiefly to get H. D.'s . . . poems a hearing without its being necessary for her to publish a whole book" (Kenner, *Pound Era*, 177). In fact, Pound began promoting the Imagist movement before he had yet seen these early poems by H. D. Believing the two necessary elements for a "Renaissance" to be "an indiscriminate enthusiasm" and "propaganda," he sent two of his own poems to Harriet Monroe, who was then in the process of developing *Poetry* magazine. One of these poems, "Middle-Aged" (sent to Monroe on 18 August 1912), was the first poem Pound labeled *imagiste*. He described it to Monroe as "an over-elaborate post-Browning 'Imagiste' affair" (Paige, *Letters of Ezra Pound*, 44).

H. D., Imagiste

Relying on the correspondence between Pound and Monroe and on the evidence of "Middle-Aged" itself, Cyrena Pondrom has demonstrated not only that Pound had not yet seen H. D.'s early Imagist writing in summer 1912, but that his own poem did not fulfill the principles of good writing he had drafted in collaboration with Aldington and H. D. the previous spring. Within days of sending Monroe "Middle-Aged," however, Pound read H. D.'s "Hermes of the Ways," and the famous scene in the British Museum tea room ensued. He edited her poem, signed it "H. D., Imagiste," and offered to send it to Harriet Monroe (H. D., *End to Torment*, 40). On 21 September 1912, he wrote to Monroe agreeing to become the magazine's "foreign correspondent," and in October he sent her his corrected version of H. D.'s "Hermes of the Ways" along with two other H. D. poems ("Priapus" and "Epigram"); a few days later he forwarded Monroe some more of his own work, poems he described as "ultra-modern, ultra-effete" (Stock, *Life of Ezra Pound*, 121). In March 1913, Pound and F. S. Flint published in *Poetry* the first descriptions of Imagist technique ("A Few Don'ts by an Imagiste" and "Imagisme"); in the gap between the self-labeling of "Middle-Aged" as *imagiste* and the publication of these Imagist prescriptives, Pound had read H. D.'s early poetic efforts. That reading, according to Pondrom, "led him . . . to re-examine his own work to find examples that approximated that standard" ("H. D. and the Origins of Modernism," 91). Further, it suggests that H. D.'s poetry crystallized the Imagist conception for him, providing a standard of poetic practice through which to define the elements of the movement he wished to found.[5]

This brief résumé of the 1912–13 events hints less at Pound's altruistic support of H. D.'s work than at his desire to found and publicize a literary movement. As Pondrom has noted, "the dates of his own actions belie Pound's claim that imagism was invented to publicize H. D.'s poetry, and the very self-absorption which could lead Pound repeatedly to claim responsibility for her career, and more, was a danger H. D. recognized and from which she withdrew" ("H. D. and the Origins of Modernism," 96). In *End to Torment* H. D. wrote that "Ezra would have destroyed me and the center they call 'Air and Crystal' of my poetry" (35). But Pound discovered in her early work something that he himself had been unable to produce under the "Imagiste" label. It seems evident, in fact, that she was two steps ahead of Pound, already producing what he would later label "Vorticist" poetry. Pound was particularly attracted to the principle of economy in her early writing. According to Noel Stock, Pound's biographer, Pound began in autumn 1912 "zealously" to apply the second principle of good writing ("to allow no word that was not essential to the presentation"), "attack[ing] with a pencil any manuscript that was offered to him for his advice or comment" (*Life of Ezra Pound*, 121). He demanded discipline, conciseness, clarity, and objectivity; he would allow no excess, no abstraction, no muddiness. In autumn 1912—after Pound had seen H. D.'s early poems—he composed "In a Station of the Metro," the most concise of Imagist poems and the one regularly anthologized as the best example of Imagism (Pondrom, "H. D. and the Origins of Modernism," 94). If one believes that reading H. D.'s first poems affected both

Pound's own writing and the emerging definition of Imagism, one would expect to discover in them evidence of a determining Imagist practice. Instead—and surprisingly—one discovers certain resistances to that practice; one even discovers evidence that H. D. was already rewriting, even subverting, Imagist claims.

That is, Pound may have seized on certain elements of H. D.'s early writing to support his own notions about the directions contemporary poetry might take. In doing so, he may have seriously misread her; and the possibility for such misinterpretation was inherent in a poetic method far more complex than Pound had initially assumed. Brendan Jackson has argued, for instance, that the qualities of concision and economy so crucial to Pound's conception of Imagism are absent in H. D.'s earliest work. "Hermes of the Ways" elaborates and extends by some fifty lines the poem on which is is based, a single quatrain by Anyte of Tegea, an Arcadian woman poet of the third century. Jackson notes that "the equation 'H. D.'s Imagism = Greek economy' has become a cliche of criticism," but he sees "her response to experience" as "far from the classical spirit" (92–93): "The additional material consists of a far more developed visualization of the scene. It is true that this is achieved by an accumulation of detail, not by an indulgence in adjectival description; nonetheless, although H. D.'s speech is indeed 'laconic,' her selection of detail is far less rigorous than that of her Greek inspiration" ("Fulsomeness of Her Prolixity," 94).

If the rendering of the Hermes subject is not classical "in spirit," neither is it entirely Imagist if one assumes this poetry to inhere in stasis. "Hermes" demonstrates the ways in which form itself can become an "image"; it is an example of a poetic practice that had not yet been elaborated by the Imagists. Only later, when describing the Vorticist operations of the image, would Pound suggest something akin to this practice. As Pondrom observes, H. D.'s first poems "actually provide early poetic models for the important transformation of the static form of imagist doctrine into vorticism" ("H. D. and the Origins of Modernism," 17). "Hermes" treats the "image" in distinctly different ways from other Imagist poems of the period, allowing the surface passivity of such poetry to be broken by the tensions inherent in the writing act. That is, the presumed objectivity and impersonality of the Imagist mode is used to render subjective, personal, and highly charged psychological subject matter. The landscape imaged by the poem is sexualized, and the narrative of the poem is structured according to sets of oppositions—forces and resistances, actions and reactions—that are themselves constructed as tensions between male and female. Passivity and violence are conceptualized in "Hermes," their oppositional forces energized in verbs that describe the force of wind and the play of water, the tensions between resistance and aggression evident in descriptive terms that offer diametrically opposed readings of the scene being visualized. The Imagist enterprise—including the not-yet-elaborated Doctrine of the Image—is both proposed and undermined by "Hermes."

Although the entire poem represents the dual effort of supposition and subversion, its effects are registered in the force of one particular stanza:

> The boughs of the trees
> are twisted
> by many bafflings;
> twisted are
> the small leafed boughs.[6]

This stanza finds its structure in chiasmus, providing a double image of the twisted boughs. The "many bafflings" serve a double function as well, existing as both the effect of a "baffling" force and an effort at resistance to that force registered in the "twisted" boughs ("baffle" here echoes both its use as a verb—to baffle—and the effect produced by the verb: to be baffled, or confounded). The "baffling" constitutes, then, both the effect of an action and a reaction; the "twisted" boughs simultaneously serve as evidence of the baffling and as images of resistance to baffling. The source of the "twisting" and "baffling" is not specified, but it apparently rests in nature (in the "sea-wind" of an earlier stanza, for instance). The poem exploits traditional concepts of nature's force and beauty, suggesting in its images a dynamic action and reaction within the universe—a dynamic in which the active is associated with masculine violence *in* nature that assaults, whose effects are doubly registered as a feminine resistance *to* nature—an attempt to ward off its force—and a being confounded or stymied by it. The poem maintains a balance between oppositions within nature through sets of images that render the *effects* of violence: the stunted, twisted trees; the torn sails of the masthead in the following stanza.

The tension between masculine and feminine, between violence and patient resistance to it, is registered as well in the original Greek poem (translated by Richard Aldington under the title "Hermes of the Ways"):

> I, Hermes, stand here at the cross-roads by the wind-beaten orchard, near the hoary-grey coast;
> And I keep a resting-place for weary men. And the cool stainless spring gushes out. (*Egoist* 2 [September 1915]: 139)

In the original poem, the orchard represents "a resting-place for weary men" in whose gardens "the cool stainless spring gushes out." The gushing spring (an image of female creativity and fecundity) is opposed to the "hoary-grey coast" that separates sea water from land. The double vision of the poem, signaled by the two "I"s, suggests a set of masculine and feminine oppositions: the first "I" belongs to Hermes; the second (also obliquely and ambiguously identified with Hermes, but feminized) situates itself in the garden with the spring. The speaking subjects of this quatrain are distinguished from each other by their relative positions within a sexualized landscape, and H. D. exploits the tensions inherent in sexual difference in her rendering of "Hermes." Although the Greek poem images the effects of natural violence in the "wind-beaten orchard," it offers relief and release from such violence in the "cool stainless spring." H. D.'s version of the quatrain, however, emphasizes the effects of violence from the sea-wind that "whips" and the sea foam that "gnashed its teeth." A stream with sweet water flows in the garden (but the stream is "small"); the orchard offers apples (that are "Too small, / Too late ripened"). The sun is "desperate" and "struggles through sea-mist," but the small and late-ripened apples give evidence that the sun's effects have been nullified. This poem provides no relief, offers no refuge from the violence. Each image of the feminine (the "sea-orchard" that "shelters" Hermes, the "white stream / Flowing below ground," the tree boughs with small apples) is countered by a violent force of nature (the wind, the sea water). Hermes waits at precisely the spot "where sea-grass tangles with / Shore-grass." (As Pondrom has remarked, the speaker belongs to the "boundary area"—a "no man's land" between sea and sand; here the female speaker meets Hermes Trismegistus, the god of writing, learning, and wisdom and the protector of travelers, "H. D. and the Origins of Modernism," 88.) The poem's final image suggests an ambiguous confusion of sea and shore, male and female, but it does not offer resolution to the oppositions set up by the poem. The verb "tangles" includes diametrically opposed and unresolvable meanings: to intermingle and to ensnare. The "sea-grass" and "shore-grass," although opposed, are not equally matched: "tangle" is itself a form of large seaweed, so that the "sea-grass" has the power to envelop—to overpower—the more vulnerable "shore-grass."

The changes H. D. wrought on the original Greek quatrain include, as Brendan Jackson has noted, a shift in speaking personae.[7] But the sum total of her changes are both different from and more significant than the ones that Jackson enumerates. H. D. does not merely extend the Greek poem, she superimposes her own poem on the earlier construct so that the Greek quatrain "shows through" the surface of her writing, thereby exposing a double text. This palimpsest unbalances the dualities implicit in the Imagist equation; it is a form that H. D. often uses in her poetry, most notably in *Helen in Egypt*. In particular, H. D.'s "Hermes" tracks the complex shifts in narrative personae proposed in the earlier poem. Jackson's claim is that "Anyte speaks for the god Hermes" in the Greek poem, while "H. D., by contrast, speaks as the wayfarer." The effect, he says, is to "render her poem less austere than the Greek original" ("Fulsomeness of Her Prolixity," 95). The Greek narrative is, however, more complex than Jackson allows. Its perspective is displaced, aligning itself first with Hermes ("I, Hermes") and next with the "wind-beaten orchard" ("And I keep a resting-place for weary men"). Moreover, the realignment suggests that Hermes is implied in the second statement (he is the keeper of the feminized "resting-place for weary men," the orchard, which is also the "wind-beaten" victim of a masculine force). Here, Hermes guards the feminine image of the "cool stainless spring." H. D.'s poem does not place Hermes as the guard who protects the orchard and oversees the spring, but as the one "whom the sea-orchard / Shelters from the west, / From the east, / Weathers sea-wind; / Fronts the great dunes."

In the later poem Hermes is not merely the guardian of the feminine, but a representative of the feminine itself (despite the continued use of masculine pronouns). The narrative perspective constantly aligns itself with Hermes ("Heu, / It whips round my ankles!"—Hermes too the victim of the masculine force of the wind) as it simultaneously separates the speaking subjects of the poem into "I" and (a doubled) "you." While the earlier poem separates the speaking subjects ("I, Hermes" . . . "And I"), H. D.'s poem incorporates the split subject into a triply feminized Hermes: Hermes "Of the triple path-ways"; the orchard, "facing three ways, / Welcoming wayfarers"; and "He whom the sea-orchard / Shelters from the west, / From the east." The earlier poem juxtaposes dualities; H. D.'s effort unsettles those dualities by offering a third possibility. This third possibility, however, does not resolve the initial opposition of the speaking subject and the orchard that provides a "resting-place" for the subject, but rather suggests an internal division within Hermes—a dubiousness, a choice of directions not yet taken—that are imaged in the split subjects of the poem. Thus "two" becomes "three," not by resolving the initial term to a third term, but by suggesting an internalized "other" *within* the initial opposition. The "Hermes, / Who awaiteth" is also the Hermes who "welcome[s] wayfarers" and the one "whom the sea-orchard / Shelters from the west, / From the east." The suggestion here is not that masculine and feminine are opposed (Hermes/the orchard) but that masculine participation in the feminine ("He whom the sea-orchard / Shelters") exposes the feminine to violence ("Hermes, Hermes / The great sea foamed, / Gnashed its teeth about me"). Feminine and masculine are not only opposed, but are placed in a hierarchy in which the feminine is submitted to the force of the masculine (as the narrative perspective of the poem submits itself to the effects of its own narration). H. D.'s effort suggests the ways in which the god Hermes embodies the masculine and participates in the feminine: he is a victim of nature's force as is the feminine.

Imagist Doctrine

In 1915, May Sinclair wrote to Charlotte Mew of her reactions to Imagism: "H. D. is the best of the Imagists (you'll observe that I don't say very much about the others). . . . The precise criticism . . . is that they lack strong human passion . . . In writing to Richard A[ldington] I said, 'some of you will have an emotion that the "image" will not carry; then where are you?'" (quoted in Guest, *Herself Defined,* 29–30). The very fact that H. D.'s conflicting emotions could not be "carried" by the "image" may have led her toward more complex poetic statements that avoided (consciously or unconsciously) the dialectical equivalence of the Imagist doctrine. If it is true that H. D. found a way to subvert Imagist principles in order to accommodate her own views, then our traditional understanding of H. D.'s relation to Imagism has not only misrepresented her poetic methods (she was not, as Friedman and DuPlessis have suggested, seeking in "the austere poetics of imagism" an "objective correlative for emotion," "Sexualities," 7), but may have also distorted our understanding of the uses she made of Greek materials and the relation of her fiction to her poetry. H. D.'s published work registered, in Claire Buck's words, "the uncertainty of sexual division itself" ("Freud and H. D.—Bisexuality and a Feminine Discourse," 58) despite its attempt to conform to the dictates of a heterosexual discourse. That the poetry registered the split of the speaking subject *in language* is something to which Pound—or H. D.'s early critics—were not sensitive: he sought in her work confirmation of the ways in which the image *clarified* relationships rather than unsettled them; her critics, for the most part, discovered in the poetry precisely what Pound had already told them they would discover there. Pound's definitions of H. D.'s poetic efforts have not until recently been challenged. Moreover, the very forms of this poetry invited Pound to read himself into the texts, to see himself in the various personae she employed.

Rather than writing from the position of Imagism (which we have assumed until recently to have been already well defined by the time H. D. drafted "Hermes of the Ways"), H. D. is seen to practice a poetics that may be allied to the Imagist enterprise but is also significantly different from it. This first poetic effort foreshadows the methods and subject matter of her later poetry, moving well beyond Imagist concerns as they had thus far been articulated: (1) H. D. expands, as Jackson has demonstrated, the Greek materials from which she works; (2) she inverts the premises of the Greek materials to offer an explicitly feminist reading of heroic and epic subjects; (3) sexual difference is rendered through images that illustrate the effects of masculine violence on the feminine in nature; (4) the images of her poetry do not resolve tensions at work in the poetic subject, nor do they rely on an equivalence of meaning between the word and its referent; rather they reveal through a linguistic "complex" a set of mutually exclusive meanings ("baffle," "tangle") that cannot be resolved in the image. Whereas Pound argued for a "fusion" through the image—defined as "that which presents an intellectual and emotional complex in an instant of time"—or juxtaposed images that "instantaneously" rendered certain effects (as "In a Station of the Metro"), H. D. used images to deny the possibility of such a "fusion": her images simultaneously concentrate and diffuse the mysterious energies they invoke. Pound's Imagist practice—if we take "In a Station of the Metro" as exemplary—enervates and renders static.

In its insistence that style and subject, form and substance, be wedded in the image and that the image be presented not as a substitute for something else (a symbol carrying a suggestive or hidden meaning) but as the thing itself, Imagism constituted a major break with earlier poetic forms. Imagism eliminated grammatical connective tissue in poetry, forcing the narrative and thematic elements of the poem to be carried through the image. The image forged a new relationship between signifier to signified, fixing a strict relation between the word and its referents, to produce meanings formerly imbedded in phrases and sentences. Although never fully elaborated by Pound and his collaborators, the Doctrine of the Image nonetheless marked a significant moment in Modernist thought, focusing attention on the role of the individual word within the agency of language. Natan Zach has suggested that Pound's Doctrine of the Image anticipated T. S. Eliot's objective correlative, which was "an 'equation' for an emotion": "The image-equation inheres in a relation between things, and is not the verbal snapshot of a thing" ("Imagism and Vorticism," 235). Pound's effort was to make poetry concrete, to avoid the abstract and prolix, to insist that "the natural object is always the *adequate* symbol" ("A Few Don'ts by an Imagiste," quoted in Perkins, *A History of Modern Poetry,* 334).[8]

H. D.'s poetic forms "unhinge" any forged alliance between signifier and signified, opening and unsettling the image construct and realigning the relationship between subject and object, form and content. Her poems only seem to establish an "image-equation . . . in a relation between things." In striving toward the Imagist doctrine of "direct treatment of the 'thing,'" they suggest that the image itself, by its presentation *in language* displaces the very reality of the "thing" that serves as the poem's subject. It is the referential nature of this poetry—and of language itself—that is opened to question here. The external object (the grains of sand, the apples, the sun, the twisted boughs, even "dubious" Hermes) is simultaneously called forth through the poem's language and displaced by that language. The Imagist effort can only signal its own failure, precisely because language itself marks a split between word and object rather than marking their equivalence. For H. D., this linguistic split was also a psychic split (indeed, the psychic constructed itself for her—as it does for all of us—*through* language). Thus her poetic practice exposed oppositions—external and internal, physical and psychic—and marked hierarchical orders within these oppositions. Rather than joining the outer and inner worlds, form and substance, the objective and subjective, *through* the image, this poetic method registered internal oppositions and hierarchical orders *within* the image. Psychic disruption or external violence was known by its effects, registered in the image, but never resolved by the image.

In finding in H. D.'s early work a "laconic speech" that seemed to reflect passivity and a subjection of will to experience, Pound overlooked subtle (but all the more important) aspects of her poetic method. He gave credit to a definition of Imagism that emphasized a mastery of experience through submission to the experience in language. For him, this poetry wore an air of disinterestedness, of existence *in absentia,* giving the impression of a distanced objectivity. The verbal tensions of the poem were overlooked by Pound, who privileged the attenuated forms that he himself would record two months later in "In a Station of the Metro." Reviewing the edition of Imagist poetry published by Amy Lowell in 1915, O. W. Firkins reacted violently against just such a definition of the Imagist enterprise. If we consider H. D.'s personal as well as poetic place in this movement, Firkins's comments suggest the psychic struggle her poetry masked:

> The loneliness in which [the Imagists] dwell is almost polar; they are exiles who have actually accomplished the traditionally impossible feat of fleeing from themselves. . . . The solitude above described is not restricted to the observer; the object likewise is a drifting, homeless, expatriated thing. It is destitute alike of a place in a charted globe and a function in a civilized order. It has no history, no prospects, no causes, no sequels, no association, no cognates, no allies. . . .
>
> The psychology of Imagism . . . contains matter of undoubted interest. Not the least conspicuous of its traits is the supineness or passivity of the attitudes which the faithful assume in relation to the overshadowing or incumbent universe. They have the air of patients, of people under treatment; they *undergo* the things which other men observe or contemplate. (from the *Nation,* 14 October 1915; quoted in "The New Movement in Poetry," in Hughes, *Imagism and Imagists,* 60–61)

The figures Firkins uses to define Imagism might also be applied to H. D.'s personal situation. She was lonely, an exile apparently fleeing herself (indeed, Imagist poetry demanded that she flee herself, erase her presence in the poem). She was drifting, expatriated, lacking a place in a charted globe, supine and passive against the conflicts that surrounded her, conflicts in which Pound, Aldington, her parents, and Frances Gregg fought over her. She seemed to have the air of someone under treatment, of disinterested absence. Moreover, the apathetic and passive pose of Imagist poetry suggested the feminine, not only in its passivity but in its effort to mask intentions and feelings. The image itself, as Natan Zach has commented, "envisages a fusion of spontaneity, intensity and critical discipline" ("Imagism and Vorticism," 234). While the image may often register the effects of emotion, movement, even aggression and violence, these actions are not themselves present in the poetry.

From Imagism to Vorticism

Whether or not Firkins's interpretation of Imagism's enforced passivity is accurate, it was on this issue—the poetics of passivity—that Pound abandoned the movement. As David Perkins explains, Pound redefined the image to make it active and energized rather than passive and incumbent:

> For although Pound's Imagist doctrine still seemed valid, he now emphasized that the Image is not mimetic. It is better thought of as a form produced by an emotional energy, as iron filings shape themselves when magnetized. It has a meaning, but the meaning is not "ascribed" or "intended"; it is variable, so the Image may be compared not to arithmetical numbers but to the letters— x, y, z,—of algebra. The Image is "a radiant node or cluster; it is what I can and must perforce call a VORTEX, from which, and through which, and into which ideas are constantly rushing." (*A History of Modern Poetry*, 465–466)

Specifically, as Zach notes, "the Vorticist insistence on movement, energy and intensity, a universal trait of pre-war (Bergson-inspired) art, strengthened Pound's conviction that the 'permanent' or 'absolute' image-complex-juxtaposition must be active rather than static or fixed—as Gautier's, H. D.'s and Aldington's word-sculpture had often tended to be" ("Imagism and Vorticism," 236). In addition, Zach remarks that Vorticism developed a strong "anti-representational bias ('We want to leave Nature and men alone')" (237). Whereas Imagism had offered a new method of representing human emotion through images often drawn from nature, Vorticism abandoned representation. The language of Vorticist manifestos, however, found equivalents for the Vorticist enterprise *outside* language structures (in physics, in music, and in the plastic and pictorial arts); thus Vorticism did not pose questions concerning the relation of the word to its referent, never investigated the hinged relation of signifier to signified. Pound's poetic experiment did not investigate principles on which language itself operated; he never puzzled over the relation of those principles to poetic modes. As Zach comments, ". . . the *image* projected by Pound's mature, but never satisfactorily resolved, doctrine can be described as content conceived as form. It provides a medium for exploration, rather than a territory to be explored. It is, in Pound's words, a 'new focus.' The combination of such a new focus with some of the old *materia poetica* is responsible for a good deal of the striking new-old physiognomy of early Imagist verse" (237). Vorticism reversed the set of properties already at work in Imagism: the "overshadowing or incumbent universe"—defined now as a set of energies that directed the construction of the image—took precedence over "the supineness or passivity" Firkins detected in the Imagist stance.

In defining Vorticism, Pound redefined Imagism as static and *passé;* he directed his energies elsewhere. Perhaps he did not recognize the Vorticist elements of H. D.'s writing, or perhaps he realized only too surely the ways in which her poetic practice had always outdistanced his theoretical speculations and prescriptive dicta. For the next thirty years of their lives, H. D. and Pound would work separately, finding each other again during World War II when H. D. learned of his imprisonment for treasonous acts in a disciplinary training center at Pisa. The questions concerning Pound's role in her poetic development still nag, however. Had she not met Pound, would she have become a poet—if so, what kind? What directions might her poetry have taken without his help? What was original about her contributions? Janice Robinson's interpretation of the crucial years in Kensington prior to the war suggests that, rather than liberating H. D.'s intellect and talent, Pound placed her in an untenable position. Having bound her to him sexually, he also bound her to him poetically, taking her poetry as testament—on the level of both subject matter and form—of his place in H. D.'s life and work:

> From her stance, the poems had been written as she came into knowledge; they were written for *her,* for herself. The poems had to do with H. D.'s own relationship to her own experiences; they were introspective studies. They were not written for public exhibition, and they were not written for Pound. Pound even acknowledges in his letters that "it was only by persistence that I got to see [these poems] at all." When H. D. presented Pound with them, he behaved as though they were his, as though they had been written to and for him. Then, like Hermes the thief, he stole her poetry: he robbed her of the right to make a decision about the publication of her own work. He took command of it. (Robinson, *H. D.,* 36)

Although one might argue that H. D.'s definition of her poetic subject and purpose was less narrow than Robinson presents it here—that poems

331

whose subject was the poet's "relationship to her own experiences" might include among those "experiences" the role of the lover-mentor—Pound's zealous appropriation of this poetry and the lack of consideration for H. D.'s feelings and disregard for her (unexpressed) concerns about publication of the poetry are probably accurately rendered by the claim that Pound "took command of" both H. D.'s writing and her public identity. Both grateful for his attention to her work and resentful of his abrupt methods, H. D. continued throughout her life to write under Pound's implied observation, remaining even at the end of her life fearful of his criticism and in need of his praise.

A Sense of Outsidership

When Pound abandoned Imagism, H. D. felt betrayed as a woman and as a poet. What she may not have seen then, but what is clear from this later perspective, is his redefinition of a literary movement in sexual terms— the feminine was exchanged for the masculine. His desertion of the movement held particular implications for H. D., all of which were associated with the feminine, with her womanhood, and with the relation of her womanhood to her creative abilities. The moment of writing always held within it the crisis of sexual identity, registered poetically in the psychic disruptions the image contained but could not resolve. The heterosexual discourse of the Imagist poems itself constituted a crisis that forced the homosexual discourse into hiding. Had H. D. ever been able to resolve her own sexual ambivalence, the dual attractions of heterosexuality and homosexuality that constantly beckoned her, perhaps the writing would have "settled" into one mode or the other. But the choice was not to be made: or, rather, the choice oscillated so that each sexual discourse participated in and directed the other—unresolvable and inseparable. Nonetheless, Janice Robinson's conclusion that in his appropriation of her poetry Pound had bound H. D. to him *through the act of writing* is undoubtedly correct. The act that might otherwise have released her from the bondage of her own psychic distress, that might have led toward an independent self-identity—an identity not forged against and through the heterosexual, patriarchal pattern—only tightened the grip of the heterosexist culture on her. The demands of that code were imposed by the world of the fathers, whose most important representative in H. D.'s adult life was Ezra Pound: "To recall Ezra is to recall my father. . . . This is not easy" (*End to Torment*, 48–49).

It is important to acknowledge the immense complexity of H. D.'s poetic and psychic "double bind." As a woman she experienced the sense of outsidership, the sense of difference from the masculine norms that all women face. But as a writer, she labored under a double penalty: her expression had to meet the expectations of the male norm and had to "pass" as male writing—that is, not draw attention to itself as having been written by a woman. Pound simultaneously imposed his normative definitions on H. D.'s work (edited her poems, told her when she was writing well and when she was not), making an exception of her *as a woman*. He rarely made exceptions for women, as his treatment of Amy Lowell, Margaret Anderson, Gertrude Stein, and Natalie Barney confirms. Two statements in a 1928 letter of advice to Louis Zukofsky on organizing a New York poetry group articulate his concerns about woman's place in the literary avant-garde. Suggesting various people who might participate, Pound wrote: "There is also . . . ole Jane Heap if she is in N. Y.; no rudder, but certain available energy, ballyhoo." Later in the letter, however, he warned Zukofsky about the pernicious influence of women in such social and intellectual gatherings: "NOT too many women, and if possible no wives at assembly. If some insist on accompanying their mariti, make sure they are bored and dont repeat offense. Also mariti shd. ignore and remain unblandished by other females *during* presence of legal consort. Cf. Cosimo medici on government" (quoted in Ahearn, "Ezra Pound and Louis Zukofsky: Letters, 1928–1930," 151). Exceptions *might* be made for women, provided they did not appear in large numbers. For Pound, as for Gertrude Stein, wives were a particular nuisance (Stein, interestingly, welcomed women to her home, provided they did not come with their spouses: she preferred women to exercise a certain independence from the men to whom they were married).

Choosing to be a "serious" writer, then, a woman must choose to write for men; she must "pass" among male writers. Her writing must follow the law of male, heterosexual discourse. Choosing otherwise would put the woman writer at risk: her audience would be other women (she would write "coterie" literature) and her reading public would be limited to a small, less well-informed, and provincial group. She would not be published by the major publishing houses; her work would not be reviewed in important journals. To write as a heterosexual male had economic and political as well as aesthetic and psychological effects. If the woman writer was lesbian and decided to write as a lesbian (as Radclyffe Hall did, for instance), grave consequences inevitably followed from her choice, unless she found some means of making the writing palatable to a heterosexual reading public. Hall succeeded in doing this by confirming lesbianism as deviancy from the heterosexual norm, making her heroine a "he," casting Stephen Gordon as an unhappy, misunderstood invert who—had genetics been less malevolent—would have been a happy heterosexual male. To celebrate lesbianism, to see it as a psychically and artistically liberating force for the woman writer was to risk censure among the heterosexual community and to invoke—as Natalie Barney did—almost uncomprehending awe among lesbian women. A third alternative offered itself in the Gertrude Stein model: to live as a lesbian in imitation of the heterosexual norm while writing encoded lesbian works that could not be decoded by a heterosexual reading public. Stein's technique traded one form of censure for another: her work was called "silly" and "nonsensical," but it was not decried as immoral because it was lesbian.

To write as a lesbian was to make a commitment to lesbianism as an artist and as a political being. In order to make this commitment, one needed to be assured of one's sexual orientation and secure in one's poetic method. As Catharine R. Stimpson has often reminded us, to "write lesbian" demands enormous courage. It was not so much courage that H. D. lacked—for she faced with great calm tremendous psychological and physical affliction during her life—but rather the knowledge that she *was* lesbian. What Sandra M. Gilbert and Susan Gubar (*Madwoman in the Attic*) would term H. D.'s "anxiety of authorship" was inextricably bound to sexual ambivalence, and the suspicion that she was lesbian—rather than liberating her writing—may have further cramped and confounded her literary efforts, as it forced the recognition that the only culturally approved texts are those that, implicitly or explicitly, underwrite the heterosexual cultural norm. As Friedman and DuPlessis state, "H. D. forged her oeuvre in persistent and profound struggles with cultural and narrative questions concerning sexuality and the domains of gender" ("Sexualities," 24). They suggest that H. D. scripted two separate selves, a heterosexual one in her printed texts, a homosexual one in her private writings: "In print, therefore, H. D. could examine her identity as a tormented heterosexual seeking non-oppressive relationships with men, the culturally approved love objects for women. In focusing on the heterosexual script, she muted often to the point of invisibility her lesbian bonds with women. In private, however, in unpublished manuscripts 'safe' as the diary where so many women's forbidden thoughts have found a half-life of secret articulation, H. D. explored her passion for women and its relation to her artistic identity" (9). Behind this analysis lurk more troubling questions, ones that surface in H. D.'s own experience, in her recurring writer's block and her continuing efforts to discover the nature of her own sexuality. Were the demands of the heterosexual norm antithetical to her creative urges—to which her lesbian writing was the real, honest alternative—or was her creativity bound to both heterosexual and homosexual identities? And were these "two selves" perfectly balanced, as Freud suggested, or did one dominate, reconstruct, even define the other?[9]

The Divided "I"

H. D.'s situation throws into relief the conditions under which all Modernist women wrote. Her case is the most extreme, the one against which the difficulties faced by other Modernist women might be measured. We read through her writing a biography constituted in a dialectical tug and pull that forces choices: between science (represented by her father) and art (represented by her mother); between heterosexuality and homosexuality; between traditionally masculine forms of art (epic poetry) and the feminine (psychological fiction); between the public and the private; between London and Paris. This dialectic, however, is not special to H. D.'s situation, but is inherent in the sets of oppositions that structure Western thought. Her writing not only shows the operations of the dialectic to work between oppositions (life/death; male/female; violence/peace; nature/society) but demonstrates that each component of the oppositional pair is defined by the other, is inhabited by the other. Thus the heterosexual/homosexual dialectic does not structure the split between public poetry and private fictions of her *oeuvre;* rather, the dialectic inhabits *all* of H. D.'s writing. The poetry and fiction, the public and private writings, are joined rather than divided by the sexual ambivalence that marked H. D.'s creative efforts.

H. D.'s fictional text, *Hermione,* follows the tortuous pathways of a sexual ambivalence that leads to psychic breakdown. Sexual division leads to an alienation—of mind from body, of identity from psyche—registered by a split in language: the word slips away from its referential moorings. This slippage—here produced as the effects of physical and psychic illness—reveals the doomed effort of Modernism to seal the space between signifier and signified, to fuse the word and referent in a single image, to eliminate oppositions. Discussing this effort to reconcile opposites in "oneness," James McFarlane comments:

> Were this all that is characteristic of Modernism—a viper's tangle in which yes and no, life and death, man and woman, terror and bliss, crime and worship, god and devil lose their separate identity and merge—there would be little real novelty. . . . What is distinctive—and difficult—about the Modernist mode is that it seems to demand the reconciliation of two distinct ways of reconciling contradictions, ways which in themselves are also contrary. On the one hand, it recognizes the validity of a largely rational, mechanistic Hegelian synthesis, a higher unity which preserves the essence of the two conflicting elements whilst at the same time destroying them as separate entities. . . . But at the same time, the Modernist mind also seems to want to acknowledge Kierkegaard's "intuitive" repudiation of this as merely shrouding everything in a great fog in which it is impossible to recognize anything, and to approve instead his concept of "either/or" in place of the Hegelian

"both/and". "Either/or", Kierkegaard claimed, should not be considered as disjunctive conjunctions; rather, they belong so inseparably together that they ought really to be written as one word. . . . Dauntingly, then, the Modernist formula becomes "both/and and/or either/or". ("The Mind of Modernism," 87–88)

H. D.'s writing, however, did not interest itself in resolving contradictions by any of these modes. Rather, her concern focused on the relation that the oppositional elements of the contradictions held with each other, in particular the ways in which a concept like "beauty" was grounded in a seeming opposition such as "violence" ("You are clear, / O rose, cut in rock, / hard as the descent of hail," "The Garden"). The crack in the Modernist facade—apparent in the images of her early poetry—corresponded to a fault in her own psychic/sexual existence; her womanhood existed on the margins of the dominant culture and served as a constant reminder that to succeed as a writer she presumably needed to reinvent herself in the image of that dominant culture. H. D. seemed aware almost from the beginning that the literary forms defined by Pound and Aldington and later by the formalism of Modernist practice could not contain the complexity of her sexual and psychic experience. Imagism, for instance, presented itself as a doctrine of technique, posing the question of the method of poetic presentation, not the subject matter of that presentation. Imagism had nothing to say about the psychological roots of poetic expression; and precisely on this ground—on the ways in which Imagism employed the aesthetic to erase the psychological—H. D. resisted the Imagist enterprise. Her own lived experiences *as a woman* (experiences later to be recorded in *Hermione*) allowed her to see both the poetic and the emotional limits of Imagism. In seemingly repeating the Imagist forms, she subverted them.

The experiences recorded in *Hermione* occurred in 1906–7 following H. D.'s return to her parents' home after her failure at Bryn Mawr. The record of those years, however, was not produced until 1927, twenty years later, and was not published until 1981—seventy-five years after the "fact." Although experimental in ways that seem typically Modernist, this fictional work little resembles any other prose work of the Modernist period. It bears some superficial resemblance, by opposition rather than imitation, to Joyce's *A Portrait of the Artist as a Young Man*. H. D.'s portrait is of the artist as a young woman, one who discovers not the keys to literary expression but the disintegration of meaning and "sense" through psychic breakdown. For most of this work, Hermione stands outside the bounds of language, desperately trying to reenter a linguistic and familial universe she had once occupied. Hers has been a flight *from* the word rather than toward it (as is Stephen Dedalus's), and she discovers through illness a means of releasing the word from predictable contexts and referential moorings. The discovery at first appears to signal liberation and freedom from patriarchal constraints, but this freedom is later redefined as yet another form of the linguistic and psychic exile that brought on the illness. Although *Hermione* is important because it serves in some sense as autobiography, its process of writing H. D.'s attempt to come to terms with the experience of her own adolescence, it is also important as a document that unwinds the Imagist enterprise, portraying in Hermione not the fictional counterpart of a young H. D. about to leave for London where Ezra Pound will transform her into "H. D., Imagiste," but of the writer H. D. reversing the principles that bound word to image from a post-Poundian, post-Imagist perspective.

The first and most striking textual sign is Hermione's name, introduced in the first sentence of the book: "Her Gart went round in circles" (3). "Her" is a shortened version of "Hermione," the name chosen for her by her father, a name too beautiful to be used in daily conversation. But "Her" is also, of course, the third-person pronoun—capitalized when it refers to Hermione Gart's shortened name, but lowercase in the text when it functions as a pronoun. Its position as the subject of a sentence ("Her stooped to the springhouse door," 11) is awkward, signaling at the surface level of text a grammatical error. Indeed, "Her" is pulled between the forces of objective and subjective, between her place as the object of others' attentions (of George Lowndes's literary plans for her, Fayne Rabb's erotic need for her, Eugenia Gart's worry about her, etc.) and her own inability to place herself as the subject of her own speech. Language itself is in some sense the "subject" of *Hermione*— the vehicle through which identity is expressed and also the mechanism that distinguishes subject from object, self from identity. But the text also mirrors woman's relation to language in Hermione's effort to become the subject of her own discourse. She struggles to say "I," to replace the third-person pronoun by the first. Hermione Gart tries, from the first sentence of the novel, to make herself the subject of her own discourse and to find her identity in language by rehearsing the *forms* of that discourse, as if by repeating the forms she might actually convince herself that she has a place in the language: "'I am Her,' she said to herself; she repeated, 'Her, Her, Her.' Her Gart tried to hold on to something; drowning she grasped, she caught at a smooth surface, her fingers slipped, she cried in her dementia, 'I am Her, Her, Her'" (3). Struggling to keep her grasp on identity through language, Hermione recognizes a multiplicity of selves that language cannot simultaneously name: "Her" is the name she holds for herself; "Hermione" is the name she has been given. These names do not *name* the same person: "She said, 'I am Hermione Gart,' but Her Gart was not that" (3).

Like Stephen Dedalus, Hermione Gart painfully realizes that words have power over the things they name. Unlike Stephen Dedalus, she fails to acquire the means by which to control things, to say what she means and mean what she says. For the duration of the novel she is poised between two signifiers ("Hermione" and "Her"), struggling to learn the relation between the two, shuttling between them. The gap in which she exists is represented in *Hermione* by two referential sign systems: geometry ("I failed in conic sections," 12) and letters ("it had not occurred to Her to try and put the thing in writing," 13). A member of a family in which the men are scientific and the women artistic, Hermione seems unable to comprehend mathematical, literary, or musical symbols.

Her Gart tries to plot the arc that joins word to meaning, pondering the relation of the Latin word for mock orange ("Philadelphus") to Philadelphia (a nearby city), tracing the root of *agoraphobia* in "fear of the marketplace" (8), puzzling over the meaning of the carnations George sends during her illness ("What do they *mean* anyway?" 206), seeing a disjunction between the name of the state (Pennsylvania) and its root meanings: "People are in things. Things are in people and people should think before they call a place Sylvania" (198). The state does not possess for Hermione the sylvan beauty its name suggests. At Gart Grange, her home, the patronym inscribes itself on the landscape: "Gart, Gart barrier. . . . She must escape Gart and Gart Grange" (24). Hermione feels the call of another country, listens carefully to the sound of foreign words on George's tongue (*agaçant, bellissimo*), practices the sound of his name in other languages ("George or Georgio. George is not Georg. . . . Georg is too hard, he is not Georg," 33). Neither does she recognize herself in the names that should identify her; she does not "fit" into the place she presumably inhabits: "I'm not at home in Gart. I'm not at home out of Gart. I am swing-swing between worlds, people, things exist in opposite dimension" (25). Hermione tries to find a word that will capture her identity, hold it for her ("I am Her exactly," 198), a word she can repeat when she feels her identity slipping away from her: "I am the word AUM" (198). Often when she repeats the word, however, it comes out as a stutter, as a clearing of the throat, rather than as an expression of identity: "Clear throat, Em, Um, Hem. Aum. It was AUM. I am the word AUM. God was in a word" (38). But she cannot hold on to her identity through language, the meanings invested in names begin to shift, displacements apparent in the grammatical malfunctions of "Her" and "her" in the text.

Hermione pursues words, tries to track down their meanings, and is pursued by them. She is in flight from George, the master of words, whose very presence reminds her that "the hounds of spring are on winter's traces" (85). Her identification as "winter's trace" in the Swinburne poem is itself a literary "trace": she recognizes herself in "winter," as her name was chosen for her from Shakespeare's *The Winter's Tale*. And George follows this literary/linguistic trail to find her, tracking her footsteps (literally) across the winter landscape, hunting her down through literature. By means of such traces, relationships are forced upon her (the hated Minnie, her sister-in-law, becomes her "sister," the name by which she is known) and, similarly, relationships are altered: "Nevertheless to hear Minnie say 'father' was a two-edged theft. It stole from Her a presence that left her (no one else had) alone and that again stole from her a presence" (16). The tug and pull of those who would master her, confine her and direct her movements, becomes a play for words. She concludes that "there were things she would never get into words" (17). But in order to understand the world she inhabits, in order to place herself in that world, she must follow the example of George and her brother Bertrand, both of whom "get things into words." Bertrand has even mastered that other, incomprehensible, sign system, mathematics. Relationships in the novel are defined and realigned through linguistic and numerical sign systems. Bertrand, for instance, explains to Hermione the origin of "Philadelphus" and the juxtaposition of "Penn" and "sylvania" in the state name, while George teaches Hermione new and foreign words, bringing them to her from Europe. Angry at George's power over her daughter, Eugenia Gart exclaims: "George Lowndes is teaching you, actually *teaching* you words, telling you what to say" (95). Each of the women of the novel stands in different relation to words and numbers than does Hermione. Minnie, whose marriage to Bertrand is beyond Her's comprehension, nonetheless "made her feel eight, nine with a page of those fractions which all have to be resolved to something different because one of them is of a different common . . . something. Denominator" (17). Hermione is unable to discover the common denominator that would bring her into relation with Minnie, but through "the lenses of the eyes of Fayne Rabb . . . things come right in geometric contour" (147).

Fayne will teach Hermione that the sense of displacement she feels *in language* reflects the homosexual difference that puts Hermione (like Fayne) under penalty of linguistic law. But first it is necessary for Fayne to discover Hermione's sexuality, to awaken her to it. After their first meeting, however, it is Fayne who cannot retrace her steps to Hermione, cannot read the landscape that would bring her back to her friend. She is forced to search over maps of the area in order to find Her: "I am sorry you never told me your name. You asked me to come see you but you never *told* me how to get to the horrid little station you said was your horrid little Werby" (128). Ambivalent about whether she really wanted to see Fayne Rabb again, Hermione very carefully withheld the crucial information—her name—that would allow Fayne to find Gart Grange. And George, too, has failed at reading sign systems of the natural world.

Even though he knows the names of things, he does not know what things are: "George doesn't know what trees are. . . . George doesn't know what I am" (84). George himself is a script, one often misread by others. He is continually misinterpreted, for instance, by Eugenia Gart, who disapproves of him. Later, when Eugenia Gart suspects that Her's relationship with Fayne includes physical passion, George Lowndes suddenly meets her approval, and she "rereads" him: "I don't understand how people so misread George Lowndes," she tells Her over breakfast (121).

Hermione places herself under George's instruction when she begins to write poetry. He pronounces favorably on her exercises, proclaiming that *"this is writing"* (149). She thinks of her writing as "my life's beginning" and sees George as the protector and nurturer of that life: "What George holds in his hands is my life's beginning. What George flutters is my life's ending" (148). He holds the power to "end" her life by pronouncing her writing to be "bad." She has looked to George to "save" her, to "make the thing an integral, herself integrity" (63). She has invested in him the power of making her whole, of uniting the diverse and contradictory elements within her, elements that divide Her from herself—and from language. In reality, the power invested in George does not exist. George defines her writing as "choriambics of a forgotten melic" (149), a phrase she does not understand that soon becomes "melic mediocrity" in her mind (150). George fails to provide her integrity; words fail to contain or define her identity; she alternately feels suffocated and exposed; words either contain too many meanings or no meanings. She turns from George to Fayne to find "meaning." Searching for Fayne's house in a small side street "where little houses all bore little numbers," Hermione cannot find her way: "The address, as Nellie said, sustains modernity or was it mediocrity? Anyhow it's melic" (150). Fayne will fail her as well—will betray her, ironically, with George. In the meantime, Her falls ill, loses three months of her life, loses her grip on the word, slips into feverish dreams in which words and meanings collide, evading each other, forming incongruous alliances that release the sacred bond between the "sign" and "sense."

Ill, Her Gart succumbs to words. She no longer has the power to control the flight of words, so they "hit or miss" (205). She instructs her nurse to call her "Hermione" (a name, according to Nurse Dennon, "too beautiful . . . to be used in conversation"), but the nurse makes a slip and calls her "Miss—yes, yes Hermione." Immediately the linguistic anchor is loosed from its hold: "Miss. I am a miss, a miss, a miss. I am as good as a mile. Now don't you see it's funny? A miss is as good as a—" (204). Although Nurse Dennon claims she sees the joke ("Yes. Yes. I see the thing is very funny," 204), she cannot in fact "see" it. Nor does she understand later when Hermione asks to "hear" the sunrise: "That odd infallible sliding-like-crystal air on water that means day's left dawn for morning" (212). George declares Hermione to be suffering from hysteria (212), but the synesthesia of Hermione's fevered mind marks the release of her bondage from words, from the game of possession for her soul— for her identity, for her future—played out by all those who surround her. In illness, Her slips out of her prescribed context in the lives of those around her just as her language slips from its "normal" contexts.

The threat of "mis-speaking" no longer holds under the pain of illness. Words mean both more and less than they were intended, utterances come out "differently," thought is reinvented through illness: released from its contextual moorings, language escapes the patriarchal law and goes "mad." This mad language offers Hermione Gart a release—through language—from those who would try to confine her, name her, and fix her in a phrase:

> The thing she realized in that moment, that fraction of waiting, was lost. Nothing could bring the thing back, no words could make the thing solid and visible and therefore to be coped with. Solid and visible form was what she had been seeking. I will put this into visible language, Amy Dennon will say this or this. Amy Dennon will say you were harassed, disintegrated, and dis- associated by preliminary erotic longings, wakened as it were in sleep, sleep- ing in a dream as in a dream we sleep and in a dream we are awakened, perceiving the dream (in the dream) to be only a dream and in the dream saying, the dream (in a dream) was the wildest of stark foreboding. In a dream, there had been a dream and it was the very valiant avid mind of Her that had started valiantly like some young Lacadaemonian alone across track- less pathways to entrap it. (213)

Hermione Gart discovers through the mad dreams of her illness the power to make herself the subject of her language. Released, her "avid mind . . . start[s] valiantly . . . along across trackless pathways." These are the trackless pathways of language released from the law, pathways that will lead her toward her own identity, an identity she can name for herself. In this process of discovery, she finds the capacity to "fix" others in her own language: "You are not Olympian, Fayne, but Delphic" (213).

The Pathways of Writing: The Grammar of Desire

Returning to the outside world after her confinement, Hermione walks through the snow to Farrand's farm. Her footprints trace a message in the snow, tracking a form of writing to be deciphered by those who follow: "the name, the word would cut its way like a snow plough, ploughing extraneous matter to this side, sweeping it to that side" (214). The white landscape becomes a blank page on which to write her name: "Her feet were pencils tracing a path through a forest. . . . Last summer Gart lawn had been a blackboard but not quite clear. Now Gart lawn and Gart for-

341

est and the Werby meadow and the Farrand forest were swept clear. . . . Now the creator was Her's feet, narrow black crayon across the winter whiteness" (223). Striking out on her first walk alone, crossing a field unmarked by human tracks, "she trailed her feet across the space of immaculate clarity, leaving her wavering hieroglyph as upon white parchment" (223–224). The signs of her footprints on the "white parchment" form hieroglyphs as she walks: she signs herself in this blank text.

Just when it seems, however, that Hermione has formed a new relationship to the word—becoming the subject of her discourse rather than the object in someone else's discourse—she is stopped dead in her tracks. The subject splits again, breaking the hieroglyph: "The ice cracked as she made tentative slipping movement. The sound it gave out suggested something beneath hammering the undersurface. . . . She stood part of next year, part of last year, not totally of either. The crack widened, actually snapped suddenly. The ice she stood on still held, did not dip further toward the tiny upward jet of running water" (225). Poised on the cracking ice, suspended above the water which might drown her, Hermione is unable to act: "Her feet were held, frozen to the cracked ice surface. Her heart was frozen, held to her cracked, somewhat injured body" (226). This crisis, like her illness to which it is connected ("I am glad I was ill"), may have real, physical consequences, but it has been brought about in part by a crisis in language that occurred just before she reached the ice pocket: "Inevitable word-reaction followed her least thought but reaction was under everything, had really been erased like last year's violets from the winter meadow. Snow had fallen, anesthetic obliterating landmarks" (224). The "anesthetic" illness has obliterated the familiar landmarks; it has erased the "writing" of the conscious world. Nevertheless, the palimpsest of the mind traces Hermione's thought through word-reaction, bringing to its surface associations that link past fears to present words. Hermione's comment to Jimmie Farrand, "You should have put on your rubbers" (228), occasions the word-reaction "black rose." Trying to trace the association in the layers of memory, Hermione recalls Mrs. Rabb coming to the house in her rubbers (201). Hermione had laughed hysterically at the vision of the woman in the rain: "I don't know what upset me. . . . My mother used to say when I laughed like that, 'It's what your grandmother used to say when I laughed like that,' (so she must have laughed like that), *there's a black rose growing in your garden*'" (201). Although the association is finally traced back through her mother's laughter to her grandmother's comment on it, the source of the youthful laughter remains inexplicable, as does the grandmother's "reading" of the laughter: "there's a black rose growing in your garden." The grandmother's explication of the laughter reinforces—rather than resolves—the unaccountable nature of the laughter. The image of the black rose suggests discordant juxtaposition (black/rose), the sign itself inexplicable.

Hermione herself suffers from an internal division, like the division marked by the jet of running water between the ice blocks or the disjunction of images in "black rose." Her illness exposes the effects of this psychic split, revealing the second name, Her, to be a sign of the illness. Under the effects of the illness "Her" splits from "Hermione": Hermione is rational, her language operating according to the law; "Her" is the mad countersign to this language, a subversion of its law that is present *even under the law*. It is Her, then, who is "mad," not Hermione. When the illness is cured, Hermione diagnoses its effects: "Hermione will say that all that was a dream" (215). In an effort to deny the internal division of language and to control its effects, Hermione Gart initially decides to repress "Her," to "keep Her under": "I will incarcerate Her. Her won't anymore be" (216). "Her" must be made to submit to the patriarchal law. Since "Hermione" is the "given" name by which she is known to society (under whose laws language operates), the private existence as "Her" (the one who dreams, who follows the slippage and seepage of language) must be sacrificed. The crucial mistake had been to let the existence of this second, internal self (Her) become known, put out "antennae" too early:

> I felt letting Her so delicately protrude prenatal antennae from the husk of the thing called Her, frost nip the delicate fibre of the starfish edges of the thing I clung to. I, Her clung to the most tenuous of antennae. Mama, Eugenia that is, Carl Gart and Lillian were so many leaves wrapped around the unborn butterfly. Outside a force wakened, drew Her out of Her. Call the thing Fayne Rabb. I clung to some sort of branch that wavered in the wind, something between Lillian and Eugenia, a sort of precise character, George Lowndes. (216)

Hermione tries secretly, however, to save "Her," to find a moment in which Her can survive. She pictures such a moment "in an infinitesimal second, the moment that divides day from dawn, that other moment that divides dawn from morning, perhaps that moment that divides early morning from exact morning, will intercede" (216). In this moment "Her will be quite sane" (216). This chrysalis identity, the "Her out of Her" who has been born of the madness inherent in language, will not be sacrificed. Rather, the new identity—one that cannot be fixed in a single word or name or situated by the rules of grammar—will live in the difference between "Hermione" and "Her."

The "Her" who "protrude[s] prenatal antennae from the husk of the thing called Her" had been "awakened" by the "outside . . . force" of Fayne Rabb. Her is defined in love for another woman, and the internal division that "Her" marks suggests split loyalties: Hermione's obedience to the patriarchal (heterosexual) law and Her's attraction to the "sister soul" in (homosexual) love. Fayne is the "sister soul" to whom Her is drawn, the two young women posing as mirror images of each other: "Her bent forward, face bent toward Her. A face bends towards me and a curtain opens" (163). The two women act out a grammar of desire, each finding her reflection in the other. Friedman and DuPlessis have read in the women's relationship a successful rewriting of the grammatical law. Lesbian eroticism serves them as an enabling mechanism that heals (and seals) the split identity of Hermione/Her through union with Fayne: "With Pound, Hermione's nickname 'her'—always grammatically awkward as a subject—signifies her object status within conventional heterosexuality. With Fayne, however, the nickname signals a fusion, one that gives birth to two selves, subject and object indistinct" ("Sexualties," 12). Suggestive as such a reading is, especially in its supposition that woman-centered love joins the erotic and linguistic subject in H. D.'s discourse, this reading overlooks some subtle—but important—complexities of the text.

Portraits of Women

Setting aside momentarily Fayne Rabb's confession of betrayal with George, we may begin by examining the more general characterization of women in the novel, especially their relations with each other. *Hermione* pays particular attention to the ways in which the patriarchy divides women from one another, a theme contained in the refrain from the Swinburne poem: "O sister my sister O singing swallow, the world's division divideth us" (179). Like Hermione Gart, Fayne Rabb is "split" in the double identities of her own name—Fayne, the name she calls herself, and Pauline (or Paulet), her mother's names for her. These sets of names mark a division between Fayne and the mother who, after having been abandoned by her husband, dedicated her life to her daughter. The world has divided Mrs. Rabb against herself ("The face does not go with the hair, the hair does not go with the face. Fayne does not go with Mrs. Rabb, not my Fayne," 155) so that mother and daughter are divided and doubled against themselves and each other. Having dedicated her life to Fayne, Mrs. Rabb now takes that daughter's life as her own, refusing to let Fayne have friends or to make alliances: "I mean mama won't let anyone come near me" (158). Threatened by the friends that Fayne made while a student at the drawing academy, Mrs. Rabb declared her daughter ill, said "that the girls at the academy were bad for me. She made me ill. . . . Then nursed me" (158). The two women, mother and daughter, "have each other" (157), sharing one life between them. Earlier, when Mrs. Rabb was courted by men, she turned them down to devote herself to her daughter, who later tells Hermione Gart that her mother refused the offer of marriage from a gentleman farmer: "He said one day if mama wouldn't marry him, he would wait for me to grow up and he would marry *me*. Then mama struck me" (157). The reaction to such an exercise of patriarchal rights—the suggestion that if the mother cannot be appropriated, the daughter will be; the suggestion that mother and daughter are interchangeable—is an ironic commentary on the mother's appropriation of her own daughter's life and the violence that she exerts against the daughter rather than the "gentleman" farmer.

Mrs. Rabb's frustration as a patriarchal victim ends in violence against her own image. The image of the daughter hides another—the image of the mother at an earlier period—and the mother has created a double image of the daughter, calling each by separate names that identify Mrs. Rabb's dual role as mother and sister to her daughter: "The voice of Mrs. Rabb strode out fearlessly; it said, I know no wrong. I love Paulet. It said I love Paulet in glittering surface, it rammed I love Pauline at you like the surface (hard and glazed) that Paulet in the showy old-fashioned photograph. The voice dressed up Paulet like the Paulet in the picture. The voice rasped I am a mother. I am her mother. I am mother, mother, mother. The voice said rather tenderly, 'But we must not make your mother anxious'" (159). Pauline hides the diminutive "Paulet" as the mother hides the woman who wants to play sister to the daughter, who is jealous of the daughter's lover, who is both devoted to and constrained by the role of mother— able to show sympathy to Hermione Gart only by calling forth Hermione's "anxious" mother. Against the double confinement in sisterhood-motherhood, the daughter tries to establish her own identity through prophetic language: Fayne made herself out some sort of Pythian priestess who has "visions, who sees, who can prophesy. She frightened me against the upstairs curtains. In her own room, she was negated. The album negated her, the window negated her. Mrs. Rabb negated Fayne Rabb. Pauline and Paulet negated Fayne Rabb. Her negated Her and all the poems I slaved over, copied out and out and out were of no use" (160). Fayne's life consists of sets of fictions: those created by her mother; those created by Hermione to "negate" the first set. These do not belong to Fayne. The effect on Fayne and Hermione of such an insidious plot to divide woman from woman is not the refusal to play out such contradictions, but the inevitable reality of repeating them. Hermione has seen Fayne play Pygmalion on the stage ("You were so exactly right as that Pygmalion," 163). In the dialogue that follows Hermione's confession, desire is expressed according to the heterosexual code by which Pygmalion creates Galatea only to fall in love with her: "Her bent forward, face bent toward Her. A face bends toward me and a curtain opens. There is a swish and swirl as of heavy parting curtains. Almost along the floor with its strip of carpet, almost across from me I feel the fringe of some fantastic wine-coloured parting curtains. Curtains part as I look into the eyes of Fayne Rabb. 'And I—I'll make you breathe, my breathless statue.' 'Statue? You—*you* are the statue'" (163). The play of pronouns in this scene—Her, I, me—preserves Hermione's perspective: it is toward her that a face bends; she feels the swish of parting curtains; she looks into the eyes of Fayne Rabb. But the dialogue is confusingly unmarked, so that statement and response can be read by either woman. The dialogue is dissembled in the exchange precisely because each woman wants to make the other the object of desire. Both play Pygmalion, both play the male lover in search of an image of desire into which he will breathe life. Their lesbian eroticism is translated into radically heterosexual terms: the male sculptor creates the image of a beautiful woman into whom he breathes life and then falls in love with her. Fayne would make Hermione her Galatea; Hermione would make Fayne *her* Galatea. Each would assume the patriarchal prerogative: neither wants to take the woman's part as the object of desire. The division of woman against woman is represented by an internalized and inscripted patriarchal code. Neither woman can find her way out of this script, just as Mrs. Rabb cannot redefine a role for herself in her daughter's life: her role is always that of mother, but that role masks another—that of the jealous sister.

The division between Hermione and her sister-in-law, Minnie, is usually seen as the negative balance to the more positive relationship Hermione establishes briefly with Fayne. But as we know from Hermione's response to the dictum that she call Minnie "sister," their relationship is scripted by fatherhood: "Nevertheless to hear Minnie say 'father' was a two-edged theft" (16). It is not Hermione's relationship with Minnie that is at stake here, but Hermione's relationship—through language—with her father. Women's alliances are scripted by fatherhood, informed by patriarchal values, and therefore carry the seeds of their own unrest.

Indeed, the role of motherhood in this novel is no happier than that of sisterhood. Only one of the several mothers presented in *Hermione*, Mim Farrand, escapes patriarchal sentencing. Eugenia Gart is concerned that her daughter do something with her life, but the "something" must be respectable, something the "university ladies" will approve. And Eugenia Gart's concern for her daughter's respectability reflects concern for her *own* place in the societal structure: mothers are judged by the behavior of their daughters. When it is clear to Eugenia that the only alternative to Hermione's deepening relationship with Fayne Rabb is her marriage to George Lowndes, she struggles to convince Hermione of the necessity to marry George by invoking *another* mother—George's own: "But—but—*Lillian*," pleads Eugenia Gart. To which Hermione replies, "Am I to marry George because of Lillian?" (184). "Lillian" is then transformed into "people"—people who gossip. Lillian's wishes are translated into the voices of the university ladies: the same women who gossiped about George Lowndes's behavior with the young woman at the Indiana college where he taught now gossip of Hermione's relationship with Fayne Rabb. Only Hermione's marriage to George will silence the gossip. Caught between George and Fayne, caught between mothers, Hermione is once again divided against herself: "Something underneath me, that isn't me, wanted George all the same to like me. I am playing not false to George, not false to Fayne. I am playing false to Her, to Her precisely. Her became an external objectified self, a thin vibrant and intensely sincere young sort of unsexed warrior. The Hermione that sat there, thought patronizingly of that Her as from an endless distance" (187). Patriarchal values once again drive a wedge between Hermione and Her, the public Hermione observing the private Her, who is now a "sort of unsexed warrior." The daughter is now not only internally divided, but has been "unsexed" by the patriarchy. Her breakdown is imminent. Later in the evening she will fall ill with the sore throat that leads to pneumonia and the three-month confinement. Later she will decide to "keep Her under" (216).

Hermione initially holds George responsible for her dilemma, for her fever and delirium. He has followed the societal script, declaring his love, judging her beautiful, "so damned decorative" (169), then leading her to the divan onto which he throws her "with a twist and deft knee movement" (173). Driven by her fever, she finally challenges his right to make her an object of his desire: "Can't you see you've tampered with me like an ill-bred child with a delicate mechanical instrument? You have no respect for science" (191). Her complaint must be made in terms that George can understand: since he cannot comprehend human conditions, she accuses him of irresponsibility on scientific grounds, finding the image for her womanhood in a "delicate mechanical instrument." Illness becomes the means by which Hermione writes herself "out" of George's script, only to discover later that Fayne Rabb uses this opportunity to write herself "into" that script. Fayne too finds it impossible to love "differently," to rewrite the patriarchal script that Hermione tries to erase in her fevered thoughts: "A white spider rose from a black mesh; there were people who loved . . . differently. There were people with suppressions; if George had let himself love, had let herself love, if George had not kissed Fayne, if George had really kissed Fayne ran its ornate pattern, made Gothic pattern" (203). The possible union of the two women has made the mothers—all the mothers—unhappy. Mrs. Rabb visits the Gart house in "floppy rubbers" to make her complaint—"We had taken, we had seduced her daughter" (211)—a complaint that forces Hermione to "range myself with everyone, with mama more exactly for the things she said were vibrous" (211).

The sisters must be divided, and it is more than ironic—it is absolutely inevitable—that it should be George Lowndes who divides Hermione and Fayne from each other: "Fayne being me, I was her. Fayne being Her I was Fayne. Fayne being Her was HER so that Her saw Fayne; there was no use trying to hide under a midnight black hat rim for out of the black hat Her saw everything. Her was Fayne, Fayne was Her so that saying to George did you love, one I love, meant nothing. I knew George saw Her, saw George, saw Fayne. Out of nothing triangles shaped Buster Brown being hit on the head sidestepping. He saw stars triangles" (210). The double image of womanhood is divided by George, who assumes the pivotal position in the triangle. In this *ménage à trois*, George has become the object of Fayne's desire, which feeds itself on Her's inability to love him properly. A theme common to all of H. D.'s prose, the inability to love "properly" is drawn, perhaps, from the suggestion that she was unable to love Pound and Aldington "properly," to fulfill their sexual needs. Fayne tells Hermione, "'If I say I love George, it isn't this flimsy thing you call love. You loved him, if you loved him, superficially. . . . You didn't know, couldn't know what love is . . . perhaps you thought you loved him'" (218–219). Fayne's accusation translates itself into a confrontation between men over a desired object: "Well then speaking man to man, Fayne, why don't you take him?" (219). In this game, women play like men, competing with each other for the love object. Hermione loses the game—she is, as the result of Fayne's intervention, rejected by George. The woman, her own double and the very image of her soul, is made the means of her rejection and failure. The patriarchy has succeeded, once again, in turning women against women.

Only one woman in this novel (a woman never actually present herself in the fiction) offers an alternative to this script: Mim Farrand, the widow with "a new lease on life" (232), whose own grown son seems to think of her as "some sort of sister or even sweetheart." Delivered from the patriarchal script by the death of her husband, Mim Farrand now writes the script of her own life. Her example allows her son to propose to Her the means of escape from Gart Grange: he invites her to join a group of people going to Europe. Jim Farrand sees in Her Gart important signs of independence when, in the gray dusk, she turns to walk back to Gart Grange alone: "She was always like that. Her knows her own way" (233). Walking home across the grange, Hermione feels her feet "winged with the winged god's sandal," thinking that she will take her grandmother's money for the trip rather than using it for the marriage trousseau for which it was meant. But Her's plans to travel, to change her situation, are blocked with Mandy's announcement on her arrival at Gart Grange that Miss Fayne is "all alone upstairs in your little workroom" (234). Fayne's

348

presence is an ominous sign that Her's victory against the domination of others for her spirit and her future has been short-lived.

Hermione constitutes H. D.'s most experimental text, a statement of discovery in a radical dissociation of word and meaning, an exploration of the deep split carved in woman by the effects of patriarchal logic. By no means is it a text that offers hope for bonds between women in a patriarchal world. Much less does it trace an enabling relation between woman-identified sexuality and the woman writer's sensibilities. *Hermione* reveals the real physical and psychic pain resulting from the struggle to achieve identity. The text itself offers evidence of one woman's victory in overcoming the external forces that create internal division. Carefully plotting the effects of self-division through language, *Hermione* suggests that language not only structures reality but is structured by reality. Thus the text does not resolve its own linguistic indeterminacy, its final words suggesting the impossibility of resolution. Her returns home from the Farrands' "practical and at one with herself, with the world, with all outer circumstance," but new divisions are suggested in the unexpected presence of "Miss Fayne all alone upstairs in [the] little workroom." As Friedman and DuPlessis have argued, "*Her* presents its main character caught in the dilemma of choice between a man and a woman. This narrative critique of heterosexist convention, however, ends in no *choice* at all" ("Sexualities," 23).

Palimpsests

Although H. D.'s work continued the critique of "heterosexist convention," with particular attention to effects of patriarchal law on the workings of language, her writings resist resolution on any of the issues raised by the investigation. It is true, as Susan Gubar has stated, that "H. D. was conscious . . . that mythic, scientific, and linguistic symbols are controlled and defined by men" and that she was fascinated with "ambiguous signs," constructing in her own writing symbols and images "with secret meanings made accessible only to those who experience either themselves or their culture as alien" ("Echoing Spell," 197). The *difference* of H. D.'s writing rests in the discovery of the gaps and contradictions, of the doubling and division, of sign systems within the parent text of Western culture. Gubar has rightly suggested that "inheriting uncomfortable male-defined images of women and of history, H. D. responds with palimpsestic or encoded revisions of male myths" (197), but her definition of the palimpsest and the suggestion that H. D. "wrote . . . verse so that it could read two ways" (198) oversimplify H. D.'s literary contributions. Although H. D.'s texts exploit the masculine perception and female perspective, it is probably not entirely accurate to say that H. D. "discovers behind the recalcitrant and threatening signs of her times a hidden meaning that sustains her quest by furnishing stories of female strength and survival" (197).

The creation of a palimpsest that would counter predominant male myths is not produced by "encod[ing] revisions of male myths" (197). Rather, the palimpsest exposes through the layers of its compositions the feminine countersign of the male myth *already present* in the culture. An understanding of the palimpsest reveals that masculine and feminine myths, male and female "texts," are not separate from each other, but entwined and encoded *in* each other by the very fact that they are culturally produced. There is not a second text ("a hidden meaning") embedded in and enclosed by the parent figure and surviving like a nut inside the shell. The second text cannot be "lifted" from the parent text complete and whole to refute the premises of the primary text. Indeed, the notions of "primary" and "secondary," "parent text" and "subtext," "surface meanings" and "hidden meanings," do not describe the operations of the palimpsest. Female experience cannot be extracted from the male experience, cannot be separately examined "in the shards / men tread upon" (*Tribute to the Angels,* 63); it is both indivisible from male experience and different from it. Indeed, in patriarchal societies, the "difference" of female experience is only known through its "indivisibility" from male cultural inscription. It is revealed in palimpsestic cultural texts that simultaneously write and erase the history they would contain. Although certain of H. D.'s writings (*Trilogy,* for example) exploit the language of enclosure (employing images of shells, cocoons, boxes, cryptograms) that would promise to reveal the "one-truth" of female experience encoded in the male world, they do so to expose the very fallacy of secret, embedded, encoded meanings that might reveal the "one-truth" to any reader—male or female.

Defining palimpsest as "a written document . . . that has been written upon several times, often with remnants of earlier, imperfectly erased writing still visible," *The American Heritage Dictionary* comments that "remnants of this kind [were] a major source for the discovery of lost literary works of classical antiquity." The palimpsest simultaneously documents and destroys its own history, preserving earlier forms in the remnants of imperfectly erased portions of its continuous text while "writing over"—rewriting—the earlier record. That the palimpsest should have served to expose lost sources of classical art is ironic, since the various reinscriptions on its surface were meant to destroy, to cover over and cover up, those sources. Indeed, a palimpsest possesses no single, identifiable source but rather raises various—often conflicting—images that present themselves as origins of the meanings the text provides. These earlier forms are read "through" the contemporary text, coexistent with it in the present moment, but are also (perhaps) discernible as relics, images of an earlier writing. The figure of the palimpsest, of course, constitutes culture as we know it and is present in all writing, since writing repeats and erases, confirms and reverses, its own historical situation. The very complexity of the figure, its undecidability, appealed greatly to H. D. In *Helen in Egypt,* for instance, H. D. exposes a palimpsest through a writing exercise that revises both classic and contemporary notions of epic and lyric.

Helen in Egypt

Helen in Egypt opens with a *Pallinode* ("a defence, explanation or apology," 1) that displaces Helen of Troy from Homer's *Iliad* to Egypt by way of a text by Stesichorus. Horace Gregory reminds us that although post-Homeric, this second text owes its "inspiration to earlier, to half-forgotten pre-Homeric sources" ("Introduction," *Helen in Egypt,* vii). Thus the source text for H. D.'s *Helen in Egypt* is itself a palimpsest whose writing both postdates and predates the circumstances it describes. And, as Gregory suggests, the fall of Troy, for which Helen was presumably responsible, constituted the beginnings of Greek literature: "In the fall of Troy was its beginning. It possessed the imagination of the poets. Troy's end became the center of a galaxy of myths, a cycle in which the present tense is in a continual process of becoming . . . in which the past becomes the future" (viii). We are immediately aware of displacements in both time and space, movements occasioned and preserved in the narrative imagination—in writing. Helen is displaced from Troy to Egypt; past and future are inverted. H. D.'s poem exploits the double sense of displacement, which is both a dislocation and a substitution. Helen is "transposed or translated from Greece to Egypt" (1) not to refute the legend of Helen of Troy but to suggest that the Helen who walked the ramparts "was but the phantom and the shadow thrown / of a reflection" (5). A second Helen is substituted for the Helen of legend. H. D.'s poem lives within the brief moment between dawn and daybreak (255–256), between the two versions of Helen (Helen/Helena), rewriting the epic history of the Trojan conflict and the fall of Troy as a "brief lyrical movement" (vii). The effects of rewriting Helen's legend, the effects of transporting her to Egypt, become a redefinition of the epic through the lyric mode.

Among its many subjects, *Helen in Egypt* addresses itself to the operations of forgetfulness and memory. The prose headnote to book II of the *Pallinode* suggests that the oppositions of forgetfulness and memory, life and death, and shadow and reality are, in fact, operations of the same principle. If *Helen in Egypt* finds its place in transposition (from Troy to Egypt) and in a single moment of time (between dawn and daybreak), it also argues that, in order for the poem to work its effects, the double elements of its spatial and temporal situation (Troy/Egypt; dawn/daybreak) must remain in place. Each defines the other: "Lethe, as we all know, is the river of forgetfulness for the shadows, passing from life to death. But Helen, mysteriously transposed to Egypt, does not want to forget. She is both phantom and reality" (3). It is this transposition of Helen to Egypt, however, that remains the central mystery of Helen's situation. The question "How was Helen transposed to Egypt" is intimately related to the question "Why does Helen not want to forget?" She was transported along the river Lethe—that is, by the operations of forgetfulness—but the potion used to induce this state also, oddly, has produced in her "everlasting memory":

> The potion is not poison,
> it is not Lethe and forgetfulness
> but everlasting memory. (3)

The "potion" and "poison," however, are one: that which produces "everlasting memory" is also that which produces death. It is her death on the stairs of the wall at Troy that Helen cannot forget, that confuses her memory now. Her death seems to have been a dream, a moment of forgetfulness, from which she will soon (in part III, *Eidolon*) awake. But the memory of Troy and the declaration of her simultaneous existence in Egypt do not contradict each other. Each a dim memory, these exist side by side, inhabiting the "continuous present" of this text. The poem explores the possibility that Helen can be in two places at the same time, and the tension held within this contradiction provides the central drama of the poem. Helen perceives the truth but cannot explain it (5). Like the reader of the poem, Helen searches for an explanation of the truth, but every explanation is but another phantom (the "shadow . . . of a reflection") that denies the existence of a "truth."

Helen of Egypt is caught, then, in a moment of time that seems to exist only in the recollection of itself; she is caught between cultures, caught between her roles as Helena of Greece and Helen of Troy (47–48), caught between interpreters (Homer and Stesichorus). She is accused of having brought such divisions into open conflict through a war in which men fought each other "cursing Helen through eternity" (4). The war is itself a contradiction, presumably fought for the love of Helen (a war begotten of love), but a war in which men forgot "women" and "cursed Helen," brothers turning against brothers. Helen, symbol of love and beauty, is also a hieroglyph that produces diametrically opposed readings: love/hate; peace/war; life/death; beauty/ugliness. Helen is a demon, the "curse of Aphrodite," whose "charm" is also an "evil philtre" (4). Placed within these contradictory interpretations, she can only discover truth in denying it, by declaring "Helen did not walk / upon the ramparts" (5). A woman who existed as a symbol (of love) in her own time is turned into a timeless symbol (of hate) as a hieroglyphic: she is scripted into art. Denying that inscription, she claims it is a "ghost," that the "real" Helen was not in Troy, but in Egypt. Refusing to credit one version of Helen's story over the other, *Helen in Egypt* suggests that both Helens were, perhaps, "ghosts" (15).

In Egypt Helen is introduced to writing, to the "temple-symbols" of the god Amen. Although such symbols may inscribe her, they are "indecipherable Amen-script" (21). She "denies an actual intellectual knowledge of the temple-symbol" whose signs constitute the writing of men. Helen "herself is the writing" (22), but she cannot read the script of self: although she was "instructed in the writ" (22), she was "not interested . . . was not instructed" (22). Thus she is vulnerable, dependent on those who *in*scribed her to *de*scribe her. She cannot explain herself to herself; she cannot answer Achilles' persistent question, "Helena, which was the dream, which was the veil of Cytheraea?" (36). She cannot say which is the "real" Helen.

If the poem follows the development of Helen from "semblance to selfhood," as L. M. Freibert has argued, *Helen in Egypt* constitutes an exercise in reading the self. The hieroglyphic text presents Helen as the demon, Hecate, the witch whose indifference to the effects of her own actions caused the Trojan war. As such, this text instructs the reader in the problems of reading a life: how to explain a life that "changed its course" (65)? How to resolve the contradictions between Helen of the *Pallinode* and Helen of the *Eidolon?* If neither Helen is the "real" one, if both are "phantoms" of each other, how do these contradictory images of womanhood resolve themselves? Must one Helen be sacrificed to the knowledge of the other? Freibert argues that the three sections of the poem trace the evolution of Helen: "the poem becomes the epic of woman evolving from the traditional passive image into the contemporary active person" ("From Semblance to Selfhood," 166). The process demands that contradictory versions of Helen—historical, inscripted versions—not be denied but be rewritten into a later version. Although Freibert argues that the poem "stop[s] time so that the real Helen can, in that finite moment, come to grips with the passive victim-image of the past, take stock of her potential, and stabilize and strengthen her identity as the creator of her own future" (175), the poem itself is less certain of its destiny—a destiny that is never entirely severed from the past. Helen as "text" is a palimpsest, whose writing both reveals and obscures its sources. Helen both writes and reads herself (reads herself *by* writing herself) throughout the poem, and the division between reading and writing, between fiction and reality, between sleeping and waking, is crossed and recrossed by Helen in her effort to understand herself.

Indeed, it is the distinction in Helen between artist and artifact, between writer and writing, that confounds the fiction. The middle section of the poem, *Leuke* ("L'Isle blanche"), incorporates two important dream sequences: the first recalls the Helen-Paris legend; in the second Theseus recalls his adventures. In these visions, Helen is both the dreamer and the dreamed. She exists outside of time, suspended in a memory of her own making and remaking. When she awakens in the *Eidolon* section, she discovers that the earlier experiences constituted a double writing, the hieroglyphs ("the old pictures") of the Egypt experience have been written over by the "marble and silver" of "Greek thought and fantasy." Superimposed, the two sets of images contradict each other, but neither entirely effaces the other. Together, they displace the notion of a final, definitive, reading of the events. Helen cannot distinguish the dream from reality ("Is this a dream / or was a lover waiting there?" 266); she does not know what phantom she pursues ("Whom did I seek? / whom did I think waited me there?" 268); the conclusion of the story is held in abeyance ("it is undecided yet," 269); the solution to the mystery is not given ("the question . . . has no answer," 276). Helen goes over the "old problem"—"how reconcile Trojan and Greek?" (297)—without discovering an answer.

Structured according to oppositions, placed between irreconcilable forces, the poem grounds itself on the shifting tensions of oppositional forces. These tensions are produced by contradictory readings of the oppositions themselves. It is Helen/Helena—a woman inscribed as hieroglyph who is confounded by the hieroglyphics of her own inscription— who tries to read the oppositions of her own experience. Her own reading would correct a misreading: she would replace Helen of Troy with Helen of Egypt. Such a reading, however, proves impossible: her evolution in the text arrives at the knowledge that she is inhabited by both Helens ("now I know the best and the worst," 303). The poem closes with a set of contradictory statements enclosed in the *Eidolon,* an image that puts into question its reality and validity. A voice gives the Message that seems to resolve all the issues put into play by the poem:

> the simple path
> refutes at last
> the threat of the Labyrinth,
>
> the Sphinx is seen,
> the Beast is slain,
> and the Phoenix-nest

> reveals the innermost
> key or clue to the rest
> of the mystery. (303)

Should we hope, however, that the complexities of the poem might be re-solved in simplicity, that the road to understanding is a "simple path" that refutes the "threat of the Labyrinth" and leads us to the hiding place of the "key or clue . . . of the mystery," the poem closes with an image that displaces such naive expectations. The poem, like Helen, exists in "a memory forgotten." Like the writing of the palimpsest, Helen is simulta-neously recalled and forgotten. Inscripted into the text of Western cul-ture, she is the very sign of writing ("I am the writing"). She exists in relation to herself as a ghost, known by her effects.

Helen in Egypt recalls H. D.'s fictional effort at another expressly pa-limpsestic text (*Palimpsest,* 1926), whose three novellas are situated in the Roman empire, London of World War I, and Egypt and whose methods collapse and extend spatial/temporal distinctions. Written in Switzerland just before her death (Bryher gave her a copy of the text on her deathbed), *Helen in Egypt* is displaced in time and space from the Modernist enterprise. Yet it explores divisions within woman that pose the question of her "proper" place: was Helen's "place" in Troy, as we have always assumed, or did she escape her destiny in Egypt? These are questions that troubled H. D. as well, questions that posed themselves *in writing* (as they do for Helen, who tries to read the writing on the Egyp-tian walls). Where was H. D.'s "place," in literature, in life? These ques-tions form the background to a series of fictional and poetic texts that weave the materials of her lived experience with rereadings of classic materials.

Troy/Paris: Egypt/London

The tension between Troy and Egypt explored in her late poem had ex-pressed itself, years earlier, in a tension between Paris and London. Drawn to the Paris experience, H. D. nonetheless felt alien to it. She "escaped" her Modernist destiny—the seeds of which were sown in London before World War I—by avoiding the Paris axis. Instead, she skirted the city, situating herself on a route between London and Switzerland. The Paris destiny avoided by both H. D. and Bryher involved for both of them issues of sexual orientation. It was a city inhabited by Ezra Pound and Robert McAlmon, H. D.'s former lover and Bryher's former husband, men whose literary activities were at the center of a masculine Modernist enterprise. Neither woman felt particularly comfortable in the Paris of High Modernism: later, in the 1930s, they were to spend more time in the

city, finding places for themselves in the side-pockets of woman's culture
there. H. D.'s earlier decision to avoid Paris, however, was not a comfortable one. Sensing the danger in placing herself on the margins of a major
literary movement, she used her writing to examine questions of displacement and marginality, to explore the effects of writing against the grain of
the dominant literary culture. She risked the serious forms of misreading
her texts have invited: like H. D., they have been excluded from Modernism. It was only by making the commitment to outsidership, however,
that H. D. could undertake her critique of Modernism, rewriting its
structures, revising its methodologies. As Ezra Pound commented in
"The Island of Paris: A Letter" (*Dial,* September 1920), "Paris, the paradise of artists irrespective of their merit or demerit . . . invites one to anything but a critical attitude" (406). H. D. needed to preserve her "critical
attitude," to resist the lure of a paradise that might lull her into forget-
ting—as Helen was lulled in Egypt—that her place in this culture was
anomalous.

10
AT THE SIGN OF THE PRINTING PRESS:
THE ROLE OF SMALL PRESSES AND LITTLE MAGAZINES

Contact Editions: Winifred Ellerman and Robert McAlmon

Winifred Ellerman proposed marriage to Robert McAlmon during tea at the Hotel Brevoort on Valentine's Day, 1921, and they were married at New York City Hall later in the day. That morning, Margaret Anderson and Jane Heap appeared before a Special Sessions Court in New York City on obscenity charges arising from their serial publication of James Joyce's *Ulysses* in the *Little Review*. Two of the three judges, however, "found incomprehensible the offending passages from *Nausikaa* read to them" and postponed the trial for a week in order to read the episode in its entirety (Litterdale and Nicholson, *Dear Miss Weaver*, 176). One week later, the court found in favor of the Society for the Suppression of Vice, and Margaret Anderson and Jane Heap were fined $100 for publishing a work declared by the court to be obscene. By the time the court had made its decision, Bryher and McAlmon were en route to London on the White Star liner *Celtic* (owned by Bryher's father). Only later, through Harriet Weaver in London, did they learn of the court decision. The coincident events in New York in February 1921 were to produce a delicate web of interrelationships that connected Bryher and McAlmon to Anderson, Heap, Weaver, and—eventually—James Joyce. Editor of the *Egoist,* Harriet Weaver was a friend of Bryher's, and when she learned that McAlmon was interested in setting up a publishing house in Paris, she provided him an introduction to James Joyce. Weaver also agreed to publish, through the Egoist Press and with money from the Ellermans, McAlmon's collected poems, entitled *Explorations* (1921). By 1923, Anderson and Heap had established the *Little Review* in Paris; within weeks Sir John Ellerman presented McAlmon with £14,000 (about $70,000 at the time) so that he could expand his limited publishing enterprise, Contact Editions. Soon James Joyce was receiving a monthly check for $150 from McAlmon.

McAlmon was later to find it ironic that "Joyce's work and acclaim should have been fostered by high-minded ladies, rather than by men" (*Being Geniuses Together*, 82), but McAlmon would find his own career aided, often in accidental or coincidental ways, by some of those same "high-minded ladies." His first Paris friendships were with expatriate women who remained loyal to him long after the men of that community had spent his money, drunk his liquor, and discovered the embittering effects of his expatriate experience. McAlmon's marriage to Bryher established him as a major publisher in Paris, the only expatriate who could afford to publish his own work and that of his friends without undue concern for printers' fees or the financial risks in publishing experimental work. Unlike John Quinn, who had more than monetary interests vested in the alternative publishing ventures he financed, Sir John Ellerman was apparently uninterested in the ways McAlmon spent the money given him. And although McAlmon reprinted Bryher's early novel *Development* and its sequel, *Two Selves,* she in no way exerted control over Contact Editions. Indeed, her father's gift provided McAlmon a Paris life that in turn freed Bryher to live her own life in London and Switzerland.

The marriage, however, was widely misunderstood, in particular by William Carlos Williams, McAlmon's close friend and publishing partner at *Contact* magazine in New York. Williams apparently thought McAlmon married for love and did not realize that Bryher's proposal was based on the need to disguise her lesbian alliance with H. D. under cover of a heterosexual union. Although McAlmon obviously felt the need to explain to Williams his reasons for marrying, he could not bring himself to explain Bryher's situation in terms that his friend would comprehend. Thus Williams and others (including McAlmon's biographer, Sanford Smoller) assumed that McAlmon had married a selfish, frigid, spoiled woman who had used McAlmon for reasons best known to herself. As the years passed, McAlmon was less inclined to correct this view of Bryher. Writing to Williams shortly after the marriage, however, McAlmon tried to explain his situation:

> Then you'd better know this, Bill. I didn't tell you in New York because I thought it wasn't mine to tell. But Bryher doesn't mind. My recklessness, as mentioned to you in a letter before our "marriage" had little to do with just that. The marriage is legal only, unromantic, and strictly an agreement. Bryher could not travel and be away from home, unmarried. It was difficult being in Greece and other wilder places without a man. She thought I understood her mind, as I do somewhat, and faced me with the proposition. Some other things I shan't mention I knew without realizing. Well, you see I took on the proposition. There are discomforts, but I don't give a damn. Bryher's a

complexity, and needs help, and appearance doesn't matter except in a way that I can think above. You can use your imagination and perhaps know what I mean. I don't like pretense, unless it's necessary for other people than myself. Because I'm a damn fool, that's what I am, and I accept it, and am not one who created the various conditions of life, and attitudes, that are displeasing to meet. So more and more I look, accept, learn not to feel morbid about things. (*The Autobiography of William Carlos Williams*, 219)

Bryher's reasons for marrying were less to protect herself than to protect H. D., as McAlmon explained to Williams three years later when Williams traveled to Paris (Ford, *Published in Paris*, 51). Whether or not McAlmon fully understood the terms of Bryher's offer, whether or not he realized her morbid fear of heterosexual advances, whether or not he had fallen in love with her, McAlmon met the terms of their agreement. The gift that allowed McAlmon to realize his dream of becoming a publisher perhaps also ruined him (as William Carlos Williams later claimed), allowing him to publish his own work without revision and making him an easy mark for expatriate drifters and spongers. Within months after their marriage, McAlmon had begun drinking heavily; within a year, he was living in Paris.

Very English in her tastes, Bryher had never been entirely comfortable in Paris (she disliked French food, for instance, preferred water to wine, and enjoyed the little English bun shops McAlmon found depressing). But it was the dissolute life led by McAlmon and his friends in Paris that she particularly detested. For his part, McAlmon hated London. Six weeks after his marriage to Bryher, he reported already having had "a bellyful of London" (Smoller, *Adrift among Geniuses*, 53). He later explained that although he "violently disliked and was depressed by London and its morale, it would be unjust to blame on the city the involved and unusually complicated household in which I found myself" (*Being Geniuses Together*, 2). But in summer 1926, after Bryher convinced him to try London again with her, he wrote to Sylvia Beach of his unhappiness: "I'm hating London so intensely that there's no use trying to work much at the moment. . . . Mould and decay and dirt and ingrown Britishness without the one time stability and dependability of it. Paris is my town, and I think after this year I'll not take on a long stretch of London again" (Ford, *Published in Paris*, 73). Although he preferred Paris, McAlmon found it difficult to enjoy the city with Bryher. She found the clubs and bars McAlmon frequented "intolerably dull." Although she claimed sympathy with the rebellion in which the expatriates had engaged themselves, she did not approve of the forms it took (*Heart to Artemis*, 222, 213). Needing a Swiss residence to avoid English taxes, Bryher had already established a quite different French environment for herself in rural Switzerland at a pension called Riant Château at Territet (near Montreux). She lived quietly and could offer accommodations to H. D. and her daughter, Perdita. Seclusion was absolutely necessary for Bryher, although both McAlmon and H. D. often felt the pressures of being closely confined with a woman who tended to "take over" other peoples' lives. But for each of them, the Swiss residence provided a place for extended periods of rest and, most importantly, offered them a place in which they could write. If McAlmon felt himself too much under the combined powers of H. D. and Bryher when visiting in Switzerland, he had occasions for revenge in London, where he turned Bryher's home into a Left Bank bohemia. He gave boisterous drinking parties, making her feel an exile in her own home.

One of the unspoken reasons that Paris was a particularly difficult environment for H. D. and Bryher in the early 1920s was that McAlmon had become a powerful figure there. Because he had money to spend and had announced his intentions to publish expatriate writing, he immediately became the center of an artistic group that included serious artists, second-rate writers, and a multitude of hangers-on. McAlmon's unhappiness at his own failure as a writer was exacerbated by the Paris environment in which Pound, Joyce, Fitzgerald, and Hemingway were constant reminders of his own limited talents. He tried to drown his disappointments in liquor and relieve his longing for intimacy in brief affairs with women of the expatriate community. His behavior was often read as frustration at an unhappy marriage, and Bryher was assumed to be a source of his despair. Thus she avoided entering a territory in which he (aided by her money) had become powerful. H. D. was even less comfortable than Bryher in Paris: the city held painful memories of her failures with Pound and Aldington; she felt old and outdated; she feared the aggressive advances of expatriate men, felt alienated by the new images of women in "fringe and belt and straps" ("Halcyon"), and was terrified of Parisian nightlife. McAlmon may not have been sensitive to H. D.'s discomfort among his Paris friends (she preferred having tea with Adrienne Monnier at her bookshop or taking quiet walks with Sylvia Beach along the *quais* at dusk), but he was sensitive to her need to escape the enclosed and rigid existence Bryher had established for her at Territet. He chided Bryher about her treatment of H. D.: "Too bad to make a bird in a gilded cage out of a person who's such a mixture of butterfly, hummingbird, giraffe, workhorse" (Guest, *Herself Defined,* 160). But rather than liberation, McAlmon's Paris life offered these women only another form of entrapment, and during his years there they avoided Paris whenever possible.

The frantic pace McAlmon established in Paris was an effort to escape the effects of his own disappointment. Although he seemed to be "everywhere" in the city, to know everyone and be included in every social and literary enterprise, McAlmon in fact was always on the margin of the Paris intellectual scene. Personable, he attracted others, but he was not given to intimate relationships, and his perceived power in the community was due more to his *largesse* than to acknowledged intellectual or literary leadership. Unlike Eugene Jolas or Ford Madox Ford, McAlmon was apparently not taken seriously as a publisher of avant-garde and experimental works, even though the Contact Publishing Company was "the leading expatriate press of the day, a showcase for new and experimental writers" (Knoll, *McAlmon and the Lost Generation,* 141). The list of writers McAlmon published through Contact Editions is retrospectively an impressive one, but the only writer whose work was a commercial and critical success at the time was Ernest Hemingway's *Three Stories and Ten Poems* (1923), his first book-length publication. For reasons that are not entirely clear, McAlmon did not publish works by the most prominent Paris writers. Instead, he took enormous risks with unknown writers, risks that were hardly noticed by the more powerful literary figures of the Left Bank. Some of the works he published were—like Robert Coates's *The Eater of Darkness*—singularly difficult and abstruse.

More than any other Paris publisher, however, McAlmon took an interest in women's writing, publishing in his Contact Collection of Contemporary Writers work by Kay Boyle, Gertrude Stein, Mina Loy, H. D., Djuna Barnes, Bryher, Mary Butts, Dorothy Richardson, May Sinclair, and Edith Sitwell. He commented that "somebody else can draw conclusions from the fact that now an amazing number of women are to be considered as artists without asking consideration as feminine authors" (Knoll, *McAlmon and the Lost Generation,* 174). (Kay Boyle excluded this statement from her revised *Being Geniuses Together,* possibly because she considered it somehow derogatory to women or, perhaps, because she felt that history had already resolved the issue of literary "greatness" for women of the Left Bank.) Unlike some of his Paris colleagues, McAlmon had never privileged male writers over women—perhaps because his own writing was not praised by the more powerful men of the Paris community. His interest in writing by expatriate women may have been stirred by Bryher, however, since she quickly formed friendships among literary women of the community, especially with lesbian writers. Although she claimed that McAlmon had a special "gift for meeting people and bringing the most incongruous groups together" (*Heart to Artemis,* 201), it was she who introduced him to some of his closest Paris friends, including Sylvia Beach. It may have been Sylvia who gently directed him to women writers in the community, providing introductions to them. She encouraged McAlmon to use Shakespeare and Company as a postal address and served him—as she did Joyce—in the capacities of literary advisor, postal clerk, accountant, and confidante. Like Joyce,

McAlmon was easily put off by strong women, and he appreciated Sylvia's loyalty, discretion, and humility. He did not assume an easy friendship with Margaret Anderson and found Jane Heap formidable (he was especially angered by her efforts to find an American publisher for Stein's *The Making of Americans* while the book was under contract to Contact Editions); Amy Lowell, a close friend of Bryher's, he thought too full of herself. McAlmon found Gertrude Stein a "much more human, indeed, a much better specimen than Amy Lowell, although the species were of the same family—doubting and spoiled rich children, hurt to discover that they can't have the moon if they want it" (*Being Geniuses Together*, 229). McAlmon's sensitivity to the "spoiled rich children" syndrome may have been a reaction to Bryher's behavior. His treatment of her in *Being Geniuses Together* is bitter, often hateful. On first meeting her parents, he was already aware of the ways in which they had "ruined her capacity for full self-expression and enjoyment of life" (3), and he watched with horror their efforts to make Bryher's 12-year-old brother, John, totally dependent on them. He later concluded that Bryher could only "repeat her own beloved complexes, aversions, inhibitions, phobias, and manias, all of which she cherished and groomed and pampered more than either Stein or Joyce do their darling words" (61).

But McAlmon himself was considered something of a spoiled child in Paris, better known for his drinking sprees and financial excesses than for his contributions to expatriate publishing. Perhaps because his wealth allowed him indulgences not available to others, McAlmon was never taken seriously by his Paris colleagues, a situation that led to increased drinking and to greater despair during the 1920s. In particular, McAlmon disappointed Pound, and, by 1920, Pound's approval was essential to success among the most intellectual and avant-garde of expatriate writers. At their first meeting Pound was condescending to McAlmon, who had introduced himself as a friend of William Carlos Williams and H. D. McAlmon resented Pound's "instructatorial" attitude and was especially angered to learn Pound had commented later to a mutual friend: "Well, well, another young one wanting me to make a poet out of him with nothing to work on" (*Being Geniuses Together*, 165–166). Deeply offended, McAlmon retaliated with a verbal portrait of Pound as the pedantic and martyred schoolmaster; although the two men were later to become friends, Pound's initial assessment of McAlmon seems to have been self-fulfilling. A writer who consistently rejected the advice of literary advisors, McAlmon recognized in Pound the "yearning for pupils to instruct" even as he claimed that "advice does nobody any good. . . . We must learn by experience" (*Being Geniuses Together*, 167).

Little Review: Margaret Anderson and Jane Heap

Another literary editor who ultimately refused Pound's advice, while accepting for publication all the manuscripts he sent her, was Margaret Anderson. Like Pound, Anderson seems to have had a sense of "her own infallibility," according to Janet Flanner, a trait that made her "insupportable to other women of spirit"—in particular to Gertrude Stein, who believed that infallibility was her gift alone (Paula R. Feldman, "Margaret Anderson," in Rood, *American Writers in Paris,* 4 : 6 – 7). Pound's record with literary women was a poor one: between 1916 and 1923, he had broken with Amy Lowell, Harriet Monroe, Harriet Weaver, Margaret Anderson, and Jane Heap, presumably for the same reason—they all lacked literary judgment. Rather, they did not always agree with his literary judgment. Writing to Anderson from London in spring 1916, Pound thanked her for the most recent issue of the *Little Review,* adding "the magazine seems to be looking up . . . though it seems to be rather scrappy and unselective" (*Little Review,* March 1916). His comments applied to Anderson herself as well as to the magazine, as she would later admit. Like McAlmon, Anderson consistently took chances in publishing experimental work, sometimes succeeding beyond her expectations and often—especially in the early years—failing very badly. She hardly needed Pound to remind her that her judgment was often wrong. Writing to Allen Tanner in March 1970, Anderson gave the credit for *Little Review* success to Joyce and Pound: "The other day, during my house-cleaning, I stumbled upon some back numbers of the L. R. They were so bad that I asked myself how such a magazine could have become the success it turned out to be. The answer to that is easy: *it was because of 'Ulysses.'* Even at the time I knew (underneath everything) that we often printed rot; but our identification with *Joyce and Pound* finally made the critics oblivious to our shortcomings." Anderson began publishing the *Little Review* when she was 28 years old, having committed herself to producing "the most interesting magazine that has ever been launched" (*My Thirty Years' War,* 36). She succeeded in printing works that would not have found a reading audience anywhere else, and her success as a sponsor of the radically experimental—even the outrageous—would earn both Pound's praise and his disapproval.

Accepting Anderson's offer to become "foreign editor" of the *Little Review* in 1917, Pound (then 32 years old) wrote an editorial in which he used the *Little Review* as weapon against Harriet Monroe's *Poetry,* the other literary journal published in Chicago, on whose staff he continued to serve as foreign correspondent. According to Pound, *Poetry* was defined by intellectual timidity, an atmosphere in which, he declared, his "voice and vote have always been the voice and vote of a minority": "*Po-*

etry has shown unflagging courtesy to a lot of old fools and fogies whom I should have told to go to hell tout pleinement and bonnement. . . . There would have been a little of this contempt to spare for that elder generation of American magazines, founded by mediocrities with good intentions, continued by mediocrities without any intentions, and now 'flourishing' under the command and the empery of the relicts, private-secretaries and ex-typists of the second regime" (*Little Review*, May 1917). Pound's success at having turned the English feminist periodical *New Freewoman* into a literary magazine entitled the *Egoist* (whose direction would soon be taken over by H. D. and Aldington) had not been matched at Harriet Monroe's *Poetry* magazine. Unlike Harriet Weaver and Margaret Anderson, Harriet Monroe was able to resist Pound's effort to take control of her journal; perhaps because she was twenty-five years Pound's senior and because she had a clear sense of both her literary audience and the directions she wanted *Poetry* to take, she often refused his suggestions and continued to publish poetry he thought outdated and uninteresting. In an effort to publicize Imagism, Pound and John Gould Fletcher had "planned an 'open move' against the localism and feminism of Dora Marsden's *The Freewoman*" (Hoffman, Allen, and Ulrich, *Little Magazine*, 22). Their effort would be, in the main, successful, forcing a change of name (Lidderdale and Nicholson, *Dear Miss Weaver*, 75), displacing Dora Marsden, its feminist founder, and Rebecca West, its most outspoken contributor, and squeezing the "local feminist" perspective of the journal into smaller and smaller space. Writing of West's involvement with the *Egoist*, Jane Marcus traces the shift in its editorial policy following Weaver's appointment as editor: "In the first five years of its publication, male writers including Ezra Pound and Ford Madox Ford [then Hueffer], dominated the *Egoist*'s pages, and while its literary content increased, the feminist writing gradually diminished. . . . [Rebecca West] saw that Ezra Pound, whom she had engaged for the paper, was determined to turn the *Egoist* into an *avant garde* paper with no special interest in feminism. . . . And so she severed her connections with the paper" (*Young Rebecca*, 8). Marsden immediately realized that "Pound and his friends . . . seemed ready to occupy almost all of the paper" (*Dear Miss Weaver*, 114). Pound guarded his domain jealously with each change of editors, and although Harriet Weaver "did not always carry out his brisk instruction," she "never lost sight of the fact that she owed . . . Pound a great deal" (*Dear Miss Weaver*, 112).

Pound enlisted John Quinn's financial support in order to buy editorial space for himself in the *Egoist* and the *Little Review*. He first secured from Quinn the promise of £120 a year to pay for his work on the *Egoist*. Pound's idea was that the *Egoist* would lease space to him to subsidize the publication of his own work and that of his friends. In fact, the section of the journal Pound wished to control was already under the editorship of Richard Aldington. When the proposal was brought to the board of directors, Dora Marsden recognized its difficulties, including the internal tensions that would be caused by a division of editorial responsibilities. Writing to Harriet Weaver in spring 1916, Marsden commented that the issue was "a question of E. P. & his friends against R. A. & his friends. . . . He reduces *our* editorial powers to zero. . . . I would never cede any rights over the space of the paper, formally, if I were you" (*Dear Miss Weaver*, 118–119). But the proposition was also not feasible on financial grounds: Pound had requested more space than he could pay for, and the acceptance of the proposal was indefinitely postponed.

When, a year later, Pound secured a similar arrangement with the *Little Review*, Marsden realized that he had been playing one journal against the other and "was furious that he wanted an announcement in *The Egoist* of his *Little Review* appointment" (*Dear Miss Weaver*, 137). Pound saw in the *Little Review* an opportunity to create a companion journal to the *Egoist* in America, a place in which work by Joyce, Eliot, Wyndham Lewis, and Pound himself might be published, and he announced in his opening editorial that "in so far as it is possible, I should like *The Little Review* to aid and abet *The Egoist* in its work" (*Little Review*, May 1917). Pound's statement was followed by a listing of all the works he had secured for the *Egoist* (including Pound's translation of Remy de Gourmont's *Chevaux de Diomedes*, *A Portrait of the Artist as a Young Man*, and Wyndham Lewis's *Tarr*). The editorial makes clear Pound's intentions to provide the same kind of intellectual direction for the *Little Review* that he had given the *Egoist* and had, against some opposition on the part of Harriet Monroe, tried to provide for *Poetry* magazine.

The first efforts to publicize Imagism in America had been through *Poetry* magazine, which, in 1913, published the early work of Pound, Aldington, and H. D. After Pound broke with the Imagists, Aldington sent their work to the *Little Review*, which printed his own work, his version of the Imagist manifesto, and exemplary work by F. S. Flint, Amy Lowell, and H. D. One of the most important *Little Review* publications, however, was a long critical essay by Aldington on the work of Hilda Doolittle. "A Young American Poet" contrasts American intellectual attitudes with European thinking, explaining that "America has this advantage over most European countries that its inhabitants are mostly willing to accept a fresh view of things." Although, in 1915, H. D. had only been publishing poetry for two years, Aldington introduced her as a "neglected" writer, one whose unconventional ways of seeing things have put her at odds with an entrenched English literary tradition in which "the critic . . . comes to judge a work of art not with an open mind but with a whole horde of prejudices, ignorances, and eruditions which he terms 'critical standards.'" It was against just such kinds of preconceived notions of art ("A work of art . . . must be this, must be that, must be the other") that the *Little Review* established itself. Aldington's subtle analysis of H. D.'s "neglect" would have found a sympathetic audience among *Little Review* readers:

> The author, who apparently possesses a great degree of self-criticism, produces a very small bulk of work and most of it is lost in magazines; such work as attained publicity was judged, before being read, from its surroundings; the work, being original, seemed obscure and wantonly destructive of classic English models (you must remember that there are very, very few people in England who have the faintest idea of what is meant by vers libre); the use of initials rather frightened people; and the author had no friends among the professional critics. (*Little Review*, March 1915)

Aldington's critique not only suggests the ways in which H. D.'s work was open to censure by a conservative English literary establishment (to which H. D.'s residence in London made her vulnerable), but it also implies that she was not well served by those who meant to promote her work: the work that has "attained publicity" has been prejudged "from its surroundings"; her writing seems "wantonly destructive of classic English models"; her initials are forbidding; she has no friends among professional critics. H. D.'s unhappy situation results not from a chance set of circumstances, but from a resistance to anything that is seen to be simultaneously revolutionary and elite.

Behind Aldington's comments emerges the shape of Ezra Pound: it is Pound's definition of the Imagist enterprise and his notion of how best to publicize its efforts that placed a shy and highly self-critical poet in an impossible position. Aldington sets himself to correcting the situation, using two of H. D.'s poems—"Hermes of the Ways" and "Sitalkas"—to explicate the Imagist method, illustrating the paradoxical complexity of her images (a condition he defines in the oxymoron "accurate mystery") and defending the juxtaposition of classic and modern materials. Unlike Pound's propaganda, Aldington's method patiently and quietly draws out the subtleties of H. D.'s work and suggests that despite the "Hellenic terms and . . . rough unaccented metres of Attic choruses and Melic lyrics," these poems belong to a "Pennsylvanian meadow" or "the New Jersey coast." Aldington strives to make H. D.'s work familiar and approachable rather than radical and inaccessible. The woman who "hides her identity under the initials H. D." is not a coldly intellectual practitioner of unknown arts but a shy American poet whose lyric poems have not yet found an appreciative audience. Aldington's hope that the *Little Review* might provide such an audience is implied rather than stated in his argument, his tone contrasting sharply with Pound's bombastic efforts on behalf of modern poetry.

Pound's enthusiasm, however, was a match for Margaret Anderson's own confidence in her enterprise; he summarized the early progress of the journal, praising its courageous efforts to resist "journalism": "*The Little Review* is now the first effort to do comparatively what *The English Review* [edited by Ford Madox Hueffer] did during its first year and a half: that is, to maintain the rights and position of literature, I do not say in contempt of the public, but in spite of the curious system of trade and traders which has grown up with the purpose or result of interposing itself between literature and the public" (*Little Review*, March 1916). It was no doubt to Pound's advantage that the editorial policy of the *Little Review* was anchored in Margaret Anderson's personality rather than in belabored critical treatises or rigid literary manifestos. Anderson wanted a magazine constituted of "inspired conversation . . . the best conversation the world has to offer" (*My Thirty Years' War*, 35). She dedicated the magazine to "Life for Art's sake," declared it to be "written for intelligent people who can feel," and defined its philosophy as "Applied Anarchism, whose policy is a Will to Splendor of Life" (Hoffman, Allen, and Ulrich, *Little Magazine*, 245). In an editorial entitled "Our First Year" (February 1916), Anderson commented on the successes and failures of such an editorial policy:

> Last March we began the publication of *The Little Review*. Now, twelve months later, we face the humiliating—or the encouraging—spectacle of being a magazine whose function is not transparent. People are always asking me what we are really trying to do. We have not set forth a policy; we have not identified ourselves with a point of view, except in so far as we have been quite ridiculously appreciative; we have not expounded a philosophy, except in so far as we have been quite outlandishly anarchistic; we have been uncritical, indiscriminate, juvenile, exuberant, chaotic, amateurish, emotional, tiresomely enthusiastic, and a lot of other things I can't remember now—all the things that are usually said about faulty new undertakings. The encouraging thing is that they are said most strongly about promising ones.

Although Pound, for instance, might have desired an editorial policy that reflected his own assured beliefs in the purpose and practice of literature, Anderson's dramatic literary gestures provided him occasions to introduce European and American writers whose work fulfilled his own literary dictum: "make it new."

The *Little Review* evolved in three distinct periods: the "formative years" (1914–April 1917), a period defined by Anderson's own interests—including anarchism, feminism, psychoanalysis, and Imagism; the "Pound period" (April 1917–1921), during which time Pound's literary discoveries (Yeats, Eliot, Hart Crane, Ford Madox Ford, and Wyndham Lewis) were published and *Ulysses* was published serially (1918–1921); the Paris years, during which time the *Little Review* became a quarterly and interested itself in new European literary movements, including Cubism and Dadaism, and published such writers as Jean Cocteau, Tristan Tzara, and Kenneth Burke (Hoffman, Allen, and Ulrich, *Little Magazine,* 245). Although the broad outlines of the three-stage development are correct, in fact Pound's involvement with the *Little Review* extended beyond 1921 (he was listed as part of the "administration" through 1924). The length and extent of Pound's association with the magazine, however, have been widely misunderstood. In a review of the 1968 reprint of the twelve-volume *Little Review,* the *Times Literary Supplement* claimed that "in the middle of 1919 Pound had left." The mistaken assumption that Pound was no longer associated with the *Little Review* may have resulted from changes in listings on the journal's masthead: beginning in September 1918 Pound was listed as "London Editor" and Jules Romains as "French Editor."

It was Margaret Anderson's firmest belief that she knew instinctively what she wanted to print and, although admitting occasional mistakes in judgment, she refused to capitulate completely to Pound's claims that he knew better what was good for the *Little Review* than she did. At separate times, both Pound and Amy Lowell offered financial assistance to the chronically impoverished journal in an effort to exert control over the editorial policy. Lowell offered Anderson $150 a month support for the journal: "you'll remain in full control, I'll merely direct your poetry department. You can count on me never to dictate." Anderson immediately recognized Amy Lowell as someone who "would dictate, uniquely and majestically, any adventure in which she had a part" (*My Thirty Years' War,* 61). Anderson politely but firmly refused Lowell's offer. Responding to the news of Amy Lowell's offer to the journal, Pound made his opinion of Lowell explicit: "Re / Amy. I DON'T want her. But if she can be made to liquidate, to excoriate, to cash in, on a magazine, ESPECIALLY in a section over which I have no control, and for which I am not responsible, THEN would I be right glad to see her milked of her money, mashed into moonshine, at mercy of monitors. Especially as appearance in U. S. section does NOT commit me to any approval of her work" (*My Thirty Years' War,* 165). Pound himself had always desired control of a section of an existing American periodical. In spring 1917, he worked with John Quinn to achieve his goal, the accomplishment of which ushered in the "Pound Era" at the *Little Review.* Quinn agreed to provide financial support for two years, giving Pound a salary of $750 per year—$300 in payment for editorial duties and $450 for his contributions. Later he increased this contribution, securing monies from other New York patrons and often giving Margaret Anderson and Jane Heap donations from his own pocket (Stock, *Life of Ezra Pound,* 203). Pound assumed a far more visible role in the direction of the journal, a situation that continued until Jane Heap took on the major editorial responsibilities.

Anderson publicly acknowledged her debt to Pound during the years of their association (even devoting a special issue to his work in November 1918) and long after their professional relationship had ended. His contributions to the *Little Review* were often not appreciated by its readership, but Anderson and Heap defended Pound's attitudes, rhetoric, and poetic accomplishments against all complaints. In December 1918, Anderson reprinted an editorial from *Poetry* in which Harriet Monroe stated that the *Little Review* was "under the dictatorship of Ezra Pound." Responding to Monroe, Jane Heap vigorously defended Pound's contributions to the journal:

> Miss Monroe is not the first to tell us that the *Little Review* is under the dictatorship of Ezra Pound. Our idea of having a foreign editor is not to sit in our New York office and mess up, censor, or throw out work sent to us by an editor in London. We have let Ezra Pound be our foreign editor in the only way we see it. We have let him be as foreign as he likes: foreign to taste, foreign to courtesy, foreign to our standards of Art. All because we believe in the fundamental idea back of our connection with Mr. Pound: the interest and value of an intellectual communication between Europe and America. If anyone can tell us of a more untiring, efficient, better-equipped poet to take over the foreign office let us hear from him.

Jane Heap, in fact, was a constant and consistent defender of Pound against his detractors. A reader had complained that "the *Little Review* is flourishing only decadent blunderings under the magical wand of the grand dervish, Mr. Ezra Pound. The fact is that most of the writings are lacking aesthetically, poetically, and philosophically." In particular, this reader complained that in his "Homage à la Langue d'Oc" (a translation from the Provençal of Daniel Arnaut's *Canzoni,* November 1918) he "picture[d] as facts the aberrations of his fancy" in these lines:

> When the nightingale to his mate
> Sings day-long and night late.

The reader commented that "if Ezra Pound had ever with his own ears heard a nightingale, he would have to admit that the bird sings to his mate only at night during the short mating period. Whether he mistook an English sparrow for a nightingale I know not; the fact remains that the poet does not know when the nightingale sings." Pound's translation not only keeps the literal sense of the Provençal, but translates its rhythm into English as well. Responding to the complaint that Pound was a poor ornithologist, Heap wrote: "It is neither necessary nor interesting for a poet to know these facts. . . . Emotion—art emotion—creates its own realities."

Although in the early years of the journal Anderson had written impassioned editorials on the subject of feminism or anarchism, she later allowed Jane Heap to speak on behalf of the *Little Review* to the readership, feeling that Heap could better articulate the concerns of the journal. Anderson consistently refused to delineate fully her conception of the *Little Review,* even as she wrote the history of the review in the first volume of her memoirs, *My Thirty Years' War.* Janet Flanner, who read portions of the manuscript before it was published, urged Anderson to address the philosophic and aesthetic concerns of the *Little Review.* An undated letter to Anderson provides Flanner's critique of the drafted manuscript:

> This chapter is necessary, you are withholding from the public information which is thrilling and interesting unless you *go into* L. R.: go into not only the esthetic theory but the practice of why and what you did.
>
> I now urge that from time to time you cease describing in delightful detail every door, shrub, painted chair and grand piano that filled your exterior (interior) life during these periods to talk about the thing which, more than the chairs surely, was truly important to you: believe me it is now also to the public: don't take for granted they know: the L. R. is already a thing of the past, a distinctly previous generation: recall that past: the clarity and good writing you failed to put into it when you *were* it emotionally you now can.

Flanner outlined a method for the kind of analysis Anderson might provide, suggesting that Anderson first include in the memoir a list of contributors as well as representative "reactions—public and private—special numbers, etc." Flanner's final suggestions returned Anderson to her stated reasons for creating the *Little Review*—to provide "the best conversation the world has to offer" (*My Thirty Years' War,* 35):

> 3rd: Every so often a mention of its growth, its blood pressure, its general health and the pressures or pains expressed in terms of the thing itself—TALK—about it, rather than the perpetual housing problems of its editor, choice and delightful, as it is—
>
> 4th: to my mind, the LR—*why* it was, what it was, why it won or failed, why America had no writers before and has it any now?—etc., etc. all the TALK.

Reacting as an experienced journalist, Flanner conceived Anderson's memoir as a *New Yorker* "Profile." Anderson, of course, was not able to provide in *My Thirty Years' War* the kind of memoir of the journal that so interested Flanner. (Flanner published a profile honoring Anderson and the *Little Review*—"A Life on a Cloud"—in June 1974, eight months after Anderson's death.)

In August 1967, when Anderson was working on the third volume of her memoirs, Flanner tried again to satisfy her curiosity about the *Little Review.* She asked her friend Solita Solano, a former journalist, to interview Anderson, hoping that direct inquiry might force Anderson to articulate her editorial policy. Solano asked Anderson to define the basis of her critical judgment "in the 1914 period of the *L.R.*": ". . . why did you take Amy Lowell, Hecht, Pound, Anderson, etc., rather than other writers? In other words, did you have any *standards* to which you adhered? I've seen letters where you turned down manuscripts—by Hart Crane, for instance. Why did you accept some of his work and not other poems? Did you reject a good number of mss. by 'faithful' contributors, or did you tend to accept almost anything Pound, Hecht, etc. sent you?" In response, Anderson exclaimed, "*Mon Dieu,* did I have any *standards?* I had nothing *but. . . .* They are the standards of a 'touchstone'—which I considered myself to be. To me a touchstone is the kind of person who can prove that, in his case, the despised term, 'I like,' or 'I don't like,' are important, authentic, 'right' (*De gustibus non est disputandum*)." She argued in this interview that Lowell, Hecht, Pound, Anderson, Hart Crane "approached in some way" her "touchstone standards" and objected to the notion of a following of the "faithful" whose work was accepted regardless of its merit: "There was never anything 'personal' about the *LR* or my ideas for it."

In Anderson's view, however, Jane Heap was responsible for the ultimate success of the *Little Review.* It was Heap who conceived the "formula" for the *Little Review:*

> To express the emotions of life is to live.
> To express the life of emotions is to make art.

Anderson found in Heap the ideal conversationalist: "my greatest ambition for the *L.R.* was to capture her talk, her ideas. As she used to say, I pushed her into the arena and she performed to keep me quiet." It was the formulation of Jane Heap's thoughts that constituted the "standards" to which the *Little Review* adhered, standards which Anderson herself recognized intuitively but felt she could not adequately express.

The *Egoist* and the *Little Review,* both founded in the year World War I broke out, were to remain the two most important English and American literary journals of the early Modernist period. Each of these journals was importantly influenced by Pound and his patronage of the Imagist and Vorticist movements. But the *Little Review,* because it continued through the 1920s and broke away from Pound's influence at the time Margaret Anderson moved to Paris, represented to a greater degree than the *Egoist* the range of literary experiments included under the Modernist rubric. Even before Anderson went to France, the *Little Review* had been publishing the most important of the avant-garde French writers—Louis Aragon, André Breton, and Philippe Soupault—and in the January–March 1921 issue published the Dadaist manifesto. Beginning in 1922, Francis Picabia joined the editorial board. Special issues of the journal that year were dedicated to Picabia and Brancusi. In 1923, Anderson became influenced by the younger Dadaists and Surrealists, including René Crevel, Paul Eluard, Jacques Baron, Tristan Tzara, Drieu de la Rochelle, and Pierre Reverdy. But within the year she had lost interest in the journal and turned its editorial direction over to Jane Heap.

transition: Eugene and Maria Jolas

By the time the *Little Review* severed its Imagist connections and turned toward European art and literature movements, Eugene Jolas was already thinking of a journal dedicated to the effects on literary language of such movements as German Expressionism, Dadaism, and Surrealism. If the *Little Review* had resisted a consciously defined editorial policy, allowing itself (like the *Egoist*) to be directed by Pound's interests and literary discoveries, *transition* would define itself as a journal devoted to Jolas's Revolution of the Word—a revolution that would overturn the principles on which Imagism and Vorticism had been founded. Pound, who himself had been the revolutionary a decade earlier, was now seen to be the conservative (even reactionary) representative of a movement that T. S. Eliot understatedly described as "a little tired" in 1927 (Dougald McMillan, *transition,* 16). If the writing of the twenties was dominated by Americans, the writing of the 1930s was European, marked by interest in the new literary movements in Germany and France. Although *transition* would publish many of the same writers whose work appeared in the *Egoist,* the *Little Review,* and under the imprints of Contact Editions, the Hours Press, and the Black Sun Press, Jolas discovered contributors who were younger and more cosmopolitan: *transition* was a journal that was markedly European rather than American or English. Moreover, *transition* was political. As Europe moved toward the inevitability of another world war, it became clearer that literary movements such as Imagism, Vorticism, Futurism, Dadaism, and Surrealism were part of larger political schemes. In particular, Jolas's strong liberalism, his commitment to literary and political revolution, was at odds with Pound's increasingly evident Fascism. The Revolution of the Word was political as well as linguistic, challenging the more conservative principles on which early Modernism based itself and opening the way to a critique of the language of power.

By mid-decade, then, a reaction had set in against the principles on which Imagism was based, and Pound—still the most articulate spokesman of the movement—had abandoned Paris for Rapallo, claiming that Paris no longer held any interest for him. In fact, it had become clear by 1924 that Pound was being displaced as the champion of the new. Indeed, the "new" was being replaced by the avant-garde, the term itself suggesting its roots in the European. A reaction against the florid forms of nineteenth-century English Romantic poetry, Imagism had always been best served by English. Its initial flowering under the French term *Imagiste* had signified not an alliance with French poetic movements but first an indebtedness to Symbolist thought and later, as Pound gained greater confidence in his literary program, an outspokenly anti-Symbolist effort. Discussions of Imagism usually focus on defining the image itself, beginning with Pound's description of the image as "that which presents an intellectual and emotional complex in an instant of time." The relation of the image to the language that represented it is rarely discussed, perhaps because this issue was of little import to Pound and his followers, who were more interested in "hardness" and "concrete objectivity." The image was the "primary pigment" of the imagination, whereas words were a "secondary and thus an inferior mode of perception," as Dougald McMillan explains:

> As Pound put it, "the image is itself speech. The image is the word beyond the formulated language." In using the image [the Imagists] are no longer dealing in mere artifice of expression but in the primary matter of the mind. The result is that the image, as the form of direct revelation, becomes an object of veneration while the word is seen as debased. As Eliot was to say in *Four Quartets* language is "shabby equipment always deteriorating." Words lack the stillness, perfection and unity of a Chinese jar (the image of the image). (*transition*, 123)

Imagism aspired to conditions in other forms of art—in sculpture and music, for instance—to geometric, mathematical, scientific forms whose exactness and specificity were free from the laxity and sentimentality inherent in language. As Natan Zach has suggested, "even the concentration on the image may be interpreted in terms of the desire for a resistant hardness, the image being one of the least 'convertible' elements of poetry" ("Imagism and Vorticism," 238). Imagism might be seen, then, as a way of using language to escape language.

In its early stages, Imagism certainly interested itself in the representational and employed language as a means of expression. And although Pound's later Vorticist convictions resisted the representational and emphasized conflict and distortion, there were no real affinities between Pound's enterprise and Jolas's Revolution of the Word. The "Revolution of the Word Proclamation" that appeared in *transition* 16/17 (1929) attacked specific tenets of the Imagist formula. For Jolas language was *not* a medium that joined the internal and external worlds ("the writer expresses, he does not communicate"); the only reality was internal ("pure poetry is a lyrical absolute that seeks an a priori reality within ourselves alone"); for Jolas, language was the "primary pigment" of the imagination ("the literary creator has the right to disintegrate the primal matter of words imposed on him by text-books and dictionaries"). For the Imagist, the imagination was "essentially visual and non-verbal" (McMillan, *transition*, 123); for Jolas, the "primal matter" of the imagination was language. Moreover, language bore no relation to external reality ("the 'litany of words' is admitted as an independent unit"). If Imagism was reductionist, forcing expression into the fewest possible words, Jolas's Revolution was expansionist: it worshipped a "litany of words" and Jolas wanted "new words, Millions of words" (McMillan, *transition*, 173).

The revolutionary power of Jolas's Word was not that it could accurately reflect reality or even reshape reality, but that it had no relationship with the external world: it sought an "a priori reality" that existed within the individual alone. The Revolution existed within the Word. The Word itself was all-powerful; it took precedence over grammatical and syntactical rules, those guardians of convention that "regulated" the Word and forced it to "communicate." Jolas's belief in the power and presence of the Word declared itself as a kind of Word-worship, the most extreme example of the Modernist faith in the Logos. Jolas believed in " 'the reality of the *universal word*'—the realization that language was the key to the instinctive realm that was common to all men of all ages" (McMillan, *transition*, 47). If Imagism shared Freud's belief in the visual nature of the imagination and the unconscious, Jolas found in Jung's "collective unconscious" a vehicle for his own belief that the key to this unconscious was to be discovered in the Word. Jolas was interested in the Word not for its capacity to visualize reality (for him the Word did not serve as a sign-symbol, a Chinese character) but in its semantic traces: for Jolas, the Word carried meanings across cultures and through time. Thus Joyce's effort in *Finnegans Wake* to record the interior reality of the unconscious in a multilingual night language was of particular interest to Jolas. Stein's exploration of the grammatical and syntactical principles and the formal relations of words to each other was not of interest to him.

Although Jolas published younger, lesser-known, writers in the pages of *transition*, he gave both Joyce and Stein prominent positions in the journal. Stein was particularly happy to have discovered a place in which to publish on a regular basis, and Joyce was pleased that his most experimental work was to appear in regular installments. The journal served as a gathering place for an eclectic literary practice; although Jolas himself was committed to the principles articulated in the various literary manifestos produced by *transition*, he did not try to hold others to his beliefs.

Like Pound's Imagist and Vorticist manifestos, Jolas's revolutionary proclamations were propaganda, designed to stir the imagination and to invite conflict. And like Pound's statements, Jolas's were personal, "tailored to his own needs" (McMillan, *transition,* 113); few would put these ideas into practice.

In a certain sense, however, Jolas and Stein were embarked on the same project. Stein investigated linguistic operations with particular concern for the language of the "everyday." Her work displaced words from their normal contexts and stripped them of their semantic signifiers in order to stop the referential process by which words "mean." Stein deliberately sought words whose meanings depended on their place in the sentence ("a," "an," "the," "it"), avoiding words—especially nouns—rich in semantic content. Jolas sought to enrich words, to create neologisms that focused meaning *in* words, finding ways to make words mean intrinsically rather than to fix "meaning" as a function of grammatical rules or syntactical place. It is not surprising, then, that Jolas admitted Stein's attitude to be "remote from anything I felt or thought. For not only did she seem to be quite devoid of metaphysical awareness, but I also found her aesthetic approach both gratuitous and lacking in substance" (McMillan, *transition,* 173). Jolas's statements about Stein do not reveal the extent to which he may not have understood the implications of her project. (He may have mistakenly thought, as Dougald McMillan does, that Stein's writing opened itself to discussion only when one compared her techniques to those in the plastic or visual arts—*transition,* 172—in which case, Jolas might have seen her work as an eccentric form of Imagism.)

Both Jolas and Stein understood linguistic "meaning" or "sense" as something quite different from conventional notions; in understanding language as something other than a medium for understanding or communication, they separated themselves from other Modernists. Nonetheless, they were not sympathetic to each other. Jolas was intimidated by Stein's sense of her own worth, was furious at her portrayal of Paris expatriate life in *The Autobiography of Alice B. Toklas,* and—with the publication of "Testament against Gertrude Stein"—broke with her entirely. She, no doubt, thought his ideas old-fashioned, rooted in a nineteenth-century Romanticism disguised under the more fashionable terms of "Dadaism," "Surrealism," and "Expressionism." While Jolas found *Finnegans Wake* the apotheosis of his Revolution of the Word, Stein remained unimpressed, feeling that the very bankruptcy of linguistic meaning was evidenced in Joyce's need to shore up meaning through multilingual puns. For Jolas, *Finnegans Wake* demonstrated the truth of the first article of the Revolution of the Word: "The revolution in the English language is an accomplished fact." For Stein, Joyce's text signaled the defeat of Jolas's Revolution.

Like its earlier counterparts in England and America, *transition* recorded the changing interests of a literary age and chronicled the various "isms" that defined European culture in these years. If the *Little Review* tried through the efforts of European-based editors like Ezra Pound, John Rodker, and Jules Romains to bring the best European and expatriate writing to America, *transition* attempted to link the best American and English writing with continental developments in aesthetics, psychology, and linguistics. According to Dougald McMillan, Jolas "considered *transition* a 'documentary organ' dedicated to what he referred to later as 'pan-romanticism'" (*transition*, 79), but the contributions to the magazine were characterized by diversity rather than rigid adherence to an aesthetic or philosophic doctrine. Nonetheless, *transition* tried to provide an historical context for the works it published, presenting not only "the authors directly involved in its own revolutionary programme, but also . . . similar movements which had preceded it and were contemporary with it" (McMillan, *transition*, 79). The revolutionary program that Jolas promoted is of less interest on its own terms—which are simultaneously vague and arbitrary, rarely situating themselves in larger philosophic contexts—than in terms of historical interest. To read the various manifestos recorded in *transition* is to get a sense of the violent upheavals that characterized a literature in transition. Against the programs outlined by the Verticalists, Surrealists, Dadaists, and Expressionists, the continuing appearance of Joyce's "Work in Progress" represents a kind of stability in an otherwise uncertain literary universe.

Jolas's own proclamations, of course, in no way saved *transition* from publishing work that today seems of little value and, even then, probably appeared to be merely eccentric. Like Margaret Anderson and Jane Heap, Jolas made mistakes, although in retrospect both the *Little Review* and *transition* offer overwhelming evidence of a literary renaissance in the first decades of the twentieth century. Jolas profited by the experience of other literary editors, including Anderson and Heap, who had, simply by establishing themselves sooner, taken enormous publishing risks. The eclectic projects that comprised Modernism were well defined, even accepted, by the time Jolas began *transition*, and he was able to continue an established publishing tradition. The publication of manifestos, for instance, had already become a literary art form, according to Malcolm Bradbury and James McFarlane:

> The manifestos of Marinetti are, for example, superbly fascinating documents in themselves. In similar fashion, Wyndham Lewis made *Blast*, the magazine of Vorticism, with its puce cover, largely a manifesto itself. And for Tzara, Breton and others, with causes to announce like the Revolution of the Word, or the Surrealist Revolution, the manifesto *was* the art form. As for the little magazine, this was often an analogue or extension of the manifesto formula.

Virtually a new phenomenon, it frequently represented a privatization of the publishing process, functioning as the logical obverse to the solemn, serious, debating Great Review. It was largely through such magazines that the evolving works of Modernism achieved their transmission, sought out their audiences, as *Ulysses* did through the American *Little Review*. ("Movements, Magazines and Manifestos," 202–203)

Certainly the manifesto was a characterizing feature of *transition*, but it was a feature importantly absent from the *Little Review*.

Editorial Policy: *Little Review*

Although Margaret Anderson published representational works from various "isms" and reprinted manifestos written by others, she assiduously resisted lengthy editorial proclamations. She declared, for instance, that "the policy of the *Little Review* has always been: a free stage for the artists," admitting that "there are moments when I believe this to be an uninteresting policy" ("The Little Review," *TLS*). Her reticence, however, invited the accusation that "the magazine had no governing idea" and that she and Jane Heap had not the "faintest clue" why, for instance, they were publishing the Baroness Else von Freytag-Loringhoven (a writer who made her way into the pages of *transition* as well). Tracking the history of the *Little Review*, the reviewer for the *Times Literary Supplement* concludes that "Pound was the only participant in the *Little Review* who knew what he was doing and had the executive force to do it. The editorial women were heroines, but at the same time children. . . . in its later years the *Little Review* was so crazy that it was useless to American writers for any important purposes." The same commitment to providing "a free stage for the artists" allowed Pound the freedom he assumed with the *Little Review*. That Margaret Anderson eschewed slavish adherence to preconceived notions of artistic excellence and literary form may as easily be seen a stroke of genius as a moral fault: the *Little Review* did not serve to promote a program conceived by Margaret Anderson (that is, the magazine did not represent a "privatization of the publishing process"), but rather served as stimulus and inspiration for her. She did not set out to put her "stamp" on modern literature but to let it put its "stamp" on *her*—a very different enterprise from those begun by Pound, Lewis, Tzara, Breton, and Jolas.

Anderson described the *Little Review* as "inspired conversation," a figure of speech that at first seems inappropriate to a literary magazine. Yet Anderson never abandoned the metaphor, allowing a free exchange of ideas within the pages of the *Little Review* through the letters to the editor column entitled "The Reader Critic." Here the editors engaged in dialogue with the readership, discussed the literary works printed in the review, and defended their artistic choices and aesthetic principles. Through *exchange* of ideas rather than insistence on an arbitrary and determined program, the *Little Review* evolved a sense of its role in the development of modern literature. Whereas the manifesto rallied sympathizers to a cause, it also provided no occasion for discussion: the very purpose of the manifesto was to bring together like-minded people. As a mechanism for promoting a movement, the manifesto was enormously successful, but its very success as a propaganda device made it inappropriate as an instrument of intellectual exchange in little magazines. Indeed, Tzara's Dadaist manifesto concluded with a "public-be-damned" clause, and Jolas's Revolution of the Word proclamation stated: "The plain reader be damned." Although Pound similarly rejected public opinion, qualifying the *Little Review* as a magazine "making no compromise with the public taste," Anderson steadfastly invited reader response. Pound declared in *Poetry* that the artist was "*not* dependent upon his audience" (*Poetry* 5:29), but Anderson was interested in discovering an audience for the artist and encouraged *Little Review* readers to define the directions the journal might take. In the winter 1922 issue of the *Little Review*, Anderson printed a letter that she said expressed her own feelings about the journal:

> I have been trying to articulate the unusual impression that the *Little Review* gives me. I placed it against the background of other reviews. They fell away into two groups: those that have had their life and are dissolving, and those that are self-consciously becoming. The *Little Review* was clear against this parting and these opposite movements. It seemed not to move. It was (is). And then I recalled your own word, "Existences." That's it: *Little Review* is an existence. It is itself germinal. It needs no anterior functioning to explain it. It is the fulfillment of its own seed. It seems not to move, yet it does move. It is vibrant within itself, as all balanced life. As art is.

The *Little Review* was born from Margaret Anderson's need to "reach people with ideas" (*Little Review*, May 1929), not from a need to impress her own ideas on others. Her motives, then, were very different from those that engendered other literary reviews of the period. Although Anderson's commitment to feminism was perhaps not as strong as Harriet Monroe's (who wanted "great audiences" for *Poetry*) or as explicit as Dora Marsden's, or as patient as Harriet Weaver's, the shape the *Little Review* assumed under her direction contrasted sharply with the literary efforts of male Modernists. Ironically, her open editorial policy left the way clear for Ezra Pound, "the master-tactician in literary politics" ("Movements, Magazines and Manifestos," 192), to establish a literary power base for himself. In providing a forum for art, Margaret Anderson was also providing a stage across which the movements that would collectively define Modernism could parade. Whereas other journals provided programs for literary revolution, hers reflected her continued commitment to anarchism.

The tensions between Socialist feminism and the literary avant-garde are evident in the histories of the *Egoist, Poetry,* and the *Little Review.* It seems hardly credible that women as committed to social change as Dora Marsden, Rebecca West, Harriet Weaver, Harriet Monroe, and Margaret Anderson could have had their journals commandeered by Pound's efforts on behalf of literary elitism. Pound was frankly not interested in the subjects discussed in the *Freewoman,* and he found Harriet Monroe's editorial policy too democratic and Margaret Anderson's too erratic. But the pull "away from social concerns and toward aesthetic issues and innovation" ("From Harriet Monroe to *AQ*," 193) evident in the *Little Review* history began not with Pound but with Jane Heap, whose contributions to this journal have been consistently underestimated. (*The Little Magazine,* for instance, does not credit Heap's contributions until 1922, although she had played an important role in "The Reader Critic" column, signing herself "jh.") In fact, Heap's involvement with the journal had begun in 1916, when she and Anderson became lovers.

Not until recently has it been acknowledged that the editors of *Little Review* were declared lesbians, itself a courageous act of independence in America during the years of the First World War. Anderson trusted Heap's judgment implicitly, declared her to be "the most interesting thing that had happened to the *Little Review*" (*My Thirty Years' War,* 102), and stated in 1967 that if she were to begin the *Little Review* again she would be happy with Jane Heap as the only contributor: "To me the expression, the formulation, of her thoughts amounted to genius" (unpublished interview with Solita Solano). Heap's views, however, often confirmed those of Ezra Pound, whose contributions to the journal she consistently defended. For some, Heap's role in the development of the *Little Review* is particularly troublesome, since her presence seemed to undercut the avowed feminism of the journal's earlier period. Heap was a strongminded, aggressive, and articulate woman whose personal presence was often threatening to both men and women. Meeting Anderson and Heap when they arrived in Paris in the early 1920s, several men of the literary community—including Pound and McAlmon—found Heap a frightening specimen of the lesbian cross-dresser. Certainly Heap's attitudes were male-identified (just as Anderson's revealed a vain and self-absorbed "femininity") and may explain "the odd biases and male-identified character" of the *Little Review* ("From Harriet Monroe to *AQ*," 193).

In reviewing woman's place in Modernism, it becomes clear that the primary avant-garde subcultures developed as "male-only" arenas of poetic endeavor. Those called by Modernist manifestos to rally to the cause were men: if women were included it was usually by the accident of their status as someone's lover (Nancy Cunard, for instance, was briefly—and uncomfortably—allied with the Surrealists). Like the "homosexual hegemony" operative in England during these same years, the small groups of literary revolutionaries became the "intellectual elite." They shared similar educational backgrounds and experiences, were drawn together by common interests, and banded together to start revolutions. Frequently these groups took on the characteristics of fraternal organizations, constructing secret communication codes, employing symbolic modes of dress, and arranging meetings in discreet locations. Robert Short explains that "surrealism required of its participants a total commitment":

> It is a corporate experience which amounts to a complete way of life: attendance at daily meetings, drawing up collective tracts, demonstrating at reactionary theatre productions, playing all manner of games that stimulate the imagination, sharing the mysteries of the capital. The Surrealist group has assumed a wide variety of guises. It has resembled in turn a magicians' coven, a bandit gang, a sect of heretics or a revolutionary cell. It is both an underground movement subverting the *status quo* and a retreat within the confines of which life can be regulated according to desire. ("Dada and Surrealism," 305)

Short then enumerates two generations of Surrealists and their imitators, a list that includes seventeen men and no women. As Anne Chisholm comments, "no woman writer or painter emerged to join their activities or sign their manifestos" (*Nancy Cunard*, 150). Although the Surrealists proclaimed radically progressive ideas about sexual practices, they held "highly conventional, even traditional, ideas about women" (*Nancy Cunard*, 150). One of their more daring manifestos, "Hands Off Love" (McMillan, *transition*, 6), written in support of Charlie Chaplin (whose wife had sued him for divorce, accusing him of asking her to perform "unnatural acts") justified fellatio and advocated abortion, child desertion, and *ménage à trois* living. No woman was among its signers. Only two women were included among the signers of the Dadaist manifesto (reprinted in the *Little Review*), both of them wives of artists already part of the Dadaist group. The Baroness Else von Freytag-Loringhoven—who had been part of the Greenwich Village group in the early years of the century, a friend of Djuna Barnes—was presented by the *Little Review* as a kind of female Dada. (And Anderson and Heap were rebuked for their continued support of the baroness, who was considered to be not even an imitation Dadaist but a thoroughly mad woman, pathetic on both scores.) Rather than testifying to her political commitment, the exceptional woman's signature to a manifesto almost always raises questions about the woman's relationship to certain men in the group. Gertrude Stein was the only woman (among sixteen men) to sign the Verticalism manifesto (*transition* 21), and only two women—Kay Boyle and Martha Foley—signed the Revolution of the Word proclamation (*transition* 16/17). Women's involvement in such movements was characterized by financial support (Nancy Cunard donated large sums to Louis Aragon and his friends) or publicity in the pages of the little magazines they edited: Margaret Anderson first published the Surrealists in America, and later Jane Heap devoted pages of the *Little Review* to various French literary movements of the mid-1920s.

Publishing Histories: The Case of Mina Loy

Literary activity in the years following World War I was characterized by variously competing "isms," and it was important for new writers to identify themselves with these movements in order to be published. Little magazines developed around such movements, and there was often a tacit requirement that contributors be ideologically identifiable in order to be published. As women were excluded from these literary subgroups—except as they served as lovers or literary patrons—they were automatically denied access to publication opportunities. Eugene Jolas had discovered, for instance, both a patron and co-editor in his wife, Maria MacDonald Jolas, who served *transition* as typist, copy editor, and business manager and began at *transition* a long and significant career as translator of French and German texts. But the Jolases were an important exception to the trend among literary editors of the period: they published a significant number of women writers, some of them not well known at the time and barely remembered now. These included Bryher, H. D., Laura Riding, Kathleen Cannell, Emily Holmes Coleman, Solita Solano, Claire Goll, Caresse Crosby, Blanche Matthias, Genevieve Taggard, Ruth Pine Furniss, Pauline Leader, as well as Gertrude Stein, Djuna Barnes, Kay Boyle, Katherine Anne Porter, and even Berenice Abbott (who was a poet as well as a photographer). Eugene Jolas had known a good number of these women from his days as a journalist for the *Chicago Tribune*, writing his "Rambles through Literary Paris" column for the Sunday edition. These women too had come to Paris to participate in the expatriate literary experiment, supporting themselves as journalists while continuing to write in their spare time. Except for Barnes and Stein, however, these writers did not contribute highly experimental work to *transition*, nor did they follow the dictates of the various manifestos printed in its pages. Some of them did not necessarily agree with Jolas's own notions about the function of language in literary expression. Despite their allegiances, Jolas found a place for their work—and his decision to publish the work of unknown women journalists was a political one.

The Paris experiences of Florence Gilliam and Solita Solano typify the woman journalist's situation. Gilliam, a journalist and theater critic, moved to Paris after her marriage to editor Arthur Moss, for whom she had worked on his Greenwich Village magazine, *Quill.* They founded *Gargoyle,* a magazine that surveyed Paris intellectual life, in Paris in 1921. Gilliam and Moss published and provided commentary on the work of such expatriates as Hart Crane, H. D., Malcolm Cowley, and Robert Coates and reproduced contemporary paintings in the journal. The magazine lasted a year and never made money: its editors supported themselves as freelance writers. According to Karen Lane Rood, Gilliam was at one time writing for all three American newspapers in Paris: she wrote "Round the Studios" and "Latin Quarter Notes" for the *Paris Herald,* a "window-shopping" column for the *Paris Times,* and feature articles for the Sunday edition of the *Paris Tribune,* the paper for which Eugene Jolas worked as well. She also served the *Tribune* as theater critic and worked as the Paris correspondent for *Theatre Magazine* and *Theater Arts,* two New York publications. When her husband became editor of Erskine Gwynne's *Boulevardier,* Gilliam joined its staff as theater critic (Rood, *American Writers in Paris,* 4:177). Gilliam's one published book was a tribute to France (*France: A Tribute by an American Woman,* 1945). Solita Solano was also a theater critic, having been named drama editor and critic for the *Boston Herald-Traveler* during World War I. Later, she served in the same capacity for the *New York Tribune,* but left that position in 1921 to travel in Europe and the Near East with Janet Flanner. She settled permanently in Paris in 1922, publishing three novels of psychological realism in her first years there. Jolas published an excerpt of her third novel, *This Way Up,* in *transition* 6, commenting that the work "had the honor of not pleasing" American critics, who disliked her "sophisticated" use of classical allusions and her "execrable" and "abhorrent" style. Solano was not a prolific writer, and her work did not fit easily into any of the categories of literary experimentalism that dominated the period. Although both Gilliam and Solano were important in their contemporary settings, their writings have been lost: Gilliam's professional journalism disappeared in the pages of newspapers and periodicals, Solano's in marginal literary publications.

It is not surprising, perhaps, that chroniclers of the period have assumed that, with the obvious exception of Gertrude Stein, there were no women writers of merit among the expatriates. When Malcolm Cowley chose to study American writers born between 1894 and 1900, he concentrated on eight men, noting: "There are no women among the eight, a fact being that the admired writers of the generation were men in the great majority. The time of famous women storytellers and poets was, in this country, either a little earlier or twenty years later. I feel a lasting gratitude for the work of Caroline Gordon, Louise Bogan, Dawn Powell, and one or two other women of the generation, but they have been less widely read than male contemporaries of no greater talent" (*A Second Flowering,* 240). The obvious question that Cowley might have asked—*why* have women been "less widely read than male contemporaries of no greater talent"?—goes unanswered, apparently beyond the scope of his study.

To discover some answers to this question, we might look at the writing and publishing career of Mina Loy. On an extended visit to Florence in 1913 with her husband and small children, Loy discovered in "Marinetti's reading of Futurist poems" the intellectual stimulation she had been seeking (Kouidis, *Mina Loy,* 7). She came to know Carlo Carrà, Marinetti, and Giovanni Papini (probably having affairs with the latter two) before World War I, and, although she was never converted to Futurism, the movement influenced her deeply and her work of this period structures itself in dialogue with Futurist beliefs. Writing to Mabel Dodge in February 1914, she admitted to being "in the throes of conversion to Futurism—but I shall never convince myself—There is no hope in any system that 'combat le mal avec le mal' . . . and that is really Marinetti's philosophy" (*Mina Loy,* 7–8). In January 1914, Loy's "Aphorisms on Futurism," her first Modernist writing, appeared in Alfred Stieglitz's journal *Camera Work.* Her interest in Futurism, oddly enough, joined an interest in feminism; later that same year, Loy composed her unpublished "Feminist Manifesto." This manifesto "owes several debts to Futurism," according to Virginia Kouidis, who suggests that "the aggressive tone and shocking defiance of convention" in Loy's declaration "echo Futurist manifestoes":

> Nevertheless, her rejection of sexual equality challenges the Futurists' program. They scorned women as the embodiment of the *amore* to which the Italian male sentimentally devoted himself at the expense of the technological world that the Futurists prized as Italy's hope for cultural and political rejuvenation. Not totally unsympathetic to women, Marinetti stated that with proper education they could become equal to men, and he supported the suffragists because, he said, "the more rights and powers they win for woman, the more will she be deprived of *Amore,* and by so much will she cease to be a magnet for sentimental passion or lust." (*Mina Loy,* 29–30)

Loy took exception to Marinetti's claims for women's equality, arguing in her manifesto that women should "leave off looking to men to find out what you are *not*—seek within yourselves to find out what you *are.*"

The preamble to the Futurist Manifesto (published in *Le Figaro,* 20 February 1909) described the process of its composition, employing in its langauge traditional images of woman—as "ideal Mistress" and "cruel Queen"—as well as degrading and disgusting notions of motherhood. In their flight from the Unknown, Marinetti and his friends race through the night, Marinetti's car capsizing in a ditch. Proclaiming against his fate, he cries: "Oh! Maternal ditch, almost full of muddy water! Fair factory drain! I gulped down your nourishing sludge; and I remembered the blessed black breast of my Sudanese nurse." Fleeing the Unknown, the adventurer falls back into the womb, a "fair factory drain" whose amniotic fluid is "nourishing sludge." Marinetti's writing also exploited images of the tight circle that represented woman's enclosure in traditional roles in contrast to "the straight line and terminal, Futurist symbols of masculine purpose and action" (*Mina Loy,* 45).

In reacting against traditional (and typically Italian) views of women as dependent creatures, Futurist thought preserved the inherent distinctions between the intellectual male and the intuitive female against which its program waged war. In "Against *amore* and Parliamentarianism," an essay from a collection entitled *War, the World's Only Hygiene,* Marinetti wrote: "It is plain that if modern woman dreams of winning her political rights, it is because without knowing it she is intimately sure of being, as a mother, as a wife, and as a lover, a closed circle, purely animal and wholly without usefulness" (Flint, *Marinetti,* 75). It was precisely such categories that structured Mina Loy's feminist thought, her writing in this period simultaneously resisting these categories and dependent upon them. A woman whose personal and intellectual development was directed by men (especially by her husband, Stephen Haweis, the British painter), Loy's early writing established a dialogue with these mentors. Energizing the intellectual, defining it as an aggressively masculine striving toward mastery and superiority, Futurist thought awakened Loy's intellectual needs, demands that she was unable to separate from her sexual desires. Pulled by the force of the Futurist movement and energized by it, Loy nonetheless feared its masculinizing effects, found herself once again caught in conflicting patriarchal structures: to be feminine was to be silent, passive, desirous; to be masculine was to speak, to act, to master (the feminine).

Mina Loy was introduced to an American reading audience through "Aphorisms on Futurism." According to Carolyn Burke, this work displays a dominant "masculine character" through which the *he* of an aggressive Futurist intellect is clearly distinguished from the "weak or subservient" *you* connected with a "reactionary public" ("Becoming Mina Loy," 142). But "Aphorisms on Futurism" also represents Loy's earliest assault on the restrictive images of womanhood, as Virginia Kouidis has explained. In this work Loy "ignores Futurist devotion to technology except as speed and energy are useful images of a positive, aggressive confrontation of life" (*Mina Loy,* 37). The aphorisms exhort the reader to abandon regressive and restrictive attitudes and to look toward the future ("THE Future is limitless"); the ego expands to dominate this broad horizon ("MAY your egotism be so gigantic that you comprise mankind in your self-sympathy"). As prescriptions for woman's liberation, the aphorisms suggest a compelling need in Loy's own circumstances to cut herself free of conventional attitudes and constraining social circumstances in order to discover herself as woman and poet. Carolyn Burke has commented that Loy "came gradually to her distinctive voice in a dialogue with Futurism," a process that helped her "reinvent a first-person singular" through which she could speak her own experience in the world ("Becoming Mina Loy," 142).

Loy's feminist/Futurist attitudes were tied in complex ways to her sexuality. Heterosexual, Loy's notions of sexual behavior were structured by the late-Victorian English thinking of her childhood: women were a valuable economic commodity on the marriage market only if they retained their virginity; men could act on their desires, women could not; propriety prevented women from achieving selfhood; women are often the victims of bodily processes (pregnancy, for instance). During the period she was influenced by Futurist thought she was also corresponding with Mabel Dodge and Carl Van Vechten on the subjects of feminism, female sexuality, and politics—subjects discussed at greater length in her "Feminist Manifesto," where she calls for the "*unconditional* surgical *destruction of virginity* throughout the female population at puberty." This enforced alteration of woman's relation to her body (a "daring" proposal, as Loy admitted to Mabel Dodge) would allow woman the possibility of emotional independence. Although Loy's manifesto separates its concerns from the economic and political discussions of the suffrage movement and, according to Virginia Kouidis, "rejects the notion that women are equal to men or that they should desire equality" (*Mina Loy,* 28), the economic system that places a "price" on woman's virginity also extracts from woman the high price of her selfhood as it is defined by emotional and sexual identity. Loy's radical proposition would, in Kouidis's words, discard "the fictive value of virginity" (*Mina Loy,* 29), put a stop to the economics of the marriage market, and divide motherhood from marriage. Virginia Woolf too saw the relation between the economic value of virginity and woman's oppression. Susan Squier reads in *The Pargiters* Woolf's suggestion that women were denied the vote in protection of their chastity: ". . . female chastity was essential because women did not have the vote, and hence could not change the law which disabled them from earning enough money to support the children which might result from sexual freedom. . . . Women were denied the vote, and hence denied the opportunity for education and a profession, because their chastity must be protected" ("Politics of City Space in 'The Years,'" 223–224). The effects of this argument are, of course, circular: woman is kept continually within that enclosed space that Marinetti termed the "purely animal and wholly without usefulness" (*Marinetti,* 75).

Loy's association with Futurism provided an occasion to mount an "assault against the restrictions upon the self" (*Mina Loy*, 37) and to imagine a female self whose potential was not constrained by restrictive economic and social conventions. Recording the loss of creative energies produced by arbitrary moral and social codes, Loy's poetry also urged the artist to independent thinking and linguistic experiment. Distinctly feminist as well as Modernist, Loy's writing suffered the same fate as did that of other Paris women (especially Emily Holmes Coleman, Kathleen Cannell, Antonia White, Solita Solano, Laura Riding, and the early work of Djuna Barnes): printed in little magazines or appearing under the imprint of small publishing houses (like McAlmon's Contact Editions, Nancy Cunard's Hours Press, or Harry and Caresse Crosby's Black Sun Press), the work was lost to later reading audiences. Reviewing the erratic publication history of Mina Loy's work, Samuel French Morse discovered only one American review of *Lunar Baedecker* (published in Paris by McAlmon in 1923), a review appearing in the *Dial* in 1926 in which Yvor Winters suggested that Loy and William Carlos Williams (one of her most enthusiastic readers) "have the most, perhaps, to offer the younger American writers" ("Rediscovery of Mina Loy," 16). However, it was Williams who influenced a younger generation of writers, not Loy.

Published in the *Little Review, Others, Dial, Pagany, Contact, Rogue, Between Worlds, Blind Man, Camera Work,* and *Transatlantic Review,* and anthologized by Alfred Kreymborg in *Others: An Anthology of New Verse* and later in *Lyric America* and *Our Singing Strength,* Loy's work was nonetheless unknown to later readers. Indeed, she was lost before she had ever been discovered, perhaps accounting for the absence of published work by Loy between 1931 and 1944. Kenneth Rexroth's tribute to Loy in *Circle* (1944) may well have encouraged the publication of work in *Accent* and *Partisan Review,* but when Jonathan Williams printed *Lunar Baedeker & Time-Tables* in 1958, the book met silence "even among the avant garde who might have been expected to profess excitement at this event" ("Rediscovery," 13). The lack of response seemed particularly discouraging, since the book included introductions to Loy's writing by William Carlos Williams, Kenneth Rexroth, and Denise Levertov as well as commentaries by Henry Miller, Edward Dahlberg, and Louis Zukofsky (among others) on the back cover. In praising the republishing of Loy's poetry, Edward Dahlberg called for the reevaluation of other women writers (such as H. D. and Mary Butts) of the Paris period.

Morse suggests that the highly experimental nature of Loy's work accounted for her disappearance from print during the 1930s. Remarking on the rediscovery of Loy in the forties, he concludes: "What is most interesting about all this is that both the older generation who are the official spokesmen and preservers of the avant garde and the avant garde itself turn time backwards in its flight to find a voice that was not only ahead of its own time but one which is still out in front. And it suggests that the newness of the new is not necessarily quite so original as it appears to be" ("Rediscovery," 14). What was new in Loy's work, however, was not merely its technical and structural experiment, but the treatment of a subject matter based in female experience. As Virginia Kouidis has commented, "few, if any, of the other female poets of the era speak so honestly about the quotidian life of woman" (*Mina Loy,* 47). Loy may have discovered the same destructive truth in woman's experience that Susan Squier suggests lurked behind Virginia Woolf's conception of *The Years:* "that male oppression causes women to cover up, whitewash, or lie about the truth of the female experience in order to avoid alienating their male audience" ("Politics of City Space," 218). Like Woolf's experience with *The Years,* the combination of a feminist subject matter and technical experimentation may have proved fatal to Loy's efforts to find a receptive reading audience. Alfred Kreymborg, perhaps her most enthusiastic supporter, admitted the particular difficulties posed by her writing: "Detractors shuddered at Mina Loy's subject-matter and derided her elimination of punctuation marks and the audacious spacing of her lines" (*Troubadour: An Autobiography,* 235). Loy's technical experiments were recognizable as a defining characteristic of Modernism, and later adopted by e. e. cummings, who was given credit for the similar use of spacing and broken lines. The subject matter of her writing, however, continued to locate itself in the female body, her poetry offering a record of brutal sexual honesty. Mina Loy's struggle, as Carolyn Burke has noted, was "to create an authentically modern woman's voice, one that speaks from the body to articulate the urgent needs of the spirit" ("Becoming Mina Loy," 149). Loy's publication record may suggest that the avant-garde effort to overturn the bourgeois and conventional may not have included an overturning of conventional male attitudes to female sexuality or have been comfortable with a woman poet who so persistently held up the contradictions of patriarchal sexual practices to inspection.

Mina Loy was, of course, a painter as well as a poet. Like other women of the Paris community who explored more than one artistic world—women who were publishers as well as poets; journalists who were critics as well as novelists—Loy's versatility made it difficult for commentators to "classify" her, a suggestion perhaps that such diversification signaled indecision, an inability to persevere in a single endeavor, or a lack of genuine talent. Exemplary to such a consideration are the women who edited little magazines or set up small presses—they were, with one or two notable exceptions, writers themselves. In general, the writings of Nancy Cunard, Caresse Crosby, Ethel Moorhead, Maria Jolas, Florence Gilliam, Margaret Anderson, Jane Heap, Sylvia Beach, and Adrienne

Monnier have not received serious attention, and although the editing and publication efforts of these women have been lauded by W. G. Rogers, Hugh Ford, and Morrill Cody (among others), the feminist implications of such efforts have not been examined. Too often women's involvement in publication has been seen as a function of their roles as wives or lovers of men who were editors or publishers (as has been the case with Gilliam, Moorhead, Crosby, and Jolas) or, in the case of Cunard, as part of a pattern of unconventional behavior. These women's efforts have been, if not trivialized, at least classified as less important than similar efforts by men (including editorial roles played by Ford Madox Ford, Pound, and Eliot, and the publishing roles played by Robert McAlmon, Edward Titus, William Bird, and Harry Crosby, for instance). If it is true, as Blanche Wiesen Cook has claimed, that the women artists, writers, and poets of this period have been "defined as eccentrics and salonists who served history by discovering and nurturing great male talents" and that an "undeniable" female talent among them (a Gertrude Stein, for instance) has been classified as "genius manqué" ("Women and Politics," 147–148), then the fate of women editors and publishers has been even more deplorable.

The political implications of women's involvement in publication have not often been acknowledged, even by the women involved. The commitments made by these women to professional editing and publishing, which involved considerable financial risk and hard physical labor, offer an alternative impression to the continuing legend that Paris expatriates spent their days in cafes and their nights in Montparnasse bars. Although none of these women edited feminist journals or set up alternative women's presses, each participated in a radically political act, engaging herself in the publication of literary work that could not have been printed through commercial presses. The tremendous successes and failures of women's alternative publishing are well known, of course: Sylvia Beach and Adrienne Monnier's efforts on behalf of Joyce's *Ulysses*; Harriet Weaver's serial publication of *A Portrait of the Artist as a Young Man,* and her conversion of the *Egoist* magazine into the Egoist Press in order to publish *Ulysses* in England; the suit against the *Little Review* that brought Margaret Anderson and Jane Heap into court in New York City. But the less sensational stories remain untold, and the more general contributions of alternative publishing—that offered artists freedom of expression, relieved them of demanding negotiations with commercial presses, and often assured them some small profit on otherwise unpublishable material—are less generally recognized. The existence of such little magazines and small presses encouraged the development of all literary genres, as Sally Dennison has pointed out, but in particular alternative publishing supported poetry (which by the first decade of the twentieth century had become "a drug on the market") and short fiction (*[Alternative] Literary*

Publishing, 5). Devoting themselves to smaller projects—to limited editions of experimental poetry and short fiction—alternative presses were often able to produce beautiful and elegant books and pamphlets. Two Paris presses—the Hours and the Black Sun—were well known for the extraordinary care with which they produced texts, their beautifully designed publications reflecting the aesthetic values of Nancy Cunard and Caresse Crosby.

The Hours Press: Nancy Cunard

In 1925, the Hogarth Press published Nancy Cunard's *Parallax.* In 1928, Cunard herself had decided to set up a hand press in France, and she wrote Leonard and Virginia Woolf to seek their advice. Surprised, and perhaps alarmed at Cunard's temerity, they exclaimed, "Your hands will always be covered with ink!" (*These Were the Hours,* 8). Like Virginia Woolf, however, Nancy Cunard enjoyed having her hands covered with ink and admitted that "the smell of printer's ink pleased me greatly, as did the beautiful freshness of the glistening pigment" (9); she too quickly mastered the technical skills and found release from tension in the physical exertion demanded by the press. For Cunard, the operation of a hand press was an aesthetic experience: she delighted in choosing typefaces and paper stock and designing covers and bindings.

The Hours Press was not conceived as a commercial publishing firm, but neither did Cunard think of it as a hobby. Her decision to open the Hours Press constituted commitment to experimental poetry, and she was willing to risk financial loss in order to publish the best verse she could find. As Hugh Ford explains, she wanted to publish good work by young writers and to reward them "in a manner more generous than that to which they were accustomed" (*Published in Paris,* 260). Many of the writers she published, however, were well known (George Moore, for instance, was in his late seventies when Cunard published his *Peronnik the Fool*), her only "discovery" being Samuel Beckett, who won the Hours poetry prize for "Whoroscope" in 1930. She also published a "poem-fresco" by the Chilean painter Alvaro Guevara; a French translation by Aragon of Lewis Carroll's *The Hunting of the Snark;* the catalogue for a Paris exhibition of work by the American painter Eugene MacCown (who had made the cover designs for Cunard's long poem *Parallax*); poems by Robert Graves, Laura Riding, Richard Aldington, Roy Campbell, Brian Howard, Bob Brown, and Harold Acton; a portion of Pound's *Cantos;* an essay by Havelock Ellis, *The Revaluation of Obscenity;* and a collection of six songs by Henry Crowder—who was Cunard's colleague at the press—based on the poetry of Beckett, Aldington, Acton, and Walter Lowenfels. Cunard's association with Crowder, a black American jazz musician, would lead to her interest in compiling the anthology *Negro,* her political involvement in the black cause, and the publication in 1931 of her pamphlet *Black Man and White Ladyship,* a public attack on Lady Emerald Cunard's racist attitudes.

Anne Chisholm has suggested that the decision to open the press may have been occasioned by Cunard's sense of dissatisfaction with her own career as a poet: "she kept on writing and publishing occasional poems, but she needed to try a more practical outlet for her energies" (*Nancy Cunard,* 190). The three years Cunard spent at the Hours Press, however, led to highly productive years of writing and publication: *Negro,* her anthology on black politics and culture, was published in 1934; she served as a journalist for the *Manchester Guardian* during the Spanish Civil War, while writing war poetry and publishing commentaries on the war; later, she served in England as a translator for the Free French during World War II, often monitoring Ezra Pound's broadcasts from Italy. In 1944, she completed an anthology of French translations of British poems about France (*Poems for France*) and had completed a collection of war poems entitled *Man-Ship-Tank-Gun-Plane.* Cunard's decision to establish a small press marked the moment in which she turned away from her own self-interest to a commitment to others in collaborative efforts. As Hugh Ford has suggested, the story of the Hours Press is one "of close personal relationships and co-operation between . . . Cunard and the authors she published, which made possible the most fruitful sort of collaboration" (*These Were the Hours,* xvi). This story is also one of an emerging political identity.

Plain Edition: Alice B. Toklas

Unlike some of her Paris contemporaries, Nancy Cunard did not use the Hours Press to publish her own writings, but rather directed her interests to the work of others. We can read in this decision a political subtext of commitment to the work of younger, avant-garde writers. But the decision by Alice Toklas to open a press through which the works of Gertrude Stein could be marketed may also be seen as political. In 1930, Gertrude Stein was 56 years old, and many of her writings were still in manuscript. The effort by McAlmon to bring out *The Making of Americans* had proved unsatisfactory; although her work continued to appear in *transition,* Stein felt the need to turn the remainder of her manuscripts into books. In order to finance the endeavor, Stein sold Picasso's *Woman with a Fan* (the loss of which made Alice Toklas cry) and established Plain Edition—the name chosen by Gertrude herself to suggest her preference for simple, inexpensive, commercial texts. Describing Alice as "the imaginary editor" in a letter to Carl Van Vechten, Stein announced the collective efforts of author and publisher "to shove the unshoveable." The first title published under the Plain Edition imprint was *Lucy Church Amiably* on 5 January 1931. Over the next two years, Stein and Toklas published *How to Write* (1931); a "translation" of Georges Hugnet's *Enfances* entitled *Before the Flowers of Friendship Faded Friendship Faded* (1931); *Operas and Plays* (1932); and *Matisse Picasso and Gertrude Stein,* a work that included two other unpublished works, *A Long Gay Book* and *Many Many Women* (1933). The publication of *The Autobiography of Alice B. Toklas,* written while Alice was producing the last of these titles under the Plain Edition imprint, eliminated the need for self-publication: Harcourt Brace published *The Autobiography,* and Bennett Cerf at Random House soon offered Stein a contract guaranteeing publication of one book a year without constraints on the author's style. Plain Edition served the important purpose of getting into print some of the later and more difficult of Stein's theoretical works—in particular, *How to Write,* the treatise on grammar—and bringing together in one volume all of Stein's theater texts.

The Black Sun: Harry and Caresse Crosby

Another Paris press established to publish the work of its founders was the Black Sun, begun by Harry and Caresse Crosby in 1924. Although it began as a noncommercial enterprise, it continued to prosper for almost thirty years under the direction of Caresse Crosby, following her husband's death. The success of this business venture was due almost entirely to her imaginative efforts in finding a market for modern literature. Alice Toklas and Gertrude Stein had not been pleased by the quality of printing in Plain Edition publications, but neither had they interested themselves to the degree that Nancy Cunard and the Crosbys did in the craft of publication. Stein wanted to see herself in print: Cunard and the Crosbys wanted to produce exquisite limited editions and to involve themselves in every aspect of the publication process. Hugh Ford comments that the history of the Hours Press is a story of "how books were made, of how ideas became the words on a printed page" (*These Were the Hours,* xv−xvi), and Millicent Bell remarks that the Crosbys "developed . . . that *responsibility to the text* which is the basis of good book design": "All of the Black Sun Press books have been notable for successful fusion of the writer's, the illustrator's, and the designer's points of view. In a few cases, the Crosbys even illustrated as well as designed books written by themselves—thus making every aspect of the book a personal expression" ("Black Sun Press," 4). Unlike Cunard, the Crosbys did not set and print their own works, but found a printer in the rue Cardinale on the Left Bank, Roger Lescaret, to produce the texts. As Nancy Cunard had done, the Crosbys involved their authors in the process of text production, often guided in their choice of illustrations, cover designs, or paper stock by the author's wishes.

Before Harry Crosby's death, the Black Sun published elegant reprints of older texts by Poe, Wilde, Sterne, and Lewis Carroll (the text of *Alice in Wonderland* accompanied by Marie Laurencin watercolors) as well as their own poetry—twelve volumes of which had appeared by 1930. After Harry Crosby's death in 1929, Caresse Crosby published her own poems in honor of her husband (*Poems for Harry Crosby*), a four-volume edition of his collected poems, each with an introductory essay by a contemporary writer—T. S. Eliot, D. H. Lawrence, Ezra Pound, and Stuart Gilbert—and several posthumous volumes of Harry Crosby's writings. In 1930, she decided to publish the work of Paris colleagues, including Hart Crane (*The Bridge*), Ezra Pound (*Imaginary Letters*), and Archibald MacLeish (*New Found Land*), as well as translations from French works, beginning with a series of unpublished letters from Marcel Proust to Walter Berry that the Crosbys had translated together. When Pound's effort to publish the complete works of Guido Cavalcanti was interrupted by the bankruptcy of the Aquila Press, Caresse Crosby took over this difficult project, hiring Wyn Henderson (who was also working for Nancy Cunard at the Hours Press), who agreed to oversee publication of the complete *Guido* without payment (Ford, *Published in Paris*, 216).

In 1931, Caresse Crosby decided to establish Crosby Continental Editions in order to publish inexpensive reprints of avant-garde literature. Pound supplied a list of possible texts, and Hemingway agreed to allow Caresse to publish *The Torrents of Spring* as the first title in the Continental Editions series. The list of writers published by the Black Sun Press under Caresse Crosby's direction is a long and impressive one that includes both important and popular European writers (such as Alain-Fournier and Charles-Louis Philippe, Antoine de Saint-Exupéry, Paul Elouard, George Grosz, Max Ernst, C. G. Jung) and such Americans as Dorothy Parker, William Faulkner, and Kay Boyle.

The Politics of Publication: Nancy Cunard

As Caresse Crosby embarked on new publishing ventures in 1931, Nancy Cunard's interest in *Negro,* for which she had begun research with Henry Crowder, displaced her interest in the press. The previous year she had moved her press from the farmhouse in Réanville, north of Paris, to a small shop at 15, rue Guénégaud, just around the corner from the Galerie Surréaliste in the rue Jacques Callot. The location was more convenient than the farm had been, but she often found herself interrupted at her work. Harold Acton, a frequent visitor to the Guénégaud address, described Nancy as harried and overworked: "The clock did not exist for her: in town she dashed in and out of taxis clutching an attaché-case crammed with letters, manifestoes, estimates, circulars and her latest African bangle, and she was always several hours late for any appointment. A snack now and then but seldom a regular meal; she looked famished and quenched her hunger with harsh white wine and gusty talk" (quoted in Chisholm, *Nancy Cunard,* 202). By 1931, Nancy had turned the actual operation of the press over to Wyn Henderson in order to continue her research for *Negro,* a decision that angered her friend Richard Aldington, who felt that Cunard's decision in opening the press had not been a wise one but who now thought that she had abandoned her responsibilities. Like other of Nancy's friends, Aldington was shocked by the publication of *Black Man and White Ladyship,* an attack on Lady Cunard, perhaps feeling that Nancy was no longer in control of her life. Anne Chisholm writes that after the publication of the pamphlet, Nancy "was in danger of being written off as someone whose bohemian eccentricity had turned into dangerous, distasteful unacceptability" (*Nancy Cunard,* 252). In 1932, Aldington published with Heinemann a collection of stories entitled *Soft Answers* that included a portrait of Nancy in "Now Lies She There." Described in the story as lacking literary talent, a sense of responsibility, and a standard of conduct, the central character desires above all else to become recognized in the world, using sexual attachments with a variety of important men to make her way. Aldington's caricature of Cunard, his revenge against what he perceived to be her lack of professional and ethical standards, can be extended to a more generalized patriarchal view of women. Its "hysterical relish" constitutes a stronger, more virulent form of an underlying assumption that women of a certain social class and economic background discovered in the expatriate experience a means of open rebellion against their families and a method of killing time. (Objecting to remarks made about him in *The Autobiography of Alice B. Toklas,* Robert McAlmon, for instance, commented that Gertrude Stein was "a pronounced example of the rich and pampered and protected child who has never been allowed to face actual hardship," *Being Geniuses Together,* 228.) Chisholm's résumé of Aldington's attitudes toward Cunard echoes similar opinions held of Natalie Barney, Zelda Fitzgerald, Mabel Dodge Luhan, Winifred Ellerman, Djuna Barnes, and Caresse Crosby: "His revenge was to turn every aspect of her character and behavior into a nightmare caricature, not allowing her any taste, brains or passion, not allowing her lovers or proteges any success or distinction, not granting her any generosity of mind or body. He painted a vicious portrait of a rich, useless erratic girl in rebellion against her family and class for want of anything better to do or be" (*Nancy Cunard,* 253–254). This portrait, of course, never raises the issue of racism, but it may well have been Cunard's relationship with Crowder, her public announcement of a preference for black men, which disgusted Aldington. Indeed, in taking a black lover—and later accompanying him to Harlem —she was making a political statement about the combined issues of racism and sexual freedom.

Nancy Cunard was already hard at work on *Negro* when the Hours Press published its last book, *The Revaluation of Obscenity* by Havelock Ellis, a man whose writing Nancy knew well and a work that supported her own views on sexuality. The decision to publish this text, however, was entirely Wyn Henderson's, although Nancy was pleased at the inclusion of Ellis's book in the Hours list. Ellis's essay explicitly raised issues relating sexuality (particularly homosexuality) to the legal definition of "obscenity," itself a subject of concern to expatriate writers, publishers, and editors. Ellis carefully distinguished in the article between two kinds of obscenity—sexual processes and excremental processes: "The taboo of the excremental obscene is only conventional and social, while that of the sexual obscene is regarded as moral and religious" (*These Were the Hours,* 190). Analyzing similar issues in a *Little Review* essay (September 1917) on James Joyce's *A Portrait of the Artist,* Jane Heap commented on a form of obscenity overlooked by Ellis's categories: "You can talk about or write about or paint or sculpt some parts of the body but others must be treated like the Bad Lands. You can write about what you see that you don't like, what you touch, taste, or hear; but you can't write about what you smell; if you do you are accused of using nasty words. I could say a lot more about the geography of the body, and how its influence goes all the way through until the censor makes a geography for your mind and soul." In a later article, "Art and the Law," Heap discussed the question of obscenity in the "Nausikaa" episode of *Ulysses,* which includes a young girl's thoughts, later considered corrupt by a New York court. Her argument was with Mr. Sumner, the head of the Society for the Prevention of Vice, who brought suit against the *Little Review* for publication of *Ulysses.* Heap concluded: "It was the poet, the artist, who discovered love, created the lover, made sex everything that it is beyond a function. It is the Mr. Sumners who have made it an obscenity" (*Little Review,* September–December 1920). A victim in England of persecution on obscenity charges for scientific works that treated the subject of human sexuality, Ellis would have agreed both with Heap's analysis of obscenity and with her observation that in seeking to protect the public against obscenity the law actually creates "an artificial market for pornography" (Ford, *Published in Paris,* 287).

The Hours Press edition of Ellis's *The Revaluation of Obscenity* sold out, presumably—according to Cunard—"owing to the great name of the author and the interest the public had in the subject" (*These Were the*

Hours, 192). The proceeds from sales, however, did not cover the outstanding debts of the press, which had risen at an alarming rate since Cunard had turned over the press to Wyn Henderson. Cunard's interest in the press had always been in production—the typesetting, choice of papers and bindings, and printing—and she had always felt burdened by publicity and accounting. However, in the first year of production she had successfully managed the business, even making a profit. As other interests had impinged on the time needed to run the business, she had dissociated herself from its operations. By the end, she was thoroughly disillusioned with the publishing trade. She wrote to Wyn Henderson, who wanted to keep the press open: "Do you really think I ever want to have anything [to do] with publishing again? You must be crazy! I despise the whole thing and am disgusted, thoroughly and permanently. . . . Damn all business!" (Ford, *Published in Paris,* 288). But Nancy Cunard was not "thoroughly and permanently" finished with publishing. In 1931, she met Edgell Rickword, an Englishman whose political views were very similar to hers. He agreed to publish *Negro,* through Wishart and Company, the publisher for whom he worked, provided that Nancy paid for its publication. Still soliciting contributions for the anthology, Nancy also spent most of 1932 and 1933 designing the book, correcting and proofreading its text, and overseeing the publication process. On 15 February 1934, the 855-page, eight-pound anthology was published, a work that included 250 contributions by 150 authors, two-thirds of whom were black. In her introduction, Nancy defined the purpose of the publication: "It was necessary to make this book—and I think in this manner, an Anthology of some one hundred and fifty voices of both races—for the recording of the struggles and achievements, the persecutions and the revolts against them of the Negro peoples." Nancy Cunard took political action through publication, first in the pamphlet *Black Man and White Ladyship,* next through the publication of *Negro,* and finally through her work on behalf of the Republicans in the Spanish Civil War and against Fascism during World War II. Her politics—and her methods of making them public—often met with disapproval. As a result, her very real contributions to the expatriate literary experience have been affected by reactions against her liberal politics, her insistence on sexual freedom, and her outspoken denouncement of the English upper class.

11
PARIS TRANSFER:
THE 1930s

Writing of England in the 1930s, Samuel Hynes comments that the decade was less determined by a "fixed and definable set of characteristics" than by a developing consciousness that changed according to circumstances (*Auden Generation*, 11–12). The circumstances directing cultural and social change were more openly political in the thirties than in the twenties, but the polarization of attitudes that retrospectively appeared to define this decade was not so clearly marked in the immediate moment. In 1931, Paris witnessed the mass emigration of American expatriates, forced to return home by the Wall Street crash. But the crash itself was not at first interpreted as part of a devastating worldwide economic crisis. Instead, it was thought to be a freak accident occasioned by the peculiarities of American investment practice. Leon Edel comments in his introduction to Edmund Wilson's notebooks and diaries from the thirties on the retrospective reevaluation demanded by this decade: "Looking backward . . . Wilson wrote that it was difficult for those born late 'to believe that it really occurred, that between 1929 and 1933 the whole structure of American society seemed to be going to pieces.' Seeking for a word in 1932, he spoke of 'the American jitters' and published a volume of that title. There was indeed a state of jitters. But later the word seemed a euphemism for disaster, and in the full light of history Wilson renamed his book, when it was revised and reprinted, *The American Earthquake*" (*The Thirties*, xv–xvi). Close up, the Wall Street crash seemed a local event, one not destined to affect farmers in Iowa or fruitgrowers and fishermen in California. But within four years, the events of October 1929 had registered shock waves in every city, small town, and rural area of America. This earthquake was not, as Wilson's title suggested, an American phenomenon, however: the crash itself was an effect of a larger, more pervasive crisis in Western culture that would result in the creation of political utopias—Communism offering one alternative world, Fascism another.

Aesthetics and Politics: From the 1920s to the 1930s

Literary histories of the interwar years usually suggest that the emphasis on aesthetics that marked the moment of High Modernism in the 1920s was replaced by an interest in politics in the 1930s. That is, art was politicized in the third decade of Modernism. Registering the literary effects of this shift, Sally Dennison comments that "the most important aspect of a writer's work became not its aesthetic soundness, but its social or political stance, and the writer's artistic role was secondary to his role as social historian" (*[Alternative] Literary Publishing*, 119). For Bernard Bergonzi, this cultural shift forced a "desirable change . . . in our model of the literary text" by insisting that the political, social, and biographical contexts of literary production be acknowledged in analyses of the literary work. The Modernist notion that the text constituted a "smooth, solid, self-enclosed, free-standing object" (*Reading the Thirties*, 4) was undermined by events that proclaimed the impossibility of an art separate from the social situation in which art is produced. In the 1930s, then, the "writer as artist" became unpopular.

As Sally Dennison's work has demonstrated, young writers who followed the tradition of experimental poetry and fiction so valued in the 1920s faced difficulties in the 1930s finding publishers for their work. Social relevance became a hallmark of thirties literature, just as artistic integrity had been the defining feature of the Modernist writing of the 1920s. Those established writers who continued the earlier tradition are often set aside in discussions of the thirties. Bernard Bergonzi does not discuss these writers, claiming that they "belong on different maps, are to be sought on different expeditions" (*Reading the Thirties*, 9). Samuel Hynes excludes "important works" written during the thirties by older writers even as he argues that "one could not be a young poet in the 'thirties and be unaffected by *Ash Wednesday* and *The Winding Stair*, or be a young novelist and unaware of *Work in Progress*" (*Auden Generation*, 9). Although some of the most experimental work of the Modernists was published in these years—Pound's *Fifth Decad of Cantos*, Eliot's "Burnt Norton," Joyce's *Finnegans Wake*, Virginia Woolf's *The Waves*, Djuna Barnes's *Nightwood*, Gertrude Stein's *Lectures in America* and *Narration*, and Wyndham Lewis's *The Revenge for Love*—Sally Dennison can still declare that the literary Modernism of the 1920s was "all but dead by the end of the thirties": "Ezra Pound allied himself with the Fascist cause in Italy, where he moved from Paris; the Bloomsbury group was dismissed as elitist; Harriet Weaver joined the Communist party; the Nobel Prize for literature went to Pearl Buck, the author of a 'proletarian' novel, *The Good Earth*" (*[Alternative] Literary Publishing*, 120). One might also add that Gide's conversion to Communism in the 1930s had a major impact on French youth; that texts by men as politically dissimilar as Céline (*Voyage to the End of Night*) and Malraux (*Man's Fate*) were published a year apart, each nominated for major French literary awards— *Man's Fate* winning the prix Goncourt in 1933, *Voyage* having been denied the prize the previous year after members of the selection committee altered their votes under political pressure from the government. Strong Fascist and Communist parties struggled against each other to gain control of popular thinking in England, France, Italy, and Spain in this decade, a period in which writers became pamphleteers and propagandists, taking sides on political issues.

Samuel Hynes has commented that the Auden Generation did not entirely reject the values of the Pound Era; rather, it revised them (*Auden Generation*, 11). In fact, the literature of the thirties exposed the political nature of the presumed apolitical literary aesthetics of early Modernism, not only uncovering the Fascist leanings of an Ezra Pound or a Wyndham Lewis but unearthing as well a reactionary T. S. Eliot and an anti-Semitic Gertrude Stein. If early Modernist writing masked political attitudes by claims to aesthetic purity, some writing of the thirties employed political rhetoric to code private messages and protect personal attitudes. Bernard Benstock argues that the political activities of such writers as Malraux, Saint-Exupéry, Gide, Céline, Aragon, Esenin, Lorca, Silone, D'Annunzio, Claudel, and Graham Greene concealed complex personal commitments to adventurism, romanticism, religious endeavor, and the international community, while W. H. Auden, Christopher Isherwood, and Stephen Spender developed poetic styles that simultaneously mapped and masked homosexuality. This latter group allowed its works to be interpreted in political rather than personal terms, preferring the "Communist" label to the discovery of a homosexual counterculture. Their writing was indeed subversive, as commentators were quick to perceive, but it was subversive in ways that eluded readers who accepted the coded political rhetoric at face value.[1]

If the revolutionary literary experiments of the 1920s were allied to conservative—even reactionary—political beliefs, the rhetoric of writing in the 1930s posed revolutionary political concepts in terms of conservative literary practice. If early Modernism had discovered the power of language to reflect the chaos, uncertainty, and meaninglessness of modern life, the 1930s discovered in language a powerful political weapon. Thus the opposition of "public" and "private" in the literary languages of these two decades reversed themselves: early Modernism made the private public, exploiting a language appropriate to investigation of the psyche, the unconscious, of dreams and nightmares. (Reader response often did not accurately assess the literary effort, however, perhaps confused by the stylistic experiment of the Modernist mode. Samuel Hynes comments, for instance, that *The Waste Land* was first "read as a work of primarily social and moral import, a public poem on public themes." Only years later was it possible "to see it as the private nightmare of a young expatriate having a nervous breakdown," *Auden Generation,* 28.) Stylistic experiment revealed a new world, the uncharted, unknown, and dark continent of the soul. Mapping the contours of this region, Modernist language perfectly suited itself to its subject: substance determined style. By the 1930s, however, such expeditions were seen as self-indulgent, and the private world of literary exploration was expanded, becoming an arena for political and social concern. According to Bernard Bergonzi, the writing of W. H. Auden and Graham Greene is defined by "two quite disparate qualities: a private, idiosyncratic, even obsessional aspect, often looking back to childhood or adolescent experience; and a keen, observant, classifying interest in contemporary mass society" (*Reading the Thirties,* 62).

These two literary periods are set at angles to each other, like photographs in a hinged frame. Obsessed by the notion of war, the literature of the 1920s reacted against the war it had just witnessed, recorded the effects of that war in modern life; the literature of the 1930s anticipated the inevitable war to come, played out fantasies of combat and secret spy missions, inverting and subverting the political rhetoric of World War I. A time of economic growth and prosperity, the 1920s richly nurtured the arts, allowing the leisure and freedom to pursue private or aesthetic pleasures, offering psychic and artistic liberation through language. Virginia Woolf's observation of an altered human character suggested, as did post-Impressionist art, the infinite possibilities held within human character. For Woolf, the surface realism of nineteenth-century fiction, with its claims to defining human character through conventional behavior traits, had reduced the complexity of the human subject to formula and cliché. For James McFarlane, it is through its definition of human character that Modernism made its "classic declaration": ". . . human nature is not to be contained by vast and exhaustive inventories of naturalistic detail arranged and sorted under prescriptive heads but instead is elusive, indeterminate, multiple, often implausible, infinitely various and essentially irreducible" ("The Mind of Modernism," 81). By definition, then, human nature thwarted efforts to catalogue and code its external manifestations; indeed, such efforts at definition through categorization become impossible. More than twenty years after Virginia Woolf's pronouncement on the state of human character, T. S. Eliot confirmed her perceptions: "a poet's mind . . . is constantly amalgamating disparate experience; the ordinary man's experience is chaotic, irregular, fragmentary" ("The Metaphysical Poets," 287). The very implausibility and infinitely various qualities of human nature made it an irresistible subject for literary experiment.

The 1930s, however, overturned the Modernist definition of human character: the notion of human nature as elusive and indeterminate was not compatible with a poetic method that operated by code to identify the enemy and expose the conspirator. Thus the elements of human character had to be identifiable and quantifiable—that is, amenable to cataloguing. Those involved in the conspiratorial revolt against reactionary institutional forms invented alternative worlds constructed by means of secret poetic languages. Reversing the value systems of the external world, these fantasy societies were populated by people who demonstrated all kinds of extravagant and eccentric behavior, but, like characters in medieval morality plays, their natures were contained in their names (e.g., Ronald Gunball, Reverend Welkin). Although such worlds constituted retreats from reality and overturned the ordering structures of the real world, they were nonetheless constructed according to predictable and recognizable principles of human behavior. Samuel Hynes defines such worlds as *parables:* "highly structured, non-realistic, significant systems that constitute[d] judgments of life as it exists" (*Auden Generation,* 36). The best known of such invented alternative societies is Mortmere, created by Edward Upward and Christopher Isherwood during their undergraduate years at Cambridge, a parable that anticipates Auden's *Paid on Both Sides* and Rex Warner's *The Wild Goose Chase.* The distinguishing features of this world are paranoia, depravity and sexual perversion, amalgamation of fact and fantasy, inexplicable violence, complex—and often incomprehensible—plot structures, the absence of any kind of creative, nurturing principle. That is, the world of Mortmere constitutes an entirely masculine invention that excludes women altogether.

The thirties has been defined as a "masculine decade," a "male preserve" in which narrowly defined class distinctions excluded "issues of gender and sexual politics." The collective experience of this generation of writers was masculine, its participants products of the English public school. The Auden Generation, like the men of Bloomsbury, shared preparatory and public school experiences, were educated at Oxford and Cambridge, and were predominantly homosexual.[2] Bernard Bergonzi comments that "never before or since have English writers been so heavily marked by the homogeneous educational formation of the English upper and upper-middle classes" (*Reading the Thirties,* 37). Indeed the integration of class values and educational values is the defining characteristic of English public school experience, and for the Auden Generation the mark of cultural homogeneity. Public schools served as models of Fascist states whose rigid forms and enforced conventions were inverted—but never entirely escaped—in fantasy worlds; private and shared, the public school experience became "a source of personal fantasies and public metaphors," the best example of which was Mortmere (*Reading the Thirties*, 32).

Entre deux guerres

The literary imagination of the period was structured by the two wars that framed its historical situation. A generation *entre deux guerres,* this group of writers was deeply affected by the series of events that linked these two international catastrophes. Not surprisingly, perhaps, the literature of this period reveals a crisis of masculine identity linked both to homosexuality and to war (English Study Group, "Thinking the Thirties," 2:6). Homosexuality was associated, of course, with public schools and perceived as a cultural and class experience that put into question traditional definitions of masculine identity. In particular, homosexuals of the period defined themselves against a romanticized image of the rugged and heroic young men who died on the battlefields in World War I. The postwar generation of public school men feared a failure of courage and conscience, imagined war as the ultimate "Test" of masculinity, and dreamed of ways to escape the death sentence meted out to those who passed the "Test." The fear of death structured the private worlds in which these poets tested their valor and masculine identity. Mortmere, for instance, defined itself as a place of deadly enchantment, the place-name (with its echo of "Mortlake" and allusion to the Dead Sea) implying the dangers inherent in the quest into the unknown. Samuel Hynes describes this place in the imagination as a "young man's Waste Land," a world that expresses "the anxiety of the valueless post-war world, which is the primary *donnée* of the time" (*Auden Generation*, 37). Importantly, the values that have been lost to this postwar generation are *masculine* values that are both mocked and mourned by the poetry of the period. It is significant that "Mortmere" marks the death of the mother (the absence of the female element is suggested by the substitution of the masculine generic form—"mort mere"—for the correct French feminine, "morte mère"). Even more significantly, perhaps, this deliberate putting to death of the maternal, with its accompanying denial of female values, is consistently overlooked by commentators.

The postwar world of the Auden Generation was "full of the Myth of War," according to Hynes (*Auden Generation*, 23); the book of war read by this generation was Eliot's *Waste Land,* the imagery of which conveyed the effects of war: ". . . the world of the poem, with its heaps of broken images and its shocked and passive and neurasthenic persons, is a paradigm of war's effects, and of a world emptied of order and meaning, like a battlefield after the battle. And the *manner* of the poem—its ironic tone, its imagery, its lack of heroes and heroism, its anti-rhetorical style—is also a consequence of the war, an application of war-poet principles to the post-war scene" (*Auden Generation,* 25). The effects of the war were particularly evident in English public schools of the period: the Old Boys had been killed; the young boys had missed their great opportunity to serve. Christopher Isherwood reports in his autobiographical work *Lions and Shadows* that "we young writers of the middle 'twenties were all suffering, more or less subconsciously, from a feeling of shame that we hadn't been old enough to take part in the European war" (74–75). The knowledge of having missed the "Test" led to obsessive worries about whether the young men of this later generation could have passed it, endured the hardships, put their lives on the line traced by the trenches across Belgium and France. The frontier between peace and war, between childhood and manhood, between the prewar civilization and the postwar world, marked psychic divisions in the imaginations of these writers that the Spanish Civil War would reopen. For the moment, these men traced an interior space within the Myth of War, a space that enclosed a private vision and recorded personal experience. This interior world Auden described as Poetry—"the formation of private spheres out of a public chaos" ("Preface," *Oxford Poetry 1927,* v). Auden's poetic definition of this interior space is to be found in "The Journal of an Airman" (*The Orators,* 1932). Involved in a secret revolutionary plot, the Airman records his plans, fears, fantasies, and recollections in the journal. His thoughts are constructed around the notion of the Enemy, a collective group that includes middle-class suburbanites as well as old men and mothers who mouth patriotic speeches. The Airman is neurotic, introspective, a sneak-thief, a homosexual, and afraid of failing the "Test." The Test, however, is not the public demonstration of bravery and courage required of the Old Boys in the Great War, but rather a private form of guerrilla warfare enacted against the self. The journal is a journey to self-knowledge and a retreat from the world of publicly enacted rituals of bravery.

Contrasting Visions: Céline and Auden

Six months after *The Orators* appeared in England, Céline's *Voyage au bout de la nuit* appeared in France. Céline's pessimism was darker and more debilitating than Auden's; his world, dominated by an incomprehensible but all-powerful and more destructive evil. Whereas Auden's universe was constructed in terms of a complex power struggle between opponents, Céline's world is structured by the dominance of evil forces that oppress and exploit their victims. The only hope for survival is escape—often through madness. The novel opens in Flanders during the First

World War, where Bardamu, a reluctant soldier, escapes the battlefield by taking refuge in hospitals and insane asylums. The battlefield is a slaughterhouse, the soldiers cannon-fodder in an irrational war in which both sides can only lose. Patrick McCarthy comments that "Celine's art aims at turning life into a series of random catastrophes" (*Celine,* 50). As one such "random catastrophe," World War I remains inexplicable, and Bardamu's role in it seems as accidental and purposeless as any of the other events in the novel. Although the title of the work suggests that the voyage it undertakes has a purpose (to the "end of night"), the novel itself subverts the notion of linear progression by asserting the randomness of narrative event: "By this technique Celine destroys cause and effect. The different episodes of the book have no internal logic. The war is fought in a wasteland with neither conquerors nor conquered. The French soldiers, who do not dislike the Germans, loathe their own officers. There is no strategy: the men are sent into the dark and told to look for their units, which they usually cannot find. 'The war, in fact, was everything that one didn't understand,' concludes Bardamu" (*Celine,* 50–51). McCarthy observes that "the supremely irrational fact of life is death," and Bardamu concludes, "The truth of this world is to die" (*Celine,* 51). But the death holds no meaning, remaining as inexplicable as the reasons for living. Like Auden, Céline exposes the bankruptcy of conventional patriotic values and reveals heroism to be little more than vanity. While *Voyage* does not restrict itself to an examination of World War I (Bardamu discovers other forms of exploitation in colonial Africa, in the modern industrial cities of America, and as a medical practitioner in Paris), the war exposes the corruption of the very values for which it was presumably fought. As in Eliot's poem, the wasteland of modern civilization is figured by No Man's Land. Céline's novel explores the wasteland of Flanders and plots its action across a landscape charted by military maps and along the time-line of documented battles. Always "under fire," constantly exposed to the possibility of imminent and painful death, Céline's characters move in a No Man's Land that is all the more frightening for its literal exactness and its historical accuracy.

By contrast, Auden's figures play out imaginary war games across a landscape that is already economically, morally, and psychologically "wasted": ". . . the derelict world is the present from which young men must start, the border is the edge of the unknown and the beginning of uncertainty, and the world beyond it is the one that the young man must enter, if he is to act. . . . reality has its frontiers, on *this* side a dead security, on the *other* side the fearful threat that is unknown, but cannot be ignored" (*Auden Generation,* 56). It is the acceptance or rejection in the "fearful threat" that constitutes the starting place of Auden poems. Unlike Céline's determinedly irrational universe in which there is no place to hide or to escape the consequences of evil, Auden Country is constructed along a zone of risk. Crossing the border, taking the risk, constitutes a *rite de passage*—the "Test." Early Auden writings (particularly, "Charade," *Paid on Both Sides*) construct the map. The "Charade" itself forms, as Hynes has commented, the large-scale map, and poems written between the years 1927 and 1932 chart the "local details, which fill in and complete Auden's alternative world" (*Auden Generation*, 55). The horror of the poems rests not in the casual and graphic brutality of Céline's universe, but rather in understated ironic effects of poems whose titles suggest the lyric or the pastoral ("This Loved One," "On Sunday Walks"). Many of the poems take a spectatorial attitude ("The Witnesses," "The Watchers") or examine those who are outside the boundaries of society ("The Exiles," "The Wanderer"). Auden Country is not plotted according to the sectors and quadrants of a military map, across which armies will march and tanks will roll. Rather, Auden's terrain is dangerous because certain areas remain mysterious, unknown and unknowable. Maps, if they exist, are not to be trusted; the enemy, if there is one, is not easily identifiable. Unable to distinguish illusion from reality in this country, the traveler cannot be assured safe passage: the seemingly innocent birds may be decoys, "trained to snaring"; even "the trained spy" may walk "into the trap / For a bogus guide, seduced by the old tricks" ("The Decoys," "The Secret Agent," *Collected Poems*, 66, 41).

Whereas Céline's war is characterized by wholesale slaughter that is both egregious and meaningless, carried out by unthinking and unfeeling participants on both sides, Auden's war is frustrated, stalemated, and dead-ending—each side posturing and posing. Céline's war is defined in frenzied activity, Auden's by debilitating stasis. Despite its grounding in the specific locale and operation of World War I, the psychology of Céline's battle is guerrilla warfare; Auden's is a cold war, fought by calculating military spies. Death in Céline's world is violent and ugly, in Auden's, internalized as numbness, defined in the Airman's journal as "impotence—cancer—paralysis." The divisions of Auden's world are reflected in dialogic poetic constructions, conversations between speaker and self, interrogations of the rider by the reader, accusations of cowardice by those who are brave. If violence is imminent and everywhere in Céline's universe, it is concealed and localized in Auden's. The whole world is a battlefield for Céline, while for Auden the world is polarized by good and evil, Communism and Fascism, the Left and the Right, the real world and the fantasy landscape, the public and the private, life and death.

Although there is negligible difference between war and peace in Céline's writings, war and peace constitute the polar oppositions by which the writings of the Auden Generation are constructed. Thus the dividing lines between these sectors—the notion of borders and frontiers, check points and passport control, barriers and fortifications—suggest psychological, social, and political alignments. Julian Symons has remarked that for Auden, Isherwood, and Upward, "a predominant image . . . is that of the frontier" (*The Thirties: A Dream Revolved*, 35), and Bernard Bergonzi has commented that the appeal of this "flexible symbol . . . derived its basic force from the historical conditions of the twenties and thirties" in which—for the first time in European experience—frontiers between countries constituted "formidable barriers" (*Reading the Thirties*, 70). The effect of political polarization was the creation of *real* frontiers that required passports and visas, but these frontiers were psychologically internalized as well ("Do not imagine you can abdicate; / Before you reach the frontier you are caught," writes Auden in "Venus Will Now Say a Few Words," *Collected Poems*, 49), and the sharp division of political attitudes increasingly suggested that the frontiers had become the "centers" of political thought and activity. Not to choose a side, not to commit oneself to one of the opposed alternatives, was, in fact, to place oneself in the vast No Man's Land between the frontiers—that is, the center itself became a frontier, a place of great risk in a world that insisted that one declare loyalties, take sides, join up.

In the 1930s, the notion of the frontier displaced the concept of the "center" that was "nowhere," an empty space between opposed areas of activities. The "center" also extended itself in time as an interim period between events: it existed *entre deux guerres*. Stephen Spender commented that "from 1931 onwards, in common with many other people, I felt hounded by external events" (*World within World*, 137). It was in this year that Janet Flanner marked the noticeable exit of Americans from Europe, the effects of the Great Depression having finally affected expatriates. Britain too was suffering an apparently "permanent" depression, and in this year the second Labour government in Britain collapsed. The revolution in Spain and the Japanese invasion of Manchuria were interpreted by some as the beginnings of another world war. As it became clear that, rather than ending future wars, the first war had merely guaranteed the occasion of a second war, Europe saw itself poised between two powerful and, to many, equally hideous alternatives: Communism and Fascism. Although ideologically opposed, the actual operation of the two political systems displayed certain similarities—the promise of economic security and political stability, the revision of existing social structures, the disregard for personal freedom, the manifest need to conquer and colonialize, the exploitation of propaganda and a rhetoric of fear, the appearance of frightening father figures who marshaled armies and paraded the machinery of war. Forced to choose sides, some saw in Fascism the only means of containing Communism (posters in London proclaimed "Better Hitler than Blum!"); others, less sure of the political terrain, occupied the center, passing silently between the extremes and waiting out the inevitable.[3] A moment that presaged the inevitable arrived in July 1936, when the popular forces in Spain defeated the generals in Madrid and Barcelona. From this moment on, the "frontier" acquired a "precise significance," as Bergonzi suggests (*Reading the Thirties*, 73): it was real, no longer imaginary, and those writers who had been waiting for the call to action were now forced to answer it.

Private Faces in Public Places

The reaction of the Auden group to the Spanish Civil War resulted in a realignment of its political views, and Virginia Woolf watched the political and poetic development of this group with some interest. In 1932, the same year the Hogarth Press published the work of Auden, John Lehmann, C. Day Lewis, and Stephen Spender in *New Signatures,* Virginia Woolf published a response to that poetry, *Letter to a Young Poet,* part of *The Hogarth Letters* series. Remembering Woolf's own efforts to track the complex indeterminacies of human character through language, her Socialist feminism, and her resentment of the Cambridge-Oxford intellectual hegemony, the particular complaints she takes up with these poets are predictable. In particular, she reacted negatively to the privacy of their writing, to the extent that it seemed to deny the "world outside." She wished for a poetry that more clearly located itself in lived experience and found it troublesome that "these modern poets should write as if they had neither ears nor eyes, neither soles to their feet nor palms to their hands, but only honest enterprising book-fed brains, uni-sexual bodies" (*Letter to a Young Poet,* 26). What Woolf apparently wanted was a more open and obvious political literature, resenting the adolescent secrecy of this encoded complaint against the modern world. She found some of the poetry undigested, even undigestible, and some of it unintelligible. In particular, she had little sympathy with the despair that seemed to inform the poetry. As Hynes has suggested, however, "the very things that she complains of become terms in a definition, and support the already existing idea of what the generation was" (*Auden Generation,* 85–86). In particular, Woolf's negative reaction to this work affirmed the separation of these young poets from the generation that immediately preceded them. Peter Quennell, an Oxford friend of Auden and Spender, replied with *A Letter to Mrs. Virginia Woolf* (published the same year by the Hogarth Press), a letter that defended his fellow poets and also further defined them. Rehearsing the familiar characteristics of this new writing—recalling the crisis in language, the polarization of political attitudes, the loss of the prewar past—Quennell conjures up, as Samuel Hynes has noted, a "mythical figure, the Thirties Poet": in citing the op-

posed political stances available to this young poet ("for all I can tell
he may be a Communist or a young Hitlerite"), he brings Hitler's name
into a literary discussion for the first time (*Auden Generation,* 86–87).
Hitler's ominous figure casts a long shadow across the poetry of this period, and it was Virginia Woolf herself who analyzed the threat of Fascism
to Western culture in *Three Guineas.*

In 1940, the year before her death, Virginia Woolf again took up the
topic of the Thirties Poets in a lecture to the Workers' Educational Association on the subject of the relation between class and creativity. As
Quentin Bell has noted, this lecture "got her into a great deal of trouble
with Left Wing intellectuals," he himself admitting that she was both
rude and, perhaps, mistaken about their poetry (*Virginia Woolf,* 2:219).
The lecture took up familiar Woolf themes, in particular the intimate relation between the history of English literature and the development of
English class structure (a theme first publicly raised in the lectures that
were to comprise *A Room of One's Own,* delivered some dozen years
earlier). In "The Leaning Tower," as the lecture was entitled when it was
later published, Woolf drew attention to the fact that even the young social writers of the thirties were the products of a bourgeois upbringing;
she insisted that their writing could not escape the boundaries of the social class and educational background of its authors. Such insecurities as
this poetry recorded, she argued, derived from the necessity to write even
as their superior position in society was crumbling: Woolf predicted that
"the world after the war will be a world without classes or towers" ("The
Leaning Tower," in *Collected Essays* 2:178): "Trapped by their education, pinned down by their capital they remained on top of their leaning
tower, and their state of mind as we see it reflected in their poems and
plays and novels [is] full of discord and bitterness, full of confusion and
compromise" (172). Her prediction that a classless society would result
from the current war was, of course, incorrect, but her analysis of the
false political and social claims of thirties poetry was both audacious and
accurate. Woolf suspected that this poetry revealed a collapse of faith in
the power of poetry to affect social circumstances; rather than a poetry
directed at persuading the masses, Woolf discovered coterie literature
constructed according to secret codes that purposely excluded from the
readership all but those already initiated to its practices. Reacting against
the presumed elitism of early Modernism, the writers of the Thirties had
adopted an even more exclusive and elitist practice that employed political metaphors to mask private concerns.

Woolf resisted the temptation to expose the secret heart of this poetry,
although she would certainly have recognized the component elements of
public school homosexuality and reaction against bourgeois values as the
defining features of the group. In *Lions and Shadows,* first published in

1938, Christopher Isherwood had already drawn the general outlines of this generation's pervasive myth: "Gradually, in the most utter secrecy, I began to evolve a cult of the public-school system. . . . I built up the daydream of an heroic school career, in which the central figure, the dream I, was an austere young prefect, called upon unexpectedly to captain a 'bad' house, surrounded by sneering critics and open enemies, fighting slackness, moral rottenness, grimly repressing his own romantic feelings towards a younger boy, and finally triumphing over all his obstacles, passing the test, emerging—a Man" (181–182). Isherwood's articulation of the public school myth lent weight to the accuracy of Woolf's perceptions. No doubt she could not publicly discuss in 1940 the private elements of this poetic imagination or expose the methods by which it undercut the very political stance it would construct.

Later analyses of the Auden Generation have not been forced to keep silent on the personal elements that comprised the public poetic stance of this group. The English Study Group at Birmingham, for instance, has examined the efforts of "ideological collapse" that Woolf herself detected in this writing:

> Much of Auden's writing in the thirties is symptomatically uncertain: ridden by guilt about its own futility ("Poetry makes nothing happen"), restricted to worlds of largely private allusion in which public schools could be offered as models of fascist states, consciously frivolous and distractingly clever. His poems combine a gestural invocation of marxism with a notable distance from any actual English politics. They are marked by a sense of literature's inferior usefulness and explanatory power next to science, and next also to the mass media, to documentary and to propaganda, to which an attenuated and facetious surrealism stands in an uneasy relation. In many texts, too, by members of that coterie, reference is made to a more widespread crisis of masculine identity, connected in one way with the war ("'War' in this purely neurotic sense meant The Test . . . 'Are you really a Man?'" Isherwood, 1938) and in another way with homosexuality, but more generally with a political skepticism offset by a craving for ambivalent strong leader-figures ("Let us now praise famous men"). Auden's poems remained incoherent and unstable, shifting awkwardly in tone and reference. In them there was a crisis of the literary discourse itself. ("Thinking the Thirties," 5–6)

Virginia Woolf's complaint with the thirties poets was not that "they became political-minded," as Hynes has described it (*Auden Generation*, 392), but that they had not become political-minded enough. Their politics did not ring true to her: they were blinded to the effects of class and education precisely because these elements had shaped their thinking. (Woolf herself was a member of the same class but had not received the same education: she was able to see the inherent contradictions of the Auden Generation in part because she was a woman.) In refusing to acknowledge their own privileged place in the social scheme, they evaded the dominant social, political, and historical issues of the period. She saw their attack on bourgeois society as both violent and halfhearted: "they are profiting by a society which they abuse. . . . It explains the destructiveness of their work; and also its emptiness" ("The Leaning Tower," 175).

The angered responses that Woolf's analysis engendered (and continues to engender) were indication enough that she had touched a raw nerve.[4] But she herself did not escape the sentence she meted out for Auden's contemporaries, as Quentin Bell explains:

> Where Virginia differed from most of the younger socialists was in her frank and unequivocal acceptance of the importance of the class structure in literature. Where others attempted to cross the barriers of class, or even to deny their existence, she frankly recognised them and, in so doing, recognised that she herself was in an isolated position within a divided society. As she makes clear in *The Leaning Tower,* she did not consider that this was a desirable state of affairs; but neither did she think that it was a state of affairs which could be altered by pretending that it did not exist. It was here that she parted company, not only with the Left, but with the Right. (*Virginia Woolf,* 2:219)

If it had ever been true, as Hynes claims, "that in the 'thirties poets did believe, or at least hoped, that poetry might alter action in . . . a fundamental way" (*Auden Generation,* 24), employing the power of language to change societal structures, these poets had long since abandoned such naive hopes by 1940. Virginia Woolf, of course, had never held out such hopes, claiming—against Benedict Nicolson's accusation that "Bloomsbury . . . had been living in a fool's paradise"—that artists had never been able to influence society substantially (*Virginia Woolf,* 2:220–221). The view that it is the artist's responsibility to try to change society was, in Virginia Woolf's opinion, politically naive. Woolf's own writing—her essays, reviews, and journalism—became markedly political as the decade wore on, and one senses in this work an increasing despair that artists and writers remain impotent in the face of political danger: they may be able to diagnose societal ills accurately, but cannot do anything to change them. Such a view, it seems, informed Woolf's decision to take her own life in spring 1941.

Patriarchal Values: The Politics of Exclusion

Polarized as European society had become by the mid-thirties, both the Left and the Right shared a view of post–World War I society as decadent, without values, and emptied of meaning. The crisis in literature Woolf perceived in the writing of Auden and his contemporaries was a "personal crisis about writing and political commitment" ("Thinking the

Thirties," 7). This crisis was experienced by writers on both the Right and the Left, suffered by Evelyn Waugh as well as by Stephen Spender, by Céline as well as Esenin. In both England and France, however, the writing of the Left was associated with experimental, "highbrow" modes in which language itself became an instrument of political revolution: the avant-garde was seen as politically revolutionary.[5] The antibourgeois pose, however, was not the sole property of the Left. There were strongly anarchistic and nihilistic strains in the writing of Céline as well as Auden, Isherwood, and Spender, while Pound and Eliot used experimental literary methods to support reactionary political ideologies. Thus the literature of the Right often looked rather like the literature of the Left: Céline's *Voyage* was at first thought to be leftist and was translated into Russian by Elsa Triolet, and Céline was invited to the Soviet Union, where the novel sold well; Auden's *The Orators* was initially perceived as Fascist, and Auden later admitted that its implicit violence confused its political thrust. The writing of both the Left and Right, as Virginia Woolf quickly observed, was produced by and for men, and its political thrust turned attention to the very institutions from which writing derived (class structures, family structures, schools, universities, and religious institutions) as well as to the considerations of publishing and marketing such writing. That is, it drew the attention of a Virginia Woolf, for instance, who immediately focused her critique on the place of women and other marginal elements excluded from or oppressed by the very organizations that defined political ethics and shaped literary aesthetics.

Woolf recognized as well the mysogyny of Fascism, with its program to build physical strength and military might, just as she was able to recognize the mysogyny of the secret public-school myth of the Auden poets: "the whole iniquity of dictatorship, whether in Oxford or Cambridge, in Whitehall and Downing Street, against Jews or against women, in England, or in Germany, in Italy or in Spain is now apparent" (*Three Guineas*, 187). Woolf correctly interpreted woman's place under Fascism: continued servitude in a state that declared women to be physically, morally, and intellectually inferior to men.[6] Hitler came to power on a political program designed to make Germany strong again and soon after his election set about establishing Order Castles to train a Nazi elite composed of young men and women who not only embodied traditional male values of strength and courage, but demonstrated sadistic aggression and violence as the outward manifestation of those values:

The *weak must be chiselled away*. In my Order Castles young people will grow up who will *frighten the world*. I want a *violent, arrogant, unafraid, cruel youth who must be made to suffer pain. Nothing weak or tender must be left in them*. Their eyes must bespeak once again the free, magnificent beast of prey. I want my young people strong and beautiful. I shall train them in all kinds of athletics, for I want youth that are athletic—that is first and foremost. Thus will I erase *a thousand years of human domestication*. Thus will I face the pure and noble raw material. Thus I can create the new. I do not want an intellectual education. (Kedward, *Fascism in Western Europe*, 230; emphasis added)

Values traditionally associated with the feminine—generosity, sympathy, kindness, tenderness, domestication—were to be systematically eliminated from the national character in the creation of "magnificent beast[s] of prey"; freedom defined itself in terms of power and aggression, enforcing its aims through terror and uncivilized, cruel actions. Intellectual values were to be replaced by indoctrination and directed belief. In their reproductive capacities, women of course were necessary to Hitler's effort to develop a master race, but individual women were dispensable and exchangeable. As Woolf explained, women were made slaves to a ferocious masculinity embodied in the state: "Here, as so often, the example of the Fascist States is at hand to instruct us—for if we have no example of what we wish to be, we have, what is perhaps equally valuable, a daily and illuminating example of what we do not wish to be" (*Three Guineas*, 207).

Woolf saw in the Fascist state a more violent and indoctrinated form of the patriarchal dominance already at work in Western society, a force that associated the female with weakness in order to keep women (and other marginal elements) outside the societal power structure. As an alternative to the masculine values enforced by the Fascist state, Woolf proposed in *Three Guineas* that women establish themselves as a Society of Outsiders, defining the goals of freedom, equality, and peace in terms radically different from those established under state patronage. Natalie Barney had already tried to create such a society in Paris, but the fragile form of this group had been broken by the political and economic climate of the 1930s. By 1939, the women who had participated in the Académie des Femmes had been forced by the Nazi invasion to flee Paris, and it was at this moment—when Barney herself was forced to take refuge in Italy—that she began to write her "Memoirs of a European American," a recollection of her expatriate years that would occupy her for the duration of the war. Chapter 13 of this unpublished manuscript ("And the Women?") is concerned with women's responses to the two wars that framed the Paris expatriate experience. Barney saw women as the particular victims of war, as did her friend Marie Laurencin, who risked her life in order to stay on in Paris in autumn 1939 to finish a set of paintings: "What a crime to have brought this on us, and the people know it, especially the women: not one of them in the shelter I went down to from my sixth floor, ceased murmuring that this was not their's nor France's war . . . but that of a manoeuvered Government, too weak to resist" ("Memoirs of a European American," 14).

Barney agreed with Laurencin that France had been unfairly maneu-
vered into the war, but she also felt that war itself was a peculiarly masculine occupation, one that destroyed woman's work and values and need-
lessly wasted the lives born of women's bodies:

> Perhaps a reign of powerful women is necessary to make, or unmake when
> need be, powerful men. Women would not waste so readily and uselessly the
> lives they had such care and pains in bearing. Why should they submit to the
> massacre of the innocent, one generation after another (and, as now, twice in
> the same) and allow them to be brought up as live-stock for the inevitable
> killing? If the voices of women are hushed up like children's—they the coura-
> geous mothers of men—if they have no worthy representatives for their
> cause, if they cannot rule equally with men over the lives they created, should
> not the stronger in the instinct of race preservation prevail, and the Ma-
> triarchal again dominate the Patriarchal? If, through all these centuries of
> patriarchal rule, this war-curse has not been averted, but increased and made
> more terrible, is it indeed madness to hope that women might stop this mad-
> ness? (66–67)

Virginia Woolf might well have supported this aspect of Barney's argument (indeed, in *Three Guineas* she argued that the "one method by
which [women] can help to prevent war is to refuse to bear children,"
266), but she defined her feminism in opposition to everything that Fascism represented. During her residence in Italy in the war years, Natalie
Barney came to admire Fascism; in particular she thought Mussolini an
admirable leader and Maréchal Pétain, head of the occupation government in France, a hero. Unlike Woolf, Barney did not see in Fascism a
particularly virulent form of patriarchal thinking and practice; thus her
feminism coexisted with a deepening commitment to the Fascist cause—
a commitment underwritten by an intense anti-Semitism.

Anti-Semitism

Not since the days of the Dreyfus Affair had so much public attention
beeen brought to bear on the Jewish question. In autumn 1940, Virginia
Woolf waited out the inevitable German invasion, relieved that Leonard
need not yet wear the yellow Star of David. Gertrude Stein and Alice
Toklas were already in Bilignin: having resisted the directive of the American Consulate in Lyon that they return home, they chose to see the war
through with their country neighbors. Adrienne Monnier and Sylvia
Beach were providing food, clothes, and lodging for Jewish friends including Gisèle Freund, Walter Benjamin (whose escape from Germany
Bryher had arranged), Arthur Koestler, and Jewish women resistance
workers. Within a year Maurice Goudeket, Colette's Jewish husband, was
arrested by the Nazis and placed in an internment camp at Compiègne,

north of Paris; in August 1942, Sylvia Beach was arrested as an enemy alien and taken to a hotel that served as a women's internment camp at Vittel, in eastern France. She was released after six months, when her old friend, Jacques Benoist-Méchin, a man with powerful ties to the German government, intervened with the authorities on her behalf. Retrospectively, then, Adrienne Monnier's essay "On Anti-Semitism," written in 1938 for her *Gazettes,* eerily forecasts a future in which the Jewish question would not only raise moral and ethical problems, but would soon affect Monnier in very personal and painful ways:

> I have thought many times about the Jewish question these recent years.
> Since the beginning of German anti-Semitism I have been striving to under-
> stand and to see clearly. . . . I do not believe I had ever seriously thought
> about it before. The Dreyfus affair, which had taken place when I was a little
> girl, had not disturbed me. And still, at the time of the affair my parents were
> living at the Place-Saint-André-des-Arts and the students used to pass
> by under our windows crying "Spit upon Zola!" My grandfather, an anti-
> Dreyfusard, and my Dreyfusard father, used to wrangle at every meal; I used
> to see them rise up over the table, ready to throw themselves upon each
> other, and the women bustle about them in order to get them to sit down
> again. (*Very Rich Hours,* 373–374)

Monnier decried the "constant degradations imposed upon [Jews] . . . through stupid and sterile national pride" (378) and was hurt that the German people, whom she admired, had undertaken a national campaign to discredit Jews. It was primarily on the question of their treatment of Jews that Monnier opposed Fascist claims. It is ironic, then, that when Ernest Hemingway came into Paris on 26 August 1944 with the liberation troops, he questioned Adrienne about her political activities during the war: hadn't she "been brought to the point of collaborating a little?" If she had, Hemingway was offering to draw her out of all possible danger. Adrienne of course had not collaborated, but Hemingway's questions forced her to examine her conscience. Sylvia, however, replied that if Adrienne had collaborated, "it was with us, the Americans" (*Very Rich Hours,* 417).

Natalie Barney did not collaborate with the Germans or Italians, but she acknowledged "no end of troubled, anguished and conflicting states of mind, which future states of mind will be surprised to recognize" ("Memoirs of a European American," iv). Some have been surprised to learn that Barney, known in Paris for her pacifist thinking, became a reactionary during the Second World War: confident in Mussolini, she derided British and American policy and enthusiastically supported Pound's radio broadcasts. Passing Rapallo on her way to Florence with Romaine Brooks in autumn 1939, Barney stopped to see Pound, giving him the radio they had brought with them from 20, rue Jacob—the first radio

Pound ever had ("Memoirs of a European American," 9). Listening to Pound's broadcasts on a radio belonging to their Italian neighbors, Barney commented that "he spoke more and more in a savoury idiom of his own and the force and frankness which he sent through won over or stung even the most smug and obdurate" (82). In earlier years, Natalie Barney had boasted of her Jewishness (she was one-quarter Jewish through the Pike family on her mother's side), but in her later years, guided primarily by Pound's writings on usury, she became anti-Semitic. In "Memoirs of a European American" Barney analyzed the effects of money-lending practices of Jews on the German state, arguing that the Star of David should be proudly displayed as a symbol of the Jew's profession (usury), a warning to Gentiles who might consider trade with such people:

> The trade of usury has proved the most lucrative and far reaching: practised openly in well-defined quarters, it was long tolerated and even found useful. But since these usurers have dissimulated themselves, that they might more easily mix with and "fix" the Gentiles, they very much resent having their manoeuvres divulged, as recently distinguished by the obligatory wearing of a yellow star. Yet other nations and trades are proud of their insignia. Should they not rather imitate that German Jewess who had her star made up of yellow diamonds and wore it as proudly as the German his swastika? (144–145)

Acknowledging that Jews "first commercialized the world," Barney believed that they "then set their wits to running it into wars that they might secure greater profits and get it all into their hands at a bargain as damaged goods" (144). Specifically, she saw Jewish greed as the cause of World War II, a war that merely extended a previous, essentially commercial, conflict: "Why all this mystery about financing the second act of this continous war? Are not its bankers secured against loss either by the victory of the Allies or assured of revenge by getting their money's worth of Aryan flesh?" (145). She blamed the present troubles on "the children of Israel" and proclaimed the necessity of "being rid of them and of our mutual bondage" (146), suggesting that America, in "welcoming a super-abundance of Jewish emigrants, profiled on her horizon" (142), had enchained itself to moneylenders who would deplete the country's riches. For Barney, as for Monnier, the immediate concern with the Jewish question recalled the Dreyfus case, in which Barney's sympathies were again with the state: "I wondered still more that so mediocre a little person could stir up an 'affaire d'Etat' and be allowed, however innocent, to damage the prestige of the French army" (170). As France moved closer to war in the late 1930s, however, Barney's allegiance to the state diminished. She thought the country weakened and corrupt; she agreed with Céline that the combination of Léon Blum's Socialist politics and his Jewish intellectualism had nearly destroyed France. She thought Fascism both acceptable and inevitable. Undecided about whether to stay on in Paris in September 1939 or to return to America as she was officially urged to do by the American Embassy and unofficially by friends, Barney said to a Paris neighbor: "I should hate to stay and witness your mistake and possible defeat" ("Memoirs of a European American," 1).

Barney's shocking views in these years would seem not only to undermine the pronounced liberal attitudes of her youth but also to cast doubt on the extent to which she fully understood the feminism she proclaimed. Hitler's theories of Aryan superiority were designed to produce a state defined by and for men who could prove themselves "pure Aryans," and the political charisma of both Hitler and Mussolini derived from a combination of male vanity and egotism especially repugnant to Barney. She continued to make a separate case for woman's situation in society, however, separating feminism from larger political and economic issues that bound women to the fate of other minorities and marginal groups (Jews, blacks, and foreigners). Only toward the end of the war, when the defeat of the Fascists was clearly forecast, would she wonder whether "the long-deferred vote now granted to French and Italian women" was given "only that they might be privileged to share the blame . . . an avowal of the failure the men have made of it all?" (337). The implication of such a comment is not at all clear, since Barney may have considered the defeat of Fascism itself to be the failure, in which case she may have been suggesting that Italian men should have secured Fascism for Italy and the French should have better served Pétain.

An Altered Perspective: Natalie Barney's Views on War

Certainly Barney found Fascism attractive and felt no sympathy with the Allies; in particular, she hated de Gaulle, was suspicious of the Free French, and thought the resistance (both in France and in Italy) Communist-inspired and politically subversive. Indeed, she praised Mussolini and Hitler for bringing Europe at last into the twentieth century, while preserving its individual customs and cultural heritage: "That Fascism and Nazism, while modernizing [Europe's] structures and improving the welfare of its populations, tried to safeguard all its traditional and local colours—and whether their joint efforts actually succeed or not—will remain to their everlasting honour" (213–213 *bis*).

Reconciling herself to the failure of Fascism, Barney nonetheless regretted its losses: "If theirs be the losing side, it must nevertheless clearly appear how right were their wrongs and how wrong the rights of their opponents" (213 *bis*). Barney's greatest fear was European Communism. After the liberation, she reported an overheard conversation: "However hard our times may be, surely anything is better than Fascism!" Barney's response was revealing: "Yet some are beginning to regret it. . . . for nothing else is likely to ensure us against Bolshevism" (315). Like many others, Barney believed that Europe was caught between the Fascists and Communists. In particular, she had been influenced by French thinking, which tended to polarize political tensions toward the extremes of Left and Right. H. R. Kedward comments that "this simplification had one significant result: those who were passionately anti-Communist were drawn irresistibly into the Fascist camp as if there were no alternative, and the same pull operated in the other direction" (*Fascism in Western Europe,* 74). Frightened by the Communist threat, convinced that Pound's economic theories were accurate and his anti-Semitism justified, Barney took sanctuary in a Fascist stronghold.

Living in a villa outside Florence during World War II, Barney and Romaine Brooks dug a trench in their garden so that they could lie in the sun on *chaises longues,* safely out of view of overhead aircraft. In World War I, they had the doubtful honor of being "the only two American women resident in Paris who did not drive an ambulance" (Chalon, *Portrait of a Seductress,* 122). In 1917, however, Natalie Barney had assembled at her Temple à l'Amitié women committed to pacifism. In her memoirs, she recounted that this endeavor included "the women of all countries, classes and professions"; she brought together a group comprised of Lucie Delarue-Mardrus, Rachilde, Madame Lara ("who abandoned her leading parts at the Comédie Française to start an emancipated career as the founder of 'Art and Action'"), the Duchesse de Clermont-Tonnerre, the Baroness of Brimont ("a descendent of Lamartine and a poet in her own right"), who brought to the meetings "a gentle, white-haired little woman who turned out to be Mrs. Pankhurst" and her daughter, Christabel ("Memoirs of a European American," 71). Barney admitted that she was "possessed of few convictions" and that this early endeavor was an attempt to "pick some up while listening attentively," but that it was the "first and last time" her literary salon "took on the colours of political inquiry" (72). On the whole, Barney was not persuaded by what she heard; she was only "momentarily impressed by those who professed" the convictions she herself desired to hold (71). She prided herself on never having "assumed any responsibilities nor duties, even conjugal," and considered herself "a free agent, having espoused neither state nor man" (79).

But during World War I, Barney's attitudes toward woman's relation to war had become firmly fixed: man found it necessary to wage battle—it was his temptation and his instinct; woman silently, courageously, with a certain fixity and without honor, was forced to see the living bodies she had created lying dead or wounded on the fields of battle. In *Pensées*

d'une amazone, Barney juxtaposed the vocabulary of combat ("mobilization," "requisition") with the official language of military strategy and di-
plomacy, allowing each to undercut the other. Dividing the page into two
columns, Barney contrasted government-sanctioned explanations and
newspaper reports:

"respected his neutrality"	"killed by an exploded shell in the femur"
"the new Pope disapproves as	"we progress on all fronts"
well of the tango"	(44, 46)

The romanticized patriarchal values that underwrote the First World
War—duty, honor, sacrifice, courage, glory—were supported by educational and religious attitudes that a woman like Natalie Barney could not
share. (Across the Channel, Virginia Woolf was later to wonder whether
England's daughters had the same reasons for loving, defending, and
being proud of England as did her sons, *Three Guineas,* 18.) Like Woolf,
Barney did not think it "sweet and fitting" *pro patria mori;* rather, she
thought it silly—even stupid. Barney did not need Eliot's *Waste Land* to
recount the effects of war, and she exempted herself—and all women—
from the pervasive guilt and remorse that characterized postwar male attitudes. The Great War did not shape her literary imagination. She coun-
teracted its images of violent death, its smell of rotting corpses, and the
feel of cold rain and slimy mud with alternative literary figures: the celebration of living things, the smell of flowers and sweet perfumes, the sight
of blue skies, green grass, and flowing rivers. In *Nouvelles pensées de
l'amazone,* Barney commented: "Women's frivolity, my own included,
disappoints me; but before the cataclysms necessitated by the seriousness
of men, I raise my head."

Faced with the inevitability of the Second World War, Barney quickly
perceived a certain unwillingness on the part of women to dedicate themselves to another war effort: "If women are not heart and soul, as well as
bodily, in this war, as they were in the former one, why don't they speak
up, instead of letting it be forced upon them? Why all this difficulty in
recruiting, which makes one doubt that they take willingly to anything
but home, or relief, or Red Cross work, or ambulance driving, in which
they distinguished themselves before? Why do the English women in particular, and in spite of their hard-gained rights, seem to have so little to
say in the matter?" ("Memoirs of a European American," 66). Barney
recognized war as a man's game—a *jeu de massacre.* Although women's
opinions were rarely solicited in the decision to make war, women's services were always needed to repair the effects of war. If English women,
for instance, thought that their valor in World War I and their success in
gaining the vote had earned them a place in the national decision-making
process, had allowed them a voice on questions of war and peace, it was

clear by 1939 that their enfranchisement was symbolic rather than functional: they succeeded, according to Virginia Woolf, in becoming *step-daughters* rather than daughters of the state (*Three Guineas,* 28). Laying the effects of violence at man's doorstep, Woolf commented in *Three Guineas* that "scarcely a human being in the course of history has fallen to a woman's rifle; the vast majority of birds and beasts have been killed by you, not by us" (13–14). Like Barney, Woolf admitted to incomprehension at man's desire—his basic need—to wage war and to kill: "Obviously there is for you some glory, some necessity, some satisfaction in fighting which we have never felt or enjoyed" (14).

War Correspondence: Nancy Cunard and the Spanish Civil War

The response of women writers to the increasingly politicized events of the 1930s suggests the significantly different ways men and women experienced this decade. For some women journalists—in particular Janet Flanner and Nancy Cunard—the events of this period provided the first real opportunity to write political analysis, to reveal their political interests and documentary skills to a reading public. Flanner's Letters from Paris not only documented events but educated an American readership to the complexities of the European situation. Unlike Virginia Woolf, however, Flanner could not openly argue her own political views. The effort required to maintain a neutral pose was particularly difficult in a period marked by extremist views, and Flanner's personal perceptions were often more sharply focused, more direct and exact, than her published opinions. To no small degree, Flanner was constrained by the editorial policy of the *New Yorker,* which avoided extremist thought. Nancy Cunard, who freelanced for various papers and journals, had far greater freedom in the expression of her political attitudes than did Flanner, whose long-standing commitment to the *New Yorker* both guaranteed an enthusiastic and dedicated reading audience and limited the ways in which she could address that readership. With the onset of the Spanish Civil War, however, Flanner's letters begin to demonstrate a noticeably less guarded and more politically committed tone. This conflict forced her, like other liberals (including those who made up the readership of the *New Yorker*), to more open support of the Communist-supported Republicans. For Nancy Cunard, the Spanish Civil War constituted a call to action and the major political and personal defeat in her life.

Cunard's early association with Aragon and the Surrealists had brought her into contact with writers who conceived of literary forms in relation to political ideology. Inevitably, the Surrealist group suffered dissension and internal division over political commitments (they were particularly obsessed with the problem of Communist doctrine in relation to literary revolution), and Cunard observed the ruptures and realignments with quiet interest. From the moment in 1932 when she began research on *Negro*, however, she turned away from literary concerns to active involvement in political causes. Never one to join organizations or to express conventional political attitudes on any subject, Cunard subscribed to no doctrinaire ideology. According to her close friend Solita Solano, Cunard's activism was more frequently motivated by the need to express anger against all forms of tyranny: "All the activities of her earliest causes—the right of a brilliant-minded child to study in her own way (three governesses whacked her on the knuckles), the injustices of governments toward the individual, the discrimination against races, servants overworked and underpaid—all such activities were set into devastating motion by a word, a look, a memory" ("Nancy Cunard," 77). Cunard described herself as an "anarchist"; that is, she claimed to subscribe to no political program. In fact, many who knew her thought her to be a Communist, a charge she vehemently denied. Friends claimed she knew nothing of Marxism, and the more politically sophisticated of her associates described her politics as personally rather than ideologically motivated. A rebellious aristocrat, Cunard would never have found a place among orthodox Communists; instead, she was part of an essentially nonprogrammed Left and was one of many in Europe in these years who sympathized with the resistance against forms of political tyranny but who held membership in no established political organization.

Cunard began her work as a journalist at the outbreak of the Ethiopian war, reporting at first for the Associated Negro Press at the League of Nations. During the Spanish Civil War she wrote for various British publications, including the *Manchester Guardian*, the most prestigious of the pro-Republican English newspapers, and practiced a form of activist journalism more common today than in the 1930s. Rather than providing a neutral reportage of events, her descriptions of suffering peoples constituted the basis of appeals for financial and political support for the victims of Fascist aggression. The *Guardian* welcomed her descriptions of the Spanish situation, was pleased with her work, printed everything she wrote, and thought her articles "admirable" (Chisholm, *Nancy Cunard*, 334). In addition to writing on behalf of the Republican cause, Cunard also took an active part in relief work, serving in the concentration camps along the French border, and organized efforts to raise monies to buy food and clothing for the war victims. In the last months of the war, she raised funds for relief of war victims through a series of appeals printed in British newspapers:

> This is an appeal to all those who realise the magnitude of the tragedy of Catalonia, to all those compassionate and generous readers of the *Manches-*

ter Guardian who may want to help alleviate the indescribable suffering of scores of thousands of refugees pouring in during the last week. To give you an idea of the number (the figures I have just verified at the Prefecture of Police here), 55,000 have come in and have been sent in from Perpignan to date. This does not include all those still in this region—10,000, 20,000? No one knows. And of those to come still less can be foretold. ("The Refugees at Perpignan," in Ford, *Nancy Cunard*, 196)

Writing from the headquarters of the Centro Espagnol, Cunard was seeking funds to assist this "entirely non-political and non-party" organization in providing food, clothing, and medical assistance to the starving refugees. Cunard traveled with the food lorries of the Centro Espagnol, an eyewitness to bombing attacks that killed women and children as they tried to escape Spain, exposed to the same dangers and living conditions as were the escaping refugees whose plight she was documenting. On 28 January 1939, when the French opened the border to allow civilian refugees to cross into France, both Nancy Cunard and Janet Flanner observed the exodus. Flanner wrote a long documentary for the *New Yorker*, describing for an American readership removed from the realities of the war the unspeakable conditions in Catalonia. On 30 January, Cunard wired her newspaper: "Beseech you open fund immediately in Guardian for possibly as much as half a million starving Spanish refugees pouring in stop situation catastrophic." The *Guardian* opened the fund, raising monies and collecting relief supplies (Chisholm, *Nancy Cunard*, 332). The conditions in the camps were so appalling, however, that the international press was asked to restrain its reporting and to avoid descriptions of the more harrowing situations. Cunard herself personally arranged for the release of five men from the camps. These men accompanied her to Réanville, where she wrote, under the pseudonym Ray Holt, an unpublished account of her efforts on their behalf (*Nancy Cunard*, 336).

Long after the Civil War had ended in defeat for the Loyalists, Spain excited Cunard's imagination and shaped her poetry. Her commitment to the Loyalist cause had been deeply emotional and led eventually to a severe mental breakdown following World War II; her interest in the internal politics of the Loyalist government, however, was absolutely minimal. Anne Chisholm reports that Cunard's initial visit to Spain left her with two unshakable convictions: "First, that the republican side was the side of the people, freedom and revolution, and that to question or criticize it was intolerable. . . . Second, she felt all 'intellectuals' everywhere were the natural allies of the republican side and that they had a duty to arouse the conscience of the world on its behalf" (*Nancy Cunard*, 314). Cunard marshaled the intellectual and literary communities of Paris and London to open support of the Republican cause. In spring 1937, she reassembled the hand press at Réanville to print a series of six pamphlets of war-inspired poems. Entitled "Poets of the World Defend the Spanish People," each pamphlet contained several poems—in English, French, and Spanish—and was sold to raise monies for the Spanish cause. Contributors included Tristan Tzara, Louis Aragon, Langston Hughes, Brian Howard, Pablo Neruda, and García Lorca. In this same spring she met W. H. Auden, whose poem "Spain" became the most famous and influential poem in the series. The poem was criticized by orthodox Communist critics as a too personal, private, and highly psychological response to the war. Auden wrote the poem after a brief visit to Spain with a medical team in winter 1937. Rather than confirming Auden's commitment to the Left, the visit to Spain actually undermined his leftist political stance while simultaneously reawakening in him a religious interest that had apparently been dormant for almost sixteen years. Although the poem does not make specific use of the tensions between the political and the religious (Auden may not have been able to articulate these tensions so soon after the visit), "Spain" does pose the dilemma of the Spanish Civil War specifically for poets. Auden was later to renounce the poem.

Whereas for Cunard and many other writers of the thirties the Spanish Civil War provided a specific cause for their leftist and liberal politics, for Auden the Civil War unraveled and undermined his political enthusiasm. Samuel Hynes suggests that while Auden's poem represents "the best of the English war-poems from Spain . . . it is also the least partisan, the least passionate, the least concerned about the actual war, and the least Spanish": "The war in Spain is indeed not so much the subject of the poem as the occasion [for it]. . . . it extends our knowledge of the crucial moral choice of the 'thirties—the choice between fascism and its opponent—by examining that choice as it was manifested in Spain in 1937. But it does not *make* the choice: its subject is moral decision, not political action" (*Auden Generation*, 252). Although for Cunard moral decision and political action were one and the same, she had no objections to Auden's poem: she found it aesthetically beautiful and was proud to have published it. Auden felt increasing discomfort with the poem, especially as it appeared in the red-covered Faber and Faber edition published in May 1937. As the violence of the war increased, as Europe moved closer to the world war for which the Spanish conflict served as a preview, the rhetoric of Auden's poetry became subdued, almost passive, even apolitical.

As Auden's political commitment lessened, Cunard's strengthened. While setting the type for the series of poems, she decided to print a broadside to be entitled *Authors Take Sides on the Spanish War*. Typeset on the Réanville press, the broadside was printed in red and black, its bold letters demanding that writers abandon "the equivocal attitude, the Ivory Tower, the paradoxical, the ironic detachment" and take sides on the Spanish question: "Are you for, or against, the legal government and the People of Republican Spain? Are you for, or against, Franco and Fascism? For it is impossible any longer to take no side."

The initial broadside appended a dozen signatures, including those of W. H. Auden, Louis Aragon, Brian Howard, Pablo Neruda, Stephen Spender, Tristan Tzara, and Cunard's own. Almost immediately after printing the broadside, Cunard decided to expand the scope of the project, and she prepared at Réanville a questionnaire distributed to about 200 writers in Europe. Cunard then edited the responses and had the questionnaire printed in Paris. Of the 148 answers eventually tabulated, 126 supported the Republic; 5 (including Edmund Blunden and Evelyn Waugh) supported Franco; 16 (including Aldous Huxley, T. S. Eliot, Ezra Pound, H. G. Wells, and Vita Sackville-West) were neutral.[7] Auden signed in favor of the Republican government, but in the letter accompanying his answer expressed doubts about her undertaking: "I have my doubts as to the value of such pronouncements, but here mine is for what it's worth" (quoted in Chisholm, *Nancy Cunard,* 318). The questionnaire was published in November 1937 (after Nancy was back in Spain) by the *Left Review* in London. The pink slip around the cover proclaimed that the document was "causing a sensation," and in fact it sold so well that Nancy had trouble procuring copies for herself. As Chisholm has remarked, however, Nancy Cunard has often not been given credit for preparing the questionnaire and editing the responses (Samuel Hynes and Peter Ackroyd, among others, do not list her as the editor).

Cunard's activist political and literary stance of the 1930s continued during the Second World War. A strongly outspoken anti-Fascist, she wanted to work with the French resistance, but by chance was in England at the time of the Nazi invasion. From London she began work with the Free French, serving as journalist and translator. Six months after France was liberated, Cunard returned to Paris, and immediately began writing her impressions of the effects of occupation on the country, the longest and most important of these articles being published in *Horizon* in June 1945. In the first months after her return, however, she had a difficult time reestablishing the pattern of her life, and over the next years she traveled extensively, finding it impossible to "settle down." As Herman Schrijver describes her in these years, Nancy always desired "to be where she was *not*. This passion—always to be in some very strange and distant land where one is not—is indeed wishing for the moon, or what the French call 'lunatique'" ("About Nancy," 268). In particular, she desired to return to Spain and made several trips there in the years following the war until, after difficulties with a pro-Franco official who refused to renew her transit visa, she was expelled. She drank heavily, ate little, smoked constantly, and her health suffered a rapid decline. The war still dominated her thoughts, and friends discovered that she had developed an obsession about Fascism, reading its effects in every form of French and Spanish life. After several years of an unstable existence punctuated by arrests, drunkenness, and severe illness, a cousin declared her insane, and she was hospitalized for what was described as a "persecution mania." According to Chisholm, Cunard's "tendency to paranoia swelled to insanity. Anyone who tried to calm or restrain her became a fascist spy, especially if they were in uniform" (*Nancy Cunard,* 408).

The resistance to order and authority that had always been a part of her character, and a central element of her political behavior, had taken control of her personality. The world had become a Fascist state whose persecutions continued even after the war had been won. John Banting, a close friend, recalls that in her last years, Nancy's only subject of conversation was the war: ". . . from angles which surprised me she seemed almost to glorify 'LaGloire' and to regard it as a genuine anti-Fascist war, so that we had some bad arguments about its aims and results. . . . It seemed to me that with her official reportage some of the 'Establishment' had infected her outlook. She had not become a 'Reactionary' or a jingoist but some of her outlook had undergone a change for the conventional, which I found unlike her with her courage and questioning revaluation of outworn and cancerous symbols" ("Nancy Cunard, 185). An aspect of Nancy's instability in these years was her insistent involvement of her friends in public scenes with the police, government officials, the press, even taxi drivers and waiters. She found it impossible to be alone and sought public places (train station lounges, cafes, parks, hotel bars) to relieve the intense pain of her existence. Her friends—especially Janet Flanner and Solita Solano—remained intensely loyal to her despite the difficult situations she created for them. They indulged her need for all-night conversation and communal reminiscences of their contributions to the war effort and sheltered and fed her when she made Paris the crossroads of a transient existence. Years of poverty, stress, overwork, unstable living conditions, and personal disappointment had destroyed Nancy Cunard's physical and mental health. When she died in the Hôpital Cochin in Paris, she was on her way to visit Janet Flanner. Weighing no more than sixty pounds, raving incoherently, and unable to walk, she was eventually turned over to the police, who had her placed in the hospital, where she demanded red wine and writing materials in order to continue working on "a long poem against all wars" (Chisholm, *Nancy Cunard,* 440). In her last hours she wrote letters recalling her life in France and Spain in the 1930s to all of her friends, letters that were delivered in the days following her death on 16 March 1965. Indeed, the commitment to humanitarian ideals her life encompassed was exceptional: no other writer of the ex-patriate group—male or female—responded as fully and as creatively as she did to the war against Fascism.

For Djuna Barnes, as for Nancy Cunard, the thirties marked a turning point in her emotional and creative life. Both women left Paris during these years to lead an essentially transient life marked by financial insecu-rity; neither of them had a "home" as such during the latter half of the decade. Each woman suffered the effects of a painful separation from a lover (Barnes separated from Thelma Wood and Cunard from Henry Crowder), and both felt that the intellectual and cultural life Paris offered in the twenties had been destroyed by terrifying forms of political and social change. In addition, the two women already displayed the symp-toms of physical illness and emotional instability that would mark the later years of their lives. While Cunard found the energy to fight the rising tide of totalitarianism and adopted experimental literary forms to politi-cal causes, Barnes retreated to an absolutely private literary world.

Barnes was not alone among women writers of this period in choosing privacy over public activism. Jean Rhys too continued writing the same kinds of self-absorbed experimental fictions she had composed in the early twenties, while Anaïs Nin began to explore the female psyche, focusing on interior and intensely private worlds that defined themselves in opposition to external realities. The living and writing patterns of Barnes, Rhys, and Nin reveal complex reactions *against* the call to social and political involvement in the period. In a political climate that de-manded social relevance in literature, these women writers experienced difficulties in finding a reading public because their fictions seemed to ex-ploit an entirely private, even secret, female experience. Rather than denying external reality, however, their fictions may be seen retro-spectively to rewrite it. Such works as Barnes's *Nightwood,* Nin's *House of Incest,* and Rhys's *Good Morning, Midnight* render the sense of im-pending catastrophe in terms of a forbidding urban landscape to be nego-tiated by female characters. A city of dreadful night, Paris no longer wel-comes and protects woman, but rather enforces her vulnerability against its inexplicable and threatening powers.

Nightwood

Djuna Barnes's *Nightwood,* for instance, is set in Paris in the twenties; written in the thirties, it concerns society's outsiders—Jews, homosexu-als, the mentally and physically weak—those whom Hitler would define as the *Untermenschen. Nightwood* records their sufferings and foreshad-ows their ultimate destruction, the spectre of Fascism casting a long shadow over its landscape. The novel opens in Vienna in 1880 at the birth of Felix Volkbein, son of Guido Volkbein—a Jew of Italian descent, "a gourmet and a dandy" (1)—who died six months before his son's birth. Felix's Viennese mother, Hedvig—a "woman of great strength and military beauty" (1)—dies moments after the child's birth, unaware that her son is a Jew or that she has perpetuated the "race which has the sanction of the Lord and the disapproval of the people" (1). Born outside the Austrian power structure under which he lived, Guido invented a noble lineage for himself ("producing, to uphold his story, the most amazing and inaccurate proofs: a coat of arms that he had no right to and a list of progenitors . . . who had never existed," 3), converted to Christianity, announced himself a baron of an old, "almost extinct" Austrian family, and through clever financial maneuvers amassed the necessary capital to buy his wife a house overlooking the Prater. Conscious of some underlying anxiety in Guido's demeanor, Hedvig had nevertheless "become a Baroness without question" (5).

Hedvig and Guido symbolize the power of the Austrian state and the vulnerability of the Jew within its circumference, and the ominous foreshadowings of Nazi militarism and aggression are apparent in even the slightest details of their characterization. Obsessed by the need to "pass" as a Gentile, Guido is nonetheless haunted by racial memory. Walking in the Prater, he tries to imitate his wife's "goose-step of a stride" (3) but carries in his "conspicuously clenched fist" (2) a yellow and black linen handkerchief in remembrance of the Medici ordinance of 1468 that marked Jews for death. While his wife's movements are masculine (she plays the piano "with the masterly stroke of a man," 5) and her bearing that of a military officer, Guido is marked by a feminized sensibility, often trembling in fear in the presence of his wife. Like his father, Felix feels himself an outcast and becomes obsessed by the traditions of Old Europe symbolized by the aristocracy, nobility, and royalty. Having "hunted down his own disqualification" among the great families of Europe (9), however, he is forced to settle for the degraded versions of aristocratic pomp and pageantry available in the circus and theater.

In the circus and theater world of Berlin in the 1920s, Felix discovers misfits and monstrosities, beings "surviving in an alien element" (13). In their "sham salons" he shares in a "splendid and reeking falsification" (11), this world of artifice providing an inverted image of the larger society on whose margins Felix tries to insinuate himself. In this setting he meets Nora Flood, a publicity agent for the circus; Matthew O'Connor, a "gynecologist" with uncertain medical credentials; Robin Vote, the "somnambule . . . who lives in two worlds—meet of child and desperado" (35), the woman by whom Felix fathers a "mentally deficient and emotionally excessive" child, described as "an addict to death" (107). It is precisely such "outsiders" as these who will become Hitler's *Unter-*

menschen, those who will be eliminated in the production of his master race. Under Hitler, it will become necessary to establish blood lines and to trace patrilineage to remote Aryan ancestors, to eliminate all forms of mental and physical weakness, to purge society of homosexuals, transvestites, and sexual perverts.

The inhabitants of Barnes's "nightwood," those forced to live outside society's boundaries in hiding from the daylight world, will be the first hunted down in the night by Hitler's Gestapo, itself a sham authority invented by the son of a minor customs official in Austria, a man who rose only to the rank of corporal in the kaiser's army, who did not have the requisite Aryan blond hair and blue eyes, who had little formal education and no social prestige.[8] H. R. Kedward comments that in the 1920s Hitler "was seen by most conservative nationalists as a vulgar street orator" (*Fascism in Western Europe,* 52); indeed, he seemed a parodic version of the very ideals and values he espoused. Seen through the eyes of the aristocratic Ernst Hanfstaengel, Hitler seems almost a character from Barnes's fiction: "Hitler lived a shadowy existence and it was very difficult to keep track of his movements. He had the Bohemian habits of a man who had grown up with no real roots. He was hopelessly unpunctual and incapable of keeping to any sort of schedule. He walked around leading a fierce alsatian named Wolf and always carried a whip with a loaded handle" (*Hitler: The Missing Years,* 44). Fearing the deracinated in himself, Hitler— like Guido Volkbein—was able to detect in others the condition of estrangement he knew well, the condition that marks each of the characters in *Nightwood.* The inhabitants of the night world instinctively recognize their compatriots; like trained dogs, they smell out perversion and expose the blood lines debilitated by inbreeding. To the larger world these misfits are frightening reminders of biological and psychological miscalculation. They serve as society's scapegoats, carrying the burdens of guilt and suffering the larger community refuses to acknowledge and cannot bear to look upon.

Recognizing the alien in himself, Matthew O'Connor diagnoses the societal illness that has produced such aliens: he is able to articulate the very argument that Hitler will later make in justifying the mass murder of those who do not fit his narrow definition of racial and social perfection. When Nora Flood does not understand the premises on which his argument is based, O'Connor asks her to consider "those who turn the day into night": ". . . the young, the drug addict, the profligate, the drunken and that most miserable, the lover who watches all night long in fear and anguish. These can never again live the life of the day. When one meets them at high noon they give off, as it were a protective emanation, something dark and muted. The light does not become them any longer. They begin to have an unrecorded look. It is as if they were being tried by the continual blows of an unseen adversary" (94). Unable to find a job in pre-war Vienna, Hitler moved among immigrants and transients, wandered the streets at night, and slept in doss-houses among vagrants and outcasts whom he hated. Recognizing in such people elements of his own frustrated and failed self, Hitler's paranoia was fed by the fear—well articulated by Matthew O'Connor—that these misfits might recognize him as one of their kind rather than as the superior person he considered himself to be. Later, as leader of a regime that made anti-Semitism the cornerstone of its economic and political program, Hitler tried to conquer his fears of social and psychological estrangement through organized purges of Jews and other marginal elements of society.

Nightwood provides a catalogue of Hitler's intended victims and an analysis of the secret fears such outcasts instill in the larger culture. The night, which has traditionally offered refuge to the displaced and outcast, serves in Barnes's novel to mark the inversion and disruption of the daylight order. The "nightwood" is not separate from that "daylight order," however: it is the creation of it. The nightwood serves as a frightening symbol of the irrational and bestial in which civilization's corruption works its effects. Nature's laws are inverted in this secret wilderness enclosed by the urban community: here, the weak dominate the strong. In such an environment Robin Vote's "primitive innocence" is considered "depraved" (117) and Guido, the child "born to holy decay" (107), is defined as "maladjusted" (116). As Felix explains to Matthew O'Connor, Guido is a sensitive, even precocious, child: ". . . he is not like other children, not cruel, or savage. For this very reason he is called 'strange.' A child who is mature, in the sense that the heart is mature, is always, I have observed, called deficient" (115). A child of the nightwood, Guido is doomed, as are all the animals that populate this medieval bestiary: they do not find sanctuary in this secret place but discover in its "shadow . . . a vast apprehension . . . toward which life and death are spinning" (117). Originally titled *Bow Down* and subtitled *anatomy of night,* Barnes's novel foreshadows the subjection of humankind to corrupt forces whose powers remain inexplicable and absolute.

Nightwood examines the underside of urban European life between the wars, drawing subtle parallels between Vienna in the 1880s and Paris in the 1920s, revealing psychic disturbances, unaccountable yearnings and fears, and a pervasive restlessness. Because the novel did not explicitly address the social and political issues of the period, however, its concerns were considered outdated and self-indulgent. The paralyzed international economy and political upheavals of the decade rendered irrelevant an experimental fiction whose subject was thought to be the social and sexual deviancy of the Paris postwar years. When Barnes returned to New York with the manuscript in 1934, America was still in the depths of the Great

Depression, and the search for a publisher was an exhausting and discouraging one. As Andrew Field has noted, the manuscript "did not even suffer the usual agonizing delays but shot in and out of the publishers' offices as though it were being ejected from a greased revolving door in an old silent movie" (*Djuna*, 207). The manuscript was also passed from one hand to another as Barnes's friends (including Dylan Thomas) read it enthusiastically and themselves tried to find a publisher sympathetic to its subject matter. In 1935, Edwin Muir convinced T. S. Eliot, then a senior editor at Faber and Faber, to put aside his reservations and print the novel. The novel was published in 1936 after Eliot had reduced its bulk by more than two-thirds, eliminating—among other things—scenes that expressed explicit lesbian rage and virulent anticlerical sentiment.[9] Worried that the book would sell poorly in England and receive negative reviews there, Eliot insisted that Barnes be paid no advance and that Faber retain American rights to offset the loss of sales in England. In fact, the English publication received excellent reviews, including a laudatory notice by Graham Greene, who praised its effort to trace a spiritual experience.

The 1937 American publication, however, was ignored. With the exception of Clifton Fadiman in the *New Yorker,* those reviewers who commented on it did so to denigrate it. The novel was thought by some reviewers to be incomprehensible and by others, like Philip Rahv (*New Masses,* 4 May 1937), to be elitist and limited to "those minute shudders of decadence developed in certain small ingrown cliques of intellectuals and their patrons, cliques in which the reciprocal workings of social decay and sexual perversion have destroyed all response to genuine values and actual things" (Field, *Djuna*, 215). Rahv did not see the larger implications of the spiritual malaise and social injustice treated in Barnes's novel, nor did he accurately locate the source of "social decay and sexual perversion" in the myth of "genuine values." Indeed, his commentary suggests that he held sacred the very "genuine values" that Barnes's novel dissected. Such misreadings of the novel in America undermined its potential as an "artistic keystone" of the period, as Field has explained:

> While its story and its spiritual crisis are both highly personal and particular, the portrait of a world in intensely still crisis and on the verge of disintegration corresponds remarkably well to the social and political age in which it was written. If one understands the spirit of the Thirties at all, it is quite clear that, in spite of its arch language and manner (which can also be seen to a lesser extent in many other works of art of the period), *Nightwood* does not speak only to the question of lesbianism or the private life of Djuna Barnes but also to its time. The Elizabethan passion is there, and so is the mood of a time when Bakelite radios first said terrible things to the world. The sudden appeal of Catholicism to many writers and intellectuals of the period is also

there. This contextual atmosphere of *Nightwood* has not been sufficiently noticed. (*Djuna*, 214)

The negative response to *Nightwood* did not at all surprise Djuna Barnes, who had never thought it possible that such a work could have commercial success. After its publication in England, Eliot tried to persuade Barnes quickly to write a follow-up book (he wanted her to do a study of the late Baroness Freytag-Loringhoven, an idea that she rejected). Instead, her return to England brought on psychological illness and bouts of alcoholism resembling those described in *Nightwood*. Suffering acute depression and the fear that she was unloved and had no future, she haunted London pubs, telling the story of her life to anyone who would listen. Like Nancy Cunard, Barnes sought relief from private fears in public places; also like Cunard, she was often quarrelsome and violent, considered insane by the staff in a nursing home where she had been sent to recover from her physical illnesses (*Djuna*, 211). Djuna Barnes was in Paris at the beginning of the Second World War in 1939, living in a nursing home where she was recuperating from the effects of a second nervous breakdown. Emily Coleman found her and convinced Peggy Guggenheim to provide the return fare to America. Although she was not yet 50 years old, Barnes's health was so damaged that her Paris friends feared she might not survive the journey to New York.

House of Incest

In this same month, Anaïs Nin left Paris to return to New York City. A great admirer of Djuna Barnes, Nin had written to her after reading *Nightwood:* "I have to tell you of the great, deep beauty of your *Nightwood*. . . . A woman rarely writes as a woman, as she feels, but you have" (Knapp, *Anaïs Nin*, 10). In the weeks before the war in Europe began, Nin had published her second work of fiction, a collection of novelettes entitled *The Winter of Artifice*. Named for Djuna Barnes, the eponymous heroine of the first of these stories would become the most important of Nin's characters, reappearing in the various novels that compose the later *Cities of the Interior* (1959). Like *Nightwood*, *Winter of Artifice* had a particularly difficult time finding a publisher. Completed in 1934, it was accepted by Jack Kahane of the Obelisk Press in 1935, but not published until 1939. In the intervening years Nin had tried unsuccessfully to place *Winter of Artifice* with New York and London publishers, but could find no one sympathetic to its subject matter or method. When Nin's friend Lawrence Durrell agreed to underwrite the costs of printing the work, Kahane finally scheduled it for publication. The last work to be published by the Obelisk Press, it was printed one week before the outbreak of World War II and nine days before Kahane's death in Paris. Founded in

1931, the Obelisk Press was a publishing house that avoided works of social and political import, specializing in literature banned in England and America, works that often concerned the sexual underworlds of urban culture. Kahane was the most daring of the Paris publishers and had accepted the most controversial and sexually explicit of experimental Modernist works, printing—among many others—Henry Miller's *Tropic of Cancer,* Radclyffe Hall's *The Well of Loneliness,* and Frank Harris's *My Life and Loves* (a book that Sylvia Beach had turned down, more appalled by its egotism than by its sexual frankness).

Nin's first fictional work, *House of Incest,* had been published in Paris three years earlier under the imprint of Siana Editions, Nin's own publishing operation. The publishing house was named for Anaïs ("Siana" reversed the letters of her name in a "baptism" effected by Alfred Perles, *Diary* II, 46). Control of the press, however, was wrested from Nin by Perles, Henry Miller, and Michael Fraenkel (who had set up the Carrefour press in Paris in 1929) soon after it was installed in the old barn next to her house in Louveciennes in 1935. Primarily interested in using the press to publish their own work, these men did agree to set the text of *House of Incest,* printing the prose poem while Nin was in Morocco in 1936. Although Fraenkel had promised to serve Nin as her publisher, distributing and marketing the book, he quickly lost interest in the enterprise. Consequently, the book received no reviews, and upon her return to Paris Nin found herself responsible for sending it to bookstores. Later that year Kahane republished *House of Incest* under the imprint of the Obelisk Press.

Nin's writing in the 1930s examined a specifically female-centered universe, its experimental literary forms tracing the psychological contours of woman's imagination. In its creation of eroticized and internalized female landscapes Nin's work was absolutely unique, but its experimental narrative methods derived from her early interest in Surrealism and her ongoing psychoanalysis. In both subject and style, then, Nin's work was clearly at odds with the predominant literary mood of the thirties and was misunderstood by the publishers and literary agents who examined it. Kahane, for instance, was interested in *House of Incest* because its title suggested forbidden sexuality. In fact, this "house" figures woman's fragmented and internally divided personality; through its rooms she wanders in search of her identity. Specifically denying the workings of the outer world, the text translates the cityscape into a dreamscape in which incest becomes a figure of stasis, a dead end, "a room without window," a "fortress . . . of love" from which the only escape is death (52).

Trapped in the "house of incest," the female narrator of the poem is shut off from the external world, able to register its workings only through her own self-division. The dissonance and dissension of external reality are internalized in the poem, evoked in images of violence, unpleasant odors, and the din of street sounds that confirm the dissociative split in the female consciousness that is the poem's subject. Awakened out of innocence, the woman perceives her psychological division in the difference between the dream world and the day world: "The day and night unglued, and I falling in between not knowing on which layer I was resting, whether it was the cold grey upper leaf of dawn, or the dark layer of night" (18). The opening sections of the poem explore the nature of lesbian love, a search for the self in the self's own image: Sabina's face appears to the narrator "suspended in the darkness of the garden" (18). This vision of woman's reflected image recalls the moment in *Nightwood* when Nora Flood, awakened from sleep, sees Robin Vote in the shadow of the garden statuary: "Nora saw the body of another woman swim up into the statue's obscurity . . . her arms about Robin's neck, her body pressed to Robin's, her legs slackened in the hang of the embrace" (64). In both subject matter and imagery, *House of Incest* parallels Barnes's *Nightwood*. In both works the female Other represents a lost and prelapsarian past: in Nin's poem, Sabina peers through the darkness with "an ancient stare, heavy luxuriant centuries flickering in deep processions" (18); she appears from another world, "the sound of her feet treading down into the blood the imprint of her face" (21). In *Nightwood* Robin Vote wears the past as "a web about her," embodying "a fearful sort of primitive innocence" (119, 117). But this radical innocence exists only as a vague memory, as "a slight drag" in her movements, and as a noticeable hesitation of speech (119). Robbed of her past, Robin has also been deprived of sexual innocence: after the birth of her son, she is estranged from her former self by sexual knowledge. In contrast, Sabina's nature is innately sensuous and sexual, her temptation resting in the physical, "in the last paroxysm of orgasm" (21) that obliterates memory and annihilates hope.

The search for self undertaken in Nin's poem is endangered by the very physical presence of Sabina, whose beauty threatens to drown the poem's speaker (25): "I feel you in me; I feel my own voice becoming heavier, as if I were drinking you in, every delicate thread of resemblance being soldered by fire and one no longer detects the fissure" (26). Rather than serving as a symbol of woman's alienation from her own physical and psychic selves—as Robin Vote served to divide Nora Flood against herself, the two women eventually divided against themselves and each other—Sabina offers the opposite, but equally deadly, temptation. One desires to merge with her, to lose one's identity in her own: "I AM THE OTHER FACE OF YOU" (28). This pull toward the other who is the image of yourself represents death: "I see two women in me freakishly bound together, like circus twins. I see them tearing away from each other. I can hear the tearing, the anger and love, passion and pity" (30). The psychic pain the narrator experiences is not the suffering of Nora Flood, who in finding Robin Vote risks losing herself: "a woman is yourself, caught as you turn in panic; on her mouth you kiss your own. If she is taken you cry that you have been robbed of yourself" (*Nightwood,* 143). The risk taken in Nin's poem is one of "dissolution," a dissolving of the self into the other. Rather than divided against herself, estranged from her own body and spirit like Nora Flood, the narrator of *House of Incest* discovers herself estranged from the reality of the surrounding environment. Awakening from the dream of innocence, she discovers that the ceiling of the room in which she sleeps threatens her "like a pair of open scissors" (31).

The images that close the opening section of Nin's poem exploit Surrealistic effects, juxtaposing violence to beauty, terror to love, laughter to torture. The room has become an iron cage. Formerly a place of refuge, the room now represents a "mortal danger" that cannot be escaped because it is internalized. Natural elements such as snow and rain become aspects of physical disintegration, the rain a slow cerebral leak, the snow causing distension of the lungs: "All the ships are sinking with fire in their bowels, and there are fires hissing in the cellars of every house. The loved one's whitest flesh is what the broken glass will cut and the wheel crush. The long howls in the night are howls of death. Night is the collaborator of torturers. Day is the light on harrowing discoveries. If a dog barks it is the man who loves wide gashes leaping in through the window. Laughter precedes hysteria. I am waiting for the heavy fall and the foam at the mouth" (31). The images of conflagration and violent death are registered by "hissing" and "howls," the night collaborating in torture by offering a protective covering for the "harrowing discoveries" the day will reveal. Cruelty and anger are signaled by laughter and hysteria as the world is overtaken by a rabid and delirious madness from which there is no escape. Waiting "for the heavy fall and the foam at the mouth," the narrator confesses her dread of the future. Although the record of an intensely private and undoubtedly painful nightmare through which Nin worked her way to psychic integration, the *House of Incest* describes an apocalyptic vision shared by all of Europe in the thirties. These poetic effects derive from the rhetoric of war, with its "howls of death," its newly discovered "collaborators" and "torturers," and the dreaded prospect of the "heavy fall" that would make Europe the victim of a fanatical and uncontrollable urge toward power.

The final section of the poem exploits an even more explicit Surrealistic rhetoric that forecasts the end of the world. Described as "noble-raced," Jeanne enters "all in fur, with fur eyelashes" (43), her "head carried high, nose to the wind," as though she were a powerful thoroughbred horse. As soon as the image of an imperious and elegant animal is established, however, it is destroyed as we see her "dragging her crippled leg," her body pulling the leg as though it were "the chained ball of a prisoner" (43). Jeanne's physical deformity balances the psychic perversion of desire for her brother, both abnormalities suggesting her alienation from a world that tolerates only physical and psychic perfection. Desiring her brother, she covets the world men inhabit and over which they rule. Thus her physical affliction becomes not only the mark of her illicit sexual urges but the sign of her degraded womanhood. Estranged from self, she tries to confirm her identity in the mirror, where she gazes at herself "with love" (44). Rather than confirming her selfhood, however, the mirror reflects an image of impending disaster: she sees there "the Four Horsemen of the Apocalypse riding through the Bois. Tragedy rolling on cord tires" (44). Registering the image of death, the mirror-world closes in on her ("the world is too small"), leaving no place for escape; the house of refuge becomes the house of incest whose rooms have interior, "spying-eyed" windows (51) from which her tragedy is observed.

Led into the most secret parts of the house by Jeanne's obsessive search for her brother, the narrator stumbles into a room of paintings in which Lot's incestuous desire for his daughter is portrayed against the background of a burning city "cracking open and falling into the sea" (52). The incestuous passions of father for daughter "heave and swell" as "the city is rent by lightning, and spits under the teeth of fire, great blocks of a gaping ripped city sinking with the horror of obscenity, and falling into the sea with the hiss of the eternally damned" (55). Nin's vision of the world's inevitable destruction is occasioned here by sexual perversion, the sin that God punishes with a reign of fire that destroys all living things. The images, however, are those of modern warfare, the Blitzkrieg from the sky; the narrator "look[s] upon a clock to find the truth" and discovers that "the minutes race on wires mounted like tin soldiers" whose heavy-treaded footsteps she hears in her dreams stepping out "the beat of time" (55). Jeanne's search for her brother and the narrator's search for self are paradigmatic efforts to escape a cultural text bounded by "the fear of death and the fear of life," a text in which love is registered as a "cold neutral absence of pain" (60).

For the narrator, the dream-book is an interior cityscape whose sharp corners can cause injury, where "pointed glass and broken bottles" suggest the particular dangers of an urban terrain. This theme is explored in the work of Djuna Barnes, Jean Rhys, and Mina Loy. Writing of Barnes and Loy, Carolyn Burke comments that both writers chose "to focus on the predicament of the modern woman adrift in the urban wasteland, where her new freedoms (which proved to be only relative) culminated in psychic disillusionment, spiritual lassitude or . . . in real or imagined suicide" ("'Accidental Aloofness'"). Nin's narrator walks out of the dream-book to discover the modern Christ, a paralytic, "wiping the perspiration which dripped over his face, as if he were sitting there in the agony of a secret torture" (68). Born without a skin, this Christ is exposed to the constant pain of the surrounding environment. The modern savior is impotent, obsessed with his own pain, hoping for release from the "darkness and night" (70) that shadow the world. The only escape from this world to the daylight world, however, is through a narrow tunnel that "would close around us, and close tighter and tighter around us and stifle us" (70). Unable to escape the "house of incest," the dreamers become spectators, watching a woman dance to the sound of castanets. Repeating the gestures of Christ—"opening her arms and her hands, permitting all things to flow away and beyond her" (71)—the dancer's movements suggest the inevitability of loss, of "the passing of things." Turning "like a disk, turning all faces to light and to darkness evenly, dancing towards daylight" (72), the dancer's movements repeat the cyclical pattern of darkness and light, daybreak and dusk, with which the poem opened.

The psychological distress registered by this poem signals a more pervasive anxiety in European culture of the 1930s. Obsessed as Nin is with psychological torment in *House of Incest,* the poem's nightmare vision produces its effects through images of physical violence, its epigraph suggesting that art is composed out of human suffering. The writing process itself is figured in "spitting out" the heart; the haunting music that soothes the misery of those trapped in the "house of incest" is produced on a flute made from the bones of the musician's dead lover. Nin has not waited for the lover's death, however; her art plays upon pain of the living body, taking pleasure in suffering. Pain and pleasure are intimately bound to each other here, the dreamer seduced by a desire that can only produce pain. "Desire which had stretched the nerve broke, and each nerve seemed to break separately, continuously, making incisions, and acid ran instead of blood. I writhed within my own life, seeking a free avenue to carry the molten cries, to melt the pain into a cauldron of words for everyone to dip into, everyone who sought words for their own pain" (32). Searching for a language in which to express pain, the narrator of this poem discovers the power of expression in images that result in "a dissolution of the soul within the body like the rupture of sweet-acid of the orgasm" (34). The sources of this art rest in a form of sadomasochism; the artistic subject, the lover, is summoned in order to be mutilated: "I came upon a forest of decapitated trees, women carved out of bamboo, flesh slatted like that of slaves in joyless slavery, faces cut in two by the sculptor's knife, showing two sides forever separate, eternally two-faced, and it was I who had to shift about to behold the entire woman" (55). Culture itself is seen to be a destructive force that registers through art a violence against nature. Woman's self-division and disfigurement are carved in "the veined docile wood" of the living tree. Nature is made to reflect "human contortions," the truncated form shaped into "fragments of bodies, bodies armless and headless" (56). This brutality is the record of cultural values registered here in an art composed by images of savagery. The psychic distress that the *House of Incest* examines signals cultural unrest and employs cultural expressions of that unease. Rather than turning its back on external reality, Nin's poem registers the subliminal effects of that reality on the individual psyche. Tracing the effects of the societal consciousness on the individual mind, of the public on the private, of civilization on art, Nin rebelled against the cultural values of her time and cried out against the pervasive violence and aggression apparent in the world around her. The mutilated forest of the dream world "trembl[es] with rebellion so bitter" that the narrator of Nin's poem can hear "its wailing within its deep forest consciousness" (56).

Although Nin refused to address the social and political issues of the 1930s directly, the psychopathology of the female spirit that is the subject of her writing in these years reflects a larger cultural paranoia and self-hatred. The women of her writings do not submit to the cultural imperative, however; like Nin, they fight against it, seeking integrity through self-awareness. Nin herself chose to live apart from the larger culture, placed herself outside the boundaries of a politicized society in an effort to protect her commitment to pacifism. In the mid-thirties she was living on a houseboat in the Seine with her lover, Gonzalo, a Peruvian musician and revolutionary. Although Gonzalo spoke passionately of the Spanish cause and was determined to take an active part on the side of the Loyalists, he was overcome by passivity. Apolitical herself, Nin felt sympathy for the Loyalist cause, but admitted that she found "fanaticism and injustice" in all political movements (Knapp, *Anaïs Nin,* 11). She did not think revolution a viable political method, arguing that revolutionaries only achieved an inevitable hierarchical inversion: those who had been downtrodden became the new tyrants and torturers. When Nin was forced to flee France in 1939, she assumed that Europe had been given over to the tyrants and torturers, that it would never escape from Fascist tyranny and was lost to her forever: "I felt every cell and cord which tied me to France snapping in me, the parting from a pattern of life I loved, from an atmosphere rich, creative and human, from intimacy with people and a city" (*Anaïs Nin,* 12). Back in New York, she felt displaced, an alien, and was tormented by guilt for friends left behind in France. She determined, however, to continue working "until the bomb falls," confessing her commitment to her diary: "I am not going to quit, abdicate, and play its game of death and power" (*Diary,* III, 177).

Shortly after the bombing of Pearl Harbor, Nin set up a small press at 144 MacDougal Street with funds provided by friends, including Frances Steloff of the Gotham Book Mart, who was then marketing Nin's books.

As America went to war against Germany and Japan, Nin and Gonzalo (who wanted to use the press to print political tracts) were buying up paper and ink for the press. Although Gonzalo was an unreliable helper and the work was physically demanding, Nin's publishing venture was a success. The engraved texts, set in unusual typefaces, received high praise, but to Nin's dismay reviewers continued to misunderstand her texts. In an effort to educate the public to her methods, she chose William Carlos Williams to review a limited edition of *The Winter of Artifice* and was shocked and disappointed when his review portrayed her as a man-hater and described the novelettes as barely disguised autobiography. The *New York Times* and *Tribune* ignored the book, while the *New Republic* apparently prevented its reviewer, Harvey Breit, from writing a more sympathetic interpretation of it (Dennison, *[Alternative] Literary Publishing,* 147). Nin's work continued to be criticized for the absence of realistic detail and fully realized characterization, its emphasis on personal and interior landscapes, and its poetic diction. By 1943, when Nin set the type for a collection of short stories published in little magazines during the previous decade, she had already decided to abandon the dream world that had served as the source of her writing and turn to realistic fiction.

Nin used the preface to the collection of short stories *Under a Glass Bell* to suggest the ways in which the seemingly separate fantasy worlds of the stories represent artistic escape from the pressing political realities of the 1930s:

> These stories represent the moment when many like myself had found only one answer to the suffering of the world: to dream, to tell fairytales, to elaborate and to follow the labyrinth of fantasy. All this I see now was the passive poet's only answer to the torments he witnessed. . . .
>
> I did not stay in the world of the isolated dream or become permanently identified with it. The Spanish war awakened me. I passed out of romanticism, mysticism and neurosis into reality. (n.p.)

A year later Nin recorded in her diary that the diary itself would be transformed "into a full, long novel of the thirty years between 1914 and 1940—between the two wars." Although Nin declared that this fiction would explore "the transition from romanticism to realism," this literary exploration was never undertaken. When Nin prepared her diaries for publication in the 1960s, she eliminated references to the project (*[Alternative] Literary Publishing,* 151). In fact, Nin was never able fully to transform her literary methods; she continued a practice influenced by psychoanalysis and literary experimentation, a practice that focused on the introspective world of woman's thought. The external world appears only in fleeting glimpses in these fictions, its powers diminished by the reality of the interior landscape. When the external world intrudes on the private world of consciousness it appears alien, unknown, inhuman, and strange.

Good Morning, Midnight

Jean Rhys's world was also introspective, but the relation of interior to exterior in her work reverses Nin's paradigm. Rhys's characters cannot escape the suffering inflicted by the external world, and they live out that suffering *in* the external world. Like the modern Christ in *House of Incest*, these women have no protective covering; they are exposed—and expose themselves—to continual torture. Thomas F. Staley comments that although "Rhys wrote precisely of what it was like to be down and out in both Paris and London, her fiction was not a literature of social engagement" (*Jean Rhys*, 84). Like Nin, Barnes, H. D., and many other women writers of the thirties (but unlike most of the male writers), Rhys did not make overt reference to the political and social situation of the interwar years in her fiction:

> Even by 1939 her writing seemed untouched by the devastating political and military events which had occurred and the even more horrendous ones which were on the horizon. A passing reference in *Good Morning, Midnight* to Franco's Spain and the fact that it is October, 1937, are the only indications that the outside world has changed very much since Marya Zelli [of *Quartet*] first came to Paris in the aftermath of World War I. . . . [Rhys's] work continued to rest on the power of style rather than new subject matter, intuition rather than analysis, the private rather than the public self. (*Jean Rhys*, 84)

Rhys had not lived in Paris since 1929, but had made frequent visits to the city in the intervening years. Taking up the circumstance of a middle-aged woman's return to the city where she had first experienced love, *Good Morning, Midnight* (1930) registers through Sasha Jansen's psychic turmoil the effects of change and passing time on the city itself. As in Nin's *House of Incest,* the cityscape of narrow streets and tall houses threatens Sasha's stability, but her survival depends on proving to herself that she can successfully negotiate this bewildering terrain. Unlike the house in Nin's poem, however, the city cannot offer any refuge: Sasha is forced to enact her private drama in public places—in hotels and shops, on the street, at cafes: "My life, which seems to be simple and monotonous, is really a complicated affair of cafes where they like me and cafes where they don't, streets that are friendly, streets that aren't, rooms where I might be happy, rooms where I never shall be, looking-glasses I look nice in, looking-glasses I don't, dresses that will be lucky, dresses that won't, and so on" (46). The city offers no safe sanctuary where Sasha can hide from the prying eyes of clerks and concierges, or escape the staring windows of the houses and the mirrors that return to her the image of a lonely, aging woman.

Paris exposes Sasha Jansen's vulnerability. She is caught both by the city spaces and by time itself: the city stirs memories of youth and of previous loves and in so doing alters the image of the present experience. Sasha exchanges one set of experiences for another, always losing something of herself in the trade, as she tries to recover the Sasha Jansen of a previous decade. The twists and turns of the city's labyrinthine streets trace the circular and involuted path of Sasha's consciousness. Trapped by time and space, she realizes at the novel's end that there is no possibility of change for her—she cannot break the circular pattern of her existence: "It doesn't matter, there I am, like one of those straws which floats around the edge of a whirlpool and is gradually sucked into the centre, the dead centre, where everything is stagnant, everything is calm" (44). Associating death with stasis, Sasha keeps moving, walking aimlessly through cold, wet streets in order to prove to herself that she is still alive. Aware that she exists at an oblique angle to her own life (she has "no pride, no name, no face, no country," 44), she constantly measures the dimensions of her existence. While this trip to Paris stirs memories of past intimacies, it also makes Sasha aware of the degree to which she is an alien being in this environment. Once the city had provided an exotic background to the promise of love; once she had walked its streets aware of herself as an object of male desire. Now she exists beyond the city's limits of desire: "Yes, I am sad, sad as a circus-lioness, sad as an eagle without wings, sad as a violin with only one string and that broken, sad as a woman who is growing old" (45).

Good Morning, Midnight recapitulates familiar Rhys themes, in particular the contrasts between London and Paris. Sasha Jansen is English, has lived most of her adult life in London, is recognizably—even predictably—*Anglaise*. Paris offers her an escape from a London life that is cold and gray, an existence without contours, without hope. But the French city also reminds her that she is English, that the English are disliked and considered a "plague" by the French, tolerated as tourists only because they spend money. In speaking the language of the country, Sasha is made even more aware of her foreignness and becomes an observer of her own actions, an eavesdropper on her own conversations. She can understand the comments made about her by those who assume her ignorance of French. She is hurt to hear herself referred to as "la vieille . . . the old one" (54).

Forced to see herself as the French see her (as a "petite dame"), she also realizes that she is as alien to the English as she is to the French. Seated at lunch in her favorite restaurant, Sasha overhears the insult made about her—in French—by the young English girl at another table: "Et qu'est-ce qu'elle fout ici, maintenant?" (50). For reasons never explained, the young English woman resents Sasha's presence in the restaurant. Angered by the remark (which is doubly distancing, as it is spoken in perfect French by an English woman), Sasha nonetheless admits that the girl's question is one she has often posed to herself: "I am asking myself all the time what the devil I am doing here" (54). Her discomfort with herself and with living is so apparent that people cannot prevent themselves from commenting on it. After a trip to Paris five years earlier, a member of her family, whom she refers to as "old devil," had remarked to her: "We consider you as dead. Why didn't you make a hole in the water? Why didn't you drown yourself in the Seine?" (41–42). These shocking remarks serve as prelude to the old devil's announcement that Sasha is to receive a small legacy that includes a weekly annuity and "a room off the Gray's Inn Road," a "place to hide in" (42). No longer wishing to be "loved, beautiful, happy or successful" (43), Sasha wants only to be left alone and slams "the lid of the coffin . . . with a bang" (42).

To no small degree, economic strictures have defined Sasha's world (as they defined Jean Rhys's own personal world), and it is significant that a chance inheritance "saves" her from drowning: "Saved, rescued, fished-up, half-drowned, out of the deep, dark river, dry clothes, hair shampooed and set. Nobody would ever know I had been in it" (10). The novel makes constant references to the cost of things, to Sasha's efforts to control her economic existence as she tries to exert a measure of control over her psychological state. Before she received the legacy, she had lived on the margins of poverty, forced to take temporary and ill-paid jobs in dress shops. Sasha has particularly painful memories of her situation in a dreary Paris dress shop where she was victimized—and later fired—by Mr. Blank, the English owner. Like the lovers who have used her, Mr. Blank has exploited her: "You represent Society, have the right to pay me four hundred francs a month. That's my market value, for I am an inefficient member of Society, slow in the uptake, uncertain, slightly damaged in the fray, there's no denying it. So you have the right to pay me four hundred francs a month, to lodge me in a small, dark room, to clothe me shabbily, to harass me with worry and monotony and unsatisfied longings till you get me to the point when I blush at a look, cry at a word" (29). Through this stream-of-consciousness monologue that Sasha later admits to never having thought, much less spoken, Rhys articulates a feminist argument based on the economic, physical, and psychological exploitation of women by a patriarchal society. All the heroines of Rhys's novels are subjected to this kind of patronage, but only Sasha is able to articulate the force of its consequences. She is able to acknowledge as well that there is a conspiracy, a "freemasonry," not only among those who exploit the poor but among the waiters, shop assistants, and "old ladies in lavabos" who "prey upon the rich." As Helen Nebeker comments, "in no other [Rhys] novel has the heroine been able to admit that exploitation is not the prerogative of the rich" (*Jean Rhys*, 89), and it is on this understanding of the mutual exploitation of the rich and poor that Sasha will establish her relationship with the gigolo René. In Sasha's view of society, capitalist and patriarchal values are inseparable, each supporting the other in a parasitical economy.

The closing scenes of the novel illustrate the workings of this economy. The young gigolo René offers her temporary release from her isolation and self-absorption in return for her money. Ironically, Sasha's economic freedom allows her to play in this relationship the role usually assigned to the male in society. As Thomas F. Staley has commented, "she need not give her feelings inauthentically in exchange for security" (*Jean Rhys*, 92). But René himself is a victim of the patriarchal economy, forced to live off rich women. A young man who looks hopefully to the future, it is clear that he soon will be affected—in ways similar to Sasha's own experience—by the necessity of living by his wits. René still has expectations; Sasha has only regrets. And when she discovers that they have shared a moment in the past, that their paths have crossed before, she becomes increasingly guarded. She resists his offer to make love to her and in so doing threatens to deny him the occasion to rob her.

Returning alone to her hotel room in the Hotel de l'Espérance, she finds René awaiting her in the corridor. On the darkened landing she takes him in her arms, leading him to her room, where they begin drinking and where he tries to force himself upon her. Unable to enact the ritual sexual scene, she begs René to take the thousand franc note from her dressing case and to leave the room. After he has gone, she discovers that he has not taken her money. Deliriously happy at this evidence of his humanity, she hallucinates his return: "Come back, come back, come back" (189). Lying on the bed in the darkened room, she awaits his return, opening her arms to the man who enters the room, a man wearing a white dressing gown. Welcoming him into her arms, she whispers "Yes— yes—yes" (190) to the occupant of the adjacent room, a man who has watched in the corridor and overheard all that has taken place with René. In embracing this salesman, Sasha opens her arms to the slow numbing of human responses that will end in death.

The final pages of *Good Morning, Midnight* offer a horrifying image of woman's sexual and emotional degradation in a society that does not value the individual and exploits the weak and economically displaced. Rhys avoids the apocalyptic visions of Nin and the displays of bestiality offered by Barnes, but in drawing the effects of woman's economic and social exploitation, she adds the final panel to a triptych of the thirties.

Unlike Sabina, who flees in fear from the terrors of the external world, or Robin Vote who is a "beast turning human," Sasha Jansen lives in the present world, caught by the cold realities of her existence. Rhys's spare, almost clinical treatment of Sasha's predicament constitutes an indictment of contemporary society all the more devastating for its understatement. Although Rhys explores in her subject matter the concerns of other women writers of the period, her lean prose style shares more with the poets of the Auden group than with Nin's expressionistic landscapes or Barnes's antiquated verbal modes. Rhys's dialectic of self and world, like that of Auden's later poetry, grounds itself in the everyday, reveals its vision in personal disappointment and discouragement.

World War II: "September 1, 1939"

Auden's poem "September 1, 1939," marking the onset of the Second World War, envisions Europe as a "haunted wood" over which night has fallen. In its description of the thirties temperament and its reaction to the announcement of war, the poem recapitulates themes already developed in the work of Barnes, Nin, and Rhys, but its situation (a "dive" on Fifty-second Street in New York City) and its terse language of despair are particularly reminiscent of Rhys. Seated at the bar, the poem's narrator is "Uncertain and afraid / As the clever hopes expire / Of a low dishonest decade" (*The Collected Poetry of W. H. Auden*, 57). He smells the "odour of death" in the September night and feels "waves of anger and fear . . . Obsessing our private lives." The "blind skyscrapers" of the city "proclaim / The strength of Collective Man," but in the bar, the "faces . . . Cling to their average day," the dailiness of existence providing a bulwark against the effects of cultural insanity. The men gathered under the bright lights of the bar protect themselves against the realization that they are "Lost in a haunted wood, / Children afraid of the night." This nightmare is the product of individual needs for love and human understanding. The Western world is acting out a truth known by all schoolchildren: "Those to whom evil is done / Do evil in return." Dictators and commuters, militants and "helpless governors," crave what they cannot have: "Not universal love / But to be loved alone." Exposed to the "neutral air" of this September evening, "defenceless under the night," the "world in stupor lies." Recumbent, the world awaits its fate, awaits the apocalypse, awaits the "tragedy rolling on cord tires" to which the history of the thirties has given the lie.

12
THE CITY THEY LEFT

On 1 September 1939, Ezra Pound was in Rapallo, where he had lived since autumn 1924. He had grown tired of France, Noel Stock reports, not simply because he felt in the mid-twenties that the country had "no writer of the first magnitude," but because he felt uncomfortable in the predominantly American expatriate community (*Life of Ezra Pound,* 256). More significantly, however, he believed that important things were happening elsewhere; in particular, he found the atmosphere of Italy after Mussolini's march on Rome in October 1922 more agreeable than that of France. During the 1930s, Pound had continued work on the *Cantos,* addressing himself in this series of poems to economic and political matters. Indeed, his interest in monetary and economic matters in these years overshadowed his interest in literature, and his political ideology was structured by his understanding of economic issues. When he received Nancy Cunard's questionnaire on the Spanish Civil War in June 1937, he replied to her that he thought little of the questionnaire and less of those who signed it ("your gang are all diarrhoea," he wrote her); personally, he was opposed to "taking sides in a sham conflict" (*Life of Ezra Pound,* 345). The outbreak of World War II confirmed for Pound the truth of his political and economic theories, the cause of the war resting in "international usury" (*Life of Ezra Pound,* 368). By late 1939, he was committed to the German and Italian point of view, was isolated by his geographical association with the Axis powers, and had taken to reading anti-Semitic tracts. Concerned about possible American intervention in the European conflict and still committed to a Jeffersonian notion of American democracy, he intended to return home. As the months passed, however, he remained in Italy and was soon to become a spokesperson for the Axis position.

Departures

The early stages of the Second World War, before Italy officially entered the conflict, did not affect Pound personally. Unlike his friends in Paris, who in autumn 1939 were desperately planning escape routes, his daily life went on unchanged. On 1 September 1939, Joyce was trying to find means to transport Lucia, his mentally ill daughter, to a *maison de santé* in Switzerland. Maria Jolas was preparing to move her Ecole Bilingue to Saint-Gerand-le-Puy, a village near Vichy, where the Joyces were to join her. Arriving at the Hotel de la Paix on Christmas eve, Joyce collapsed with stomach pains, the first signs of the duodenal ulcer that would kill him thirteen months later—six weeks after F. Scott Fitzgerald's death in Hollywood. On 1 September 1939, Georgette Leblanc was scheduled for cancer surgery at the American Hospital in Paris. But with news of the war, the hospital planned its evacuation to Etretat on the Normandy coast. Like characters in an Auden poem, Georgette Leblanc and her lover, Margaret Anderson, fled the city, convinced that the Germans would immediately begin bombing Paris: "We were tense in the car, thankful for every kilometre gained without being halted . . . imaginary dramas of pursuit and capture that mark a war's beginning" (Anderson, *The Fiery Fountains*, 170–171). On their way to the Normandy coast, where the American hospital was to be relocated, the two women were forced to make frequent stops, taking several days for the journey, because Leblanc was weak and in great pain. By Saturday, 2 September, the hospital had been relocated in the Golf Hotel in Etretat and its patients transferred from Neuilly. The following Tuesday Leblanc underwent surgery for the cancer from which she would die a year later at Le Cannet, a small village on the French Riviera where the two women had gone to wait out the war.

In the week that Leblanc and Anderson left Paris for Normandy, their friend Romaine Brooks returned from America, where she had discovered little interest in her painting. Very much aware that war was coming to Europe, Brooks returned to Paris on purpose, determined that "wherever and whenever" the war took place, she would spend it with Natalie Barney (Secrest, *Between Me and Life*, 356). Within days of Brooks's return, the two women set out for Italy, hastily packing a few things into trunks, hoping to return to Paris before Christmas. Brooks was 66 years of age and Barney 62, almost exactly the ages of Gertrude Stein and Alice Toklas, who were still at their summer place in Bilignin. Like Colette, who was *en vacances* on the Riviera, Stein and Toklas decided to extend their summer holidays. Apart from one midnight trip to Paris to bring to Bilignin Picasso's portrait of Gertrude, the two women did not return to the newly redecorated rue Christine apartment until 1945, by which time Stein was 71 years old and already stricken with cancer.

By 1939, however, there were few expatriates left in Paris—most had already been gone for some time. When Henry Miller arrived in Paris on 4 March 1930, many of his compatriots were already packing to return home. Hemingway had gone back in 1929, not to return until 26 August 1944 with the liberation troops. Cummings was in New York, living in Patchin Place, where Djuna Barnes would soon establish residence. Kay Boyle was living with Lawrence Vail in Haute Savoie, near Gertrude Stein, and would not return to America until August 1941. Mina Loy was in New York and Katherine Anne Porter in Texas. Malcolm Cowley was in New York, where he had been since 1929 (he had returned to America in 1923), an associate editor of the *New Republic,* and Caresse Crosby was living with her new husband in a plantation house in Virginia. By 1 September 1939, Henry Miller himself had left the city, staying long enough to see the Obelisk Press publication of *The Tropic of Capricorn* on 10 May of that year. He first traveled to Athens and then returned to Corfu for several months before returning to America in 1940 to stay briefly with Caresse Crosby in Virginia. Writing to Anaïs Nin from Corfu on 9 September 1939, Miller reported "a week of war and here I am in the dead silence of a tiny village—Kalami—writing you tonight. Strangest of all is that I feel absolutely tranquil, sure somehow that everything will turn out all right" (*Henry Miller: Letters to Anaïs Nin,* 184).

In February 1939 (on the occasion of Joyce's fifty-seventh birthday), the long-delayed final issue of *transition* that included the "Russian General" section of *Finnegans Wake* was printed, and within weeks the complete edition of the *Wake* was published in London by Faber and Faber. Aware that the war was imminent, Joyce had hurried to complete the text, confessing to Jolas that "this book of mine must appear before the war breaks out or no one will read it" ("Man from Babel," ms. p. 257). The war presented a final, and insurmountable, obstacle for Jolas as well. He knew that the community of writers whose work had been published in *transition* would soon be forced to leave Paris. Born in Alsace-Lorraine, the product of a combined German-French culture, Jolas was a man who had been bred on the linguistic and political frontier separating Germany and France (he referred to himself as a "frontier man"). By 1936, it was clear to him that a second world war was imminent and that Paris itself was in jeopardy. In the last years of the decade, he considered making *transition* into an anti-Fascist political magazine, but by summer 1939 had decided against such a plan. Instead, he and Maria Jolas moved to New York in 1940 to join a community of other writers and artists working against Fascism; in 1941, Eugene Jolas joined the United States Office of War Information, and he was to stay in government service until 1950.

The Sounds of War

In 1938, Waverly Root, Jolas's friend and co-journalist from the *Chicago Tribune* days in Paris, had been fired by United Press for predicting a Nazi invasion of Austria in mid-May of that year (the takeover took place on 13 May 1938). Later that year Root joined the staff of the Mutual Broadcasting System, making his final radio broadcast from Bordeaux on 22 June 1940, the day Pétain declared an armistice with Germany. From her home in Switzerland, Bryher listened to this broadcast, which asked nurses, radio technicians, and engineers to mobilize under the auspices of the French army in Bordeaux (*Heart to Artemis,* 293). In the days that followed, Swiss radio warned of imminent invasion of the country, and Bryher devoted both money and her own personal services to helping refugees escape. At the last moment, she found an escape route through Portugal, the same route taken by Robert McAlmon, her former husband, who by this time was ill with tuberculosis. Bryher went to London, where she was expected by H. D. and her daughter, Perdita, and McAlmon left by boat for New York. From London, Bryher wrote to Sylvia Beach in remembrance of the Paris years and of her role in the literary revolution that took place there: "I . . . tried always to do what [I] could for the real artists, and especially for the woman artist" (Fitch, *Sylvia Beach,* 400). On 7 June 1940, seven days before the occupation of Paris began, Adrienne Monnier took Gisèle Freund to the Gare d'Austerlitz, the first stage of a journey that would bring the German Jewish woman to safety in Argentina. On Thursday, 13 June, the day before the occupation of Paris began, Sylvia Beach tried to leave Paris, only to learn that it was by then too late. On this evening, Adrienne recorded in her "occupation journal" that the "black rain" had begun. Four days later, she reported: "I feel defeat and that it's going to be fascism" (*Very Rich Hours,* 397).

In August 1940, Colette and her husband, Maurice Goudeket, tried to return to Paris from Coreze. Arriving at the border control for the Occupied Zone, Colette was accused of being Jewish by the German officers, at which point her husband replied (in German), "You're making a mistake . . . I'm the only one here of Jewish birth." After some consultation among the officers, Colette and her husband were turned back. They returned to Lyon, obtained a letter of recommendation from the Swedish consulate, and were allowed to pass into the Occupied Zone a few days later. Sixteen months after this incident at the border, on 12 December 1941, Goudeket was among hundreds of "prominent French Jews" arrested. The Gestapo arrived at 7:20 in the morning, awakening the sleeping couple. Colette, aged 68, helped her husband pack a small suitcase and watched from the top of the stairs as he was taken away. It was a moment from which she would never recover: ". . . the sound of foreign voices, the noise of nailed boots, and the ringing of the bell . . . and then the softer sound of the footsteps of the man descending the stairs, his little suitcase in his hand. . . . When they went away, that man and the two hundred others they had picked up, they joined the anonymous dead. Frozen and silent as the dead. There were no voices, there was no writing, nothing was left to show they were alive" (*The Evening Star: Recollections*, in Sarde, *Colette*, 418). Just before Sylvia Beach was interned in August 1942, Goudeket was released. He returned to the second-floor apartment on the Palais-Royal and was almost immediately forced into hiding. Jews in occupied France were being deported by truck, from the Pont de la Tournelle and sent to extermination camps. Goudeket hid himself first in the south of France and later in Paris, where he slept in the attic, just under the eaves of the Palais-Royal apartment building. Alone, two stories below, Colette waited for the sound of nailed boots and the knock on the door. In hiding throughout the remainder of the war, Goudeket managed to survive.

At sunrise on the morning of 10 May 1940, Louis Aragon was interrupted as he tried to complete a poem by the delivery of official orders that he join an armored detachment of the French army on its way into Belgium ahead of the Allied forces. "The Interrupted Poem" comments on the present war by recalling the previous one ("Curtains are drawn this morning / Once more falls the Flanders mist") and asks, rhetorically, "What dream in the heavens outrides / The night that will not be gone?" (Josephson and Cowley, *Aragon*, 32). The long night of "black rain" that lasted from June 1940 until August 1944 was about to set in, forcing Paris into hiding from itself. In these years of enforced solitude, those who had elected to stay on in the city lived on past memories and hopes for a future in which Paris would again be the city of light. Ashamed of their defeat by the Germans, Parisians turned to French classical literature in an effort to recover national pride. Adrienne Monnier reported in her *Gazette* that "it [was] to these sixteenth and seventeenth centuries that we have all gone with the same urge to find once more the person of France, to take her in our arms and weep upon her shoulder" (*Very Rich Hours*, 406). Facing what seemed the collapse of civilization, contemporary French writers had little idea how to respond, either as poets or as patriots, to the consequent disaster. Most retreated behind closed doors, keeping in private journals a record of the pain this chapter in French history brought them. An activist, Aragon joined the resistance and wrote love poems to the city of Paris. "More Beautiful Than Tears" describes the city as the "heart of our grief" and prays that she "not cry in vain." A later poem ("Paris") celebrates the liberation, imagining Paris as the heart "of our motherland" whose beauty is born of defiance:

Nothing before made my heart to beat thus
Nothing my laughter with my tears so mated
As this cry of my people victorious
Nothing is so vast as a shroud torn and shed
Paris, Paris, of herself liberated. (*Aragon*, 72)

In this moment of victory the city frees herself from those who would possess her but is liberated as well *of* herself. No longer given to grief, no longer spilling her heart's blood in the streets, she emerges from her torn shroud independent and strong.

The Patriarchal Perspective: Paris Is a Woman

Like other poets before and since, Aragon imagined Paris to be a woman. Stretched out along the Seine, she is a seductive and mysterious woman, her body both "landscape" and "sleep-charmer" ("More Beautiful Than Tears," *Aragon*, 57). Twenty-five years earlier, in a previous war, e. e. cummings had thought Paris a whore, "the putain with the ivory throat," who sold her wares in the streets: "bon dos, bon cul de Paris" ("little ladies more," *Collected Poems*). From the trenches, "Marie Louise with queenly legs" had called to him to dance with her and forget the war: "ladies skilfully / dead precisely dance / where has danced la / guerre" ("little ladies more"). Earlier, cummings envisioned Paris against an April sky: "the mauve / of twilight . . . slenderly descends / . . . carrying in her eyes the dangerous first stars." A seductive, nubile mistress, Paris at twilight "daintily carries" a new moon of promise behind which is shadowed "the lithe indolent prostitute / Night" ("Paris"). Flirtatious ingenue and indolent prostitute, Paris is both eroticized and adulterated in this heterosexual poetic economy that envisions the city landscape in a woman's body. Like Jane Avril, her skirts raised before an audience of males, Paris dances for the male imagination, tempts man to her sexual delights. The male poet yields to her as a figure of sexual desire, a woman who can make him forget both past and future and for whose pleasures he would sell his soul.

Paris never danced so enticingly before the female literary imagination, however, and it is perhaps ironic that so many women writers were drawn to its borders in the early years of this century. For some, like Jean Rhys, Paris offered sunlight and warmth, an escape from the dreary coldness of London, a city that more than one expatriate woman writer visualized as the patriarchy incarnate. For Edith Wharton, Paris epitomized the cultural values of Old Europe. For Gertrude Stein, the city offered respite from the puritanism of America. For Natalie Barney, Paris extended sisterhood. For all of these women, Paris offered a place to write, releasing

447

them from the patriarchal cultural script of marriage and motherhood enforced in other cities of the world. And in these years Paris itself underwent cultural re-vision by the women who participated in its communities of writers, painters, and musicians. Rejecting the image of Paris as an object of man's lustful desires, these women rewrote the cultural script through their own lives, making Paris complicit in their effort to establish a female culture on the landscape of a city that had been feminized and sexualized by a masculine literary poetic.

Not surprisingly, the women who undertook this project stood outside the heterosexual dialectic that had constructed the Paris of man's erotic imagination. Committed both emotionally and erotically to other women, Natalie Barney, Sylvia Beach, and Adrienne Monnier established bonds with other women within the physical boundaries of Paris: that is, within the city's borders they created female-centered worlds. And in the privacy of their gardens and reading rooms modern culture was created and nurtured. Indeed, so powerful was the influence of these internal spaces within the city walls—20, rue Jacob; 27, rue de Fleurus; 7 and 12, rue de l'Odéon—that they dominated the landscape of the Paris literary experiment. These communities had the effect of redesigning the city map and reversing the referential status of the Left Bank. Once known in relation to the Right Bank as *l'autre côté,* the Left Bank in these years displaced (and dismissed) the power and prestige, the conservative traditionalism and expansive capitalism, of the Right Bank.

The Literary Left Bank

In his commentary on *The Left Bank,* a collection of Jean Rhys's short stories written after the First World War, Ford Madox Ford tried to establish the political and imaginative boundaries of the Left Bank in the Modernist period, suggesting not only that the Left Bank represented the psychological and intellectual inverse of its opposite territory across the river, but that it symbolized all the "Left Banks of the world" ("Preface," *The Left Bank,* 23). It was a place inhabited by all those on the margin of culture, a place for the dislocated, even the dispossessed. And precisely such *marginaux* populate the stories of *The Left Bank.* Rhys was particularly concerned with those on the economic periphery of society, of young women vulnerable to commercial and sexual exploitation and old women whose bodies and spirits bear the scars of such mistreatment. Like the women of her fiction, Jean Rhys did not find a place for herself on the literary Left Bank; she was an outsider among outsiders, neither part of the cafe crowd nor an occasional visitor to Sylvia Beach's bookshop. Rhys lived outside the bounds of society, outside even the bounds of so loosely constructed and open a society as that of the Left Bank. She discovered there no island havens, no communities of writers, no women friends who might support her talent. Even the relationship with Ford Madox Ford, who had served as both mentor and publisher to her (printing some of her stories in *Transatlantic Review*), was destroyed when Ford fell in love with her. Like many of Rhys's relationships with men, this one ended in disappointment and bitterness and left Rhys, in Thomas F. Staley's words, "desperate and dependent": "his relationship with her . . . confirmed her deepest suspicions about her own feminine vulnerability and male exploitation" (*Jean Rhys,* 12–13).

Rhys was not destined, then, to discover on the Paris Left Bank the "perfection" that Ford claimed existed there. Instead, she discovered its outer regions where streets smelled of poverty and hunger and lives were desperate and embittered. In the thirteenth *arrondissement,* southeast of what Ford termed "the living heart" of Paris in the Latin Quarter ("Preface," *The Left Bank,* 13), Rhys spent long days of aimless walking through mean and uninteresting quarters, passed nights in cheap hotels, and made weekly visits to the Santé prison (where her husband, Jean Lenglet, was interred for trafficking in art objects of questionable ownership). In short, she discovered a part of the Left Bank unknown to other of its residents. Stella Bowen, Ford's mistress at the time of his affair with Rhys, described Rhys in these years as "a really tragic person" whose literary talent was offset by "bad health, destitution, shattered nerves, an undesirable husband, lack of nationality, and a complete absence of any desire for independence." It was precisely these qualities, listed rather uncharitably by her rival, that Rhys examined in her fiction. According to Bowen, Rhys's fiction "took the lid off the world that she knew, and showed us an underworld of darkness and disorder, where officialdom, the bourgeoisie and the police were the eternal enemies and the fugitive the only hero. . . . She regarded the law as the instrument of the 'haves' against the 'have nots' and was well acquainted with every rung of that long and dismal ladder by which the respectable citizen descends towards degradation" (*Drawn from Life,* 166–167). In Rhys's fiction, the Left Bank was not the setting of an exciting literary revolution in which writers enjoyed the ease of cafe life. Rather, the Left Bank represented exhausting and degrading efforts to provide the necessities of survival.

Rhys represents an extreme example of woman's marginality in the modern urban environment. Although Paris provided the backdrop for many of her fictions—*Quartet; After Leaving Mr Mackenzie; Good Morning, Midnight*—and although she continued to prefer Paris to London, Rhys herself was never comfortable in the city setting. The city's margins, its peripheral limits, drew Rhys like a magnet: disgusted by the sordid, she was nonetheless incapable of resisting it. Sharing much with the women of her fictions, she too admitted to being marked by a fundamental passivity, the only means by which she was able to exert some measure of control over the environment around her. Paris induced in Rhys an extreme form of this lassitude; she discovered in Paris that she was unable to direct her own movements—and it was for this that she loved the city. Again and again in her life she was drawn to the Paris Left Bank, recalled to the memory of its power over her. As Ford Madox Ford had earlier observed, Rhys knew intimately the psychology of Left Bank existence:

> I should like to call attention to her profound knowledge of the life of the Left Bank—of many of the Left Banks of the world. For something mournful— and certainly hard up!—attaches to almost all uses of the word *left*. The left hand has not the cunning of the right: and every great city has its left bank. London has, round Bloomsbury, New York has, about Greenwich Village, so has Vienna. . . . And coming from the Antilles, with a terrifying insight and a terrific . . . passion for stating the case of the underdog, [Rhys] has let her pen loose on the Left Banks of the Old World—on its gaols, its studios, its salons, its cafes, its criminals, its midinettes—with a bias of admiration for its midinettes and of sympathy for its law-breakers. ("Preface," *The Left Bank,* 24)

Rhys wrote the underside of heterosexual woman's Paris existence as Djuna Barnes wrote the underside of the homosexual woman's experience in Paris. Each of their worlds is populated with outsiders, composed of people who live out their existences at an oblique angle to the larger culture. By comparison with Rhys, however, Barnes was a central figure in the expatriate literary community, an active participant in its cultural life, and her fiction represents a knowledge of the "outside" as seen from the "inside" of expatriate culture. Djuna Barnes spent fifteen years in Paris; Rhys made two brief appearances on the Paris scene, the first in the years immediately following World War I, a second time in the early 1920s. She moved like a ghost among the expatriates. Whether by choice or by chance, she remained at the furthest fringes of intellectual and literary activity during her Paris residence.

Within the Patriarchy: Heterosexual Women of the Left Bank

Rhys's experience describes in the extreme the situation of heterosexual women in the Paris community. Attached to men who were journalists, editors, or writers themselves, these women often found themselves in satellite roles to the more successful careers of their husbands or lovers or found their desire to write eclipsed altogether by the requirements of home and family. The most tragic case was Zelda Fitzgerald's, and while the sources of her mental illness were complex, her continuing breakdowns were caused in part by her husband's jealousy of her own desire to write and the inability to discover a place for herself among the resident artist community in Paris. More common to the expatriate woman's experience were the situations of Kay Boyle, Caroline Gordon, and Maria Jolas, women who continued writing, editing, and translating activities while raising children and assisting in furthering their husbands' literary careers. Katherine Anne Porter is perhaps the single example of an expatriate woman writer whose career was fostered and furthered by marriage. She married Eugene Pressly, who worked for the American diplomatic corps, in 1933, spending the next four years living in Paris. As Joan Givner explains, "The marriage to Pressly must . . . be counted among the favorable conditions which contributed to Porter's creativity during her Paris period. While the marriage was far from satisfactory, the relationship was the longest she maintained with any man, and it represented the nearest compromise she ever achieved between her conflicting desires for a domestic life and the solitary existence necessary for her work" ("Katherine Anne Porter," in Rood, *American Writers in Paris*, 4:313). In general, however, heterosexual women of the expatriate community did not find in marriage the enriching and supportive relationships that homosexual women of the community found with each other. Even presumably "liberated" marriages—like those of Harry and Caresse Crosby or Scott and Zelda Fitzgerald—were often painful and ultimately destructive to one or both partners. Even more debilitating were the serial relationships and brief encounters that characterized Nancy Cunard's and Peggy Guggenheim's expatriate existences or the relationships based on economic need and sexual dependence described in Jean Rhys's fiction and experienced by Rhys herself in the early years of her writing career.

The individual circumstances of heterosexual women tended to confirm the normative pattern by which the interests of men took precedence over those of women. By choosing alternative erotic existences, homosexual women found it somewhat easier to redefine the emotional and psychological dynamics of their relationships with each other, often moving away from the standard of heterosexual behavior in which one partner assumed authority and control over the other. Moreover, homosexual women of necessity were forced to define and create their own communities of friends; they could not assume that such support groups were a "given" in the culture of any urban environment, although the city itself provided the meeting ground—in cafes, restaurants, bars—for these women. Paris lesbians, however, avoided public spaces and created their own private places within the city, redefining the nineteenth-century salon for their own emotional and intellectual purposes. These environments served, in fact, as power bases for women in Paris, threatening at certain times to overthrow the androcentric culture of the Modernist patriarchy. While homosexual women writers were *de facto* on the margins of the heterosexual and paternalistic expatriate society, they were far less marginalized than heterosexual women who were unable (even unwilling) to establish any firm power base within the masculine culture and who were threatened by the company of homosexual women. For the "wives"—as Stein so astutely defined all women who attached themselves to a dominant partner—the Paris community did not provide the occasion to rewrite the paternalistic law but offered a further reinforcement of it, the more painful because masked by many illusory freedoms, the most seductive (and destructive) of which was the freedom to explore erotic and emotional relationships outside the bounds of marriage. In this, as Jean Rhys discovered, woman opened herself to further exploitation by men and, often, the censure of other women.

Redefining Paris: The Female Poetic

If Paris offered herself to men as a mistress of carnal delights, women discovered in the folds of her recumbent body confirmation of their own contradictory experience as women. Paris, like woman, was simultaneously desired and detested, courted and corrupted. The Modernist men who came to Paris in the early twentieth century had been seduced by her charms; in establishing within her embrace one of the most powerful literary movements in history, although their literary claims would separate politics and poetics, sexuality and aesthetics, it is clear that Modernism staked its claims on political and sexual grounds. The politics of Modernism were too closely allied with the reactionary for comfort (only the Russian Futurists were able to turn Modernism's poetics into Communist politics), whereas the patriarchal and heterosexual imperative of Modernism was implicit in even the most "neutral" of aesthetic principles. It was Modernist women writers who, in Sandra M. Gilbert's words, exposed in this "asexual poetics" a submerged—even repressed—"sexual politics" ("From *Patria* to *Matria*," 195).

If the experience of expatriate women writers in Paris tells us anything, it tells us that poetics and politics are never separate and that the very notion of the "asexual" incorporates the concept of the "sexual." Further, it has shown us the ways in which some Modernist women writers fused "asexual poetics" and "sexual politics" in the continuation of a female poetic tradition that extended back to Sappho and forward to H. D.'s rewriting of the classical tradition. That is, these women established on the body politic of Paris a female landscape that redefined—both in life and in literature—the role that city has traditionally played for the male literary imagination. With the exception of Gertrude Stein, Modernist women writers did not take Paris itself as a subject for their writing, revising and rewriting the standard metaphors applied to the city, but rather discovered in its dimensions a pattern of life that allowed literature itself to be re-visioned. They recalled through Paris the ancient matriarchal Minoan civilization and the long-lost sisterhood in Mytilène: Paris served as both *matria* and *sororitas*.

Natalie Barney turned her energies to reestablishing a Sapphic sisterhood, while Adrienne Monnier envisioned in her house of books a country of memory that would resurrect a mother whose memory had been effaced by patriarchal civilization. She imagined Odéonia as a female place whose heart and hearth welcomed all who crossed the threshold of 7, rue de l'Odéon. Those expatriate women who decided to "stay on" during the occupation of the Second World War came to La Maison des Amis des Livres seeking friendship and conversation. Adrienne Monnier was later to remember that this small band of American women "shared our sufferings and privations with love and underwent a more or less long captivity" in the war years because, "having settled in Paris, [they] never wanted to leave it" (*Very Rich Hours*, 413). Worried for their safety, Adrienne was also heartened by their intense loyalty to France. One among them, Florence Gilliam, returned to New York in 1941. In her only published book, *France: A Tribute by an American Woman* (1945), she reported that in leaving Paris she felt the past slip away: "I felt something like the snapping of a continuity. Life had always seemed a chain . . . or quicksilver perhaps, which defies sharp beginnings and endings. Never was there a point at which to stop and look back, or peer ahead. That day, time seemed for once to stand still" (quoted in "Florence Gilliam," *American Writers in Paris: 1920–1939*, 177). For Colette, however, the past was recalled by the events of World War II. Her writings of the 1930s anticipate the inevitability of another war, and her journals of the early days of the war and occupation recall to her mind the experiences of an earlier time. In particular, she regrets the effects of that earlier period on women, dreaming of a romanticized past in which woman was domesticated:

> Twenty-six years ago, a long and murderous war called women to fill the place of the men who were fighting or sacrificed. They held it by the physical and moral effort which is well-known and of which they did not believe themselves capable. Since then woman has not thought, has refused to think, that a day might come when she might be asked to seek her full stature in home and hearth. Gallant, often ambitious, having lost the habit of idleness and modesty, women have no longer been tempted by obscure goals and have turned away from their ancient mission: to organize and distribute a homely happiness.
>
> The great change for women a quarter of a century ago was to adopt a mode of existence where, initially, everything was injurious to her. . . . But she had to adapt herself to every hasty apprenticeship, accept the atmosphere of the factory, get used to cloakrooms, refectories, the hubbub of communal labor, the hostility of fellow-workers, the unfeelingness of administration. But

just admire what she made of herself in so few years! Seasoned she certainly is. But she no longer has any acquaintance with laborious solitude and silence. . . . The communal work imposed by the epoch has guided woman to communal leisure and pleasure and she has demanded them. (*Looking Backwards,* 111–112)

Hitler closed the door on the communal life of literary Paris. Women like Colette and Adrienne Monnier were to remember the Second World War as a time of enforced solitude, the present moment of that war constructed in reminiscences of the past and vague hopes for the future. Frequently their thoughts and writing turned to other women, to mothers and older sisters, to women of an earlier time. They placed themselves in a woman's tradition from which they constructed a bravery and endurance that inhered in a female identity. Those women who stayed on or who returned to the Left Bank following the war created for themselves an afterlife that recalled the country of memory, a powerful mother culture beyond the bounds of patriarchy. Recalled to the country of memory, Adrienne Monnier remembered an earlier war, during which she had established her bookshop. Her memories rekindled the spirit of womanhood that nurtured the early years of twentieth-century culture: "Here then, built in a time of destruction, is La Maison des Amis des Livres. Adrienne Monnier wrote these pages there in August 1918. Outside, the menace is less great, but here, in the midst of books that guard all living forms like the animals of the ark, she was preserved from revolt and from fear, she acquired the certainty that everything abides and grows beyond the nights of sleep and death, and that everything is faithful to the best will" ("La Maison des Amies des Livres," 75).

NOTES

1. Women of the Left Bank

1. *Staying On Alone: Letters of Alice B. Toklas,* ed. Edward Burns. Janet Flanner captured the poignancy of Toklas's later existence in a *New Yorker* "Profile" entitled, "Memory Is All" (*Janet Flanner's World*), 334–341.

2. The effort to construct a feminist poetics for female Modernists has just begun. Feminist critics have drawn on work in history, psychoanalytic theory, Marxism, and poststructuralism as the bases for approaches to Modernist women's writing. Sandra M. Gilbert and Susan Gubar's *The Madwoman in the Attic,* Elaine Showalter's *A Literature of Their Own,* Nina Auerbach's *Communities of Women* and *Woman and the Demon,* among others, have used feminist critical approaches to illuminate women's writing in the nineteenth century. Of undoubted importance to a reexamination of twentieth-century women writers will be Sandra M. Gilbert and Susan Gubar's forthcoming study, *No Man's Land: The Place of the Woman Writer in the Twentieth Century.* The controlling thesis of the latter work is adumbrated by Susan Gubar in "Sapphistries" (*Signs,* 10 [1984]: 43–62). Contrasting the experience of the twentieth-century woman writer to that of her nineteenth-century precursors, Gubar addresses herself to the situation of women writers who are both sexually and domestically expatriated. For Gubar, lesbian women writers "replac[ed] the schizophrenic doubling Sandra Gilbert and I have traced throughout Victorian women's literature with euphoric coupling [between women] in which the other is bound to the self as a lover" (47); "living . . . *ex patria,* outside of their fathers' country, they represent their exile as a privileged marginalization that paradoxically exposes the homogeneity of heterosexual culture, the heterogeneity of homosexual coupling" (62).

Recent work on individual women writers, especially work on Djuna Barnes, Natalie Barney, Colette, H. D., Mina Loy, Renée Vivien, Virginia Woolf, Katherine Anne Porter, Jean Rhys, and Edith Wharton, has demonstrated the rich interpretive resources available to feminist critics in their re-visionary efforts. Of central importance to much of this work has been the attempt by the scientific and social science communities to redefine the nature of female sexuality, particularly the relationship between mothers and daughters, and the work of historians, political analysts, and psychologists in examining the effects on women of living within patriarchal cultures. Of particular importance is "The Lesbian Issue" of *Signs* (9:1984) devoted to these questions. References to individual works are included below under "Works Cited and Consulted."

3. The underlying assumptions about women that inform feminist and deconstructive practice as described here are examined by Nina Baym in "The Madwoman and Her Languages" (*Tulsa Studies in Women's Literature* 3 [1984]: 45–60). In particular, Baym isolates work on women's language, suggesting that *écriture féminine* conspires with deconstructive descriptions of the otherness of women's languages: "A theory of uniquely female language emerges. Descriptions and prescriptions result from a common procedure: features of the dominant language, masculine because dominant, are identified; opposite features are advanced as appropriate for women. . . . The theory is also applied by certain especially ingenious critics to discover the mandated language in canonical women's texts via deconstruction. Deconstruction, however, is a procedure whose vocabulary, shared by non-feminists and men, yields identical results no matter whose texts it analyzes" (49). Because the features "advanced as appropriate for women" are also features of what has been termed Modernist or experimental writings (in Christiane Makward's terms, "open, linear, unfinished, fluid, exploded, fragmented, polysemic, attempting to speak the body, i.e., the unconscious, involving silence, incorporating the simultaneity of life as opposed to or clearly different from pre-conceived, oriented, masterly or 'didactic' languages," "To Be or Not to Be . . . a Feminist Speaker," in Eisenstein and Jardine, *The Future of Difference*, 96), Baym's argument—which may be seen by some as not accurately describing French poststructuralist logic—has relevance to the use of these methodologies in this text. That is, Baym is not alone in making such claims against feminist and deconstructive logic. A similar argument is put forth by Carolyn G. Heilbrun, "Presidential Address 1984," Modern Language Association (*PMLA*, 100, 281–282).

4. Some of the more important contributions include Gloria Feman Orenstein, "The Salon of Natalie Clifford Barney: An Interview with Berthe Cleyrergue" (*Signs* 4 [1979]: 484–496); Susan Gubar, "Blessings in Disguise: Cross-Dressing as Re-Dressing for Female Modernists" (*Massachusetts Review* 22 [1981]: 477–508); Elyse Blankley, "Return to Mytilène: Renée Vivien and the City of Women" (in Squier, *Women Writers and the City*); Karla Jay, "The Disciples of the Tenth Muse: Natalie Clifford Barney and Renée Vivien" (unpublished dissertation), and Susan Gubar, "Sapphistries." Of particular import in this emerging discussion is Gloria Feman Orenstein's forthcoming study of *salonières, Salon Women: Creators of Culture.*

5. See Monique Wittig, "Paradigm" (in Stambolian and Marks, *Homosexualities*), and Blanche Wiesen Cook, "'Women Alone Stir My Imagination'" (*Signs* 4 [1979]: 718–739) and *Women and Support Networks,* for evidence of the ways in which lesbian culture has been erased, obscured, or trivialized. Both Wittig and Cook argue the political necessity behind the scientific and moral labeling of lesbianism as perversion, situated in the need to use women's bodies for reproductive

purposes. Lesbian resistance to the dominant heterosexual and heterosocial codes resulted in mass cultural censorship.

6. Works that reflect such bias include Susan Gubar's "Blessings in Disguise," which her "Sapphistries" tries to redress, suggesting a heterogeneity of homosexual experience (see note 3); Bertha Harris's "The More Profound Nationality of Their Lesbianism" in Birky, et al., *Amazon Expedition;* George Wickes, *The Amazon of Letters;* and Jean Chalon, *Portrait of a Seductress.* More recent work on the general subject of the lesbian communities in Paris during these years and on individual women (particularly work by Elyse Blankley, Blanche Wiesen Cook, Karla Jay, Jane Marcus, Gloria Feman Orenstein, and Catharine R. Stimpson) has helped to revise some of these stereotypes.

7. All quotations are from Hugh Ford, ed., *The Left Bank Revisited.*

8. Gloria Feman Orenstein's current work on Stein's salon is relevant here; in particular, see "Gertrude Stein: Decoding the Amusing Muse" (1984 MLA), where she argues that Toklas's role was to make Stein the centerpiece of the salon. Toklas promoted Stein as earlier French *salonières* had promoted their lions (Anatole France or Marcel Proust, for instance). In this reading, Toklas and Stein play out the heterosexual dialectic of their homosexual life together—Gertrude as male literary genius, Toklas as *salonière.*

9. *Paris Tribune,* 7 April 1931, quoted in *The Left Bank Revisited,* 141. Another version is quoted by Samuel Putnam, *Paris Was Our Mistress,* 153. This version differs radically from that printed in the *Tribune* and corrects the error that Stein made in naming as her first publication *The Making of Americans* in 1905 (in fact, it was published in 1925): "Joyce is good. He is a good writer. People like him because he is incomprehensible and nobody can understand him. But who came first, Gertrude Stein or James Joyce? Do not forget that my first great book, *Three Lives,* was published in 1908. That was long before *Ulysses.*" Stein herself is mistaken about the publication date of *Three Lives,* which appeared in 1909.

10. See particularly Benjamin Reid's *Art by Subtraction;* Frederick J. Hoffman, *Gertrude Stein;* and B. F. Skinner, "Has Gertrude Stein a Secret?" (*Atlantic Monthly* 153 [January 1934]: 50-57). Only recently, and under the auspices of feminist criticism, has a reevaluation of Stein's personal and artistic complexities begun. See "Works Cited and Consulted" for references to Blanche Wiesen Cook, Ulla Dydo, Marianne DeKoven, Lillian Faderman, Elizabeth Fifer, Cynthia Secor, Catharine R. Stimpson, and Jayne L. Walker.

11. Cook notes Barney's disapproval of Stein's "male-derived attitudes toward women," quoting a letter Barney wrote to Romaine Brooks on the subject: "Alice T. is withering away under the stress of moving into a new flat. . . . I am afraid 'the bigger one,' who gets fatter and fatter, will sooner or later devour her" ("'Women Alone Stir My Imagination,'" 734, quoted from Meryle Secrest, *Between Me and Life,* 327-328).

12. On the question of the Beach/Joyce finances and profits from *Ulysses,* see Maria Jolas, "The Joyce I Knew and the Women around Him" (*Crane Bag* 4 [1980]: 86), and Noel Riley Fitch, *Sylvia Beach and the Lost Generation,* 316-323. For a more general consideration of Joyce's working relationship with Beach, see Bonnie Kime Scott, *Joyce and Feminism.*

13. Sandra M. Gilbert and Susan Gubar define woman's place in twentieth-century writing in terms of the "no man's land" of trench warfare in World War I. See Gilbert's "Soldier's Heart" (*Signs* 8 [1983]: 422–450) and Jane Marcus's response to it, "Asylums of Antaeus: Women, War and Madness" (1985 SCMLA).

14. Paul Fussell makes this issue the central subject of his study *The Great War and Modern Memory*.

15. See Maurice Beebe, "Joyce and the Meanings of Modernism" (in Bates and Pollock, *Litters from Aloft*), especially 16–17, where Beebe delineates four characteristics of Modernism: formalism; irony; mythic ordering; self-reflexiveness. A somewhat more complex explanation of Modernism is provided by Malcolm Bradbury and James McFarlane in "The Name and Nature of Modernism" (in Bradbury and McFarlane, *Modernism*). As they suggest, Modernism changed its premises and practices from one European city to another and from one period to another. In "Struggling Westward," Bradbury delineates four stages of Modernism: Modernism I (1890s); Modernism II (1900–1912); Modernism III (1913–1930); Modernism IV (1930s). Descriptions that share some—but not all—of these defining elements are Hugh Kenner's "The Making of the Modernist Canon" (*Chicago Review* 34 [1984]: 49–61) and David Antin's "Some Questions about Modernism" (*Occident* 8 [1974]: 7–38).

16. For a discussion of the ways in which Gertrude Stein, Virginia Woolf, and Edith Sitwell worked toward the development of an aesthetic and psychology of eccentricity in both their lives and writings, see Susan Hastings, "Two of the Weird Sisters" (*Tulsa Studies in Women's Literature* 4 [1985]: 101–123).

2. Secret Passages: The Faubourg St. Germain

1. The story of Edith Wharton's marriage, and of the effects of that marriage on the mental and physical health of both partners, is told by R. W. B. Lewis in his biography of Wharton. Married twenty-eight years at the time of their divorce, both Edith and Edward suffered the effects of a union that was sexless, without common interests or aspirations, and marked by lengthy separations and long periods of depression. It should not be assumed, however, that in choosing a life for herself in Paris Edith Wharton was consciously preparing a life in which her husband could not—and would not—fully participate, although it is certainly possible to read the ensuing events as the result of a subconscious effort to rid herself of middle-class marital conventions. Had her husband's deteriorating health, extramarital affairs, and consequent mismanagement of their estate and her earned income not been enough reason for Wharton seriously to consider a legal separation, her passionate affair with Morton Fullerton and the discovery of herself as a sexual being in the years preceding the divorce made more obvious to her the need to cut the marriage bond. Nonetheless, the decision for divorce—which was entirely hers—was an exceedingly difficult one that brought with it guilt, self-recrimination, and a further sense of personal failure.

2. Kay Boyle has remarked recently that the younger generation of Modernists was in "revolt against all literary pretentiousness, against weary, dreary rhetoric, against all the outworn literary and academic conventions. Our slogans were 'Down with Henry James, down with Edith Wharton, down with the sterility of

"The Waste Land"''" (Leo Litwak, "Kay Boyle—Paris Wasn't Like That," *New York Times Book Review* [15 July 1984], 2).

3. Disillusioned with the *haut-monde*, Proust nonetheless found ways in *A la recherche* to redeem certain of its participants. He wrote to a friend: "The nicest people sometimes go through hateful periods. I promise you that in the following volume, when he becomes a Dreyfusard, Swann will begin once more to be sympathetic" (Rivers, *Proust and the Art of Love*, 154).

4. George Stambolian and Elaine Marks emphasize the "pluralism and diversity" of homosexual experience as it is recorded in literature by and about homosexuals (*Homosexualities and French Literature*, 24–25). The effects of compulsory heterosexuality on homosexual women are explored by Adrienne Rich in "Compulsory Heterosexuality and Lesbian Existence" (*Signs* 5 [1980]: 631–660). See also Wittig, "Paradigm," 118–119.

5. On lesbian images, see Elaine Marks, "Lesbian Intertextuality" in *Homosexualities and French Literature*, 360ff. The definitions of the female in homosexual ideology are from Eric Bentley's essay in the same volume, "We Are in History," 132–133. He describes what he calls the "Uncle Tomism" of an earlier stage of male homosexual ideology whose definition rested on the scientific notion that male homosexuals had a female soul trapped inside a male body. It is the female soul that is weak, sickly, and that the man must deny in order to behave as a "normal" heterosexual male. See Hélène Cixous on *la folle*, "Rethinking Differences," in the same volume, 76–77.

6. See Esther Newton, "The Mythic Mannish Lesbian: Radclyffe Hall and the New Woman" (*Signs* 9 [1984]: 557–575). See also the discussion of this and related theories (by Brouardel, Krafft-Ebing, Havelock Ellis, and others) in Rivers, *Proust and the Art of Love*, 156–158, 164–165, 184–188. Such scientific theories replaced, temporarily, other models for women's behavior such as those apparent in mythology. An alternative reading to the notion that all homosexual women of this period believed themselves to be victims of a biological malfunction is available in Jane Marcus, "Liberty, Sorority, Misogyny" (in Heilbrun and Higgonet, *The Representation of Women in Fiction*), and in Martha Vicinus, "Distance and Desire: English Boarding School Friendships" (*Signs* 9 [1984]: 600–622), as well as in Elyse Blankley's subtle reading of Renée Vivien, "Return to Mytilène." The model for this alternative vision of lesbian homosexuality was, of course, Natalie Barney. Sandra M. Gilbert discusses the "liberating" aspects of the third sex in "Costumes of the Mind" (*Critical Inquiry* 7 [1980]: 416–417).

7. J. E. Rivers discusses the various scientific theories that associated male homosexuality with feminine characteristics. The work of Tardieu, Carpenter, and Krafft-Ebing finds feminine tendencies a consistent feature of male homosexuals. To quote Carpenter, "In the male of this kind we have a distinctly effeminate type, sentimental . . . mincing in gait and manners, something of a chatterbox, skillful in woman's work, sometimes taking pleasure in dressing in woman's clothes; his figure not unfrequently betraying a tendency towards the feminine, large at the hips, supple, not muscular, the face wanting in hair, the voice inclining to be high-pitched" (*Proust and the Art of Love*, 182). Proust employed such stereotyped images of homosexual men in *A la recherche*, where a hatred of these tendencies is internalized by the male homosexual. As Rivers points out, "in *A la recherche*, of

course, Charlus is notorious for his self-conscious attempt to banish any trace of the flamboyant or feminine from his outfits. . . . As for the feminine gestures and postures of men who are homosexually inclined, Jupien, in his attempt to attract Charlus, 'placed with grotesque impertinence his fist on his hip, stuck out his derriere, struck poses with the same coquetishness [*sic*] the orchid could have displayed to the bees' (2:604)" (183). The modifying terms in this quotation from Proust ("grotesque impertinence," "coquetishness") suggest a use of culturally ascribed femininity to burlesque it.

8. Martin Green (*Children of the Sun*) links dandyism to an emphasis on style in Modernist art and finds the psychological sources of dandyism in an unwillingness to grow up and accept responsibility. Such definitions have important implications for Modernist art that are overlooked by Green, in particular the implied analogy between women's "style" and the burlesque of it in dandyism and the childishness Green suggests is part of the dandy's rebellion. Similar analogies have been used to suggest that women's writing of the Modernist period was not to be taken seriously because of its marked "style" (and implied lack of substance) and because of its rebellion against the patriarchal virtues of the Modernist undertaking. These issues are taken up at greater length in later chapters and in my essay on Gertrude Stein, "Beyond the Reaches of Feminist Criticism" (*Tulsa Studies in Women's Literature* 3 [1984]: 5–27), but it is important to note here the degree to which dandyism marked its rebellion against Victorian literary fathers by a blatant form of misogyny. More significant, perhaps, is the blindness of Martin Green and of Ellen Moers (*The Dandy: Brummell to Beerbohm*) to the misogynistic element in dandyism. The inversion of sexual stereotypes for subversive purposes extends in mythology back to the Greeks: Amazons were little boy/girls who refused to grow up (see Tyrrell, *Amazons*, 40–55).

9. This incident is recorded in Rivers, *Proust and the Art of Love,* 31. The confession was apparently made on 13 May 1921 and recorded by Gide in his *Journal* the following day. The tone in which Gide claims the confession to have been made, however, may owe more to his need to make Proust confess his homosexual inclinations and to have Proust as a fellow homosexual than to Proust's own declaration. Gide's comments cannot be accepted at face value, since they were written without Proust's knowledge and published after his death, Gide taking for himself the "last word" on the subject of Proust's homosexuality.

10. As J. E. Rivers comments, Painter's reading of Proust's sexuality is a heavily Freudian one in which the overanxious love of a mother is the root cause of the son's sexual abnormality (*Proust and the Art of Love,* 17–18). None of the underlying assumptions about homosexuality are examined by Painter, nor does he question the use of sexual stereotypes in Proust's texts (particularly *A la recherche*). He seems to accept these stereotypes at face value (as does Michèle Sarde, in her discussion of the Sodom and Gomorrah sections of those texts in *Colette,* 227–229). Painter thus sees the homosexual experience as an inevitable descent into degradation and is unable to draw distinctions among a variety of homosexualities—both male and female.

11. See Carroll Smith-Rosenberg, "The New Woman and the Mannish Lesbian: Gender Disorder and Social Control," in *Disorderly Conduct: Visions of Gender*

in Victorian America, and Newton, "The Mythic Mannish Lesbian." See also Wittig, "Paradigm," and Cook, "'Women Alone Stir My Imagination.'"

12. See J. E. Rivers's discussion of Painter's reading of Proust's descent into decadence for an alternate reading of male homosexual behavior in these years in *Proust and the Art of Love,* 15–21.

13. This misperception has been repeated by several critics (including Millicent Bell and George Painter) whose work was published prior to R. W. B. Lewis's biography of Wharton. Painter describes Berry as a "steadying influence on the passionate Mrs. Wharton" (*Marcel Proust,* 2:253), suggesting Wharton's lust for Berry was "deplored" by Berry's friends. The major shock produced by that publication, however, was the identification of Morton Fullerton, an American journalist resident in Paris prior to World War I, as the secret lover of Wharton's diary. Among many unpublished and private papers to which Lewis had access was the fragment of a highly erotic fiction, "Beatrice Palmato," whose sexual explicitness betrays the notions of Edith Wharton as a rather stiff, highly proper lady of the "old school." The subject of this fragment is father-daughter incest, and while no one suggests that Wharton had personal experience with this taboo form of sexuality, it is clear from this narrative that she had a fuller range of sexual knowledge than had previously been thought. Wharton's relationship with Morton Fullerton is outlined by Alan Gribben in "'The Heart Is Insatiable'" (*Library Chronicle of the University of Texas at Austin* n.s. 31 [1985]:7–20) and in "Edith Wharton Letters" (ibid., 21–72). Clare Colquitt examines the importance of this relationship for Wharton in "Unpacking Her Treasures" (ibid., 73–107).

3. Simultaneous Existences: Four Lives in St. Germain

1. In the section of this work entitled "The Faubourg," Lewis situates the solidity and tradition of Faubourg life against the changes in French culture and the undercurrent of unrest in the early years of this century in Paris itself. The disjunction between the cloistered world of old society and the unstable character of European life in these years is crucial to understanding the events that follow (e.g., World War I) and the reaction of the 1920s to prior forms and codes of French life.

2. Jane Lilienfeld discusses the various roles played by Willy and Colette's mother, Sido, in Colette's literary creativity. She concludes that it was the relationship with her mother that was essential to Colette's writing, Sido not only serving as a model artist but playing a central role in Colette's use of language and imagery. For Lilienfeld, "Willy was accident. Sido was necessary" ("The Magic Spinning Wheel: Straw of Gold—Colette, Willy, and Sido," in Perry and Brownley, *Mothering the Mind,* 165–177).

3. R. W. B. Lewis seems to have thought that Natalie Clifford Barney was a widow and that "Barney" was her married name. He perhaps followed the erroneous *New York Times* obituary, which indicated that she was briefly married to a Mr. Clifford. But Clifford was Barney's father's middle name (Albert Clifford Barney); she was never married.

4. See Françoise Mallet-Joris, "A Womanly Vocation," in Eisinger and Mc-

Carty, *Colette: The Woman, The Writer,* 7–15, especially the description of Colette's ambivalence about writing.

4. From the Left Bank to the Upper East Side: Janet Flanner's Letter from Paris

1. Janet Flanner's "Letter from Paris" appeared fortnightly in the *New Yorker* from October 1925 until September 1975. This study examines the letters written between 1925 and 1939, dividing those that deal with the Paris cultural and political scene from those that focus primarily on the rise of Fascism and its implications for France. All parenthetical notations are to the issue of the *New Yorker* in which the letters appeared.

2. All Flanner letters (here edited) are to be found in the Library of Congress collection under her name.

3. The extent to which Paris lesbians internalized homophobia is considered further in chapters 8 and 9.

4. It is important to note that the assumptions that underlie Gilbert's assessment of the effects of World War I on English women may not necessarily hold for French women. That France was occupied by German troops during the First World War, and that these troops were quartered in the most heavily populated industrial sections of the country, constituted a primary difference in the living experience between the two countries. While English women worked in munitions factories, taking over men's jobs and performing essential services for the Allied military operation, in France these very industries were located near the trenches and suffered almost continual German bombardment. For the most part, there were no industries in France in which women could serve. Instead, French women went about preserving the notion that life away from the war zone went on as usual: they fought against the very notion of a debilitating war by the pretense that the war had no effect on daily life (see Richard Cobb, *French and Germans,* 14–15). Like English women, however, French women cared for the sick and wounded, served as nurses and aides in hospitals, and drove ambulances.

5. Gertrude Stein and Alice B. Toklas: Rue de Fleurus

1. *The Autobiography of Alice B. Toklas,* 6. Neil Schmitz, *Of Huck and Alice: Humorous Writing in American Literature,* discusses the implications of a narrative method that makes Alice Toklas the observer in order to render Gertrude Stein absent from her own story. He suggests that Stein is an escaped slave, that the *Autobiography* is a fugitive narrative in which Stein is the one sought after but never found: "I am not here" (see particularly chapter 7, "The Genius of Gertrude Stein," 200–240).

2. B. L. Reid, *Art by Subtraction: A Dissenting Opinion of Gertrude Stein,* 19, 168. See also Edmund Wilson's comment on visiting Gertrude Stein at the rue Christine apartment in "Gertrude Stein Old and Young" (in *The Shores of Light,* 585): "this reviewer met Miss Stein only once, but he received, in the course of that interview, an agreeable first impression of a quick and original intelli-

gence dealing readily from the surface of the mind with the surfaces presented by life . . . but a chilling second impression of (to resort to an overworked metaphor) a great iceberg of megalomania that lay beneath this surface and on which, if one did not skirt around it, conversations and personal relations might easily crash and be wrecked."

3. "Gertrude and I are not just contrary. She's basically stupid and I'm basically intelligent" (Leo Stein, *Journey into Self*, 149). Among the marginal notes Leo Stein included in his personal copy of *Paris France* (published in 1940, his copy part of the Stein materials in the American Literature Collection at Yale University) are these: "Gertrude like all stupid people is given to the post hoc propter hoc kind of reasoning because they haven't more than one thing in their minds at a time" (*Paris France*, 7). Appended to her comment "so familiarity did not breed contempt" (14), Leo wrote: "Of course the proverb means that the extraordinary becomes ordinary with familiarity. Gertrude doesn't know English."

4. The chronology of the affair and the composition of *Q.E.D.* is complicated; it is outlined by Katz's "Introduction"; by Mellow, *Charmed Circle*, 56–68, 73–83; and by Bridgman, *Gertrude Stein in Pieces*, 37–47.

5. I am indebted for the insight to Jan Calloway's unpublished paper "The Patriarchal Portraits of H. D. and Gertrude Stein." Stein uses the occasion to reflect upon the experience that necessitated her flight.

6. The extant Radcliffe themes from English Composition 22 (which Stein took in 1894–95 and in which she received a C) are collected in Rosalind S. Miller, *Gertrude Stein: Form and Intelligibility*. Many of these seem to be early efforts at fiction based on experiences in Stein's own life; they often have a meditative quality, as though they are simultaneously exploring the situation and the possibility for rendering situation through writing. A surprising number are narratives, rather traditionally set forth, suggesting that in her earliest writings Stein was interested in storytelling. Bridgman sees the autobiographical elements in these essays: "in them she held a mirror before her face" (22).

7. See also Pamela Hadas's comments on Leo's "incessant need to lecture" in "Spreading the Difference: One Way to Read Gertrude Stein's *Tender Buttons*" (*Twentieth Century Literature* 24 [1978]: 61). It should be noted that *Everybody's Autobiography*, like the *Autobiography of Alice B. Toklas*, is a shifting fictional terrain whose surface is composed of self-justifications, fantasies, even lies. As such, it reveals a great deal about Stein's psychic economy.

8. *Two: Gertrude Stein and Her Brother and Other Early Portraits*, 9. Manuscript copies of *Two* (available in the American Literature Collection at Yale University) suggest that these lines reflect the similarity of personality and modes of communication between Sally and Leo Stein. The title of this piece places Gertrude in relation to Leo, however. I suggest that the word portrait incorporates Sally and Leo as a unit, making Gertrude the observer, the listener, the "other." The relationship examined here is that of brother and sister, with the sister-in-law allied to the brother. As the notes to Jayne L. Walker's chapter on *Two* as a transitional text in Stein's work indicate, Stein was in the process of trying to separate herself from her brother during the time she was at work on *Two* (in 1911). Her notebooks contain "a long, devastatingly critical analysis of her brother" (*The*

Making of a Modernist, 104), written as she was completing *The Making of Americans* and beginning work on *Two* (see *The Making of a Modernist,* 159, fn. 4, and 160, fn. 15).

9. Jan Calloway makes an interesting observation in "Patriarchal Portraits," suggesting that because the pronominal referents are so obscure here, the "I" may also refer to Leo Stein, making his anger at Gertrude's writing due to her exclusion of him as the reason for her success (22).

10. Among those who have read failure in Stein's work are Edmund Wilson (who praised the early work and found the later, more experimental writing unintelligible), Katherine Anne Porter, B. F. Skinner, B. L. Reid, and many others.

11. The most extended version of this complaint with Stein has been articulated by B. L. Reid, *Art by Subtraction: A Dissenting Opinion of Gertrude Stein.* Although the title of this work suggests that it is a minority view of Stein, in fact the principles of Reid's investigation inform much of earlier Stein criticism.

12. The later, more experimental, Stein texts have systematically been avoided by critics, perhaps because they are just too difficult. Richard Kostelanetz, in his perceptive introduction to *The Yale Gertrude Stein,* notes that "the enterprise of American literary criticism has scarcely noticed Stein's work, and too many literary professionals honor and teach the simpler books, such as *Three Lives* and *The Autobiography of Alice B. Toklas,* to the neglect of the more extraordinary ones—those whose special qualities have never been exceeded" (xxix–xxx). The best work on Stein has been published within the last two years, but even these texts (by DeKoven, Dubnick, Schmitz, and Walker) avoid confronting those Stein texts that address the issue of language itself.

13. Those who have worked to explicate Stein's sexual language include Richard Bridgman, *Gertrude Stein in Pieces;* Linda Simon, *The Biography of Alice B. Toklas;* Catharine R. Stimpson; "The Mind, the Body, and Gertrude Stein" (*Critical Inquiry* 3 [1977]: 491–506), "Gertrice/Altrude: Stein, Toklas, and the Paradox of the Happy Marriage" (in Perry and Brownley, *Mothering the Mind*), and "The Somagrams of Gertrude Stein" (*Poetics Today* 6 [1985]: 67–80); Cynthia Secor, "Gertrude Stein: The Complex Force of Her Femininity" (in *Women, the Arts,* edited by Wheeler and Lussier, 27–35); Elizabeth Fifer, "Is Flesh Advisable? The Interior Theater of Gertrude Stein" (*Signs* 4 [1979]: 472–483). Catharine R. Stimpson is at work on a book-length study of Stein that will further explicate the lesbian contexts of her works.

14. See Catharine R. Stimpson, "The Somagrams of Gertrude Stein" and my "Beyond the Reaches of Feminist Criticism: A Letter from Paris."

15. Using Stein and Toklas as examples, Adrienne Rich cautions us against such readings in "Compulsory Heterosexuality and Lesbian Existence" (*Signs* 5 [1980]: 648). Jane Marcus, in "Carnival of the Animals" (*Women's Review of Books* 8 [May 1984]: 6–7), a review of Andrew Field's biography of Djuna Barnes, makes an issue of distinguishing the kinds of ritual love acts among Paris lesbians and the uses to which they put costuming.

16. Bertha Harris, in "The More Profound Nationality of Their Lesbianism" (in Birky, et al., *Amazon Expedition*), recounts the anecdote from William Carlos Williams's autobiography that recalls the behavior of a member of the Chamber of

Deputies at Natalie Barney's. George Wickes's account tells of female couples "silently slipping away" during Barney's Friday evening salons. Barney made an effort on these occasions to include both men and women, homosexuals and heterosexuals. Although we have little evidence of what took place at such events, apart from the confused and contradictory memories of those who attended them, the separate meetings of the salon, the Académie des Femmes, and groups of women who came to the Temple à l'Amitié should be carefully distinguished from each other.

17. Natalie Barney, for instance, was particularly interested in the Burne-Jones image of beauty. On the subject of Burne-Jones and misogyny, see Joseph Kestner, "Edward Burne-Jones and the Nineteenth-Century Fear of Women" (*Biography* 7 [1984]: 95–122).

18. "From Dark to Day," *Vogue*, November 1945: "I suppose there at the opening, we were the only ones who had been clothed in all those long years in Pierre Balmain's clothes, we were proud of it. It is nice to know the young man when he is just a young man and nobody knows, and now well I guess very soon now anybody will know. And we were so pleased and proud." See also Pierre Balmain, *My Years and Seasons:* Stein and Toklas attended Balmain's first Paris opening with Cecil Beaton (113).

19. See Katherine Anne Porter, "Gertrude Stein: A Self-Portrait" (*Harper's* 195 [December 1947]: 519–527); Catharine R. Stimpson, "The Mind, the Body, and Gertrude Stein"; and Cynthia Secor, "The Question of Gertrude Stein" (in *American Novelists Revisited*); as well as Linda Simon, *The Biography of Alice B. Toklas.*

20. In "Gertrude Stein: A Self-Portrait" Katherine Anne Porter questions Stein's patriotism and the means by which she survived both wars in Europe:

> She and Alice B. Toklas enjoyed both the wars. The first one especially being a lark with almost no one getting killed where you could see, and it ended so nicely too, without changing anything. The second was rather more serious. She lived safely enough in Bilignin throughout the German occupation, and there is a pretty story that the whole village conspired to keep her presence secret. She had been a citizen of the world in the best European tradition; for though America was her native land, she had to live in Europe because she felt at home there. (527)

From others there were actual suggestions that she had collaborated. One of her closest friends during the second war, Bernard Fay (who was appointed director of the Bibliothèque Nationale under the Vichy government) had assured official protection of Gertrude and Alice in Bilignin and had saved Stein's valuable art collection in the rue Christine apartment from confiscation by the Nazis. After the war he was imprisoned for his wartime activities. Stein's proximity to him led those who resented Stein, including Maria Jolas, to speculate that Stein herself had collaborated in order to protect herself. Such suspicions have not been confirmed and perhaps tell us more about the animosities toward Stein among others of the expatriate Paris community than about Stein's possible wartime activities. Those who allied themselves with anti-Fascist organizations or who worked with the resistance especially resented Stein's apparent ease and comfort during the war, leading to speculation—later proved true—that she was protected at the highest levels of the Vichy government.

21. See Catharine R. Stimpson, "Gertrude Stein and the Ideology of America," presented at the 1984 MLA (Washington, D.C.) and "Gertrude Stein: American Writer," presented at the 1985 SCMLA (Tulsa, Oklahoma).

22. See Ulla Dydo, "To Make a Sentence in Vincennes," presented at the 1984 MLA (Washington, D.C.). Dydo argues for a reading of Stein's poetry that is inflected and nuanced with French puns that operate on both the verbal and visual levels. She suggests the ways in which Stein's writing has absorbed the spoken French around her, rendered in an English that has a French subtext.

6. Sylvia Beach and Adrienne Monnier: Rue de l'Odéon

1. Monnier's *Gazette,* as McDougall explains, appeared irregularly in ten short issues from January 1938 until May 1940: "As the voice of La Maison des Amis des Livres, it was [Monnier's] vehicle not only for expressing herself directly to her own public on whatever topics she chose, but also a means of disseminating a bibliography, which she published serially from the second issue through that of July 1939, the last before the outbreak of the war" (469). Further references to essays in this collection are cited parenthetically in the text according to essay title. Contributions by McDougall are cited parenthetically as *Very Rich Hours.*

2. Letter from Noel Riley Fitch to author, September 1983.

3. Until the publication of Fitch's *Sylvia Beach and the Lost Generation,* Richard Ellmann's biography of James Joyce provided most of the factual information about Joyce's relation with Beach and was in part responsible for continuing the myth that Beach dedicated herself happily and unquestioningly to Joyce's career. Although it would have been of great interest to students of Joyce to know precisely his financial indebtedness to Beach, the relevant materials were not examined by Ellmann. The recent publication of Beach's biography has made apparent the risks that Shakespeare and Company incurred in its efforts to support Joyce through his various financial difficulties; until publication of Maria Jolas's article "The Joyce I Knew and the Women around Him," Monnier's angry letter received only casual allusion. The letter altered Joyce's working relationship with Monnier and Beach (as it was intended to do) by addressing the previously unexpressed tensions that had existed on both sides of the Beach-Joyce partnership. Ellmann's avoidance of such issues suggests that he took Adrienne Monnier and Sylvia Beach less seriously than did his biographical subject.

A portion of the letter is reproduced in Ellmann's revised and expanded biography of Joyce (1982). Maria Jolas contends that the letter quoted by Ellmann is not the letter Joyce showed her in 1931 (conversation with author, July 1984).

4. Letters documenting Beach's relationships with Bryher and with Camilla Steinbrugge are among those in the Beach papers at Princeton. My thanks to Noel Riley Fitch for documentation of Beach's relationship with Steinbrugge, information that is not contained in *Sylvia Beach and the Lost Generation.*

7. Djuna Barnes: Rue St.-Romain

1. Reading literature as biography is a common feature of critical analyses of expatriate writing. Memoirists of the period emphasize the *roman à clef* aspects of these literary works, identifying the circumstances and characters of the Paris setting. More than other such works, however, *Nightwood* has been subjected to readings that suggest its reality in Djuna Barnes's own lived experience. Andrew Field, for instance, suggests that in order to write the novel Barnes had only to listen to and observe the group of eccentric expatriates around her; see *Djuna,* particularly 137–141. An alternate reading is provided by Carolyn Burke, who comments of Djuna Barnes and Mina Loy: "It is my contention that their lapidary language actually prefigures their reclusiveness and that, for this reason, both their work and their lives illustrate tensions inherent in Modernism for women of their generation" ("'Accidental Aloofness,'" in Broe, *Silence and Power*).

2. In "To Make Her Mutton at Sixteen" (in Broe, *Silence and Power*), Louise A. DeSalvo discusses the theme of father-daughter incest in *The Antiphon,* calling the play a "chilling, utterly realistic and highly accurate portrayal of the psychodynamics and sexual pathology that operate with a family organized so that each child (but especially Miranda, the daughter) will be available for routinized and ritualized sexual molestation which their father, Titus Higby Hobbs, disguised (with the collusion of his dim-witted wife, Augusta) as religious ceremony."

In "'Tom Take Mercy'" (in Broe, *Silence and Power*), Linda Curry demonstrates through the successive drafts of *The Antiphon* the ways in which the incest theme is transformed from realism to ritual and complicates the character portrayal of the mother, especially her complicity in (or at least knowledge of) incestuous acts. These changes were the results of cuts asked by T. S. Eliot, Barnes's editor at Faber and Faber, cuts that very nearly erased information necessary to an understanding of character motivation. Barnes's own anxieties and ambivalences about the play may stem from its subject, which probably retraces her own situation as the victim of incest in the parental home.

3. Kannenstine reveals these contradictory positions in *Art of Djuna Barnes,* 30–31, 47–49.

4. Wickes describes the *Almanack* as a "satiric spoof [that] pokes good-natured fun at some of the better-known lesbians of Paris" (*Amazon of Letters,* 180). He suggests that Barnes "makes fun of her heroine's [Dame Evangeline Musset] pontifical manner and missionary zeal" (181). One suspects that Morrill Cody's reading of the *Almanack* is based on that of Wickes, although Cody gives no credit to Wickes in his paraphrase. Contrasting *Ladies Almanack* with *The Well of Loneliness,* Cody writes: "Djuna Barnes . . . presented similar material in her *Ladies Almanack,* but treated it satirically rather than tragically. She poked fun at the well-known lesbians in Paris, singling out particularly a character she called Evangeline Musset, a patron saint of lesbians, whose pontifical manner and apostolic zeal she ridiculed" (*The Women of Montparnasse,* 137). Cody's book (coauthored with Hugh Ford) is a memoir-cum-critique of the postwar Paris years that relies on the research of others, repeats the clichéd notions of Paris life, and provides factually inaccurate thumbnail sketches of the participants. As such, *Women of Montparnasse* can only remind serious scholars of the period of the

ways in which women's contributions continue to be overlooked and misinterpreted. Cody's memoir is not unlike William Wiser's study, *The Crazy Years: Paris in the Twenties,* another book that can only repeat clichéd opinions and perpetrate new historical errors concerning the period.

5. In an essay on a quite different subject, Gayatri Chakravorty Spivak provides a critique of inherent forms of patriarchal ideology in literary critical practice; see "Draupadi" (*Critical Inquiry* 8 [1981]: 381–402).

6. As Susan Sniader Lanser suggests, *Ladies Almanack* also responds to (and rewrites) Hall's *The Well of Loneliness,* published in the same year. By demonstrating lesbianism to be "normative," Barnes's text undercuts the homophobia and paranoia inherent in Hall's text: "*The Well of Loneliness* is a passionate plea and cry of rage; audacious in the clarity with which it portrays lesbian existence, it cannot afford to dare in structure, language, or tone. It is only in privacy that *Ladies Almanack* was able to exist in 1928." There is only one heterosexual female character in *Ladies Almanack,* Patience Scalpel (based on Mina Loy), herself eventually tempted to lesbian experience. Even Dame Musset does not escape the mark of the heterosexual scalpel (the name "patience" suggests the inevitable nature of this mark): she admits to having been "deflowered by the Hand of a Surgeon" at age ten (*Ladies Almanack,* 24).

7. Jane Gallop discusses Lacan's reading of "difference" and "sameness" in *The Daughter's Seduction,* chapters 2–4. See also the introduction by Juliet Mitchell and Jacqueline Rose to *Jacques Lacan and the Ecole Freudienne,* 1–57. Adopting Lacan's language, Susan Sniader Lanser comments that for Dame Musset in *Ladies Almanack* "the psychotragedy of femininity, the Phallic Lack, becomes nothing short of the signifier of superiority" ("Speaking in Tongues," in Broe, *Silence and Power*). That Dame Musset's tongue is still flicking on her funeral pyre suggests to Lanser the ways in which "the Tongue—the Word—outlives the flesh. Female sexuality and female word coalesce to form the Last Signifier, displacing the Phallus in its pre-eminence."

8. C. A. Tripp writes: "Only in popular thinking are homosexuality and inversion synonymous. For several decades biologists and experimental psychologists have recognized that these are distinctly different phenomena, though they may or may not occur together. Homosexuality refers to any sexual activity between members of the same sex. Inversion, on the other hand, implies nothing about the sex of the partner; it refers to a reversal of the commonly expected gender-role of the individual" (*The Homosexual Matrix,* 22).

9. In "Costumes of the Mind," Sandra Gilbert argues that the literary works of Barnes and other female Modernists (in particular, Virginia Woolf) find a kind of "redemption . . . in the symbolic chaos of transvestism" (415). For Gilbert, the "third sex" represents an escape from heterosexual, patriarchal gender-bound categories:

> Such political devotees of "the third sex" wish to say "I am not that fixed self you have restrained in those nettight garments; I am all selves and no selves." Given even a modicum of power, as they were, for example, by the Great War, these women . . . will enact their ceremonies of ritual transvestism with what we might call a "vengeance." Those to whom the social order has tradi-

tionally given power, however, will inevitably use ceremonies of transvestite misrule to recapture rule: they seek not a third sex but a way of subordinating the second sex, and in their anxiety they play with costumes to show that costumes are merely plays, seeking reassurance in what they hope is the reality behind appearances. (416)

Susan Gubar extends this argument for female cross-dressing and the inherent misrule in the order of the "third sex" in "Blessings in Disguise." In positing a "third sex beyond gender," both Gilbert and Gubar employ late-nineteenth-century scientific terminology, constructed by a patriarchal medical community to suggest the abnormality and perversion of homosexuality. The "third sex," even in Gilbert and Gubar's application of the term, represents no alternative to the imposed gender hierarchical dialectic (male/female; heterosexual/homosexual). Indeed, the third sex constitutes a further—and deleterious—insistence on the validity of the two biological sexes. As Gilbert herself suggests, the patriarchy ("those to whom the social order has traditionally given power") "will inevitably use ceremonies of transvestite misrule to recapture rule." Such efforts can only result in failure. In no way do they offer an alternative to or an escape from enforced heterosexuality and obedience to a dress and behavior code. For the patriarchy that enforced this code, efforts to invert it (through cross-dressing) became pathetic attempts that could only reveal the ways in which homosexuals were doubly bound under the law: they could invert the dress code, but they could not undo it. In calling attention to the oppositions of dress and behavior, participants in transvestism could only proclaim themselves misfits, parading themselves in the clothes of their oppressors.

8. Natalie Barney: Rue Jacob

1. Writing about Les Ruches in *Olivia,* Dorothy Strachey Bussy described an atmosphere conducive to repressed lesbian sexuality that had operated in the school prior to Barney's arrival there. Wickes, among others, suggests that the intensity of female relationships at Les Ruches was still apparent in Barney's time (*Amazon of Letters,* 28–29).

Marie Souvestre, the co-headmistress on whom one of Strachey's major characters is based, left Les Ruches to open Allenswood, a fashionable school for girls near Wimbledon, which Eleanor Roosevelt attended and where Dorothy Strachey taught Shakespeare. Marie Souvestre's feminism had a powerful effect on her young female students; Beatrice Webb, for instance, considered her to be brilliant. See Cook, "'Women Alone Stir My Imagination,'" 722–723, and Martha Vicinus's examination of women's relationships in similar English boarding schools in "Distance and Desire: English Boarding-School Friendships" (*Signs* 9 [1984]: 600–622).

2. Virginia Woolf had two Greek tutors, both of them women: Clara Pater, sister of Walter Pater (who may have taught his sister Greek), and Janet Case. Case was the more demanding, insisting that Virginia master grammatical concepts. That Woolf was instructed by women—rather than by her father or brothers—is anomalous, but it suggests, perhaps, the desire by women of her class to learn the

languages considered essential to an educated person. Virginia Woolf continued her tutoring in Greek even after Janet Case thought she might have lost interest, and the two women continued to be close friends. Like Violet Dickinson, Case served as an important role model for Woolf. For accounts of the ways in which Virginia Woolf was shaped by powerful female figures around her, see Elizabeth French Boyd, *Bloomsbury Heritage,* and Jane Marcus "Tintinnabulations" (*Marxist Perspectives* 2 [1979]: 150–151).

3. Jane Marcus discusses the search for Sappho in Virginia Woolf's essay "A Society" (*Monday or Tuesday*). The essay turns on a philosophic dispute concerning Sappho's sexuality. One scholarly view argues her chastity, another her sexual lasciviousness. See "Liberty, Sorority, Misogyny," 80–81, and Susan Gubar, "Sapphistries," 45.

4. Karla Jay suggests the ways in which Barney's "errors" in style—her poor rhymes and unbalanced metrics—may have been an effort to mock the forms of nineteenth-century verse. In particular, she argues that the division Wickes sees between "banality of style and the daring candor of the subject matter" (*Amazon of Letters,* 45) may not in reality exist (see chapter 1, "The Language of Expatriatism," in "Disciples of the Tenth Muse"). She discusses the ways in which both Barney and Vivien overturned the religious and courtly conventions of Western poetry in chapter 3, "The Inversion of Christian Imagery and Courtly Love."

5. In "Sapphistries" Susan Gubar provides a model by which this reflection of images and the verification of woman's own experience was effected through Sappho:

> Precisely because so many of her original Greek texts were destroyed, the modern woman poet could write "for" or "as" Sappho and thereby invent a classical inheritance of her own. In other words, such a writer is not infected by Sappho's stature with a Bloomian "anxiety of influence" because her precursor is paradoxically in need of a contemporary collaborator, or so the poetry of Renee Vivien and H. D. seems to suggest. What Sandra Gilbert would call a "fantasy precursor" or what I would term a "fantastic collaboration" simultaneously heals the anxiety of authorship and links these two women poets to an empowering literary history they could create in their own image. (46–47)

6. George Wickes refers to the chapter on Renée Vivien in Barney's *Souvenirs indiscrets* when he comments: "Looking back, Natalie found their love ill-matched from the start, her own based on desire while Renee seemed hardly aroused physically. Natalie's love was fired by her senses: Renee's, flamed by her imagination" (*Amazon of Letters,* 57). The distinction between a sensual Natalie and an intellectual Renée seems oversimplified. These two women were drawn to each other by a set of complex forces allied to their differences from each other. As Wickes points out, Vivien—for all her efforts to rediscover Lesbos and a pagan culture—rebelled against a deeply ingrained puritanism by cultivating decadence. Barney was not herself afflicted by such self-divisions, was not estranged from her body in the same ways as Vivien, and often found it difficult to cope with the forms of Vivien's illnesses. That Vivien died from self-induced star-

vation and chronic alcoholism suggests far more serious divisions between mind and body than mere disinterest in physical passion. Barney, by contrast, always protected her health, refrained from taking alcohol or drugs, never used cigarettes, and believed that sleep and good food were protections against illness.

7. Unless otherwise noted, all the translations from Barney's French texts are my own.

8. In particular, one needs to look at the changes wrought in Vivien's vision of Mytilène between 1904 and her death in 1909 and examine more carefully the intricate and highly subtle tapestry of images that constitute Vivien's poetic Sappho. By no means is it clear that Vivien adopted wholesale the Sappho created by the decadents or that she unleashed "the demonic power that drew Baudelaire and Swinburne to the lesbian femme fatale" (Gubar, "Sapphistries," 49). Certainly Natalie Barney set aside such literary versions of lesbianism—if, indeed, she had ever taken them seriously—as soon as she began her search for a literary heritage that rested in Sappho's work. The relationship of both these poets to the nineteenth-century decadent tradition and their internship with Pierre Louÿs in the study of classic literatures requires further investigation. Karla Jay, for instance, traces a quite different trajectory of literary influences in "Disciples of the Tenth Muse."

9. André Germain writes in *Les fous de 1900* that Barney planted a carpet of *lys* in her garden at 20, rue Jacob—a garden that was "arid" until her arrival (159). Translations from Germain's text are my own.

9. H. D. and Bryher: *En passant*

1. These forms are discussed at length in Friedman and DuPlessis, "'I Had Two Loves Separate': The Sexualities of H. D.'s *Her*" (*Montemora* 8 [1981]: 7–30). Further references to this text are included parenthetically as "Sexualities." My text refers to H. D.'s novel as *Hermione*. The New Directions publication prints the title *HERmione*, drawing attention to the double references to "Hermione" and "Her."

2. Hueffer at least probably did not need much convincing: "the fact remains that [Hueffer] . . . threw in his lot with the new movements" (Wees, *Vorticism*, 76).

3. The Paris influence on the development of Vorticism is generally overlooked. Imagism had set itself against French Symbolism, but Vorticism aligned itself with contemporary French thinking. In 1913, Paris became for Pound "the standard against which all contemporary writing was to be measured," according to Richard Sieburth ("Ezra Pound," 321). In "Approach to Paris" Pound wrote: "If our writers would keep their eye on Paris instead of on London—the London of today or yesterday—there might be some chance of their doing work that would not be demode before it gets to the press. Practically the whole development of the English verse-art has been achieved by steals from the French, from Chaucer's time to our own, and the French are always twenty to sixty years in advance" ("Ezra Pound," 321). Like many other Poundian pronouncements, this one is marked by overstatement and bravado. In fact, at the time Pound knew

little of Paris developments, but the statement itself is a sign of his enthusiasm for what he had recently learned.

4. Imagism has always elicited somewhat contradictory interpretations of its aesthetic stance. For some, like O. W. Firkins, it had about it an air of effete and enervated disinterestedness, a passivity, that associated it with the feminine; for others, especially for Pound on occasion, it exemplified a move away from the feminine, if the feminine is defined in a language of directionless prolixity. Indeed, Pound felt that the hard clarity of early Imagist work was replaced by a laxity and flaccidness when it came under the influence of Amy Lowell. In adopting the Vorticist stance, Pound emphasized the energy and movement, which he would later claim had always inhered in Imagism (see note 8 below), but the very change in terminology—from that which connotes the fixed to that which defines itself in a rush of energy—indicates an effort to reemphasize, if not redefine, the earlier project.

5. Pound had published in June 1912 a poem that he would later include in the anthology *Des Imagistes* (a replacement for "Middle-Aged"). Although Pound did not label "The Return" as Imagist in 1912, in fact this poem seems to meet Imagist requirements. Its writing and publication preceded H. D.'s first poems, and Barbara Guest assumes that H. D.'s writing in summer 1912 was influenced by "The Return," which perhaps served to "inspire" her (*Herself Defined*, 45). We can only speculate on the ways H. D. might have been affected by "The Return," but the existence of the poem—which examines the effects of psychic violence—suggests that Pound himself had begun composing the slight, tight forms that Imagism would call for. Considering the direction of his poetic concerns that summer, it seems odd that he apparently did not think of this poem in Imagist terms—intimating, perhaps, that his recognition of Imagism came only later.

6. The complete text of "Hermes of the Ways" follows:

> The hard sand breaks,
> And the grains of it
> Are clear as wine.
> Far off over the leagues of it,
> The wind,
> Playing on the wide shore,
> Piles little ridges,
> And the great pines
> Break over it.
>
> But more than the many-foamed waves
> Of the sea,
> I know him
> Of the triple path-ways,
> Hermes,
> Who awaiteth.

Dubious,
Facing three ways,
Welcoming wayfarers,
He whom the sea-orchard
Shelters from the west,
From the east,
Weathers sea-wind;
Fronts the great dunes.

Wind rushes
Over the dunes,
And the coarse, salt-crusted grass
Answers.
Heu,
It whips round my ankles!

Small is
The white stream,
Flowing below ground
From the poplar-shaded hill,
But the water is sweet.

Apples on the small trees
As hard,
Too small,
Too late ripened
By a desperate sun
That struggles through sea-mist.

The boughs of the trees
Are twisted
By many bafflings;
Twisted are
The small-leafed boughs.

But the shadow of them
Is not the shadow of the mast head
Nor of the torn sails.
Hermes, Hermes
The great sea foamed,
Gnashed its teeth about me;
But you have waited,

Where sea-grass tangles with
Shore-grass.

7. Jackson carefully documents the ways H. D. expanded the classical materials in her early poems. However, he does not approve of her methods, using his evidence to undercut her status as the foremost Imagist. Moreover, he seems to feel that only under Pound's careful guidance was H. D. able to control her prolix style. Once under the influence of Amy Lowell, H. D. abandoned the strict, sparse forms of Pound's Imagism and indulged herself in a "fulsome prolixity":

> The expansive subjectivity manifested in H. D.'s rhapsodies on the Sapphic fragments, and in her "Lais," "Nossis," and "Heliodora," was no doubt fostered by her allegiance to Amygism: to the Imagist group of the official anthologies organized by Amy Lowell after Pound's defection, or deposition. Pound himself noted as much. But the seeds were there. One recalls that it was H. D.'s poems in *Poetry* which persuaded the far from laconic Amy Lowell that she, too, was an "Imagiste." A comparison of one of those first Imagist poems, "Hermes of the Ways," with Anyte's brief original forces a revaluation of H. D.'s reputation for ascêsis, for ruthless pruning, for a relentless artistic conscience. ("Fulsomeness of Her Prolixity," 102)

Unfortunately, Jackson uses his careful and intelligent analysis of H. D.'s method to undercut her poetic contributions. His evidence suggests that the woman "regularly acknowledged as the prime exemplar of Imagism [and] conventionally credited with a demanding, even a ruthless economy" (91) exploited a more expansive poetic method. Rather than assuming that the label "Imagist" might be incorrectly applied to H. D.'s work (or, perhaps, that Imagism has been broadly misunderstood), he assumes H. D. to be a failed Imagist, her best work accomplished only under Pound's strict guidance. Such attitudes have structured evaluations of H. D.'s work for almost sixty years and have only recently, under feminist critical practice, begun to be revised. Part of the feminist revisionist exercise directs itself, of course, to the misogyny apparent in the assessments of Amy Lowell's role in the Imagist movement.

8. Imagist poetics have traditionally been understood to inhere in stasis, but Pound himself suggested that this notion rests on a misunderstanding of Imagist principles. In *The ABC of Reading* (1934) he commented:

> The defect of earlier imagist propaganda was not in misstatement but in incomplete statement. The diluters took the handiest and easiest meaning, and thought only of the STATIONARY image. If you can't think of imagism or phanopoeia as including the moving image, you will have to make a really needless division of fixed image and praxis or action.
>
> I have taken to using the term phanopoeia to get away from irrelevant particular connotations tangled with a particular group of young people who were writing in 1912. (52)

In part this explication of the moving image might be seen as an effort to link Imagism to the later Vorticist efforts, but it also places responsibility for misreading Imagism on the "diluters," those who would reduce the poetic power of Imagism, and those who associated themselves with Imagism after Pound had left the group. Pound distinguishes the "group of 1912" (*his* group, which included H. D. and Aldington) from those to come later. Even so, this emphasis on the moving image does not treat the specific techniques of movement that inhere in H. D.'s poetry of the period, in particular her use of verbs (very different from Pound's use of verbal forms) or her exploitation of etymological dissonances within single word forms. That is, Pound's description of the ways in which Imagism was not stationary does not take into consideration H. D.'s poetic practice.

9. An important contribution to these concerns is Claire Buck's "Freud and H. D.—Bisexuality and a Feminine Discourse" (*m/f* 8 [1983]: 53–66). Buck recapitulates Lacan's rereading of Freud's concerns with the split subject and the question of sexual difference, subjects taken up at greater length in Juliet Mitchell and Jacqueline Rose's edition of the relevant Lacan texts ("Introduction," *Jacques Lacan*, 1–57). Buck comments that in "'Woman Is Perfect,'" DuPlessis and Friedman are silent on "the problematic nature and status of the 'I' in women's writing, of what constitutes the 'I' of the texts, or whom this 'I' is addressing. In the absence of any such discussion the projection of this 'I' back onto the author anterior to the text, to H. D. as the subject of analysis with Freud, becomes a way of evading the problem of how the subject uses a language which already speaks it, and which does so as a negative inscription of women" (56). The effects of the split speaking subject are registered all through H. D.'s work—in the poetry and the prose—but this condition is specifically addressed in *Hermione*, written, significantly, prior to H. D.'s work with Freud.

11. Paris Transfer: The 1930s

1. See Bernard Benstock, "Private Faces in Public Places: Writers and Political Commitment in the 1930s," a work in progress.

2. There were exceptions to this general rule. George Orwell, who was not homosexual, also did not attend either Oxford or Cambridge, joining the Indian Imperial Police after he left Eton. For a fuller discussion of the individual characteristics among these groups, see Bergonzi, *Reading the Thirties*, 10–11.

3. Herbert R. Lottman examines the widening split between Right and Left in the 1930s, a division based not only on ideological divergences but on the link between anti-Semitism and the economic difficulties experienced by western European countries in the 1930s (see *The Left Bank*, part II, "The Thirties," 47–140).

4. Virginia Woolf's comments continue to rankle. Samuel Hynes, for instance, summarized Woolf's objections: she found them "class-conscious, self-pitying, angry; they became political-minded; they sought out scapegoats on whom to cast the blame; they attacked bourgeois society; they preached; they wrote a 'bastard language'" (*Auden Generation*, 392). In fact, Hynes misreads Woolf's argument and states that her disappointment in these writers stemmed from her desire to find "beauty and fine language" in poetry rather than "politics and polemics" (393). He claims as well that Woolf's judgments constituted "orthodox elements

in the Thirties Myth" (393); the elements he lists may well be pertinent to that myth, but most of them are not to be found in a careful reading of Woolf's text; see Marcus, "The Canonization."

5. This argument, made by Julia Kristeva in *Revolution in Poetic Language,* is summarized in *The Politics of Modernism* 1:257–260. Kristeva's claims are specious to the extent that reactionary political forms are also associated with the avant-garde (Pound, Lewis, and Eliot in English; Céline in French).

6. Woolf's argument in *Three Guineas* has been examined by Blanche Wiesen Cook, "'Women Alone Stir My Imagination,'" (*Signs* 4 [1979]: 718–739); Berenice Carroll, "'To Crush Him in Our Own Country': The Political Thought of Virginia Woolf" (*Feminist Studies* 4 [1978]: 99–131); Phyllis Rose, *Woman of Letters: A Life of Virginia Woolf;* and Jane Marcus, "'No More Horses,'" (*Women's Studies* 4 [1977]: 265–289), and "Tintinnabulations" (*Marxist Perspectives* 2 [1979]: 145–167). Virginia Woolf expressed strong anti-Fascist opinions in *The Years,* and the essays in the special issue of the *Bulletin of the New York Library* on *The Years* is pertinent to the study of Woolf's feminist and anti-Fascist politics.

For a comprehensive study of women's place in Nazi Germany, see Jill Stephenson, *The Nazi Organization of Women,* especially 11–15, where Stephenson describes Hitler's efforts to return women to hearth and home after they had been "deflected from their destiny" by World War I and tempted by Marxism toward an unhealthy liberation. Direct political activity by women under the Third Reich was exceptional; in almost every case, individual women supported Nazi causes by working behind the scenes (often through husbands, brothers, lovers) to achieve National Socialist goals. For most of this period, women were forbidden to join the Nazi party and until the last months of the war were discouraged from active participation in the war. Thus the situation of German women in World War II contrasts strikingly with that of women in England and America, for instance, who were actively involved in the war effort, working in factories and in all branches of the armed services.

7. Peter Ackroyd writes that Eliot had not expected his response to the questionnaire would be published. He wrote: "While I am naturally sympathetic I still feel convinced that it is best that at least a few men of letters remain silent." As Cunard's letter requesting written responses clearly stated that those responses would be published, Eliot's surprise at the publication is itself surprising (*T. S. Eliot,* 243).

8. Jane Marcus treats this subject at length in "Laughing at Leviticus," arguing that Barnes creates in *Nightwood* an "outsiders' society" under threat.

9. Jane Marcus is currently examining the edited portions of the *Nightwood* manuscript. Her preliminary findings suggest that Eliot was particularly uncomfortable with the connections Barnes drew between the expression of lesbian anger and societal institutions, particularly the church. Moreover, Marcus is the only critic to my knowledge who has examined *Nightwood* as a text that presages the war and, particularly, the endangered situation of European Jews ("Laughing at Leviticus").

Barnes claimed to be apolitical, her only political act preparation of some antiwar drawings for the pacifist movement prior to World War I in America. According to Andrew Field, she claimed to have made these drawings under the influence of Courtenay Lemon. Field reports that "in later years she reacted violently to suggestions that the 'decadence' of *Nightwood* had anything at all to do with the spirit of Nazism and remained absolutely apolitical through the decades of depression, communism, fascism, war and McCarthyism" (*Djuna*, 15). Despite Barnes's disclaimers, the evidence of *Nightwood* itself suggests an accurate, even diagnostic reading of the spirit of the thirties.

WORKS CITED AND CONSULTED

Selected Primary Sources

ANDERSON, MARGARET (1886–1973). Publisher, editor, journalist, critic, auto-biographer, memoirist.

My Thirty Years' War. New York: Covici Friede, 1930; London: Knopf, 1930.

The Fiery Fountains. New York: Hermitage House, 1951; London: Rider, 1953.

The Little Review Anthology [edited by]. New York: Hermitage House, 1953.

The Unknowable Gurdjieff. London: Routledge and Paul, 1962.

The Strange Necessity. New York: Horizon, 1970.

Papers: Library of Congress, Washington, D.C.

BARNES, DJUNA (1892–1982). Novelist, short story writer, poet, playwright, journalist, theatrical columnist.

The Book of Repulsive Women: 8 Rhythms and 5 Drawings. New York: Bruno Chap Books, 1915.

A Book. New York: Boni and Liveright, 1923; London: Faber and Faber, 1958.

Ladies Almanack. Paris: Privately Printed [Robert McAlmon], 1928; New York: Harper and Row, 1972.

Ryder. New York: Liveright, 1928.

A Night among Horses. New York: Liveright, 1929.

Nightwood. London: Faber and Faber, 1936; New York: Harcourt Brace, 1937.

The Antiphon. New York: Farrar, Straus and Cudahy, 1958; London: Faber and Faber, 1958.

Selected Works of Djuna Barnes: Spillway/The Antiphon/Nightwood. New York: Farrar, Straus and Cudahy, 1962.

Spillway. London: Faber and Faber, 1962; New York: Harper and Row, 1972.

Smoke and Other Early Stories. Edited by Douglas Messerli. College Park: Sun and Moon Press, 1982.

Papers: McKeldin Library, University of Maryland.

479

BARNEY, NATALIE (1876–1972). Poet, playwright, novelist, essayist, memoirist, epigrammatist.

Quelques portraits-sonnets de femmes. Paris: Ollendorf, 1900.

Cinq petits dialogues grecs. Paris: La Plume, 1901.

"Lettres à une connue." Unpublished novel. *Eparillements [Scatterings].* Paris: Sansot, 1910.

Actes et entr'actes. Paris: Sansot, 1910.

Pensées d'une amazone. Paris: Emile Paul Frères, 1920.

Aventures de l'esprit. Paris: Emile Paul Frères, 1929.

The One Who Is Legion. London: Eric Partridge, 1930.

Nouvelles pensées de l'amazone. Paris: Mercure de France, 1939.

In Memory of Dorothy Ierne Wilde. Dijon: Darantière, 1951.

Souvenirs indiscrets. Paris: Flammarion, 1960.

"Memoirs of a European American." Unpublished manuscript.

Selected Writings. Edited with an introduction by Miron Grindea. London: Adam, 1963.

Traits et portraits. Paris: Mercure de France, 1963.

Papers: Fonds Littéraire Jacques Doucet, Paris; Beinecke Rare Book and Manuscript Library, Yale University.

BEACH, SYLVIA (1887–1962). Publisher, bookseller, editor, literary entrepreneur, translator, memoirist.

Our Exagmination Round His Factification for Incamination of Work in Progress. Edited with an introduction by Sylvia Beach. Paris: Shakespeare and Company, 1929.

Catalogue of a Collection Containing Manuscripts and Rare Editions of James Joyce, Etc. Paris: Shakespeare and Company, 1935.

Les années vingt: Les écrivains américains à Paris et leurs amis: 1920–1930. Paris: Centre Culturel Américain, 1959.

Shakespeare and Company. New York: Harcourt, Brace, 1959; Faber and Faber, 1960.

Papers: Princeton University; Beach's James Joyce Collection is at the State University of New York at Buffalo.

BOYLE, KAY (1902–). Novelist, short story writer, poet, essayist, editor, translator, ghostwriter, children's story writer, memoirist.

Short Stories. Paris: Black Sun Press, 1929.

Wedding Day and Other Stories. New York: Cape and Smith, 1930; London: Pharos Editions, 1932.

Plagued by the Nightingale. New York: Cape and Smith, 1931; London: Cape, 1931.

Year before Last. London: Faber and Faber, 1932; New York: Harrison Smith, 1932.

Gentlemen, I Address You Privately. New York: Smith and Haas, 1933; London: Faber and Faber, 1934.

My Next Bride. New York: Harcourt, Brace, 1934; London: Faber and Faber, 1935.

Death of a Man. London: Faber and Faber, 1936; New York: Harcourt, Brace, 1936.

The White Horses of Vienna and Other Stories. New York: Harcourt, Brace, 1936; London: Faber and Faber, 1937.

A Glad Day. Norfolk, Conn.: New Directions, 1938.

Monday Night. New York: Harcourt, Brace, 1938; London: Faber and Faber, 1938.

The Crazy Hunter. London: Faber and Faber, 1940; New York: Harcourt, Brace, 1940.

Avalanche. New York: Simon and Schuster, 1944; London: Faber and Faber, 1944.

Thirty Stories. New York: Simon and Schuster, 1946; London: Faber and Faber, 1948.

His Human Majesty. New York: McGraw Hill, 1949; London: Faber and Faber, 1950.

The Smoking Mountain: Stories of Postwar Germany. New York: McGraw Hill, 1951; London: Faber and Faber, 1952.

The Seagull on the Step. New York: Knopf, 1955; London: Faber and Faber, 1955.

Three Short Novels. Boston: Beacon Press, 1958.

Generation without Farewell. New York: Knopf, 1960.

Collected Poems. New York: Knopf, 1962.

Being Geniuses Together [with Robert McAlmon]. New York: Doubleday, 1968; London: Joseph, 1970.

The Long Walk at San Francisco State and Other Essays. New York: Grove Press, 1970.

Papers: Morris Library, Southern Illinois University.

BRYHER, WINIFRED (ANNIE WINIFRED ELLERMAN) (1894–1983). Novelist, short story writer, editor, critic, poet, autobiographer, travel writer, translator, children's story writer.

Region of Lutany [as A. W. Ellerman]. London: Chapman and Hall, 1914.

Amy Lowell: A Critical Appreciation. London: Eyre and Spottiswoode, 1918.

Development. London: Constable, 1920; New York: Macmillan, 1920.

Two Selves. Paris: Contact Publishing, 1923; New York: Chaucer Head, 1927.

Arrow Music [with others]. London: Bumpus, 1924.

A Picture Geography for Little Children: Asia. London: Cape, 1925.

West [on the U.S.A.]. London: Cape, 1925.

Civilians. Territet, Switzerland: Pool, 1927; London: Pool, 1930.

Film Problems of Soviet Russia. Territet, Switzerland: Pool, 1929.

Paris 1900. Translated into French by Sylvia Beach and Adrienne Monnier. Paris: Shakespeare and Company, 1929.

The Light-Hearted Student [with Trude Weiss]. Dijon: Pool, 1930.

Cinema Survey [with Robert Herring and Dallas Bower]. London: Brendin, 1937.

The Fourteenth of October. New York: Pantheon, 1952; London: Collins, 1954.

The Player's Boy. New York: Pantheon, 1953; London: Collins, 1957.

Roman Wall. New York: Pantheon, 1954; London: Collins, 1955.

Beowulf. New York: Pantheon, 1956.

Gate to the Sea. New York: Pantheon, 1958; London: Collins, 1959.

Ruan. New York: Pantheon, 1960; London: Collins, 1961.

The Heart to Artemis: A Writer's Memoirs. New York: Harcourt, Brace, 1962; London: Collins, 1963.

The Coin of Carthage. New York: Harcourt, Brace, 1963; London: Collins, 1964.

Visa for Avalon. New York: Harcourt, Brace, 1965.

This January Tale. New York: Harcourt, Brace, 1966; London: Secker and Warburg, 1968.

The Colors of Vaud. New York: Harcourt, Brace, 1969.

The Days of Mars: A Memoir 1940–1946. New York: Harcourt, Brace, 1972; London: Calder and Boyars, 1972.

COLETTE, SIDONIE GABRIELLE (1873–1954). Novelist, short story writer, journalist, essayist, memoirist.

Claudine à l'école. Paris: Ollendorff, 1900.

Claudine à Paris. Paris: Ollendorff, 1901.

Claudine en ménage. Paris: Ollendorff, 1902.

Claudine s'en va. Paris: Ollendorff, 1903.

Dialogues de bêtes. Paris: Mercure de France, 1904.

Sept dialogues de bêtes. Paris: Mercure de France, 1905.

La retraite sentimentale. Paris: Mercure de France, 1907.

L'Ingénue libertine. Paris: Ollendorff, 1909.

La vagabonde. Paris: Ollendorff, 1911.

L'Entrave. Paris: Libraire des Lettres, 1913.

L'Envers du music-hall. Paris: Flammarion, 1913.

Mitsou ou Comment l'esprit vient aux filles. Paris: Arthème Fayard, 1918.

Chéri. Paris: Arthème Fayard, 1920.

La maison de Claudine. Paris: Ferenczi et fils, 1922.

Le blé en herbe. Paris: Flammarion, 1923.

La femme cachée. Paris: Flammarion, 1924.

La fin de Chéri. Paris: Flammarion, 1926.

La naissance du jour. Paris: Flammarion, 1928.

Renée Vivien. Abbéville: F. Paillart, 1928.

Sido. Paris: Editions Krâ, 1929.

Ces plaisirs. Paris: Ferenczi et fils, 1932.

Mes apprentissages. Paris: Ferenczi et fils, 1936; English translation by Helen Beauclerk, *My Apprenticeships,* New York: Farrar, Straus and Giroux, 1957.

Journal à rebours. Paris: Arthème Fayard, 1941.

Mes cahiers. Paris: Aux Armes de France, 1941.

De ma fenêtre. Paris: Aux Armes de France, 1942.

Gigi et autres nouvelles. Lausanne: La Guilde du Livre, 1944.

L'Etoile vesper. Geneva: Editions du Milieu du Monde, 1946; English translation by David Le Vay, *The Evening Star: Recollections,* New York: Bobbs-Merrill, 1974.

Le fanal bleu. Paris: Ferenczi et fils, 1949.

The Pure and the Impure. Translated by Herma Briffault. New York: Farrar, Straus and Giroux, 1966.

Looking Backwards. Translated by David le Vay. Bloomington: Indiana University Press, 1975.

CROSBY, CARESSE (1892–1970). Publisher, editor, poet, translator, autobiographer.

Crosses of Gold. Paris: Privately Printed [by Harry and Caresse Crosby, 1925]; enlarged edition, Paris: Messein, 1925.

Graven Images. Boston and New York: Houghton Mifflin, 1926.

Painted Shores. Paris: Editions Narcisse, 1927.

Impossible Melodies. Paris: Editions Narcisse, 1928.

The Stranger. Paris: Editions Narcisse, 1928.

Poems for Harry Crosby. Paris: Black Sun Press, 1931.

The Passionate Years. New York: Dial, 1953; enlarged edition, London: Redman, 1955.

Papers: The Black Sun Press archives, Morris Library, Southern Illinois University Library.

CUNARD, NANCY (1896–1965). Publisher, editor, journalist, poet, translator, memoirist.

Outlaws. London: Elkin, Matthews and Marrot, 1921.

Sublunary. London: Hodder and Stoughton, 1923.

Parallax. London: Hogarth Press, 1925.

Black Man and White Ladyship: An Anniversary. London: Utopía Press, 1931.

Negro. Edited by Nancy Cunard. London: Wishart, 1934.

Authors Take Sides on the Spanish War. Edited by Nancy Cunard. London: Left Review, 1937.

Man-Ship-Tank-Gun-Plane. London: New Books, 1944.

Poems for France. Edited by Nancy Cunard. Paris: La France Libre, 1944.

Grand Man: Memories of Norman Douglas. London: Secker and Warburg, 1954.

G. M.: Memories of George Moore. London: Rupert Hart-Davis, 1956.

These Were the Hours. Carbondale: Southern Illinois University Press, 1966.

Papers: Humanities Research Center, University of Texas at Austin.

DOOLITTLE, HILDA (H. D.) (1886–1961). Poet, novelist, editor, translator, avant-garde film critic, essayist.

Sea Garden. London: Constable, 1916; Boston and New York: Houghton Mifflin, 1916.

Hymen. London: Egoist Press, 1921; New York: Holt, 1921.

Heliodora and Other Poems. Boston: Houghton Mifflin, 1924; London: Cape, 1924.

Collected Poems. New York: Boni and Liveright, 1925.

Palimpsest. Paris: Contact Editions, 1926; Boston: Houghton Mifflin, 1926.

Hippolytus Temporizes. Boston: Houghton Mifflin, 1927.

Hedylus. Boston: Houghton Mifflin, 1928; Oxford: Blackwell, 1928.

Borderline—A Pool Film with Paul Robeson. London: Mercury, 1930.

Red Roses for Bronze. London: Chatto and Windus, 1931; Boston and New York: Houghton Mifflin, 1931.

The Hedgehog. London: Brendin, 1936.

Tribute to the Angels. London and New York: Oxford University Press, 1945.

The Walls Do Not Fall. London and New York: Oxford University Press, 1945.

The Flowering of the Rod. London and New York: Oxford University Press, 1946.

By Avon River. New York: Macmillan, 1949.

Tribute to Freud. New York: Pantheon, 1956.

Selected Poems. New York: Grove, 1957.

Bid Me to Live. New York: Grove, 1960.

Helen in Egypt. New York: Grove, 1961.

Hermetic Definition. New York: New Directions, 1972.

Trilogy. New York: New Directions, 1973.

End to Torment. New York: New Directions, 1979.

HERmione. New York: New Directions, 1981.

Notes on Thought and Vision. San Francisco: City Lights, 1982.

"Notes on Recent Writing." Unpublished manuscript at Beinecke Library, Yale University.

Papers: Beinecke Library, Yale University.

FLANNER, JANET (1892–1978) Journalist, novelist, essayist, translator, memoirist.

The Cubical City. New York and London: Putnam, 1926; reprint, Carbondale and Edwardsville: Southern Illinois University Press, 1974 [includes an afterword by Janet Flanner].

✓*An American in Paris, Profile of an Interlude between Two Wars*. New York: Simon and Schuster, 1940; London: Hamilton, 1940.

Pétain: The Old Man of France. New York: Simon and Schuster, 1944.

Men and Monuments. New York: Harper, 1957; London: Hamilton, 1957.

✓*Paris Journal: 1944–1965*. Edited by William Shawn. New York: Atheneum, 1965; London: Gollancz, 1966.

Paris Journal: Volume II, 1965–1971. Edited by William Shawn. New York: Atheneum, 1971.

Paris Was Yesterday: 1925–1939. Edited by Irving Drutman. New York: Viking, 1972; London: Angus and Robertson, 1973.

London Was Yesterday: 1934–1939. Edited by Irving Drutman. New York: Studio Book/Viking, 1975; London: Joseph, 1975.

Janet Flanner's World: Uncollected Writings, 1932–1975. Edited by Irving Drutman. New York: Harcourt Brace Jovanovich, 1979.

HEAP, JANE (?–1964). Editor, journalist, painter. No published books. Her writings are in the *Little Review*.

Papers: Library of Congress, Washington, D.C.

JOLAS, MARIA (1893–). Publisher, editor, translator, critic, journalist.
  A James Joyce Yearbook. Edited by Maria Jolas. Paris: Transition Press, 1949.
  Her writings and translations appear in *transition, Mercure de France, New Republic, Paris Review,* and others.

LOY, MINA (1882–1966). Poet, experimental playwright, prose writer, pamphleteer.
  Auto-Facial Constructions. Sociétaire du Salon d'Automne. Florence: Tipografia Giuntina, 1919.
  Psycho-Democracy. Florence: Tipografia Peri and Rossi, 1920.
  Lunar Baedecker. Paris: Contact Editions, 1923.
  Lunar Baedeker & Time-Tables. Highlands, N.C.: Jargon, 1958.
  Papers: Beinecke Library, Yale University.

MONNIER, ADRIENNE (1892–1955). Publisher, editor, poet, diarist, critic, travel writer, experimental prose writer, bibliographer, memoirist, autobiographer.
  Fableaux. Paris: La Maison des Amis des Livres, 1932.
  Les gazettes d'Adrienne Monnier, 1925–1945. Paris: René Juilliard, 1953.
  Rue de l'Odéon. Paris: Editions Albin Michel, 1960.
  Trois agendas d'Adrienne Monnier. Paris: Privately Printed, 1960.
  Dernières gazettes et écrits divers. Paris: Mercure de France, 1961.
  Les poésies d'Adrienne Monnier [including *La figure,* 1923, and *Les vertus,* 1926]. Paris: Mercure de France, 1962.
  The Very Rich Hours of Adrienne Monnier. Translated, with an introduction and commentaries by Richard McDougall. New York: Scribners, 1976; London: Millington Books, 1976.
  Papers: Fonds littéraire Jacques Doucet, Paris.

NIN, ANAÏS (1903–1977). Publisher, editor, diarist, novelist, short story writer, essayist, critic.
  D. H. Lawrence: An Unprofessional Study. Paris: Black Manikin Press, 1932; London: Spearman, 1961; Denver, Swallow, 1964.
  House of Incest. Paris: Sianna Editions/Obelisk Press, 1936; New York: Gemor, 1947.
  The Winter of Artifice. Paris: Villa Seurat Editions/Obelisk Press, 1939; New York: Gemor, 1942.
  Under a Glass Bell. New York: Gemor, 1944; London: Editions Poetry, 1947.
  Realism and Reality. New York: Alicat Book Shop, 1946.
  Children of the Albatross. New York: E. P. Dutton, 1947; Denver, Swallow, 1966.
  On Writing. Hanover, N.H.: Daniel Oliver Associates, 1947.
  The Four-Chambered Heart. New York: Duell, Sloan and Pearce, 1950; Denver: Swallow, 1966.
  A Spy in the House of Love. New York: British Book Centre, 1954; Denver: Swallow, 1966.
  Solar Baroque. N.p.: Edwards Brothers, 1958.

Cities of the Interior. Denver: Swallow, 1959.

Seduction of the Minotaur. Denver: Swallow, 1961.

Collages. Denver: Swallow, 1964.

The Diary of Anaïs Nin, 1931–1934. Edited by Gunther Stuhlmann. New York: Harcourt, Brace and World, 1966; London: Owen, 1966.

The Diary of Anaïs Nin, 1934–1939. Edited by Gunther Stuhlmann. New York: Harcourt, Brace and World, 1967; London: Owen, 1967.

The Novel of the Future. New York: Macmillan, 1968.

The Diary of Anaïs Nin, 1939–1944. Edited by Gunther Stuhlmann. New York: Harcourt, Brace and World, 1969; London: Owen, 1970.

The Diary of Anaïs Nin, 1944–1947. Edited by Gunther Stuhlmann. New York: Harcourt Brace Jovanovich, 1971; London: Owen, 1972.

The Diary of Anaïs Nin, 1947–1955. Edited by Gunther Stuhlmann. New York: Harcourt Brace Jovanovich, 1974; London: Owen, 1974.

A Photographic Supplement to the Diary of Anaïs Nin. New York and London: Harcourt Brace Jovanovich, 1974.

A Woman Speaks: The Lectures, Seminars and Interviews of Anaïs Nin. Edited by Evelyn J. Hinz. Chicago: Swallow Press, 1975.

The Diary of Anaïs Nin, 1955–1966, Edited by Gunther Stuhlmann. New York and London: Harcourt Brace Jovanovich, 1976; London: Owen, 1977.

In Favor of the Sensitive Man, and Other Essays. New York: Harcourt Brace Jovanovich, 1976.

The Diary of Anaïs Nin, 1966–1977. Edited by Gunther Stuhlmann. New York and London: Harcourt Brace Jovanovich, 1980.

RHYS, JEAN (1894–1979). Novelist, short story writer, essayist, translator, autobiographer.

The Left Bank [with a preface by Ford Madox Ford]. London: Jonathan Cape, 1927; New York: Harper and Row, 1928.

Quartet [originally published as *Postures*]. London: Chatto and Windus; published as *Quartet,* New York: Simon and Schuster, 1929.

Good Morning, Midnight. London: Constable, 1930; New York: Harper and Row, 1939.

After Leaving Mr Mackenzie. London: Jonathan Cape, 1931; New York: Alfred Knopf, 1931.

Voyage in the Dark. London: Constable, 1934; New York: William Morrow and Company, 1934.

Wide Sargasso Sea. London: Andre Deutsch, 1966; New York: W. W. Dutton, 1966.

Tigers Are Better-Looking. London: Andre Deutsch, 1968; New York: Harper and Row, 1974.

My Day. New York: Frank Hallman, 1975.

Sleep It Off, Lady. London: Andre Deutsch, 1976; New York: Harper and Row, 1976.

Smile Please: An Unfinished Autobiography. London: Andre Deutsch, 1979; New York: Harper and Row, 1980.

The Letters of Jean Rhys. Edited by Francis Wyndham and Diana Melly. New York: Viking, 1984.
Papers: McFarlin Library, University of Tulsa.

SOLANO, SOLITA (1888–1975). Novelist, journalist, essayist.
The Uncertain Feast. New York and London: Putnam, 1924.
The Happy Failure. New York and London: Putnam, 1925.
This Way Up. New York and London: Putnam, 1927.
Statue in a Field. Paris[?], 1934.

STEIN, GERTRUDE (1874–1946). Novelist, poet, playwright, opera librettist, memoirist, autobiographer, travel writer, literary theorist, critic.
Three Lives. New York: Grafton Press, 1909; London: Bodley Head, 1915.
Tender Buttons. New York: Claire Marie, 1914.
Geography and Plays. Boston: Four Seas, 1922; New York: Something Else Press, 1968.
The Making of Americans. Paris: Contact Editions, 1925; New York: Boni, 1926; London: Owen, 1968.
Composition as Explanation. London: Hogarth Press, 1926.
Lucy Church Amiably. Paris: Plain Edition, 1931; New York: Something Else Press, 1969.
Before the Flowers of Friendship Faded Friendship Faded. Paris: Plain Edition, 1931.
How to Write. Paris: Plain Edition, 1931; Barton: Something Else Press, 1971.
Operas and Plays. Plain Edition, 1932.
The Autobiography of Alice B. Toklas. New York: Harcourt, Brace, 1933; London: Bodley Head, 1933.
Matisse Picasso and Gertrude Stein with Two Shorter Pieces. Paris: Plain Edition, 1933; Barton, Berlin, and Millerton: Something Else Press, 1972.
Four Saints in Three Acts, an Opera to Be Sung. New York: Random House, 1934.
Portraits and Prayers. New York: Random House, 1934.
Lectures in America. New York: Random House, 1935.
Narration. Chicago: University of Chicago Press, 1935.
The Geographical History of America. New York: Random House, 1936.
Everybody's Autobiography. New York: Random House, 1937; London and Toronto: Heinemann, 1938.
Picasso. Paris: Libraire Floury, 1938; republished with English translation by Alice B. Toklas, London: Batsford, 1938; New York: Scribners.
√*Paris France*. London: Batsford, 1940; New York: Scribners, 1940.
What Are Masterpieces. Los Angeles: Conference Press, 1940.
Ida. New York: Random House, 1941.
Brewsie and Willie. New York: Random House, 1945.
Wars I Have Seen. New York: Random House, 1945; enlarged edition, London: Batsford, 1945.

Selected Writings of Gertrude Stein. Edited by Carl Van Vechten. New York: Random House, 1946.

Four in America. New Haven: Yale University Press, 1947.

The Mother of Us All [with Virgil Thomson]. New York: Music Press, 1947.

Blood on the Dining Room Floor. Pawlet, Vt.: Banyan Press, 1948.

Last Operas and Plays. Edited by Carl Van Vechten. New York and Toronto: Rinehart, 1949.

Things as They Are. Pawlet, Vt.: Banyan Press, 1950.

Two: Gertrude Stein and Her Brother and Other Early Portraits (1908–1912). Foreword by Janet Flanner. New Haven: Yale University Press, 1951.

Bee Time Vine and Other Pieces, 1913–1927. New Haven: Yale University Press; London: Cumberlege/Oxford University Press, 1953.

Painted Lace and Other Pieces (1914–1937). New Haven: Yale University Press, 1955; London: Cumberlege, 1956.

Stanzas in Meditation and Other Poems (1929–1933). New Haven: Yale University Press, 1956; Cambridge: Oxford University Press, 1956.

A Novel of Thank You. New Haven: Yale University Press, 1958.

"Rich and Poor in English." *Mercure de France* 349 (August–September 1963): 95–98 [also in *Painted Lace*].

Gertrude Stein on Picasso. Edited by Edward Burns. New York: Liveright, 1970.

Fernhurst, Q.E.D., and Other Early Writings. New York: Liveright, 1971; London: Owen, 1971.

Papers: Major repository, Beinecke Library, Yale University. Significant collections: Bancroft Library, University of California at Berkeley; Humanities Research Center, University of Texas at Austin.

TOKLAS, ALICE B. (1877–1967). Publisher, memoirist, translator, journalist.

Alice B. Toklas Cookbook. New York: Harper, 1954; London: Joseph, 1954.

Aromas and Flavors of Past and Present. Edited by Poppy Cannon. New York: Harper, 1958; London: Joseph, 1958.

What Is Remembered. New York: Holt, Rinehart and Winston, 1963; London: Joseph, 1963.

Staying On Alone: Letters of Alice B. Toklas. Edited by Edward Burns. New York: Liveright, 1973.

Papers: Beinecke Library, Yale University; Bancroft Library, University of California at Berkeley.

VIVIEN, RENEE [BORN PAULINE TARN] (1877–1909). Poet, novelist.

Cendres et poussières. Paris: Alphonse Lemerre, 1902.

Du vert au violet. Paris: Alphonse Lemerre, 1903.

Evocations. Paris: Alphonse Lemerre, 1903.

La dame à la louve. Paris: Alphonse Lemerre, 1904.

Etudes et préludes. Paris: Alphonse Lemerre, 1904.

Une femme m'apparut. Paris: Alphonse Lemerre, 1904. English translation by Jeannette H. Foster, *A Woman Appeared to Me.* Tallahassee, Fla.: Naiad Press, 1979.

A l'heure des mains jointes. Paris: Alphonse Lemerre, 1906. English translation by Sandia Belgrade, *At the Sweet Hour of Hand in Hand*. Tallahassee, Fla.: Naiad Press, 1979.

Chansons pour mon ombre. Paris: Alphonse Lemerre, 1907.

Flambeaux éteints. Paris: Sansot, 1908.

Sillages. Paris: Sansot, 1908.

Poèmes en prose. Paris: Sansot, 1909.

Dans un coin de violettes. Paris: Sansot, 1910; English translation by Margaret Porter and Catherine Kroger, *The Muse of Violets,* Tallahassee, Fla.: Naiad Press, 1977.

Hallions. Paris: Sansot, 1910.

Poésies complètes, I. Paris: Alphonse Lemerre, 1934.

Poésies complètes, II. Paris: Alphonse Lemerre, 1934.

Papers: Fonds littéraire Jacques Doucet, Paris.

WHARTON, EDITH (1862–1937). Novelist, short story writer, poet, critic, travel writer, nonfiction writer, autobiographer.

Italian Villas and Their Gardens. New York: Century, 1904; London: Lane/ Bodley Head, 1904.

The House of Mirth. New York: Scribners, 1905; London: Macmillan Ltd./ New York: Macmillan, 1905.

Italian Backgrounds. New York: Scribners, 1905; London: Macmillan, 1905.

The Fruit of the Tree. New York: Scribners, 1907.

Madame de Treymes. New York: Scribners, 1907; London: Macmillan, 1907.

A Motor-Flight through France. New York: Scribners, 1908.

Ethan Frome. New York: Scribners, 1911; London; Macmillan, 1911.

The Reef. New York: Appleton, 1912; London: Macmillan, 1912.

The Custom of the Country. New York: Scribners, 1913; London: Macmillan, 1913.

Fighting France from Dunkerque to Belfort. New York: Scribners, 1915; London: Macmillan, 1915.

Summer. New York: Appleton, 1917; London: Macmillan, 1917.

The Marne. New York: Appleton, 1918; London: Macmillan, 1919.

French Ways and Their Meanings. New York and London: Appleton, 1919; London: Macmillan, 1919.

The Age of Innocence. New York and London: Appleton, 1920.

A Son at the Front. New York: Scribners, 1923; London: Macmillan, 1923.

The Writing of Fiction. New York and London: Scribners, 1925.

Twilight Sleep. New York and London: Appleton, 1927.

The Children. New York and London: Appleton, 1928.

Hudson River Bracketed. New York and London: Appleton, 1929.

The Gods Arrive. New York and London: Appleton, 1932.

A Backward Glance. New York and London: Appleton-Century, 1934.

The Buccaneers. New York and London: Appleton-Century, 1938.

The Collected Short Stories. Edited by R. W. B. Lewis. 2 vols. New York: Scribners, 1968.

Fast and Loose [under pseudonym of David Olivieri]. Edited by Viola Hopkins Winner. Charlottesville: University of Virginia Press, 1977.

Secondary Sources

Books, Dissertations, and Works in Progress

Abel, Elizabeth. *Writing and Sexual Difference*. Chicago: University of Chicago Press, 1982.

————, and Emily K. Abel, eds. *The Signs Reader: Women, Gender and Scholarship*. Chicago: University of Chicago Press, 1983.

Ackroyd, Peter. *T. S. Eliot: A Life*. New York: Simon and Schuster, 1984.

Acton, Harold. *Memoirs of an Aesthete*. London: Methuen, 1948.

Adam, H. Pearl. *Paris Sees It Through: A Diary, 1914–1919*. London: Hodder and Stoughton, n.d.

Aldington, Richard. *Life for Life's Sake*. London: Cassell, 1968.

Ammons, Elizabeth. *Edith Wharton's Argument with America*. Athens: University of Georgia Press, 1980.

Anderson, Margaret, ed. *The Little Review Anthology*. New York: Horizon, 1953.

Les années vingt: Les écrivains américains à Paris et leurs amis, 1920–1930. Exposition du 11 Mars au 25 Avril 1959. Paris: Centre Culturel Américain, 1959.

Auden, W. H. *Collected Poems*. Edited by Edward Mendelson. New York: Random House, 1976.

————. *The Collected Poetry of W. H. Auden*. New York: Random House, 1945.

————. *The Orators: An English Study*. New York: Random House, 1967.

Auerbach, Nina. *Communities of Women: An Idea in Fiction*. Cambridge: Harvard University Press, 1978.

————. *Woman and the Demon: The Life of a Victorian Myth*. Cambridge: Harvard University Press, 1982.

Baker, Carlos. *Ernest Hemingway: A Life Story*. New York: Scribners, 1969.

————. *Hemingway: The Writer as Artist*. Princeton: Princeton University Press, 1972.

Balmain, Pierre. *My Years and Seasons*. New York: Doubleday, 1965.

Barker, Francis, et al. *1936: The Sociology of Literature*. 2 vols. Colchester: Hewitt-Photo-Lith, 1979.

Bates, Ronald, and Harry J. Pollock. *Litters from Aloft*. Tulsa: University of Tulsa, 1971.

Bell, Millicent. *Edith Wharton and Henry James*. New York: Braziller, 1965.

Bell, Quentin. *Virginia Woolf: A Biography*. New York: Harcourt, 1976.

Benstock, Bernard, "Private Faces in Public Places: Writers and Political Commitment in the 1930s." Work in progress.

Benstock, Shari. "The Private Self: Theory and Practice in Women's Autobiographical Writings." Forthcoming.

Bergonzi, Bernard. *Reading the Thirties: Texts and Contexts*. Pittsburgh: University of Pittsburgh Press, 1978.

Bernikow, Louise. *Among Women*. New York: Crown, 1980.

Birky, Phillis, et al., eds. *Amazon Expedition: A Lesbian Feminist Anthology*. New York: Times Change, 1973.

Bloch, Marc. *Memoirs of War, 1914–15*. Ithaca: Cornell University Press, 1980.

Bowen, Stella. *Drawn from Life*. London: Collins, 1941.

Boyd, Elizabeth French. *Bloomsbury Heritage: Their Mothers and Their Aunts*. New York: Taplinger, 1976.

Bradbury, Malcolm, and James McFarlane, eds. *Modernism: 1890–1930*. Harmondsworth: Penguin, 1976.

Brassai. *The Secret Paris of the 30's*. Translated by Richard Miller. New York: Pantheon, 1976.

Bridgman, Richard. *Gertrude Stein in Pieces*. New York: Oxford, 1970.

Brinnin, John Malcolm. *The Third Rose: Gertrude Stein and Her World*. Boston: Little, Brown, 1959.

Broe, Mary Lynn, ed. *Silence and Power: Djuna Barnes, a Revaluation*. Carbondale: Southern Illinois University Press, 1986.

Brooks, Romaine. *Thief of Souls*. Washington, D.C.: National Collection of Fine Arts, 1971.

Brown, Cheryl L., and Karen Olson, eds. *Feminist Criticism: Essays on Theory, Poetry and Prose*. Metuchen: Scarecrow, 1978.

Callahan, Morley. *That Summer in Paris*. New York: Coward-McCann, 1963.

Caudwell, Christopher. *Illusion and Reality: A Study of the Sources of Poetry*. London: Lawrence, 1937.

Céline, Louis-Ferdinand. *Voyage au bout de la nuit*. Paris: Gallimard, 1952.

Chalon, Jean. *Portrait of a Seductress: The World of Natalie Barney*. Translated by Carol Barko. New York: Crown, 1979.

Chapon, François, Nicole Prévot, and Richard Sieburth. *Autour de Natalie Clifford Barney*. Paris: Universités de Paris, 1976.

Chisholm, Anne. *Nancy Cunard*. London: Penguin, 1981.

Cobb, Richard. *French and Germans, Germans and French: A Personal Interpretation of France under Two Occupations 1914–1918/1940–1944*. Hanover: University Press of New England, 1983.

Cody, Morrill, with Hugh Ford. *The Women of Montparnasse: The Americans in Paris*. New York: Cornwall, 1984.

Cook, Blanche Wiesen. *Women and Support Networks*. New York: Out and Out, 1979.

Cowley, Malcolm. *Exile's Return: A Literary Odyssey of the 1920's*. New York: Viking, 1951.

———. *A Second Flowering: Works and Days of the Lost Generation*. New York: Viking, 1973.

Crosland, Margaret. *Colette: The Difficulty of Loving*. New York: Reynal, 1973.

cummings, e. e. *Collected Poems*. New York: Harcourt, Brace, 1945.

DeKoven, Marianne. *A Different Language: Gertrude Stein's Experimental Writing*. Madison: University of Wisconsin Press, 1983.

Dennison, Sally. *(Alternative) Literary Publishing: Five Modern Histories*. Iowa City: University of Iowa Press, 1984.

Derrida, Jacques. *Dissemination*. Translated by Barbara Johnson. Chicago: University of Chicago Press, 1981.

Dickson, Lovat. *Radclyffe Hall at the Well of Loneliness: A Sapphic Chronicle*. New York: Scribners, 1975.

Douglas, Ann. *The Feminization of American Culture*. New York: Knopf, 1977.

Dubnick, Randa. *The Structure of Obscurity: Gertrude Stein, Language and Cubism*. Urbana: University of Illinois Press, 1984.

DuPlessis, Rachel Blau. *Writing Beyond the Ending: Narrative Strategies of Twentieth-Century Women Writers*. Bloomington: Indiana University Press, 1984.

Earnest, Ernest. *Expatriates and Patriots: American Artists, Scholars and Writers in Europe*. Durham: Duke University Press, 1968.

Eisenstein, Hester, and Alice Jardine, eds. *The Future of Difference*. Boston: Hall, 1980.

Eisinger, Erica Mendelson, and Mari Ward McCarty, eds. *Colette: The Woman, the Writer*. University Park: Pennsylvania State University Press, 1981.

Ellmann, Richard. *James Joyce*. New York: Oxford University Press, 1982.

Faderman, Lillian. *Surpassing the Love of Men: Romantic Friendship and Love between Women from the Renaissance to the Present*. New York: William Morrow, 1981.

Field, Andrew. *Djuna: The Life and Times of Djuna Barnes*. New York: Putnam, 1983; Austin: University of Texas Press, 1985.

Fitch, Noel Riley. *Sylvia Beach and the Lost Generation: A History of Literary Paris in the Twenties and Thirties*. New York: Norton, 1983.

Fleischmann, Fritz, ed. *American Novelists Revisited: Essays in Feminist Criticism*. Boston: G. K. Hall, 1982.

Flint, R. W., ed. *Marinetti: Selected Writings*. Translated by R. W. Flint and Arthur A. Coppotelli. New York: Farrar, Straus and Giroux, 1972.

Ford, Hugh, ed. *The Left Bank Revisited: Selections from the Paris Tribune, 1917–1934*. University Park: Pennsylvania State University Press, 1979.

———. *Nancy Cunard: Brave Poet, Indomitable Rebel, 1896–1965*. Philadelphia: Chilton, 1968.

———. *Published in Paris: American and British Writers, Printers, and Publishers in Paris, 1920–1939*. New York: Macmillan, 1975.

Foster, Jeannette. *Sex Variant Women in Literature*. Baltimore: Diana, 1975.

Franks, Claudia Stillman. *Beyond the Well of Loneliness*. Atlantic Highlands: Humanities, 1982.

Friedman, Susan Stanford. *Psyche Reborn: The Emergence of H. D.* Bloomington: Indiana University Press, 1981.

Fussell, Paul. *The Great War and Modern Memory*. New York: Oxford, 1975.

Gage, John T. *In the Arresting Eye: The Rhetoric of Imagism*. Baton Rouge: Louisiana State University Press, 1981.

Gallop, Jane. *The Daughter's Seduction: Feminism and Psychoanalysis*. Ithaca: Cornell University Press, 1982.

Gallup, Donald, ed. *The Flowers of Friendship: Letters Written to Gertrude Stein*. New York: Knopf, 1953.

Gass, William H. *The World within the Word*. New York: Knopf, 1979.

Germain, André. *Les fous de 1900*. Paris: Palatine, 1954.

———. *Renée Vivien*. Paris: Cres, 1917.

Gilbert, Sandra M., and Susan Gubar. *The Madwoman in the Attic: The Woman*

Writer and the Nineteenth-Century Imagination. New Haven: Yale University Press, 1979.

Gilliam, Florence. *France: A Tribute by an American Woman*. New York: Dutton, 1945.

Givner, Joan. *Brave Voyage: The Life of Katherine Anne Porter*. New York: Harper, 1981.

Glassco, John. *Memoirs of Montparnasse*. New York: Oxford, 1970.

Goodman, Bernice. *The Lesbian: A Celebration of Difference*. Brooklyn: Out and Out, 1977.

Gramont, Elizabeth de. *Souvenirs du monde*. Paris: Grasset, 1966.

Grant, Jane. *Ross, The New Yorker and Me*. New York: Reynal/Morrow, 1968.

Green, Martin. *Children of the Sun: A Narrative of Decadence in England after 1918*. New York: Basic, 1976.

Guest, Barbara. *Herself Defined: The Poet H. D. and Her World*. New York: Doubleday, 1984.

Hall, Radclyffe. *The Well of Loneliness*. New York: Avon, 1980.

Hanfstaengel, Ernst. *Hitler: The Missing Years*. London: Eyre and Spottiswoode, 1957.

Harrison, Gilbert A., ed. *Gertrude Stein's America*. Washington: Luce, 1965.

Harrison, Nancy. "An Introduction to the Writing Practice of Jean Rhys: The Novel as Women's Text." Diss., University of Texas, 1984.

Hawkins, Eric, with Robert N. Sturdevant. *Hawkins of the Paris Herald*. New York: Simon and Schuster, 1963.

Heilbrun, Carolyn G., and Margaret R. Higgonet. *The Representation of Women in Fiction*. Baltimore: Johns Hopkins University Press, 1983.

Hemingway, Ernest. *A Moveable Feast*. New York: Scribners, 1964.

———. *Selected Letters: 1917–1961*. Edited by Carlos Baker. New York: Scribners, 1981.

Hinz, Evelyn J. *The Mirror and the Garden: Realism and Reality in the Writings of Anaïs Nin*. Columbus: Ohio State University Press, 1971.

Hobhouse, Janet. *Everybody Who Was Anybody: A Biography of Gertrude Stein*. New York: Putnam, 1975.

Hoffman, Frederick J. *Gertrude Stein*. Minneapolis: University of Minnesota Press, 1961.

———. *The Twenties: American Writing in the Postwar Decade*. New York: Collier, 1962.

———, Charles Allen, and Carolyn F. Ulrich. *The Little Magazine: A History and Bibliography*. Princeton: Princeton University Press, 1946.

Hoffman, Michael J. *The Development of Abstractionism in the Writings of Gertrude Stein*. Philadelphia: University of Pennsylvania Press, 1965.

Huddleston, Sisley. *Back to Montparnasse: Glimpses of Broadway in Bohemia*. Philadelphia: Lippincott, 1931.

———. *Paris Salons, Cafes, Studios*. New York: Blue Ribbon, 1928.

Hughes, Glenn. *Imagism and Imagists: A Study in Modern Poetry*. New York: Humanities, 1931.

Hynes, Samuel. *The Auden Generation: Literature and Politics in England in the 1930s*. London: Bodley Head, 1976.

Isherwood, Christopher. *Lions and Shadows*. London: Hogarth, 1938.

Jacques, Jean-Pierre. *Les malheurs de Sapho*. Paris: Grasset, 1981.

Jay, Karla. "The Disciples of the Tenth Muse: Natalie Clifford Barney and Renée Vivien." Diss., New York University, 1984.

Jenkins, Alan. *The Twenties*. New York: Universe, 1974.

Jolas, Eugene. "Man from Babel." Unpublished biography.

———, ed. *Transition Workshop*. New York: Vanguard, 1949.

Joost, Nicholas. *Ernest Hemingway and the Little Magazines: The Paris Years*. Barre: Barre, 1968.

Josephson, Hannah, and Malcolm Cowley, eds. *Aragon: Poet of the French Resistance*. New York: Duell, 1945.

Josephson, Matthew. *Life among the Surrealists: A Memoir*. New York: Holt, 1962.

Joyce, James. *Ulysses*. New York: Random House, 1961.

———. *Letters of James Joyce*. Edited by Stuart Gilbert. New York: Viking, 1957.

———. *Letters of James Joyce*. Edited by Richard Ellmann. 2 vols. New York: Viking, 1966.

Kannenstine, Louis F. *The Art of Djuna Barnes: Duality and Damnation*. New York: New York University Press, 1977.

Katz, Johnathan. *Gay American History: Lesbians and Gay Men in the USA*. New York: Crowell, 1976.

Katz, Leon, ed. *Fernhurst, Q.E.D., and Other Early Writings*. New York: Liveright, 1971.

Kawin, Bruce. *Telling It Again and Again*. Ithaca: Cornell University Press, 1972.

Kedward, H. R. *Fascism in Western Europe 1900–45*. New York: New York University Press, 1971.

Kenner, Hugh. *A Homemade World: The American Modernist Writers*. New York: Knopf, 1975.

———. *The Poetry of Ezra Pound*. New York: New Directions, 1951.

———. *The Pound Era*. Berkeley: University of California Press, 1971.

Kert, Bernice. *The Hemingway Women*. New York: Norton, 1983.

Kiely, Robert, ed. *Modernism Reconsidered*. Harvard: Harvard University Press, 1983.

King, Michael, ed. *H. D.* New York: National Poetry Foundation, 1986.

Klaich, Dolores. *Woman plus Woman*. New York: Morrow, 1974.

Knapp, Bettina L. *Anaïs Nin*. New York: Ungar, 1978.

Knoll, Robert E., ed. *McAlmon and the Lost Generation: A Self-Portrait*. Lincoln: University of Nebraska Press, 1962.

Kostelanetz, Richard, ed. *The Yale Gertrude Stein*. New Haven: Yale, 1982.

Kouidis, Virginia M. *Mina Loy: American Modernist Poet*. Baton Rouge: Louisiana State University Press, 1980.

Kreymborg, Alfred. *Troubadour: An Autobiography*. New York: Liveright, 1925.

Kristeva, Julia. *Revolution in Poetic Language*. Translated by Margaret Waller. New York: Columbia University Press, 1984.

Laney, Al. *Paris Herald: The Incredible Newspaper*. New York: Appleton-Century, 1947.

Lewis, R. W. B. *Edith Wharton: A Biography*. New York: Harper, 1975.

Liberman, M. M. *Katherine Anne Porter's Fiction*. Detroit: Wayne State University Press, 1971.

Liston, Maureen R. *Gertrude Stein: An Annotated Critical Bibliography*. Kent: Kent State University Press, 1979.

Lidderdale, Jane, and Mary Nicholson. *Dear Miss Weaver: Harriet Shaw Weaver, 1876–1961*. New York: Viking, 1970.

Loeb, Harold. *The Way It Was*. New York: Criterion, 1959.

Lopez, Enrique Hank. *Conversations with Katherine Anne Porter*. Boston: Little, Brown, 1981.

Lorenz, Paul. *Sapho, 1900: Renée Vivien*. Paris: Julliard, 1977.

Lottman, Herbert R. *The Left Bank: Writers, Artists, and Politics from the Popular Front to the Cold War*. Boston: Houghton Mifflin, 1982.

McAlmon, Robert. *Being Geniuses Together: 1920–1930*. Revised with additional material by Kay Boyle. Garden City: Doubleday, 1968.

McCarthy, Harold T. *The Expatriate Perspective: American Novelists and the Idea of America*. Rutherford: Fairleigh, 1974.

McCarthy, Patrick. *Celine: A Biography*. London: Penguin, 1975.

McConnell-Ginet, Sally, Ruth Borker, and Nelly Furman, eds. *Women and Language in Literature and Society*. New York: Praeger, 1980.

McDougall, Richard, ed. *The Very Rich Hours of Adrienne Monnier*. New York: Scribner, 1976.

McMillan, Dougald. *transition: The History of a Literary Era, 1927–1938*. New York: Braziller, 1976.

Marcus, Jane, ed. *New Feminist Essays on Virginia Woolf*. Lincoln: University of Nebraska Press, 1981.

———, ed. *The Young Rebecca: Writings of Rebecca West 1911–17*. London: Macmillan, 1982.

Mellow, James R. *Charmed Circle: Gertrude Stein and Company*. New York: Avon, 1975.

Mellown, Elgin W. *Jean Rhys: A Descriptive and Annotated Bibliography of Works and Criticism*. New York: Garland, 1984.

Mendelson, Edward, ed. *W. H. Auden: Collected Poems*. New York: Random House, 1976.

Messerli, Douglas. *Djuna Barnes: A Bibliography*. Rhinebeck: Lewis, 1975.

———. *Djuna Barnes Interviews*. Washington, D.C.: Sun and Moon Press, 1985.

Meyerowitz, Patricia, ed. *Look at Me Now and Here I Am: Writings and Lectures 1909–45 by Gertrude Stein*. Harmondsworth: Penguin, 1971.

Meyers, Jeffrey. *Homosexuality and Literature, 1890–1930*. Montreal: McGill-Queen's University Press, 1977.

Miller, Henry. *Henry Miller: Letters to Anaïs Nin*. Edited by Gunther Stuhlman. New York: Putnam, 1965.

———. *Tropic of Cancer*. Paris: Obelisk, 1934.

Miller, Rosalind S. *Gertrude Stein: Form and Intelligibility*. New York: Exposition, 1949.

Mitchell, Juliet, and Jacqueline Rose, eds. *Jacques Lacan and the Ecole Freudienne: Feminine Sexuality*. London: Macmillan, 1982.

Mitchell, Yvonne. *Colette: A Taste for Life.* New York: Harcourt Brace Jovanovich, 1975.

Moers, Ellen. *The Dandy: Brummell to Beerbohm.* New York: Viking, 1960.

Nance, William L. *Katherine Anne Porter and the Art of Rejection.* Chapel Hill:
University of North Carolina Press, 1964.

Nebeker, Helen. *Jean Rhys: Woman in Passage.* Montreal: Eden, 1981.

Orenstein, Gloria Feman. "Salon Women: Creators of Culture." Work in progress.

Ostriker, Alicia. *Writing Like a Woman.* Ann Arbor: University of Michigan
Press, 1983.

Oxford Poetry 1927. Oxford: Blackwell, 1927.

Painter, George D. *Marcel Proust: A Biography.* 2 vols. London: Chatto, 1965.

Paul, Elliot. *The Last Time I Saw Paris.* New York: Random, 1942.

Perkins, David. *A History of Modern Poetry.* Cambridge: Harvard University
Press, 1957.

Perry, Ruth, and Martine Watson Brownley. *Mothering the Mind: Twelve Studies
of Writers and Their Silent Partners.* New York and London: Holmes and
Meier, 1984.

Pondrom, Cyrena N. *The Road from Paris: French Influence on English Poetry,
1900–1920.* Cambridge: Cambridge University Press, 1974.

Porter, Katherine Anne. *The Days Before.* New York: Harcourt Brace, 1952.

———. *The Collected Essays and Occasional Writings of Katherine Anne Porter.*
New York: Delacorte, 1970.

Pound, Ezra. *The ABC of Reading.* London: Routledge, 1934; New York: New
Directions, 1960.

———. *The Cantos.* New York: New Directions, 1948.

———. *A Draft of XVI Cantos.* Paris: Three Mountains Press, 1925.

———. *A Draft of XXX Cantos.* Paris: Hours Press, 1930; New York: Farrar and
Rinehart, 1933; London: Faber and Faber, 1933.

———. *Exultations.* London: Matthews, 1909.

———. *Ezra Pound Speaking: Radio Speeches of World War II.* Edited by Leonard
Doob. Westport: Greenwood, 1978.

———. *The Fifth Decad of Cantos.* London: Faber, 1937.

———. *The Letters of Ezra Pound.* Edited by D. D. Paige. New York: Harcourt,
1950.

———. *Personae.* London: Matthews, 1909.

———. *Poems 1918–21.* New York: Boni and Liveright, 1922; London: Casa-
nova Society, 1926.

———. *Ripostes.* London: Swift, 1912.

———, ed. *Des Imagistes: An Anthology.* New York: Shay, 1917.

Putnam, Samuel. *Paris Was Our Mistress: Memoirs of the Lost and Found Generation.* New York: Viking, 1947.

Quennell, Peter. *Letter to Mrs. Virginia Woolf.* London: Hogarth, 1932.

Reid, B. L. *Art by Subtraction: A Dissenting Opinion of Gertrude Stein.* Norman: University of Oklahoma Press, 1958.

Reilly, Catherine, ed. *Scars upon My Heart: Women's Poetry and Verse of the First
World War.* London: Virago, 1981.

Resnick, Margery, and Isabelle de Courtivron. *Women Writers in Translation: An*

Annotated Bibliography, 1948–1982. New York: Garland, 1984.

Rich, Adrienne. *On Lies, Secrets and Silence: Selected Prose, 1966–1978*. New York: Norton, 1979.

Rivers, J. E. *Proust and the Art of Love: The Aesthetics of Sexuality in the Life, Times, and Art of Marcel Proust*. New York: Columbia University Press, 1980.

Robinson, Janice S. *H. D.: The Life and Work of an American Poet*. Boston: Houghton Mifflin, 1982.

Rogers, W. G. *When This You See Remember Me: Gertrude Stein in Person*. New York: Rinehart, 1948.

Rood, Karen Lane, ed. *American Writers in Paris, 1920–1939*. Dictionary of Literary Biography. Detroit: Gale, 1980.

Root, Waverly. *The Secret History of the War*. 2 vols. New York: Scribners, 1945.

Rose, Phyllis. *Woman of Letters: A Life of Virginia Woolf*. New York: Oxford, 1978.

Rudnick, Lois Palken. *Mabel Dodge Luhan: New Woman, New Worlds*. Albuquerque: University of New Mexico Press, 1984.

Sachs, Maurice. *The Decade of Illusion, Paris 1918–1928*. New York: Knopf, 1933.

Said, Edward. *Selected Papers from the English Institute, Literature and Society*. Baltimore: Johns Hopkins University Press, 1978.

Saillens, E[mile]. *Facts about France*. London: Adelphi Terrace, 1918.

Sarde, Michèle. *Colette: Free and Fettered*. Translated by Richard Miller. New York: Morrow, 1980.

Schmitz, Neil. *Of Huck and Alice: Humorous Writing in American Literature*. Minneapolis: University of Minnesota Press, 1983.

Schneidau, Herbert. *Ezra Pound: The Image and the Real*. Baton Rouge: Louisiana State University Press, 1969.

Scott, Bonnie Kime. *Joyce and Feminism*. Bloomington: Indiana University Press, 1984.

Scudder, Janet. *Modeling My Life*. New York: Harcourt, 1925.

Secrest, Meryle. *Between Me and Life: A Biography of Romaine Brooks*. Garden City: Doubleday, 1974.

Sedgwick, Eve Kosofsky. *Between Men: English Literature and Male Homosocial Desire*. New York: Columbia University Press, 1985.

Shattuck, Roger. *The Banquet Years: The Arts in France 1885–1918*. New York: Harcourt Brace, 1955.

Showalter, Elaine. *A Literature of Their Own: British Women Novelists from Bronte to Lessing*. Princeton: Princeton University Press, 1977.

Sieburth, Richard. *Investigations: Ezra Pound and Remy de Gourmont*. Cambridge: Harvard University Press, 1978.

Simon, Linda. *The Biography of Alice B. Toklas*. Garden City: Doubleday, 1977.
———, ed. *Gertrude Stein: A Composite Portrait*. New York: Avon, 1974.

Sitwell, Edith. *Taken Care of: Edith Sitwell's Autobiography*. London: Hutchinson, 1963.

Smith-Rosenberg, Carroll. *Disorderly Conduct: Visions of Gender in Victorian America*. New York: Knopf, 1984.

Smoller, Sanford J. *Adrift among Geniuses: Robert McAlmon, Writer and*

Publisher of the Twenties. University Park: Pennsylvania State University Press, 1975.

Spears, Monroe K. *Dionysus and the City: Modernism in Twentieth-Century Poetry*. New York: Oxford, 1970.

Spencer, Sharon. *Collage of Dreams: The Writings of Anaïs Nin*. Chicago: Swallow, 1977.

Spender, Stephen. *World within Word*. London: Hamilton, 1951.

Sprigge, Elizabeth. *Gertrude Stein: Her Life and Work*. New York: Harper, 1957.

Squier, Susan Merrill, ed. *Women Writers and the City: Essays in Feminist Literary Criticism*. Knoxville: University of Tennessee Press, 1984.

Staley, Thomas F. *Jean Rhys: A Critical Study*. Austin: University of Texas Press, 1979.

Stambolian, George, and Elaine Marks, eds. *Homosexualities and French Literature: Cultural Contexts/Critical Texts*. Ithaca: Cornell University Press, 1979.

Stein, Leo. *Journey into Self: Being the Letters, Papers and Journals of Leo Stein*. Edited by Edmund Fuller. New York: Crown, 1950.

Steiner, Wendy. *Exact Resemblance to Exact Resemblance: The Literary Portraiture of Gertrude Stein*. New Haven: Yale University Press, 1978.

Stephenson, Jill. *The Nazi Organization of Women*. London: Croom, 1981.

Steward, Samuel. *Dear Sammy: Letters from Gertrude Stein and Alice B. Toklas*. New York: Houghton Mifflin, 1977.

Stewart, Allegra. *Gertrude Stein and the Present*. Cambridge: Harvard University Press, 1967.

Stock, Noel. *The Life of Ezra Pound*. New York: Pantheon, 1970.

Sutherland, Donald. *Gertrude Stein: A Biography of Her Work*. New Haven: Yale University Press, 1951.

Symons, Julian. *The Thirties: A Dream Revolved*. London: Faber, 1975.

Tripp, C. A. *The Homosexual Matrix*. New York: McGraw-Hill, 1975.

Troubridge, Lady Una. *The Life of Radclyffe Hall*. New York: Arno, 1975.

Tyrrell, William Blake. *Amazons: A Study in Athenian Mythmaking*. Baltimore: Johns Hopkins University Press, 1984.

Walker, Jayne L. *The Making of a Modernist: Gertrude Stein from "Three Lives" to "Tender Buttons."* Amherst: University of Massachusetts Press, 1984.

Wees, William C. *Vorticism and the English Avant-Garde*. Toronto: University of Toronto Press, 1972.

Wheeler, Kenneth W., and Virginia Lee Lussier, eds. *Women, the Arts, and the 1920s in Paris and New York*. New Brunswick: Transaction Books, 1982.

White, Ray Lewis. *Gertrude Stein and Alice B. Toklas: A Reference Guide*. Boston: G. K. Hall, 1984.

Wickes, George. *The Amazon of Letters: The Life and Loves of Natalie Barney*. London: Allen, 1977.

———. *Americans in Paris*. Garden City: Doubleday, 1969.

Williams, Ellen. *Harriet Monroe and the Poetry Renaissance: The First Ten Years of "Poetry": 1912–22*. Urbana: University of Illinois Press, 1977.

Williams, William Carlos. *The Autobiography of William Carlos Williams*. New York: Random, 1951.

Wilson, Edmund. *Axel's Castle: A Study in the Imaginative Literature of 1890–1930*. New York: Scribners, 1931.

———. *The Shores of Light: A Literary Chronicle of the Twenties and Thirties*. New York: Farrar, 1952.

———. *The Thirties*. Edited by Leon Edel. New York: Farrar, Straus and Giroux, 1980.

Wilson, Ellen. *They Named Me Gertrude Stein*. New York: Farrar, 1973.

Wiser, William. *The Crazy Years: Paris in the Twenties*. New York: Atheneum, 1983.

Wolff, Charlotte. *Bisexuality: A Study*. New York: Horizon, 1978.

———. *Love between Women*. New York: Harper, 1972.

Wolff, Cynthia Griffin. *A Feast of Words: The Triumph of Edith Wharton*. New York: Oxford, 1976.

Wolff, Geoffrey. *Black Sun: The Brief Transit and Violent Eclipse of Harry Crosby*. New York: Random House, 1976.

Woolf, Virginia. *Collected Essays*. 4 vols. New York: Harcourt, 1966–1967.

———. *The Diaries of Virginia Woolf*. Edited by Anne Olivier Bell. 5 vols. New York: Harcourt Brace Jovanovich, 1977–1984.

———. *Letter to a Young Poet*. London: Hogarth, 1932.

———. *Moments of Being*. Edited by Jeanne Schulkind. New York: Harcourt Brace Jovanovich, 1976.

———. *A Room of One's Own*. London: Hogarth, 1929.

———. *Three Guineas*. New York: Harcourt, 1968.

———. *The Waves*. New York: Harcourt, 1931.

Zeldin, Theodore. *France: 1848–1945*. 2 vols. Oxford: Clarendon, 1973.

Essays

Ahearn, Barry. "Ezra Pound and Louis Zukofsky: Letters 1928–1930." *Montemora* 8 (1981): 149–183.

Allen, Carolyn. "'Dressing the Unknowable in the Garments of the Known': The Style of Djuna Barnes' *Nightwood*." In *Women and Language*, edited by McConnell-Ginet, Barker, and Furman, 106–118.

———. "Writing toward *Nightwood*: Djuna Barnes' Seduction Stories." In *Silence and Power*, edited by Broe.

Antin, David. "Some Questions about Modernism." *Occident* 8 (1974): 7–38.

Aron, Jean-Paul, and Roger Kempf. "Triumphs and Tribulations of the Homosexual Discourse." In *Homosexualities and French Literature*, edited by Stambolian and Marks, 141–160.

Auden, W. H., and C. Day Lewis. "Preface." In *Oxford Poetry 1927*. Oxford: Blackwell, 1926.

Auerbach, Nina. "Magi and Maidens: The Romance of the Victorian Freud." *Critical Inquiry* 8 (1981): 281–300.

Banting, John. "Nancy Cunard." In *Nancy Cunard*, edited by Ford, 179–185.

Barrett, Michele, and Jean Radford. "Modernism in the 1930s: Dorothy Richardson and Virginia Woolf." In *1936: The Sociology of Literature*, edited by Barker et al., 1:252–272.

Bassoff, Bruce. "Gertrude Stein's 'Composition as Explanation.'" *Twentieth Century Literature* 24 (1978): 76–80.

Baym, Nina. "The Madwoman and Her Languages: Why I Don't Do Theory." *Tulsa Studies in Women's Literature* 3 (1984): 45–60.

Beach, Sylvia. "'Ulysse' à Paris." *Mercure de France* 309 (May–August 1950): 12–29.

Beebe, Maurice. "Joyce and the Meanings of Modernism." In *Litters from Aloft*, by Bates and Pollock, 15–25.

Bell, Millicent. "The Black Sun Press to the Present." *Books at Brown* 17 (1955): 2–24.

Benstock, Shari. "Beyond the Reaches of Feminist Criticism: A Letter from Paris." *Tulsa Studies in Women's Literature* 3 (1984): 5–27.

———. "The Feminist Critique: Mastering Our Monstrosity." *Tulsa Studies in Women's Literature* 2 (1983): 137–150.

———. "*Les Liaisons dangereuses:* The Grammar of Sexuality in the Works of James Joyce." Paper presented at 1984 MLA, Washington, D.C.

———. "Reading Women Writing." *Tulsa Studies in Women's Literature* 4 (1985): 5–15.

Bentley, Eric. "We Are in History." In *Homosexualities and French Literature*, edited by Stambolian and Marks, 122–140.

Blankley, Elyse. "Return to Mytilène: Renée Vivien and the City of Women." In *Women Writers and the City*, edited by Squier, 45–67.

Bloom, Lynn Z. "Gertrude Is Alice Is Everybody: Innovation and Point of View in Stein's Autobiographies." *Twentieth Century Literature* 24 (1978): 81–93.

Bock, Gisela. "Racism and Sexism in Nazi Germany: Motherhood, Compulsory Sterilization, and the State." *Signs: Journal of Women in Culture and Society* 8 (1983): 400–421.

Bradbury, Malcolm. "London 1890–1920." In *Modernism*, edited by Bradbury and McFarlane, 172–190.

———. "Struggling Westward: America and the Coming of Modernism (1)." *Encounter* 50 (January 1983): 55–60.

———, and James McFarlane. "Movements, Magazines and Manifestos: The Succession from Naturalism." In *Modernism*, edited by Bradbury and McFarlane, 192–205.

———. "The Name and Nature of Modernism." In *Modernism*, edited by Bradbury and McFarlane, 19–56.

Bryher. "For Sylvia." *Mercure de France* 349 (August–September 1963): 17–21.

Buck, Claire. "Freud and H. D.—Bisexuality and a Feminine Discourse." *m/f* 8 (1983): 53–66.

Burke, Carolyn G. "'Accidental Aloofness': Barnes, Loy and Modernism." In *Silence and Power*, edited by Broe.

———. "Becoming Mina Loy." *Women's Studies* 7 (1980): 137–150.

———. "Gertrude Stein, the Cone Sisters, and the Puzzle of Female Friendship." In *Writing and Sexual Difference*, by Abel, 221–242. Originally published in *Critical Inquiry* 8, 3 (1982): 543–564.

———. "The Last Lunar Baedeker." Revision of *The Last Lunar Baedeker*, edited by Roger L. Conver. *San Francisco Review of Books* (November–December 1982): 28–29.

Burke, Kenneth. "Engineering with Words." *Dial* 74 (April 1923): 410.

———. "The Impartial Essence." *New Republic* 83 (July 1935): 227.

———. "Version, Con-, Per-, and In-: Thoughts on Djuna Barnes' Novel *Nightwood*." *Southern Review* 2 (1966–67): 329–346.

Cahm, Eric. "Revolt, Conservatism and Reaction in Paris: 1905–25." In *Modernism*, edited by Bradbury and McFarlane, 162–171.

Calloway, Jan. "The Patriarchal Portraits of H. D. and Gertrude Stein." Unpublished essay.

Carroll, Berenice. " 'To Crush Him in Our Own Country': The Political Thought of Virginia Woolf." *Feminist Studies* 4 (1978): 99–131.

Cixous, Hélène. "The Laugh of the Medusa." Translated by Keith Cohen and Paula Cohen. In *The Signs Reader*, edited by Abel and Abel, 279–297.

———. "Rethinking Differences: An Interview." In *Homosexualities*, edited by Stambolian and Marks, 70–86.

Cody, E. Morrill. "Shakespeare and Company—Paris." *Publishers Weekly* 12 (April 1924): 1261–1263.

Colquitt, Clare. "Unpacking Her Treasures: Edith Wharton's 'Myterious Correspondence' with Morton Fullerton." *Library Chronicle of the University of Texas at Austin* n.s. 31 (1985): 73–107.

Cook, Blanche Wiesen. "The Historical Denial of Lesbianism." *Radical History Review* 20 (1979): 60–65.

———. " 'Women Alone Stir My Imagination': Lesbianism and the Cultural Tradition." *Signs: Journal of Women in Culture and Society* 4 (1979): 718–739.

———. "Women and Politics: The Obscured Dimension." In *Women, the Arts*, edited by Wheeler and Lussier, 147–152.

Coombes, Anna. "Virginia Woolf's *The Waves*: A Materialist Reading of an Almost Disembodied Voice." In *1936: The Sociology of Literature*, by Barker et al., 1:228–251.

Cowley, Malcolm. "The Twenties in Montparnasse." *Saturday Review* (11 March 1967): 51–55, 98–101.

———. "When a Young American." *Mercure de France* 349 (August–September 1963): 57–59.

Cunard, Nancy. "Letter From Paris." *Horizon* 11 (June 1945): 397–407.

———. "The Refugees at Perpignan: Miss Cunard's Appeal." In *Nancy Cunard*, edited by Ford, 196–197.

Curry, Linda. " 'Tom, Take Mercy': Djuna Barnes' Drafts of *The Antiphon*." In *Silence and Power*, edited by Broe.

Davidson, Arnold E. "The Art and Economics of Destitution in Jean Rhys's *After Leaving Mr. Mackenzie*." *Studies in the Novel* 16 (1984): 215–237.

DeSalvo, Louise A. "To Make Her Mutton at Sixteen: Rape, Incest, and Child Abuse in Djuna Barnes's *The Antiphon*." In *Silence and Power*, edited by Broe.

Doolittle, Hilda. "Will this reach you . . ." *Mercure de France* 349 (1963): 158–159.

DuPlessis, Rachel Blau. "Family, Sexes, Psyche: An Essay on H. D. and the Muse of the Woman Writer." *Montemora* 6 (1979): 137–156.

————. "Romantic Thralldom in H. D." *Contemporary Literature* 20 (1979): 178–203.

————, and Susan Stanford Friedman. "'Woman Is Perfect': H. D.'s Debate with Freud." *Feminist Studies* 7 (1981): 417–429.

Dydo, Ulla E. "Landscape Is Not Grammar." Unpublished essay.

————. "Must Horses Drink; or, 'Any Language Is Funny If You Don't Understand It.'" *Tulsa Studies in Women's Literature* 4 (1985): 272–280.

————. "To Make a Sentence in Vincennes." Paper presented at 1984 MLA, Washington, D.C.

Eagleson, Harvey. "Gertrude Stein: Method in Madness." *Sewanee Review* (April 1936): 164–177.

Eliot, T. S. "The Metaphysical Poets." In *Selected Essays: 1917–1932*. London: Faber and Faber, 1932.

————. "Miss Sylvia Beach." *Mercure de France* 349 (August–September 1963): 9–12.

English Study Group, Centre for Contemporary Studies, Birmingham. "Thinking the Thirties." In *1936: The Sociology of Literature*, by Barker et al., 2: 1–20.

Faderman, Lillian. "The Morbidification of Love between Women by 19th Century Sexologists." *Journal of Homosexuality* 4 (1978): 73–90.

Fassler, Barbara. "Theories of Homosexuality as Sources of Bloomsbury's Androgyny." *Signs: Journal of Women in Culture and Society* 5 (1979): 237–251.

Feldman, Paula R. "Margaret Anderson." In *American Writers in Paris*, edited by Rood, 3–10.

Fifer, Elizabeth. "Is Flesh Advisable?: The Interior Theater of Gertrude Stein." *Signs: Journal of Women in Culture and Society* 4 (1979): 472–483.

Fifield, William. "Pablo Picasso: The Dynamic of Creation." *Paris Review* 32 (1965–66): 37–71.

Flanner, Janet. "Foreword." In *Colette: The Difficulty of Loving*, by Crosland, ix–xxx.

————. "The Great Amateur Publisher." *Mercure de France* 349 (1963): 46–54.

————. "The Greatest Refreshment." *New Yorker* (11 March 1972): 32–36.

————. "Profiles: A Life on a Cloud." *New Yorker* 50 (June 1974): 46–67.

————. "Then and Now." *Paris Review* 9 (1965–66): 158–170.

Ford, Ford Madox. "Preface." In *Left Bank*, by Rhys, 7–27.

Freibert, L. M. "Conflict and Creativity in the World of H. D." *Journal of Women's Studies in Literature* 8 (1979): 258–271.

————. "From Semblance to Selfhood: The Evolution of Woman in H. D.'s Neo-Epic *Helen in Egypt*." *Arizona Quarterly* 36 (1980): 165–175.

Friedman, Susan Stanford. "Creating a Woman's Mythology: H.D.'s *Helen in Egypt*." *Women's Studies* 5 (1977): 163–198.

————. "Creativity and the Childbirth Metaphor: Gender Differences in Literary Discourse." In "The Private Self," by Benstock.

————. "Modernism of the 'Scattered Remnant': Race and Politics in H. D.'s Development." In *H. D.*, edited by King.

————. "Psyche Reborn: Tradition, Re-Vision, and the Goddess as Mother-Symbol in H. D.'s Epic Poetry." *Women's Studies* 6 (1979): 147–160.

————. "Who Buried H. D.? A Poet, Her Critics, and Her Place in the Literary Tradition." *College English* 36 (1975): 801–814.

————, and Rachel Blau DuPlessis. "'I Had Two Loves Separate': The Sexualities of H. D.'s *Her*." *Montemora* 8 (1981): 7–30.

"From Harriet Monroe to *AQ*." *13th Moon* 8 (1984): 183–215.

Gass, William H. "Gertrude Stein and the Geography of the Sentence." In *The World within the Word*, by Gass, 63–123.

————. "Three Photos of Colette." In *The World within the Word*, by Gass, 124–146.

Gilbert, Sandra M. "Costumes of the Mind: Transvestism as Metaphor in Modern Literature." *Critical Inquiry* 7 (1980): 391–418.

————. "From *Patria* to *Matria*: Elizabeth Barrett Browning's Risorgimento." *PMLA* 99 (1984): 194–211.

————. "Soldier's Heart: Literary Men, Literary Women, and the Great War." *Signs: Journal of Women in Culture and Society* 8 (1983): 422–450.

Givner, Joan. "Katherine Anne Porter." In *American Writers in Paris*, edited by Rood, 311–314.

Gregory, Horace. "Introduction." In *Helen in Egypt*, by H. D., vii–xi.

Gribben, Alan. "Edith Wharton Letters Selected, Transcribed, and Annotated." *Library Chronicle of the University of Texas at Austin* n.s. 31 (1985): 21–72.

————. "'The Heart Is Insatiable': A Selection from Edith Wharton's Letters to Morton Fullerton, 1907–1915." *Library Chronicle of the University of Texas at Austin* n.s. 31 (1985): 7–20.

Gubar, Susan. "Blessings in Disguise: Cross-Dressing as Re-Dressing for Female Modernists." *Massachusetts Review* 22 (1981): 477–508.

————. "The Echoing Spell of H. D.'s *Trilogy*." *Contemporary Literature* 19 (1978): 196–218.

————. "Sapphistries." *Signs: Journal of Women in Culture and Society* 10 (1984): 43–62.

Hadas, Pamela: "Spreading the Difference: One Way to Read Gertrude Stein's *Tender Buttons*." *Twentieth Century Literature* 24 (1978): 57–75.

Hahn, Emily. "Salonists and Chronicity." In *Women, the Arts*, edited by Wheeler and Lussier, 56–64.

Harris, Bertha. "The More Profound Nationality of Their Lesbianism: Lesbian Society in the 1920's." In *Amazon Expedition*, edited by Birky et al., 77–88.

Haslinger, Regina. "Gertrude Stein and *écriture féminine*." Unpublished essay.

Hastings, Susan. "Two of the Weird Sisters: The Eccentricities of Gertrude Stein and Edith Sitwell." *Tulsa Studies in Women's Literature* 4 (1985): 101–123.

Heilbrun, Carolyn G. "Presidential Address 1984." *PMLA* 100 (1985): 281–286.

Hoffman, Frederick. "Conversation and Experiment: *The Little Review* in Modern Literature." Available in Manuscripts Division, Library of Congress.

Jackson, Brendan. "The Fulsomeness of Her Prolixity." *South Atlantic Quarterly* 83 (1984): 91–102.

Jolas, Maria. "The Joyce I Knew and the Women around Him." *Crane Bag* 4 (1980): 82–87.

Katz, Leon. "Introduction." In *Fernhurst, Q.E.D., and Other Early Writings by Gertrude Stein*, by Katz, ix–xlii.

Katz, Leslie. "Meditations on Sylvia Beach." *Mercure de France* 349 (1963): 82–88.

Kenner, Hugh. "The Making of the Modernist Canon." *Chicago Review* 34 (1984): 49–61.

Kestner, Joseph. "Edward Burne-Jones and the Nineteenth-Century Fear of Women." *Biography* 7 (1984): 95–122.

Kolodny, Annette. "Dancing through the Minefield: Some Observations on the Theory, Practice and Politics of a Feminist Literary Criticism." *Feminist Studies* 6 (1980): 1–25.

———. "Some Notes on Defining a 'Feminist Literary Criticism.'" In *Feminist Criticism,* edited by Brown and Olson, 37–58.

Lanser, Susan Sniader. "Speaking in Tongues: *Ladies Almanack* and the Discourse of Desire." In *Silence and Power,* edited by Broe.

———. "Speaking in Tongues: *Ladies Almanack* and the Language of Celebration." *Frontiers: A Journal of Women's Studies* 4 (1979): 39–46.

Lilienfeld, Jane. "The Magic Spinning Wheel: Straw of Gold—Colette, Willy, and the Sido." In *Mothering the Mind,* by Perry and Brownley, 165–178.

"The Little Magazine—VIII: 'The Little Review.'" *TLS* (25 April 1968).

Litwak, Leo. "Kay Boyle—Paris Wasn't Like That." *New York Times Book Review,* 15 July 1984.

McFarlane, James. "The Mind of Modernism." In *Modernism,* edited by Bradbury and McFarlane, 71–93.

Makward, Christiane. "To Be or Not to Be . . . a Feminist Speaker." In *The Future of Difference,* edited by Eisenstein and Jardine, 95–105.

Mallet-Joris, Françoise: "A Womanly Vocation." In *Colette,* edited by Eisinger and McCarty, 7–15.

Marcus, Jane. "Asylums of Antaeus: Women, War, and Madness." Paper presented at 1985 SCMLA, Tulsa Oklahoma.

———. "The Canonization." Review of *The Auden Generation* by Samuel Hynes. *Minnesota Review* 15 (1978): 117–120.

———. "Carnival of the Animals." *Women's Review of Books* 8 (May 1984): 6–7.

———. "Laughing at Leviticus: *Nightwood* as Woman's Circus Epic." In *Silence and Power,* edited by Broe.

———. "Liberty, Sorority, Misogyny." In *Representation of Women in Fiction,* by Heilbrun and Higgonet, 60–97.

———. "'No More Horses': Virginia Woolf on Art and Propaganda." *Women's Studies* 4 (1977): 265–289.

———. "Thinking Back through Our Mothers." In *New Feminist Essays on Virginia Woolf,* edited by Marcus, 1–30.

———. "Tintinnabulations." *Marxist Perspectives* 2 (1979): 145–167.

———. "Virginia Woolf and Her Violin: Mothering, Madness, and Music." In *Mothering the Mind,* by Perry and Brownley, 181–201.

Marinetti, F. T. "Against *Amore* and Parliamentarianism." In *War, the World's Only Hygiene* in *Marinetti: Selected Writings,* edited by Flint.

Marks, Elaine. "Foreword: Celebrating Colette." In *Colette,* edited by Eisinger and McCarty, ix–xi.

———. "Lesbian Intertextuality." In *Homosexualities and French Literature*, edited by Stambolian and Marks, 353–377.

Miller, Nancy K. "The Anamnesis of a Female 'I': In the Margins of Self-Portrayal." In *Colette*, edited by Eisinger and McCarty, 164–175.

Monnier, Adrienne. "Americans in Paris." In *The Very Rich Hours*, edited by McDougall, 413–416.

———. "La Maison des Amis des Livres." In *The Very Rich Hours*, edited by McDougall, 69–74.

———. "Les Amies des Livres." In *The Very Rich Hours*, edited by McDougall, 183–185.

———. "Lectures chez Sylvia." *Mercure de France* 349 (1963): 133–135.

———. "A Letter to André Gide about the Young." In *The Very Rich Hours*, edited by McDougall, 407–410.

———. "A Letter to Friends in the Free Zone." In *The Very Rich Hours*, edited by McDougall, 403–406.

———. "Letter to a Young Poet." In *The Very Rich Hours*, edited by McDougall, 186–192.

———. "Lunch with Colette." In *The Very Rich Hours*, edited by McDougall, 196–199.

———. "Lust." In *The Very Rich Hours*, edited by McDougall, 169–172.

———. "Memories of London." In *The Very Rich Hours*, edited by McDougall, 315–327.

———. "Number One." In *The Very Rich Hours*, edited by McDougall, 136–152.

———. "On Anti-Semitism." In *The Very Rich Hours*, edited by McDougall, 373–378.

———. "On War." In *The Very Rich Hours*, edited by McDougall, 367–372.

———. "The Swastika." In *The Very Rich Hours*, edited by McDougall, 365–366.

———. "'Unkindness.'" In *The Very Rich Hours*, edited by McDougall, 173–174.

———. "A Visit to T. S. Eliot." In *The Very Rich Hours*, edited by McDougall, 200–203.

———. "With Gide at Hyères." In *The Very Rich Hours*, edited by McDougall, 93–97.

Moore, Marianne. "How do justice . . ." *Mercure de France* 349 (August–September 1963): 13.

Morse, Samuel French. "The Rediscovery of Mina Loy and the Avant Garde." *Wisconsin Studies in Contemporary Literature* 2 (1961): 12–19.

Mortimer, Raymond. "Nancy Cunard." In *Nancy Cunard*, edited by Ford, 48–49.

Newton, Esther. "The Mythic Mannish Lesbian: Radclyffe Hall and the New Woman." *Signs: Journal of Women in Culture and Society* 9 (1984): 557–575.

Orenstein, Gloria Feman. "Gertrude Stein: Decoding the Amusing Muse." Paper presented at the 1984 MLA, Washington, D.C.

———. "Natalie Barney's Parisian Salon." *13th Moon* 5 (1980): 76–93.

———. "The Salon of Natalie Clifford Barney: An Interview with Berthe Cley-rergue." *Signs: Journal of Women in Culture and Society* 4 (1979): 484–496.

Patterson, Celia. "Gertrude Stein and the Patriarchal Umbrella." Unpublished essay.

Perloff, Marjorie. "Poetry as Word System: The Art of Gertrude Stein." *American Poetry Review* 8 (1979): 33–42.

Pinckney, Darryl. "Sweet Evening Breeze." *New York Review of Books* (December, 1984).

Pondrom, Cyrena N. "H. D. and the Origins of Modernism." *Sagetrieb* 4 (Spring 1985): 73–100.

———. "Selected Letters from H. D. to F. S. Flint: A Commentary on the Imagist Period." *Contemporary Literature* 10 (1969): 557–569.

Ponsot, Mary. "A Reader's *Ryder.*" In *Silence and Power,* edited by Broe.

Porter, Katherine Anne. "Gertrude Stein: A Self-Portrait." *Harper's* 195 (December 1947): 519–527.

———. "Tell me about Adrienne . . ." *Mercure de France* 349 (1963): 154–157.

Pound, Ezra. "De Gourmont: A Distinction." In *Little Review Anthology,* edited by Anderson, 255–257.

———. "This Island of Paris: A Letter." *Dial* 69 (1920): 406–411.

Raymont, Henry. "From the Avant-Garde of the Thirties, Djuna Barnes." *New York Times,* 24 May 1971.

Rich, Adrienne. "Compulsory Heterosexuality and Lesbian Existence." *Signs: Journal of Women in Culture and Society* 5 (1980): 631–660.

———. "It Is the Lesbian in Us." *Sinister Wisdom* (1977): 6–9.

Riddel, Joseph. "H. D.'s Scene of Writing—Poetry as (and) Analysis." *Studies in the Literary Imagination* 12 (1979): 41–59.

———. "'Spiritual Realism.'" *Contemporary Literature* 10 (1969): 447–473.

Robbins, Bruce. "Modernism in History, Modernism in Power." In *Modernism Reconsidered,* edited by Kiely, 229–246.

Roberts, Helene E. "The Exquisite Slave: The Role of Clothes in the Making of the Victorian Woman." *Signs: Journal of Women in Culture and Society* 2 (1977): 554–569.

Rood, Karen L. "Florence Gilliam." In *American Writers in Paris,* edited by Rood, 176–177.

Ruddick, Lisa. "William James and the Modernism of Gertrude Stein." In *Modernism Reconsidered,* edited by Kiely, 47–64.

Sahli, Nancy. "Smashing: Women's Relationships before the Fall." *Chrysalis* 8 (1979): 17–27.

Saillet, Maurice. "Mots et locutions de Sylvia." *Mercure de France* 349 (August–September 1963): 75–81.

Sarde, Michèle Blin. "The First Steps in a Writer's Career." In *Colette,* edited by Eisinger and McCarty, 16–21.

Schmitz, Neil. "Gertrude Stein as Post-Modernist: The Rhetoric of *Tender Buttons.*" *Journal of Modern Literature* 3 (1975): 1203–1218.

———. "Portrait, Patriarchy, Mythos: The Revenge of Gertrude Stein." *Salamagundi* (1978): 70–91.

Schrijver, Herman. "About Nancy." In *Nancy Cunard,* edited by Ford, 268–270.

Secor, Cynthia. "Gertrude Stein: The Complex Force of Her Femininity." In *Women, the Arts,* edited by Wheeler and Lussier, 27–35.

———. "The Question of Gertrude Stein." In *American Novelists Revisited,* edited by Fleischmann, 299–310.

Short, Robert. "Dada and Surrealism." In *Modernism,* edited by Bradbury and McFarlane, 292–308.

Sieburth, Richard. "Ezra Pound." In *American Writers in Paris,* edited by Rood, 315–333.

Sitwell, Edith. "Modernist Poets." *Echanges* 2 (1930): 77–82.

———. "The Works of Gertrude Stein: A Modern Writer Who Brings Literature Nearer to the Apparently Irrational World of Music." *Vogue* (London) 66, no. 11 (October 1925): 98.

Skinner, B. F. "Has Gertrude Stein a Secret?" *Atlantic Monthly* 153 (January 1934): 50–57.

Smith-Rosenberg, Carroll. "The Female World of Love and Ritual." *Signs: Journal of Women in Culture and Society* 1 (1975): 1–30.

Solano, Solita. "Nancy Cunard: Brave Poet, Indomitable Rebel." In *Nancy Cunard,* edited by Ford, 76–77.

———. "Paris between the Wars: An Unpublished Memoir by Solita Solano." *Quarterly Journal of the Library of Congress* 34 (October 1977): 306–351.

Spivak, Gayatri Chakravorty. "Draupadi." *Critical Inquiry* 8 (1981): 381–402.

Squier, Susan. "The Politics of City Space in 'The Years': Street Love, Pillar Boxes, and Bridges." In *New Feminist Essays,* edited by Marcus, 216–237.

Stein, Gertrude. "From Dark to Day." *Vogue* (London) (November 1945): 52.

———. "Rich and poor in English . . ." *Mercure de France* 349 (1963): 95–98.

Stimpson, Catharine R. "Ad/d Femininam: Women, Literature, and Society." In *Selected Papers from the English Institute,* by Said, 174–192.

———. "The Androgyne and the Homosexual." *Women's Studies* 2 (1974): 23–47.

———. "Gertrice/Altrude: Stein, Toklas, and the Paradox of the Happy Marriage." In *Mothering the Mind,* by Perry and Brownley, 123–139.

———. "Gertrude Stein: American Writer." Paper presented at 1985 SCMLA, Tulsa, Oklahoma.

———. "Gertrude Stein and the Ideology of America." Paper presented at the 1984 MLA, Washington, D.C.

———. "The Mind, the Body, and Gertrude Stein." *Critical Inquiry* 3 (1977): 491–506.

———. "Reading Gertrude Stein." *Tulsa Studies in Women's Literature* 4 (1985): 265–271.

———. "The Somagrams of Gertrude Stein." *Poetics Today* 6 (1985): 67–80.

———. "Women Writers and Gertrude Stein: The Possibility of Another American Revolution." Paper presented at the Austrian American Studies Association, Salzburg, Austria, 1983.

———. "Zero Degree Deviancy: The Lesbian Novel in English." In *Writing and Sexual Difference,* by Abel, 243–260.

Stockinger, Jacob. "The Test of Love and Nature: Colette and Lesbians." In *Colette,* edited by Eisinger and McCarty, 75–84.

Sutherland, Donald. "Alice and Gertrude and Others." *Prairie Schooner* 45 (1971): 284–299.

Toklas, Alice B. "Fifty Years of French Fashions." *Atlantic* (June 1958): 55–57.

———. "Sylvia and Her Friends." *New Republic* 19 (October 1959): 24–26.

"Two Acorns, One Oak." Review of *The Little Review Anthology*, edited by Margaret Anderson. *New Yorker* (23 January 1954).

Vicinus, Martha. "Distance and Desire: English Boarding-School Friendships." *Signs: Journal of Women in Culture and Society* 9 (1984): 600–622.

Weisstein, Ulrich. "Beast, Doll, and Woman: Djuna Barnes' Human Bestiary." *Renascence* 15 (1962): 3–11.

Wescott, Glenway. "Memories and Opinions." *Prose* 5 (1972): 177–206.

Weston, Ruth Deason. "*Poète Maudit:* The Publishing History of Anaïs Nin." Unpublished essay.

Wickes, George. "Natalie Barney." In *American Writers in Paris*, edited by Rood, 23–28.

Wilson, Edmund. "Gertrude Stein Old and Young." In *The Shores of Light*, by Wilson, 575–586.

Wittig, Monique. "Paradigm." In *Homosexualities and French Literature*, edited by Stambolian and Marks, 114–121.

Woolf, Virginia. "The Leaning Tower." In *Collected Essays*, by Woolf, 162–181.

Zach, Natan. "Imagism and Vorticism." In *Modernism*, edited by Bradbury and McFarlane, 228–242.

INDEX

Abbott, Berenice, 110, 381
Adam, George, 72, 92
Adam, Pearl, 72
aesthetics (Modernist), xii, 4, 31,
    34, 121, 153 (Stein, Picasso), 242
    (Barnes), 278, 286, 290–294, 296
    (Barney), 302, 312, 313 (H. D.),
    317 (Vorticism), 336, 397–398,
    410, 452, 472 n.4 (Imagism)
Aldington, Richard, 63, 249, 312,
    314, 315–316, 317, 318, 320, 321,
    324, 327, 330, 348, 360, 364, 365,
    389, 393, 394, 475 n.8
Aldrich, Mildred, 169
Anderson, Margaret, 2, 6, 21, 22–23,
    114, 120, 165, 175, 236, 239, 267,
    333, 357, 362, 363, 364, 367, 368,
    369, 370–371, 372, 376, 377, 378,
    379, 380, 381, 387, 388, 443
Anderson, Sherwood, 15, 88, 169
anti-Semitism, xii, 19, 31, 45–46, 55,
    63, 121, 123–124, 127–128,
    129–139, 214, 410, 412–415,
    416, 425, 427, 442, 446, 475 n.3
Apollinaire, Guillaume, 63, 85, 95, 169
Aragon, Louis, 217, 372, 381, 389,
    398, 418, 421, 422, 446–447
art, women's contributions to, 109–
    110, 117, 122–123, 175, 178, 243,
    270, 281, 387, 445

Auden, W. H., 398, 399, 400, 401–
    405, 406, 408, 409, 410, 421, 422,
    441, 443

Baker, Josephine, 4, 13, 114
Balmain, Pierre, 110, 169, 465 n.18
Barnes, Djuna, xi, 2, 4, 6, 9, 10, 25,
    28, 29, 31, 32, 34, 88, 110, 113,
    115, 120, 174, 175, 230–267, 268,
    313, 361, 380, 386, 393, 397, 424–
    429, 433, 437, 440, 441, 444, 450,
    455 n.2, 464 n.15, 467–468 n.4;
    The Antiphon, 233, 236, 237, 247,
    467 n.2; The Book of Repulsive
    Women, 235, 240, 241–242, 252;
    Ladies Almanack, 115, 233, 235,
    238, 241, 245, 246, 247, 248, 249,
    250–253, 255, 259, 260–267,
    467 n.4, 468 n.6; Nightwood, 231,
    232, 233, 234, 235, 236, 237, 238,
    240, 241, 243, 246, 247, 248, 252,
    254–267, 424–429, 431–432;
    Ryder, 233, 235, 238, 241, 243,
    245, 246–247, 250, 253
Barney, Albert Clifford, 89, 91, 268,
    269, 270, 272, 273–274, 461 n.3
Barney, Alice Pike, 9, 268, 269, 270,
    272, 273, 279
Barney, Natalie, 2, 6, 8–12, 15, 18,
    22, 25, 31, 34, 48, 49, 53, 54, 59,

61, 62, 63, 65, 77, 78, 79–80, 82,
86–89, 91, 93, 97, 98, 115, 120,
125, 165, 174, 175, 179, 182, 188,
232, 233–234, 235, 236, 249, 250,
251, 253, 255, 256, 257, 268–307,
311, 318, 320, 333, 393, 411, 413–
418, 443, 447, 448, 453, 455 n.2,
456 n.4, 457 n.11, 459 n.6,
464 n.16, 465 n.17, 469 nn.1–2,
470–471 n.6; *The One Who Is
Legion,* 298–301, 302
Beach, Cyprian (sister), 201, 203,
204, 209, 227
Beach, Eleanor (mother), 200, 201,
202–203, 205, 209, 223, 227
Beach, Holly (sister), 202, 203
Beach, Sylvester, 200, 201, 202–203,
214
Beach, Sylvia, 2, 6, 10, 17, 20–21,
31, 112, 114, 132, 165, 169, 174,
176, 194, 196, 197, 198, 200, 201–
204, 206–215, 217–229, 230,
234, 313, 320, 359, 360, 361–362,
388, 412, 413, 430, 445, 446, 448,
457 n.12, 466 nn.3–4; *Shakespeare
and Company,* 201, 202, 212, 221,
224
belle époque, xii, 44, 47, 48, 50, 52–
54, 55, 56, 57, 59, 69, 70–76, 80,
82, 183, 306
Berenson, Bernard, 65
Bernhardt, Sarah, 72
Berry, Walter, 64, 392, 461 n.13
Black Sun Press, 113, 372, 386, 389,
391–392
Blanche, Jacques Emile, 63, 65
Blast, 23, 24, 376
Blum, Léon, 120, 121, 128–130, 136,
405, 414
body (female), 253–256, 286–289,
301–304, 305–307, 411, 412
Bonnierre, Suzanne, 204, 207, 208,
209, 210
Bookstaver, May, 147, 148–149, 150,
151, 155, 192
Bourget, Paul, 38, 46, 71

Boyle, Kay, 2, 6, 9, 10, 120, 235, 361,
381, 392, 444, 451, 458 n.2
Breton, André, 216, 217, 372, 376,
377
Brooks, Romaine, 88, 173, 175, 181,
256, 298, 304–307, 413, 416, 443,
457 n.11
Bryher. *See* Ellerman, Winifred

Céline, Louis Ferdinand, 109, 129,
398, 402–404, 409, 410, 414,
476 n.5; *Voyage au bout de la nuit,*
109, 398, 402–403, 410
censorship, 91, 267, 394, 457 n.5
Chanel, Coco, 74–75, 111, 112, 114,
118, 183
Chaplin, Charles, 117, 380
Chicago Tribune, 4, 21, 35–36, 126,
381, 382, 445
Claudel, Paul, 79
clothing, 37–38, 62, 74–75, 76, 85,
164, 177–184, 210, 253, 304,
468–469 n.9
Cocteau, Jean, 52, 61, 63–64, 69, 88,
108, 110, 116, 169, 214, 368
Cody, Morrill, 4, 29, 206, 388, 467–
468 n.4
Colette, 2, 6, 48, 54–59, 61, 71, 74,
76, 79, 80–84, 88, 89–91, 96–98,
112, 114, 125, 127, 174, 175, 180,
196, 204, 205, 251, 270, 412, 445–
446, 453, 454, 455 n.2, 461–
462 n.4; *The Pure and the Impure,*
48, 56, 175, 251, 277, 307
collaboration (Nazi), 123, 413, 432
Communism/Marxism, 108, 127,
128, 129, 132, 133, 135, 138, 379,
397, 398, 404, 407, 415–416, 418,
419, 421, 452, 476 n.6
communities of women, xii, 10, 12,
34, 54, 56, 58–59, 97–98, 102,
115, 116, 125, 140, 174–175, 189,
233, 249, 252, 270, 271, 282, 284,
304, 319, 448, 449, 451, 457 n.6
Cone, Claribel, 146, 166, 167, 169
Cone, Etta, 148, 166, 167, 169

Coty, François, 126
courtesans, 11, 48, 82, 276, 290
Cowley, Malcolm, 120, 212, 382, 444
Crane, Hart, 120, 368, 371, 382, 392
Crosby, Caresse, 2, 9, 21, 113, 381,
    386, 387, 388, 389, 391–392, 393,
    444, 451
Crosby, Harry, 9, 109, 120, 219, 386,
    388, 391–392, 451
cross-dressing, 11, 47, 48, 50, 54, 55,
    58–59, 60, 84, 173, 177–184,
    188, 266, 307, 379, 468–469 n.9
Cubism, 112, 160, 184, 368
cummings, e. e., 35, 120, 267, 387,
    444, 447
Cunard, Lady Emerald, 115, 390, 393
Cunard, Nancy, 2, 6, 9, 21, 31, 34,
    112, 113, 114, 120, 129, 172, 217,
    237, 278, 281, 386, 387, 389, 391,
    392–395, 418; *Black Man and
    White Ladyship*, 390, 393, 395;
    Negro, 114, 120, 380, 390, 392,
    393, 394, 395, 419–424, 429, 442,
    451

Dadaism, 368, 372, 375, 376, 378,
    380
dandyism, 52, 84, 180, 460 n.8
Daudet, Léon, 46, 120, 121
David, Hermine, 113, 114
Davidson, Jo, 17, 169
de Belbeuf, Marquise (Missy), 48, 58,
    83, 84, 98, 173, 180
de Castellane, Boni, 46, 102, 103
de Clermont-Tonnerre, Duchesse
    (Elizabeth de Gramont), 48, 79,
    305, 307, 416
de Fitz-James, Comtesse, 41, 42, 46
de Gourmont, Remy, 59, 61, 63, 77,
    80, 94, 283, 320, 365
Delarue-Mardrus, Lucie, 48, 59, 79,
    307, 416
de Montesquiou, Robert, 46, 52, 60,
    61
de Noailles, Comtesse, 61, 68–70, 75,
    79, 81, 87, 114

de Pougy, Liane, 48, 59, 82, 273,
    274–275, 276–277, 283, 307
Depression, 126, 227, 405. *See also*
    economics
Dodge, Mabel, 169, 172, 236, 383,
    385, 393
Doolittle, Hilda (H. D.), 2, 6, 22, 23,
    24, 25, 28, 29, 30–31, 32, 121,
    125, 175, 176, 233, 311–356,
    357–362, 364, 365–366, 381,
    382, 386, 437, 445, 452, 455 n.2,
    470 n.5, 471 n.1, 472 n.5, 474 n.7,
    474–475 nn.8–9; *End to Tor-
    ment*, 24, 322; *Helen in Egypt*,
    325, 351–356; "Hermes of the
    Ways," 322, 323–327, 366, 472–
    474 nn.6–7; *Hermione*, 335–349,
    471 n.1
Dreyfus, Alfred (Dreyfus Affair), 41,
    45, 46, 55, 69–70, 80, 127, 412–
    413, 414
Duncan, Isadora, 108, 112, 117, 180
Duncan, Raymond, 85

economics, 9, 12, 13, 19 (Stein), 21,
    35, 47–48, 61, 75, 76, 86, 91,
    96–97, 100, 107, 110–111, 113,
    116, 117–118, 127, 129, 133, 134,
    150, 181, 195, 205, 208, 209,
    217–220, 223–225, 237, 269,
    321, 385, 386, 393, 396, 399, 405,
    411, 414, 415, 427, 439, 440, 442,
    448, 449, 466 n.3, 475 n.3. *See also*
    Depression
education, 9–10, 16, 25–26, 28,
    145–147, 202, 204–205, 212–
    214, 273, 278–285, 292–293,
    313–314, 315–316, 318–319,
    385, 407, 408, 410, 411. *See also*
    public schools
Egoist (*New Freewoman*), 22, 23,
    364–365, 371, 372, 379, 388
Eliot, T. S., xii, 21, 22, 23, 25, 29, 33,
    184, 198, 213, 214, 222, 226, 231,
    232, 233, 242, 266, 316, 328, 365,
    368, 372, 373, 388, 392, 397, 398,

399–400, 403, 410, 417, 422, 428, 429, 467n.2, 476nn.5 & 9

Ellerman, John, 10, 357, 358

Ellerman, Winifred (Bryher), 2, 4, 6, 9, 10, 21, 125, 176, 222, 228, 229, 233, 246, 269, 278, 311–313, 315, 318, 319, 355, 357, 358–362, 381, 393, 412, 445; *Two Selves*, 312, 358

Ellis, Havelock, 11, 177, 459n.6

expatriate, 3, 5, 6, 8, 10, 13, 14, 15, 30, 32, 34–36, 37, 78–79, 89, 99, 100–101, 103, 106–107, 114, 120, 124, 143–144, 149, 168, 176, 180, 189, 190–193, 197, 211, 212, 226, 230, 231, 233, 234, 245, 266, 311, 329, 330, 358, 359, 360, 362, 376, 381, 382, 388, 393, 394, 395, 396, 399, 405, 411, 424, 450, 452, 455n.2, 467n.1

expatriate community, 9, 11, 12, 19, 34–36, 100, 108, 113, 116, 158, 159, 175, 176, 188, 225, 236, 244, 249, 266, 359, 360–361, 442, 450, 451, 465–466n.20

Fargue, Léon-Paul, 4, 276

Fascism, 4, 119, 121, 124–126, 127–128, 130–140, 372, 395, 397, 398, 400, 404, 405, 407, 410, 411, 412, 413, 415, 416, 419, 422, 423, 424, 435, 444, 445, 462n.1, 476n.6

fashion, 72–73, 74–75, 110–112, 246, 274, 307

Faubourg society, xii, 34, 37–49, 61–70, 79, 81, 92, 114, 461n.1

Fauset, Jessie, 13

feminine, 20–21, 29–30, 44, 52, 62, 67, 77, 177, 178, 181, 182, 184, 188, 189, 251, 263, 277, 284, 295, 297, 298, 307, 313, 317, 324–325, 326–328, 330, 332, 335, 350, 361, 401, 411, 425, 449, 459–460n.7, 472n.4

feminism, xii, 12, 15, 19, 31, 59, 65–67, 75, 99–100, 103, 110, 116–117, 173, 177, 179, 189, 194,

210, 238, 249, 262, 268, 274, 277, 278, 281, 283, 290, 291, 292, 293, 295, 297, 306, 327, 364, 367, 370, 378, 379, 383, 384–385, 386, 387, 388, 406, 412, 415, 439, 469n.1, 476n.6

feminist criticism, 6, 7, 8, 10, 11, 12, 18, 20, 90, 179, 242, 243–244, 245, 246, 455n.2, 457n.10, 474n.8

Fitzgerald, F. Scott, 4, 9, 21, 29, 120, 360, 443, 451

Flanner, Janet, xii, 2, 6, 9, 10, 16, 21, 88, 99–140, 169, 171, 173, 174, 175, 176, 180, 183, 215, 222, 228, 236, 237, 239, 307, 363, 370–371, 382, 405, 418, 420, 455n.1, 462nn.1–4; "Letter from Paris," 4, 21, 31, 99–140, 422, 462n.1

Flint, F. S., 23, 314, 316, 322, 365

Ford, Ford Madox, 63, 88, 232, 314, 316, 361, 364, 367, 368, 388, 448–450, 471n.2

France, Anatole, 43, 47, 79, 81, 457n.8

Franco, Francisco, 130, 134, 136, 437

Freud, Sigmund, 26, 52, 247, 251, 327, 334, 375, 460n.10, 475n.9

Freund, Gisèle, 110, 228–229, 412, 445

Friedlander, Benedict, 51

Fuller, Loïe, 113

Fullerton, Morton, 69, 92, 93, 458n.1, 461n.13

Futurism, 31, 372, 383, 384–385, 386–387

Gaudier, Henri, 24

Gauthier-Villars, Henri, 49, 55, 76, 79, 81–84, 89, 90–91, 96–98, 205, 461n.2

Gautier, Théophile, 51, 279, 283, 285, 330

gender, principle of, xi, 4, 6, 8, 31–32, 174, 175, 178, 181, 188, 189, 193, 266, 302, 460–461n.11, 468–469n.9

Gide, André, 21, 55, 64, 79, 88, 105,

106, 108, 110, 121, 198, 214, 215–216, 219, 222, 398, 460 n.9
Gilliam, Florence, 9, 381–382, 387, 388, 453
Gordon, Caroline, 4, 6, 382, 451
Grant, Jane, 105, 106, 110
Gregg, Frances, 314, 315, 316, 330
Gris, Juan, 108, 169
Guggenheim, Peggy, 230, 234, 236, 256, 429, 451

Hall, Radclyffe, 35, 51, 59, 87, 115, 173, 175, 177, 180, 182, 303, 305, 306, 307, 333, 430, 467 n.4, 468 n.5
Haynes, Mabel, 148, 150
H. D. See Doolittle, Hilda
Heap, Jane, 2, 21, 22, 23, 176, 232, 236, 239, 333, 357, 362, 363, 369, 370, 371, 372, 376, 377, 379, 380, 387, 388, 394
Hemingway, Ernest, 4, 15, 21, 29, 105, 107, 109, 120, 132, 165, 169, 170, 171–173, 222, 360, 361, 392, 413, 444
heterosexuality, xii, xiii, 6, 10, 12, 18, 19, 32, 40, 47, 50–53, 54–60, 74, 115, 150, 157, 162, 166, 172, 173, 174, 176, 179, 180, 181, 186, 188, 189, 209, 210–211, 244, 245, 247, 249, 250, 252, 254, 256, 258, 260, 264, 265, 272, 275, 277, 284, 287, 288, 289, 290, 300, 306, 307, 312, 313, 314, 327, 332, 333, 335, 344, 345, 346, 349, 358, 359, 385, 447, 448, 450–451, 457 nn.5 & 8, 459 n.4, 461 n.12, 465 n.16, 468 n.6, 468–469 n.9
Hitler, Adolf, 119, 122–123, 124, 126, 127, 128, 130, 132, 133, 134, 135, 136, 137, 138, 139, 405, 407, 415, 424, 425–426, 454, 476 n.6
homophobia, xii, 11, 50–62, 115, 292, 303, 459 nn.6–7, 462 n.3, 468 n.6
homosexuality, xii, 10, 11, 12, 18, 19, 22, 30, 32, 45, 46–62, 83, 108,

145, 152, 157, 163, 166–168, 172–173, 174, 179, 180, 181, 185–190, 210–211, 215, 235, 236, 244, 245, 247–248, 259, 260, 261, 264, 280, 281, 283, 285, 289, 302, 306, 312, 313, 314, 319, 332, 333, 335, 339, 344, 380, 394, 398, 401, 402, 408, 424, 426, 451, 452, 457 nn.5 & 8, 459–460 n.7, 465 n.16, 468 n.8, 475 n.2
Hours Press, 113, 372, 386, 389–390, 391, 392, 394
Hueffer, Ford Madox. See Ford, Ford Madox
Huysmans, Joris-Karl, 52, 60, 82, 317

Imagism, 23–24, 31, 242, 314, 316, 317, 318, 319, 321, 322–324, 327–330, 336, 337, 364, 365, 366, 367, 371, 372, 373, 374, 375, 471 n.3, 472 n.4, 474 n.7, 474–475 n.8
inversion, 11, 54, 173–174, 178, 179, 181, 247, 248, 251, 261, 262, 264, 333, 425, 427, 468 n.8
Isherwood, Christopher, 398, 400, 402, 405, 408, 410

James, Henry, 25, 37, 62–65, 88, 89, 458 n.2
James, William, 89, 146, 147
Jolas, Eugene, 4, 17, 107, 120, 361, 372–377, 378, 381, 382, 444, 445
Jolas, Maria, 2, 4, 6, 9, 17, 21, 120, 219, 235, 372, 381, 387, 388, 443, 444, 451, 457 n.12, 465 n.20, 466 n.3
Josephson, Matthew, 16, 120
journalism, 4, 20, 98–140, 176, 235, 237–239, 245–246, 370–371, 381–382, 387, 390, 409, 418–420, 450
Joyce, James, xii, 16–18, 20, 21, 22, 23, 25, 29, 33, 35, 110, 120, 158–159, 161, 184, 198, 208, 209, 212, 213, 214, 216, 217–221, 222, 223, 224, 227, 231, 236, 242, 266, 313,

357, 358, 360, 362, 363, 365, 374, 376, 388, 394, 443, 444, 457 n.12, 466 n.3; *Finnegans Wake,* 109, 158, 218, 219, 220, 229, 374, 375, 376, 377, 444; *A Portrait,* 16, 23, 336, 365, 388; *Ulysses,* 5, 16, 17, 18, 20, 21, 22–23, 214, 217, 218, 220, 221, 223, 224, 225, 227, 228, 266, 357, 368, 388, 394, 397, 457 n.9

Kahane, Jack, 219, 429–430
Kiki of Montparnasse (Alice Prin), 4, 109
Krafft-Ebing, Richard von, 11, 177, 459 nn.6–7

Larbaud, Valéry, 63, 198, 217, 226
Laurencin, Marie, 85, 110, 112, 114, 392, 411–412
Lee, Vernon, 69, 87
Left Bank, xi, xii, 3, 9, 15, 16, 30, 34–36, 37, 59, 70, 88, 89, 108, 115, 119, 120, 125, 140, 158, 189, 200, 204–205, 206, 208, 220, 221, 225, 228, 315, 361, 448, 449, 450, 454
lesbianism, xii, 10–11, 12, 13, 15, 18, 19, 22, 30, 32, 40, 47–52, 53–62, 79, 83, 88, 97–98, 115, 145, 147–152, 155–156, 161, 162–169, 170–184, 187–189, 192–193, 204, 207, 208–211, 220, 233, 236, 237, 244–245, 246–256, 258–267, 268–294, 300–307, 312–313, 315, 333–336, 344–346, 358, 361, 379, 428, 431, 451, 455 n.2, 456–457 n.5, 457 n.6, 459 nn.5–6, 462 n.3, 464 n.13, 468 n.5, 469 n.1, 476 n.9
Lesbos, 11, 12, 47, 53, 55, 56–60, 98, 173, 246, 281, 284, 285, 286, 287, 288, 292, 302, 306
Lewis, Wyndham, 21, 22, 23, 24, 365, 368, 376, 377, 398, 476 n.5
Little Review, 18, 22, 23, 104, 120, 217, 232, 357, 363–372, 376–381, 386, 388, 394

Logos (Word), 26, 28, 32, 158–159, 162, 186, 331, 340, 342, 374, 468 n.7; agency of language (Stein), 158–161
Lorrain, Jean, 46
Louÿs, Pierre, 51, 53, 282–285, 471 n.8
Lowell, Amy, 21, 23, 28, 329, 333, 362, 363, 365, 368, 371, 472 n.4, 474 n.7
Loy, Mina, 2, 6, 29, 120, 236, 253, 361, 381, 383–389, 433, 455 n.2, 467 n.1, 468 n.6

McAlmon, Robert, 10, 29, 120, 230, 231–232, 235, 246, 312, 313, 355, 357–362, 363, 379, 388, 390, 393, 445
Malraux, André, 130, 132, 398
manifestos, xii, 32, 330, 365, 376, 378, 379, 380, 381, 383, 385, 393
mannish women, 51, 60, 87, 173, 174, 182, 210, 303, 460–461 n.11
marginality, xii, 20, 26, 27, 30–31, 47–49, 54, 63–64, 189–190, 193, 311–313, 409–412, 433–435, 437–441, 448–450
Marinetti, Filippo, 376, 383–384
marriage, xii, 10, 18–19, 38–39, 42–43, 64, 66–68, 76, 80–84, 92–93, 98, 100, 116, 175, 177, 181, 184, 195, 210, 229, 246, 268–271, 272–273, 274, 296, 358–359, 385, 448, 450–451, 452
Marsden, Dora, 23, 364, 365, 378, 379
masculinity, 19–21, 23, 26–27, 29, 30, 51, 52, 67, 89, 125, 172–173, 174, 177–181, 184, 188, 189, 195, 210, 211, 241, 245, 251, 252, 264, 277, 284, 296, 297, 302, 303, 305, 307, 312, 317, 318, 324–325, 326–328, 332, 335, 349, 355, 384, 400, 401, 410, 411, 412, 425, 448, 452, 459–460 nn.6–7
Maurras, Charles, 46
Miller, Henry, 120, 386, 430, 440

misogyny, xii, 30, 50–52, 53, 115, 180, 217, 246, 263, 280, 281, 283, 302, 303, 410, 460 n.8, 465 n.17, 474 n.7

Mistinguette, 72, 114

Modernism, xi, xii, xiii, 3, 4, 6, 7, 9, 12, 15, 19, 20, 23, 24–29, 30–34, 62–63, 71, 100, 108, 110, 112, 125, 157–158, 159, 162, 176, 177–179, 183, 184, 186, 187, 192, 204, 206, 215, 221, 222, 231, 234, 242, 243, 253, 266, 267, 293, 305, 311, 312, 313, 316, 317, 319, 322, 328, 335, 336, 355, 356, 371, 372, 374, 375, 376, 377, 378, 379, 383, 386, 387, 397, 398–399, 400, 407, 430, 448, 451, 452, 455 n.2, 456 n.3, 458 n.15, 458–459 n.2, 460 n.8, 467 n.1, 468 n.9

Monnier, Adrienne, 2, 6, 10, 21, 31, 114, 126, 169, 176, 184, 194–201, 204–221, 223–229, 230, 360, 387, 388, 412, 413, 414, 445, 446, 448, 453, 454, 466 nn.1, 3, & 4

Monnier, Marie, 114

Monro, Harold, 203, 314, 316

Monroe, Harriet, 22, 321, 322, 363, 364, 365, 369, 378, 379

Moore, Marianne, 29, 221

Morand, Paul, 118

Mussolini, Benito, 119, 124, 126, 130, 134, 135, 138, 412, 413, 415, 442

Nazis, 121–126, 130, 133–140, 228, 410–411, 412, 415, 422, 425, 445, 477 n.9. See also collaboration

New Freewoman. See Egoist

New Yorker, 4, 21, 100, 106, 112, 113, 126, 127, 132, 228, 237, 241, 370, 418, 420, 428, 462 n.1

New York Herald, 4, 21, 35, 126, 139

Nin, Anaïs, xi, 2, 5–6, 31, 120, 174, 253, 424, 429–437, 440, 441, 444; House of Incest, 429–435, 437; The Winter of Artifice, 429, 436

Obelisk Press, 429–439, 444

palimpsest, 25, 312, 325, 349–351, 353, 355

Palmer, Eva, 53, 182, 273, 277, 279, 291, 307

Paris Herald. See New York Herald
Paris Tribune. See Chicago Tribune

patriarchy, xii, 3, 7–8, 15, 25, 30, 31, 32, 33, 47, 48, 52, 57, 58, 65, 84, 91, 102, 124, 125, 162, 163, 166, 174, 176, 178, 181, 184–187, 188, 189, 190, 192, 212, 221, 241–242, 243, 246, 247, 249, 250, 251, 252, 253, 255, 258, 259, 261, 262, 263, 264–267, 268, 271–272, 274, 276, 280, 281, 285–286, 287, 288, 289, 291, 292, 297, 300, 306, 312, 332, 337, 341, 343, 344, 345, 346, 347, 348, 349, 350, 384, 387, 409, 411, 412, 417, 439, 440, 447–448, 450, 453, 454, 460 n.8, 468 n.5, 468–469 n.9

perversion, 11, 50, 54, 55–56, 59–60, 179, 181, 240, 245, 257, 258–260, 261, 263, 264, 265, 400, 426, 428, 433, 456–457 n.5, 468–469 n.9

Pétain, Henri Philippe, 126, 412, 415, 445

Picasso, 17, 21, 63, 72, 85, 96, 108, 119, 121, 131–132, 136, 151, 153–154, 160, 169, 182, 188–189, 390, 443

Plain Edition, 165, 390–391

Poetry, 22, 321, 322, 363–364, 365, 369, 378, 379, 474 n.8

politics, xi, xii, 4, 10, 12, 19, 31, 63, 74, 79–80, 81–82, 104, 106, 111, 113, 116–117, 119, 121, 122–140, 179, 384, 385, 393–394, 429, 435, 437, 452, 475–477 nn.4–9

Porter, Katherine Anne, 4, 6, 120, 161–162, 187, 244, 248, 251, 260, 381, 444, 451, 455 n.2, 464 n.11, 465 n.20

post-Modernism (literary theory), 7–8, 20, 185–186, 246, 297–298, 299–301, 325–329, 335–344,

349, 350–351, 375, 456 n.3, 475 n.9

Pound, Ezra, xii, 4, 21–22, 23, 24, 25, 29, 33, 62–63, 77, 88, 120, 184, 232, 233, 242, 283, 311, 312, 313, 315, 316, 317, 318, 320, 323, 328, 329, 330–333, 337, 344, 348, 355, 356, 360, 362, 363–369, 371, 372–373, 375, 376, 377, 378, 379, 388, 389, 390, 392, 397, 398, 410, 413–414, 416, 422, 442–443, 471 n.1, 472 nn.4–5, 474 n.7

prostitution, 50–51, 53, 54, 90, 96, 274–275, 276. *See also* courtesans

Proust, Marcel, 21, 40, 41, 43, 45, 46, 47, 52, 53, 54–60, 69, 79, 88, 107–108, 215, 246, 285, 392, 457 n.8, 459 n.3, 459–460 n.7, 460 n.10, 461 n.12

public schools, 400–402, 407, 410. *See also* education

puritanism, xii, 12, 18, 30, 68, 99, 101, 117, 209, 210, 217, 246, 260–264, 265, 268, 287, 447, 470 n.6

Rachilde, 81–82, 205, 416

Revolution of the Word, 372, 373, 375, 376, 377, 381. *See also* Logos

Rhys, Jean, xi, 2, 4, 6, 9, 31, 253, 424, 433, 437–441, 447, 448–450, 451, 452, 455 n.2; *Good Morning, Midnight*, 437–441, 449; *The Left Bank*, 448–449

Riefenstahl, Leni, 122–123

Right Bank, 34–36, 119, 204–205, 448

Rose, Francis, 116, 169

Rosenshine, Annette, 166

Ross, Harold, 100, 104, 106, 108, 126

Saillet, Maurice, 213

salons, 3, 9, 10, 12, 15, 17, 34, 37, 39–48, 53, 55, 60–68, 70, 72, 81–82, 83–88, 101, 158, 180, 197, 226, 307, 388, 451, 456 n.4, 457 n.8

Sappho, 11, 25, 53, 180, 190, 250, 271, 277, 278, 281, 283, 284, 285, 286, 287, 288, 290–292, 294, 302, 304, 306, 452, 453, 470 nn.3 & 5, 471 n.8, 474 n.7

Schliemann, Heinrich, 25

Scudder, Janet, 116, 169

sexual difference, 11–12, 173–177, 246–253, 256–257, 264–265, 276–277, 288–289, 300, 307, 312, 313, 325, 328, 334, 475 n.9

sexuality, female, 10, 14, 58, 91, 174–184, 192, 248, 252, 255, 259, 260, 264, 272, 276–277, 283–284, 292–293, 302, 319, 333–335, 384–385, 387, 411, 430, 448, 455–456 n.2, 468 n.7

sexual orientation, 11, 12, 13, 19, 48, 79, 91, 115, 155, 163, 166, 170–171, 173, 175, 176, 179, 180, 181, 183, 184, 188, 189, 192, 208–209, 231, 244–245, 248, 269, 273, 289, 290, 306, 312, 319, 321, 334, 355

sexual pathology, 51–54, 57, 59–60, 83–84, 173, 174, 181, 182, 233, 240, 245, 427

sexual stereotypes, 21, 52, 110, 111, 170–171, 173–177, 179, 183, 248, 283, 457 n.6, 459–460 n.7, 460 n.10

Shakespeare and Company, 17, 20–21, 196, 197, 198, 201, 202, 203, 205, 206, 207, 208, 211, 212, 213, 218, 221, 223, 224, 225, 226, 227, 228, 229, 230, 361, 466 n.3

Shawn, William, 104, 105, 108, 133

Sinclair, May, 31, 124, 314, 319, 361

Sitwell, Edith, 17, 29, 32, 33–34, 153, 361, 458 n.16

social class, 7, 9, 10–12, 37–38, 39–43, 47–49, 53–54, 55, 56, 57, 60–62, 63–64, 66–68, 71, 74–76, 79, 84, 89–91, 96–98, 102, 103, 104, 111, 113, 114, 133, 143, 150, 174, 177, 180–181, 182, 204, 217, 246, 274, 280, 297, 386, 393, 400,

407, 408, 410, 416, 425, 426, 475–476 n.4

Solano, Solita, 2, 9, 10, 23, 88, 108–109, 115, 132–133, 176, 236, 371, 379, 381, 382, 386, 419, 422

Spanish Civil War, 110, 128–129, 130–132, 136, 390, 395, 402, 406, 418–422, 434, 442

Spender, Stephen, 398, 405, 406, 410, 422

status of women, 3, 6, 7–8, 11–12, 20–21, 27–29, 33–34, 38, 44, 50–51, 56–59, 61–62, 65–68, 74–76, 78–79, 96–98, 99, 101, 113, 116–117, 139, 143–144, 153, 194–195, 214, 266, 274, 295, 297, 333, 383, 462 n.4

Stavisky, Alexandre, 127–128

Stein, Gertrude, xi, 2, 4, 6, 8, 9, 10, 12–20, 26, 27, 29, 31, 34, 63, 72, 74, 77, 78, 79, 84–86, 88–91, 94–96, 97, 98, 108, 109, 110–111, 112, 114, 116, 120, 125, 130, 133, 143–193, 197, 198, 208, 209, 210, 222, 236, 243, 244, 248, 254, 255, 260, 281, 284, 311, 312, 313, 318, 320, 333, 334, 361, 362, 363, 374, 375, 380, 381, 382, 388, 390–391, 393, 397, 398, 412, 443, 444, 447, 452, 457 nn.8–12, 458 n.16, 462–466 nn.1–22; "Arthur A Grammar," 185–186; *The Autobiography of Alice B. Toklas*, 16, 120, 144, 154, 156, 162, 170, 171, 371, 375, 393, 462 n.1, 463 n.7, 464 n.12; *Everybody's Autobiography*, 120, 152, 153, 154, 191, 463 n.7; isolation, 151, 157, 158, 169, 181–182, 244; *The Making of Americans*, 16, 18, 152–153, 157, 160, 161, 164, 167, 192, 243, 362, 390, 464 n.8; medical school, 14, 16, 84, 144, 145, 146–147; *A Novel of Thank You*, 163, 171; *Q.E.D.*, 14, 147, 148, 149–152, 155, 178, 192; *Tender Buttons*, 154, 160, 161, 162, 176, 187; *Three Lives*, 148, 152, 153, 160, 457 n.9; *Two*, 152, 154–155, 463 n.8

Stein, Leo, 13, 14, 15, 16, 20, 84, 89, 91, 144–157, 159, 162–164, 166, 167, 168, 179, 254, 255, 463 nn.3, 7, & 8, 464 n.9

Stein, Michael, 55, 94, 145, 191

Stein, Sally, 154, 463

Stephen, Leslie, 65

Stieglitz, Alfred, 154, 169, 383

Straus, Mme., 43, 46

style, 179, 183, 185, 240, 241, 242–244, 245, 254, 257–258, 399, 430

Surrealism, 31, 216–217, 372, 375, 376, 380, 418, 430, 432

Sutherland, Donald, 169, 170

Swinburne, Charles, 281, 338, 344, 471 n.8

Tchelitchev, Pavel, 169

technology, 71, 73–74, 102, 383, 385

third sex, 52, 60, 177–178, 261, 266, 281, 459 n.6, 468–469 n.9

This Quarter, 18

Thomson, Virgil, 169

Toklas, Alice B., 2, 4, 6, 9, 10, 14, 15, 17, 18, 19, 20, 94, 95, 114, 120, 144, 148, 151, 152, 153, 154, 155–158, 162–177, 182, 183, 184, 188, 189, 190, 192, 193, 198, 209, 210, 213, 254, 255, 390–391, 412, 443, 457 nn.8 & 11, 462 n.1, 464 n.15, 465 n.20

transition, 4, 18, 113, 372–377, 381, 390, 444

transvestism. *See* cross-dressing

Troubridge, Lady Una, 34, 270, 304, 307

Ulrichs, Karl Heinrich, 51

Valéry, Paul, 73, 79, 88, 113, 136, 216, 222

Vivien, Renée, 2, 25, 49, 53, 59, 61,

83, 94, 98, 182, 276, 277, 279, 283–284, 285–294, 299, 301, 302, 303, 304, 307, 455 n.2, 470 n.5, 470–471 n.6, 471 n.8

Vorticism, 23–24, 31, 317, 318, 323, 330, 371, 372, 373, 375, 376, 471 n.3, 472 n.4, 474–475 n.8

voyeurism, 49, 50, 53, 54, 56, 252, 281, 283, 447

Weaver, Harriet, 21, 23, 208, 220, 227, 357, 363, 364, 365, 378, 379, 388, 398

Weeks, Mabel, 148, 156

West, Rebecca, 23

Wharton, Edith, xii, 2, 5, 6, 27, 37–45, 60, 61–70, 77, 78, 79, 80, 86–93, 94, 95, 97, 99, 102, 103, 108, 114, 124, 140, 231, 269, 270–271, 278, 447, 455 n.2, 458 nn.1–2; *A Backward Glance*, 39, 40, 41–48, 64–65, 66, 68, 90; *French Ways and Their Meanings*, 66, 67, 68, 100; *The House of Mirth*, 97; *Madame de Treymes*, 40

Wharton, Edward, 38, 39, 42, 92–93

Wilde, Dolly, 88, 103, 180, 256, 307

Wilde, Oscar, 52, 82, 103, 180, 271, 295

Wilder, Thornton, 88

Williams, William Carlos, 22, 25, 29, 184, 357–359, 362, 386, 436, 464 n.16

Wood, Thelma, 10, 175, 235, 236, 255–256, 260, 424

Woolf, Virginia, 25, 28, 29, 31, 33, 34, 65, 125, 212, 214, 280, 281, 284, 311, 312, 313–320, 385, 387, 389, 397, 399, 406–409, 410, 411, 412, 417, 418, 455 n.2, 458 n.16, 468 n.9, 469–470 n.2, 470 n.3, 475 n.4, 476 n.6

World War I, 5, 24–25, 26–28, 30–31, 42, 45, 52, 66, 71–72, 75, 78, 99, 100, 111, 117–118, 119, 124, 125, 126, 135, 137, 168, 183, 189, 203, 205–206, 211, 297, 306, 317, 318, 319–320, 371, 379, 381, 382, 383, 399, 401–403, 404, 409, 416, 417, 453–454, 458 n.14, 461 n.1, 462 n.4, 468–469 n.9, 476 n.6, 476–477 n.9

World War II, 31, 104, 124–125, 319, 331, 390, 395, 405, 413, 414, 416, 417, 420, 421, 429, 441, 442, 453, 454, 476 n.6

writing practice, women's, xi, 3, 10–11, 13–14, 32, 42, 43–44, 53, 59, 64–65, 76–79, 80, 81–82, 88, 90–91, 98, 100–101, 102–103, 106, 107–108, 109, 123–124, 133, 139–140, 143, 156–158, 162–164, 168–169, 188, 190, 191, 200, 213, 214–215, 233–234, 236, 237, 271, 283–290, 294–301, 311, 322, 334, 349, 409, 434, 436, 447–448, 452